MW01031217

Baseball Cyclopedia

Table of Contents

Editors' Note

Ernest Lanigan once told sportswriting great Fred Lieb, "All my interest in baseball is in its statistics. I want to know something about every major league ball player, not only what he is hitting, but his full name with all middle names and initials, where they were born, and where they now live." Years later, in 1973, it was this fascination with the numbers, the names and the fine-pointed details of the sport that Lieb must have had in mind when he called Lanigan the "patron saint of SABR." That year, the centennial of his birth, was proclaimed by the Society for American Baseball Research as the "Year of Ernest J. Lanigan."

Ernest John Lanigan was born January 4, 1873, to George Lanigan, a newspaperman and poet, and Berthan Spink Lanigan, one-time editor of *Ladies Home Journal*. Berthan's brothers Alfred and Charles Spink started the *Sporting News*, where a 15-year-old Ernest did his first baseball writing. Lanigan had a brother, Harold, who was also a baseball writer and editor.

He remained at the *Sporting News* for three years before taking a job as a bank clerk. After eight years in banking, during which time he continued to publish his baseball work, he came down with what he described as a "weak lung" (according to a November 24, 1938, article in the *Sporting News* he had three bouts with pneumonia). He would eventually spend two years convalescing in the Adirondack Mountains where, in the three hours a day he was allowed to work, he compiled statistics for the *Sporting News* and began keeping track of runs batted in, which he persuaded the National and American Leagues to record as an official statistic. The box scores he created soon included not only runs batted in, but the winning and losing pitchers, and the runners thrown out by catchers—details that had previously been omitted. The abbreviations RBI, WP and LP would become standard elements in the modern box score. He also began the feature *This Day in Baseball*, which newspapers still run.

While he was continually drawn back to jobs in and around baseball, his resume was full and remarkably diverse. In addition to his banking and stats-keeping, and despite his ill health, he served a brief stint as the Eastern League's secretary during its transition to the International League and later as the league's historian. He was a sometime contributor to *Baseball Magazine* and other publications; baseball editor of the *New York Press* and *Cleveland Leader;* auditor and press agent for the Syracuse Chiefs; business manager for the Fort Wayne and Dayton clubs in the St. Louis Cardinals' farm system; Hall of Fame curator and then official historian; treasurer, press representative and manager of the Philadelphia Symphony Orchestra; and press representative of Washington and Lee University; he performed on occasion as a drama and music critic. He even spent time farming along the Hudson River.

In 1922, when he was with the Syracuse International League club, his *Baseball Cyclopedia* was published by the Baseball Magazine Company. The first ever encyclopedia for the sport, it was a forerunner to the modern *Baseball Encyclopedia* and *Total Baseball,* sharing with those later volumes a full player register that included full names (beginning with the American League's rise to major league status in 1901), season summaries for the leagues, great feats by major leaguers (minor leaguers were also covered in the *Baseball Cyclopedia*), team histories (Lanigan added seating capacities for the stadiums, franchise records, and pennant-winning rosters), World Series summaries, all-time record holders and a general baseball history. It was said by many to be his greatest contribution to baseball. Assembled from scattered and often contradictory sources, the *Baseball Cyclopedia* was a remarkably comprehensive record and a pioneering feat of research. Today, first editions run in the hundreds of dollars.

Ernest Lanigan (National Baseball Hall of Fame Library, Cooperstown, N.Y.)

The McFarland edition of Ernest J. Lanigan's *Baseball Cyclopedia* exactly reproduces the text of the original, including any peculiarities of spelling and punctuation, and any historical inaccuracies. The pagination has of course been adjusted to fit series specifications. An index, table of contents and this note have been added. Any additional modifications are enclosed in brackets.

The editors gratefully acknowledge the contributions of Steve Gietschier, author and senior managing editor of the Sporting News Research Center, who generously shared historical articles about E.J. Lanigan; Loretta Holland, office manager of the International League, who cleared up conflicting information about the dates of Lanigan's early stint as league secretary; and Joanne Kemp, adult services librarian of the Ashe County (N.C.) Library, whose patience and skill we've relied on throughout this series.

Finally, we thank Roger Erickson of the SABR Bibliography Committee for volunteering his fine indexing skills, and Andy McCue, who put us in touch with Roger.

Ernest John Lanigan

Ernest J. Lanigan was born in Chicago, Illinois, January fourth, eighteen hundred and seventy-three. Early in life he developed a fondness for baseball which has been his leading characteristic. Lanigan's interest, however, was centered in the press box rather than the diamond, for at an age when most young fellows are busy scooping up grounders and batting safe hits, Lanigan was already engaged in the varied experiences of a scribe. And almost from the first his activities were directed to ferreting out obscure facts and tabulating statistics, an occupation in which he has won a place at the very head of baseball statisticians.

Lanigan's first job was with the Philadelphia Record away back in 1887. The next year he was with Sporting News in St. Louis where he remained through 1891. The following eight years he was a bank clerk. But whatever his occupation he retained his interest in baseball and spent his spare time in tabulating and writing for numerous publications.

Lanigan's health gave way in 1901 and he was obliged to spend most of the next two years in the Adirondack Mountains nursing a weak lung. But he was never for a moment out of touch with baseball and continued his researches and investigations wherever he chanced to be located. In 1903 and 1904 he was Treasurer and Press Representative of the Philadelphia Symphony Orchestra. He was manager of this Orchestra in 1905, but was obliged to lay off most of the following season because of an attack of pneumonia to which his infected lungs seemed to render him peculiarly susceptible. In fact, Lanigan has had no fewer than three attacks of pneumonia. These attacks put him out of the running temporarily, but they couldn't hold him back very long. In 1907, Lanigan became baseball editor of the New York Press, a job which he held for four years. He gave it up to accept the position of Secretary of the Eastern League in 1911. The following two years saw him mixed up in numerous business enterprises. In 1914, he was press representative of Washington and Lee University. In 1915, he was farming on the Hudson River. In 1916, he became baseball editor of the

Cleveland Leader. All these years, however, he was writing syndicate articles and keeping up his statistical researches. In 1917, Lanigan devoted his time mainly to catching up with his numerous assignments with various papers. That job, in fact, has kept him busily occupied ever since. However, for the past three seasons he has found time to be press representative and auditor of the Syracuse Baseball Club in the International League.

In his long career, as a statistician, Lanigan has introduced various novelties into the records. Perhaps the most prominent innovation for which he is responsible is the column in the batting records now maintained by most professional leagues which indicates the number of runs batted in by every player during the season. Lanigan has written baseball very steadily since 1888 and though somewhat worn and weather beaten by his numerous bouts with ill health, still feels game for many more seasons with the big show.

Lanigan is perhaps the most independent sport writer in the business. He loves his work much more than any financial consideration. More than one good job has been offered him only to be turned down because he didn't want to spare the time. An inflated bank roll means very little to Lanigan. Personal independence means everything. He has been called, with good reason, the fearless writer, and yet he has few or no enemies. He is uncompromisingly honest, hard working, accurate. Baseball is under lasting obligations to him for the clear, concise and correct manner in which he has for years presented striking facts and figures of the game for popular approval. No more original or sturdily independent character ever penned a column for a sport sheet. And it can be stated without fear of contradiction, that baseball has produced no abler statistician than Ernest John Lanigan.

PART I

The National Pastime

Many thousands of words could be used by the historian in telling the story of Baseball. The career of the National Game, the National Pastime, or whatever else you desire to call it might occupy volumes but filling them would get the subject little further than it has been carried before.

The World Almanac, to which the constant seeker after information turns when he desires certain necessary data, says that ball playing was popular in Egypt 4,000 years ago and a leather ball has been used ever since in almost every country including China.

"But batting the ball," continues the W. A., "is a modern innovation. According to the Commission appointed at A. G. Spalding's suggestion in 1907 baseball originated in the United States, and the first scheme for playing it was devised by Major General Abner Doubleday in 1839, at Cooperstown, N. Y. The game was developed from Town Ball into a diamond-shaped field, and a code of playing rules was adopted by the Knickerbocker Baseball Club of New York in 1845. In 1858 the National Association of Baseball Players was formed and the first game with an admission fee

was played July 20, at the Fashion Race Course, near Jamaica, L. I., between the New York and Brooklyn clubs. The first tour of an organized club was made through New York State, in 1860, by the Excelsiors of Brooklyn. The first Eastern club to tour the west was the National of Washington, D. C. The first professional baseball club (1869) was the Cincinnati (Red Stockings), formed in 186 as an amateur organization. The National Association of Professional Baseball Players was formed in 1871 (with ten clubs); the National League of Professional Baseball Clubs, in 1876; the American Association, in 1882; the American League, in 1902."

Further condensed data about The National Pastime, or The National Obsession, as it frequently becomes, can be found in The Little Red Book, which is Part III of Spalding's Official Baseball Record of 1922. The tabloid information begins on Page 75. On the title page it is stated by Editor John B. Foster and Compiler Charles D. White that the accurate facts gathered came from about 30 reference books. Messrs. Foster and White might have stated, at the same time, that very few people have the

30 reference books in question and they might have added that to gather these facts required only about fifteen years of hard, hard work.

This contribution to baseball literature represents the unpaid and enthusiastic cooperation of a lot of persons connected with, involved in or interested in, The National Pastime. Attempt has been made to furnish the public with a handy reference book on Baseball and the effort will be made to keep it strictly up-to-date by issuing annual supplements.

All the facts that follow are guaranteed under the Pure Dope Act, and a great many of them have been supplied by people who have obtained nothing out of The National Pastime except the keen interest gained in following it.

To Charles W. Mears of Cleveland, Bradshaw H. Swales of Washington, Al Munro Elias of New York, Charles D. White of the Spalding Forces, Charles J. Foreman of Baltimore, Gerald E. Price of Elmira, Carroll B. Mayon and Arthur J. Shean of Springfield, Mass., and to a flock of present and past members of the Baseball Writers' Association of America, is due the credit if the reading public finds this book a help; to the writer is due the blame if it doesn't.

More Early History

Previous to 1870 baseball was indulged in more for its healthful exercise and the sport it furnished than as a business enterprise or profession, which it has now become. Harry Wright's renowned Red Stockings of Cincinnati were the first regularly organized professional team in the country and they played through their first season in 1869 without sustaining a defeat, following this up by winning the championship in 1870.

George Leonard Moreland's Balldom, Page Nos. 13 to 15 inclusive, gives the remarkable record of the Reds, who didn't know what defeat was until they met the Atlantics of Brooklyn at Brooklyn on June 14, 1870. Then they were beaten in 11 innings, 8 to 7. Their highest score game was 108 to 3, against the Unions, at Urbana, Ohio, in 1870. The year before, in Cincinnati, the Unions, who certainly represented Lansingburg and who may not have been the Unions who pastimed in Urbana, played a 17 to 17 tie game with the Roystering Reds.

Mr. Moreland figures that in the two years of their glory the Reds traveled 11,877 miles to play 57 combats, but there is something wrong in his calculations, for the record of games presented shows that at least 80 were run off and there probably were more.

The grand total of the Reds for 1869 and 1870, as shown by Mr. Moreland, undoubtedly should apply to 1869 only. George Wright batted at a .518 clip then and the team made 169 home runs. The highest salaried player, George Wright, signed for $1400 a season; the lowest salaried players drew $800 a year. Nowadays a college player of repute will get twice the last named sum just to sign with a major league team.

The Earliest League

The World Almanac, quoted previously as an authority, gives the number of the clubs in the earliest of the leagues, the National Association of Professional Base Ball Players, or the National Professional Association, as Frances C. Richter, who ought to know, calls it, as ten, but apparently there were only nine. These were Boston, Chicago, the Athletic of Philadelphia, the Mutual of New York, the Olympic of Washington, the Haymakers of Troy, the Forest City of Cleveland, the Kekionga of Fort Wayne and the Forest City of Rockford. The first year the N. P. A. functioned was 1871 and it continued to function for five years.

Spalding's Official Base Ball Record has the National League starting in 1871 and includes among that organization's pennant winners the Athletics of 1871 and the Bostons of the next four years.

Mr. Richter, founder of the earliest baseball paper, The Sporting Life, and a man who sacrificed time and money to help make baseball what it now is, gives a very interesting and authentic account of the activities of what we are calling the National Professional Association in his Sporting Life Base Ball Guide and Hand-Book, published in 1891.

From this hand book, which the fans of the time were able to buy for one small dime, the records of the contesting clubs, the players on the champion teams and the leading batsmen for each of the five years, have been lifted and are presented below. That no percentages are given the clubs will be explained later, when certain remarks are made about the first rival of the National League, said rival being the American Association. The records in question:

Records of National Professional Association Operated Five Years

Season of 1871

Club	Won	Lost
Athletic of Philadelphia	22	7
Boston	22	10
Chicago	20	9
Mutual of New York	17	18
Olympic of Washington	16	15
Haymakers of Troy	15	15
Forest City of Cleveland	10	19
Kekiongas of Fort Wayne (a)	7	21
Forest City of Rockford	6	21
Kekiongas of Fort Wayne (a)	7	21
Forest City of Rockford	6	21

A—Disbanded in July. Vacancy filled by Eckford club of Brooklyn, but games not counted.

Season of 1872

Club	Won	Lost
Boston	39	8
Lord Baltimore of Baltimore	34	19
Mutual of New York	34	20
Athletic of Philadelphia	30	14
Haymakers of Troy	15	10
Atlantic of Brooklyn	8	27
Forest City of Cleveland	6	15
Mansfield of Middletown, Conn. (a)	5	19
Eckford of Brooklyn	3	26
Olympic of Washington	2	7
National of Washington	0	11

A—Disbanded.

Season of 1873

Club	Won	Lost
Boston	43	16
Philadelphia	36	17

Club	Won	Lost
Baltimore	33	22
Mutual of New York	29	24
Athletic of Philadelphia	28	23
Atlantic of Brooklyn	17	17
National of Washington	8	31
Resolute of New Jersey	2	21
Maryland of Baltimore	0	5

Season of 1874

Club	Won	Lost
Boston	52	18
Mutual of New York	42	23
Athletic of Philadelphia	33	23
Philadelphia	29	29
Chicago	27	31
Atlantic of Brooklyn	23	33
Hartford	17	37
Baltimore	9	38

Season of 1875

Club	Won	Lost
Boston	71	8
Athletic of Philadelphia	53	20
Hartford	54	28
St. Louis	39	29
Philadelphia	37	31
Chicago	30	37
Mutual of New York	29	38
New Haven (a)	7	39
Red Stockings of St. Louis (b)	4	14
National of Washington (c)	4	22
Centennial of Philadelphia (d)	2	13
Atlantic of Brooklyn	2	42
Western of Keokuk (e)	1	12

A, B, C, D and E—Disbanded.

The champion teams were made up as follows:

1871, Athletic—McBride, pitcher; Malone, catcher; Fisler, Reach, and Meyerle, on the bases; Radcliff, shortstop; Cuthbert, Sensenderfer and Heubel, outfielders; Bechtel and Pratt, substitutes.

1872, Boston—Spalding, pitcher; McVey, catcher; Gould, Barnes and Schafer, on the bases; George Wright, shortstop; Leonard, Harry Wright and Rogers, outfielders; Birdsall and Ryan, substitutes.

1873, Boston—Spalding, pitcher; White, catcher; James O'Rourke, Barnes and Schafer, on the bases; George Wright, shortstop; Leonard, Harry Wright and Manning, outfielders; Birdsall, Addy and Sweasy, substitutes.

1874, Boston—Spalding, pitcher; McVey, catcher; White, Barnes and Schafer, on the bases; George Wright, shortstop; Leonard, Hall and James O'Rourke, outfielders; Harry Wright and Beals, substitutes.

1875, Boston—Spalding, pitcher; White, catcher; McVey, Barnes and Schafer, on the bases; George Wright, shortstop; Leonard, James O'Rourk and Manning, outfielders; Harry Wright, Beals, Helfert and Latham, substitutes.

And the leading batsmen each year were:

1871, Levi Meyerle, third baseman Athletics, .403 in 37 games.

1872, Ross Barnes, second baseman Boston, .404 in 44 games.

1873, Ross Barnes, second baseman Boston, .453 in 60 games.

1874, William McMullin, left field Athletics, .387 in 55 games.

1875, Ross Barnes, second baseman Boston, .386 in 78 games.

More About the N. P. A.

Mr. Richter, in telling about the last season of the National Professional Association (1875), says that it had become permeated with dishonesty in its ranks and therefore unpopular with the public. The wind-up found 13 clubs competing for the championship, St. Louis being the only one of the new entries that did not disband before the season closed.

Philadelphia had three clubs—the Athletic, Philadelphia and Centennials. Regarding the latter, Mr. Richter says:

The Centennials played but few games, and their brief existence is only noteworthy for the fact that with them began the sale of players, a custom that has grown to tremendous proportions since. The Centennial Club contained but two first-class players—Carver and Bechtel. The rival Philadelphia club, the Athletics, wanted these two, and two wealthy members of the club paid an official of the Centennial to have the two players released and transferred to the Athletic Club. This was done and shortly after the Centennial Club was disbanded. It was a peculiar fact that the first sale of players brought retribution with it, as Crayer turned out to be crooked, and Bechtel took Anson's place so often that the latter became dissatisfied and later seceded to the Chicago Club.

The National League

The National League is now 46 years old, NOW being 1922. It was organized February 2, 1876, in New York City, with William A. Hulbert of Chicago doing most of the organizing and with Albert G. Spalding, who had gone from Boston to the Windy City, doing a great deal of the suggesting. The pioneer clubs were Chicago, managed by A. G. Spalding; Hartford, managed by Robert Ferguson; St. Louis, managed by S. W. Graffen; Boston, managed by Harry Wright (William Henry Wright his real name was, unless certain historians have been misinformed); Louisville, managed by John C. Chapman; Mutual of Brooklyn, managed by G. W. H. Cannmyer; Athletic of Philadelphia, managed by Al H. Wright, and Cincinnati, managed by C. H. Gould. They finished in the order named and played a 70-game schedule.

To stick on through 46 years was not the easiest task in the world for the parent body. The National League rescued the game from disrepute, and then later some National League politicians acted in such a manner that many fans would have been pleased had the organization received a death blow from some of its rivals.

The National, until the advent of the American League, always was considered a bit better than its rivals. It survived wars with the American Association, the Players' League, the Union Association, the Federal League and the American League, the last named being the only one that practically made the senior league sue for peace. In the fight with the Federals, the American League stood with the National and in the fight with the Players' League, the American Association also lined up with the 46 (going on 47) year old organization.

The National League had the assistance of the American Association in battling the Union Association, it being the habit of the senior leaguers to suggest plans for their associates they wouldn't follow themselves. Looking backward on the baseball trail, it seems strange that the word bonehead wasn't introduced into our national game at the time the early overlords of baseball were blundering.

And digressing for a minute the first trace of bonehead in baseball came during the George Stallings regime in Philadelphia, which was in 1897 and 1898. Then the present half owner of the Rochester International League club commanded a hard hitting and slow thinking team. His athletes played extremely poorly in Pittsburg one day and one of the public prints of the Smoky City the following morning carried an interview with George of Georgia in which he alluded to his pastimers as a set of boneheads.

The National Leaguers, up to the time the American League decided it wished to be a national organization and not merely a sectional body, always were far superior thinkers to their peaceful or warring rivals. They would lose a battle at the turnstiles and win every decision in the council chamber.

Some of the council chamber decisions cost certain club owners heavily (pioneer club owners are meant, not those of today), and frequently to own a National League has stuck pretty constantly to the scheme of its founders. They were for honest sport.

Where the National League got into jams and into disfavor was where one or

two men considered themselves greater than the game. Never did the National League welcome a rival. It was against the American Association at the start and it turned down a proposition from the American League in 1901 when Mr. Byron Bancroft Johnson's organization desired to go into certain cities peaceably. The American Leaguers went anyhow, and baseball was benefited in every way because the Johnsonians didn't drop their plans when permission to push them through was denied.

The First War

War No. 1 for the National Leaguers was in 1884 with the Union Association. Henry V. Lucas of St. Louis, possessed of large means, was the leader of the Unions, who, of course, were called Onions by the sarcastic and loyal scribes of the time. The Unions lasted one year and retired from business when the National League gave Mr. Lucas permission to place his club in the American Association territory of St. Louis.

Naturally Chris Von der Ahe, Der Boss President of the Conquering Browns, protested vigorously against Henry V. being recognized by O. B., but the protest got him nothing, for this good and sufficient reason:

The Brooklyn club of the American Association had, buying certain players from the Cleveland National League club, which was going to quit, negotiated for their purchase before the legal time.

The dear old agreement under which the majors were operating had been violated and the National League wanted Brooklyn expelled. When the Association let Lucas acquire a National League franchise in St. Louis, the National Leaguers whitewashed the Brooklyn–Cleveland transaction. Another victory for the National Leaguers in the chamber council and a costly victory for Lucas, as he lost more in the National League than he did in his Union (or Onion) Association.

When the Unions (or Onions) were being fought the National Leaguers suggested that it would be a good idea for the American Association to have a 12-club circuit to shut out the invaders, the result being that the younger league had an unwieldy wheel and lost out in a couple of places where there was competition. Washington was one of these, the Senators having to quit and Richmond getting into fast company.

Scrap the Second

Scrap II in which the National League was involved came six years later (in 1890), and was with the members of the Baseball Brotherhood. These, the stars of their time, had previously wanted certain concessions from the magnates and got them not. Rather irritated and seeing that the turn-stiles were clicking merrily, the athletes turned to capitalists for cash and consolation—and got both.

Financiers were found able and willing to put up cash to erect new plants, some players putting up money, too, and most of the stars being with the movement to leave the magnates flat and to share the profits of the season of 1890 with their new employers.

Like all wars the players suffered, except those who were wise or weak enough to listen to arguments of high priced lawyers that the reserve clause bound them to their old clubs, which were ready to pay them to rubberleg back. The players who stuck got no profits and shared in the losses. Business for the National League clubs was poor and it was poor for the Brotherhood (or Players' League) clubs.

Had the players stuck together the National League today would not be in existence, for at the annual meeting of the National League in New York, on November 13, 1889, the club owners, counting the number of athletes they had on hand, found but one—Adrian Constantine Anson. Then came deserters from the Brotherhood movement, then some minor leaguers were picked up and eventually the National League had enough talent to supply its eight clubs.

These, in 1890, played with the standard Spalding ball and the Brotherhood played with a ball of its own make. The ball was lively and the scores of games in the new league were large, the public getting the idea the brand of ball played was very inferior to that of 1889 and not being able to digest all the games set before it.

In cities where there were two clubs, these clubs competed for patronage, the schedules being practically duplicates. No one had sense enough to see that two clubs for one city would be all right if 140 games of ball could be played on 140 days instead of 70.

At the end of the season the National League was licked, so was the Players' League, and the American Association, an innocent bystander, had been licked, too, and was but a shade of its former powerful self.

Worst off of all the organizations, though, was the National, for the Players' League people had pulled a coup by buying the Cincinnati National League club.

Here was the National League with seven clubs, practically ready for the count, but it never got it.

The millionaires, or near millionaires, who had backed the Players' League listened to the talk of the National League club owners and there was a consolidation. Before that the strong clubs in the weakened American Association had spurned overtures to go in with the strong clubs of the Players' League.

Tussle the Third

In baseball, as well as in real life, virtue is its own reward and the virtuous American Association clubs soon got what the fan public considered a raw deal from the law abiding National League clubs. This raw deal led to Baseball War No. 3, with the National League battling the American Association, whose strong clubs it always was ready to make room for.

Before going on to Tussle the Third see how much truth there is to the foregoing statement. The National League, in 1891, had this circuit: Boston, Brooklyn, Chicago, Cincinnati, Cleveland, New York, Philadelphia and Pittsburgh.

Boston and Chicago had been in the parent organization since its birth, in 1876, and New York and Philadelphia were legitimate National League cities, too, the career of both dating from 1883.

What of the other four, though?

Brooklyn and Cincinnati joined the National League in 1890, Cleveland in 1889 and Pittsburgh in 1887.

All four resigned from the American Association in order to get into the National League.

They were baseball cities that had been developed in the American Association and under its regime.

So when the American Association is thought of think of it as a real league.

It was.

Getting on to Tussle the Third, that came about because of an eminently unjust, but perfectly legal, ruling on the part of the Board of Control in the cases of Players Harry D. Stovey and Louis Bierbauer, who were stars of the Athletic American Association team in 1889 and who cast their fortunes with the Brotherhood the next year. The Athletics, after peace was declared between the National League and American League, neglected to reserve these men, thinking such a procedure unnecessary.

Harry Pulliam's motto of "Take nothing for granted in baseball" wasn't in existence then.

It ought to have been.

The Boston National Leaguers sent a man out and signed Stovey and the Pittsburgh National Leaguers shot a chap out and snared Bierbauer. The Board of Control promptly decided that the National League clubs were within their rights in doing this, the decision giving general dissatisfaction. The poor A's had been innocent bystanders in the war of the previous year and had been terribly treated, and now with the dove of peace hovering around they had gotten a rawer deal.

So the American Association deposed its lawyer president, girded up its loins and went out and battled the National League. When October 1891, rolled round both sides were ready for peace, there were a flock of depleted bank rolls and the National League became the National League and American Association of Professional Base Ball Clubs, with a 12-club circuit.

As to who got the decision in the war of 1891, National League or American Association, most people living in those times would say neither did.

American League Delivers Kayo

There was no question as to the winner of the Baseball War of 1901 and 1902, in which the National League went to the mat with the young and sturdy American League. The American League, which was never going to start in 1901 (see numerous predictions by National Leaguers in the public prints winter of 1900-1901), started and went through the season, placing competing clubs in Boston and Philadelphia and occupying the vacant territory of Washington and Baltimore.

The Johnsonites first asked for permission to invade Boston and Philadelphia and occupy Washington and Baltimore, and when they didn't get it went ahead and did so anyway. In 1900 a club had been placed in Chicago and another one in Cleveland and at the time the circuit of the Western League was changed its title was also changed to the American League.

The American League of 1900 was not a major league and did not pretend to be, but the A. L. of the following year was and boldly announced it was going to be, when the National Leaguers were predicting that it wouldn't start. It started and went right through, getting more than its share of patronage where there were competing clubs and becoming more popular by the innovations introduced.

In 1902 the junior leaguers dropped Milwaukee from their wheel and substituted St. Louis and a year later New York took Baltimore's place. In July, 1902, the Orioles were wrecked by the National Leaguers, but said National Leaguers, owning the franchise, forgot to protect their property rights by placing a team in the field and Mr. Johnson, hurrying to the scene, had a ball club in action the next day. Thus the American League obtained for nothing a franchise that National League capital had paid for.

What ended the battle between the National and American Leaguers was the fact that the Johnsonites accomplished the impossible by getting a location for a park in New York. Everybody in Gotham and in National League circles was positive this couldn't be done—but it was done.

When the senior leaguers discovered this it was only a question of getting together and straightening out a few differences.

So from 1903 on the National and American Leagues worked in harmony.

Occasionally the two leagues have had disagreements and there have been paper wars and phantom circuits perpetrated on the public, but the differences always have been amicably settled.

The Last War

Baseball, described by Charles H. Ebbets of the Brooklyn club as being in its infancy in 1908, began to get noticeably popular and profitable a few years later and in the winter of 1913 there was an impression that all one had to do in order to make a fortune was to erect a ball park in a major league city, hire some major leaguers and some Class AA men, announce the formation of a new league—and then sit back and divide the profits.

As a consequence the Federal League was formed, Harry Sinclair, the oil king, and Robert B. Ward, the Brooklyn baker, being its principal backers. The league functioned for two years—1914 and 1915—lost a lot of money for itself and made the major leaguers lose a lot of money at the same time. Mr. Ward died just as he was thoroughly interested in the game and just as he knew how tremendous would be the cost of establishing a third major league. Mr. Sinclair was already to continue the fight in 1916, and operate a club himself in New York, when Federal Leaguers and O. B. got together and wiped out of existence the

majors' new rival, the settlement pleasing everybody except Baltimore. That club sued Organized Baseball over the settlement, in which it was not taken care of.

This brings our history down pretty nearly to the point where fast work can be done in throwing some realistic facts at the fan populace.

Realistic Fact No. 1

The first of the realistic facts would seem to be that in the six major (or near major leagues) that have operated from 1876 on there have been more than 45,000 championship games played, the exact number of those decided being 45,419. Later you can find out what cities lead in victories, defeats, percentage and pennants, but right here that information is just carried by leagues, the grand total being due later on.

Here is the record for the National League, the American League, the American Association, the Federal League, the Players' League and the Union Association, the American League figures starting with 1901, when the junior organization claimed rivalry with the National League:

National League

Operating 46 Years

Pennants	Club	Won	Lost	Pc.
0	Hartford	71	45	.612
2	Providence	434	276	.611
3	Baltimore	642	443	.592
9	New York	3106	2341	.570
11	Chicago	3390	2583	.568

Pennants	Club	Won	Lost	Pc.
4	Pittsburgh	2674	2359	.531
9	Boston	2998	2957	.504
1	Philadelphia	2717	2715	.500
1	Detroit	426	437	.494
1	Cincinnati	2427	2568	.486
5	Brooklyn	2224	2371	.484
0	Buffalo	312	333	.484
0	Cleveland	977	1061	.479
0	St. Louis	1936	2768	.412
0	Troy	134	191	.412
0	Louisville	477	739	.392
0	Mutuals	21	35	.375
0	Indianapolis	170	285	.374
0	Washington	572	1032	.357
0	Worcester	90	159	.361
0	Syracuse (a)	15	27	.000
0	Milwaukee	15	45	.250
0	Kansas City	30	91	.248
0	Athletics	14	45	.237
46	Totals	25906	25906	.500

A—Did not finish, no percentage awarded:
Note—

American League

Operating 21 Years

Pennants	Club	Won	Lost	Pc.
4	Chicago	1700	1417	.545
6	Boston	1695	1418	.544
1	Cleveland	1631	1497	.521
3	Detroit	1605	1511	.515
1	New York	1414	1412	.500
6	Philadelphia	1545	1548	.499
0	Washington	1383	1727	.445
0	St. Louis	1307	1674	.438
0	Baltimore	118	153	.435
0	Milwaukee	48	89	.350
21	Totals	12446	12446	.500

American Association

Operating 10 Years

Pennants	Club	Won	Lost	Pc.
1	Boston	93	42	.689

Pennants	Club	Won	Lost	Pc.
4	St. Louis	780	433	.643
0	Milwaukee	26	16	.619
1	Cincinnati	587	451	.566
1	Philadelphia	632	566	.529
1	Brooklyn	436	427	.505
0	Rochester	63	63	.500
0	Columbus	301	313	.490
0	Toledo	114	122	.483
1	Louisville	577	635	.476
1	New York	270	309	.466
0	Baltimore	489	602	.448
0	Pittsburgh	235	297	.442
0	Syracuse	55	72	.433
0	Kansas City	98	171	.364
0	Cleveland	89	174	.338
0	Richmond	12	30	.286
0	Washington	56	141	.284
0	Indianapolis	29	78	.271
10	Total	4942	4942	.500

Federal League

Operated 2 Years

Pennants	Club	Won	Lost	Pc.
1	Indianapolis	88	65	.575
1	Chicago	173	133	.565
0	Newark	80	72	.526
0	Buffalo	154	149	.508
0	Pittsburgh	150	154	.493
0	Kansas City	149	156	.489
0	St. Louis	149	156	.489
0	Brooklyn	147	159	.480
0	Baltimore	131	177	.425
2	Totals	1221	1221	.500

Players' League

Pennants	Club	Won	Lost	Pc.
1	Boston	81	48	.850
0	Brooklyn	76	56	.576
0	New York	74	57	.565
0	Chicago	75	62	.547
0	Philadelphia	68	63	.519
0	Pittsburgh	60	68	.469

Pennants	Club	Won	Lost	Pc.
0	Cleveland	55	75	.423
0	Buffalo	36	96	.273
1	Totals	525	525	.500

Union Association

Operated One Year

Pennants	Club	Won	Lost	Pc.
1	St. Louis	91	16	.850
0	Cincinnati	68	35	.660
0	Baltimore	56	48	.538
0	Boston	58	51	.532
0	Washington	47	66	.416
0	Kansas City	14	63	.182
0	Chicago	33	35	.000
0	Philadelphia	21	46	.000
0	Milwaukee	8	3	.000
0	Pittsburgh	7	10	.000
0	Altoona	6	19	.000
0	St. Paul	2	6	.000
0	Wilmington	2	15	.000
1	Totals	413	413	.500

Note—No percentages are given the last seven clubs, as they did not finish the season.

Realistic Fact No. 2

Distributing the six tables previously presented and putting them on an adding machine produces Realistic Fact No. 2 about the National Pastime—produces a flock of Realistic Facts, in fact. One is that 30 cities have at various times had teams in the major (or near major) leagues, that two of these teams won only two games and that the teams of one city up to the close of 1921 have won 5371 games and the teams of another city have lost 5047 contests.

Later in this book the major league career of each city is sketched and right now the totals for each city are given, the names of the cities and the number of leagues (major and near major) they were in. No city has held membership in all six of the organizations which have claimed they were the salt of the land. Baltimore, Boston, Chicago, Philadelphia, Pittsburgh and St. Louis were in five of the six leagues of high degree that have operated, Baltimore and St. Louis not having been in the Players' League, Boston and Philadelphia not having been in the Federal League, Chicago not having been in the American Association and Pittsburgh not having been in the American League.

St. Paul had major league ball only very briefly, for its Union Association team merely played eight games.

Against this note the fact that Chicago's major league teams have won 5371 games and note also that St. Louis' major league teams have let 5047 games escape.

This table carries the victories and defeats of each major league city from 1876 to 1921, inclusive, being arranged alphabetically for the busy reader or the quick seeker after information:

Table Showing All Cities That Have Had Major League Clubs, Number of Leagues They Have Been in and Games Won and Lost by the Teams of Each—

1876 to 1921, Inclusive

City	State	Leags	Victories	Defeats
Altoona	Pennsylvania	1	6	19
Baltimore	Maryland	5	1436	1423
Boston	Massachusetts	5	4925	4516
Brooklyn	New York	4	2904	3048
Buffalo	New York	3	502	578
Chicago	Illinois	5	5371	4230
Cincinnati	Ohio	3	3082	3054
Cleveland	Ohio	4	2752	2807
Columbus	Ohio	1	301	313
Detroit	Michigan	2	2031	1948
Hartford	Connecticut	1	71	45
Indianapolis	Indiana	3	287	428
Kansas City	Missouri	4	291	481
Louisville	Kentucky	2	1054	1374
Milwaukee	Wisconsin	4	97	153
Newark	New Jersey	1	80	72
New York	New York	4	4864	4119
Philadelphia	Pennsylvania	5	4997	4983
Pittsburgh	Pennsylvania	5	3126	2888
Providence	Rhode Island	1	434	276
Richmond	Virginia	1	12	30
Rochester	New York	1	63	63
St. Louis	Missouri	5	4263	5047
St. Paul	Minnesota	1	2	6
Syracuse	New York	2	70	99
Toledo	Ohio	1	114	122
Troy	New York	1	134	191
Washington	District Col.	4	2058	2966
Wilmington	Delaware	1	2	15
Worcester	Massachusetts	1	90	159
Total		6	45419	45453
National League		1	25872	25906
American League		1	12446	12446
American Association		1	4942	4942
Federal League		1	1221	1221
Players' League		1	525	525
Union Association		1	413	413
Total		6	45419	45453

Note—Difference of 34 between victories and defeats accounted for through National League record of 1877, when Cincinnati's games were thrown out.

The Pennant Winners

The present life time totals of victories and defeats of the clubs of the major league cities has already been thrown into type and now come the lists of the pennant winners and certain information as to them. In another section of this book the names of the players on the winning clubs are given and there also is shown how these clubs fared in series for the championship of the universe or in series for the one time famed Temple Cup.

Just now the big league teams are competing for the 82nd and 83rd championships, 81 having previously been settled. Boston clubs have finished in front 17 times, Chicago clubs have led the pack on 16 occasions. New York has owned 11 pennant winners, Philadelphia eight, Brooklyn six, St. Louis five, Detroit and Pittsburgh four, Baltimore three, Cincinnati and Providence two, Cleveland, Indianapolis and Louisville, one.

The following table shows the champion teams:

City	Natl	AL	AA	FL	PL	UA	Totl
Boston	9	6	1	0	1	0	17
Chicago	11	4	0	1	0	0	16
New York	9	1	1	0	0	0	11
Philadelphia	1	6	1	0	0	0	8
Brooklyn	5	0	1	0	0	0	6
St. Louis	0	0	4	0	0	1	5
Detroit	1	3	0	0	0	0	4
Pittsburgh	4	0	0	0	0	0	4
Baltimore	3	0	0	0	0	0	3
Cincinnati	1	0	1	0	0	0	2
Providence	2	0	0	0	0	0	2
Cleveland	0	1	0	0	0	0	1
Indianapolis	0	0	0	1	0	0	1
Louisville	0	0	1	0	0	0	1
Totals	46	21	10	2	1	1	81

Abbreviations used—Natl, for National League; AL, for American League; AA for American Association; FL, for Federal League; PL, for Players' League; UA, for Union Association.

The Tail-Enders

There have been 82 tail-enders in the major leagues, for once, when the returns all were in, two clubs, finishing last, had the same percentage. Those clubs were St. Louis and Cincinnati of the National League, in 1916. St. Louis has a clear claim to the Subway Championship, with either 14 or 13½ tail-enders. No Chicago team ever has wound up at the bottom.

This table shows the tail-end teams:

City	Natl	AL	AA	FL	PL	UA	Totl
St. Louis	9	4	0	1	0	0	14
Philadelphia	5	7	1	0	0	0	13
Washington	4	4	1	0	0	0	9
Baltimore	1	1	4	1	0	0	7
Cincinnati	6	0	0	0	0	0	6
Boston	5	1	0	0	0	0	6
New York	3	2	0	0	0	0	5
Louisville	3	0	1	0	0	0	4
Pittsburgh	3	0	0	0	0	0	3
Cleveland	1	1	1	0	0	0	3
Worcester	2	0	0	0	0	0	2
Milwaukee	1	1	0	0	0	0	2
Indianapolis	1	0	1	0	0	0	2
Kansas City	0	0	1	0	0	1	2
Brooklyn	1	0	0	0	0	0	1
Buffalo	0	0	0	0	1	0	1
Detroit	1	0	0	0	0	0	1
Syracuse	1	0	0	0	0	0	1
Totals	*47	21	10	2	1	1	*82

*Two tail-enders in National League in 1916.

Lists of the Flag Winners

The one major league team to win four pennants in a row was St. Louis of the American Association, from 1885 to 1888, inclusive. The Browns, managed by Charles Comiskey, were stopped by Brooklyn.

Clubs that have won three championships in succession were Chicago of the National League twice, 1880–1882 inclusive and 1906–1908 inclusive (stopped by Boston and Pittsburgh); Boston of the National League, 1891–1893 inclusive (stopped by Baltimore); Baltimore of the National League, 1894–1896 inclusive (stopped by Boston); Pittsburgh of the National League, 1901–1903 inclusive (stopped by New York); New York of the National League, 1911–1913 inclusive (stopped by Boston), and Detroit of the American League, 1907–1909 inclusive (stopped by Philadelphia).

The highest percentage on record for a major league flag winner is .850, acquired by the St. Louis Maroons, in the Union Association, in 1884; the lowest, .566, obtained by the Chicago Whales, in the Federal League, in 1915.

The greatest number of victories for a major league flag winner is 116, Chicago's Cubs attaining that mark in the National League in 1906.

This is the list of the major league pennant winners, their personnel being given in the section of this book devoted to the 30 cities that have been (or are) in fast company:

National League Pennant Winners

Year	Club	Won	Lost	Pc.
1876	Chicago	52	14	.788
1877	Boston	31	17	.648
1878	Boston	41	19	.707
1879	Providence	55	23	.705
1880	Chicago	67	17	.798
1881	Chicago	56	28	.667
1882	Chicago	55	29	.655
1883	Boston	63	35	.643
1884	Providence	84	28	.750
1885	Chicago	87	25	.776
1886	Chicago	90	34	.725
1887	Detroit	79	45	.637
1888	New York	84	47	.641
1889	New York	83	43	.659
1890	Brooklyn	86	43	.667
1891	Boston	87	51	.630
1892	Boston	102	48	.680
1893	Boston	86	43	.667
1894	Baltimore	89	39	.695
1895	Baltimore	87	43	.669
1896	Baltimore	90	39	.698
1897	Boston	93	39	.705
1898	Boston	102	47	.685
1899	Brooklyn	88	42	.677
1900	Brooklyn	82	54	.603
1901	Pittsburgh	90	49	.657
1902	Pittsburgh	103	36	.741
1903	Pittsburgh	91	49	.650
1904	New York	106	47	.693
1905	New York	105	48	.686
1906	Chicago	116	36	.763
1907	Chicago	107	45	.704
1908	Chicago	99	55	.643
1909	Pittsburgh	110	42	.724
1910	Chicago	104	50	.676
1911	New York	99	59	.614
1912	New York	103	48	.682
1913	New York	101	51	.664
1914	Boston	94	59	.614
1915	Philadelphia	90	62	.592
1916	Brooklyn	94	60	.610
1917	New York	98	56	.636
1918	Chicago	84	45	.651
1919	Cincinnati	96	44	.686
1920	Brooklyn	93	61	.604
1921	New York	94	59	.614

American League Pennant Winners

Year	Club	Won	Lost	Pc.
1901	Chicago	83	53	.610
1902	Philadelphia	83	53	.610
1903	Boston	91	47	.659
1904	Boston	95	59	.617
1905	Philadelphia	92	56	.621
1906	Chicago	93	58	.616
1907	Detroit	92	58	.613
1908	Detroit	90	63	.588
1909	Detroit	98	54	.645
1910	Philadelphia	102	48	.680
1911	Philadelphia	101	50	.669
1912	Boston	105	47	.691
1913	Philadelphia	96	57	.627
1914	Philadelphia	99	53	.651
1915	Boston	101	50	.669
1916	Boston	91	63	.591
1917	Chicago	100	54	.649
1918	Boston	75	51	.595
1919	Chicago	88	52	.629
1920	Cleveland	98	56	.636
1921	New York	98	55	.641

American Association Pennant Winners

Year	Club	Won	Lost	Pc.
1882	Cincinnati	54	26	.675
1883	Athletic	66	32	.673
1884	Metropolitan	75	32	.701
1885	St. Louis	79	33	.705
1886	St. Louis	93	46	.669
1887	St. Louis	95	40	.704
1888	St. Louis	92	43	.681
1889	Brooklyn	93	44	.679
1890	Louisville	88	44	.667
1891	Boston	93	42	.689

Federal League Pennant Winners

Year	Club	Won	Lost	Pc.
1914	Indianapolis	88	65	.575
1915	Chicago	86	66	.566

Players' League Pennant Winner

Year	Club	Won	Lost	Pc.
1890	Boston	81	48	.628

Union Association Pennant Winner

Year	Club	Won	Lost	Pc.
1884	St. Louis	91	16	.850

PART II

A Brief Outline
of the History of Baseball
in the Cities of the
Leading Professional Circuits

Boston

Population—748,060.

Seating capacity of Braves' Field, opened in 1915, 45,000; of Fenway Field, opened in 1912, 30,000.

Major league experience—Constantly in National and American Leagues, one year in Players' League, on year in American Association and one year in Union Association.

BOSTON holds the record for champion teams, for world's champion teams and according to many, for fairness and knowledge of the game among its fan population.

The Boston National League club started the practice, back in 1887, of paying large sums of money to other clubs (the other club was Chicago) for high grade talent and recently H. H.

Frazee, owner of the Red Sox, has been doing the opposite and in consequence is persona non grata with the enthusiasts. They fail to remember how they praised the old Triumvirate for doing just what Frazee isn't doing.

In Boston they say that the only Boston club that never won a world's series was the New York American League team of 1921 and they lay that incident to the fact that on the opposing Giant combination was a left-hander who won his spurs at the Hub—one Arthur Nehf.

The personal unpopularity of the original owners of the Boston National League club paved the way for the American League in Boston. They had economy reduced to a fine science.

Many wonderful players have made their reputations in Boston—and been put up to the highest bidder.

The passing of Babe Ruth did not irritate the fans so much as the sale of Hooper.

Record of Boston's major league teams to 1921, inclusive:

VICTORIES, 4925—2998 in National League, 1695 in American, 93 in Association, 81 in Players', 58 in Union.

DEFEATS, 4516—2957 in National League, 1418 in American, 51 in Union, 48 in Players', 42 in Association.

Boston—National League

Year	Position	Won	Lost	Pc.
1878	First	41	18	.707
1897	First	93	39	.705
1898	First	102	47	.685
1892	First	102	48	.680
1893	First	86	43	.667
1877	First	31	17	.648
1883	First	63	35	.653
1891	First	87	51	.630
1914	First	94	59	.614
1884	Second	73	38	.658
1889	Second	83	45	.648
1879	Second	49	29	.628
1899	Second	95	57	.625
1915	Second	83	69	.546
1894	Third	83	49	.629
1916	Third	89	63	.586
1882	Third (a)	45	39	.536
1902	Third	73	64	.533
1896	Fourth	74	57	.565
1876	Fourth	39	31	.557
1888	Fourth	70	64	.522
1921	Fourth	79	74	.516
1900	Fourth	66	72	.478
1890	Fifth	76	57	.571
1895	Fifth (b)	71	60	.542
1887	Fifth	61	60	.504
1901	Fifth	69	69	.500
1886	Fifth	56	61	.478

Year	Position	Won	Lost	Pc.
1913	Fifth	69	82	.457
1885	Fifth	46	66	.410
1880	Sixth	40	44	.474
1917	Sixth	72	81	.471
1881	Sixth	38	45	.458
1903	Sixth	58	80	.420
1919	Sixth	57	82	.410
1908	Sixth	63	91	.409
1918	Seventh	53	71	.427
1920	Seventh	62	90	.408
1907	Seventh	58	90	.392
1904	Seventh	55	98	.360
1905	Seventh	51	103	.331
1910	Eighth, Last	53	100	.346
1912	Eighth, Last	52	101	.340
1906	Eighth, Last	49	102	.324
1909	Eighth, Last	45	108	.294
1911	Eighth, Last	44	107	.291

(a) Tied with Buffalo
(b) Tied with Brooklyn.

Boston—American League

Year	Position	Won	Lost	Pc.
1912	First	105	47	.691
1915	First	101	50	.669
1903	First	91	47	.659
1904	First	95	59	.617
1918	First	75	51	.595
1916	First	91	63	.591
1914	Second	91	62	.595
1917	Second	90	62	.592
1901	Second	79	57	.581
1909	Third	88	63	.583
1902	Third	77	60	.562
1910	Fourth	81	72	.529
1913	Fourth	79	71	.527
1905	Fourth	78	74	.513
1911	Fifth	78	75	.509
1921	Fifth	75	79	.487
1908	Fifth	75	79	.487
1920	Fifth	72	81	.471
1919	Sixth	66	71	.482
1907	Seventh	59	90	.396
1906	Eighth, Last	49	105	.318

Boston—Union Association

Year	Position	Won	Lost	Pc.
1884	Fourth	58	51	.532

Boston—Players' League

Year	Position	Won	Lost	Pc.
1890	First	81	48	.628

Boston— American Association

Year	Position	Won	Lost	Pc.
1891	First	93	42	.689

Boston's Pennant Winners

1877, National League, William Henry Wright, manager—Thomas H. Bond and William H. White, pitchers; Lewis J. Brown, catcher; Timothy Hayes Murnane, George Wright, Ezra B. Sutton, John F. Morrill and Andrew J. Leonard, infielders; James H. O'Rourke, Harry C. Schaefer, John E. Manning and James L. White, outfielders. White also caught.

1878, National League, William Henry Wright, manager—Thomas H. Bond, pitcher; Charles N. Snyder, catcher; John F. Morrill, John J. Burdock, Ezra B. Sutton and George Wright, infielders; John E. Manning, Andrew J. Leonard and James H. O'Rourke, outfielders. Harry C. Schaefer, substitute.

1883, National League, John F. Morrill, manager—Charles G. Buffington and James E. Whitney, pitchers; Michael P. Hines and Merton M. Hackett, catchers; John F. Morrill, Lewis J. Brown, John J. Burdock, Ezra B. Sutton and Samuel W. Wise, infielders; Joseph Hornung, Paul Revere Radford and Charles A. Smith, outfielders. Buffington and Whitney alternated in center field most of the time.

1890, Players' League, Michael J. Kelly, manager—William Daley, Addison C. Gumbert, Matthew Gilroy, Charles A. Radbourne and Michael Joseph Madden, pitchers; Morgan Murphy, Charles A. Sweet and Michael J. Kelly, catchers; Dennis Brouthers, Joseph J. Quinn, William M. Nash and Arthur Albert Irwin, infielders; A. Harding Richardson, Thomas T. Brown, Harry D. Stovey and Richard F. Johnson, outfielders. As the Players' and National Leagues were at war, no world's series was played.

1891, National League, Frank G. Selee, manager—John G. Clarkson, Charles A. Nichols, Harry F. Staley, Charles H. Getzein and James Sullivan, pitchers; Charles W. Bennett, Charles W. Gannel, Michael J. Kelly and Frederick N. Lake, catchers; Thomas J. Tucker, Joseph J. Quinn, William M. Nash and Herman A. Long, infielders; Robert Lincoln Lowe, Walter Stephenson Brodie, Harry D. Stovey, Martin C. Sullivan, Joseph James Kelley and George Rooks, outfielders. As the National League and American Association were at war, no world's series was played.

1891, American Association, Arthur Albert Irwin, manager—George S. Haddock, Charles G. Buffington, John F. O'Brien, William Daley, John J.

Fitzgerald and Clark Calvin Griffith, pitchers; Morgan G. Murphy, Thomas Cotter and Michael J. Kelly, catchers; Dennis Brouthers, John A. Stricker, William O. Joyce, Charles A. Farrell and Paul Revere Radford, infielders; A. Harding Richardson, Hugh Duffy, John C. McGeachy and Thomas T. Brown, outfielders; John Irwin, substitute. As the American Association and National League were at war, no world's series was played.

1892, National League, Frank G. Selee, manager—Charles A. Nichols, John E. Stivetts, John G. Clarkson, Harry F. Staley and Leon Viau, pitchers; Charles W. Bennett, Charles W. Ganzel, Michael J. Kelly and Daniel Burke, catchers; Thomas J. Tucker, Joseph J. Quinn, William M. Nash and Herman A. Long, infielders; Hugh Duffy, Harry D. Stovey, Robert Lincoln Lowe and Thomas F. McCarthy, outfielders. National League had a split season, Boston being ahead at end of first half and Cleveland at end of second. On the year, Boston won more games than anyone else. In the play-off Boston won five straight games from Cleveland after engaging in an 11-inning runless draw.

1893, National League, Frank G. Selee, manager—Charles A. Nichols, John E. Stivetts, Harry F. Staley, Henry C. Gastright and William H. Quarles, pitchers; Charles W. Bennett, Charles W. Ganzel and William H. Merritt, catchers; Thomas J. Tucker, Robert Lincoln Lowe, William M. Nash and Herman A. Long, infielders; Hugh Duffy, Thomas F. McCarthy, S. Clif-

ford Carroll and William J. VanDyke, outfielders.

1897, National League, Frank G. Selee, manager—John E. Stivetts, Charles A. Nichols, F. Klobedanz, Edward M. Lewis, James Sullivan and Charles Hickman, pitchers; Martin Bergen, Charles W. Ganzel, Fred N. Lake and George Yeager, catchers; Frederick C. Tenney, Thomas J. Tucker, Robert Lincoln Lowe, James J. Collins, Herman A. Long and Robert G. Allen, infielders; Hugh Duffy, William R. Hamilton and Charles Sylvester Stahl, outfielders. Failed to become world's champions by losing four out of five games to Baltimore in Temple Cup series.

1898, National League, Frank G. Selee, manager—Charles A. Nichols, F. Klobedanz, Victor G. Willis, Edward M. Lewis, John E. Stivetts, Charles Hickman and Michael Sullivan, pitchers; Martin Bergen, George Yeager and William E. Bransfield, catchers; Frederick C. Tenney, Robert Lincoln Lowe, James J. Collins, Herman A. Long, James Joseph Stafford and William H. Keister, infielders; Hugh Duffy, Charles Sylvester Stahl, William R. Hamilton and David Pickett, outfielders.

1903, American League, James J. Collins, manager—Denton J. Young, William Henry Dinneen, George L. Winter, Thomas J. Hughes and Norwood Gibson, pitchers; Charles A. Farrell, Louis Criger and J. Garland Stahl, catchers; George LaChance, Hobart Ferris, James J. Collins and Fred N. Parent, infielders; Patrick Henry Dougherty, Charles Sylvester Stahl and John C. Freeman, outfielders; John O'Brien, substitute. Became world's champions by winning five out of nine games from Pittsburgh.

1904, American League, James J. Collins, manager—Denton J. Young, William Henry Dinneen, George L. Winter, Jesse Niles Tannehill and Norwood Gibson, pitchers; Charles A. Farrell, Louis Criger and Thomas Doran, catchers; George LaChance, Hobart Ferris, James J. Collins and Fred N. Parent, infielders; Patrick Henry Dougherty, Charles Sylvester Stahl and John C. Freeman and Albert C. Selbach, outfielders; Robert Unglaub and William J. O'Neill, substitutes. Claimed world's championship by default because of New York's refusal to play for title.

1912, American League, J. Garland Stahl, manager—Joseph Wood, Hugh Bedient, Charles Hall, Ray W. Collins, Thomas J. O'Brien, Edward V. Cicotte, Benjamin H. VanDyke and Lawrence A. Pape, pitchers; William F. Carrigan, Forrest L. Cady, Chester D. Thomas and Leslie G. Nunamaker, catchers; J. Garland Stahl, Hugh F. Bradley, Stephen D. Yerkes, William Lawrence Gardner and Charles Wagner, infielders; George Edward Lewis, Tris Speaker, Harry B. Hooper and Olaf Henricksen, outfielders; Neal Ball, Arthur Clyde Engel and Martin Krug, substitutes. Became world's champions by winning four out of seven games from New York, second game of series being an 11-inning tie.

1914, National League, George Tweedy Stallings, manager—Richard Rudolph, George Albert Tyler, William

Lawrence James, Otto C. Hess, Richard L. Crutcher, Paul E. Strand, Eugene Cocrehan, Hub Perdue, Ensign S. Cottrell, Thomas Hughes, George A. Davis, Jr., and Adolfo Luque, pitchers; Harry M. Gowdy, Fred Tyler and Bert Whaling, catchers; Charles John Schmidt, John J. Evers, James Carlisle Smith, Walter James Vincent Maranville and Charles Albert Deal, infielders; George B. Whitted, Theodore H. Cather, Joshua Devore, J. Herbert Moran, Leslie Mann, Lawrence W. Gilbert and Joseph Connolly, outfielders; Oscar J. Dugey, Clarence O. Kraft, John C. Martin, W. G. Martin, Wilson Collins, James O. Murray and Thomas H. Griffith, substitutes. Became world's champions by winning four straight games from Philadelphia.

1915, American League, William F. Carrigan, manager—Ray W. Collins, Ralph Comstock, Guy E. Cooper, George Foster, Sylveanus Gregg, Hubert B. Leonard, Carl W. Mays, Herbert J. Pennock, George Herman Ruth, Ernest G. Shore and Joseph Wood, pitchers; William F. Carrigan, Forrest L. Cady, R. E. Haley and Chester D. Thomas, catchers; Richard Carleton Hoblitzel, Del Gainer, John J. Barry, Harold C. Janvrin, William Lawrence Gadner and L. Everett Scott, infielders; George Edward Lewis, Tris Speaker, Harry B. Hooper and Olaf Henricksen, outfielders; Michael J. McNally, William K. Rodgers, Charles H. Shorten and Charles Wagner, substitutes. Became world's champions by winning four out of five games from Philadelphia.

1916, American League, William F. Carrigan, manager—George Foster, Sylveanus Gregg, Samuel Pond Jones, Hubert B. Leonard, Carl W. Mays, Martin Joseph McHale, Herbert J. Pennock, George Herman Ruth, Ernest Shore and J. Weldon Wyckoff, pitchers; Samuel L. Agnew, Forrest L. Cady, William F. Carrigan, R. E. Haley and Chester D. Thomas, catchers; Richard Carleton Hoblitzel, Del Gainer, John J. Barry, Harold C. Janvrin, William Lawrence Gardner and L. Everett Scott, infielders; George Edward Lewis, Clarence Walker, Harry B. Hooper and Olaf Henricksen, outfielders; Michael J. McNally, Charles Wagner, Charles H. Shorten and James Walsh, substitutes. Retained world's championship by winning four out of five games from Brooklyn.

1918, American League, Edward Grant Barrow, manager—Loren V. Bader, Leslie Joseph Bush, John A. Dubuc, Samuel Pond Jones, Walter Kinney, Hubert B. Leonard, Carl W. Mays, Vincent Molyneaux, Richard McCabe, William Pertica, George Herman Ruth and J. Weldon Wyckoff, pitchers; Samuel L. Agnew, Walter Mayer and Walter H. Schang, catchers; Richard Carleton Hoblitzel, John McInnis, David W. Shean, Fred Thomas, George Cochrane and L. Everett Scott, infielders; George Whiteman, Amos Strunk and Harry B. Hooper, outfielders; Walter Barbare, John Francis Coffey, E. Gonzales, John Stansbury, Frank Truesdale, Charles Wagner, Bluhm and Lawrence Miller, substitutes. Became world's champions by winning four out of six games from Chicago.

Chicago

Population—2,701,705.

Seating capacity of Comiskey Park, opened in 1910, 35,000. Seating capacity of Cub Park, opened in 1914, 16,000.

Major League experience—Constantly in National and American Leagues, two years in Federal League, one year in Players' League, part of one year in Union Association.

CHICAGO has been in every major (or near major) league except the American Association and the Association once had permission, which wasn't granted at all willingly, to place a team there. The only ball club of the Windy City that fell by the wayside was the Union Association outfit of 1884. That moved on to Pittsburgh.

If there is one city more than another that has made baseball, it is Chicago. The old White Stockings, managed by Anson, started the pastime on the way up. Adrian Constantine saw to it that his men stopped at the best hotels and they drove to the parks in open faced carriages. Certain hostelries barred the able athletes, but never those representing Chicago.

Anson was loyal to the National League in its fight with the Brotherhood, but no life-time job was ever made for him by the club's owner or owners and he quit the machine he had built up in 1898. His successful successors were Frank Leroy Chance, working under Charles Webb Murphy, and Fred L. Mitchell, working under Charles Henry Weeghman, the Dough Nut King.

Charles Comiskey, Chicagoan himself, always insisted that there was room in his native city for two clubs and in 1900 he moved his St. Pauls in there, first against the wishes of Jim Hart and then with that gentleman's permission. The Old Roman's theory turned out to be correct and the new White Sox soon had their own clientele and at once a pennant. The Chicago Feds also won a pennant, but it is doubtful if they made any money. They were consolidated with the Cubs.

Chicago's major league record to 1921, inclusive:

VICTORIES, 5371—3390 in National League, 1700 in American, 173 in Federal, 75 in Players', 33 in Union Association.

DEFEATS, 4230—2583 in National League, 1417 in American, 133 in Federal, 62 in Players', 35 in Union Association.

Chicago—National League

Year	Position	Won	Lost	Pc.
1880	First	67	17	.798
1876	First	52	14	.788
1885	First	87	25	.776
1906	First	116	36	.763
1886	First	90	34	.725
1907	First	107	45	.704
1910	First	104	50	.676
1881	First	56	28	.667
1882	First	55	29	.655
1918	First	84	45	.651
1908	First	99	55	.643
1909	Second	104	49	.680
1890	Second	83	53	.610
1904	Second	93	60	.608
1891	Second	82	53	.607
1883	Second	59	39	.602
1911	Second	92	62	.597
1888	Second	77	58	.578
1912	Third	91	59	.607
1905	Third	92	61	.601
1903	Third	82	56	.594
1887	Third	71	50	.587
1879	Third (a)	44	32	.579
1913	Third	88	65	.575
1919	Third	75	65	.536
1889	Third	67	65	.508
1898	Fourth	85	65	.567
1895	Fourth	72	58	.554
1884	Fourth (b)	62	50	.554
1914	Fourth	78	76	.506
1878	Fourth	30	30	.500
1915	Fourth	73	80	.477
1896	Fifth	71	57	.555
1902	Fifth	68	69	.496
1920	Fifth (c)	75	79	.487
1917	Fifth	74	80	.481
1900	Fifth (d)	65	75	.464
1916	Fifth	67	86	.438
1877	Fifth	18	30	.375
1901	Sixth	53	86	.381
1892	Seventh	70	76	.479
1921	Seventh	64	89	.418
1899	Eighth	75	73	.507
1894	Eighth	57	75	.432
1897	Ninth	59	73	.447
1893	Ninth	57	71	.445

(a) Tied with Buffalo.
(b) Tied with New York.
(c) Tied with St. Louis.
(d) Tied with St. Louis.

Chicago—American League

Year	Position	Won	Lost	Pc.
1917	First	100	54	.649
1919	First	88	52	.629
1906	First	93	58	.616
1901	First	83	53	.610
1920	Second	96	58	.623
1905	Second	92	60	.605
1916	Second	89	65	.578
1915	Third	93	61	.604
1908	Third	88	64	.579
1904	Third	89	65	.578
1907	Third	87	64	.576
1902	Fourth	74	60	.552
1909	Fourth	78	74	.513
1911	Fourth	77	74	.509
1912	Fourth	78	76	.506
1913	Fifth	78	74	.513
1918	Sixth	57	67	.460
1914	Sixth (a)	70	84	.455
1910	Sixth	68	85	.444
1903	Seventh	60	77	.438
1921	Seventh	62	92	.403

(a) Tied with New York

Chicago—Union Association

Year	Position	Won	Lost	Pc.
1884	Did not finish	33	35	

Chicago—Players' League

Year	Position	Won	Lost	Pc.
1890	Fourth	75	62	.547

Chicago—Federal League

Year	Position	Won	Lost	Pc.
1915	First	86	66	.566
1914	Second	87	67	.565

Chicago's Pennant Winners

1876, National League, Albert Goodwill Spalding, manager—Albert Goodwill Spalding, pitcher; James L. White, catcher; Calvin Alexander McVey, Ross Barnes, Adrian Constantine Anson and John P. Peters, infielders; Paul A. Hines, John W. Glenn, Robert Addy and Oscar Bielaski, outfielders; J. F. Cene and F. H. Andrus, substitutes.

1880, National League, Adrian Constantine Anson, manager—Lawrence J. Corcoran and Fred E. Goldsmith, pitchers; Frank Sylvester Flint, catcher; Adrian Constantine Anson, Joseph L. Quest, Edward N. Williamson and Thomas Everett Burns, infielders; Abner F. Dalrymple, George F. Gore and Michael J. Kelly, outfielders; Thomas L. Beals, substitute.

1881, National League, Adrian Constantine Anson, manager—Lawrence J. Corcoran and Fred E. Goldsmith, pitchers; Frank Sylvester Flint, catcher; Adrian Constantine Anson, Joseph L. Quest, Edward N. Williamson and Thomas Everett Burns, infielders; Abner F. Dalrymple, George F. Gore, Michael J. Kelly and Hugh Nicol, outfielders; Piercey, substitute.

1882, National League, Adrian Constantine Anson, manager—Lawrence J. Corcoran and Fred E. Goldsmith, pitchers; Frank Sylvester Flint, catcher; Adrian Constantine Anson, Joseph L. Quest, Edward N. Williamson and Thomas Everett Burns, infielders; Abner F. Dalrymple, George F. Gore, Michael J. Kelly and Hugh Nicol, outfielders.

1885, National League, Adrian Constantine Anson, manager—John G. Clarkson, James McCormick, Lawrence J. Corcoran and Kennedy, pitchers; Frank Sylvester Flint, Elmer E. Sutcliffe and John A. McCauley, catchers; Adrian Constantine Anson, N. Fred Pfeffer, Edward N. Williamson and Thomas Everett Burns, infielders; Abner F. Dalrymple, George F. Gore, Michael J. Kelly and William Ashley Sunday, outfielders; James Ryan and William F. Kreig, substitutes. Kelly also caught. Won three and lost three games in series with St. Louis for world's championship, another game ending in a draw.

1886, National League, Adrian Constantine Anson, manager—John G. Clarkson, James McCormick and John A. Flynn, pitchers; Frank Sylvester Flint, Lewis Hardie and George H. Moolic, catchers; Adrian Constantine Anson, N. Fred Pfeffer, Edward N. Williamson and Thomas Everett Burns, infielders; James E. Ryan, Abner F. Dalrymple, George F. Gore, William Ashley Sunday and Michael J. Kelly, outfielders. Kelly also caught. Failed to win world's championship, losing four out of six games to St. Louis.

1901, American League, Clark Calvin Griffith, manager—Clark Calvin Griffith, James J. Callahan, Roy Patterson, Wiley Piatt, John Katoll, Erwin K. Harvey and Skopec, pitchers; William D. Sullivan and Joseph Sugden, catchers; W. Frank Isbell, Samuel Mertes, Fred Hartman and Frank Shugart, infielders; Hermas McFarland, William E. Hoy and Fielder Allison Jones, outfielders; James Burke, Clarence Foster and David L. Brain, substitutes. As the American League and National League were at war, no world's series was played.

1906, American League, Fielder Allison Jones, manager—Nicholas Altrock, Louis Fiene, Frank M. Owen, Roy Patterson, Frank Elmer Smith, Edward Armstrong Walsh and Guy Harris White, pitchers; William D. Sullivan, Frank Roth, Edward McFarland, James H. Hart and Jay King Towne, catchers; Frank Leroy Chance, John J. Evers, Harry M. Steinfeldt and Joseph B. Tinker, infielders; Samuel James Tilden Sheckard, James F. Slagle, Frank Schulte and Harry H. Gessler, outfielders; L. O. Smith and Arthur F. Hofman, substitutes. Failed to become world's champions by losing four out of six games to Chicago.

1907, National League, Frank Leroy Chance, manager—Mordecai Peter Centennial Brown, Blaine Dubin, Charles C. Fraser, Carl Lundgren, Orval Overall, John A. Pfiester, Edward M. Reulbach and John W. Taylor, pitchers; John G. Kling, Patrick Joseph Moran, Michael Kahoe and Harty, catchers; Frank Leroy Chance, John J. Evers, Henry Zimmerman, Harry M. Stein-Tinker, infielders; Samuel James Tilden Sheckard, James F. Slagle, Frank Schulte and Arthur F. Hofman, outfielders; William J. Sweeney, Henry Zimmerman, George Elmer Howard and Newton J. Randall, substitutes. Became world's champions by winning four straight games from Detroit after the first had resulted in a 3 to 3 twelve-inning draw.

1908, National League, Frank Leroy Chance, manager—Mordecai Peter

Centennial Brown, Andrew J. Coakley, Charles C. Fraser, Floyd M. Kroh, Carl Lundgren, W. F. Mack, Orval Overall, John A. Pfiester, Edward M. Reulbach and Sponsberg, pitchers; John G. Kling, Patrick Joseph Moran, W. R. Marshall and Vincent Campbell, catchers; Frank Leroy Chance, John J. Evers, Harry M. Steinfeldt and Joseph B. Tinker, infielders; Samuel James Tilden Sheckard, James F. Slagle, Frank Schulte and John F. Hayden, outfielders; Henry Zimmerman, George Elmer Howard, Arthur F. Hofman and Blaine Durbin, substitutes. Retained world's championship by winning four out of five games from Detroit.

1910, National League, Frank Leroy Chance, manager—Mordecai Peter Centennial Brown, Leonard L. Cole, Andrew J. Carson, William A. Foxen, Floyd M. Kroh, Harry M. McIntire, Orval Overall, John A. Pfiester, Frank Xavier Pfeffer, Edward Marvin Reulbach, Lewis Richie and Orlie F. Weaver, pitchers; John G. Kling, James Peter Archer and Thomas J. Needham, catchers; Frank Leroy Chance, John J. Evers, Henry Zimmerman, Harry M. Steinfeldt and Joseph B. Tinker, infielders; Samuel James Tilden Sheckard, Arthur F. Hofman and Frank Schulte, outfielders; Fred Luderus, John F. Kane, Clarence Beaumont and Roy Miller, substitutes. Failed to become world's champions by losing four out of five games to Philadelphia.

1915, Federal League, Joseph B. Tinker, manager—Mordecai Peter Centennial Brown, William Bailey, Claude Ray Hendrix, A. Rankin Johnson, Leo Pren-

dergast, Addison F. Brennan, David Black, George McConnell and Henry Rasmussen, pitchers; Arthur Earl Wilson, William Charles Fischer and C. L. Clemons, catchers; Fred T. Beck, Harry K. Fritz, Joseph B. Tinker, John S. Farrell, Arnold J. Hauser, Rollie Zeider, James Lawrence Smith, Charles E. Pechous, George J. Westerzil, William R. Jackson, Michael J. Doolan and Weiss, infielders; Leslie Mann, Max O. Flack, Albert Wickland, Edward H. Zwilling and Charles J. Hanford, outfielders. As the Federal League was not recognized by Organized Ball, Whales did not participate in world's series.

1917, American League, Clarence Henry Rowland, manager—Joseph D. Benz, Edward V. Cicotte, David C. Danforth, Urban C. Faber, E. A. Russell, James Scott, Claude Preston Williams and Meldon G. Wolfgang, pitchers; Ray W. Schalk, Joseph Jenkins and Byrd Lynn, catchers; C. Arnold Gandil, Edward Trowbridge Collins, Fred McMullin, Charles A. Risberg and George Davis Weaver, infielders; Joseph Jackson, Oscar Felsch, Harry Leibold and John F. Collins, outfielders; Joseph Jackson, Oscar Felsch, Harry Leibold and John F. Collins, outfielders; Jacques Frank Fournier, Robert Byrne, William Gleason, R. L. Hasbrook, T. Jourdan, Zebulon A. Terry and J. Edward Murphy, substitutes. Became world's champions by winning four out of six games from New York.

1918, National League, Fred L. Mitchell, manager—Grover Cleveland Alexander, Victor Aldridge, Paul Carter, Philip Brooks Douglas, Claude Ray

Hendrix, E. C. Martin, Samuel Leroy Napier, George Albert Tyler, James L. Vaughn, James R. Walker and Harry A Weaver, pitchers; William Killefer, Jr., Harold H. Elliott, Thomas D. Daly, Thomas A. Clarke and Robert J. O'Farrell, catchers; Fred C. Merkle, Rollie Zeider, Charles Pick, Charles Albert Deal and Charles J. Hollocher, infielders; Leslie Mann, Max O. Flack, George H. Paskert and Turner Barber, Outfielders; Peter Kilduff, William L. Wortman, William Francis McCabe and Fred F. Lear, substitutes. Failed to become world's champions by losing four out of six games to Boston.

1919, American League, William Gleason, manager—Joseph D. Benz, Edward V. Cicotte, David C. Danforth,

Urban C. Faber, William Henry James, Richard Kerr, Grover Cleveland Alexander, J. Erskine Mayer, McGuire, W. C. Noyes, Don Carlos Patrick Ragan, Robertson, E. A. Russell, Frank Shellenback, John Jeremiah Sullivan, Roy Hamilton Wilkinson and Claude Preston Williams, pitchers; Ray W. Schalk and Byrd Lynn, catchers; C. Arnold Gandil, Edward Trowbridge Collins, Charles A. Risberg and George Davis Weaver, infielders; Joseph Jackson, Oscar Felsch, Harry Leibold and John F. Collins, outfielders; Fred McMullin and J. Edward Murphy, substitutes. Failed to become world's champions by losing (or throwing) five out of eight games to Cincinnati.

Cincinnati

Population—401,247.

Seating capacity of Redland Field, opened in 1902, 24,000.

Major league experience—37 years in National League, nine years in American Association, one year in Union Association.

CINCINNATI, expelled from the National League once for failure to pay championship dues, later was reinstated and later was invited back into the parent organization—much later. The reason for the invitation to come back was that in the meantime the Queen City had developed into one of baseball's

strongholds. The Reds rejoined the National in 1890 and have been in it ever since. The year their due weren't paid was 1877.

From 1882 to 1889, Cincinnati was in the American Association—very much in it—for during only one of eight years did the Reds fail to win more games than they lost, and the first year they won the pennant. Joining the National, Cincinnati could not boast a flag winner until 1919, and then the Reds, with Pat Moran driving them, got going so fast that they didn't even stop when the championship season closed, but kept right on and whaled the daylights out of the White Sox, possibly getting some aid from certain members of the Comiskey-owned troupe, who looked under their pillows before retiring.

Cincinnati, before the National League was dreamed of, was famed for its Red Stockings, who won 56 out of 57 games in 1869 and 1870. During the days of the Association it was famed for its ball clubs and for its scribes, among the latter being Byron Bancroft Johnson, Ren Mulford, Jr., and Harry Weldon. These gentlemen could recognize a bit of baseball news before it bit them. They set a standard for baseball writing in Cincinnati that has been kept up to by their successors.

Cincinnati was the spot where Charles Webb Murphy broke into the pastime and where John Talleyrand Brush got his real start in baseball. They game him the Reds for practically nothing and later he was in New York.

Record of Cincinnati's major league teams to 1921, inclusive:

VICTORIES, 3082—2427 in National League, 587 in Association, 68 in Union.

DEFEATS, 3054—2568 in National League, 451 in Association, 35 in Union.

Cincinnati—National League

Year	Position	Won	Lost	Pc.
1919	First	96	44	.686
1878	Second	37	23	.617
1896	Third	77	50	.606
1898	Third	92	60	.605
1904	Third	88	65	.575
1920	Third	82	71	.536
1918	Third	68	60	.531
1890	Fourth	78	55	.586

Year	Position	Won	Lost	Pc.
1897	Fourth	76	56	.576
1903	Fourth	74	65	.532
1917	Fourth	78	76	.506
1909	Fourth	77	76	.504
1902	Fourth	70	70	.500
1912	Fourth	75	78	.490
1892	Fifth	82	68	.547
1905	Fifth	79	74	.516
1879	Fifth	38	36	.514
1910	Fifth	75	79	.487
1908	Fifth	73	81	.474
1899	Sixth	83	67	.553
1893	Sixth (a)	65	63	.508
1921	Sixth	70	83	.458
1911	Sixth	70	83	.458
1907	Sixth	66	87	.431
1906	Sixth	64	87	.424
1877	Sixth, Last	19	53	.268
1915	Seventh	71	83	.461
1900	Seventh	62	77	.446
1913	Seventh	64	89	.418
1891	Seventh	56	81	.409
1916	Seventh (b), Last	60	93	.392
1895	Eighth	66	64	.508
1914	Eighth, Last	60	94	.390
1901	Eighth, Last	52	87	.374
1880	Eighth, Last	21	59	.263
1876	Eighth, Last	9	56	.135
1894	Tenth	54	75	.419

(a) Tied with Brooklyn.
(b) Tied with St. Louis.

Cincinnati—American Association

Year	Position	Won	Lost	Pc.
1882	First	54	26	.675
1887	Second	81	54	.600
1885	Second	63	49	.563
1883	Third	62	36	.633
1888	Fourth	80	54	.597
1889	Fourth	76	63	.547
1884	Fifth	68	41	.624
1886	Fifth	65	72	.471
1891	Did not finish	38	56	

Cincinnati— Union Association

Year	Position	Won	Lost	Pc.
1884	Second	68	35	.660

Cincinnati's Pennant Winners

1882, American Association, Oliver Perry Caylor, manager—Will H. White and Harry F. McCormick, pitchers; Charles N. Snyder and Phillip J. Powers, catchers; Daniel E. Stearns, John Alexander McPhee, William W. Carpenter and C. Fulmer, infielders; Joseph A. Sommer, James F. Macullar and Harry E. Wheeler, outfielders; Rudolph Kemmler and Harry T. Luff, substitutes.

1919, National League, Patrick Joseph Moran, manager—Raymond Bloom Bressler, Horace Owen Eller, Ray L. Fisher, Edward F. Gerner, Adolfo Luque, A. Roy Mitchell, Michael John Regan, James Joseph Ring, Walter Henry Ruether and Harry Franklin Sallee, pitchers; Artemus Ward Allen, William A. Rariden and Iby Brown Wingo, catchers; Jacob Ellsworth Daubert, Morris C. Rath, Henry Knight Groh and William L. Kopf, infielders; Sherwood Robert Magee, Louis Baird Duncan, Edward J. Roush and Alfred Earle Neale, Outfielders; Henry Schreiber, James Lawrence Smith, Manuel Cueto, Walter P. Rehg, Charles H. See and William A. Zitman, substitutes. Became world's champions by winning five out of eight games from Chicago.

St. Louis

Population—772,897.

Seating capacity of Sportsman's Park, where both clubs play, 20,600.

Major league experience—34 years in National League, 20 years in American League, 10 years in American Association, two years in Federal League, one year in Union Association.

St. Louis still has to win a National or American League pennant. In the days when Chris Von der Ahe owned the Browns and Charles A. Comiskey managed them, the Mound City's Association team won four championships in succession and previously Henry V. Lucas' costly and ill-fated Maroons had landed the Union Association standard of supremacy.

Eighteen eighty-eight was the last year St. Louis' fans had opportunity to gloat, but frequently they have had chances to get excited, and did so. In 1908 the Browns, managed by Jim McAleer now leading a life of luxuriant ease in Youngstown, Ohio, put in a strong bid for the championship and last year the Clouting Cardinals, directed by Branch Rickey, threatened to slug their way to the top. Fielder Jones' St. Louis Feds, in 1915, almost reached the peak.

Some managers say that a St. Louis' team, in order to win, has to be at least 20 per cent. stronger than any of its rivals, because of the well-known and torrid Missouri climate.

Comiskey's old Browns became famous despite the climate and won the last of their flags after having sold a bevy of stars to Brooklyn.

One manager's complaint about St. Louis is that it harbors too many critics. At the present time it harbors George Harold Sisler, one of the greatest pastimers in captivity. Criticism doesn't seem to have hurt him.

Record of St. Louis' major league teams to 1921, inclusive:

VICTORIES, 4263—1936 in National League, 1307 in American, 780 in Association, 149 in Federal, 91 in Union.

DEFEATS, 5047—2768 in National League, 1674 in American, 433 in Association, 158 in Federal, 16 in Union.

St. Louis—National League

Year	Position	Won	Lost	Pc.
1876	Third	45	19	.703
1921	Third	87	66	.569
1917	Third	82	70	.539
1914	Third	81	72	.529
1901	Fourth	76	64	.543
1877	Fourth	19	29	.396
1899	Fifth	83	66	.557
1911	Fifth	75	74	.503
1820	Fifth (a)	75	79	.487
1900	Fifth (b)	65	75	.464
1904	Fifth	75	79	.422
1915	Sixth	72	81	.471
1902	Sixth	56	78	.418

Year	Position	Won	Lost	Pc.
1912	Sixth	63	90	.412
1905	Sixth	58	96	.377
1886	Sixth	43	79	.352
1910	Seventh	63	90	.412
1919	Seventh	54	83	.394
1916	Seventh (c), Last	60	93	.392
1909	Seventh	54	98	.355
1906	Seventh .	52	98	.347
1918	Eighth, Last	51	78	.395
1907	Eighth, Last	52	101	.340
1913	Eighth, Last	51	99	.340
1885	Eighth, Last	36	72	.333
1908	Eighth, Last	49	105	.318
1903	Eighth, Last	43	94	.314
1894	Ninth	56	76	.424
1893	Tenth	57	75	.432
1892	Eleventh	56	94	.373
1896	Eleventh	40	90	.308
1895	Eleventh	39	92	.298
1898	Twelfth, Last	39	111	.260
1897	Twelfth, Last	29	102	.221

(a) Tied with Chicago.
(b) Tied with Chicago.
(c) Tied with Cincinnati.

St. Louis—American League

Year	Position	Won	Lost	Pc.
1902	Second	78	58	.574
1921	Third	81	73	.526
1908	Fourth	83	69	.546
1920	Fourth	76	77	.497
1916	Fifth	79	75	.513
1906	Fifth	76	73	.510
1918	Fifth	60	64	.484
1919	Fifth	67	72	.482
1914	Fifth	71	82	.464
1903	Sixth	65	74	.468
1907	Sixth	69	83	.454
1904	Sixth	65	87	.428
1915	Sixth	63	91	.409
1909	Seventh	61	89	.407
1917	Seventh	57	97	.370
1912	Seventh	53	101	.344
1913	Eighth, Last	57	96	.373
1905	Eighth, Last	54	99	.354
1910	Eighth, Last	47	107	.305
1911	Eighth, Last	45	107	.296

St. Louis— American Association

Year	Position	Won	Lost	Pc.
1885	First	79	33	.705
1887	First	95	40	.704
1886	First	93	46	.669
1888	First	92	43	.681
1889	Second	90	45	.667
1883	Second	65	33	.663
1891	Second	85	52	.620
1890	Third	78	58	.574
1884	Fourth	67	40	.626
1882	Fifth	36	43	.456

St. Louis— Union Association

Year	Position	Won	Lost	Pc.
1884	First	91	16	.850

St. Louis—Federal League

Year	Position	Won	Lost	Pc.
1915	Second.	87	67	.565
1914	Eighth, Last	62	89	.411

St. Louis Pennant Winners

1884, Union Association, Ted P. Sullivan, manager—Charles Sweeney, Henry P. Boyle, Perry W. Werden, Charles Hodnett and William Taylor, pitchers; Thomas J. Dolan, John J. Brennan and George F. Baker, catchers; Joseph J. Quinn, Fred C. Dunlap, John Gleason and Milton P. Whitehead, infielders; David E. Rowe, George Shaffer, Lewis C. Dickerson and Fred Lewis, outfielders. As the Union Association had no standing in organized ball, Maroons played in no world's series.

1885, American Association, Charles A. Comiskey, manager—Robert Lee Carruthers, David L. Foutz and George McGinnis, pitchers; A. J. Bushong, Calvin C. Broughton, Nickolas Drissel and Daniel C. Sullivan, catchers; Charles A. Comiskey, Samuel W. Barkley, Walter Arlington Latham and William G. Gleason, infielders; James F. O'Neill, Curtis Benton Welch, Hugh Nicol and William H. Robinson, outfielders. Robinson was caught. Won three and lost three games in series with Chicago for world's championship, another game ending in a draw.

1886, American Association, Charles A. Comiskey, manager—Robert Lee Carruthers, David L. Foutz, Nathaniel P. Hudson and George McGinnis, pitchers; A. J. Bushong and Rudolph Kemmler, catchers; Charles A. Comiskey, William H. Robinson, Walter Arlington Latham and William G. Gleason, infielders; James F. O'Neill, Curtis Benton Welch and Hugh Nicol, outfielders. John B. McSorley, substitute. Became world's champions by winning four out of six games from Chicago.

1887, American Association, Charles A. Comiskey, manager—Robert Lee Carruthers, David L. Foutz, Charles F. King, Nathaniel P. Hudson and Edward Knouff, pitchers; A. J. Bushong and John J. Boyle, catchers; Charles A. Comiskey, William H. Robinson, Walter Arlington Latham and William G. Gleason, infielders; James F. O'Neill, Curtis Benton Welch and Louis J. Sylvester, outfielders. Michael J. Goodfellow and Harry P. Lyons, substitutes. Carruthers and Foutz alternated in right field for 95 games. Failed to retain world's championship by losing 10 out of 15 games to Detroit.

1888, American Association, Charles A. Comiskey, manager—Charles F. King, Nathaniel P. Hudson, James Devlin, Elton Chamberlain and Edward Knouff, pitchers; John Boyle, John Milligan and Thomas J. Dolan, catchers;

Charles A. Comiskey, William H. Robinson, Walter Arlington Latham, James B. McGarr, Joseph Herr and William White, infielders; James F. O'Neill, Harry P. Lyons and Thomas F. McCarthy, outfielders. Failed to become world's champions by losing six out of 10 games to New York.

Brooklyn

Population—2,018,356.

Seating capacity of Ebbets Field, opened in 1913, 30,000.

Major league experience—32 yeas in National League, seven years in American Association, two years in Federal League, one year in Players' League.

BROOKLYN went from the American Association to the National League in 1890 after having been in the younger organization since 1884. Before that the Superbas, who got their present nickname when Ned Hanlon became their manager, had been in the Inter-State League. Charles Hercules Ebbets, their principal owner, has been about everything with them, starting as a ticket-seller, has even been their manager.

The last thing Brooklyn did in the American Association was to win the pennant in 1890 on entering the National League. It needed additional strength for 1885 and then the best of the Cleveland stars were bought. More strength was needed for 1888 and

Charles H. Byrne one of the early really great baseball men, bought for Brooklyn, from St. Louis, Dave Foutz, Bob Carruthers and Doc Bushong. The pennants of 1889 and 1890 were the result of the purchases from the Browns.

In 1899 the Brooklyn owners maneuvered a deal with Baltimore whereby the two clubs were consolidated, or at least jointly owned—Brooklyn to get most of the good players and Ned Hanlon. Two more pennants were annexed, but the last never would have been captured if it had not been for Joe McGinnity, one of the unknowns the Baltimored Brooklyns had let escape in the spring of 1899.

Robert B. Ward backed the Federal Leaguers in Brooklyn and the team lost a raft of money.

Brooklyn's record in the major leagues to 1921, inclusive:

VICTORIES, 2883—2224 in National League, 436 in Association, 147 in Federal, 76 in Players'.

DEFEATS, 3013—2371 in National

League, 427 in Association, 159 in Federal, 45 in Players'.

Brooklyn—
National League

Year	Position	Won	Lost	Pc.
1899	First	88	42	.677
1890	First	86	43	.667
1916	First	94	60	.610
1920	First	93	61	.604
1900	First	82	54	.603
1902	Second	75	63	.543
1892	Third	95	59	.617
1901	Third	79	57	.581
1915	Third	80	72	.527
1895	Fifth (a)	71	60	.542
1894	Fifth	70	61	.534
1903	Fifth	70	66	.515
1921	Fifth	77	75	.507
1919	Fifth	69	71	.493
1914	Fifth	75	79	.487
1918	Fifth	57	69	.452
1907	Fifth	65	83	.439
1893	Sixth (b)	65	63	.508
1897	Sixth (c)	61	71	.462
1891	Sixth	61	76	.445
1913	Sixth	65	84	.436
1910	Sixth	64	90	.416
1904	Sixth	56	97	.366
1909	Sixth,	55	98	.359
1917	Seventh	70	81	.464
1911	Seventh	64	86	.427
1912	Seventh	58	95	.379
1908	Seventh	53	101	.344
1905	Eighth, Last	48	104	.316
1896	Ninth (d)	58	73	.443
1898	Tenth	54	91	.372

(a) Tied with Boston.
(b) Tied with Cincinnati.
(c) Tied with Washington.
(d) Tied with Washington.

Mutual—National League

Year	Position	Won	Lost	Pc.
1876	Sixth	21	35	.375

Brooklyn—
National Association

Year	Position	Won	Lost	Pc.
1889	First	93	44	.679
1888	Second	88	52	.629
1886	Third	76	61	.555
1885	Fifth (a).	53	59	.473
1887	Sixth	60	74	.448
1884	Ninth	40	64	.385
1890	Did not finish	26	73	

(a) Tied with Louisville.

Brooklyn—Players' League

Year	Position	Won	Lost	Pc.
1890	Second	76	56	.576

Brooklyn—Federal League

Year	Position	Won	Lost	Pc.
1914	Fifth	77	77	.500
1915	Seventh	70	82	.461

Brooklyn's Pennant Winners

1889, American Association, William H. McGunnigle, manager—William H. Terry, Robert Lee Carruthers, Michael F Hughes and Thomas Joseph Lovett, pitchers; A. J. Bushong, Joseph P. Visner, Robert H. Clark and Charles L. Reynolds, catchers; David L. Foutz, Hubert B. Collins, George Burton Pinckney and George J. Smith, infielders; William D. O'Brien, John S. Corkhill and Thomas P. Burns, outfielders. Failed to become world's champions by losing six out of nine games to New York.

1890, National League, William H. McGunnigle, manager—William H.

Terry, Robert Lee Carruthers, Michael F. Hughes and Thomas Joseph Lovett, pitchers; A. J. Bushong, Thomas P. Daly, Robert H. Clark, Charles L. Reynolds and George Tweedy Stallings, catchers; David L. Foutz, Hubert B. Collins, George Burton Pinckney and George J. Smith, infielders; William D. O'Brien, John S. Corkhill, Thomas P. Burns and Patrick Joseph Donovan, outfielders. Won three and lost three games in world's series with Louisville, third game of set being a tie and series being called off without decision being reached on account of bad weather and lack of public interest.

1899, National League, Edward H. Hanlon, manager—William Kennedy, John Dunn, James Hughes, James Mc-James, Joseph Yeager, William Edward Donovan, William Reidy and Albert Maul, pitchers; James Thomas McGuire, Alexander Smith and Charles H. Farrel, catchers; Hugh Ambrose Jennings, Peter J. Cassidy, Daniel F. McGann, Thomas P. Daly, James P. Casey and William Frederick Dahlen, infielders; William H. Keeler, Fielder Allison Jones, Joseph James Kelley and John J. Anderson, outfielders; George W. Wrigley and Erve T. Beck, substitutes.

1900, National League, Edward H. Hanlon, manager—Joseph Jerome McGinnity, William Kennedy, John Dunn, Harry Howell, Frank Kitson, William Edward Donovan, Joseph Yeager, August P. Weyhing and Jerry Nops, pitchers; James Thomas McGuire and Charles H. Farrel, catchers; Hugh Ambrose Jennings, Thomas P. Daly, Eugene Napoleon Demontreville, Lafay-ette Napoleon Cross and William Frederick Dahlen, infielders; William H. Keeler, Fielder Allison Jones, Joseph James Kelley and Samuel James Tilden Sheckard, outfielders; James B. Casey and Alexander Smith, substitutes.

1916, National League, Wilbert Robinson, manager—Edward Samuel Appleton, Leon J. Cadore, Lawrence D. Cheney, John Wesley Coombs, W. G. Dell, John Walter Mails, Richard W. Marquard, Edward Joseph Pfeffer, George Napoleon Rucker and Sherrod M. Smith, pitchers; John T. Meyers, Otto Lowell Miller, McKinley D. Wheat, Lewis McCarty and Arthur Dede, catchers; Jacob Ellsworth Daubert, George William Cutshaw, Fred C. Merkle, Harry H. Mowrey and Ivan M. Olson, infielders; Henry Harrison Myers, Zachary D. Wheat, Charles D. Stengel and James Harl Johnston, outfielders; Lavern Fabrique, Gustave Getz, J. P. Kelleher, Oliver O'Mara, James Daniel Smythe, David James Hickman, Jr., Lawrence Miller and Albert Nixon, substitutes. Failed to become world's champions by losing four out of five games to Boston.

1920, National League, Wilbert Robinson, manager—Leon J. Cadore, Burleigh A. Grimes, Albert Mamaux, Richard W. Marquard, John Kenneth Miljus, Clarence E. Mitchell, George B. Mohart, Edward Joseph Pfeffer and Sherrod M. Smith, pitchers; Otto Lowell Miller, Ernest George Krueger, James Wren Taylor and Harold Elliott, catchers; Edward J. Konetchy, Peter J. Kilduff, Raymond H. Schmandt, James Harl Johnston and Ivan M. Olson, infielders; Zachary D. Wheat, Henry Harrison Myers, Thomas Herman Griffith and Bernard Edmund Neis, outfielders; William Francis McCabe, John Thomas Shehan, Charles W. Ward, Eugene Sheridan, H. Douglas Baird, Wallace Hood and William G. Lamar, Jr., substitutes. Failed to become world's champions by losing five out of seven games to Cleveland.

Philadelphia

Population—1,823,779.

Seating capacity of Shibe Park, opened in 1909, 22,000. Seating capacity of Philadelphia National Park, opened in 1887, 18,000.

Major league experience—40 years in National League (Athletics' year included), constantly in American League, 10 years in American Association, one year in Players' League, part of one year in Union Association.

PHILADELPHIA, up to the time the glad hand of welcome was extended to the American League, had few pennants in its trophy room. To be exact, there was one, gained by the old Athletics of the old American Association back in 1883. Fans had the impression the owners of the Phils preferred to finish second or third. The new organization, warmly welcomed because of the non-popularity of one of the Phillies' owners, the militant Colonel John I. Rogers, supplied the Quaker City with gonfalons in 1902, 1905, 1910, 1911, 1913 and 1914, and then when the Athletics were sold and torn apart the National Leaguers surprised everyone by leading the pack of flag aspirants. Since 1915 the

Philadelphia teams evidently imagine that eighth place, not first, is the desired position.

The Athletics were in the National League at the start and then were thrown out on their noble necks for failure to make the second Western trip of 1876. The Phillies came into existence in 1883 and into the National League, too. A year before that the Athletics had joined the newly organized American Association.

Philadelphia spurned Union Association ball in 1884, one of the men entangled in this disaster being William J. Shettsline, the demon fire marshal of Glenolden, Pa., and ever since then identified with the Phils.

Connie Mack reached Philadelphia in 1901 and until 1915 his Athletics always satisfied their clientele. Since then they have disappointed it.

Philadelphia's major league record to 1921, inclusive:

VICTORIES, 4997—2731 in National League (including 14 by Athletics in 1876), 1545 in American, 632 in Association, 68 in Players' League, 21 in Union.

DEFEATS, 4983—2760 in National League (including 45 by Athletics in 1876), 1548 in American, 566 in Association, 63 in Players', 46 in Union.

Philadelphia— National League

Year	Position	Won	Lost	Pc.
1915	First	90	62	.592
1887	Second	75	48	.610
1916	Second	91	62	.595
1901	Second	83	57	.593
1913	Second	88	63	.583
1917	Second	87	65	.572
1899	Third	94	58	.618
1890	Third	78	53	.595
1895	Third	78	53	.595
1907	Third	83	64	.566
1900	Third	75	63	.543
1888	Third	69	61	.531
1885	Third	56	54	.509
1886	Fourth	71	43	.622
1892	Fourth	87	66	.569
1894	Fourth	71	56	.559
1893	Fourth	72	57	.558
1905	Fourth	83	69	.546
1908	Fourth	83	71	.539
1911	Fourth	79	73	.520
1910	Fourth	78	75	.510
1891	Fourth	68	69	.496
1889	Fourth	63	64	.496
1906	Fourth	71	82	.464
1909	Fifth	74	79	.484
1912	Fifth	73	79	.480
1898	Sixth	78	71	.523
1914	Sixth	74	80	.481
1918	Sixth	55	68	.447
1884	Sixth	39	73	.348
1902	Seventh	56	81	.409
1903	Seventh	49	86	.363
1896	Eighth	62	68	.477
1920	Eighth, Last	62	91	.405
1919	Eighth, Last	47	90	.343
1904	Eighth, Last	52	100	.342
1921	Eighth, Last	51	103	.331
1883	Eighth, Last	17	81	.173
1897	Tenth	55	77	.417

Philadelphia— American League

Year	Position	Won	Lost	Pc.
1910	First	102	48	.680
1911	First	101	50	.669
1914	First	99	53	.651
1913	First	96	57	.627
1905	First	92	56	.621
1902	First	83	53	.610
1909	Second	95	58	.621
1907	Second	88	57	.607
1903	Second	75	60	.556
1912	Third	90	62	.592
1901	Fourth	74	62	.544
1906	Fourth	78	67	.538
1904	Fifth	81	70	.536
1908	Sixth	68	85	.444
1918	Eighth, Last	52	76	.402
1917	Eighth, Last	55	98	.359
1921	Eighth, Last	53	100	.346
1920	Eighth, Last	48	106	.312
1915	Eighth, Last	43	109	.283
1919	Eighth, Last	36	104	.257
1916	Eighth, Last	36	117	.235

Philadelphia— American Association

Year	Position	Won	Lost	Pc.
1883	First	66	32	.673
1888	Third	81	52	.609
1889	Third	75	58	.564
1882	Third	40	35	.533
1885	Fourth	55	57	.491
1891	Fifth	73	66	.525
1887	Fifth	64	69	.481
1886	Sixth	63	73	.467
1884	Seventh	61	46	.570
1890	Eighth, Last	54	78	.409

Athletic—National League

Year	Position	Won	Lost	Pc.
1876	Seventh	14	45	.237

Philadelphia— Union Aassociation

Year	Position	Won	Lost	Pc.
1884	Did not finish	21	46	

Philadelphia— Players' League

Year	Position	Won	Lost	Pc.
1890	Fifth	68	63	.519

Philadelphia's Pennant Winners

1883, American Association, Charles Mason and Alonzo Knight, managers— Robert Matthews, Fred Corey, George Washington Bradley, John Jones and Edward Bakely, pitchers; John O'Brien, Edward Bowen and Hubbard, catchers; Harry D. Stovey, John Stricker, Robert J. Blakiston and Michael Moynahan, infielders; A. J. Birchal, William W. Crowley and Alonzo Knight, outfielders.

1902, American League, Cornelius McGillicuddy (Connie Mack), manager—William Bernhard, Andrew J. Coakley (under alias of J. McAllister), William Duggleby, Barthold J. Husting, Edward B. Kenna, Frederick L. Mitchell, Edward S. Plank, Porter, Clarence Quinn, George Edward Waddell, Lewis D. Wiltse, Thomas Walker and Howard P. Wilson, pitchers; Ossee F. Schreckengost, Maurice R. Powers and Morris Steelman, catchers; Harry H. Davis, Napoleon Lajoie, Daniel F. Murphy, Lafayette Napoleon Cross and Montford Cross, infielders; T. F. Hartsel, David L. Fultz, Ralph O. Seybold and Elmer Harrison Flick, outfielders; Louis Castro and Frank J. Bonner, substitutes. As the American and National Leagues were at war, no world's series was played.

1905, American League, Cornelius McGillicuddy (Connie Mack), manager—Charles Albert Bender, Andrew J. Coakley, James H. Dygart, Weldon Henley, Edward S. Plank and George Edward Waddell, pitchers; Ossee F. Schreckengost, Maurice R. Powers and Harry Barton, catchers; Harry H. Davis, Daniel F. Murphy, Lafayette Napoleon Cross and Montford Cross, infielders; T. F. Hartsel, Bristol Lord, Ralph O. Seybold and Daniel Hoffman, outfielders; John W. Knight, substitute. Failed to become world's champions by losing four out of five games to New York.

1910, American League, Cornelius McGillicuddy (Connie Mack), manager—T. Atkins, Charles Albert Bender, John Wesley Coombs, James H. Dygart, Harry Krause, Harry R. Morgan, Edward S. Plank and Clarence Dickson Russell, pitchers; John W. Lapp, J. Ira Thomas, Patrick J. Livingston, Earl Mack and Patrick Donohue, catchers; Harry H. Davis, Edward T. Collins, John Franklin Baker, John J. Barry and John McGinnis, infielders; Reuben Noshier Oldring, T. F. Hartsel, Amos Strunk and Daniel F. Murphy, outfielders; Ben Houser, Maurice C. Rath, Claude Derrick, Bristol Lord and Henry Heitmuller, substitutes. Became world's champions by winning four out of five games from Chicago.

1911, American League, Cornelius McGillicuddy (Connie Mack), manager—Armstrong, Charles Albert Bender, Carroll Brown, John Wesley Coombs, A. E. Collamore, David C. Danforth, Emerson, Harry Krause, Hubert B. Leonard, Long, Martin, Harry R. Morgan, Edward S. Plank and Clarence Dickson Russell, pitchers; John W. Lapp, J. Ira Thomas, Patrick J. Livingston and Earl Mack, catchers; Harry H. Davis, John McGinnis, Edward Trowbridge Collins, John Franklin Baker and John J. Barry, infielders; Reuben Noshier Oldring, Amos Strunk, T. F. Hartsell, Daniel F. Murphy, and Bristol Lord, outfielders; Hogan and Claude Derrick, substitutes. Retained world's championship by winning four out of six games from New York.

1913, American League, Cornelius McGillicuddy (Connie Mack), manager—Charles Albert Bender, Leslie Joseph Bush, Charles L. Boardman, Carroll Brown, Pat Bohen, Ensign S. Cottrell, John Wesley Coombs, Byron Houck, David B. Morey, Edward S. Plank, Herbert J. Pennock, Robert J. Shawkey, J. G. Taff and J. Weldon Wyckoff, pitchers; John W. Lapp, J. Ira Thomas, Walter H. Schang and James McAvoy, catchers; John McGinnis, Harry H. Davis, Edward Trowbridge Collins, John Franklin Baker, John J. Barry and John J. Lavana, infielders; Daniel F. Murphy, J. Edward Murphy, James Walsh, Amos Strunk and Reuben Noshier Oldring, outfielders; William Orr, Harry K. Fritz, Pfeffer, Carruthers, T. F. Daley and Guy V. Brickley, substitutes. Became world's championship

by winning four out of five games from New York.

1914, American League, Cornelius McGillicuddy (Connie Mack), manager—Charles Albert Bender, Leslie Joseph Bush, Carroll Brown, Raymond Bloom Bressler, Charles L. Boardman, John Wesley Coombs, Lloyd Davies, Byron Houck, Jensen, Edward S. Plank, Herbert J. Pennock, Robert J. Shawkey and J. Weldon Wyckoff, pitchers; John W. Lapp, Walter H. Schang, J. Ira Thomas, and Earl Mack, catchers; Harry H. Davis, John McGinnis, Edward Trowbridge Collins, John Franklin Baker and John J. Barry, infielders; James Walsh, Reuben Noshier Oldring, Amos Strunk, and J. Edward Murphy, outfielders; Samuel Byren Crane, William L. Kopf, Carruthers, T. F. Daley and C. Thompson, substitutes. Surrendered world's championship by losing four straight games to Boston.

1915, National League, Patrick Joseph Moran, manager—Grover Cleveland Alexander, Stanwood F. Baumgartner, George Chalmers, Albert Wentworth Demaree, George Washington McQuillan, J. Erskine Mayer, Joseph Oeschger, Eppa J. Rixey and Ben Tincup, pitchers; William Killefer, Jr., Edward J. Burns and John B. Adams, catchers; Fred Luderus, John Albert Niehoff, Milton J. Stock and David James Bancroft, infielders; George B. Whitted, George H. Paskert, C. C. Cravath and Beals Becker, outfielders; Robert Byrne, Oscar J. Dugey and Harry Weiser, substitutes. Failed to become world's champions by losing four out of five games to Boston.

New York

Population—5,620,048.

Seating capacity of Polo Grounds, where both clubs play (Yankees will have new park by 1923)—38,000. The Polo Grounds were re-opened in 1911 after having been destroyed by fire.

Major league experience—40 years in National League (Mutuals' year included), 19 years in American League, five years in American Association, one year in Players' League.

NEW YORK, like Philadelphia, was one of the original members of the National League and its first club, the Mutuals, got the same treatment as the Quaker City's pioneer big league team—banishment for failure to make the second Western trip of 1876. The Giants—not Giants then—got back into the parent organization in 1883 and at the same time the Metropolitans joined the American Association. Whenever a Met went well he joined the Giants and whenever a Giant went badly he joined the Mets. The Mets won a pennant before the John B. Day and Jim Mutrie scheme got working perfectly, Tim Keefe, who helped win it, becoming a Giant in 1885. Three years later the Giants, almost all of them big men, won the National League championship and they repeated in 1889.

Then came the Brotherhood scrap and Day and Mutrie lost about all they had made in the pastime. The club had a career of ups and downs until John T. Brush became its president and John J.

McGraw its manager, the little Napoleon going to Gotham when Andrew Freedman was its principal owner. Ever since 1904 the Giants have been on the crest or extremely near thereto. They are the best known team in the world and that made it hard for the Yankees to break in. Not until the two Colonels—Ruppert and Huston—acquired Babe Ruth for $100,000 plus did the American Leaguers begin to do anywhere near the business that always has been the Giants' portion.

New York's record in the major leagues to 1921, inclusive:

VICTORIES, 4885—3127 in National League (including 21 by Mutuals in 1876), 1414 in American, 270 in Association, 74 in Players'.

DEFEATS, 4154—2376 in National League (including 35 by Mutuals in 1876), 1412 in American, 309 in Association, 57 in Players'.

New York—National League

Year	Position	Won	Lost	Pc.
1904	First	106	47	.693
1905	First	105	48	.686
1912	First	103	48	.682
1913	First	101	51	.664
1889	First	83	43	.659
1911	First	99	54	.647
1888	First	84	47	.641
1917	First	98	56	.636
1921	First	94	59	.614
1885	Second	85	27	.758
1894	Second	88	44	.677
1908	Second (a)	98	56	.636

Year	Position	Won	Lost	Pc.
1906	Second	96	56	.632
1919	Second	87	53	.621
1903	Second	84	55	.604
1910	Second	91	63	.591
1918	Second	71	53	.573
1920	Second	86	68	.558
1914	Second	84	70	.545
1897	Third	83	48	.634
1886	Third	75	44	.630
1909	Third	92	61	.601
1891	Third	71	61	.538
1916	Fourth	86	66	.566
1884	Fourth (b)	62	50	.554
1887	Fourth	68	55	.553
1907	Fourth	82	71	.536
1893	Fifth	68	64	.515
1890	Sixth	63	68	.481
1883	Sixth	46	50	.479
1898	Seventh	77	73	.513
1896	Seventh	64	67	.489
1901	Seventh	52	85	.380
1892	Eighth	71	80	.470
1915	Eighth, Last	69	83	.454
1900	Eighth, Last	60	78	.435
1902	Eighth, Last	48	88	.353
1895	Ninth	66	65	.504
1899	Tenth	60	86	.411

(a)—Tied with Pittsburgh.
(b)—Tied with Chicago.

New York—American League

Year	Position	Won	Lost	Pc.
1921	First	98	55	.641
1904	Second	92	59	.609
1906	Second	90	61	.596
1910	Second	88	63	.583
1920	Third	95	59	.617
1903	Fourth	74	62	.544
1916	Fourth	80	74	.519
1918	Fourth	60	63	.488
1909	Fifth	74	77	.490
1907	Fifth	70	78	.473
1915	Fifth	69	83	.454
1911	Sixth	76	76	.500
1905	Sixth	71	78	.477
1917	Sixth	71	82	.464

Year	Position	Won	Lost	Pc.
1914	Sixth (a)	70	84	.455
1913	Seventh	57	94	.377
1908	Eighth, Last	51	103	.331
1912	Eighth, Last	50	102	.329

(a)—Tied with Chicago.

New York— American Association

Year	Position	Won	Lost	Pc.
1884	First	75	32	.701
1883	Fourth	54	42	.563
1885	Seventh	44	64	.407
1886	Seventh	53	82	.393
1887	Seventh	44	89	.331

New York—Players' League

Year	Position	Won	Lost	Pc.
1890	Third	74	57	.565

New York's Pennant Winners

1884, American Association, James J. Mutrie, manager—Timothy J. Keefe and John H. Lynch, pitchers; William H. Holbert and Charles Reipschlager, catchers; David L. Orr, Thomas J. Esterbrook, John J. Troy and John Nelson, infielders; Edward Kennedy, J. J. Roseman and Stephen A. Brady, outfielders; Grayson S. Pearce, substitute. Failed to become world's champions by losing three straight games to Providence.

1888, National League, James J. Mutrie, manager—Timothy J. Keefe, Michael Welch, Ledell Titcomb, Edward N. Crane, William M. George and George E. Weidman, Pitchers; William Ewing, William Brown and Patrick J. Murphy, catchers; Roger Connor, Daniel Richardson, Arthur W. Whitney and John Montgomery Ward, infielders; James H. O'Rourke, Michael J. Slattery, George F. Gore and Michael Tiernan, outfielders; Gilbert Hatfield, Elmer Cleveland and Elmer E. Foster, substitutes. Became world's champions by winning six out of ten games from St. Louis.

1889, National League, James J. Mutrie, manager—Timothy J. Keefe, Michael Welch, Ledell Titcomb, Edward N. Crane, and Henry F. O'Day, Pitchers; William Ewing and William Brown, catchers; Roger Connor, Daniel Richardson, Arthur W. Whitney and John Montgomery Ward, infielders; James H. O'Rourke, Michael J. Slattery, George F. Gore and Michael Tiernan, outfielders; Gilbert Hatfield, substitute. Retained world's championship by winning six out of nine games from Brooklyn.

1904, National League, John J. McGraw, manager—Christopher Mathewson, Joseph Jerome McGinnity, George Leroy Wiltse, Leon Kessling Ames, Luther H. Taylor, Claude Elliott and William J. Milligan, pitchers; Frank Bowerman, John J. Warner and William R. Marshall, catchers (James H. O'Rourke caught one game); Daniel L. McGann, William Oliver Gilbert, Arthur Devlin and William Frederick Dahlan, infielders; Samuel Mertes, Roger P. Bresnahan, Michael J. Donlin and George Browne, outfielders; John Dunn and Harry Ellwood McCormick, substitutes. Refused to meet Boston to determine world's championship.

1905, National League, John J. Mc-

Graw, manager—Christopher Mathewson, Joseph Jerome McGinnity, George Leroy Wiltse, Leon Kessling Ames, Luther H. Taylor, and Claude Elliott, pitchers; Frank Bowerman, Roger P. Bresnahan and William J. Clarke, catchers; Daniel L. McGann, William Oliver Gilbert, Arthur Devlin and William Frederick Dahlan, infielders; Samuel Mertes, George Browne and Michael J. Donlin, outfielders; Samuel Strang Nicklin and Robert P. Hall, substitutes. Became world's champions by winning four out of five games from Philadelphia.

1911, National League, John J. McGraw, manager—Christopher Mathewson, Richard W. Marquard, George Leroy Wiltse, Leon Kessling Ames, Arthur L. Raymond, Otis Crandall, J. A. Maxwell, Louis Drucke and Richard Rudolph, pitchers; John T. Meyers, George Schlei, Grover Cleveland Hartley and Arthur Earl Wilson, catchers; Fred C. Merkle, Lawrence Joseph Doyle, Arthur Devlin, Charles Lincoln Herzog, Arthur Fletcher and Albert H. Bridwell, infielders; John J. Murray, Frederick C. Snodgrass, Beals Becker and Joshua Devore, outfielders; Charles Victory Faust, Harry M. Gowdy, J. Eugene Paulette, George J. Burns and Michael J. Donlin, substitutes. Failed to become world's champions by losing four out of six games to Philadelphia.

1912, National League, John J. McGraw, manager—Christopher Mathewson, Richard W. Marquard, George Leroy Wiltse, Leon Kessling Ames, Otis Crandall, Charles Monroe Tesreau, Albert Wentworth Demaree, Loren V.

Bader, Theodore Goulait, Larue Kirby, Louis Drucke and Ernest Shore, pitchers; John T. Meyers, Arthur Earl Wilson and Grover Cleveland Hartley, catchers; Fred C. Merkle, Lawrence Joseph Doyle, Charles Lincoln Herzog and Arthur Fletcher, infielders; John J. Murray, Frederick C. Snodgrass, Joshua Devore and Beals Becker, outfielders; Henry Knight Groh, Davis O. Robertson, Arthur Shafer, George Joseph Burns and Harry Ellwood McCormick, substitutes. Failed to become world's champions by losing four out of seven games to Boston, second game of series being an 11-inning tie.

1913, National League, John J. McGraw, manager—Christopher Mathewson, Richard W. Marquard, George Leroy Wiltse, Leon Kessling Ames, Albert Wentworth Demaree, Otis Crandall, Arthur Fromme, Ferdinand Maurice Schupp, Alexander J. Schauer, Charles Monroe Tesreau and Bunn Hearne, pitchers; John T. Meyers, Arthur Earl Wilson, Grover Cleveland Hartley and John Bannerman McLean, catchers; Fred C. Merkle, Lawrence Joseph Doyle, Charles Lincoln Herzog and Arthur Fletcher, infielders; George Joseph Burns, Frederick C. Snodgrass, Arthur Shafer and John J. Murray, outfielders; Edward Grant, Henry Knight Groh, Milton J. Stock, Joseph F. Evers, Harry Elwood McCormick, Joshua Devore, H. Merritt, Claude Cooper and James Thorpe, substitutes. Failed to become world's champions by losing four out of five games to Philadelphia.

1917, National League, John J. Mc-

Graw, manager—Fred Anderson, John C. Benton, Albert Wentworth Demaree, John B. Middleton, William Dayton Perritt, Harry Sallee, Ferdinand Maurice Schupp, George Allen Smith, Adam Swigler and Charles Monroe Tesreau, pitchers; Lewis McCarty, William A. Rariden, Ernest George Krueger, George Gibson and John J. Onslow, catchers; Walter Holke, Charles Lincoln Herzog, Henry Zimmerman and Arthur Fletcher, infielders; George Joseph Burns, Benjamin Michael Kauff and Davis O. Robertson, outfielders; Al W. Baird, Jr., Edson M. Hemingway, George Lange Kelly, Peter J. Kilduff, Jose Rodriguez, James Lawrence Smith, John J. Murray, James Thorpe, Joseph William Wilhoit and Ross Young, substitutes. Failed to become world's champions by losing four out of six games to Chicago.

1921, National League, John J. McGraw, manager—Arthur N. Nehf, Philip Brooks Douglas, Fred Toney, Jesse L. Barnes, John C. Benton, Cecil Algernon Causey, Claude Jonnard, William Dayton Perritt, Wilfred D. Ryan, Harry Franklin Sallee, Patrick Shea and Walter Zink, pitchers; Earl Smith, Frank Snyder, Alexander N. Gaston and Miguel Gonzales, catchers; George Lange Kelly, John William Rawlings, Joseph Aloysius Rapp, Frank Francis Frisch and David James Bancroft, infielders; George Joseph Burns, Emil Frederick Meusel, Ross Young, Lee King, Curtis Walker and Charles D. Stengel, outfielders; John A. Monroe, William J. Patterson, Edward Brown, William A. Cunningham, J. Howard Berry, Jr., Joseph Connolly, William H. Heine,

Walter J. Henline, Walter H. Kopf, James B. Mahady and Henry W. Schreiber, substitutes. Became world's champions by losing five out of eight games from New York.

1921, American League, Miller J. Huggins, manager—Carl William Mays, Waite Charles Hoyt, Harry C. Harper, Harry Warren Collins, William Piercy, Robert J. Shawkey, John Quinn, Alexander Ferguson and Thomas Rogers, pitchers; Walter H. Schang, Fred Hoff-

mann and Al Devormer, catchers; Walter Charles Pipp, Aaron Lee Ward, Michael J. McNally, Wilson Fewster, John Franklin Baker and Roger Peckinpaugh, infielders; George Herman Ruth, Frank L. Bodie, Elmer J. Miller, Robert William Meusel, Robert Frank Roth and Nelson Hawks, outfielders. Failed to become world's champions by losing five out of eight games to New York.

Pittsburgh

Population—588,343.

Seating capacity of Forbes' Field, opened in 1909—24,500.

Major league experience—35 years in National League, two years in American Association, two years in Federal League, one year in Players' League, part of one year in Union Association.

PITTSBURGH has been continuously among the baseball select since 1882. The Smoky City, with a team known as the Alleghenys, was in the American Association from the start, resigning from that organization to go into the National League at the end of the season of 1886.

The Pirates of 1882, 1883 and 1884 were more or less jokes, but became strengthened when the star players of the Columbus club were bought in 1884, these stars including Ned Morris, Fred Carroll, Billy Kuehne and Pop

Smith. This purchase did not supply Pittsburgh with a pennant winner, but later another big deal did.

The deal in question was the consolidation of the Pittsburgh and Louisville clubs after the 1899 season closed. The Pirates got Fred Clarke, Hans Wagner, Tom Leach, Deacon Phillippe and others then, and in another year had a pennant. The American League helped the Corsairs in their quest for first honors, since the Johnsonites took most of Ned Hanlon's Brooklyn stars away from him.

The best clubs Pittsburgh had were when Clarke was managing them and when Hans Wagner was playing for them. The worst team representing Dreyfussville was that of 1890, nine years before Barney went there. It was in the National League, sailed under the alias of J. Palmer O'Neill's Innocents and was so bad that neither at home nor abroad would many people turn out to see it. Only 114 games did this collection of jokes lose and it lost them in a season when 140, not 154 games, were scheduled.

Record of Pittsburgh's major league teams to 1921, inclusive:

VICTORIES, 3126—2674 in National League, 235 in Association, 150 in Federal, 60 in Players', 7 in Union.

DEFEATS, 2888—2359 in National League, 297 in Association, 154 in Federal, 68 in Players', 10 in Union.

Pittsburgh—National League

Year	Position	Won	Lost	Pc.
1902	First	103	36	.741
1909	First	110	42	.724
1903	First	91	49	.650
1901	First	90	49	.647
1908	Second (a)	98	56	.636
1893	Second	81	48	.628
1905	Second	96	57	.627
1912	Second	93	58	.616
1907	Second	91	63	.591
1921	Second	90	63	.588
1900	Second	79	60	.568
1906	Third	93	60	.608
1910	Third	86	67	.562
1911	Third	85	69	.552
1904	Fourth	87	66	.569
1913	Fourth	78	71	.523
1918	Fourth	65	60	.520
1920	Fourth	79	75	.513
1919	Fourth	71	68	.511
1915	Fifth	73	81	.474
1889	Fifth	61	71	.462
1892	Sixth	80	73	.516
1896	Sixth	66	63	.512
1888	Sixth	66	68	.493
1887	Sixth	55	69	.444
1916	Sixth	65	89	.422
1895	Seventh	71	61	.538
1894	Seventh	76	73	.510

Year	Position	Won	Lost	Pc.
1914	Seventh	69	85	.448
1898	Eighth	72	76	.486
1897	Eighth	60	71	.458
1891	Eighth, Last	55	80	.407
1891	Eighth, Last	51	103	.331
1890	Eighth, Last	23	114	.168

(a)—Tied with New York.

Pittsburgh— American Association

Year	Position	Won	Lost	Pc.
1886	Second	80	57	.584
1885	Third	56	55	.505
1882	Fourth	39	39	.500
1883	Seventh	30	68	.306
1884	Eleventh	30	78	.278

Pittsburgh—Federal League

Year	Position	Won	Lost	Pc.
1915	Third	86	67	.562
1914	Seventh	64	87	.424

Pittsburgh— Union Association

Year	Position	Won	Lost	Pc.
1884	Did not finish	7	10	

Pittsburgh—Players' League

Year	Position	Won	Lost	Pc.
1890	Sixth	60	68	.469

Pittsburgh's Pennant Winners

1901, National League, Frederick C. Clarke, manager—John Dwight Chesbro, Edward R. Doheny, Samuel Leever,

Charles Louis Phillippe, Jesse Niles Tannehill, George Edward Waddell, George Merritt, Edward Poole and Lewis D. Wiltse, pitchers; Charles L. Zimmer, John O'Connor, George Yeager and John Augustin Donohue, catchers; William E. Bransfield, Claude C. Ritchey, W. Fred Ely and John Peter Wagner, infielders; Frederick C. Clarke, Clarence H. Beaumont, Alfonzo D. Davis and Thomas W. Leach, outfielders; James Timothy Burke, Judson Smith, Terrence Lamont Turner and Elmer J. Smith, substitutes. As the National and American Leagues were at war, no world's series was played.

1902, National League, Frederick C. Clarke, manager—John Dwight Chesbro, Edward R. Doheny, Samuel Leever, Charles Louis Phillippe, Jesse Niles Tannehill, Warren A. McLaughlin, Edward Poole and ____ Cushman, pitchers; Charles L. Zimmer, John O'-Connor, Edward J. Phelps, Harry Smith, Lee Alexander Fohl and ____ Hopkins, catchers; William E. Bransfield, Claude C. Ritchey, Thomas W. Leach, John Peter Wagner and William E. Conroy, infielders; Frederick C. Clarke, Clarence H. Beaumont, Alfonzo D. Davis, Fred Crolius and James D. Sebring, outfielders; James Timothy Burke, William Miller and George Merritt, substitutes. As the National and American Leagues were at war, no world's series was played.

1903, National League, Frederick C. Clarke, manager—Edward R. Doheny, Fred P. Falkenberg, William Kennedy,

Samuel Leever, George Merritt, Charles Louis Phillippe, John A. Pfiester, William Dennis Scanlan, Fred W. Veil, Irwin K. Wilhelm, Lafayette S. Winham, ____ Moran and ____ Thompson, pitchers; Edward J. Phelps, Harry Smith, Fred B. Carisch and A. C. Weaver, catchers; William E. Bransfield, Claude C. Ritchey, Thomas W. Leach, and John P. Wagner, infielders; Frederick C. Clarke, Clarence H. Beaumont and James D. Sebring, outfielders; John H. Lobert, Arthur F. Hofman, Otto Krueger, Eugene Curtis, William Gray, J. H. Marshall and Charles Gertenrich, substitutes. Failed to become world's champions by losing five out of eight games to Boston.

1909, National League, Frederick C. Clarke, manager—Charles B. Adams, S. Howard Camnitz, Samuel Lever, Albert Peter Leifield, Nicholas Maddox, Charles Louis Phillippe, Harry Camnitz, Victor G. Willis, Chester M. Brandom, Samuel W. Frock, Eugene Moore, William B. Powell and C. Wacker, pitchers; George Gibson, Patrick F. O'Connor and Michael E. Simon, catchers; William Abstein, John Barney Miller, Robert Byrne and John Peter Wagner, infielders; Frederick C. Clarke, Thomas W. Leach and J. Owen Wilson, outfielders; Alan Storke, Edward J. Abbaticchio, W. J. Barbeau, R. Hamilton Hyatt, Blaine Durbin and Ward T. Miller, substitutes. Became world's champions by winning four out of seven games from Detroit.

Cleveland

Population—796,841.

Seating capacity of Dunn Field, opened in 1910—22,091.

Major league experience—Constantly in American League, 17 years in National League, two years in American Association, one year in Players' League.

CLEVELAND had many ups and downs in baseball before it became firmly established as one of the strongholds of the pastime, the decision of James C. Dunn, formerly of Marshalltown, Iowa, to put in a pile of his own money and all he could borrow to buy the Indians in 1916 having helped a lot to establish this condition.

In the National League from 1879 on, the Forest City sold its best players to Brooklyn of the Association six years later and retired to the minors. Two years of Association ball, in 1887 and 1888, showed the National Leaguers that Cleveland was a valuable spot and they induced the Babes to rejoin them.

Under Oliver P. Tebeau and with Cy Young as their war horse, the Babes became Indians and then the Robison's, owning them, sent them to St. Louis and foisted a joke team on the Sixth City. Cleveland was dropped from the League at the end of the season of 1899 and fell back into slow company—into the American League, which had just asked for waivers on its old title of Western League. By 1901 the American League was a major league. That it so became was due in art to the capital

supplied by Charles W. Somers, from whom James C. Dunn brought the club in 1916.

Cleveland always was a good baseball city and under the Dunn regime it became a great one. Tris Speaker, the world's greatest outfielder, became an Indian private in 1916 and the Indian chieftain in 1919. A year later he led the Tribe to a pennant and to the world's championship.

The old Indians, of the National League, once finished first in a section of a split season. Tebeau was their leader and aggressiveness was the keynote of their campaigns. Their aggressiveness had so much voltage it was termed rowdyism.

Record of Cleveland's major league teams to 1921, inclusive:

VICTORIES, 2752—1631 in American League, 977 in National, 89 in Association, 55 in Players'.

DEFEATS, 2807—1497 in American League, 1061 in National, 174 in Association, 75 in Players'.

Cleveland—American League

Year	Position	Won	Lost	Pc.
1920	First	98	56	.636
1921	Second	94	60	.610
1919	Second	84	55	.604
1908	Second	90	64	.584
1918	Second	73	56	.566
1906	Third	89	64	.582
1917	Third	88	66	.571
1913	Third	86	66	.566

Year	Position	Won	Lost	Pc.
1903	Third	77	63	.550
1911	Third	80	73	.523
1904	Fourth	86	65	.570
1907	Fourth	85	67	.559
1902	Fifth	69	67	.507
1905	Fifth	76	78	.494
1912	Fifth	75	78	.490
1910	Fifth	71	81	.467
1916	Sixth	77	77	.500
1909	Sixth	71	82	.464
1901	Seventh	54	82	.397
1915	Seventh	57	95	.375
1914	Eighth, Last	51	102	.333

Cleveland—National League

Year	Position	Won	Lost	Pc.
1895	Second	84	46	.646
1896	Second	80	48	.625
1892	Second	93	56	.624
1893	Third	73	55	.570
1880	Third	47	37	.559
1883	Fourth	55	42	.567
1898	Fifth	81	68	.544
1897	Fifth	69	62	.527
1882	Fifth	42	40	.512
1891	Fifth	65	74	.468
1894	Sixth	68	61	.527
1889	Sixth	61	72	.459
1879	Sixth	24	53	.312
1881	Seventh	36	48	.429
1890	Seventh	44	88	.333
1884	Seventh	35	77	.313
1899	Twelfth, Last	20	134	.129

Cleveland— American Association

Year	Position	Won	Lost	Pc.
1888	Sixth	50	82	.378
1887	Eighth, Last	39	92	.298

Cleveland—Players' League

Year	Position	Won	Lost	Pc.
1890	Seventh	55	75	.423

Cleveland's Pennant Winning Team

1920, American League, Tris Speaker, manager—James Charles Jacob Bagby, J. Joseph Boehling, Raymond B. Caldwell, Robert William Clark, Stanley Coveleskie, H. Ellison, Tony Joseph Faeth, John Walter Mails, Guy Morton, Tim Murchison, Richard J. Niehaus and George Ernest Uhle, pitchers; Stephen Francis O'Neill, Leslie G. Nunamaker and Chester D. Thomas, catchers; George Henry Burns, Wheeler Rodgers Johnston, William A. Wambsganss, Raymond Johnson Chapman, Joseph Wheeler Sewell and William Lawrence Gardner, infielders; Charles D. Jamieson, John Gladstone Graney, Tris Speaker, Elmer John Smith and Joseph Wood, outfielders; Joseph Patton Evans and Harry Lunte, substitutes. Became world's champions by winning five out of seven games from Brooklyn.

Cleveland's Near Pennant Winner

1892, National League, Oliver P. Tebeau, manager—Denton J. Young, Henry Gruber, George B. Cuppy, John H. Shearon, Leon Viau, John G. Clarkson and George Davies, pitchers; John O'Connor, Charles L. Zimmer and John Joseph Doyle, catchers; Jacob Virtue, Clarence L. Childs, Oliver P. Tebeau and Edward J. McKean, infielders; Jesse C. Burkett, James Robert McAleer and George Stacey Davis, outfielders. Finished first in second part of season, second on whole of season. Failed to become champions by losing five games to Boston, first game of series having been 11-inning runless tie.

Detroit

Population—993,678.

Seating capacity of Navin Field, opened in 1912—25,000.

Major league experience—Eight consecutive years in National League, constantly in American League.

DETROIT became a National League city before it really had population enough to support a team, and eventually the City of Straits had to drop out of the parent organization and into slower company. When the old Western League was reorganized, in 1894, Detroit got back on the baseball map and it has been a most important spot on it ever since. The city has four championships and one world's title to show for its activities in fast company.

William H. Watkins' National League team of 1887 cleaned up the St. Louis Browns in the world's series, but the Hugh Jennings managed American League clubs of 1907, 1908 and 1909 never could win the blue ribbon event.

In its National League days, Detroit was famed for its hitters, particularly after the Big Four of Richardson, White, Rowe and Brouthers were bought from Buffalo (the entire Bisou outfit was brought to get these men), and in its American League career the city was first noted for the scrappy teams it had and later for Tyrus Raymond Cobb.

A new era in baseball dawned for Detroit when the Georgia Peach got really going, which was in 1907, under the handling and encouragement of Hugh Jennings. Jennings' most famous predecessor as manager of the Tigers was George Stallings. The National League nickname of the Detroits was Wolverines.

Record of Detroit's major league teams to 1921, inclusive:

VICTORIES, 2031—1605 in American League, 426 in National.

DEFEATS, 1948—1511 in American League, 437 in National.

Detroit—American League

Year	Position	Won	Lost	Pc.
1909	First	98	54	.645
1907	First	92	58	.613
1908	First	90	63	.588
1915	Second	100	54	.649
1911	Second	89	65	.578
1916	Third	87	67	.565
1910	Third	86	68	.558
1901	Third	74	61	.548
1905	Third	79	74	.516
1919	Fourth	80	60	.571
1914	Fourth	80	73	.523
1917	Fourth	78	75	.510
1903	Fifth	65	71	.478

Year	Position	Won	Lost	Pc.
1906	Sixth	71	78	.477
1921	Sixth	71	82	.464
1912	Sixth	69	84	.451
1913	Sixth	66	87	.431
1918	Seventh	55	71	.437
1904	Seventh	62	90	.408
1920	Seventh	61	93	.396
1902	Seventh	52	83	.385

Detroit—National League

Year	Position	Won	Lost	Pc.
1887	First	79	45	.637
1886	Second	87	36	.707
1881	Fourth	41	43	.488
1888	Fifth	68	63	.519
1882	Sixth	42	41	.506
1885	Sixth	41	67	.379
1883	Seventh	40	58	.408
1884	Eighth, Last	28	84	.250

Detroit's Pennant Winners

1887, National League, William Henry Watkins, manager—Charles H. Getzein, Charles B. Baldwin, George E. Weidman, Henry Gruber, Edward A. Beatin, Peter J. Conway and W. R. Burke, pitchers; Charles W. Bennett, Charles W. Ganzel and Charles Briody, catchers; Dennis L. Brouthers, Fred Dunlap, James L. White, William Shindle and John Charles Rowe, infielders; Edward H. Hanlon, A. Harding Richardson, Samuel L. Thompson and Lawrence C. Twitchell, outfielders; Thomas Flanigan, substitute. Became world's champions by winning 10 out of 15 games from St. Louis.

1907, American League, Hugh Ambrose Jennings, manager—William Edward Donovan, John Eubanks, Elijah Jones, Edward Henry Killian, George Mullin, Edward Siever, Robert Edgar Willett and _____ Malloy, pitchers; Charles Schmidt, James Peter Archer, Fred Payne and Ross E. Erwin, catchers; Claude Rossman, Herman Schaefer, Jeremiah Downs, William Coughlin and Charles T. O'Leary, infielders; David Jefferson Jones, Matthew McIntyre, Tyrus Raymond Cobb and Samuel Crawford, outfielders; Wade Hampton Killefer, substitute. Failed to become world's champions by losing four straight games to Chicago after playing 3 to 3 twelve-inning tie in first game of series.

1908, American League, Hugh Ambrose Jennings, manager—William Edward Donovan, Edward Henry Killian, George Mullin, Edward Siever, Oren Edgar Summers, George Franklin Suggs, Robert Edgar Willett, George L. Winter and _____ Malloy, pitchers; Charles Schmidt, J. Ira Thomas and Fred Payne, catchers; Claude Rossman, Herman Schaefer, Jeremiah Downs, William Coughlin and Charles T. O'Leary, infielders; David Jefferson Jones, Tyrus Raymond Cobb, Samuel Crawford and Matthew McIntyre, outfielders; Wade Hampton Killefer, substitute. Failed to become world's champions by losing four out of five games to Chicago.

1909, American League, Hugh Ambrose Jennings, manager—William Edward Donovan, Elijah Jones, Edward Henry Killian, Edward Francis Lafitte, George Mullen, Oren Edgar Summers, George Franklin Suggs, Robert Edgar Willett, Ralph Tecumseh Works, _____ Lelivelt and _____ Speer, pitchers;

Charles Schmidt, Oscar Stanage, Joseph Felix Casey and Henry Beckendorf, catchers; Thomas Jones, Claude Rossman, James C. Delehanty, Herman Schaefer, George J. Moriarty and Owen Bush, infielders; David Jefferson Jones, Tyrus Raymond Cobb, Samuel Crawford and Matthew McIntyre, outfielders; Charles T. O'Leary, Wade Hampton Killefer and Del Gainer, substitutes. Failed to become world's champions by losing four out of seven games to Pittsburgh.

Washington

Population—437,571.

Seating capacity of American League Park, 15,300.

Major league experience—Constantly in American League, 12 years (not consecutive) in National League, two years (not consecutive) in American Association, one year in Union Association.

WASHINGTON still has to float its first major league pennant. The National League gonfalon never was seriously menaced, but twice have the Senators, or the Nationals, as they call them now, made a noise like flag winners in the American.

The remark of Charles Dryden's about Washington being "First in war, first in peace and last in the American League," had force and truth to it until Clark Griffith's loyalty to the American League was rewarded by his being permitted to buy stock in the club. That was in 1912. That year and the next the Senators (Nationals, rather) finished second. They haven't been so high since and they never got nearly that high in the National. In the Association once they didn't finish (that was when the Unions drove them to Richmond on the run) and once they finished last.

Washington's baseball history has mainly to do with Walter Johnson. He has been pitching for that city's teams since 1907 and everybody has wanted to see him operate in a world's series. It is doubtful if he ever will. The Idaho Phenom had to wait until 1920 to pitch his first no-hit game. Without him baseball in Washington would not have flourished as it has.

Washington's most popular pitcher before Johnson was Jimmy McJames, a handsome Carolinian. He was sold for a song. Selling players for a song was what soured the fans on the men who ran National League teams there—the Wagners of Philadelphia.

Record of Washington's major league teams to 1921, inclusive:

VICTORIES, 2058—1383 in American League, 572 in National, 56 in Association, 47 in Union.

DEFEATS, 2966—1727 in American League, 1032 in National, 141 in Association, 66 in Union.

Washington— American League

Year	Position	Won	Lost	Pc.
1912	Second	91	61	.599
1913	Second	90	64	.584
1918	Third	72	56	.563
1914	Third	81	73	.526
1915	Fourth	85	68	.556
1921	Fourth	80	73	.523
1917	Fifth	74	79	.484
1901	Sixth	61	72	.459
1902	Sixth	68	84	.447
1916	Seventh	76	77	.497
1908	Seventh	67	85	.441
1910	Seventh	66	85	.437
1905	Seventh	64	87	.421
1911	Seventh	64	90	.416
1919	Seventh	56	84	.400
1906	Seventh	55	95	.367
1907	Eighth, Last	49	102	.325
1903	Eighth, Last	43	94	.314
1909	Eighth, Last	42	110	.276
1904	Eighth, Last	38	113	.251

Washington— National League

Year	Position	Won	Lost	Pc.
1897	Sixth (a)	61	71	.462
1887	Seventh	46	76	.377
1888	Eighth, Last	48	86	.358
1889	Eighth, Last	41	83	.331
1886	Eighth, Last	28	92	.233
1896	Ninth (b)	58	73	.443
1892	Tenth	58	93	.384
1895	Tenth	43	85	.336
1899	Eleventh	53	95	.358
1894	Eleventh	45	87	.341
1898	Eleventh	51	101	.335
1893	Twelfth, Last	40	90	.308

(a) Tied with Brooklyn.
(b) Tied with Brooklyn.

Washington— American Association

Year	Position	Won	Lost	Pc.
1891	Eighth, Last	44	90	.328
1884	Did not finish	12	51	

Washington— Union Association

Year	Position	Won	Lost	Pc.
1884	Fifth	47	66	.416

Washington's Near Pennant Winners

TEAMS FINISHING SECOND

1912, American League, Clark Calvin Griffith, manager—Walter Perry Johnson, Robert B. Groom, Thomas J. Hughes, J. Carl Cashion, James L. Vaughn, Joseph W. Engel, Barney Pelty, J. Joseph Boehling, Paul Musser, Nicholas Altrock, Melvin Albert Gallia, E. Walker, Jerry Akers, Becker, Schehg, Herring and White, pitchers; John P. Henry, Edward Ainsmith, Alva G. Williams and John B. Ryan, catchers; C. Arnold Gandil, Ray Caryll Morgan, Edward Cunningham Foster and George Florian McBride, infielders; Howard S. Shanks, Daniel E. Moeller, Jesse Clyde Milan and Clarence Walker, outfielders; John Anthony Flynn, Herman Schaefer, John W. Knight, Wilbur Roach, Joseph A. Agler, Frank Laporte, William B. Kenworthy and Cunningham, substitutes.

1913, American League, Clark Calvin Griffith, manager—Walter Perry Johnson, Robert B. Groom, Thomas J. Hughes, Joseph W. Engel, J. Joseph Boehling, Nicholas Altrock, Melvin Albert Gallia, Yancey W. Ayers, John Needles Bentley, George Mullin, E. C. Love, Harry C. Harper, Thomas Drohan and James Aloysius Shaw, pitchers; John P. Henry, Edward Ainsmith, Alva G. Williams, catchers; C. Arnold Gan-

dil, Ray Caryll Morgan, Edward Cunningham Foster and George Florian McBride, infielders; Howard S. Shanks, Daniel E. Moeller and Jesse Clyde Milan, outfielders; Frank Laporte, Herman Schaefer, Joseph Gedeon, Balmadero Acosta and Jacinto Calvo, substitutes.

Baltimore

BALTIMORE (population 733,826), now in the International League, firmly believes it belongs in fast company. Barring a brief time spent in the Atlantic Association in 1890, the city was always in the American Association; it had a team in the National League when that organization had a 12-club circuit; it was a Federal League stronghold, so much so that John Dunn had to move his International League team to Richmond; it supported American League ball well for two years and it went through the Union Association season successfully.

Still no place can be found in the majors for Babe Ruth's home town and the fans of that city, in consequence, have no use for the big fellows and foam at the mouth whenever the draft is talked of.

Baltimore, under Ned Hanlon, won three National League pennants in succession in the middle nineties, then finished twice in succession and then most of the stars were sold to Brooklyn

and consolidated with that club. John McGraw and Wilbert Robinson were left and the Little Napoleon promptly proceeded to develop a club that made trouble for everyone.

When the National League and the American League split in 1901, McGraw and Robinson got the Baltimore franchise, McGraw had trouble with B. B. Johnson, left the junior league and finally most of the stars jumped. John T. Brush, acting for the National pulled a coup and a bone at the same time in getting the franchise and then failing to operate it.

Baltimore's Record in the majors:

VICTORIES, 1436—National 642, Association 489, Federal 131, American 118, Union 56.

DEFEATS, 1423—Association 602, National 443, Federal 177, American 153, Union 48.

Baltimore—National League

Year	Position	Won	Lost	Pc.
1896	First	90	39	.698
1894	First	89	39	.695
1895	First	87	43	.669
1897	Second	90	40	.693
1898	Second	96	53	.644
1899	Fourth	84	58	.591
1893	Eighth	60	70	.462
1892	Twelfth, Last	46	101	.313

Baltimore—American League

Year	Position	Won	Lost	Pc.
1901	Fifth	68	65	.511
1902	Eighth, Last	50	88	.362

Baltimore— American Association

Year	Position	Won	Lost	Pc.
1887	Third	77	58	.570
1891	Fourth	71	64	.526
1889	Fifth	70	65	.519
1888	Fifth	57	80	.416
1884	Sixth	63	43	.594
1890	Sixth	15	19	.441
1882	Sixth, Last	19	54	.260
1885	Eighth, Last	41	68	.376
1886	Eighth, Last	48	83	.366
1883	Eighth, Last	28	68	.292

Baltimore—Federal League

Year	Position	Won	Lost	Pc.
1914	Third	84	70	.545
1915	Eighth, Last	47	107	.305

Baltimore— Union Association

Year	Position	Won	Lost	Pc.
1884	Third	56	48	.538

Baltimore's Pennant Winners

1894, National League, Edward H. Hanlon, manager—Charles Esper, William Gleason, William V. Hawke, George Earl Hemming, Albert Preston Inks, John J. McMahon, A. J. Mullane, _____ Brown and _____ Horner, pitchers; Wilbert Robinson and William J. Clarke, catchers; Dennis L. Brouthers, Henry P. Reitz, John J. McGraw and Hugh Ambrose Jennings, infielders; Joseph James Kelley, Walter Stephenson Brodie and William H. Keeler, outfielders; Frank J. Bonner, substitute. Failed to become champions of the world by losing all four games of Temple Cup series to New York.

1895, National League, Edward H. Hanlon, manager—Arthur Clarkson, Charles Esper, George Earl Hemming, William L. Hoffer, _____ Kissinger, John J. McMahon, and _____ Pond, pitchers; Wilbert Robinson and William J. Clarke, catchers; Dennis L. Brouthers, George Carey, Henry P. Reitz, William Gleason, John J. McGraw and Hugh Ambrose Jennings, infielders; Joseph James Kelley, Walter Stephenson Brodie and William H. Keeler, outfielders; Frank J. Bonner, substitute. Failed to become champions of the world by losing four out of five games of Temple Cup series to Cleveland.

1896, National League, Edward H. Hanlon, manager—Joseph Corbett, Arthur Clarkson, Charles Esper, George Earl Hemming, William L. Hoffer, John J. McMahon, Jeremiah Nops and

_____ Pond, pitchers; Wilbert Robinson and William J. Clarke, catchers; John Joseph Doyle, Henry P. Reitz, James J. Donnelly, John J. McGraw and Hugh Ambrose Jennings, infielders; Joseph James Kelley, Walter Stephenson Brodie and William H. Keeler, outfielders; Joseph J. Quinn, substitute. Became champions of the world by winning four straight games of Temple Cup series from Cleveland.

Buffalo

BUFFALO (population 506,775), now in the International League, had three flings at big league ball. Each was costly for the men who footed the bills. The Bisons were in the National for seven years, dropping out at the end of the 1885 season, when Detroit purchased the Big Four—Richardson, White, Rowe and Brouthers. Buffalo was in the Players' League the one year of its existence and that club, with Connie Mack as one of its catchers and stockholders, lost money and drove the rival International League to Montreal and then to Bay City. The Federal League, operating for two years in Buffalo, made no money, but did bankrupt the rival Ints. No Buffalo major league team ever got higher than third. The record of the city's fast set teams:

VICTORIES, 502—312 in National League, 154 in Federal, 36 in Players'.

DEFEATS, 578—333 in National League, 149 in Federal, 96 in Players'.

Buffalo—National League

Year	Position	Won	Lost	Pc.
1879	Third (a)	44	32	.579
1884	Third	64	47	.577
1881	Third	45	38	.542
1882	Third (b)	45	39	.536
1883	Fifth	52	45	.536
1885	Seventh	38	74	.339
1880	Seventh	24	58	.293

(a)—Tied with Chicago.
(b)—Tied with Boston.

Buffalo—Federal League

Year	Position	Won	Lost	Pc.
1914	Fourth	80	71	.530
1915	Sixth	74	78	.487

Buffalo—Players' League

Year	Position	Won	Lost	Pc.
1890	Eighth, Last	36	96	.273

Buffalo's Nearest Pennant Winner

1879, National League—James F. Galvin, pitcher; Clapp, catcher; Walker, C. Fulmer, A. Harding Richardson and David Force, infielders; Joseph Hornung, Eggler and Crowley, outfielders.

Columbus

COLUMBUS (population 237,031), now in the American Association, had five years of big league ball, all in one organization—the old American Association. The Senators never won a pennant in that, but twice they finished second. The Columbus team of 1884 was practically sold entire to Pittsburgh. Ned Morris was its star pitcher, Fred Carroll its star catcher and Tom Brown its star outfielder and base runner. Said team was too expensive a luxury for Columbus in those days. Columbus teams won 301 and lost 313 games in the old Association for an average of .490.

Columbus— American Association

Year	Position	Won	Lost	Pc.
1884	Second	69	39	.639
1890	Second	79	55	.590
1891	Sixth	61	76	.445
1889	Sixth	60	78	.435
1883	Sixth	32	65	.330

Columbus' Near Pennant Winners

TEAMS FINISHING SECOND

1884, American Association, Gustavus Heinrich Schmelz, manager—Edward Morris, Frank H. Mountain and Edward J. Dundon, pitchers; Fred H. Carroll and Rudolph Kemmler, catchers; James Field, Charles M. Smith, William J. Kuehne and John Richmond, infielders; Thomas T. Brown, Fred T. Mann, John Patrick Cahill and Thomas Mansell, outfielders.

1890, American Association, Albert C. Buckenberger, manager—Frank Knauss, Henry C. Gastright, Elton T. Chamberlain, John E. Easton and William W. Widner, pitchers; John O'Connor, John Joseph Doyle and Edward F. Bligh, catchers; Michael M. Lehane, Charles John Crooks, Charles T. Reilly, Harry Esterday and Warren H. Wheelock, infielders; James McTamany, J. Ralph Johnson and John L. Sneed, outfielders.

Indianapolis

INDIANAPOLIS (population 314,194), now in the American Association, was in the National League a couple of times, in the old Association for one year and in the Federal League for one year. The Feds of 1914 were the only collection of athletes Hoosier fans could be proud of, but their pride profited them little, as the next season Roush, Kauff & Co. had been moved Eastward. The cellar, or distinctly near it, was the reposing place of most of Indianapolis' major league clubs. Frank Flint, great catcher, was a graduate of an Indianapolis club, so was Amos Rusie, wonderful pitcher. Benny Kauff and Ed Roush got their chances to deliver in Indianapolis while the Feds were presenting the pastime to the objection and horror of O. B.—and delivered.

The record of Indianapolis' major league teams:

VICTORIES, 287—170 in National League, 88 in Federal, 29 in Association.

DEFEATS, 428—285 in National League, 78 in Association, 65 in Federal.

Indianapolis—
National League

Year	Position	Won	Lost	Pc.
1878	Fifth	24	36	.400
1889	Seventh	59	75	.440
1888	Seventh	50	85	.370
1887	Eighth, Last	37	89	.294

Indianapolis—
Federal League

Year	Position	Won	Lost	Pc.
1914	First	88	65	.575

Indianapolis—
American Association

Year	Position	Won	Lost	Pc.
1884	Twelfth, Last	29	78	.271

Indianapolis' One
Pennant Winner

1914, Federal League, William Phillips, manager—Harry P. Billiard, George Kaiserling, Fred Harter, Earl Victor Mosely, Fred P. Falkenberg, Edward Henderson, Kiefer, George Mullin, A. J. McConnaughey, Charles Whitehouse, Ossendorf and Wood, pitchers; William A. Rariden, George Texter and W. H. Warren, catchers; Charles C. Karr, William B. McKechnie, Frank Rooney, Carl Vandergrift, Frank Laporte, James J. Esmond and M. L. Dolan, infielders; Benjamin Michael Kauff, Edward J. Roush, A. Vincent Campbell, Al Scheer and Albert Kaiser, outfielders. As Federal League was not recognized by Organized Ball, team played in no world's series.

Kansas City

KANSAS CITY (population 324,410), now in the American Association, never has particularly cared for major league baseball, because its major league teams never have been anywhere nearly as good as its minor league teams. The Federals of 1915 alone finished in the first division and stand alone of the six Cowboy teams of supposed major league caliber in having won more games than they lost. Kansas City furnished Herman Long, great shortstop, and William Hamilton, equally great base runner, to fast company. The record of Kansas City's major league teams:

VICTORIES, 291—Federal 149, Association 98, National 30, Union 14.

DEFEATS, 481—Association 171, Federal 156, National 91, Union 63.

Kansas City— National League

Year	Position	Won	Lost	Pc.
1886	Seventh	30	91	.247

Kansas City— American Association

Year	Position	Won	Lost	Pc.
1889	Seventh	55	82	.401
1888	Eighth, Last	43	89	.326

Kansas City—Federal League

Year	Position	Won	Lost	Pc.
1915	Fourth	81	72	.533
1914	Sixth	68	84	.447

Kansas City— Union Association

Year	Position	Won	Lost	Pc.
1884	Sixth, Last	14	63	.182

Kansas City's Nearest Pennant Winner

TEAM FINISHING FOURTH

1915, Federal League, George Thomas Stovall, manager—Norman A. Cullop, George Johnson, Eugene Packard, Miles Main and Henning, pitchers; Theodore Harrison Easterly and D. Brown, catchers; George Thomas Stovall, George Perring, William J. Bradley, William B. Kenworthy, John William Rawlings and Goodwin, infielders; Grover Gilmore, Chester Chadbourne, Krueger and Shaw, outfielders.

Louisville

LOUISVILLE (population 234,891), now in the American Association, was relegated to slow company when the National League reduced its circuit from twelve to eight clubs at the end of the season of 1899. Thus did Barney Dreyfuss acquire the Pirates and the Pirates acquired John Peter Wagner, better known as Honus Wagner. The Falls City was constantly in the old American Association and put in 10 years in the National, too. Some Colonels of the early days were like certain White Socks of 1919—guilty of throwing games. Early in its big league career Louisville had a wonderful batting pitcher in Hecker and before Sir Guy lost either his clouting or curving ability another top-notcher joined them in the person of Thomas Ramsey, eminent strike-out king. However, neither Hecker nor Ramsey could pitch the Colonels to a pennant, but they got one in 1890. Louisville's major league teams won 1054 and lost 1374 games for an average of .434. Their record:

VICTORIES, 1054—577 in American Association, 477 in National League.

DEFEATS, 1374—739 in National League, 634 in American Association.

Louisville—National League

Year	Position	Won	Lost	Pc.
1877	Second	28	20	.583
1876	Fifth	30	36	.455
1899	Ninth	75	77	.493

Year	Position	Won	Lost	Pc.
1898	Ninth	70	81	.464
1892	Ninth	63	89	.414
1897	Eleventh	52	78	.400
1893	Eleventh	50	75	.400
1896	Twelfth, Last	38	93	.290
1894	Twelfth, Last	36	94	.277
1895	Twelfth, Last	35	96	.267

Louisville— American Association

Year	Position	Won	Lost	Pc.
1890	First	88	44	.667
1882	Second	44	35	.557
1884	Third	68	40	.630
1887	Fourth	76	60	.559
1886	Fourth	66	70	.485
1883	Fifth	52	45	.536
1885	Fifth (a)	53	59	.473
1891	Seventh	55	84	.396
1888	Seventh	48	87	.360
1889	Eighth, Last	27	111	.195

(a)—Tied with Brooklyn.

Louisville's One Pennant Winner

1890, American Association, John Curtis Chapman, manager—C. Scott Stratton, Herbert F. Goodall, Edward M. Daily, Philip H. Ehret and George C. Meakin, pitchers; John B. Ryan, Edward F. Bligh and Peter Weckbecker, catchers; Harry L. Taylor, Timothy J. Shinnick, Harry H. Raymond, Philip H. Tomney and Harry Esterday, infielders; Charles M. Hamburg, William B. Weaver and William V. Wolf, outfielders;

J. J. Roseman, substitute. Won three and lost three games in world's series with Brooklyn, third game of set being a tie and series being called off without decision being reached on account of bad weather and lack of public interest.

Newark

NEWARK (population 414,524), now in the International League, had a major league club for one year, in the Federal League of 1915, and it still has a major league plant, at Harrison. The Newark Feds were not a paying proposition, but their owner—Harry F. Sinclair—did not assign for the benefit of creditors after the season closed. The Jerseymen, in their one year in fast company, won 80 and lost 72 games for an average of .526. One of said Jerseymen was Edward J. Roush, noted hitter, noted holdout.

agers—Chester M. Brandom, George Mullin, Harry Moran, George Kaiserling, Harry P. Billiard, Fred P. Falkenberg, Charles E. Whitehouse, Thomas Gordon Seaton, Earl Victor Mosely, Edward Marvin Reulbach and Trautman, pitchers; William A. Rariden, Lawrence Pratt, W. H. Warren and George Texter, catchers; Emil Huhn, William B. McKechnie, James J. Edmond, Herman Schaefer, Hugh F. Bradley, Rupert Mills, Frank Laporte, John Lawrence Strands and Reed, infielders; Edward J. Roush, A. Vincent Campbell, Al Scheer and George Whitehouse, outfielders.

Newark—Federal League

Year	Position	Won	Lost	Pc.
1915	Fifth	80	72	.526

Newark's One Major League Team

FINISHED FIFTH

1915, Federal League, William Phillips and William B. McKechnie, man-

Milwaukee

MILWAUKEE (population 457,147), now in the American Association, has supported minor league clubs better than it has major league clubs. The Brewers were in the National League for one year, in the American League for one (being replaced by St. Louis), in the old American Association for part of one season and in the Union Association for possibly two weeks. Milwaukee, when it entered the American Association (the old Association) in 1891, took Cincinnati's place. That club was the most successful major league club the city ever had, the Union Association team not being considered because of the fact it did not finish its season. However, even if Milwaukee cannot support fast set teams it has furnished the majors of the past and present with some of their greatest stars, notably Clark Griffith, Jim McAleer, Rube Waddell and Ray Schalk. And Connie Mack came back to fast company from Milwaukee, too. Milwaukee's major league teams won 97 and lost 153 games for a percentage of .388.

Milwaukee— National League

Year	Position	Won	Lost	Pc.
1878	Sixth, Last	15	45	.250

Milwaukee— American League

Year	Position	Won	Lost	Pc.
1901	Eighth, Last	48	89	.350

Milwaukee— American Association

Year	Position	Won	Lost	Pc.
1891	Third	26	16	.619

Milwaukee— Union Association

Year	Position	Won	Lost	Pc.
1884	Did not finish	8	3	

Milwaukee's Nearest Pennant Winner

TEAM FINISHED THIRD

1891, American Association—John Francis Dwyer, Frank B. Killen, James Hughey, William Mains and George Davies, pitchers; Harry Vaughn and John H. Grim, catchers; John J. Carney, James Canavan, Robert H. Pettit and George Schoch, infielders; Abner F. Dalrymple, Edward Burke and William Earle, outfielders.

Rochester

ROCHESTER (population 295,750), now in the International League, put in one full season in the majors as a member of the American Association in 1890, which was the year of the fight between the players and the magnates. When the war ended Rochester dropped back to its natural place on the baseball map. Patrick T. Powers, for years president of the organization Rochester now is in, managed its city's only big league team. Rochester, in 1921, under the Stallings–Hapgood regime, showed major league attendance, with a total of over 250,000.

Rochester's Only Major League Team

1890 American Association, Patrick T. Powers, manager—Robert M. Barr, William T. Callihan, Ledell Titcomb, John J. Fitzgerald and Robert Miller, pitchers; James Thomas McGuire, David J. McKeough and John H. Grim, catchers; James Field, Thomas H. O'Brien, William D. O'Brien, William H. Greenwood, James Knowles and Marr B. Phillips, infielders; T. C. Griffin, Harry P. Lyons, Theodore J. Scheffler and Daniel L. Burke, outfielders; George Smith, substitute.

Rochester— American Association

Year	Position	Won	Lost	Pc.
1890	Fifth	63	63	.500

St. Paul

ST. PAUL (population 234,698), now in the American Association, had an eight game career in the Union Association in 1884, joining that outlaw organization after the Northwestern League season closed. Of the eight games played by the Apostles two were won and six lost for a percentage of .250. Charles Ganzel, catcher, and Joseph Werrick, shortstop, were the best known players of St. Paul's one and only major league club.

St. Paul—Union Association

Year	Position	Won	Lost	Pc.
1884	Did not finish	2	6	

St. Paul's Only
Major League Team

DID NOT FINISH

1884, American Association, George Kasson Frazer, manager—Daniel M. Casey, Charles McCulloch, Michael Morrison, Edward Mars, Toby A. Lyons, J. T. Keefe and Sullivan, pitchers; Grant Briggs, Herman Pitz and Patrick E. Dealy, catchers; William Max McQuery, Clarence L. Childs, Tim O'Rourke, Joseph V. Battin, Marr B. Phillips and Barney McLaughlin, infielders; Henry Simon, Michael J. Dorgan, Patrick H. Friel, W. Fred Ely, William H. Wright and Peltz, outfielders.

Toledo

TOLEDO (population 243,164), now in the American Association, put in two years in that organization when it was competing with the National League for patronage. One of these years was 1884, the other 1890. The earliest Toledo club was a flivver in every way, but the last fared well on the diamond and was well supported in a year when the baseball business was decidedly off. A star Toledo pitcher back in 1884 was Hank O'Day, veteran umpire now. Hank wasn't as good, though, as his box associate—Tony Mullane. Toledo's fast set teams won 114 and lost 122 games for an average of .483.

Toledo's Nearest
Pennant Winner

FINISHED FOURTH

1890 American Association, Charles M. Morton, manager—Edward L. Cushman, Fred C. Smith, Charles W. Sprague and John Healy, pitchers; Harry Sage, Emmett Rogers and James T. Welch, catchers; Perry W. Werden, Thomas C. Nicholson, William Alvord and Frank Shiebeck, infielders; John Peltz, George E. Tebeau, William H. VanDyke, John L. Sneed and Charles Edward Swartwood, outfielders.

Toledo—
American Association

Year	Position	Won	Lost	Pc.
1890	Fourth	68	64	.515
1884	Eighth	46	58	.442

Hartford

HARTFORD (population 138,036), now in the Eastern League, was a charter member of the National League, lasted two years in it and its teams always were in the running. It was in Hartford that two games in one day were played for the first time in the National League, and as the attendance at each was miserable perhaps the backers of the Hartford club then saw the handwriting on the wall. It was a Hartford team that ran into the first no-hit game in the National League and it would have been a Hartford player—Bob Ferguson—who first made a triple play unassisted but for one trifling thing—there was one man defunct when he put out three of his opponents without aid. Hartford's National League teams won 71 and lost 45 games for a percentage of .612.

Hartford—National League

Year	Position	Won	Lost	Pc.
1876	Second	47	21	.691
1877	Third	24	24	.500

Hartford's Nearest Pennant Winner

TEAM FINISHING SECOND

1876 National League—Thomas Bond and W. A. Cummings, pitchers; Douglas Allison and W. H. Harbridge, catchers; E. Mills, John J. Burdock, Thomas J. Carey and Robert Ferguson, infielders; J. J. Remsen, Thomas York and R. Higham, outfielders.

Worcester

WORCESTER (population 179,754), with no representation in professional baseball now, had three years' experience in the National in the early days of that organization. The team never threatened to win the championship, but it was feared by its opponents because of its wonderful left-handed pitcher—J. Lee Richmond, first of the really great southpaws. Worcester's victories in three years in the National numbered 90, as against 159 defeats, for a percentage of .361.

Worcester—National League

Year	Position	Won	Lost	Pc.
1880	Fifth	40	43	.482

Year	Position	Won	Lost	Pc.
1881	Eighth, Last	32	50	.390
1882	Eighth, Last	18	66	.214

Worcester's Nearest Pennant Winner

TEAM FINISHING FIFTH

1880, National League—J. Lee Richmond and Fred Corey, pitchers; Charles W. Bennett and A. J. Bushong, catchers; Sullivan, Creamer, Arthur Albert Irwin and Arthur W. Whitney, infielders; Harry D. Stovey, George A. Wood, Lewis Dickerson, Michael J. Dorgan and Alonzo Knight, outfielders; Nichols, substitute.

Richmond

RICHMOND (population 171,667), now in the Virginia League, kept company with the big fellows for part of one year—1884. Then Washington showed its preference for Union Association as against American Association ball and Richmond, with its team known as the Virginias, seceded from the Eastern League to take the Senators' place. Two good players among the Virginias were Billy Nash, third baseman, and Dick Johnston, outfielder. The Virginias played their first game in the American Association on August 5 and finished with a record of .285, derived from 12 victories and 30 defeats. Pittsburgh (the Alleghenys then) and Indianapolis didn't do so well.

Richmond— American Association

Year	Position	Won	Lost	Pc.
1884	Tenth	12	30	.286

Richmond's Only Major League Team

1884, American Association—Edward Dugan, Peter Meegan and Curry, pitchers; William Dugan, Marshall Quinton, Henry Morgan and W. V. Hanna, catchers; Abner F. Powell, Ford, A. J. Swann, Frank Larkins, William M. Nash and William G. Schenck, infielders; Edward C. Glenn, Richard F. Johnston, Walton H. Goldsby, Michael R. Mansell and W. Williams, outfielders.

Altoona

ALTOONA (population 60,331), nowhere on the baseball map now, was a major league city for a trifle over a month back in 1884. It had a team in the Union Association, said team lasting until May 31 and then disbanding after having won six and lost 19 games for a percentage of .240. The Pennsylvanian's shortstop—George J. Smith—later was a major league head-liner for years.

Altoona—Union Association

Year	Position	Won	Lost	Pc.
1884	Did not finish	6	19	

Altoona's Only Major League Team

DID NOT FINISH

1884, Union Association, E. Curtis, manager—James W. Brown and Jerry Moore, pitchers; George W. Noftsker and Carroll, catchers; John Grady, Charles Dougherty, Charles Berry, Harry Coons and George J. Smith, infielders; Harris, Frank Shaffer and John Leary, outfielders.

Providence

PROVIDENCE (population 237,595), with no representation anywhere in professional baseball now, spent eight artistically successful seasons in the National League and twice its teams finished in front, carrying off the red ribbon three times and never occupying a lower position in the pennant pursuit than fourth. The Rhode Islanders' best known club was that of 1884, when Charles Radbourne, compelled to pitch almost all its games after the defection of Charles Sweeney to the St. Louis Union Association team, did so and hung up a wonderful record for endurance. Providence occasionally is represented in the International League now (in the winter time); it belongs somewhere on the baseball map. Providence National League teams won 434 and lost 276 games for a percentage of .611.

Providence— National League

Year	Position	Won	Lost	Pc.
1884	First	84	28	.750
1879	First	55	23	.705
1880	Second	52	32	.619
1882	Second	52	32	.619

Year	Position	Won	Lost	Pc.
1881	Second	47	37	.559
1883	Third	58	40	.592
1878	Third	33	27	.550
1885	Fourth	53	57	.481

Providence's Pennant Winners

1879, National League, George Wright, manager—Robert Matthews and John Montgomery Ward, pitchers; Lewis J. Brown, Emil M. Gross and Kemmler, catchers; Joseph Start, Michael H. McGeary, William L. Hague, John Farrell and George Wright, infielders; Thomas York, James H. O'Rourke, Paul Hines and O'Leary, outfielders.

1884, National League, Frank C. Bancroft, manager—Charles Radbourne and Charles Sweeney, pitchers; Vincent Nava and Barney Gilligan, catchers; Joseph Start, John Farrell, Jeremiah Denny and Arthur Albert Irwin, infielders; Paul Hines, S. Clifford Carroll and Paul Revere Radford, outfielders; Conley, Harry Arundel and Daily, extra battery men, Conley and Arundel each pitching one game and Daily catching one game. Became world's champions by winning three straight games from New York (Metropolitans).

Troy

Troy (population 72,013), with no representation on a minor league circuit now, was for four years in the National League, the Trojans never being able to win half their games. They ceased being big leaguers at the end of the season of 1882, and thereafter Troy and the National League have only been associated in the thoughts of the fans as having been equally concerned in the career of John J. Evers, now Kid Gleason's assistant on the Chicago American League club. Troy's National League teams won 134 and lost 191 games for a percentage of .253.

Troy—National League

Year	Position	Won	Lost	Pc.
1880	Fourth	41	42	.494

Year	Position	Won	Lost	Pc.
1881	Fifth	39	45	.464
1882	Seventh	34	48	.422
1879	Seventh	19	56	.253

Troy's Nearest Pennant Winners

TEAM FINISHING FOURTH

1880, National League—Michael Welch and Larkin, pitchers; William Ewing, William H. Holbert and W. H. Harbridge, catchers; Roger Connor, Robert Ferguson, Coggswell and W. H. Caskin, infielders; Patrick Gillespie, Lewis Dickerson, Tobin and Cassidy, outfielders.

Wilmington

WILMINGTON (population 110,168) was a major league city for less than a month. That was in 1884. The Delawareans started the year in the Eastern League and deserted that organization to go into the Union Association, the Federal League of its time, on August 18. On September 12 Wilmington's stay in the majors terminated. The team won two of the 16 games it played in fast company for an average of .118.

Wilmington—Union Association

Year	Position	Won	Lost	Pc.
1884	Did not finish	2	15	

Wilmington's Only Major League Team

1884, Union Association, Joseph Simmons, manager—Thomas P. Burns, Dan P. Casey, James D. McElory, Edward T. Nolan and E. Bakely, pitchers; Andrew Cusick, McCloskey and Lynch, catchers; Snyder, Charles J. Bastian, Say, Cullen, Myers, Murphy and Fisher, infielders; Dennis Casey, Munce, Ryan, Benners and Tenney, outfielders.

◆ PART III ◆

Baseball's Leaders
and Title Holders

When the fan mentions baseball's leaders he doesn't speak of Judge Kenesaw Mountain Landis, Byron Bancroft Johnson, John Arnold Heydler or John Conway Toole, but he does speak of the able athletes who are at the top in hitting and other things and who have been the pace setters. One feature put out by an able dopester, "The Five Leading Hitters of the Big Leagues," appears probably in over one thousand papers each day of the playing season and the rabid fan of any small hamlet generally is as promptly informed as to the men who are setting the pace in swatting in the majors as the rabid fan of places of immensely greater population.

Most of the title holders of baseball are known by the record keepers, but there are still certain gaps in the archives to be pieced out, for the public prints, in the early days of the game, did not give it the prominence it now commands and the men who made out the averages were not as thorough in their work as they now are. Even if some of them did turn out complete sets of averages, these averages were quite likely to be edited almost to the vanishing point by those whose job it was to preserve the figures for posterity.

Gallant work on the part of certain archeologists in the last 15 years has brought to light a mass of valuable information, but much more still remains to be turned up before the statistical side of the game can be deemed near perfect.

Now one knows positively the batting leaders for all time in the major leagues, the men who have annually made the most sacrifices, and the men who have stolen the most bases annually, but that is all one does know positively.

With the data at their command the record keepers have been able to establish certain marks for the able athletes to keep shooting at, but only in a few isolated instances are the records complete.

One record that is complete is that of the leading hitters of the major leagues, for the compiling of averages dates as far back as 1865.

On Page 247 of Balldom, George Leonard Moreland says that prior to 1879 there was no record of how many hits a batter made in the National League. "All that can be found is the batting average for the first three seasons. * * * It was in 1881 when players were credited with having scored a run. Not until 1886 is any credit given for stealing a base. It was three years later when sacrifice hits were credited."

Mr. Moreland was right in his remarks about steals and sacrifices, but wrong in his comments as to hits and runs.

The National League averages of 1878 did carry the runs and hits and it is possible that this information was carried in the two earlier years as well—and eliminated from the guides by that demon eliminator—Henry Chadwick.

Mr. Chadwick edited the National League averages so thoroughly several years that now, when National League headquarters is asked for certain early data said queries have to be passed on to others to be answered.

However, all the batting leaders of the major leagues are known, though all authorities do not agree as to their identity. Pitchers have led the National League in hitting, but historians pass them up when writing on this subject and award the place of honor to a regular.

The World Almanac names Zach Wheat of Brooklyn as the leading hitter of the National League in 1918 and yet William H. Southworth of Pittsburgh that year had an average six points higher than the Superba, playing in 64 games to his 105.

For the American League season of ten years earlier the World Almanac makes Dode Criss of St. Louis the Mauling Monarch in preference to Tyrus Raymond Cobb. Criss was in 64 games, Cobb in 150, and in a majority of the games Criss was in, he was merely a pinch-hitter.

And around that time, unless the writer is mistaken, the National League didn't count a man as being in a game unless he was in it as a defensive participant as well as an offensive performer.

Any 12 men, making up lists of the leading hitters of the major leagues for all time from the baseball guides, will make up 12 different lists.

O'Neill's Mark of .492 Not a Real Mark

The highest batting average credited to a major league player—the .492 belonging to James F. O'Neill of the St. Louis Browns of 1887 is really not the highest real mark, for that year batters received base hits when they got passes. Once the writer checked, as far as he could, the performance of Tip the First and found that if the passes were taken away from him he would have batted in the neighborhood of .400.

And if Babe Ruth in 1921 had received a hit for every pass he received and had been charged with a time at bat his record, instead of being merely .378, would have been .509.

Furthermore, O'Neill, in 1887, was getting four strikes instead of three.

In 1888, with the strikes numbering three again and with bases on balls no longer counting as hits, O'Neill, who was a Canadian, a native of Woodstock, Ontario, was able to acquire an average of only .332.

There was no question about O'Neill not being a hard hitter. He batted right handed and could slam them against the fences. There was a trace of tuberculosis in his family and Jim always was afraid he would get the dread disease. He never did and died of heart failure in Montreal about 15 years ago, quitting the game in 1892 and thereafter never doing anything in it except umpire. O'Neill was originally a pitcher and as such was more or less a failure with the old Mets. He is generally called Tip the First by the writers, but Norris L. O'Neil, former president of the Western League, says that he was Tip I and that James F. was Tip II. Tip III was William John O'Neill, infield and outfielder, briefly with the Boston Red Sox and the Chicago White Sox (and

with Washington, too) in the early days of the American League.

Tip O'Neill III wasn't much of a hitter in the majors and he didn't startle the populace as fielder, either, for on May 21, 1904, when he was subbing for Fred Parent at short, he committed six misplays in a 13-inning game in which the Red Sox and Browns engaged.

Getting back to the subject of batting leaders, Hugh Duffy's .438 in 1894 is the real Simon pure high mark, with Tyrus Raymond Cobb's .420 in 1911 as the modern mark. When Duff was on the rampage the pitchers had just been set back ten and a half feet and when the Peach was going at his fastest clip the cork centered sphere had just made its appearance.

The averages of the leading hitters range from .492 to .320, and in the list presented below you will find the name of Tyrus Raymond Cobb 12 times. The figures:

Year	Player	Club	League	Pc.
1887	James F. O'Neill	St. Louis	Association	*.492
1894	Hugh Duffy	Boston	National	.438
1897	William H. Keeler	Baltimore	National	.432
1895	Jesse C. Burkett	Cleveland	National	.423
1887	Adrian C. Anson	Chicago	National	*.421
1884	Fred C. Dunlap	St. Louis	Union	.420
1911	Tyrus R. Cobb	Detroit	American	.420
1896	Jesse C. Burkett	Cleveland	National	.410
1912	Tyrus R. Cobb	Detroit	American	.410
1893	Jacob Stenzel	Pittsburgh	National	.409
1884	Thomas Esterbrook	New York	Association	.408
1899	Edward J. Delahanty	Philadelphia	National	.408
1879	Adrian C. Anson	Chicago	National	.407
1920	George H. Sisler	St. Louis	American	.407
1901	Napoleon Lajoie	Philadelphia	American	.405
1876	Ross Barnes	Chicago	National	.403
1881	Adrian C. Anson	Chicago	National	.399
1921	Rogers Hornsby	St. Louis	National	.397

Year	Player	Club	League	Pc.
1921	Harold E. Heilmann	Detroit	American	.394
1890	Louis R. Browning	Cleveland	Players'	.391
1913	Tyrus R. Cobb	Detroit	American	.390
1886	Michael J. Kelly	Chicago	National	.388
1916	Tris E. Speaker	Cleveland	American	.386
1877	James L. White	Boston	National	.385
1910	Tyrus R. Cobb	Detroit	American	.385
1919	Tyrus R. Cobb	Detroit	American	.384
1917	Tyrus R. Cobb	Detroit	American	.383
1882	Louis R. Browning	Louisville	Association	.382
1901	Jesse C. Burkett	St. Louis	National	.382
1918	Tyrus R. Cobb	Detroit	American	.382
1904	Napoleon Lajoie	Cleveland	American	.381
1900	John P. Wagner	Pittsburgh	National	.380
1898	William H. Keller	Baltimore	National	.379
1905	J. Bentley Seymour	Cincinnati	National	.377
1909	Tyrus R. Cobb	Detroit	American	.377
1902	Edward J. Delahanty	Washington	American	.376
1889	Thomas J. Tucker	Baltimore	Association	.375
1889	Dennis L. Brouthers	Boston	National	.373
1912	Henry Zimmerman	Chicago	National	.372
1883	Dennis L. Brouthers	Buffalo	National	.371
1885	Roger Connor	New York	National	.371
1915	Tyrus R. Cobb	Detroit	American	.370
1920	Rogers Hornsby	St. Louis	National	.370
1883	Charles E. Swartwood	Pittsburgh	Association	.368
1914	Tyrus R. Cobb	Detroit	American	.368
1882	Dennis L. Brouthers	Buffalo	National	.367
1885	Louis R. Browning	Louisville	Association	.367
1890	William V. Wolfe	Louisville	Association	.366
1914	Benjamin M. Kauff	Indianapolis	Federal	.366
1880	George F. Gore	Chicago	National	.365
1906	Jay J. Clarke	Cleveland	American	.358
1906	George R. Stone	St. Louis	American	.358
1902	Clarence H. Beaumont	Pittsburgh	National	.357
1878	Abner F. Dalrymple	Milwaukee	National	.356
1903	Napoleon Lajoie	Cleveland	American	.355
1903	John P. Wagner	Pittsburgh	National	.355
1908	John P. Wagner	Pittsburgh	National	.354
1884	James H. O'Rourke	Buffalo	National	.350
1907	Tyrus R. Cobb	Detroit	American	.350
1907	John P. Wagner	Pittsburgh	National	.350
1913	Jacob E. Daubert	Brooklyn	National	.350
1891	Dennis L. Brouthers	Boston	Association	.349
1904	John P. Wagner	Pittsburgh	National	.349
1886	David Orr	New York	Association	.346
1915	Benjamin M. Kauff	Brooklyn	Federal	.344
1888	Adrian C. Anson	Chicago	National	.343
1917	Edward J. Roush	Cincinnati	National	.341

Year	Player	Club	League	Pc.
1918	William H. Southworth	Pittsburgh	National	.341
1919	C. C. Cravath	Philadelphia	National	.341
1906	John P. Wagner	Pittsburgh	National	.339
1909	John P. Wagner	Pittsburgh	National	.339
1916	Harold H. Chase	Cincinnati	National	.339
1891	William R. Hamilton	Philadelphia	National	.338
1890	John W. Glasscock	New York	National	.336
1892	Clarence L. Childs	Cleveland	National	.335
1892	Dennis L. Brouthers	Brooklyn	National	.335
1911	John P. Wagner	Pittsburgh	National	.334
1888	James F. O'Neill	St. Louis	Association	.332
1910	Sherwood R. Magee	Philadelphia	National	.331
1905	Napoleon Lajoie	Cleveland	American	.329
1914	Jacob E. Daubert	Brooklyn	National	.329
1908	Tyrus R. Cobb	Detroit	American	.324
1915	Lawrence J. Doyle	New York	National	.320

*Four strikes; bases on balls counted as hits and charged as at bats.

Leading Robbers All Identified, Too

The major league master robbers can all be identified, too, stolen bases having been introduced into the summaries of the box scores and into the averages during the season of 1886. The rules as to thefts have been changed from time to time, and when the scorers first began to record stolen bases some of them didn't just know how. Players used to get a stolen base when they took two bases on an infield out and they used to get a stolen base when they scored from third on a fly ball. They used to get steals when they were retired after having overslid the bag they set out for, and they used to get steals when one section of a double pilfering expedition met disaster.

Also, until 1920, a notable athlete, with his team miles in the rear, could skip round the circuit in the ninth, or a late inning and, though unmolested, receive credit for a group of stolen sacks.

Tighter scoring rules have changed things in stolen bases so that no longer do any huge records crop up. The last bid for a century performance was Cobb's, in 1915, the Peach that year outwitting the backstops 96 times.

Harry D. Stovey, outfielder and first baseman, holds the major league record for steals in one season with 156. This number of bags Stovey, who hailed from New Bedford, Mass., and who played with Worcester in the National League before going to the Athletics, filched in 1888. The year before Stovey perpetrated 143 robberies, but some of them would not have been O. K.'d by the scorers of the present day. Stovey was a great big fellow, fleet of foot and a quick thinker.

Another flyer produced in the National League's first real rival was William R. Hamilton. He displaced Stovey as the Association's Ty Cobb in 1889, and then going into the National led the base stealers of that organization the next two years, his 1891 performance on the paths being the banner one for the senior organization. Some information on Hamilton is contained later in certain matter relative to the demon run makers of the fast set, and Stovey's name will be found associated with the baseball war of 1891.

Ty Cobb's name appears six times in the list of leading base runners and so does Max Carey's. Hans Wagner's is in evidence five times. George Moriarty's isn't in evidence at all, but the present American League umpire probably beat his way from third to the plate oftener than any other man who ever was in the junior organization.

These are the leading base stealers of the major leagues from 1886 on, the list of the champion flyers being complete.

Leading Base Stealers of Major Leagues
(Stolen bases introduced into summaries of box scores in 1886.)

Year	Player	Club	League	Stolen Bases
1888	Harry D. Stovey	Philadelphia	Association	156
1887	Harry D. Stovey	Philadelphia	Association	143
1889	William R. Hamilton	Kansas City	Association	117
1891	William R. Hamilton	Philadelphia	National	115
1887	John M. Ward	New York	National	111
1891	Thomas T. Brown	Boston	Association	110
1890	William R. Hamilton	Philadelphia	National	102
1896	William A. Lange	Chicago	National	100
1889	James G. Fogarty	Philadelphia	National	99
1894	William R. Hamilton	Philadelphia	National	99
1886	Harry D. Stovey	Philadelphia	Association	96
1915	Tyrus R. Cobb	Detroit	American	96
1890	Curtis B. Welch	Phila.-Balto.	Association	95
1895	William R. Hamilton	Philadelphia	National	95
1892	John M. Ward	Brooklyn	National	94
1912	J. Clyde Milan	Washington	American	88
1890	Thomas T. Brown	Boston	Players'	87
1897	William A. Lange	Chicago	National	83
1911	Tyrus R. Cobb	Detroit	American	83
1888	William E. Hoy	Washington	National	82
1910	Edward T. Collins	Philadelphia	American	81
1911	Robert H. Bescher	Cincinnati	National	80
1899	James T. Sheckard	Baltimore	National	78
1909	Tyrus R. Cobb	Detroit	American	76
1914	Benjamin M. Kauff	Indianapolis	Federal	75
1913	J. Clyde Milan	Washington	American	74
1914	Fritz C. Maisel	New York	American	74
1893	John M. Ward	New York	National	72
1910	Robert H. Bescher	Cincinnati	National	70

Year	Player	Club	League	Stolen Bases
1916	Tyrus R. Cobb	Detroit	American	68
1903	Frank L. Chance	Chicago	National	67
1903	James T. Sheckard	Brooklyn	National	67
1912	Robert H. Bescher	Cincinnati	National	67
1898	Fred C. Clarke	Louisville	National	66
1916	Max Carey	Pittsburgh	National	63
1914	George J. Burns	New York	National	62
1920	Edgar S. Rice	Washington	American	62
1907	John P. Wagner	Pittsburgh	National	61
1913	Max Carey	Pittsburgh	National	61
1905	William A. Maloney	Chicago	National	59
1905	Arthur Devlin	New York	National	59
1918	Max Carey	Pittsburgh	National	58
1906	Frank L. Chance	Chicago	National	57
1886	George E. Andrews	Philadelphia	National	56
1917	Tyrus R. Cobb	Detroit	American	55
1902	T. F. Hartsel	Philadelphia	American	54
1909	Robert H. Bescher	Cincinnati	National	54
1915	Benjamin M. Kauff	Brooklyn	Federal	54
1904	John P. Wagner	Pittsburgh	National	53
1908	John P. Wagner	Pittsburgh	National	53
1920	Max Carey	Pittsburgh	National	52
1907	Tyrus R. Cobb	Detroit	American	49
1921	Frank F. Frisch	New York	National	49
1901	John P. Wagner	Pittsburgh	National	48
1901	Frank Isbell	Chicago	American	48
1908	Patrick H. Dougherty	Chicago	American	47
1900	James E. Barrett	Cincinnati	National	46
1903	Harry D. Bay	Cleveland	American	46
1905	Daniel Hoffman	Philadelphia	American	46
1917	Max Carey	Pittsburgh	National	46
1918	George H. Sisler	St. Louis	American	45
1902	John P. Wagner	Pittsburgh	National	43
1904	Elmer H. Flick	Cleveland	American	42
1919	George J. Burns	New York	National	40
1906	Elmer H. Flick	Cleveland	American	39
1906	John Anderson	Washington	American	39
1915	Max Carey	Pittsburgh	National	36
1921	George H. Sisler	St. Louis	American	35
1919	Edward T. Collins	Chicago	American	33

Sacrificers Also All Known

The leading sacrificers of the major leagues are known, too, and all that the fans don't find out now about the suicides are how many are of the land type and how many of the air variety. The sacrifice fly was introduced into the code in 1908, William J. Murray, then manager of the Phillies and now a Pirate scout, urging its adoption so that batters who scored men from third on fly balls could get proper credit in the averages. For a time the sacrifice flies and the sacrifice bunts were reported separately in the summaries, but they never were distributed in the averages and now it is hard to tell from the records whether the leader is a good bunter or whether he has the faculty of being able to bring a man home on a long fly.

A Harding Richardson, better known to the fans of his time as Hardy Richardson, living somewhere in New York State now, holds the ancient record for sacrificing, with 68 hits, said record having been made as a member of the Boston American Association team in 1891.

Ray Chapman, killed by a ball pitched by Carl Mays in 1920, set the modern record three years before that disaster with 67. The Cleveland shortstop, in 1917, was sacrifice bunting more than sacrifice flying and his immediate predecessor in the Indian lineup—John Gladstone Graney—was opening about every game by getting on, being partially responsible for Chappy's great record in suicides.

Kid Gleason, White Sox manager now, was an able sacrificer and so was Franz Otto Knabe, an associate of the Kid's on the Philadelphia National League team when it was managed by the inventor of the sacrifice fly rule and now the leader of the Kansas City American Association team.

Knabe, who pronounces his name entirely different from the way the Baltimore piano makers do, led the tap brigade four years. His name appears more frequently in the list below than anyone else's, this list being complete:

Leading Sacrifice Hitters of Major Leagues
(Sacrifice hitting introduced into summaries of box scores in 1889.)

Year	Player	Club	League	Sacrifice Hits
1891	A. Harding Richardson	Boston	Association	68
1817	Raymond J. Chapman	Cleveland	American	67
1893	Jacob C. Beckley	Pittsburgh	National	64
1890	Charles J. Crooks	Columbus	Association	63
1890	Albert Myers	Philadelphia	National	62
1892	William B. Weaver	Louisville	National	60
1908	William J. Bradley	Cleveland	American	60
1891	George S. Davis	Cleveland	National	54
1891	Edward J. Delehanty	Philadelphia	National	54
1890	Daniel Richardson	New York	Players'	53
1889	Michael J. Kelly	Boston	National	52
1909	Owen Bush	Detroit	American	52
1919	Raymond J. Chapman	Cleveland	American	50
1889	Oliver P. Beard	Cincinnati	Association	48
1913	Raymond J. Chapman	Cleveland	American	48
1920	Joseph Gedeon	St. Louis	American	48
1920	Owen Bush	Detroit	American	48
1907	William J. Bradley	Cleveland	American	46

Year	Player	Club	League	Sacrifice Hits
1909	James T. Sheckard	Chicago	National	46
1916	George D. Weaver	Chicago	American	44
1905	William Gleason	Philadelphia	National	43
1921	William A. Wambsganss	Cleveland	American	43
1905	William H. Keeler	New York	American	42
1908	Franz O. Knabe	Philadelphia	National	42
1915	Robert T. Fisher	Chicago	National	42
1915	Robert Vaughn	St. Louis	Federal	42
1915	Oscar J. Vitt	Detroit	American	42
1915	George D. Weaver	Chicago	American	42
1913	Franz O. Knabe	Philadelphia	National	41
1906	Thomas Jones	St. Louis	American	40
1906	James T. Sheckard	Chicago	National	40
1907	Franz O. Knabe	Philadelphia	National	40
1916	Max O. Flack	Chicago	National	39
1919	Jacob E. Daubert	Cincinnati	National	39
1911	John B. Lobert	Philadelphia	National	38
1914	Charles Arnold Gandil	Washington	American	38
1914	Terrence L. Turner	Cleveland	American	38
1910	Franz O. Knabe	Philadelphia	National	37
1912	Max Carey	Pittsburgh	National	37
1920	George W. Cutshaw	Pittsburgh	National	37
1904	Fielder A. Jones	Chicago	American	36
1914	William B. McKechnie	Indianapolis	Federal	36
1918	David W. Shean	Boston	American	36
1921	Milton J. Stock	St. Louis	National	36
1902	David L. Fultz	Philadelphia	American	35
1904	William Gleason	Philadelphia	National	35
1914	Lee C. Magee	St. Louis	National	35
1903	William L. Lush	Detroit	American	34
1910	Harry B. Hooper	Boston	American	34
1911	James P. Austin	St. Louis	American	34
1896	William E. Hoy	Cincinnati	National	33
1918	Edward J. Roush	Cincinnati	National	33
1898	Claude C. Ritchey	Louisville	National	31
1912	George E. Lewis	Boston	American	31
1897	Thomas L. McCreery	Louis.—N. Y.	National	30
1903	Daniel L. McGann	New York	National	30
1899	Fred W. Ely	Pittsburgh	National	29
1901	William Hallman	Philadelphia	National	29
1902	Fred C. Tenney	Boston	National	29
1917	Charles A. Deal	Chicago	National	29
1895	Hugh Jennings	Baltimore	National	28
1900	James F. Slagle	Philadelphia	National	27
1894	Patrick J. Donovan	Pittsburgh	National	26
1901	William Nance	Detroit	American	24

Lists That Are Incomplete

Now one starts to strike lists of leaders that are incomplete, all those printed hereafter in this section being shy certain data that may be turned up in years to come. The omissions are noted at the top of each list.

Toured Circuit 196 Times

William R. Hamilton of Clinton, Mass., an outfielder who got his first chance in fast company with Kansas City of the American Association, is at present the record holder for runs scored in one season with 196. He got this total of tallies in 1894, when he was with the hard hitting Phillies of the National League and just after the pitcher had been set back.

Babe Ruth's 177 markers in 1921 is the nearest approach to the Hamilton performance.

George Joseph Burns, now with Cincinnati, and Tyrus Raymond Cobb, still with Detroit, have each led their leagues five years in scoring.

Hamilton was a leader four years.

Babe Ruth, Michael J. Kelly and Edward Trowbridge Collins each have been the best scorers in three campaigns.

The run figures so far as available, from 1876 to 1921, inclusive, and a hint as to the years in which the dope is missing:

Leading Run Scorers of Major Leagues

(Figures for National League for 1876 and 1877, for Union Association of 1884 and for American Association of 1882, 1883, 1884, 1885, 1887 and 1888 not available.)

Year	Player	Club	League	Runs
1894	William R. Hamilton	Philadelphia	National	196
1921	George H. Ruth	New York	American	177
1891	Thomas T. Brown	Boston	Association	170
1895	William R. Hamilton	Philadelphia	National	166
1890	Hugh Duffy	Chicago	Players'	161
1896	Jesse C. Burkett	Cleveland	National	159
1920	George H. Ruth	New York	American	158
1886	Michael J. Kelly	Chicago	National	155
1889	Harry D. Stovey	Philadelphia	Association	154
1886	Walter A. Latham	St. Louis	Association	153
1887	Dennis L. Brouthers	Detroit	National	153
1897	William R. Hamilton	Boston	National	153
1893	Hugh Duffy	Boston	National	149
1893	Herman C. Long	Boston	National	149
1890	Hubert Collins	Brooklyn	National	148
1911	Tyrus R. Cobb	Detroit	American	147
1889	Michael J. Tiernan	New York	National	146
1901	Napoleon Lajoie	Philadelphia	American	145
1915	Tyrus R. Cobb	Detroit	American	144
1891	William R. Hamilton	Philadelphia	National	142
1898	John J. McGraw	Baltimore	National	142

Year	Player	Club	League	Runs
1899	William H. Keeler	Brooklyn	National	141
1901	Jesse C. Burkett	St. Louis	National	139
1903	Clarence H. Beaumont	Pittsburgh	National	137
1912	Edward T. Collins	Philadelphia	American	137
1892	Clarence L. Childs	Cleveland	National	135
1890	Thomas F. McCarthy	St. Louis	Association	134
1900	Roy Thomas	Philadelphia	National	131
1921	Rogers Hornsby	St. Louis	National	131
1909	Thomas W. Leach	Pittsburgh	National	126
1913	Edward T. Collins	Philadelphia	American	125
1885	Michael J. Kelly	Chicago	National	124
1905	Michael J. Donlin	New York	National	124
1914	Edward T. Collins	Philadelphia	American	122
1911	James T. Sheckard	Chicago	National	121
1884	Michael J. Kelly	Chicago	National	120
1912	Robert H. Bescher	Cincinnati	National	120
1888	Dennis L. Brouthers	Detroit	National	118
1914	Benjamin M. Kauff	Indianapolis	Federal	118
1909	Tyrus R. Cobb	Detroit	American	116
1920	George J. Burns	New York	National	115
1904	Patrick H. Dougherty	Bos.-N.Y.	American	113
1916	Tyrus R. Cobb	Detroit	American	113
1917	Owen Bush	Detroit	American	112
1902	David L. Fultz	Philadelphia	American	110
1910	Sherwood R. Magee	Philadelphia	National	110
1903	Patrick H. Dougherty	Boston	American	108
1993	Joseph W. Hornung	Boston	National	106
1910	Tyrus R. Cobb	Detroit	American	106
1902	John P. Wagner	Pittsburgh	National	105
1908	Matthew McIntyre	Detroit	American	105
1916	George J. Burns	New York	National	105
1907	Porter B. Shannon	New York	National	104
1906	Frank L. Chance	Chicago	National	103
1906	John P. Wagner	Pittsburgh	National	103
1917	George J. Burns	New York	National	103
1919	George H. Ruth	Boston	American	103
1907	Samuel Crawford	Detroit	American	102
1908	Fred C. Tenney	New York	National	101
1914	George J. Burns	New York	National	100
1882	George F. Gore	Chicago	National	99
1904	George Browne	New York	National	99
1913	Thomas W. Leach	Chicago	National	99
1913	Max Carey	Pittsburgh	National	99
1915	W. Baker Borton	St. Louis	Federal	99
1906	Elmer H. Flick	Cleveland	American	98
1905	Harry H. Davis	Philadelphia	American	92
1880	Abner F. Dalrymple	Chicago	National	90
1915	C. C. Cravath	Philadelphia	National	89
1918	Henry K. Groh	Cincinnati	National	88

Year	Player	Club	League	Runs
1881	George F. Gore	Chicago	National	86
1919	George J. Burns	New York	National	86
1879	Charles Jones	Boston	National	85
1918	Raymond J. Chapman	Cleveland	American	84
1878	Joseph Start	Chicago	National	58
1878	Richard Higham	Providence	National	58

Modern Player Released Most Base Hits

A modern player—George Harold Sisler, of the St. Louis Browns—holds the record for releasing the most base hits in one year, said record being 257 and having been made in 1920. H. Dennis Lyons, a heavy weight third baseman and a star in the old American Association, got credit for obtaining 284 blows in 1887 as a member of the Athletics, but in 1887 passes were included with legitimate hits and Denny didn't acquire as many wallops as Michigan's best known graduate.

Tyrus Raymond Cobb has been the pace setter in the American League in safeties in eight seasons, the list of nearly all the major league's leading manufacturers of base hits being given below:

Leading Manufacturers of Base Hits

(National League, for 1876 and 1877; Union Association for 1884, and American Association, for 1882, not reported.)

Year	Player	Club	League	Base Hits
1887	H. Dennis Lyons	Philadelphia	Association	*284
1920	George H. Sisler	St. Louis	American	257
1911	Tyrus R. Cobb	Detroit	American	248
1897	William H. Keeler	Baltimore	National	243
1896	Jesse C. Burkett	Cleveland	National	240
1887	Dennis L. Brouthers	Detroit	National	*239
1921	Harold E. Heilmann	Detroit	American	237
1894	Hugh Duffy	Boston	National	236
1895	Jesse C. Burkett	Cleveland	National	235
1921	Rogers Hornsby	St. Louis	National	235
1899	Edward J. Delahanty	Philadelphia	National	234
1901	Jesse C. Burkett	St. Louis	National	228
1910	Napoleon Lajoie	Cleveland	American	227
1912	Tyrus R. Cobb	Detroit	American	227
1917	Tyrus R. Cobb	Detroit	American	225
1893	Samuel L. Thompson	Philadelphia	National	220
1901	Napoleon Lajoie	Philadelphia	American	220
1905	J. Bentley Seymour	Cincinnati	National	219
1920	Rogers Hornsby	St. Louis	National	218
1909	Tyrus R. Cobb	Detroit	American	216

Year	Player	Club	League	Base Hits
1898	Jesse C. Burkett	Cleveland	National	215
1906	Napoleon Lajoie	Cleveland	American	214
1916	Tris E. Speaker	Cleveland	American	211
1914	Benjamin M. Kauff	Indianapolis	Federal	210
1889	John W. Glasscock	Indianapolis	National	209
1903	Clarence H. Beaumont	Pittsburgh	National	209
1915	Tyrus R. Cobb	Detroit	American	208
1912	Henry Zimmerman	Chicago	National	207
1908	John P. Wagner	Pittsburgh	National	201
1890	William V. Wolfe	Louisville	Association	200
1889	Thomas J. Tucker	Baltimore	Association	198
1892	Dennis L. Brouthers	Brooklyn	National	197
1913	Joseph Jackson	Cleveland	American	197
1886	David Orr	New York	Association	196
1903	Patrick H. Dougherty	Boston	American	195
1890	Hugh Duffy	Chicago	Players'	194
1902	Clarence H. Beaumont	Pittsburgh	National	194
1902	Charles Hickman	Cleveland	American	194
1914	Tris E. Speaker	Boston	American	193
1911	Roy Miller	Boston	National	192
1919	Tyrus R. Cobb	Detroit	American	191
1919	Robert H. Veach	Detroit	American	191
1886	A. Harding Richardson	Detroit	National	189
1915	Lawrence J. Doyle	New York	National	189
1908	Tyrus R. Cobb	Detroit	American	188
1905	George R. Stone	St. Louis	American	187
1907	Clarence H. Beaumont	Pittsburgh	National	187
1915	John Tobin	St. Louis	Federal	186
1884	Thomas Esterbrook	New York	Association	185
1916	Harold H. Chase	Cincinnati	National	184
1888	James Ryan	Chicago	National	182
1917	Henry K. Groh	Cincinnati	National	182
1900	George VanHaltren	New York	National	181
1891	William R. Hamilton	Philadelphia	National	179
1904	Jacob C. Beckley	St. Louis	National	179
1913	C. C. Cravath	Philadelphia	National	179
1910	Robert M. Byrne	Pittsburgh	National	178
1910	John P. Wagner	Pittsburgh	National	178
1918	George H. Burns	Philadelphia	American	178
1885	Louis R. Browning	Louisville	Association	176
1888	James F. O'Neill	St. Louis	Association	176
1906	Henry Steinfeldt	Chicago	National	176
1890	John W. Glasscock	New York	National	172
1890	Samuel L. Thomason	Philadelphia	National	172
1909	Lawrence J. Doyle	New York	National	172
1914	Sherwood R. Magee	Philadelphia	National	171
1885	Roger Connor	New York	National	169
1919	Rogers Hornsby	St. Louis	National	163
1918	Charles J. Hollocher	Chicago	National	161

Year	Player	Club	League	Base Hits
1884	Abner F. Dalrymple	Chicago	National	160
1891	Dennis L. Brouthers	Boston	Association	160
1883	Dennis L. Brouthers	Buffalo	National	156
1883	Charles E. Swartwood	Pittsburgh	Association	149
1879	Paul M. Hines	Providence	National	145
1881	Adrian C. Anson	Chicago	National	137
1882	Dennis L. Brouthers	Buffalo	National	129
1880	Abner F. Dalrymple	Chicago	National	123
1878	Joseph Start	Chicago	National	97

* Bases on balls counted as hits.

Delehanty the Demon Doubler

Edward J. Delahanty, a tremendously hard hitting right-hander, probably set the major league mark for doubles in 1899, when he was with the Philadelphia National League club. That year he pounded out 56. The leaders in two base hits have passed or reached the half century mark six times, Tris Speaker claiming three of these performances, Napoleon Lajoie two and Delahanty one. Delahanty first gained fame in the old Tri-State League in 1887 and 1888. Later he went to the Phillies, then he put in a season with Cleveland of the Players' League and then he went back to the Quackers, jumping to the American League in 1902 and playing with Washington that year and part of 1903. Put off a train near the Niagara River in July, 1903, he apparently tried to cross that river on a bridge and fell off.

Cleveland players, or Cleveland born players. Delahanty having been a native of what used to be called the Forest City, have distinguished themselves as manufacturers of two base hits. Speaker, later manager of the Indians, excelled in hits of this type for six years, two of these when he was with Boston. Lajoie, former manager of the Tribe, ranked first, five campaigns, twice when he was employed by some other club.

But the real doubling demon is (or was) John Peter Wagner of Pittsburgh. This perennial pitcher pounder was the leading releaser of hits good for half the distance during seven seasons, four of these being in succession.

The two base hit figures so far as available and a hint as to the years in which the dope is missing.

Leading Two Base Hitters of Major Leagues

(National League from 1898 on, American League from 1901 on, Players' League for 1890.)

Year	Player	Club	League	2BH
1899	Edward J. Delahanty	Philadelphia	National	56
1912	Tris E. Speaker	Boston	American	53
1921	Tris E. Speaker	Cleveland	American	52

Year	Player	Club	League	2BH
1910	Napoleon Lajoie	Cleveland	American	51
1904	Napoleon Lajoie	Cleveland	American	50
1920	Tris E. Speaker	Cleveland	American	50
1906	Napoleon Lajoie	Cleveland	American	49
1901	Napoleon Lajoie	Philadelphia	American	48
1905	Harry H. Davis	Philadelphia	American	47
1911	Tyrus R. Cobb	Detroit	American	47
1914	Tris E. Speaker	Boston	American	46
1900	John P. Wagner	Pittsburgh	National	45
1914	Benjamin M. Kauff	Indianapolis	Federal	45
1919	Robert H. Veach	Detroit	American	45
1904	John P. Wagner	Pittsburgh	National	44
1917	Tyrus R. Cobb	Detroit	American	44
1920	Rogers Hornsby	St. Louis	National	44
1921	Rogers Hornsby	St. Louis	National	44
1898	Napoleon Lajoie	Philadelphia	National	43
1902	Harry H. Davis	Philadelphia	American	43
1903	Ralph O. Seybold	Philadelphia	American	43
1910	Robert M. Byrne	Pittsburgh	National	43
1916	John A. Niehoff	Philadelphia	National	42
1890	Louis R. Browning	Cleveland	Players'	41
1890	Jacob C. Beckley	Pittsburgh	National	41
1912	Henry Zimmerman	Chicago	National	41
1916	Tris E. Speaker	Cleveland	American	41
1916	John G. Graney	Cleveland	American	41
1905	J. Bentley Seymour	Cincinnati	National	40
1913	J. Carlisle Smith	Brooklyn	National	40
1915	Robert H. Veach	Detroit	American	40
1915	Lawrence J. Doyle	New York	National	40
1901	Jacob C. Beckley	Cincinnati	National	39
1908	John P. Wagner	Pittsburgh	National	39
1909	John P. Wagner	Pittsburgh	National	39
1913	Joseph Jackson	Cleveland	American	39
1914	Sherwood R. Magee	Philadelphia	National	39
1917	Henry K. Groh	Cincinnati	National	39
1906	John P. Wagner	Pittsburgh	National	38
1907	John P. Wagner	Pittsburgh	National	38
1911	Edward J. Konetchy	St. Louis	National	38
1907	Harry H. Davis	Philadelphia	American	37
1908	Tyrus R. Cobb	Detroit	American	36
1909	Samuel Crawford	Detroit	American	35
1915	Harold H. Chase	Buffalo	Federal	33
1918	Tris E. Speaker	Cleveland	American	33
1902	John P. Wagner	Pittsburgh	National	32
1903	Fred C. Clarke	Pittsburgh	National	32
1903	Harry Steinfeldt	Cincinnati	National	32
1903	Samuel Mertes	New York	National	32
1919	Ross Young	New York	National	31
1918	Henry K. Groh	Cincinnati	National	28

Pirates Pound Out Triples

There must be something in the air of Pittsburgh that fills players with ambition to land on pitchers for triples. J. Owen Wilson, right fielder for the Pirates, probably owning the major league record for hits of this kind through the 36 he made in 1912.

An earlier Pirate with a penchant for tripling was James Thomas Williams, one of the few players who deserted the Dreyfuss craft for life aboard the American League cruiser, which went where it wanted to despite warnings from Freedman, Brush & Co. The first year Williams was with the Pittsburgh club he made his presence felt by slamming out 27 three baggers and the record stood for the National League until J. Owen, Texan by birth and a player who had a tremendous pair of hands, broke it in 1912.

Digressing for a moment, another Texan—Harry Ables, left handed pitcher, briefly seen in the American League with the Browns and with the Yankees— was another player who had extremely large paws and another pastimer in the same class with Wilson and Ables is Joseph B. B. Benes, now second basing for the Newark Internationals. The smallest hands possessed by a big league athlete were those belonging to J. Bentley Seymour, and it was because he had small hands that the left-hander had to desert the box for the suburbs, he being unable to control the ball.

When Wilson was having his great year in triples in 1912 there were some parties who thought that he would have to make 43 in order to establish a major league record for the Reach Guide for 1903 gave Lajoie 43 through a typographical error. This fact is mentioned again should anyone question Wilson owning the record for triples.

Wilson when he was setting the major league mark for triples, made seven against Chicago and Cincinnati, six against Boston, five against St. Louis (he finished his major league career with the Cardinals), and New York, and three against Philadelphia and Brooklyn. The only high grade hurler who was not touched for a three bagger by the Chief, as J. Owen was called, was George Napoleon Rucker of Brooklyn.

The list of the leading triplers of the major leagues, Sam Crawford's name being in it six times, Ty Cobb's four, Joe Jackson's three, Hans Wagner's three, Jimmy William's three and Elmer Flick's three. Michael F. Mitchell's name is in the list twice, but it would have been in oftener than that if Sir Michael had not been compelled to play the blinding sun field in Cincinnati, said field reported to be the worst of its kind in the world. The dope:

Leading Three Base Hitters of Major Leagues

(National League from 1898 on, American League from 1901 on, Players' League and Federal League complete.)

Year	Player	Club	League	3BH
1912	J. Owen Wilson	Pittsburgh	National	36

Year	Player	Club	League	3BH
1899	James T. William	Pittsburgh	National	27
1912	Joseph Jackson	Cleveland	American	26
1914	Samuel Crawford	Detroit	American	26
1890	William Shindle	Philadelphia	Players'	25
1903	Samuel Crawford	Detroit	American	25
1911	Lawrence J. Doyle	New York	National	25
1915	Thomas A. Long	St. Louis	National	25
1911	Tyrus R. Cobb	Detroit	American	24
1902	Samuel Crawford	Cincinnati	National	23
1902	James T. Williams	Baltimore	American	23
1913	Samuel Crawford	Detroit	American	23
1917	Tyrus R. Cobb	Detroit	American	23
1901	James T. Williams	Baltimore	American	22
1904	Charles S. Stahl	Boston	American	22
1906	Elmer H. Flick	Cleveland	American	22
1920	Henry H. Myers	Brooklyn	National	22
1900	John P. Wagner	Pittsburgh	National	21
1901	James T. Sheckard	Brooklyn	National	21
1905	J. Bentley Seymour	Cincinnati	National	21
1913	Victor S. Saier	Chicago	National	21
1916	Joseph Jackson	Chicago	American	21
1898	John Anderson	Brooklyn	National	20
1908	Tyrus R. Cobb	Detroit	American	20
1920	Joseph Jackson	Chicago	American	20
1903	John P. Wagner	Pittsburgh	National	19
1905	Elmer H. Flick	Cleveland	American	19
1908	John P. Wagner	Pittsburgh	National	19
1909	J. Franklin Baker	Philadelphia	American	19
1910	Samuel Crawford	Detroit	American	19
1915	Leslie Mann	Chicago	Federal	19
1915	Joseph H. Kelly	Pittsburgh	Federal	19
1915	Samuel Crawford	Detroit	American	19
1921	Howard S. Shanks	Washington	American	19
1904	Harry G. Lumley	Brooklyn	National	18
1907	Elmer H. Flick	Cleveland	American	18
1910	Michael F. Mitchell	Cincinnati	National	18
1921	Rogers Hornsby	St. Louis	National	18
1921	Raymond Powell	Boston	National	18
1909	Michael F. Mitchell	Cincinnati	National	18
1914	Max Carey	Pittsburgh	National	17
1917	Rogers Hornsby	St. Louis	National	17
1919	Robert H. Veach	Detroit	American	17
1907	John H. Ganzel	Cincinnati	National	16
1907	Charles A. Alperman	Brooklyn	National	16
1916	William W. Hinchman	Pittsburgh	National	16
1914	Louis R. Evans	Brooklyn	Federal	15
1918	Jacob E. Daubert	Brooklyn	National	15
1918	Tyrus R. Cobb	Detroit	American	14
1919	Henry H. Myers	Brooklyn	National	14

Year	Player	Club	League	3BH
1919	William H. Southworth	Pittsburgh	National	14
1906	Fred C. Clarke	Pittsburgh	National	13
1906	Frank Schulte	Chicago	National	13

Will Ruth Keep His Laurels?

One of the questions that will be answered by October, 1922, will be as to whether or not George Herman Ruth will be able to keep his title of the Home Run King. The Babe violated baseball law, last fall, in going on a barnstorming trip after having played in the World's Series and a decision of Commissioner Kenesaw M. Landis's kept him on the side lines this year until May 20th.

While he was idle, Kenneth Roy (or Ray) Williams, outfielder of the St. Louis Browns, took it on himself to start a general survival of the fittest at the expense of the pitchers, and by the time Ruth was eligible to play again the young man from Grants Pass, Oregon, had emitted 11 circuit blows. These 11 homers were merely incidental, according to Kenneth who told Burt Whitman of the Boston Herald that he hadn't set any goal for four-baggers and that he was out there to hit the ball in order to help the club to win.

Ruth, to May 20, 1921, made a dozen belt line blows and during the year made 59, breaking his 1920 record by five. In 1919 George Herman sent into the Never Never Land, Edward N. Williamson's 1884 record of 27 homers, raising the major league figure to 29 and then doubling it inside of two years.

There was much hullabaloo among the dopesters as to who discovered that Williamson had made 27 home runs 38 years ago, the fact having been mentioned quite frequently, previously, and having been forgotten. Whenever Father Chadwick wrote on the subject of home runs, which variety of hits he detested, he called attention to the great number of homers made by the Ansonites in 1884 and to their position in the race, which was fourth.

Nobody discovered Williamson's 1884 record, it merely had been forgotten by those whose business it was to remember it.

As for Ruth's 1921 home run record, that is printed in nearly every baseball publication and will not be reprinted here, for this fall there may be a new one to spread before the populace.

This is a list of the home run kings of the major leagues, not complete, but fairly so. In the list the name that most frequently appears is not Ruth's, but Cravath's. C. C's cognomen crops up half a dozen times. The dope:

Leading Home Run Hitters

(National League from 1898 on and for 1884, American League complete, Federal League complete, Players' League complete, Union and American Associations incomplete.)

Year	Player	Club	League	Home Runs
1921	George H. Ruth	New York	American	59
1920	George H. Ruth	New York	American	54
1919	George H. Ruth	Boston	American	29
1884	Edward N. Williamson	Chicago	National	27
1899	John C. Freeman	Washington	National	25
1915	C. C. Cravath	Philadelphia	National	24
1921	George L. Kelly	New York	National	23
1911	Frank Schulte	Chicago	National	21
1913	C. C. Cravath	Philadelphia	National	19
1914	C. C. Cravath	Philadelphia	National	19
1915	Harold H. Chase	Buffalo	Federal	17
1901	Samuel Crawford	Cincinnati	National	16
1902	Ralph O. Seybold	Philadelphia	American	16
1914	Edward Zwilling	Chicago	Federal	16
1898	James J. Collins	Boston	National	15
1920	Fred C. Williams	Philadelphia	National	15
1912	Henry Zimmerman	Chicago	National	14
1890	Roger Connor	New York	Players'	13
1890	A. Harding Richardson	Boston	Players'	13
1901	Napoleon Lajoie	Philadelphia	American	13
1903	John C. Freeman	Boston	American	13
1900	Herman Long	Boston	National	12
1906	Timothy J. Jordan	Brooklyn	National	12
1906	Harry H. Davis	Philadelphia	American	12
1908	Timothy J. Jordan	Brooklyn	National	12
1913	J. Franklin Baker	Philadelphia	American	12
1916	Walter C. Pipp	New York	American	12
1917	Davis O. Robertson	New York	National	12
1916	Fred C. Williams	Chicago	National	12
1917	C. C. Cravath	Philadelphia	National	12
1917	Davis O. Robertson	New York	National	12
1919	C. C. Cravath	Philadelphia	National	12
1918	George H. Ruth	Boston	American	11
1918	Clarence Walker	Philadelphia	American	11
1904	Harry H. Davis	Philadelphia	American	10
1907	David L. Brain	Boston	National	10
1910	Frank Schulte	Chicago	National	10
1910	Fred T. Beck	Boston	National	10
1910	J. Garland Stahl	Boston	American	10
1912	J. Franklin Baker	Philadelphia	American	10
1903	James T. Sheckard	Brooklyn	National	9
1904	Harry G. Lumley	Brooklyn	National	9
1905	Fred Odwell	Cincinnati	National	9

Year	Player	Club	League	Home Runs
1909	Tyrus R. Cobb	Detroit	American	9
1911	J. Franklin Baker	Philadelphia	American	9
1917	Walter C. Pipp	New York	American	9
1905	Harry H. Davis	Philadelphia	American	9
1907	Harry H. Davis	Philadelphia	American	8
1914	Samuel Crawford	Detroit	American	8
1914	J. Franklin Baker	Philadelphia	American	8
1918	C. C. Cravath	Philadelphia	National	8
1908	Samuel Crawford	Detroit	American	8
1909	John J. Murray	New York	National	7
1915	Robert F. Roth	Chicago–Cleveland	American	7
1902	Thomas W. Leach	Pittsburgh	National	6

Most Attacking Lists Cleared Up

Most of the attacking lists have been cleared up previously, one that remains to be printed being the attack of the pitchers on the batters. For leaders in other departments of the game, readers are referred to The Little Red Book, part of the Spalding Baseball Record, the writer having helped Charles D. White with this publication for years.

Here is some tabloid information on the other subjects:

RUNS BATTED IN—As far back as 1879 a Buffalo paper used to include the runs batted in in the summary of the box score of the home game. Henry Chadwick urged the adoption of this feature in the middle 80's and by 1891 carried his point so that the National League scorers were instructed to report this data. They reported it grudgingly and finally were told they wouldn't have to report it. The New York Press in 1907 revived the runs batted in feature and the writer worked the figures up annually until the major leagues, on the re-

quest of the Baseball Writers' Association, incorporated the data in the averages in 1920. Most runs batted in in one season—170, by George H. Ruth, New York Americans, in 1920.

REACHED FIRST ON ERRORS—National League has reported this once or twice.

BASES TOUCHED—National League reported this in 1880 under the heading of total bases run. Abner F. Dalrymple, Chicago, leader in that respect, with 501.

REACHED FIRST BASE—National League reported this in 1879, Paul M. Hines, Providence, being leader, with 193.

STRIKE OUTS—Reported first by Clarence Dow of the Boston Globe in averages for American Association in 1891. Occasionally reported by National League in middle nineties and reported steadily by senior organization since 1909. Only baseball book that contains figures for 1911, the Spalding Guide. William H. Keeler of Baltimore is said to have gone one full season in the National League without whiffing. Player striking out oftenest in one season—Gus Williams, St. Louis Americans, 120 times in 1914.

BASES ON BALLS—Reported first by Mr. Dow. Remarks on strike outs apply to passes. Player walking oftenest in one season—George H. Ruth, New York Americans, 148 times in 1920.

HIT BY PITCHED BALLS—Never reported steadily. Dopesters have amused themselves occasionally by doing work of this kind and Hugh Jennings is thought to have been hit oftener in one year than anyone else getting 49 casualty complimentaries in 1896 when he was with the Baltimore Nationals. Some writers are in favor of consolidating the passes and Red Cross walks, the league presidents don't seem to be interested in the matter.

PLAYERS THROWN OUT STEALING—First work of this character done at request of Charles Schmidt, catcher of Detroit team, in 1912. Done in desultory and scientific fashion since. Data on this vague, but all of it may be assembled within the next few years.

HITTING INTO DOUBLE PLAYS—Done by some scribes for their amusement. Data vague.

PLAYERS LETTING IN RUNS ON ERRORS—Done by one scribe after reading this bit of doggerel by George E. Phaire of Chicago:

> Red Corriden was figuring the cost of livelihood.
> "'Tis plain," he said. "I do not get the money that I should.
> According to my figurin, I'd be a millionaire
> If I could sell the boots I make for 30 cents a pair."

Corriden had a bad year in 1914, and when investigation was made it was found he led the players of both big leagues in giving runs to the enemy, presenting them with 20, either on boots, muffs or wild throws.

The Strikeout Kings

It isn't the fault of the major league presidents or secretaries that the fans knock quite a little about the strikeout kings. The first year the whiffs were reported in the National League was 1889. During a couple of seasons later, much later, in 1903 and 1904—all that the National informed the fans about the pitchers' strikeouts was that they averaged so many to the game. Fortunately for the fan populace there were scribes and enthusiasts who cared for the strikeout data and they kept plugging away after it and now the strikeout records are complete from 1882 on. That they are complete is due to MacLean Kennedy of Detroit, Michigan, who is the strikeout authority of the country and who supplied the writer with much of the material that comes later.

Balldom is right in giving Matthew Kilroy, left hander of the Baltimore American Association team of 1886, credit for fanning more men in one year than anyone else. His total was 505. The little Red Book is wrong in saying that Amos Rusie holds the strikeout record for the National League with his 345 in 1890. Charles Radbourne, of Providence claimed 411 victims in 1884.

Walter Perry Johnson of the Washington Americans is likely to go thundering down to posterity as the world's greatest strikeout king. He has led his league, in what Charles Dryden termed navy yard home runs, 10 seasons, five of these in succession.

George Edward Waddell, left hander, was the Fanning Monarch of the big leagues for seven years, leading the American League for six consecutive years—or one more in succession than the great right hander of the Senators, who was coming in as he was getting ready to go out.

Amos Rusie, the Hoosier Thunder-bolt, reigned supreme in the National League as the Whiffing Monarch for six straight years, then laid off for a season because of a salary dispute and after-wards never was his great, glorious self.

Grover Cleveland Alexander was the Nationals' pace setter in strikeouts for six seasons, four in succession and Christopher Mathewson, now fighting tuberculosis at Saranac was its hero for five, three of these coming consecu-tively.

The list of the leaders, this list being the most complete one ever presented:

Leaders in Strike-Outs
(National League from 1882 on, all other major leagues complete)

Year	Pitcher	Club	League	Strike Outs
1886	Matthew Kilroy	Baltimore	Association	505
1884	Hugh Daly	Chicago–Pitts.	Union	464
1884	Charles Radbourn	Providence	National	411
1884	Guy Hecker	Louisville	Association	368
1889	Mark Baldwin	Columbus	Association	368
1883	Timothy J. Keefe	New York	Association	360
1887	Thomas Ramsey	Louisville	Association	*348
1890	Amos W. Rusie	New York	National	345
1904	George E. Waddell	Philadelphia	American	343
1886	Charles B. Baldwin	Detroit	National	340
1888	Timothy J. Keefe	New York	National	334
1885	John G. Clarkson	Chicago	National	333
1891	Amos W. Rusie	New York	National	321
1910	Walter P. Johnson	Washington	American	313
1883	James E. Whitney	Boston	National	308
1885	Edward Morris	Pittsburgh	Association	303
1892	Amos W. Rusie	New York	National	303
1912	Walter P. Johnson	Washington	American	303
1903	George E. Waddell	Philadelphia	American	301
1889	John G. Clarkson	Boston	National	292
1882	Timothy J. Keefe	Troy	National	289
1905	George E. Waddell	Philadelphia	American	286
1882	Anthony J. Mullane	Louisville	Association	281
1908	Edward A. Walsh	Chicago	American	269
1903	Christopher Mathewson	New York	National	267
1908	Christopher Mathewson	New York	National	259
1911	Edward A. Walsh	Chicago	American	255

Year	Pitcher	Club	League	Strike Outs
1898	J. Bentley Seymour	New York	National	249
1914	W. F. Falkenberg	Indianapolis	Federal	245
1913	Walter P. Johnson	Washington	American	243
1915	Grover C. Alexander	Philadelphia	National	241
1901	Frank L. Hahn	Cincinnati	National	237
1911	Richard W. Marquard	New York	National	237
1890	Thomas Ramsey	St. Louis	Association	234
1891	John Stivetts	St. Louis	Association	232
1915	Arthur D. Davenport	St. Louis	Federal	228
1916	Walter P. Johnson	Washington	American	228
1887	John G. Clarkson	Chicago	National	*227
1907	George E. Waddell	Philadelphia	American	226
1914	Walter P. Johnson	Washington	American	225
1888	Edward Seward	Philadelphia	Association	219
1902	Victor G. Willis	Boston	National	219
1914	Grover C. Alexander	Philadelphia	National	214
1904	Christopher Mathewson	New York	National	212
1902	George E. Waddell	Philadelphia	American	210
1903	Amos W. Rusie	New York	National	208
1905	Christopher Mathewson	New York	National	206
1909	Orval Overall	Chicago	National	205
1894	Amos W. Rusie	New York	National	204
1906	George E. Waddell	Philadelphia	American	203
1915	Walter P. Johnson	Washington	American	203
1917	Grover C. Alexander	Philadelphia	National	201
1890	Mark Baldwin	Chicago	Players'	200
1899	Amos W. Rusie	New York	National	199
1912	Grover C. Alexander	Philadelphia	National	195
1910	Earl L. Moore	Philadelphia	National	185
1917	Walter P. Johnson	Washington	American	185
1907	Christopher Mathewson	New York	National	178
1909	Frank E. Smith	Chicago	American	177
1920	Grover C. Alexander	Philadelphia	National	173
1906	Fred L. Beebe	Chicago–St. Louis	National	171
1913	Thomas Seaton	Philadelphia	National	168
1916	Grover C. Alexander	Philadelphia	National	167
1901	Denton J. Young	Boston	American	163
1918	Walter P. Johnson	Washington	American	162
1897	James M. McJames	Washington	National	161
1918	James L. Vaughn	Chicago	National	148
1899	Frank L. Hahn	Cincinnati	National	147
1919	Walter P. Johnson	Washington	American	147
1921	Walter P. Johnson	Washington	American	143
1919	James L. Vaughn	Chicago	National	141
1896	Denton J. Young	Cleveland	National	137
1921	Burleigh A. Grimes	Brooklyn	National	136
1900	George E. Waddell	Pittsburgh	National	133
1920	Stanley Coveleskie	Cleveland	American	133

*Four strikes.

PART IV

Famous Games—
Famous Players
Famous Feats

Remarkable That So Much Is Known

In many ways it is remarkable that so much is known about Baseball, for the National Pastime never has had any store house for its information or for its records and it doesn't seem likely that it ever will have. The most enthusiastic collectors of dope get discouraged sometimes and give up, and what they have gathered together goes into the discard.

Earlier in this book it was shown that there had been over 45,000 games played in the major leagues, or in the near major leagues.

Does anyone know everything unique about these games?

Positively, NO.

Some people know something about some of them.

No one knows something about all of them.

There isn't in existence a complete roster of the major league players for all time, unless some sterling collector is hiding under a bushel.

When something sensational is done in a major league game, a quick way to find out if it has been done before is to consult the guides or handbooks and then all the previous instances of the feat may not be in the authorities searched.

The time probably will never come when everything will be known about baseball as it has been exemplified in the major leagues and the time certainly never will come when everything that has happened in the minor leagues will be catalogued and ready for the seeker after information.

Sure About Home Runs

The historians feel that they have the absolute low down on the number of major leaguers who have made four home runs in one game, there having been two such men—Robert Lincoln Lowe of Boston and Edward J. Delahanty of Philadelphia. Both were National Leaguers. Lowe made his four homers at home, Delahanty away from home.

The Bean Eater faced Elton Chamberlain of Cincinnati and the Quaker batted against William H. (Adonis) Terry of Chicago. Each man made a single at the same time. Lowe batted six times, Delahanty five times, Lowe's homers being in succession and two of them coming on one inning—the third. The first time Lowe batted against Chamberlain he failed to hit safely.

The game in which Lowe made his four homers was played on the former Brotherhood grounds in Boston, the National League park having been visited by fire earlier in the playing season.

And the game in which Delahanty made his four four-baggers his team lost on the basis of 9 to 8.

All of Delahanty's home runs were inside the park; all of Lowe's hits for the full distance went over the fences. These are the box scores of the two games:

Four Home Runs for Lowe

National League Game

Played at Boston—May 30, (P.M.) 1894

Boston	AB	R	BH	PO	A	E
Lowe, 2b	6	4	5	2	2	1
Long, ss	3	5	2	2	4	2
Duffy, cf	5	0	1	1	0	0
T. McCarthy, lf	6	2	3	3	0	0
Nash, 3b	4	3	3	1	1	0
Tucker, 1b	2	1	0	11	2	0
Bannon, rf	4	2	2	1	0	0
Ryan, c	5	2	2	4	0	0
Nichols, p	5	1	1	2	3	0
Totals	40	20	19	27	12	3

Cincinnati	AB	R	BH	PO	A	E
Hoy, cf	6	1	1	3	0	0
J. McCarthy, 1b	5	2	2	9	1	1
Latham, 3b	4	3	2	0	8	2
Holliday, lf	4	3	2	1	0	0
McPhee, 2b	5	0	2	4	4	0
Vaughn, c	5	1	2	3	5	1
Canavan, rf	5	1	1	2	0	0
Smith, ss	5	0	1	1	4	0
Chamberlain, p	5	0	2	0	1	0
Totals	44	11	15	24	23	4

Boston	2	0	9	0	1	5	2	1	x—20
Cincinnati	2	0	0	0	4	0	0	0	5—11

Two base hits—Latham, 2; Long, T. McCarthy, Ryan, Chamberlain. Home runs—LOWE, 4; Holliday, 2; Long, Vaughn, Canavan. Sacrifice—Duffy. Stolen bases—Long, Duffy, Nash, Latham. Bases on balls—Off Chamberlain, 8; off Nichols, 2. Struck out—By Nichols, 1; by Chamberlain, 1. Wild pitches—Nichols, 1; Chamberlain, 1. Umpire—Charles Edward Swartwood. Time—2.15.

Four Home Runs for Delahanty

National League Game

Played at Chicago—July 13, 1896

Philadelphia	AB	R	BH	PO	A	E
Cooley, lf	3	1	1	1	0	0
Hulen, ss	4	1	1	1	4	0
Mertes, cf	5	1	0	1	0	0
Delehanty, 1b	5	4	5	9	0	0
Thompson, rf	5	0	1	2	0	0
Hallman, 2b	4	1	1	5	3	0
Clements, c	2	0	0	5	3	0
Nash, 3b	4	0	0	0	3	1
Garvin, p	4	0	0	0	1	0
Totals	36	8	9	24	14	1

Chicago	AB	R	BH	PO	A	E
Everett, 3b	3	1	2	1	3	0
Dahlen, ss	2	2	0	0	0	0
Lange, cf	4	2	2	4	0	0
Anson, 1b	3	0	1	12	2	0
Ryan, rf	4	1	1	2	0	1
Decker, lf	4	1	1	0	0	1
Pfeffer, 2b	4	0	2	1	4	0
Terry, p	4	1	2	2	3	0
Donohue, c	3	1	0	5	0	0
Totals	31	9	11	27	12	2

Philadelphia	2	1	0	0	3	0	1	0	1— 8
Chicago	1	0	4	0	4	0	0	0	x—9

Two base hits—Lange, Terry, Thompson, Decker. Three base hits—Lange, Pfeffer, Home runs—DELAHANTY, 4. Stolen bases—Everett, 2; Dahlen, 2; Lange, Anson, Mertes, Thompson. Sacrifices—Hulen, Everett. Double play—Hulen, Hallman and DELAHANTY. Bases on balls—Off Garvin, 5; off Terry, 3. Struck out—By Garvin, 4; by Terry, 5. Hit by pitcher—By Terry, 1. Umpire—Robert Emslie. Time—2.15.

Note—The Philadelphia catcher and Philadelphia shortstop in this game both were left handed throwers.

George Kelly Once Made Four Homers

George Lange Kelly, nephew of the famous Bill Lange and first baseman of the New York Giants, made four home runs and a double in one game before he became permanently connected with the McGraw forces. That game was played at Reading, Pa., on June 24, 1919, between the Rochester and Reading International League clubs. Kelly was with Rochester then and this is how the Rochester club happened to procure him.

Kelly had been with the Giants in 1916 and 1917 and hadn't shown much. Loaned to the Pirates, they returned him with thanks. Arthur Irwin was managing Rochester and the owner of that club was not keenly anxious to spend very much money for talent or even for railroad fare. He agreed, however, to pay Kelly's railroad fare from California to the training camp if he made good and in the meantime Irwin had to advance the railroad fare. Kelly made good and Irwin got the cash he had advanced for transportation back and Rochester got something like $7,000 from New York for a player it once had owned and had given away.

Kelly got four home runs, all in succession, struck out and doubled once in six times at bat off Dean Barnhardt of Reading—a pitcher who has a submarine ball. The inning in which Kelly fanned was the eighth and Barnhardt, on instructions of John Hummel, then used slow balls on him. In the ninth Dean used his fast delivery again and Kelly doubled off one of the submarine artist's speedy serves.

Rochester won the game, 19 to 0, this being the score of said game:

Four Home Runs for Kelly

International League Game

Played at Reading—June 24, 1910

Rochester	AB	R	BH	PO	A	E
Carris, 2b	6	2	4	2	4	0
Rodriguez, ss	6	1	1	1	2	0

Rochester	AB	R	BH	PO	A	E
Moran, cf	6	4	3	3	0	0
See, rf	6	4	5	1	0	0
KELLY, 1b	6	5	5	8	1	0
Nagle, 3b	6	2	4	5	2	0
Matthews, lf	6	0	1	4	0	0
O'Neil, c	5	1	2	1	0	0
Shinault, c	1	0	0	1	0	0
Clifford, p	5	0	0	1	2	0
Totals	53	19	25	27	11	0

Reading	AB	R	BH	PO	A	E
Altenberg, rf	4	0	0	2	0	0
Burns, cf	4	0	0	3	0	0
Walsh, 3b	4	0	1	2	6	2
Hummel, 2b	4	0	1	2	1	0
Kennick, 1b	4	0	2	9	0	0
Sheridan, ss	4	0	2	3	2	0
Ritter, lf	4	0	0	0	0	1
Crossin, c	3	0	0	5	0	1
Barnhardt, p	3	0	1	1	4	0
Totals	24	0	7	27	13	4

Rochester	0	2	3	0	3	0	5	0	6—19
Reading	0	0	0	0	0	0	0	0	6— 0

Two base hits—Nagle, Carris, Kelly, Matthews. Three base hit—O'Neil. Home runs—KELLY, 4; See, 2; Nagle. Double play—Barnhardt and Nagle. Struck out—By Barnhardt, 5; by Clifford, 2. Wild pitches—Barnhardt. Umpires—Carpenter and Wilson. Time—2.06.

An Earlier International Hero

Long before Bill Lange's nephew made four home runs and a double in one game, an International League player had done the same thing. This player was William Bottenus, outfielder, of Buffalo. He collected four home runs and one double off Campfield of Wilkes-Barre in a seven inning game at Buffalo on May 12, 1895, the International League then being called the Eastern League and having a Class A rating.

Bottenus batted five times in this game and scored four runs. The Bisons won the fray, 18 to 13. The only player involved in it still prominent in baseball is William J. Clymer, who started the present season as manager of the Newark International League club. Clymer went hitless.

Bottenus hit like a fiend in the minor leagues, but for some reason never was promoted.

Another Four Homer Man

Still another member of the I Made Four Homers in One Game Club was Charles John Crooks, an infielder who played in the American Association and National League in the late eighties and the early nineties. Crooks, called Jack when he played in the majors, emitted four home runs and one single for the Omaha Western Association club in a game played against St. Paul, Willie Mains pitching, at St. Paul on June 8, 1889.

The striking thing about Crook's performance, and one not noted previously when said performance was commented on, was that the day he made four home runs he batted in thirteen tallies. That is two more than the major league record, held by Wilbert Robinson.

Frank Selee, later at the head of the Boston and Chicago National League clubs managed Omaha the year Crooks slashed out four homers (and one single) in one game, and in the game in question the pitching was done by William H. Clark and Charles A. Nichols. Old-time fans will speak of them as Dad and Kid. Clark holds the International League record for consecutive victories with John Mahlon Ogden of Ogden, Pa., in the winter time and of Baltimore, Md., in the summer time.

The score of the game in which Crooks distinguished himself:

Four Home Runs for Crooks

Western Association Game

Played at St. Paul—June 8, 1889

Omaha	AB	R	BH	PO	A	E
Cooney, ss	3	2	0	0	3	0
Cleveland, 3b	5	2	2	5	4	2
Strauss, rf	3	3	1	0	0	0
CROOKS, 2b	5	5	5	4	3	1
Nagle, c	5	2	3	4	1	1
Willis, cf	5	0	0	2	0	2
Andrews, 1b	4	1	1	11	1	0
Canavan, lf	4	2	1	1	0	2
Clark, p	3	2	0	0	1	0
Nichols, p	1	0	0	0	0	0
Totals	38	19	13	27	13	7

St. Paul	AB	R	BH	PO	A	E
Hawes, 1b	5	2	1	8	0	0
Murphy, cf	5	2	0	1	0	0
Carroll, rf	4	4	2	5	2	0
Reilly, 3b	6	2	2	0	0	0
Werrick, 2b	6	2	3	2	2	0
Daly, lf	5	2	2	1	0	2
Farmer, ss	5	0	2	0	0	3
Broughton, c	4	1	1	7	3	0
Mains, p	5	0	3	0	1	1
Totals	45	15	16	24	8	6

Omaha	205	513	21x—19
St. Paul	203	324	100—15

Home runs—CROOKS, 4; Nagle, 2; Andrews, Carroll, Reilly. Two base hits—Werrick, 2; Daly. Stolen bases—Carroll, Reilly, Canavan. Double plays—Cleveland, CROOKS and Andrews; Carroll and Hawes. Struck out—By Mains, 6; by Clark, 2; by Nichols, 2. Bases on balls—Off Mains, 8; off Clark, 4; off Nichols, 1. Wild pitch—Mains. Passed ball—Nagle. Umpire—Andrew Cusick. Time—2.05.

Williams Was Number 11

When the major league seasons of 1922 started, ten players stood credited with the feat of having made three home runs in one game, Kenneth Williams of the St. Louis Browns raising the number of these athletes to 11 soon after the campaigns got under way. Baseball's expert accountants feel pretty sure that from 1876 to 1921, inclusive, they have all the individuals of the fast set who did what Mr. Williams did. Of the ten men nine were National Leaguers, one was employed in the American Association. The list printed in The Little Red Book is all right except that 1886 is given as the year in which Roger Connor made his three home runs in one game, when the year happened to be 1888. Compiler White probably will have this error corrected in the next issue of the child of his brain.

These were the ten major leaguers who made three home runs in one game previous to 1922 and certain accurate information as to the contest in question:

The Earlier Williamses

EDWARD N. WILLIAMSON, Chicago Nationals, against Detroit at Chicago. May 30 (P.M.). 1884—Williamson batted four times and made four runs and four hits. The other blow obtained by the man whose record Ruth smashed in 1919 was a double. The Detroit pitchers were George Weidman and Frank W. Meinke, Chicago winning the game by a score of 12 to 2. Williamson caught this game for the White Sox, and an account of the combat credits him with handling Fred Goldsmith without a flaw.

ADRIAN CONSTANTINE ANSON, Chicago Nationals, against Cleveland at Chicago, August 6, 1884—Anson batted five times, his home runs being in succession. Cleveland pitcher, Moffatt; score of game, 13 to 4 in favor of Chicago. The previous day, against the same club and on the same grounds, Anson made two home runs off James McCormick, making a total of five circuit drives in two successive games—a red letter performance for the majors.

JOHN E. MANNING, Philadelphia Nationals, against Chicago at Chicago, October 9, 1884—Manning right fielder and lead-off man for the Quakers, batted five times. Not known whether or not his circuit drives were in succession. Chicago pitcher, John G. Clarkson; score of game, 19 to 7 in favor of Chicago.

GUY HECKER, Louisville American Association, against Baltimore at Louisville, August 15, (P.M.), 1886—Hecker, pitching, batted seven times and made six hits, his other safeties being two doubles and one single, according to one score, and three singles, according to another. Louisville won this game, 22 to 5, the Orioles' battery being Richard Conway and William Conway. The pitcher who lost this game now is a resident of Lowell, Mass., and the score of this game and certain other information pertaining to it is given later.

DENNIS L. BROUTHERS, Detroit Nationals, against Chicago at Chicago, September 10, 1886—Brouthers batted five times and scored four runs, making a single and a double in addition to his three drives for the full distance. Chicago pitcher, James McCormick, who that year won 16 games in succession. Score of this game, 14 to 8 in favor of Chicago.

ROGER CONNOR, New York Nationals, against Indianapolis at Indianapolis, May 9, 1888—Connor batted five times, scored three runs and had a single in addition to his three homers. The Hoosier pitchers were Egyptian John Healy and John McGeachy, the latter deserting his post in right to relieve Healy, who had a lame arm. Score of this game, 18 to 4 in favor of New York. It is carried in The Little Red Book as having been played in 1886, but Indianapolis was not in the National League then.

W. FRANK SHUGART, St. Louis Nationals, against Cincinnati at Cincinnati, May 10, 1894—Shugart batted five times, scored three runs and had a single in addition to his three homers.

Cincinnati pitcher, Thomas W. Parrott; score of game, 18 to 9 in favor of Cincinnati. One of Shugart's home runs was made in the sixth inning and was followed by hits of the same kind from the bats of George (Doggy) Miller and Heinie Peitz. Shugart was a shortstop, but he covered center in this game.

WILLIAM JOYCE, Washington Nationals, against Louisville at Washington, August 20, 1894—Joyce batted five times, scored four runs and had a single in addition to his three homers, the four hits being made on his first four trips to the plate. The Senators needed the able bludgeoning of Scroppy Bill in this combat, for they fielded poorly in the seventh and the Colonels almost tied the score, which, at the end, was 8 to 7 in favor of Washington. Louisville pitcher in this game, Phil Knell.

THOMAS L. MCCREERY, Louisville Nationals, against Philadelphia at Louisville, July 12, 1897—McCreery, who had been in a batting slump, made four trips to the plate and scored three runs. Philadelphia pitcher, John B. Taylor, (Jack Taylor, I); score of game, 10 to 7 in favor of Louisville. The Colonels had two Clarkes in their lineup—Frederick C., later Louisville and Pittsburgh manager, and William Winfield, who began the season of 1922 as manager of the Norfolk Virginia League club. In this game Edward J. Delahanty of the Phillies started a hitting streak that placed his name among the immortals.

JACOB C. BECKLEY, Cincinnati Nationals, against St. Louis, at St. Louis, September 26, 1897—Beckley batted five times against Wee Willie Sudhoff

and scored three runs, the Reds winning this game by a score of 10 to 4. The Ohioans' pitcher was John Francis Dwyer, now a member of the Boxing Commission of New York. Dwyer was always alluded to as Frank Dwyer by the baseball writers and the guide books carried his name as Frank J. Dwyer, but John Francis Dwyer is correct.

Williams Once Obliged with Three

Before passing on to the subject of the major leaguers who have made two home runs in one game (and disposing of that subject isn't going to take long), it seems pertinent to remark here that Kenneth Williams, who made three home runs in one major league game this year, had done the same thing before he started drawing salary from Philip DeCatesby Ball of the St. Louis American League club.

The date when Williams first inserted three home runs into one and the same conflict was June 3, 1917, at Portland, Ore., in a Pacific Coast League game between Portland and Vernon, Williams' team winning, 4 to 3, in 14 innings, entirely through his work with the willow. John Walter Mails, now with Cleveland, worked in this game against A. Roy Mitchell, who saw service in the American League with St. Louis and Chicago and in the National League with Cincinnati. This was Williams' record in this game:

Second inning—Made home run with man on base, tying score.

Ninth inning—Made home run.

Eleventh inning—Doubled, but failed to score.

Fourteenth inning—Made home run, winning game.

Williams, on his other two trips to the plate, failed to hit safely.

A Raft of Them

Once upon a time a gentleman whose business it is to compile a baseball guide conceived the bright idea of publishing in said guide a list of the major leaguers who had made two home runs in one game. He didn't have this information himself and went to another person for it. This person tried to side-step the request and told the demon compiler the list would be a terribly large one and that it would take a terribly long time to get it up and that when it was gotten up it wouldn't be complete. He spoke with authority on the subject and spoke with bitterness, but his words had no effect on the demon compiler, who told him to get busy and assemble the data.

For the next two weeks the demon compiler was receiving the information he asked for and when he had it all he decided that with the cost of white paper where it is and with the number of pages at his command it would be impossible to print this list, and as said before the list was incomplete.

Nobody knows how many players have made two home runs in major league games, but probably the player who has turned the trick oftenest is George Herman Ruth.

It is not at all certain that the record

keepers have all the major leaguers who have made two home runs in one inning.

Robert Lincoln Lowe did this on May 30, 1894, for Boston against Cincinnati, and the score is printed elsewhere in this book.

Charles Jones of the Boston Nationals turned the trick on June 10, 1880, against Buffalo in the eighth inning and the score isn't going to be printed in this book, for the writer doesn't happen to have it. Possibly Charles W. Mears of Cleveland, Ohio, who bought the Will Rankin collection, has it and, if he has, it will see the light of day sometime.

Another Error for the L. R. B.

Another error for The Little Red Book is not including in the list of major leaguers who have made two home runs in one inning the name of Edward (Jumbo) Cartwright, first baseman of the St. Louis American Association team of 1890. Mr. White has Cartwright down as having the major league record for batting in runs in one inning on Page 44, but his name also belongs on Page 43, along with the monikers of Robert Lincoln Lowe, Charles Jones and Louis Bierbauer.

This is supposed to be a complete list of the major leaguers who have made two home runs in one inning:

CHARLES JONES, Boston Nationals, against Buffalo, at Boston, June 10, 1880—eighth inning. Score not printed in this book and information on feat vague.

LOUIS BIERBAUER, Brooklyn Players', against Buffalo, at Brooklyn, July 12, 1890—third inning. Score of this game printed in this book, for game happened to contain more runs than any other major league contest.

EDWARD CARTWRIGHT, St. Louis American Association, against Philadelphia, at St. Louis, September 23, 1890—third inning. Score of this game printed in this book, for Cartwright seems to have been the only major leaguer who ever knocked in seven tallies in one session. He did this by making one homer with three on and one with two on. Before and after he did nothing.

ROBERT LINCOLN LOWE, Boston Nationals, against Cincinnati, at Boston, May 30, (P.M.), 1894—third inning. Score of this game printed previously in this book, Lowe making two other homers in it.

Howley a Hero

Daniel Philip Howley, who coaches the Detroit pitchers and who assists Tyrus Raymond Cobb in directing the Tigers, frequently tells Heilmann & Co. they are not in his class as hitters. Howley holds a minor league record, for when Dan was manager of the Montreal Internationals he made two home runs with the bases filled in one game—the first off Walter (Rube) Manning, once of the Yankees, and the second off Fred Cook. These drives so jarred the mental poise of the Toronto manager—William J. (Derby Day) Clymer, now with Newark—that he threatened to quit the pastime, believing it was time to do so

when Howley could cause such havoc.

Two Home Runs with Bases Filled

International League Game

Played at Montreal—July 24, 1915

Montreal	AB	R	BH	PO	A	E
Nash, ss	4	0	0	2	3	0
Irelan, 2b	5	3	2	3	3	0
Whiteman, ef	4	2	1	4	0	1
Flynn, 1b	5	1	2	7	0	0
Almeida, 3b	5	3	3	0	1	1
Smith, rf	4	2	3	2	0	0
Holden, lf	1	2	0	2	0	0
HOWLEY, c	4	2	2	7	0	0
Miller, p	4	0	1	0	1	0
Totals	36	15	14	27	8	2

Toronto	AB	R	BH	PO	A	E
Gilbert, cf	4	1	1	3	0	0
Rath, 2b	4	3	4	2	2	0
Graham, 1b	4	1	2	11	1	1
Williams, lf	3	1	1	3	0	0
Daley, rf	3	0	1	0	0	0
Cather, 3b	1	0	1	1	4	0
Kocher, c	4	0	0	1	3	0
Wares, ss	4	0	1	3	4	1
Manning, p	1	0	0	0	2	0
Cook, p	3	0	0	0	1	0
Totals	31	6	11	24	17	2

Montreal	0	4	3	0	0	0	6	2	x—15
Toronto	0	0	3	0	1	0	1	0	1— 6

Two base hits—Smith, Whiteman, Flynn, Almeida. Three base hits—Gilbert, Graham. Home runs—HOWLEY 2, Irelan 2, Flynn. Sacrifices—Holden, Graham, Williams. Stolen bases—Almeida 3, Daley 2, Williams 2. Bases on balls—Off Miller 3, off Manning 3, off Cook 2. Struck out—By Miller 5, by Cook 1. Wild pitch—Miller. Hits—Off Manning, 6 in 2 and 1–3 innings. Umpires—Eckman and Freeman. Time—1.59.

Player Once Made Eight Homers

Balldom, disseminating information on players who made many home runs in one game, placed the limit for one battle as seven, with Harry Wright of the Cincinnati Reds as their author on June 12, 1867, against the Holt club, at or of Newport, Ky.

Catching for the Reading International League club when this season of 1922 started was a man who struck eight circuit blows in one game, this individual being J. J. Clarke, better known as Nig Clarke, who was with Cleveland for several years and who once led the American League in batting.

Clarke got his eight homers while playing with the Corsicanna Texas League team in a game played at Ennis, Texas, on July 14, 1902, against Texarkana. The game was a regularly scheduled game and had been transferred to Ennis. For years nobody saw the score, but J. Doak Roberts, who once tried to sell a promising young outfielder named Tris Speaker to the St. Louis Browns, always vouched for it and finally sent it to the writer, getting it, we surmise, from Dude Ransom of Corsicana, Tex.

Anyhow the present president of the Texas League, who claims to have every score of every Texas League game, sent the score on and it showed that Clarke's team won the game in which he made

eight homers by a score of 51 to 3. The victors struck 53 blows, totaling 109 bases. J. Walter Morris, later a Cardinal shortstop under the McCloskey regime and still later president of the Texas League, played with the winners, who went through the season without being shut out and who once had a string of 27 straight victories.

Don't forget that to go through a season without being whitewashed is some record.

Eight Home Runs for One Player

Texas League Game

Played at Ennis—July 14, 1902

Corsicana	AB	R	BH	PO	A	E
Maloney, cf	6	5	3	5	0	0
Alexander, 2b	8	5	8	4	5	0
Ripley, rf	8	6	5	0	0	0
Pendleton, lf	8	6	8	1	2	0
Markley, 3b	7	7	6	3	4	0
O'Connor, 1b	8	7	7	8	0	0
CLARKE, c	8	8	8	3	1	0
Morris, ss	8	6	6	3	4	0
Wright, p	4	1	2	0	2	0
Totals	65	51	53	27	18	0

Texarkana	AB	R	BH	PO	A	E
Deskin, cf	5	1	2	6	1	0
Mulkley, 2b	4	0	1	0	2	1
Wolter, 3b	4	0	1	2	2	2
Wolf, c	4	1	1	2	2	0
Murphy, lf	4	0	1	3	1	0
DeWitt, p	3	0	1	0	2	0
Tackaberry, 1b	4	1	1	9	0	0
Dillon, rf	4	0	1	1	0	0
Burns, ss	4	0	0	4	3	2
Totals	36	3	9	27	13	5

Two base hits—Maloney, Alexander, Morris, Ripley. Three base hits—Markley, O'Connor. Home runs—CLARKE 8, O'Connor 3, Pendleton 2, Alexander 2, Maloney. Stolen bases—Maloney, Alexander, Morris, Ripley. Double plays—Morris, Alexander and O'Connor; Alexander, Morris and O'Connor; Morris and Alexander; Burns and Tackaberry. Bases on balls—Off Wright 3, off DeWitt 13. Struck out—By Wright 2, by DeWitt 1. Umpires—Method and Cavendar. Time—2.10.

More Home Run Data

Quite a few minor leaguers have made three home runs in a game, but no list is complete. The first International League player to accomplish the feat was Joseph W. Knight, left fielder of the Hamilton club, at Buffalo and against Buffalo on July 4, 1887. The Bison pitcher on this occasion was John J. Fanning and he was beaten 15 to 4, Knight having a single besides his three drives for the full distance.

Probably the first Eastern League player (the present Dan O'Neil directed organization is meant) to make three home runs in one game was Outfielder William Murphy of Hartford, at New Haven and against New Haven on May 9, 1889. At that time the Eastern was known as the Atlantic Association. Sworback was the New Haven pitcher in this game. The Weissmen of that time lost this game by a score of 10 to 4.

The American Association of the present time has a circuit that includes quite a few of the clubs that made p the old Northwestern League, and apparently the first Northwestern Leaguer to

make three home runs in one game was George Rooks, outfielder of Oshkosh, against Eau Claire on June 16, 1886.

Outfielder William Bottenus of the Springfield Eastern League club made three home runs in two innings of the game with Binghamton at Binghamton, Barnett and Carey pitching, on July 25, 1893, and he might have made more only that he got into a row with the umpire—Herman Doescher—and got fired out of the combat. The Eastern League of that time is practically the International of today.

Scouting on the International League circuit at the present time is a man who made three home runs in one of its championship games, that scout being James Thomas McGuire of the Tigers. McGuire caught for Toronto in 1889 and on September 2 of that year against Hamilton and in Toronto made three home runs and a single off Pitcher Gibbs, the Maple Leafs winning by a score of 22 to 5.

Not Sure on Three Homers in One Inning Data

It is not at all certain that the figure hounds have run to earth all the instances in which three batters have successively made home runs in one inning, but the list is fairly complete and is presented below:

May 31, 1890, Players' League— George Gore, William (Buck) Ewing and Roger Connor of New York, in eighth inning, off John Kinley Tener of Pittsburgh. New York made 12 tallies in this inning and 23 in the game, winning

23 to 3. John Kinley Tener later became governor of Pennsylvania, president of the National League and now is president of the Permanent Highways Corporation, having his office in New York and being extremely willing to furnish a reason for the whaling he got in this fracas.

May 10, 1894, National League—W. Frank Shugart, George B. Miller and Henry Peitz of St. Louis, in sixth inning, off Thomas W. Parrott of Cincinnati. Reds won game, 18 to 9.

June 2, 1902, American League—Edward J. Delehanty, William Coughlin and George (Scoops) Carey of Washington in third inning off Clark Calvin Griffith of Chicago. After Wyatt Lee doubled in this session the Old Fox took himself out.

June 30, 1902, American League— Napoleon Lajoie, Charles Hickman and William J. Bradley of Cleveland in sixth inning off Charles W. (Jack) Harper of St. Louis. Home runs made on three pitched balls. Indians won game, 17 to 2.

Nine Homers the Game Limit

For a major league game the home run limit is nine, that number having cropped up in the contest in which Robert Lowe gathered four circuit clouts and the score of which is printed previously and it also having appeared in a seven inning game between Chicago and Cincinnati of the National League on the afternoon of July 4, 1895.

For one club the greatest number of

home runs in a contest on the fast time circuits is seven. The data:

June 12, 1886, National League—Detroit, seven home runs off Charles Sweeney and Al Bauer of St. Louis, Wolverines winning, 14 to 7.

June 6, 1894, National League— Pittsburgh, seven home runs off William Lampe and Thomas Smith of Boston, Pirates winning, 27 to 11.

June 3, 1921, American League— Philadelphia, seven home runs off Hubert Leonard, Carl Holling and Bert Cole of Detroit, White Elephants winning, 15 to 9.

Made a Grand Beginning

William Duggleby, called Frosty Bill by some of the experts, is suspected to have been the one major leaguer to break in with a circuit drive that scored four runs. Duggleby's first National League game was on April 21, 1898, for the Phillies, in Philadelphia. In the second inning he came to bat with the bases filled, Monte Cross, Ed Abbaticchio and Ed McFarland having been walked just previously by the opposing pitcher—J. Bentley Seymour of the Giants. Frosty Bill at once knocked the ball out of the lot, scoring everybody including himself.

A Capable Substitute

Charles Albert Bender, directing the destinies of the Reading International League club this year, possibly is the one pitcher who, in a game in an emergency capacity, helped himself to a brace of four-baggers. The Chief did this on May 8, 1906, at Boston against the pitching of Left-hander Jesse Tannehill when he took Topsy Hartsel's place in left field. Bender, at the time, was with the Athletics.

For the present no more remarks on home runs.

Triples by Wholesale

The wholesale triplers of the profession thus far have been George A. Strief, shortstop of the old Athletics, and William (Scrappy) Joyce, third baseman of the New York Giants. Each man jammed into one contest four three baggers and the American Association player, when he was doing this, also inserted for good measure a double, thus flushing five long hits in one afternoon.

Nowadays one hears quite a lot about lively balls and on June 25, 1885, when Strief was distinguishing himself there was used, according to a writer of that time, "an unusually hard and elastic ball." With it the Brooklyns, against whom Strief played, made 29 hits and the Athletics 15. The pitcher against whom Strief batted was John J. Harkins.

Scrappy Bill Joyce, when he made his four triples, faced two boxmen, these being Emerson (Pink) Hawley and James A. Gardner of the Pirates. Like Harkins these men were right-handers. Joyce made his four triples a dozen years after Strief did.

One of Joyce's 1897 companions was William (Kid) Gleason, now manager of the Chicago White Sox, and the day Scrappy Bill made four triples, Comis-

key's field general handled fifteen out of sixteen chances at second.

Further information about the two tripling feats can be obtained from the box scores:

Four Triples for Strief

American Association Game

Played at Brooklyn—June 25, 1885

Athletic	AB	R	BH	PO	A	E
Purcell, lf	6	0	0	5	0	0
Stovey, 1b	6	2	2	10	0	0
Larkin, cf	5	2	3	3	0	2
Coleman, rf-p	5	1	2	1	0	0
Corey, 3b	5	1	1	1	2	0
Quinton, c	5	2	0	3	2	1
STRIEF, ss	5	4	5	3	0	0
Stricker, 2b	4	2	1	0	5	1
Matthews, p-rf	5	0	1	1	2	1
Totals	46	14	15	27	11	5

Brooklyn	AB	R	BH	PO	A	E
Hotaling, cf	7	1	2	2	0	0
McClellan, 3b	7	1	3	0	2	2
Swartwood, lf	7	1	2	2	0	0
Phillips, 1b	7	4	4	8	1	2
Cassidy, rf	6	3	4	1	0	0
Pinckney, 3b	6	5	6	2	3	2
Smith, ss	6	3	2	1	4	0
Harkins, p	6	1	2	1	9	0
Krieg, c	3	1	2	4	2	1
Hayes, c	3	1	2	6	0	1
Totals	58	21	29	27	21	8

Athletic	0	0	0	5	1	2	3	1	2—14
Brooklyn	0	3	0	0	5	10	0	3	0—21

Two base hits—STRIEF, Hotaling, Hayes. Three base hits—STRIEF 4, McClellan, Phillips, Smith, Harkins. Home runs—Larkin 2, Stovey. Struck out—Athletics 9, Brooklyn 2. Wild pitches—Matthews 2, Coleman 1. Passed balls—

Quinton 4, Hayes 2, Krieg 2. Umpire—John Kelly. Time—2.30.

Four Triples for Joyce

National League Game

Played at Pittsburgh—May 18, 1897

New York	AB	R	BH	PO	A	E
VanHaltren, cf	5	1	1	1	0	0
Tiernan, rf	5	2	2	0	0	1
JOYCE, 3b	5	2	4	4	2	0
G. Davis, ss	5	2	2	2	3	1
Gleason, 2b	4	0	1	8	7	1
Holmes, lf	4	1	0	0	0	0
Clark, 1b	4	2	2	10	0	1
Warner, c	5	0	3	2	2	0
Doheny, p	5	1	1	0	6	0
Totals	36	5	9	27	13	4

Pittsburgh	AB	R	BH	PO	A	E
Smith, lf	5	0	2	0	0	2
Ely, ss	5	0	1	0	2	0
H. Davis, 1b	5	1	2	11	0	0
Donnelly, 3b	4	1	0	2	2	0
Brodie, cf	5	0	2	2	0	0
Donovan, rf	3	1	0	0	0	0
Padden, 2b	4	0	2	2	2	0
Merritt, c	1	0	0	3	1	0
Leahey, c	1	1	0	7	2	1
Hawley, p	1	0	0	0	2	1
Gardner, p	2	1	0	0	2	0
Totals	36	5	9	27	13	4

New York	103	301	201—11
Pittsburgh	010	020	200— 5

Two base hits—Brodie, Padden. Three base hits—JOYCE 4. Home runs—Tiernan, G. Davis. Double plays—Doheny, G. Davis and Clark; Doheny, G. Davis and Gleason. Bases on balls—Off Doheny 4, off Gardner 2. Struck out—By Gardner 4, by Hawley, 3, by Doheny 1. Hit by pitched balls—Gleason, Dono-

van. Wild pitch—Doheny. Passed ball—Merritt. Umpire—Robert Emslie. Time—2.20.

The Doubling Demons

There appear to have been only nine major leaguers able to acquire four doubles in one game, but there probably were more. One of the men in question—Frank Isbell of the Chicago Americans—got his quartets of four baggers in a contest for the championship of the universe. The nifty nine:

ADRIAN CONSTANTINE ANSON and ABNER F. DALRYMPLE, Chicago Nationals, against Buffalo on July 3, 1883. Bison pitcher, George H. Derby, who wasn't a hatter, but a shoemaker. Score, 31 to 7 in favor of the White Stockings, who crossed the plate so frequently because the Empire Staters spurned chances to retire them. Not one of Chicago's six runs in the fourth, nine in the eighth and four in the ninth was scored before chances had been offered to put the side out.

THOMAS J. TUCKER, Boston Nationals, on July 22, 1893, against New York.

JOSEPH JAMES KELLEY, Baltimore Nationals, against Cleveland, on September 3 (second game), 1894. Cleveland pitcher, Denton J. Young (Cy the First). Kelley, now a scout for the New York Americans, made five hits in five times at bat in this game and four hits in four times at bat in the first game of the double header—a total for the day of nine. Cleveland pitcher in earlier controversy—Sullivan.

EDWARD J. DELEHANTY, Philadelphia

Nationals, against New York on May 13, 1899.

FRANK DILLON, Detroit Americans, against Milwaukee, on April 25, 1901, two of the hits coming in the ninth inning and the last winning the game, 14 to 13. Milwaukee pitchers—Emerson P. Hawley, Harry Peter Dowling and Berthold J. Husting. Detroit team, managed by George Stallings, took this game from Milwaukee, managed by Hugh Duffy, by scoring ten runs in ninth and by score of 14 to 13.

FRANK ISBELL, Chicago Americans, against Chicago Nationals, in world's series' game, on October 13, 1906. Cub pitchers, Edward M. Reulbach, John A. Pfiester and Orval Overall.

SHERWOOD ROBERT MAGEE, Philadelphia Nationals, against St. Louis on June 17, 1914. The last of Magee's blows was a home run, but as there was a man on second and only one run was needed to decide game he only received credit for a two-bagger. Present rule relative to home runs in ninth or extra inning put into code in 1920.

C. C. CRAVATH, Philadelphia Nationals, against Cincinnati on August 8, 1915. Two of Wooden Shoes' doubles emptied the bases of their three tenants. Harry H. Davis, now a scout for the Philadelphia Americans, scored six players with two doubles when he was with the New York Giants on June 27, 1896, game being against Brooklyn, innings in which he cleaned up being the fifth and ninth and the pitchers who suffered being Ed Stein and Bert Abbey.

Heywood Broun
Once a Scribe

Heywood Broun, dramatic editor of the New York World, once was a baseball scribe, breaking into the pastime in 1909 or 1910 in Gotham on the Morning Telegraph. A couple of years later, when he had shifted over to the Tribune, he went South with the Giants as a war correspondent and it was soon after this that the fans were properly informed as to who held the major league record for the greatest number of hits in one game. The individual who held and who holds it—Wilbert Robinson, then coach for the McGrawites—told Broun he once had made seven hits in one game. Broun wrote that fact up, the matter was investigated and it was discovered that Uncle Wilbert was not a member of the Ananias Club and that once he had struck seven blows in a championship game.

That game was played on June 10, 1892, in Baltimore, the St. Louis club being the Orioles' opponents at the time and the pitching for the Missourians being done by Charles (Pretzel) Getzein, once a world's series' hero; one J. P. Young and by Theodore Breitenstein, a left-hander who lasted a long time. Robby batted seven times and made six singles and a double, his club winning on the basis of 25 to 4.

Did the Baltimore papers devote much space to this stunt of Your Uncles?

Extremely little.

A promising young dopester of the Monumental City searched through all the public prints of the time to get the absolute low down on Whaling Wilbert's feat and discovered this:

NOT ONE PAPER PAID ANY
ATTENTION TO THE STUNT.

It is an accepted fact, however, that when Robinson made his seven hits he batted in 11 runs, which is a major league record.

Seven Hits for Robinson

National League Game

Played at Baltimore—June 10, 1892

Baltimore	AB	R	BH	PO	A	E
Shindle, 3b	7	2	2	1	2	2
VanHaltren, rf	5	5	2	2	0	0
Halligan, 1b	5	3	2	13	0	0
Shoch, ss	6	4	5	0	4	1
Welch, cf	6	3	2	3	0	0
Gunson, lf	5	4	2	2	0	2
McGraw, 2b	6	3	3	3	7	1
ROBINSON, c	7	1	7	3	0	0
McMahon, p	7	0	0	0	3	0
Totals	54	25	25	27	16	6

St. Louis	AB	R	BH	PO	A	E
Crooks, 2b	2	1	0	3	2	3
Carroll, lf	5	0	1	1	0	2
Werden, 1b	4	1	1	10	1	1
Glasscock, ss	4	1	1	2	1	0
Brodie, cf	4	0	2	2	1	0
Caruthers, rf	4	0	0	0	1	1
Pinckney, 3b	4	0	1	3	0	1
Buckley, c	4	0	0	2	1	0
Getzein, p	1	0	0	0	1	0
Young, p	2	0	0	0	0	0
Bird, c	1	0	0	2	2	0
Stricker, 2b	3	0	1	2	2	0
Breitenstein, p	2	1	0	0	2	0
Totals	40	4	7	27	14	8

Baltimore	554	623	000 —25
St. Louis	100	002	100 — 4

Two base hits—ROBINSON, Shindle, Shoch, Glasscock. Three base hit—Shindle. Sacrifices—Werden, Glasscock, Brodie, Bird, Caruthers, Halligan, McMahon. Stolen bases—ROBINSON, McGraw, Welch. Struck out—By McMahon 3, by Breitenstein 2, by Young 1. Bases on balls—Off Young 2, off Getzein 3, off McMahon 1, off Breitenstein 1. Hit by pitched balls—Gunson 2, Welch. Wild pitch—Young. Double play—Shindle, McGraw and Halligan. Passed ball—ROBINSON. Umpire—Timothy Hurst. Time—1.50.

Crooks, who played second for St. Louis in this game (they then were known as the Browns), was the player who batted in 13 runs for Omaha in one game, that score having been previously published, and Perry Werden, first baseman for the Missourians, was the world's home run king, by virtue of his 45 circuit drives for Minneapolis of the Western League in 1895, until Babe Ruth dethroned him in 1920.

Back to the Runs Batted In

Wilbert Robinson having batted in 11 runs in this game, a major league record, the time seems ripe to present the score of the contest in which Edward (Jumbo) Cartwright of the St. Louis American Association team established the major league record for the greatest number of markers driven in in an inning, that number being seven and the incident having been alluded to previously.

Cartwright was the headliner in the game played on September 23, 1890, in St. Louis between the Browns and the

Athletics. Then, in the third inning, he assaulted a young Quaker pitcher named Green for two home runs, the first being made with three on the runway, the second with two. He made no more hits during the game, which lasted only seven innings and which resulted in a St. Louis victory, 21 to 2. The Athletics, in this game, were held hitless by a newcomer to the Browns, a youth named Nichols, from some place in Illinois. The A's of September 23, 1890, were a terrible joke team—about as bad as the Pirates of the same era.

Batted in Seven Runs in One Inning

American Association Game

Played at St. Louis—September 23, 1890

St. Louis	AB	R	BH	PO	A	E
McCarthy, rf	4	3	2	2	0	0
Fuller, ss	5	2	3	1	2	0
CARTWRIGHT, 1b	4	3	2	9	1	0
Duffee, cf-3b	4	3	3	0	1	1
Munyan, c	3	2	2	9	1	2
Campau, lf	4	2	0	0	0	0
Higgins, 2b	4	2	1	0	1	1
Gerhardt, 3b	2	1	1	0	0	0
Miller, cf	2	0	0	0	0	0
Nichols, p	3	3	1	0	0	0
Totals	35	21	15	21	6	4

Athletic	AB	R	BH	PO	A	E
Carman, 2b	4	0	0	1	1	1
Sweeney, cf	3	0	0	1	0	0
Riddle, lf	4	0	0	3	0	1
Daily, c	3	0	0	4	0	1
Snyder, rf	3	0	0	0	0	0
Knox, 1b	3	0	0	7	0	0
Sowders, 3b	2	0	0	2	0	1
Conroy, ss	3	1	0	3	3	1
Green, p	2	1	0	0	2	1
Totals	27	2	0	21	6	6

St. Louis	0	1	11	0	6	1	2—21
Athletic	0	0	2	0	0	0	0— 2

Two base hit—Nichols. Home runs—CARTWRIGHT 2, Munyan, Duffee. Stolen bases—Campau 2, Fuller 2, McCarthy, Munyan. Double plays—Conroy, Carman and Knox; CARTWRIGHT and Fuller. Bases on balls—Off Nichols 9, off Green 9. Struck out—By Nichols 7, by Green 4. Wild pitches—Green 4. Passed ball—Munyan. Umpire—Herman Doescher.

Game Containing Most Runs

The major league game that contained the greatest number of runs was played in the Players' League, Brooklyn won it and Buffalo lost it and the score was 28 to 16. The Bisons, whose right fielder on July 12, 1890, was Cornelius McGillicuddy (better known as Connie Mack), were hard up for pitchers on their second trip through the East and in the game in Brooklyn called on a youth named Lewis to perform. He lasted three innings, yielded 20 runs and then retired to left field, Ed Beecher finishing the contest. In the last inning Lewis worked, Louis Bierbauer, second baseman of Ward's Wonders, made two home runs. Brooklyn's scrambled lineup was due to injuries to George Andrews and Dave Orr. This is the score of the major league game that contained the greatest number of runs:

Heaviest Scoring Event

Players' League Game

Played at Brooklyn—July 12, 1890

Brooklyn	AB	R	BH	PO	A	E
Ward, ss	5	5	3	5	4	4
Joyce, 3b	5	3	3	0	1	1
Andrews, cf	4	2	2	0	0	0
Orr, 1b	3	2	3	8	0	0
Bierbauer, 2b	5	3	2	3	9	2
VanHaltren, lf	6	3	1	0	1	2
McGeachy, rf	5	5	2	0	0	0
Daily, c-1b	5	3	3	10	0	1
Sowders, p	5	2	2	0	2	0
Sunday, cf	2	1	2	0	0	0
Hayes, c	4	0	0	1	1	1
Murphy, p	1	0	0	0	1	0
Totals	50	28	23	27	19	11

Buffalo	AB	R	BH	PO	A	E
Hoy, cf	6	3	2	3	0	0
Mack, rf	6	1	1	2	0	0
Wise, 2b	4	2	4	2	5	1
Beecher, lf-p	3	4	1	2	1	1
Rowe, ss	6	2	2	3	3	1
Rainey, 3b	6	2	1	1	1	1
Halligan, c	5	1	5	2	2	2
Carney, 1b	5	0	0	10	1	2
Lewis, p-lf	5	1	1	2	2	0
Totals	46	16	17	27	15	8

Brooklyn	668	015	200—28
Buffalo	401	020	414—16

Two base hits—Ward 2, McGeachy 2, Sunday, Hoy, Beecher, Halligan. Three base hits—Orr 2, Joyce, Sunday. Home runs—Bierbauer 2. Sacrifices—Joyce, VanHaltren, Mack, Wise, Halligan, Carney. Stolen bases—Ward 2, Daily 2, Joyce, Andrews, Sowders, VanHaltren, Hoy. Bases on balls—Off Lewis 7, off Murphy 3, off Beecher 3, off Sowders 2. Struck out—By Sowders 2, by Lewis 1. Double plays—Ward and Bierbauer; Rowe, Wise and Carney 2. Balk—Beecher. Wild pitches—Murphy 1, Lewis 1. Umpires—Knight and Jones.

Ansonites Scored 36 Runs

Thirty-six is the record number of runs scored by a major league club in one game, Anson's Chicago team of 1897 running up this huge total against Louisville on June 29th. The Colonels acquired seven counters. Charles C. Fraser, commonly called "Chick," started to pitch for Louisville the day Anson's team went run mad and was replaced in the third by a young man from Paducah named Jones. The Ansonites scored in every inning, they all made runs and they all made hits. Barry McCormick, National League umpire now, was the leading swatter of the huge afternoon, with six blows. The score of this classic:

A Record for Runs

National League Game

Played at Chicago—June 29, 1897

Chicago	AB	R	BH	PO	A	E
Everett, ss	7	3	2	0	3	0
McCormick, ss	8	5	6	4	1	0
Lange, cf	7	4	4	4	0	0
Anson, 1b	4	4	1	10	1	0
Ryan, rf	6	5	2	0	0	0
Decker, lf	4	2	3	0	0	0
Connor, 2b	6	4	4	2	3	0
Callahan, p	7	4	5	1	2	0
Donohue, c	6	3	3	5	1	0
Thornton, lf	2	2	2	1	0	1
Totals	57	36	32	27	11	1

Louisville	AB	R	BH	PO	A	E
Clarke, lf	4	0	3	2	1	0

Louisville	AB	R	BH	PO	A	E
McCreery, rf	4	1	0	0	0	0
Pickering, cf	5	1	2	1	3	3
Stafford, ss	5	2	0	3	8	0
Werden, 1b	5	1	3	14	1	1
Dexter, 3b	5	0	4	2	6	1
Butler, c	5	0	0	3	0	2
Johnson, 2b	0	0	0	0	0	0
Fraser, p	0	0	0	1	2	0
Jones, p	3	2	1	0	0	0
Delahanty, 2b	3	1	1	1	1	2
Totals	39	7	14	27	22	9

Chicago	357	121	278—36
Louisville	001	050	100— 7

Two base hits—Callahan 2, Werden 2, Dexter 2, Everett, Ryan, Decker, Jones, Donohue, Delehanty. Three base hits—Lange, McCormick, Connor. Home runs—Ryan, McCormick. Sacrifices—Everett, McCreery. Stolen bases—McCormick 2, Lange 2, Connor, Callahan, Donohue. Bases on balls—Off Callahan 2, off Fraser 5, off Jones 5. Struck out—By Callahan 4. Hit by pitched balls—Ryan, Decker. Passed balls—Butler. Umpire—John Sheridan. Time—2.15.

More Games with 30 Runs

Here are the other major league games in which one team rang the scoring gong 30 or more times:

July 22, 1876, National League—Chicago 30, Louisville 7.

July 24, 1882, National League—Chicago 35, Cleveland 4, White Sox getting 15 singles, 10 doubles, one triple and three home runs.

June 9, 1883, National League—Boston 30, Detroit 8, Beaneaters making 28 hits for a total of 46 bases off Weidman and Mansell.

July 3, 1883, National League—Chicago 31, Buffalo 7, White Sox making 32 hits for a total of 50 bases off George H. Derby.

June 26, 1890, Players' League—Philadelphia 30, Buffalo 12, Quakers making 28 hits for a total of 41 bases off Charles B. (Lady) Baldwin, who, in the world's series of 1887, won six out of seven games for Detroit from Comiskey's St. Louis Browns.

September 10, 1891, American Association—Milwaukee 30, Washington 3, Brewers making 23 hits for a total of 31 bases off Frank Foreman and Gilbert Hatfield. Milwaukee had just taken Cincinnati's place in the American Association and it was the team's first appearance at home. Does anyone know of a more auspicious debut?

June 18, 1893, National League—Cincinnati 30, Louisville 12, Reds making 19 singles, four doubles, five triples and three home runs off Rhodes. Flying start obtained by winners, who made 14 runs in first inning.

A 41 to 9 Game

St. Paul, of the Western League, a team managed by Charles Comiskey, defeated Minneapolis 41 to 9 at Minneapolis on July 5, 1896, Byron Bancroft Johnson being the party to whom the official score was sent, as he then was president, secretary and treasurer of the Western League, which was the forerunner of the American League. In this clouting classic the Apostles scored in every inning and emitted eight home runs, the Miller pitchers being John Healy, Carney and Connor. Jack Glasscock, Comiskey's shortstop, batted nine times in this scrap, scored seven runs and made eight hits, two being doubles and one being a home run. Anyone interested in heavy scoring events would do well to look up the Western League of this period.

Another Game Almost as Large

Nine years earlier—on June 15, 1887—Lowell of the New England League won over Haverhill of the same organization 41 to 7 in a game that lasted only 7 innings. Tim Shinnick, who was one of the stars of the New York State League when John Conway Toole, now president of the International, umpired in it, played with the winners, while Fred Doe, who probably knows more about New England baseball than anyone else, pastimed with the losers.

There are plenty of large scores to be found in minor league games if one takes the trouble to look for them. The two cited above are among the largest.

Pitched When Hecker Was Heavy Scorer

In Lowell at the present time lives the man who pitched the day Guy Hecker set the major league game record for runs scored at seven. That pitcher was Richard Conway of Baltimore. Hecker, in the game in question, made according to some scribes, three home runs, two doubles and a single; according to others, he made three home runs and three singles.

If Sir Guy did what his most ardent admirers claimed he did he hit for a total of 17 bases on Conway. Frank Fennelly of the Atlantic City club, on May 25, 1882, obtained one double, three triples and two home runs in one game—an aggregate of 19. Fennelly had plenty of chances to bat against Hecker later, for he played with Cincinnati and the Athletics.

The last season Sir Guy put in with the Louisville team was 1889 and that year the Colonels lost 111 games. Then he went to the Pittsburgh National League club and it promptly lost 114. Both teams Hecker was with established records for their leagues for consecutive defeats and Guy was regarded as a Jonah.

However, on August 15, 1886, he was not a Jonah to himself, for witness what he did:

Seven Runs for Hecker

American Association Game

Played at Louisville—August 15, 1886

Louisville	AB	R	BH	PO	A	E
Kerins, 1b	5	3	2	9	0	0
HECKER, p	7	7	6	0	0	0
Browning, lf	7	2	3	4	0	0
Cross, c	7	0	2	4	1	0
Werrick, 3b	4	1	0	1	2	0
Wolf, rf	6	1	1	0	0	1
White, ss	5	3	4	3	2	1
Mack, 2b	6	2	2	3	7	2
Sylvester, cf	5	3	3	3	0	0
Totals	52	22	23	27	12	4

Baltimore	AB	R	BH	PO	A	E
O'Connell, cf	4	1	0	6	0	0
Manning, rf	4	0	0	1	0	1
Muldoon, 2b	4	0	1	2	1	1
Sommer, lf	4	0	0	4	0	0
Davis, 3b	3	0	0	0	0	2
R. Conway, p	3	1	0	0	2	0
Scott, 1b	4	1	2	9	0	0
Macullar, ss	4	1	1	1	3	0
W. Conway, c	4	1	0	4	1	1
Totals	34	5	4	27	7	5

Louisville	150	104	245—22
Baltimore	020	030	000— 5

Two base hits—HECKER 2, Cross, White, Macullar. Home runs—HECKER 3. Struck out—By HECKER 4, by Conway 4. Bases on balls—Off Conway 6, off HECKER 4. Passed balls—Cross 1, Conway 1. Umpire—Walsh.

Scored Six Runs in Games

Here are some, but not all, of the major leaguers who have scored six runs in games:

JAMES E. WHITNEY, Boston Nationals—June 9, 1883, in game with Detroit. Whitney's team made 30 runs.

MICHAEL J. TIERNAN, New York Nationals—June 15, 1887, in game with Philadelphia. Tiernan's team made 29 runs.

MICHAEL J. KELLY and EZRA B. SUTTON, Boston Nationals—August 27, 1887, in game with Pittsburgh. Their team made 28 runs.

ROBERT LINCOLN LOWE, Boston Nationals—May 3, 1895, in game with Washington. Lowe's team made 27 runs.

CLARENCE H. BEAUMONT, Pittsburgh

Nationals—July 22, 1899, in game with Philadelphia. Beaumont's team made 18 runs. "Ginger" laid down and beat out in this game six infield bunts. Wiley Piatt being the Quaker pitcher and "Chick" Fraser filling in at third.

Walked Six Times, Scored Six Times

Harry Hulen of the Minneapolis Western League club, on August 1, 1895, scored six runs in a game against Grand Rapids without being at bat once. Every time he was up he was passed by the Michigan pitchers, who were George Borchers, Tommy Miland and Jimmy Callopy. The last named is now in Holyoke, Mass. Hulen additionally stole five bases.

Also Got Six Passes

Walter Wilmot of the Chicago Nationals got six passes in a game with Cleveland on August 22, 1891, but he didn't score six runs. Before that and since the record number of gifts for a major league player in one contest was and is five.

Men Who Have Made Six Hits

Thirty-three names now adorn the list of major leaguers who, batting six times in games, have made six hits—and the list doesn't include all the men who have done so. Each year brings discoveries along this line and the last of the published lists omitted Jack Boyle, originally a catcher and then a first baseman of the Phillies, and John McTamany, outfielder of the Kansas City American Association team.

Edward J. Delahanty is the only major leaguer who twice made six hits in games, doing so once with the Cleveland Players' League club and once as a member of the Phillies.

Clarence Beaumont of the Pirates ranks in a class by himself as having scored six runs when he was making his six hits, all these being bunts, by the way.

Daniel Murphy of the Athletics is the one pastimer to get six blows when he was making his first appearance in the American League. He had previously played in the National, so Danny cannot be credited with tearing off half a dozen blows on the occasion of his major league debut.

Only for a bit of misfortune Murphy might have made seven hits the day he made six. The bit of misfortune lay in his train being late and his not arriving at the park of the Boston Americans until the first inning had been played.

In their collection of safeties, five men—one from the National and one from the American Leagues and three from the American Association—included hits of each kind. Larry Twitchell had five long hits and one short one; Ted Larkin, Buck Weaver and Dave Orr, four long ones and two short ones, and Bobby Veach, three long ones and the same number of short ones. Guy Hecker either made three long hits or five long hits, whichever score one desires to use.

Using the score in which he is given five extra base smashes entitled Sir Guy to a total of 17 bases on his six drives. The aggregate of Larry Twitchell's drives is 16, of Weaver's 14, of Orr's 13, and of Larkin's 13. Veach's blows were worth 12 bases.

Lew Dickerson of Worcester seems to have been the first big leaguer to make six hits in six times at bat in one game, doing so in 1881. Possibly somebody did the same thing before that.

Only once did two players make six hits in the same controversy. The players were Jack Doyle and Billy Keeler of Baltimore.

This is the most complete list of six-hit men ever published, but it isn't a complete list:

The Six-Hit Manufacturers
(Arranged Alphabetically)

DID ACT TWICE

EDWARD J. DELAHANTY, Cleveland Players' and Philadelphia National—June 2, 1890, three singles, two doubles and one triple off Mark Baldwin, Chicago; June 16, 1894, five singles and one double off Pfann and McGuire, Cincinnati.

ONLY ONE APPEARANCE

DAVID JAMES BANCROFT, New York Nationals—June 28, 1920, six singles off Lee Meadows, Philip Weinert and Walter Betts, Philadelphia.

CLARENCE H. BEAUMONT, Pittsburgh Nationals—July 22, 1899, six infield singles off Wiley Piatt, Philadelphia. Also scored six runs.

JOHN J. BOYLE, Philadelphia Nationals—July 6, 1893 (11 inning game), five singles and one double off William F. Hutchinson, Chicago.

WALTER S. BRODIE, Baltimore Nationals—July 9, 1894, three singles, two doubles and one triple off Frank Killen and Thomas Colcolough, Pittsburgh. Pirates had a nine run lead at end of fourth on Orioles, who then started hitting and won out, 14 to 10.

ROGER CONNOR, St. Louis Nationals—June 1, 1895, three singles, two doubles and one triple off Jouett Meekin, New York. Meekin had a sore arm, but the Giants' manager made him pitch. He yielded 30 hits and his team was beaten, 23 to 2.

GEORGE WILLIAM CUTSHAW, Brooklyn Nationals—August 9, 1915, six singles off George Pierce and Alfred (Pete) Standridge, Chicago.

GEORGE STACEY DAVIS, New York Nationals—August 15, 1895, three singles, two doubles and one triple off Wilfred Carsey, John B. Taylor and Albert Orth, Philadelphia. Phillies won this game, 23 to 9, Orth then making his first National League appearance. William J. Shettsline, business manager of the Phillies, was the scout who discovered the Curveless Wonder.

JEREMIAH DENNY, Indianapolis Nationals—May 4, 1889, four singles, one double and one home run off James Galvin and Harry Staley, Pittsburgh.

LEW P. DICKERSON, Worcester Nationals—June 16, 1881, five singles and one triple off John Lynch, Buffalo.

MICHAEL J. DONLIN, Baltimore Americans—June 24, 1901, two singles, two doubles and two triples off C.

Roscoe Miller, Detroit. Donlin now dallies with the drama and the movies.

JOHN JOSEPH DOYLE, Baltimore Nationals—September 3, 1897, four singles and two doubles off Frank Donahue and Coleman, St. Louis.

JOHN W. GLASSCOCK, New York Nationals—September 27, 1890, six singles off Anthony J. Mullane, Cincinnati.

RICHARD HARLEY, St. Louis Nationals—June 24, 1897 (12 inning game), five singles and one double off James Hughey and Jesse Tannehill, Pittsburgh. Harley practically ended John McGraw's playing career when he spiked him unintentionally in the knee in 1901. Harley had 11 putouts in the outfield in a game against Washington, June 30, 1898.

ERWIN K. HARVEY, Cleveland Americans—April 25, 1902, six singles off William Reidy, St. Louis, Harvey is now an entomologist on the Pacific Coast.

GUY HECKER, Louisville Association—August 15, 1886, one single, two doubles and three home runs off Richard Conway, Baltimore.

WILLIAM H. KEELER, Baltimore Nationals—September 3, 1897, five singles and one triple off Frank Donahue and Coleman, St. Louis.

TED LARKIN, Philadelphia Association—June 16, 1885, two singles, two doubles, one triple, and one home run off Edward Morris, Pittsburgh.

JAMES J. M'TAMANY, Kansas City Association—July 15, 1888, five singles and one home run off Elmer Smith and John Corkhill, Cincinnati.

DANIEL F. MURPHY, Philadelphia Americans—July 8, 1902, five singles and one home run off George Prentiss, Denton J. Young and Merle Theron Adkins, Boston, in his first American League game. Murphy reached park late and did not play until second inning. Castro played his position in first inning.

WILLIAM G. NANCE, Detroit Americans—July 13, 1901, five singles and one double off August Weyhing, Harry Peter Dowling, James R. McAleer and William J. Bradley, Cleveland.

WILLIAM D. O'BRIEN, Brooklyn Association—August 8, 1889, three singles and three doubles off William Widner and Henry Gastright, Columbus.

DAVID L. ORR, New York Association (Metropolitans)—June 12, 1885, two singles, two doubles, one triple and one home run off Robert Lee Caruthers, St. Louis.

GEORGE B. PINCKNEY, Brooklyn Association—June 25, 1885, six singles off Robert Matthews and John Coleman, Athletics. "An unusually hard and elastic ball was used," says a scribe.

WILLIAM SHINDLE, Philadelphia Players'—August 26, 1890, three singles, two doubles and one triple off William McGill and Enoch Bakely, Cleveland.

CHARLES SYLVESTER STAHL, Boston Nationals—May 31, 1899, six singles off Hugh Hill, John Stivetts and James Hughey, Cleveland.

JACOB STENZEL, Pittsburgh Nationals—May 14, 1896, six singles off Harry Dolan and Sullivan, Boston.

THOMAS J. TUCKER, Washington Nationals—July 15, 1897, five singles and one double off Philip (Red) Ehret and William P. Rhines, Cincinnati.

Rhines was one of the first submarine artists.

LAWRENCE TWITCHELL, Cleveland Nationals—August 15, 1889, one single, one double, three triples and one home run off Michael J. Madden, Boston, Twitchell pitched part of this game for the Indians of old, they scoring in every inning and winning 19 to 8.

ROBERT H. VEACH, Detroit Americans—September 17, 1920 (12 inning game), three singles, one double, one triple and one home run off Samuel Pond Jones, Harry C. Harper and Benjamin Karr, Boston.

WILLIAM B. WEAVER, Louisville Association—August 12, 1890, two singles one double, two triples and one home run off Lincoln and Mars, Syracuse. The next day, off Titcomb of Rochester, Weaver made four hits in five trips to the plate.

JAMES THOMAS WILLIAMS, Baltimore Americans—August 25, 1902, four singles, one double and one triple off Clark Calvin Griffith and Dummy Leitner, Chicago.

CHARLES L. ZIMMER, Cleveland Nationals—July 11, 1894, (10 inning game), four singles and two doubles off George B. (Win) Mercer, Washington.

Most Hits in Game—36

Thirty-six hits seem to be the most for a major league game, the Phillies getting this number off a Colonel curver named Wadsworth on August 17, 1894, and winning then 29 to 4. Some other individual probably would have had the misfortune to have yielded the greatest number of safeties if Wadsworth's back-stop—Weaver—only had clung to a third strike in the first inning. He didn't, and after this the Phillies scored six runs.

Every Philadelphia batter made one or more hits in which the club batting record for the major leagues was set, Sam Thompson acquiring six—three singles, a double, a triple and a home run. He batted seven times.

This is the score of the major league game in which the largest number of hits was made by one club:

Thirty-Six Safeties for Phillies

National League Game

Played at Philadelphia—August 17, 1894

Philadelphia	AB	R	BH	PO	A	E
Hamilton, cf	7	3	5	1	0	0
Boyle, 1b	8	3	3	9	2	0
Cross, 3b	8	1	1	2	5	1
Delahanty, lf-2b	7	5	4	4	3	0
Thompson, rf	7	4	6	0	0	0
Hallman, 2b	1	2	1	1	2	0
Buckley, c	1	1	1	0	0	0
Sullivan, ss	7	4	5	3	0	0
Carsey, p	7	3	4	3	0	0
Grady, c	6	3	5	3	0	0
Turner, lf	5	0	1	1	0	0
Totals	64	29	36	27	12	1

Louisville	AB	R	BH	PO	A	E
Brown, cf	4	1	1	3	0	0
Clarke, lf	3	2	2	3	0	1
Grim, 2b	4	1	1	4	4	2
Flaherty, 3b	4	0	1	1	4	0
Smith, rf	4	0	1	1	4	0
Lutenberg, 1b	4	0	0	9	4	0
Richardson, ss	4	0	1	1	3	0
Weaver, c	1	0	0	1	0	1
Wadsworth, p	4	0	1	1	1	0
Zahner, c	2	0	0	0	0	0
Totals	34	4	8	27	17	4

Philadelphia	606	231	524—29
Louisville	000	202	000— 4

Two base hits—Carsey, Boyle, Thompson, Grady, Sullivan, Brown. Three base hit—Thompson. Home runs—Thompson, Cross, Grim. Stolen bases—Boyle 3, Hamilton, Delahanty. Double plays—Cross, Hallman and Boyle; Grim and Lutenberg. Bases on balls—Off Carsey 3, off Wadsworth 2. Struck out—By Carsey 1, by Wadsworth 1. Wild pitch—Wadsworth. Passed balls—Weaver 2. Umpire, Timothy J. Keefe. Time—2.05.

The Courteous Western Union

Detroit's nine young men had 18 runs scored on them in one inning by Anson's Chicago White Stockings once and naturally the public prints of that place wanted quite a few of the harrowing details. The score for the *Free Press* came in minus the assists and errors for the vanquished and it was printed that way, the sporting editor (who may have been Charles F. Mathison, now of the New York Herald) making this comment:

The *Free Press* would be pleased to submit the full score of this remarkable game to its readers, but the Western Union Telegraph Company, which has now no excuse for poor service, has furnished it bobtailed and in ludicrous deformity it is submitted below. The company was requested to supply the missing links, but the head operator declined to do so.

In the large inning, which is the largest on record in a major league game, 23 men batted and 18 scored. Fourteen runs were scored before a man was put out and before Manager Dan O'Leary changed pitchers. Chicago got 18 hits in this inning and Thomas Everett Burns made three of them—two doubles and one home run.

The score of this remarkable game, said score being from the *Chicago Tribune*:

Majors' Largest Inning

National League Game

Played September 6, 1883, at Chicago

Chicago	AB	R	BH	PO	A	E
Dairymple, lf	6	3	2	1	0	1
Gore, cf	7	2	3	3	0	0
Kelly, c-2b	7	3	3	4	2	1
Anson, 1b-c-p	6	3	4	13	0	0
Williamson, 3b-p-c	6	3	3	0	4	0
Burns, ss	6	4	4	3	5	1
Pfeffer, 2b-3b	6	2	3	1	4	0
Goldsmith, p-1b	6	3	3	1	4	0
Sunday, rf	6	3	3	1	0	1
Totals	56	26	28	27	19	4

Detroit	AB	R	BH	PO	A	E
Wood, cf	4	2	3	4	0	0
Farrell, 3b	5	0	1	1	1	2
Powell, 1b	5	1	0	11	1	0
Hanlon, 2b	4	2	0	0	7	0
Bennett, lf	5	1	1	1	0	0
Houck, ss	4	0	1	0	0	0
Trott, ss	4	0	1	0	0	0
Weidman, p-rf	4	0	0	1	4	1
Burns, rf-p	4	0	1	2	0	2
Totals	38	6	8	*23	14	5

*Sunday out, interfering with fielder.

Chicago 1 0 3 1 2 1 18 0 x—26
Detroit 3 0 0 0 0 0   0 2 1— 6

Two base hits—Burns (Chicago) 3, Anson 2, Goldsmith 2, Pfeffer 2, Kelly, Houck, Gore, Wood, Williamson, Bennett Trott. Three base hit—Gore. Home runs—Burns (Chicago). Bases on balls—Chicago 1, Detroit 2. Passed Balls—Trott 3, Kelly 2, Anson 2. Wild pitches—Goldsmith 1, Williamson 1. Struck out—Bennett, Kelly, Williamson, Hanlon, Houck, Sunday. Umpire—Decker. Time—2.25.

A Fruitful First Round

Boston's National League representatives, on the morning of Bunker Hill Day, 1894 (the date was June 18), gave Baltimore's Orioles the warmest welcome on record in fast company by scoring 16 runs against them in the pry-off period. One pitcher worked all through this session for the Marylanders, this pitcher being Tony Mullane, frequently referred to in this history (or whatever you call it) as Anthony J. Mullane.

Twenty-two men faced the Count in this large inning, 11 hits being made, seven passes being given and one athlete being vaccinated. Mullane's catcher—Wilbert Robinson, Brooklyn manager now—took himself out at the end of the opening round in order to be in shape for the afternoon game, which game the Orioles, recuperating, won then, 9 to 7. In the morning they lost 24 to 7, Mullane being relieved in the seventh by Bert Inks, a young left-hander.

This is what happened in the largest first inning ever played in a major league:

Lowe singled to right; Long singled to right; Duffy walked; McCarthy doubled; Nash singled; Tucker singled; Bannon made a home run; Ganzel flied to Brodie; Stivetts made a home run; Lowe was hit by a pitched ball; Long singled; Duffy made a home run; McCarthy walked; Nash fanned; Tucker walked; Bannon walked; Ganzel walked; Stivetts singled; Lowe singled; Long walked; Duffy walked; McCarthy forced Duffy at second.

Boston and Baltimore also were involved in the largest closing inning on record in the National League and involved in it just previously to their meeting of June 18, 1894.

On April 24th of that year, in Baltimore, the Orioles, taking their last turn at bat against Boston, were behind, 3 to 1. They went after Charley Nichols so viciously he was pulled and then kept up their rough work when Jack Stivetts supplanted the Kid, scoring 14 runs before the third out was recorded. Many of the tallies the Orioles got in the ninth that day proved superfluous, managers then not having learned the wisdom of having their teams, when at home, but last. It used to be thought an advantage to bat first, for then one got the initial crack at the new ball.

In some leagues—smaller ones, of course—a club could go through the season with a dozen balls. Each game would be started with the same new ball and woe be to the player who hit at the first ball, for it came right out of play after the pitcher had flung it once to the backstop.

The first extra inning that was a real large one was the eleventh, in the game between Kansas City and Detroit, of the National League, on July 21, 1886. Then the Cowboys broke up the game properly, scoring 10 runs off Charles (Pretzel) Getzein. The blow-up of the Wolverines so exasperated their manager—William Henry Watkins—that he tacked a $25 fine on Ned Hanlon, his center fielder and a $100 fine on Getzein, each run Kansas City scored in the eleventh period thus costing the Detroit pitcher $10.

Authority for the Gore Feat

George Gore of Chicago and William R. Hamilton of Philadelphia, National Leaguers both, are credited with the greatest number of stolen bases in one game—seven—and quite a few inquiries have been made as to how Gore got credit for stealing seven bases in 1881 when stolen bases were not reported then.

The S. B.'s were not in the summaries then, but the able athletes were filching sacks at that time and here is the authority for the feat:

Story from the *Chicago Tribune* of June 26, 1881—Chicago won over Providence by virtue of superiority in every point of play, but notably so in base running. Gore's performances in this line were something phenomenal. Out of four times at bat, once getting his base on balls, he made three clean hits, stole second base five times and stole third base twice—a record which as a whole has probably never been equaled in a league game. The final score was 12 to 8.

So Gore did steal seven bases on June 25, 1881, even if the score doesn't show it.

The date Hamilton stole seven bases was August 31, 1894, the Phillies playing Washington that day. The game lasted only eight innings. The Senators' battery consisted of Wynne, a newcomer to the National League, and Dugdale.

To make up for having a Washington battery responsible for the greatest number of steals by a player in a major league game, Charles A. (Duke) Farrell, catcher of the District of Columbia team nailed eight Orioles who tried to steal second in a game played three years later.

Win Mercer was the Washington pitcher in this game, which was played on May 11, 1897, in Washington, with Baltimore winning 6 to 3 despite Farrell's great throwing.

The Pirates could have used a catcher of the Farrell type 17 years earlier in their game at the Polo Grounds. On May 23, 1890, the Giants stole 17 bases on the Pittsburgh battery of Schmitt and Miller, Joe Hornung getting six of these steals.

Schmitt was a note-book pitcher. He had a little memorandum book in which he used to jot down the peculiarities of the men who batted against him, but evidently on May 23, 1890, the studious twirler must have mislaid this book or forgotten when he had written, for the Giants pestled him for 19 hits and had as many stolen bases as runs.

Twenty-two years elapsed in the major leagues before another player swiped six cushions in a game (Hamilton swiped seven, not six). Then Edward Trowbridge Collins of the Athletics, who played under the alias of Sullivan when he first pastimed in the American League, twice did what Joe (Ubbo) Hornung had done once. The two feats came close together. The dope on them:

Eddie Collins Twice Steals Six Bases

September 11, 1912, at Detroit—Six stolen bases against Detroit, Joe Lake being Tiger pitcher and Bradley Kocher, Tiger catcher.

September 22, 1912, at St. Louis—Six stolen bases against St. Louis, Mack Allison, Samuel Leroy Napier and Roy Mitchell being Brown pitchers and James Stephens and Walter Alexander Brown, catchers. Collins stole second, third and home in the seventh inning.

Joshua Devore, midget outfielder and a world's series' star in 1912, never stole his way from first to the plate in one inning during his career in the National, but on June 12th of the same year in which Collins got a dozen thefts in two games, Joshua pinched four hassocks in one stanza. That stanza was the ninth of a game with Boston, Bradley Hogg and Whitehouse constituting the Braves' battery then. Devore got on twice in the ninth and each time stole second and third. He had no steals previously.

Literature on Sacrificing Slight

There isn't much sacrifice-hitting literature in existence. A man might be the most wonderful bunter in the world and yet fans wouldn't get deeply excited over him nor would special stories be written about him.

The most notable feats in sacrifice bunting were when players advanced their men four times in one game in this manner. William Hallman the First got credit for four sacrifice hits in a game in the Players' League in 1890, but perhaps all these were not bunts.

Athletes who have laid down four taps that advanced runners in one game are as follows:

WADE HAMPTON KILLEFER, Washington Americans—Against Detroit, August 27, 1910, in first game and then in second, he bunted first time up, making five sacrifices in a row.

JACOB ELLSWORTH DAUBERT, Brooklyn Nationals—Against Philadelphia, August 15, 1914, four sacrifice bunts.

JOHN J. BARRY, Boston Americans—Against Cleveland, August 21, 1916, four sacrifice bunts.

RAYMOND JOHNSON CHAPMAN, Cleveland Americans—Against Chicago, August 31, 1919, four sacrifice bunts.

August, you will observe, is the favorite month for sacrifice bunting feats to be pulled off in.

As for anything out of the ordinary in sacrifice flies, there is just one performance worth mentioning. On May 5, 1909, Harry Steinfeldt of the Cubs scored Heinie Zimmerman from third three times with fly balls, the game being against Cincinnati and Chicago winning it, 3 to 2.

The Gallant Defenders

Much attention so far has been paid to the heroes of the attack, little to the bulwarks of the defense. The principal bulwark, of course, is the pitcher and now he seems to be coming into his own again after a couple of years when the batsman reigned supreme.

Major league presidents, minor league presidents, too, seem to think that the dear old public, which pays the freight, loves earned run data on the boxmen whereas, as a matter of fact, the d.o.p. cares very little for information of this kind. No pitcher, because he has allowed only a small percentage of earned runs to his opponents, ever has attracted many cash customers to a ball park. On the contrary, a strikeout king or a man who is downing everybody with great ease will bring the fans to the orchards.

Elimination of freak deliveries has reduced the number of whiffing monarchs to such an extent that now there are practically none. Walter Johnson seems to be about the last of them. Urban Shocker of the St. Louis Browns occasionally does something out of the ordinary in the whiffing line, but he doesn't do it on purpose and he does do it with the spit ball.

Shocker originally was a catcher and when he started pitching knew nothing about the moist delivery. His curve ball wasn't much, and it looked as if he would have to return to mask and mit work if he intended to remain in the pastime.

At this time Shocker was with the Ottawa club of the Canadian League, that club being managed by Frank Joseph Shaughnessy, Notre Dame graduate and present leader of the Syracuse Internationals. Shaughnessy suggested that Shocker try to spit ball and Urban J. did, winning over his opponents 5 to 0 the first time he used it. And the first time he used it he didn't use it all the time, faking the spitter a good deal just as Edward Armstrong Walsh used to do.

Shocker, recently called by Alfred Damon Runyan of the New York American, the greatest pitcher in captivity, kept plugging away at his new delivery until he was able to control it and at the same time kept perfecting himself in fielding until it was suicide to try and bunt on him. Shaughnessy, a hard worker himself, says that he never saw such a faithful worker as the present Brownie, and if the real history of the successful pitchers ever were written it would be found that their success was due to work, work and then still more work.

When the time came to sell Shocker, Detroit was asked to take him. Back came the word:

"Mr. Jennings does not like spit ball pitchers."

The Yankees finally got him and they nearly lost him once before they traded him to St. Louis. That was in 1916, when someone in the New York club office, not knowing the American League constitution, forgot to recall waivers on

Shocker after these had been asked so they could send him out. Cleveland claimed Shocker at the time and would have obtained him only that President James C. Dunn of the Indians did not desire to benefit by a rival's mistake.

Walter Perry Johnson, who never pitched in organized ball before the afternoon of August 22, 1907, seems likely to hold the world's strikeout record, for the majors, unless someone discovers some new and baffling kind of ball.

When this season of 1921 started, Johnson stood credited with 2827 strikeouts, these obtained in 15 years. Denton J. Young (Cy I) fanned 2784 men from 1890 to 1911 inclusive—a space of 22 years.

George Edward Waddell, left-hander, who began in the major leagues with the Louisville Nationals in 1897, pitched later for the Pirates and the Cubs and then put in almost 10 years in the American League with the Athletics and the Browns, was a wonderful man in fanning players. His speed was terrific and his curve broke sharply. When he was right he needed little more than an infield and a backstop and in exhibition games it was his practice to call in the outfielders in the ninth inning—and then strike out the side. The Rube died of tuberculosis some years back. His greatest pitching was done for the Athletics from 1902 to 1907, inclusive, and in the first named of these years he had a lot to do with saving the American League, just as Christy Mathewson had a lot to do with saving the National League in 1901.

What kind of a world's series' pitcher

Waddell was, never was determined, as in 1905, just before the battles for the championship of the universe started, he hurt his priceless salary wing in a playful scuffle with some team-mates and he could not operate against the Giants. In 1902, there was no world's series, and when the Athletics won pennants later he was not with them.

Doing his best pitching for the Athletics, it was with the Browns, in 1908, that Waddell had his largest strikeout afternoon. That afternoon was on July 29, 1908, when the Browns, led by James Robert McAleer, were making a great bid for the pennant they never have won and when they were playing the Rube's old team.

On that July afternoon he hung up the American League, right-handed pitcher of the St. Louis club, is supposed to have fanned 16 men in a game against Washington on July 18, 1904. J. Sidney Mercer, now one of the baseball editors of the New York Journal and then the road secretary of the Browns, saying he did and the box scores saying he didn't. Thomas S. Rice, now baseball editor of the Brooklyn Eagle and then a baseball writer in Washington, probably could tell whether Glade fanned 15 or 16 men that day, but Glade's record, until real evidence to the contrary is produced, will stand at 15 — one less than Waddell's. Glade's arm went back on him in 1908, when he was with the Yankees, and he retired from the pastime then to devote himself to his milling interests in Grand Island, Neb.

The day Waddell fanned 16 he almost was beaten, the Browns coming strong

in the ninth and turning a three-run deficit then into a one-run asset. The only Athletic regular in the game who didn't strike out was Captain Harry Davis. Topsy Hartsel and Rube Oldring each fanned three times; Eddie Collins, Danny Murphy, Simon Nicholls and Rube Vickers each fanned twice and Jimmy Collins and Ossee Schreck each fanned once. In the second and fifth spasms, Waddell fanned everybody.

The score of the game in which Waddell hung up the American League (but not the major league) record for strikeouts:

Waddell Strikes Out Sixteen

American League Game

Played at St. Louis — July 29, 1908

St. Louis	AB	R	BH	PO	A	E
Stone, lf	4	0	0	1	1	0
Hartzell, rf	4	0	1	0	0	0
Williams, 2b	4	2	1	2	1	1
Wallace, ss	4	1	2	0	1	0
Ferris, 3b	4	1	1	1	1	0
Schweitzer, cf	1	0	0	0	0	0
C. Jones, cf	2	0	0	1	0	0
*Criss	1	1	1	0	0	0
T. Jones, 1b	4	0	2	6	0	0
Spencer, c	4	0	1	16	1	0
Waddell, p	3	0	0	0	3	0
Totals	35	5	9	27	8	1

Philadelphia	AB	R	BH	PO	A	E
Hartsel, lf	4	1	1	4	0	0
E. Collins, 2b	4	0	1	0	5	1
Davis, 1b	3	1	0	11	2	0
Murphy, rf	4	1	1	0	1	0
Nicholls, ss	4	0	0	1	2	1
Oldring, cf	4	0	0	0	0	0
Coombs, cf	0	0	0	0	0	0
J. Collins, 3b	4	0	2	0	2	0
Schreck, c	4	1	2	8	1	0

Philadelphia	AB	R	BH	PO	A	E
Vickers, p	4	0	1	1	1	0
Dygert, p	0	0	0	0	0	0
Totals	35	4	8	†25	14	2

* Singled for C. Jones in 9th
† One out when winning run was scored.

St. Louis	000	100	004—5
Philadelphia	000	003	100—4

Two base hits—T. Jones, Murphy. Three base hit—Schreck. Stolen base—Wallace. Sacrifice—E. Collins. Bases on balls—Off WADDELL 2. Struck out—By WADDELL 16 (Hartsel 3, Oldring 3, E. Collins 2, Murphy 2, Nicholls 2, Vickers 2. J. Collins, Schreck). Umpire—Thomas H. Connelly. Time—1.58.

The Same Three Victims Three Times

Waddell, when he pitched his first game at the home the Athletics had before they moved to Shibe Park, did something unique by fanning the same three men in three different innings. These three were members of the Baltimore American League club and were William Oliver Gilbert, who started the season of 1922 managing the Waterbury Eastern League club; Harry Howell and Jack Cronin, and the innings in which they fanned were the third, sixth and ninth. The date was July 1, 1902. The Spalding Record Book names the swinging three as members of the New York club, but New York didn't happen to enter the American League until a year later.

Another absolutely unique feat for the major leagues is the property of Cy Young I. When the Peoli O., agriculturist whiffed nine of the Pirates in the first game of 1900, he distributed the strikeouts one to the inning.

Charles Pick, former major leaguer, now on the Coast, says that once, for a semi-pro team, he struck out 18 men in a game and lost that game 10 to 0. That game would deserve a place in baseball history if it could be located.

And another former major leaguer who also is out on the Slope—William Mitchell of Sardis, Miss.—says that in a Texas League game for San Antonio he once fanned seven men in one inning, that four runs were scored on him in that inning, and that his catcher, Dolly Stark, later with the Superbas, had about eight passed balls. He also says the game was against Houston.

Official Statistician Ruggles of the Texas League might investigate this game of Mitchell's, for it certainly belongs inside covers if it wasn't a phantom combat.

National League's Strikeout Record

Waddell, holder of the American League strikeout record for a game, was pitching on the Coast when Connie Mack, hard up for hurlers, got B. B. Johnson to get the Rube for the Athletics, and it was from the Slope that the holder of the National League whiffing record for a contest came. Charles Sweeney was that individual. He pitched for Providence in 1883 and 1884, and it was in the last named year, on June 7th, that he wrote his name indelibly on the pages of baseball history by striking out 19 of the Bostons, this game being played in Boston.

Of the nine Bean Eaters who batted against Sweeney, just one refused to fan, that player being Ezra Sutton, for whom Larry Sutton, Brooklyn scout, is frequently taken. John Burdock supplied four of the Californian's strikeout string.

Sweeney had to go some to get the decision in the contest in which he fanned 19, for Grasshopper Jim Whitney, Boston's boxman, was in fine fettle, too, and fanned 10 of the Grays. One of the game's features was a triple play.

Sweeney deserted the Providence club later, to go with the St. Louis Maroons of the Union Association, and thus Charles Radbourne got his chance to pitch 22 consecutive games—and to pitch Providence to her second and last National League pennant at the same time.

When Sweeney came back to the National League, in 1885, he had no more 19 strikeout games in his system. The score of the game in which he was a hero:

Nineteen Strikeouts for Sweeney

National League Game

Played at Boston—June 7, 1884

Providence	AB	R	BH	PO	A	E
Hines, cf	4	0	1	1	0	0
Farrell, 2b	4	1	1	0	0	1
Radbourne, 1b	4	0	1	5	0	1
SWEENEY, p	4	0	1	1	19	1
Irwin, ss	3	1	1	0	1	0
Denny, 3b	3	0	1	0	1	0
Carroll, lf	3	0	0	1	0	1
Nava, c	3	0	0	19	3	0
Radford, rf	3	0	0	0	0	0
Totals	31	2	6	27	24	4

Boston	AB	R	BH	PO	A	E
Hornung, lf	4	0	0	2	0	0
Sutton, 3b	4	0	1	1	2	0
Burdock, 2b	4	0	0	2	2	0
Whitney, p	3	1	1	0	11	0
Morrill, 1b	4	0	1	11	1	0
Manning, cf	4	0	0	1	1	1
Crowley, rf	4	0	1	2	0	0
Hines, c	3	0	0	7	6	2
Wise, ss	3	0	0	1	1	1
Totals	33	1	4	27	24	4

Providence	000	011	000—2
Boston	000	000	100—1

Two base hits—Sutton, Crowley. Triple play—Manning, Morrill and Sutton. Base on balls—Off SWEENEY. Struck out—By SWEENEY 19, by Whitney 10. Passed ball—Hines. Umpire—Burns. Time—1.32.

One-Armed Man Fans 19

Another major leaguer who fanned 19 men was Hugh Daily, the one-armed pitcher of the Chicago Union Association club. He made a carbon copy of Sweeney's exploit one month later and in the same city, then winning over the Boston Unions, 5 to 0, and holding them to one hit—a triple by Ned Crane, later a Giant hurler, who made the trip around the world with the Spalding tourists in 1888–1889. Timothy Hayes Murnane, later a well-known baseball writer, who died in 1917, was the first baseman on the team Daily baffled. The score of this game:

Nineteen Strikeouts
for Daily

Union Association Game

Played at Boston—July 7, 1884

Chicago	AB	R	BH	PO	A	E
Ellick, rf	4	0	0	0	0	0
Shoenick, 1b	4	2	2	5	0	0
Horan, cf	4	0	0	1	0	0
Kreig, c	4	0	2	18	1	4
Fisher, 3b	3	1	2	1	0	1
Briggs, 2b	4	1	1	1	1	1
Suck, ss	4	0	0	0	1	0
Householder, lf	3	0	0	1	0	0
DAILY, p	3	1	1	0	22	1
Totals	33	5	8	27	25	7

Boston	AB	R	BH	PO	A	E
Irwin, 3b	4	0	0	1	3	0
Crane, c	4	0	1	9	2	5
Hackett, ss	3	0	0	1	1	1
Murnane, 1b	4	0	0	9	0	0
Slattery, cf	4	0	0	1	0	0
Burke, p	3	0	0	0	12	3
Scannell, lf	3	0	0	2	0	0
Butler, 2b	3	0	0	1	2	0
McKeever, rf	3	0	0	0	0	0
Totals	31	0	1	24	20	9

Chicago	101	210	00x—5
Boston	000	000	000—0

Two base hit—Shoenick. Three base hits—Briggs, Crane. Base on balls—Off Burke. Struck out—By DAILY 19, by Burke 10. Wild pitches—Burke 2. Passed balls—Crane 3, Kreig 1. Umpire—Mr. Dutton. Time—1.55.

Fanned 18—and Lost

A curving contemporary of Daily's and Sweeney's in the Union Association of 1884 was Fred L. (Dupee) Shaw, connected with the Boston club, and on July 19th he must have imagined he was a life member of the Hoodoo club for these apparently good and sufficient reasons:

In the game at Boston against the St. Louis Unions, July 19, 1884, Shaw fanned 18 of the Maroons, let them have one hit, a single by Joe Quinn, later to make his mark in the National as a second baseman with Selee's Bostons, and got beaten nevertheless, 1 to 0.

The game's bachelor count developed in the sixth inning from a muffed third strike by Brown on Gleason, Dave Rowe's sacrifice hit and a wild pitch.

Of Shaw's 18 strikeouts four were supplied by Orator George Shaffer, three by Jack Brennan, catcher by profession, but right fielding that afternoon, and three by Shortstop Whitehead.

Henry Boyle pitched for the winners. He allowed five blows and fanned 11 men.

Another Great Left-Hander

Dupee Shaw was a left-hander and so was Thomas Ramsey, commonly called the Toad, who set the strikeout record for the American Association at 17 in 1886 and then went out a year later, when four strikes had to be obtained in order to retire a man, and equaled his own record.

Ramsey began his Association career with Louisville and finished it with St. Louis. It was as a Colonel that he did his deadliest work against the batters. A brick-layer before he took up the pastime, Ramsey seemed to have acquired phenomenal strength in his arm and fingers laying brick and he used this to good advantage when he pitched. His speed was nothing terrible, but he had a drop ball that would break a foot at least.

The first time Ramsey fanned 17 men was on August 9, 1886, at Louisville, when the Colonels had as their opponents the Metropolitans. One man who refused to whiff was Dave Orr, New York first baseman, he getting four hits in four trips to the plate. Frank Hankinson third baseman, struck two blows and Barney McLaughlin, second basemen, one, but the seven swats gained nothing useful for the Mets, who were beaten, 6 to 0. In this game the Mets' pitcher was a chap named Mays, and if he was related to Carl of the Yankees no one knows about the matter.

When Ramsey equaled his own strikeout record, on June 21st of the next year, with the Clevelands as his victims, the incident created no visible impression on the Forest City representative of the A. P., whose lead for the game read thus:

"CLEVELAND, June 21, 1887 — The fielding of the home players was the worst conceivable and they walked to the bat like innocents going to the slaughter."

One of the innocents of the team of that year, but not of the team of that day, was Robert Gilks, now a scout for

the Yankees and then about everything on the Cleveland club. Said club, with Billy Crowell pitching, was beaten 21 to 1 making 11 errors and getting five safe hits and two hits that weren't safe because they were bases on balls.

In 1887, don't forget that the batter had four strikes before he was retired.

Nine days later, Ramsey came through with another strikeout stunt of large dimensions and this time one of the news associated got quite enthusiastic over the Toad. Witness this lead from St. Louis on June 30, 1887, after Ramsey had fanned 16 of Comiskey's clouting Browns:

"ST. LOUIS, June 30, 1887 — Ramsey's record of 16 strikeouts against the St. Louis Browns took the country by surprise. He beat it by one point, however, in a game against the Clevelands. There is no doubt about it, Ramsey is the greatest pitcher on the diamond and his invincible left arm is worth a fortune to the Louisville club."

The day Ramsey took the country by surprise and 16 of the Browns by the strikeout route his team won 11 to 4, Nat Hudson being the Missourian's moundsman.

When he was taking the country by surprise and taking 16 of the Browns on strikes, these were the men whom Ramsey fanned:

William H. (Yank) Robinson, three times, A. J. (Doc) Bushong, Walter A. (Dude) Latham, William Gleason, Curt Welch and Nat Hudson, twice.

Dave Foutz, Charles Comiskey and James F. (Tip) O'Neill, once.

Nobody escaped.

Seven Chances— Seven Boots

Robinson, fanned oftener by Ramsey on June 30, 1887, than any of the other Browns, became a world's record holder on May 26, 1891, when playing second for the Cincinnati American Association team against Boston, he spurned every one of the seven chances he was offered. John Francis Dwyer, now one of the members of the boxing commission of New York State, pitched this game for Kelly's Killers and won it, 21 to 16, despite the fact that on seven chances Robinson made seven errors.

The Robinson of the Browns of 1887 and of Kelly's Killers of 1891 was the Robinson of the Saginaw team of 1883 mentioned on Page 257 of Balldom as having made two doubles and a triple in the sixth inning of a game against Dayton on April 21st in which the Michigan combination scored 20 runs.

Neither a No-Hit Hero

Neither Ramsey nor Waddell, left-handers, who put Louisville on the major league map, even if they didn't keep the city there, ever pitched a no-hit game in the major leagues. The Toad emitted a one-hit classic at Baltimore on July 31, 1886, for the game went 12 innings and he won it 2 to 1 with Matt Kilroy opposing him. Ramsey then fanned 16 men. The safety off him was a double by Fulmer.

Waddell pitched several one-hit games, but the one in which his chance of getting among the immortals van-

ished most quickly was against Detroit at Columbia Park, Philadelphia, on May 17, 1906. Then the first Tiger batter laid down a bunt and beat it out. After that nobody in the Michigan team's lineup got a hit or anything that resembled it.

The name of the cruel young Tiger who beat Waddell out of a no-hit game at the start of the combat was Tyrus Raymond Cobb.

Fanned 16—and Lost

One would think that if a pitcher fanned 16 men his chances of winning a game in which he did so would be bright, but history shows at least two contests where men have whiffed 16 and been beaten.

One of the unfortunates was a National Leaguer, the other was identified with the then rival American Association. Each ran into this harrowing experience in 1886, more information on these two games being furnished below:

At Philadelphia, August 24, 1886, American Association game—Matt Kilroy of Baltimore fanned 16 of the Athletics and held them to two hits, yet lost 3 to 0. The lead-off man of the winners was Uncle Wilbert Robinson of Brooklyn. Robby whiffed three times.

At Washington, September 28, 1886, National League game—F. T. (Shadow) Gilmore of Washington fanned 16 of the St. Louis club and yet lost 5 to 2. The safeties of the Maroons numbered six, three being for extra bases. The catcher for the losers was Connie Mack, now manager of the Athletics and then about a month old as a major leaguer. Mack got two of his team's six safeties.

Won While Fanning 16

Among the major league pitchers who have fanned 16 men and won their games while getting strikeouts by the wholesale are John Clarkson, Frank (Noodles) Hahn and Christy Mathewson, of the National League, and Tom Ramsey, of the American Association.

Clarkson, in 1886, pitching for Chicago against Kansas City, fanned 16 men and won his game, the date being August 14th.

Ramsey, in 1886, pitching for Louisville (American Association) against Baltimore, fanned 16 men and won his game, 6 to 0, allowing one hit—a single by O'Connell, Oriole center fielder. Date of this game, July 29th; on July 31st, as previously shown, Ramsey came through with another one-hit game at the expense of the Marylanders, this one going 12 innings and 16 men being fanned in it, too.

Hahn, in 1901, pitching for Cincinnati against Boston, fanned 16 men and won his game, 4 to 3, setting every member of the Massachusetts team down on strikes. These were his victims: Herman Long, three times; Fred Tenney, Gene Demont, Daff Gammons, Elmer Smith and Victor Willis, twice; Pat Moran (now manager of the Cincinnati club), Malachi Kittredge and Billy Hamilton, once. The date was May 22nd.

Mathewson, in 1904, pitching for New York against St. Louis, fanned 16

men and won his game, 3 to 1. The date was October 3rd. This was Matty's largest strikeout afternoon in the majors, but possibly not in his baseball career. When Big Six was playing around Factoryville, Pa., in 1897 and 1898, (possibly a bit earlier), he used to get one dollar for pitching one ball game—and he was perfectly satisfied with his pay.

When Matty Started Out

Mathewson, in his first season as a professional, got $30 more a month than Tris Speaker did, Spoke signing for $50 a month and the contract being preserved and shown to Texas Leaguers later who had exalted ideas about salaries. J. Doak Roberts, now president of the Texas League, probably has the contract still. Speaker promised to get it for the writer once, but never carried out his threat.

Mathewson's salary with the Taunton, Mass. Club of the New England League in 1899 was for $80 a month, to be paid in eight installments of $10 each, but when the season closed there still was owing to him several of these $10 installments.

In his first season out Big Six pitched nine full games for the Tauntons, who were tailenders, winning two and losing seven. Right now it should be stated that the authority on Matty when he was a New England Leaguer is P. E. Shirley of the *Boston Herald*.

Both Matty's win in the New England League were over Portland, one of the strong teams of the organization.

These triumphs were at home and away from home. The leader of the strong team that Matty beat twice was John (Phenomenal) Smith and Smith later was Matty's manager at Norfolk. However, that is getting ahead of the story, which has to do with what Big Six did when he was in the New England League.

Christopher the Crafty pitched his first game in professional ball on July 21, 1899, at Manchester, N. H. and lost it 6 to 5, allowing nine hits. His team came strong at the finish and made three runs and it might have won the game had Big Six been able to get a hit or so in his four trips to the plate. However, on two of these Matty fanned. This is the score of the game in which Mathewson made his debut in professional baseball:

Mathewson's First Appearance

New England League Game

Played at Manchester—July 21, 1899

Taunton	AB	R	BH	PO	A	E
Grant, cf	3	0	1	3	0	0
Kellogg, 2b	2	1	1	3	1	1
Geissenger, ss	3	1	0	3	1	0
Vought, lf	4	2	1	1	0	0
Burrill, 1b	4	0	0	5	0	0
King, rf	5	1	2	0	0	0
Smith, 3b	5	0	2	3	0	0
Curtis, c	4	0	0	4	3	2
*Russell	1	0	0	0	0	0
MATHEWSON, p	4	0	0	2	3	0
Totals	35	5	7	24	8	3

Manchester	AB	R	BH	PO	A	E
Hickey, 2b	4	0	2	2	2	2

Manchester	AB	R	BH	PO	A	E
Fitzmaurice, cf	4	0	0	4	0	0
Murphy, ss	4	1	1	2	1	1
Carney, 1b	3	1	1	6	0	0
Lake, c	4	1	2	9	2	1
Shay, 2b	4	0	1	2	1	1
Cotter, lf	3	1	0	1	0	0
Morrissey, rf	3	1	1	0	1	0
Smith, p	3	1	1	0	2	0
Totals	32	6	9	26	9	5

* Batted for Curtis in ninth.
† MATHEWSON out on infield fly.

Taunton	000	000	203—5
Manchester	032	000	01x—6

Two base hits—King 2, Shay, Morrissey, Grant. Three base hit—Vought. Stolen bases—Kellogg 3, Hickey, Lake, Cotter. Double play—Lake, Carney and Hickey. Bases on balls—Off MATHEWSON 1, off Smith 9. Struck out—By MATHEWSON 5, by Smith 3. Hit by pitcher—By MATHEWSON 2. Wild pitch—Smith. Passed balls—Curtis 2. Umpire—Jack Leighton. Attendance—200. Time—2.15.

Lack of control was Mathewson's fault when he was in the New England League and it was his fault when he first went to the Giants in July of 1900. The early part of that season he spent at Norfolk in the Virginia League, his manager down there being Phenomenal Smith, now a police sergeant at Manchester.

Smith signed Mathewson for the Norfolk club in the fall of 1899 in Philadelphia, Big Six being in the Quaker City with the Bucknell football team, for which he kicked two field goals from placement in the game against Pennsylvania.

Matty, in the winter of 1900, either accepted terms or signed a contract with Connie Mack to pitch for the Athletics, but when the season started he was with the Giants. They had turned him back to Norfolk and Cincinnati had acquired him and he got back to the Polo Grounds because the Reds traded him to the Giants for Amos Rusie.

Balldom is balled up on the first appearance in fast company of one of the world's greatest pitchers. Mathewson did not start the game of July 17, 1900, in Brooklyn, nor did he lose it by a score of 13 to 7. That was the score of the game, but Ed Doheny started the battle and Matty only came in after the Superbas had scored enough runs (or near runs) to cancel an early lead the Giants had obtained off Joe McGinnity.

The score of the game in which Mathewson made his National League debut was 5 to 2 in New York's favor when the Superbas took their turn at bat in the fifth. They made three runs off Doheny, got two men on the bags and then Manager George Stacey Davis yanked the left-hander and put Mathewson in. This is how Big Six pitched in the first inning he was at work:

Joe Kelley, Yankee scout now, walked, filling the bases.

Bill Dahlen flied to center, Jimmy Sheckard scoring.

Lave Cross singled, filling the bases.

Joe McGinnity struck out.

Score of the game in which Mathewson made his first appearance in the National League:

Mathewson's First Appearance in Majors

National League Game

Played at Brooklyn—July 17, 1900

New York	AB	R	BH	PO	A	E
VanHaltren, cf	5	2	3	6	0	0
Selbach, lf	5	0	1	2	0	0
Doyle, 1b	5	1	2	10	0	0
Smith, rf	3	1	2	1	0	0
Davis, ss	3	1	0	1	0	2
Grady, 2b	4	1	1	2	0	0
Hickman, 3b	4	1	0	0	5	2
Bowerman, c	4	0	2	2	1	1
Doheny, p	2	0	0	0	0	0
MATHEWSON, p	2	0	0	0	2	0
Totals	37	7	11	24	8	5

Brooklyn	AB	R	BH	PO	A	E
Jones, cf	4	2	1	2	0	0
Sheckard, rf	2	3	0	2	0	1
Demont, 3b	3	2	2	1	2	1
Kelley, lf	3	2	2	4	0	0
Dahlen, ss	4	0	0	3	2	0
Cross, 3b	4	1	1	3	1	0
Daly, 1b	4	1	0	6	1	0
Farrell, c	4	0	0	5	1	1
McGinnity, p	5	2	3	1	1	1
Totals	33	13	9	27	8	4

New York	200	301	001— 7
Brooklyn	001	155	10x—13

Two base hits—Smith 2, Doyle, Demont, Van Haltren. Sacrifices—Demont 2. Stolen bases—Selbach, Grady, Bowerman, Cross, Kelley, Demont. Double play—Dahlen and Daly. Bases on balls—Off Doheny 4, off McGinnity 2, off MATHEWSON 2. Struck out—By McGinnity 4, by MATHEWSON 1. Hit by pitcher—By MATHEWSON 3, by McGinnity 1, by Doheny 1. Wild pitch—Doheny. Passed balls—Bowerman 2.

Umpire—Charles Edward Swartwood. Time—2.31.

Lost Both Classics

Mathewson had the misfortune to lose both the most important games in which he worked—the play-off game with the Cubs for the championship in 1908 and the final game for the championship of the world in 1912 with the Red Sox. In the earlier contest Big Six, according to some, went down to defeat because J. Bentley Seymour did not play properly for Joe Tinker, who probably hit Matty harder than any player who batted against him, and certainly in the world's title game of 1912, unfortunate errors, the most costly by Fred Snodgrass, kept Bucknell's best known graduate from conquering the Red Sox.

Baseball is full of curiosities, and one of these is that Mathewson, when he pitched his last game in the National League, had as his box rival the man who probably beat him oftener than anyone else. That man was Mordecai Peter Centennial Brown, the three-fingered marvel of the Cubs.

Brown, graduate of the coal mines, like Edward Armstrong Walsh, now umpiring in the American League, came into the National three years after Matty, being with the Cardinals in 1903 and being traded to Chicago the next year.

It was Brown who pitched against Mathewson in the play-off game of 1908, the Miner being called in after Jack Pfiester, left-hander, known at that time as Jack the Giant Killer, had opened

wildly and ineffectively. Brown stopped the Giants practically in their tracks and Chicago later had one large inning on Mathewson and then settled the issue as to whether New York or Chicago would play against Detroit in the worlds' series.

National League players of the era of Brown and Mathewson have told the writer that at throttling rallies there was no one quite like Mordecai P. C. "He could go in without warming up and stop you," says John Hummel, now managing Springfield of the Eastern League. "You'd see Brown sitting on the bench one instant and then, when you had started hitting a pitcher, he would desert that spot and be right in there, needing no preparatory work in the bull pen."

Brown generally beat Mathewson, but one time that he didn't do so was June 13, 1905. Then Big Six held the Cubs hitless and won over Mordecai P. C., 1 to 0. Brown pitched wonderfully in this game, too, for until the ninth he let the McGrawites have only one hit. Then he weakened and four blows gave New York the needed run.

That no-hit game of Matty's in 1905 was his second. On July 15, 1901, Christy held the Cardinals hitless and runless. The victory should have pleased him, for it was the Cards who gave him his first defeat of the year after he had won eight in a row. The score of that game was 1 to 0, it was played Decoration Day and John Powell was Mathewson's vis-à-vis.

September 4, 1916, closed the major league careers (as players) of both

Mathewson and Brown. They hooked up in Chicago and both were hit freely, Matty winning, 10 to 8, in a game in which 17 of the runs were earned. The score of this game:

Farewell for Brown and Mathewson

National League Game

Played at Chicago—September 4, 1916

Cincinnati	AB	R	BH	PO	A	E
Neale, lf	6	2	2	3	0	0
Groh, 3b	3	1	1	0	3	0
Roush, cf	3	1	2	2	0	0
Chase, 2b	5	1	2	2	0	0
Griffith, rf	5	1	2	4	0	0
Wingo, c	4	3	4	4	2	0
Louden, ss	5	0	2	3	0	0
Huhn, 1b	5	0	2	7	1	0
MATHEWSON, p	5	1	3	1	3	0
Totals	41	10	19	27	13	1

Chicago	AB	R	BH	PO	A	E
Flack, rf	4	2	1	1	0	0
Doyle, 2b	5	1	3	2	5	0
Kelly, lf	5	2	1	4	0	0
Saier, 1b	4	1	2	10	0	0
Williams, cf	5	0	4	2	0	0
Wilson, c	5	0	1	3	0	1
Pechous, 3b	4	0	1	2	2	0
Wortman, ss	4	0	0	3	5	1
BROWN, p	4	2	2	0	2	0
*Mollwitz	1	0	0	0	0	0
Totals	41	8	15	27	14	2

* Batted for Pechous in ninth.

Cincinnati	012	122	011—10
Chicago	201	020	003— 8

Two base hits—Griffith, Doyle, Groh, Saier, MATHEWSON, Neale, Pechous. Three base hits—Kelly, Roush, Flack. Home run—Saier. Stolen bases—Neale, Groh, Roush. Sacrifices—Groh, Saier, Wingo, Roush. Bases on balls—Off BROWN 1, off MATHEWSON 1. Hit by pitcher—By BROWN (Roush). Struck out—By MATHEWSON 3, by BROWN 2. Wild pitch—MATHEWSON. Umpires—Rigler and Eason. Time—2.10.

Everything Not Known

That the record keepers are not thoroughly conversant with every page of no-hit literature was proved in 1922 after Charley Robertson of the White Sox sent 27 Tigers back to the bench without any of them reaching first base. When a perfect game is pitched there is at once thrust before the palpitating populace the previous performances of this kind and the list printed in 1922 had on it the name of George Washington Bradley, who now is a policeman in Philadelphia. And the reason Bradley's name was on the list of authors of perfect games was that the record books have been giving him credit for a perfect game that wasn't a perfect game.

It is stated in Balldom, that the first major league game, nine innings long, in which a pitcher kept all 27 men from reaching first base was pitched by J. Lee Richmond of the Worcester Nationals against Cleveland in 1880. That fact is right, even if the date given in Balldom (July 12) is wrong.

Bradley was the first National League pitcher to become a no-hit hero, but when he pitched his no-hit game for St. Louis against Hartford he passed one man (Tom York), and three errors were made behind him. At least one Hartford player, possibly two, reached first in this game, which was played at St. Louis on July 15, 1876.

John M. Greene, sporting editor of the Hartford *Courant*, turned up the score of the no-hit game of Bradley's from the files of the *Courant* and it is printed below. The introduction to the game would be printed, too, only for this reason — there wasn't any introduction. The score came over the wire alone. Here it is:

First No-Hit Game in Majors

National League Game

Played at St. Louis — July 15, 1876

St. Louis	R	B	PO	A	E
Cuthbert, lf	1	0	2	0	0
Clapp, c	0	3	3	0	2
McGeary, 2b	0	0	3	6	0
Pike, cf	0	1	1	0	0
Battin, 2b	0	0	1	4	0
Blong, rf	1	1	0	2	0
BRADLEY, p	0	1	0	3	0
Dehlman, 1b	0	1	17	0	0
Pearce, ss	0	1	0	3	1
Totals	2	8	27	18	3

Hartford	R	B	PO	A	E
Remsen, cf	0	0	3	0	0
Burdock, 2b	0	0	3	0	0
Higham, rf	0	0	1	0	0
Ferguson, 3b	0	0	2	1	0
Carey, ss	0	0	0	2	0
Bond, p	0	0	0	1	0
York, lf	0	0	3	0	1
Mills, 1b	0	0	11	0	1
Harbridge, c	0	0	4	2	2
Totals	0	0	27	6	4

St. Louis	110	000	000—2
Hartford	000	000	000—0

Earned runs — None. Base on called balls — York. Umpire — Charles Daniels. Time — 2.00.

Robertson Was the Fifth— Not Sixth

So young Mr. Robertson was the fifth author of a flawlessly pitched major league game, not the sixth, as every public print in the land had it after he had distinguished himself against the Tigers.

The first real, honest-to-goodness no-hit hero was J. Lee Richmond of the Worcester Nationals; the second, John Montgomery Ward of the Providence Nationals; the third, Denton J. Young of the Boston Americans, and the fourth, Adrian C. Joss of the Cleveland Americans.

The scores of all four curving classics can be found later if Mr. Charles W. Mears of Cleveland comes through with that of Ward's game. John Montgomery pitched his flawless contest five days after Richmond pitched his. Richmond won over Cleveland, 1 to 0; Ward over Buffalo, 6 to 0.

Twenty-four years elapsed before Cy Young I got into the glory circle. He won over the Athletics, 3 to 0, on May 5, 1904, in Boston, eight men being retired on strikes, ten on fly balls and nine "groundering" out, as I. E. Sanborn, former president of the Baseball Writers' Association of America, was in the habit of saying, of writing rather.

Four years later — on October 2, 1908 — Addie Joss of Cleveland let only 27 of the White Sox come to bat and won over Ed Walsh, 1 to 0, the Big Reel striking out 15 men in eight innings and still being beaten. Cleveland got its run on Birmingham's single. Isbell's wild throw after Walsh had caught Joe off first and Schreck's passed ball. George Stovall, with a star play on John Anderson in the ninth, kept Joss in the real no-hit class.

The scores of the four classics:

Richmond's Perfect Game

National League Game

Played at Worcester—June 12, 1880

Worcester	AB	R	BH	PO	A	E
Wood, lf	4	0	0	0	0	0
RICHMOND, p	3	0	1	0	6	0
Knight, rf	3	0	0	1	1	0
Irwin, ss	3	1	2	2	3	0
Bennett, c	2	0	0	8	0	0
Whitney, 3b	3	0	0	1	2	0
Sullivan, 1b	3	0	0	14	0	0
Corey, cf	3	0	0	1	0	0
Creamer, 2b	3	0	0	0	4	0
Totals	27	1	3	27	16	0

Cleveland	AB	R	BH	PO	A	E
Dunlap, 2b	3	0	0	4	2	0
Hankinson, 3b	3	0	0	0	0	0
Kennedy, c	3	0	0	9	1	2
Phillips, 1b	3	0	0	7	0	0
Shaffer, rf	3	0	0	2	0	0
McCormick, p	3	0	0	0	10	0
Gilligan, cf	3	0	0	1	0	0
Glasscock, ss	3	0	0	0	2	0
Hanlon, lf	3	0	0	1	0	0
Totals	27	0	0	24	15	2

Worcester	000	010	00x—1
Cleveland	000	000	000—0

Left on bases—Worcester 3. Struck out—By McCormick 7 (RICHMOND 2, Corey 2, Sullivan, Wood, Bennett); by RICHMOND 5 (Shaffer, Hanlon, Dunlap, Phillips, Glasscock). Base on balls—Off McCormick. Double play—Glasscock, Dunlap and Phillips. Umpire—Bradley. Time—1.26.

Ward's Perfect Game

National League Game

Played at Providence—June 17, 1880

Providence	AB	R	BH	PO	A	E
Hines, cf	5	0	2	2	0	0
Start, 1b	5	1	1	14	0	0
Dorgan, rf	5	0	2	0	0	0
Gross, c	5	0	0	5	1	0
Farrell, 2b	4	3	3	0	2	0
WARD, p	4	0	1	2	6	0
Peters, ss	4	0	1	0	6	0
York, lf	4	0	2	3	0	0
Bradley, 3b	4	1	1	1	4	0
Totals	40	5	13	27	19	0

Buffalo	AB	R	BH	PO	A	E
Crowley, rf-c	3	0	0	4	0	2
Richardson, 3b	3	0	0	0	1	0
Rowe, c-rf	3	0	0	3	1	0
Walker, lf	3	0	0	3	0	1
Hornung, 2b	3	0	0	2	3	0
Mack, ss	3	0	0	3	3	1
Esterbrook, 1b	3	0	0	10	0	0
Poorman, cf	3	0	0	2	0	1
Galvin, p	3	0	0	0	5	2
Totals	27	0	0	27	13	7

Providence	010	100	111—5
Buffalo	000	000	000—0

Two base hit—Farrell. Three base hits—Start, York, Bradley. First base on error—Providence. Earned runs—Providence 3. Struck out—By WARD 2, by Galvin 2. Wild pitch—Galvin. Passed ball-Crowley. Umpire Daniels.

Young's Perfect Game

American League Game

Played at Boston—May 5, 1904

Boston	AB	R	BH	PO	A	E
Dougherty, lf	4	0	1	1	0	0
Collins, 3b	4	0	2	2	0	0
Stahl, cf	4	1	1	3	0	0
Freeman, rf	4	0	1	2	0	0
Parent, ss	4	0	2	1	4	0
LaChance, 1b	3	0	1	9	0	0
Ferris, 2b	3	1	1	0	3	0
Criger, c	3	1	1	9	0	0
YOUNG, p	3	0	0	0	2	0
Totals	32	3	10	27	9	0

Philadelphia	AB	R	BH	PO	A	E
Hartsel, lf	1	0	0	0	0	0
Hoffman, lf	2	0	0	2	1	0
Pickering, cf	3	0	0	1	0	0
Davis, 1b	3	0	0	5	0	1
L. Cross, 3b	3	0	0	4	1	0
Seybold, rf	3	0	0	2	0	0
Murphy, 2b	3	0	0	1	2	0
M. Cross, ss	3	0	0	2	2	0
Schreck, c	3	0	0	7	0	0
Waddell, p	3	0	0	0	1	0
Totals	27	0	0	24	7	1

Boston	000	001	20x—3
Philadelphia	000	000	000—0

Two base hits—Collins, Criger. Three base hits—Stahl, Freeman, Ferris. First base on error—Boston. Left on bases—Boston 5. Sacrifice hit—LaChance. Struck out—By YOUNG 8 (Davis 2, M. Cross 2, Murphy, Waddell, Seybold, Hartsel); by Waddell 6. Double plays—Hoffman and Schreck; L. Cross and Davis. Umpire—John Francis Dwyer. Time—1.23.

Joss's Perfect Game

American League Game

Played at Cleveland—October 2, 1908

Cleveland	AB	R	BH	PO	A	E
Goode, rf	4	0	0	1	0	0
Bradley, 3b	4	0	0	0	1	0
Hinchman, lf	3	0	0	3	0	0
Lajoie, 2b	3	0	1	2	8	0
Stovall, 1b	3	0	0	16	0	0
Clarke, c	3	0	0	4	1	0
Birmingham, cf	3	1	2	0	0	0
Perring, ss	2	0	1	1	1	0
JOSS, p	3	0	0	0	5	0
Totals	28	1	4	27	16	0

Chicago	AB	R	BH	PO	A	E
Hahn, rf	3	0	0	1	0	0
Jones, cf	3	0	0	0	0	0
Isbell, 1b	3	0	0	6	1	1
Dougherty, lf	3	0	0	0	0	0
Davis, 2b	3	0	0	0	0	0
Parent, ss	3	0	0	1	3	0
Schreck, c	2	0	0	13	0	0
Shaw, c	0	0	0	3	0	0
*White	1	0	0	0	0	0
Tannehill, 3b	2	0	0	0	0	0
†Donohue	1	0	0	0	0	0
Walsh, p	2	0	0	1	3	0
§Anderson	1	0	0	0	0	0
Totals	27	0	0	24	7	1

* Grounded out for Shaw in 9th.
† Fanned for Tannehill in 9th.
§ Grounded out for WALSH in 9th.

Cleveland	001	000	00x—1
Chicago	000	000	000—0

Stolen base—Lajoie. Struck out—By WALSH 15 (Goode 4, Clarke 3, JOSS 3, Lajoie 2, Birmingham, Bradley, Hinchman); by JOSS 3 (Jones, Dougherty, Donohue). Base on balls—Off WALSH (Perring). Passed balls—Schreck 2. Umpires—Connolly and O'Loughlin.

Only One of Its Kind

Fred Toney, right-hander of Cincinnati, and Jim Vaughn left-hander of Chicago, collaborated in the greatest major league box duel on record, when, on May 2, 1917, in Chicago, each traveled nine innings without allowing a hit. The Reds' northpaw pitched hitless ball against the Cubs in the tenth, too, after his team had scored a run on Kopf's single, Fred Williams' two-base muff of Hal Chase's fly and Thorpe's slow hit to the box. Kopf's safety came after one man had been retired. The score of this famous game:

Double No-Hit Game

National League Game

Played at Chicago—May 2, 1917

Cincinnati	AB	R	BH	PO	A	E
Groh, 3b	1	0	0	2	2	0
Getz, 3b	1	0	0	2	1	0
Kopf, ss	4	1	1	1	4	1
Neale, cf	4	0	0	1	0	0
Chase, 1b	4	0	0	12	0	0
Thorpe, rf	4	0	1	1	0	0
Shean, 2b	3	0	0	3	2	0
Cueto, lf	2	0	0	5	0	0
Huhn, c	3	0	0	3	0	0
TONEY, p	3	0	0	0	1	0
Totals	30	1	2	30	10	0

Chicago	AB	R	BH	PO	A	E
Zeider, ss	4	0	0	1	0	1
Wolter, rf	4	0	0	0	0	0
Doyle, 2b	4	0	0	5	4	0
Merkle, 1b	4	0	0	7	1	0
Williams, cf	2	0	0	2	0	1
Mann, lf	3	0	0	0	0	0
Wilson, c	3	0	0	14	1	0
Deal, 3b	3	0	0	1	0	0
Vaughn, p	3	0	0	0	3	0
Totals	30	0	0	39	9	2

Cincinnati	000	000	000	1—1
Chicago	000	000	000	0—0

Stolen base—Chase. Double plays—Doyle, Merkle and Zeider; VAUGHN, Doyle and Merkle. Left on bases—Chicago 2, Cincinnati 1. Bases on balls—Off TONEY 2 (Williams 2), off VAUGHN 2 (Groh, Cueto). Struck out—By VAUGHN 10, by TONEY 3. Umpires—Orth and Rigler. Time—1.50.

Does King Belong?

Charles King (Koenig his right name was and he was a bricklayer before he made his living playing baseball) once was given credit for pitching a ten-inning no-hit game for the Chicago Players' League club against Brooklyn in Chicago on June 21, 1890, and then it was discovered the game went only nine innings and now it is learned that King only pitched eight innings, so probably his name will be wiped off the list of no-hit heroes.

King lost this no-hit game, 1 to 0, because of errors by Darling, who was doing his best at short in the absence of the regular guardian of that position. Del made a double-barreled error on Van Haltren in the seventh, fumbling first and then throwing to the grandstand, the Californian going to second. He advanced to third when Cook bunted and scored when Hugh Duffy, covering right, threw Lou Bierbauer out at first.

Gus Weyhing, now a policeman in Louisville and no longer eligible to the title of the Human Hatpin, pitched for Brooklyn in this game and Ward's Wonders batted last. So King only had to hurl eight rounds of ball against them. He passed three men and whiffed two, and seven misplays were made by the Comiskeyites.

King ought to come out of the ranks of the no-hit heroes and the record keepers probably will take his name off the list of these individuals.

Here is some information about each of the no-hit games pitched in the major leagues up to 1921, inclusive, arranged by leagues and arranged alphabetically:

American Association's Hitless Games—15

EDWARD ATKISSON, Athletics, (twice)— May 24, 1884, at Pittsburgh, Atkisson, a right-hander won over Fox of the Alleghenys, 10 to 1, Pirates of early days escaping runless defeat because Atkisson hit their first batter—Charles Edward Swartwood. He stole second, took third on an out and scored on Jack Milligan's passed ball. Atkisson hit one man, whose name has been furnished, and fanned one man—Short-stop Will White. Atkisson, in his second hitless game, at Philadelphia, against the Metropolitans, on May 1, 1886, also failed to hand out ciphers, the New Yorkers scoring twice and being beaten, 3 to 2. Possibly this game wasn't a no-hit game, for in the box score there is an annotation that Orr was out, hit by batted ball. Chief Roseman scored the Mets' first

run on a pass. O'Brien's passed ball and Coleman's muff of a fly and Orr registered the second on Bradley's bad error (from account of game) and the outs of Hankinson and Brady). Cushman, a left-hander, pitched against Atkisson. Atkisson apparently didn't strike out anyone, he passed three men (Behel, Roseman and Brady) and three errors were made behind him.

THEODORE BREITENSTEIN, St. Louis— October 4, 1891, at St. Louis, Breitenstein, a left-hander, won over Meekin of Louisville, 8 to 0, striking out three men (Justice Harry L. Taylor of New York State was one of them) and passing one man. He received errorless support. Account of this game says: "Browns and Louisville closed season, playing two games. In the first, Comiskey put in Breitenstein, an amateur, and he pitched the most remarkable game ever played here or in fact anywhere else, not a hit being secured off him." Breitenstein graduated from the lots of St. Louis to the Browns. He used to pitch for the Sporting News team in St. Louis. His first appearance in fast company was on April 28, 1891, when he replaced Jack Stivetts in a game against Louisville. The Colonels could do nothing with him that day and they did less than nothing with him later in the season. Hugh Jennings was one of the players who failed to get a hit.

GUY HECKER, Louisville—September 19, 1882, against Pittsburgh. Hecker was a right-hander.

MATTHEW KILROY, Baltimore—October 6, 1886, at Pittsburgh, Matthew Kilroy, left-hander, won over Pittsburgh,

Ed Morris pitching, 60 to 0. Kilroy struck out 11 men, walked one and four errors were made behind him. Certain pundits of the pastime, James R. Price, formerly of the New York Press among them, always have insisted that Kilroy's no-hit game came just after he had received a terrible beating from the Pirates, but they were wrong, for the day before he had held Pittsburgh to two hits in a 5-inning 3 to 3 tie. Kilroy was born in Philadelphia on June 21,1866. He joined Nashville when he was 18 and then went to Baltimore, his nickname in the Association being the Phenomenal Kid. Kilroy's arm went lame after he joined the Boston Players' League club in 1890. Matt was the best man in the country at picking men off the bases. It was suicide to take a lead of more than a foot off first.

EDWARD KIMBER, Brooklyn—October 4, 1884, at Brooklyn, Kimber pitched 10 hitless and runless innings against Toledo. Darkness stopped the game just as play started in the eleventh.

EDWARD MORRIS, Columbus—May 29, 1884, at Pittsburgh, Morris, a left-hander, won over Pittsburgh (team called the Alleghenys), Neagle pitching, 5 to 0, fanning seven men, issuing one pass (to Joe Battin, third baseman) and getting errorless support. No Pittsburgher was left on base. The Alleghenys protested vigorously over the ball Morris used against them, claiming that the overhead delivery was illegal, but Umpire Valentine didn't agree with them.

FRANK H. MOUNTAIN, Columbus—June 5, 1884, at Washington, won over Washington, Bob Barr pitching, 12 to 0,

striking out eight men, walking four and having three errors made behind him. Just a week before Mountain's box associate—Ed Morris—had pitched a no-hit game against Pittsburgh. Mountain in his greatest game, procured a home run.

ANTHONY J. MULLANE, Louisville—September 11, 1882, against Cincinnati. Mullane was a right-hander.

HENRY PORTER, Kansas City—June 6, 1888, at Baltimore, won over Baltimore, Matt Kilroy pitching, 4 to 0, striking out one man, walking one and having four errors made behind him. Says one who saw this game: "Porter was particularly steady and cautious. No less than 15 fly balls were caught. Baltimore had but one man on second base and but five on first. Two were left and the others were thrown out."

EDWARD W. SEWARD, Athletics—July 26, 1888, Seward, a right-hander, won over Cincinnati, Tony Mullane pitching, 12 to 2, striking out 6 men, passing four and having six errors made behind him. Seward's backstop in this game was Wilbert Robinson, Brooklyn manager now. Cincinnati's runs, scored in the eighth inning, were due to errors by Harry Stovey and Brudder Bill Gleason.

WILLIAM H. TERRY, Brooklyn (twice)—July 24, 1886, at Brooklyn, Terry, a right-hander, won over Dave Foutz of St. Louis, 1 to 0, passing two men, striking out two and having three errors made behind him. Brooklyn's run was scored in the eighth by Swartwood who then singled, took second on a passed ball and registered on Phillip's double.

May 27, 1888, at Brooklyn, Terry won over Tom Ramsey of Louisville, 4 to 0, passing two men and striking out eight. Brooklyn was charged with six errors in this game, Terry having four, Jimmy Peoples, his catcher, one, and Bill Mc-Clellan, second baseman, one. Terry was from Westfield, Mass., and was the Chicago pitcher the day Ed Delahanty made four home runs in one game.

LEDELL TITCOMB, Rochester—September 15, 1890, at Rochester, Titcomb, a left-hander, won over Syracuse, Edward Mars pitching, 7 to 0, striking out seven men, passing two and having three errors made behind him.

AUGUST P. WEYHING, Athletics—July 31, 1888, at Philadelphia, Weyhing, a right-hander, won over Kansas City, Sullivan pitching, 4 to 0, striking out five men, passing one, hitting one and getting errorless support. The men who got on through Weyhing's wildness were Monk Cline and Cowboy Jim Davis. Weyhing's no-hit game came five days after a similar contest by his pitching associate, Seward. Weyhing and George Stallings, Rochester manager now, formed one of the early toothpick batteries. Both were with the Phillies in the spring of 1887 and both got released shortly after the series with the Athletics ended, Weyhing joining the Philadelphia Association team and Stallings going to Toronto.

American League Hitless Games—31

THE AMERICAN'S HEROES

(Note—No account is taken of the no-hit games pitched in the American League of 1900, for then it was not and did not claim to be a major league.)

CHARLES ALBERT BENDER, Philadelphia—Bender, a right-hander, won over Cleveland, 4 to 0, at Philadelphia on May 12, 1910, missing a perfect game by passing Terry Turner. He fanned four men and walked no one except the player who closed his American League career known as the Aged Albino, receiving perfect support.

JOSEPH D. BENZ, Chicago—Benz, a right-hander, won over Cleveland, Abe Bowman and Fred Blanding, pitching, 6 to 1, at Chicago on May 31, 1914. He then fanned four men and passed two, three errors being made behind him. Cleveland's run was scored in the fourth by Roy Wood, who took two bases on Buck Weaver's wild throw, advanced to third on a fielder's choice and came in while a double play was being pulled off.

LESLIE JOSEPH BUSH, Philadelphia—Bush, a right-hander won over Cleveland, Stanley Coveleskie and Fred Coumbe pitching, 5 to 0, at Philadelphia on August 26, 1916. A pass to Graney, first Indian batter, was the only thing that marred Bush's game, as he received perfect support. The previous day Bush had been knocked out of the box in three innings by the Indians, his come-back being as quick as Leonard's against St. Louis the same year.

RAYMOND B. CALDWELL, Cleveland—Caldwell, a right-hander, won over New York (his old team), 3 to 0, at New York on September 10, 1919. This was the first time Caldwell ever had pitched against his old team. He began the season of

1919 with Boston and was unconditionally released in July. Caldwell fanned five men, passed one (Hannah) and one (Baker) reached first on a fumble by Wambsganss, who made Cleveland's only error. Mays opposed Caldwell on the mound in this game.

JAMES J. CALLAHAN, Chicago—Callahan, a right-hander won over Detroit, 3 to 0, at Chicago on September 20, 1902, fanning two men, passing two and having one error made behind him.

EDWARD V. CICOTTE, Chicago—Cicotte, a right-hander, won over St. Louis (Earl Hamilton, Jim Park and Tom Rogers pitching), 11 to 0 at St. Louis on April 14, 1917, striking out five men, passing three, hitting one and having one error made behind him—a fumble by Gandil that allowed Austin to reach first.

WILLIAM HENRY DINNEEN, Boston—Dinneen, a right-hander, won over Chicago (Frank Owen pitching), 2 to 0, at Boston on September 27, 1905, fanning six men, walking two, hitting one and getting perfect support. Seventeen of the White Sox were retired on easy flies or fouls. Held hitless in the first game, the Chicagoans, in the second, tore off a flock of safeties and won as they pleased in six innings, 15 to 1.

GEORGE FOSTER, Boston—Foster, a right-hander, won over New York (Bob Shawkey pitching), to 2 to 0 at Boston on June 21, 1916, fanning three men, passing three and getting perfect support.

ROBERT B. GROOM, St. Louis—Groom, a right-hander, won over Chicago (Joe Benz pitching), 3 to 0, at St.

Louis on May 6, 1917, in the second game of a double header, the White Sox the day before also having failed to get a safe blow. Groom fanned four men, passed three, hit one and got perfect support.

EARL HAMILTON, St. Louis—Hamilton, a left-hander, won over Detroit (Jean Dubuc pitching), 5 to 1, at Detroit on August 30, 1912, the Browns, in their previous game against the Tigers, played July 4th, having failed to get a safety. Hamilton walked two men and two errors were made behind him. Cobb scored in the fourth on a walk, Pratt's boot and a fielder's choice.

WELDON HENLEY, Philadelphia—Henley, a right-hander, won over St. Louis, 6 to 0, at St. Louis on July 22, 1905, fanning two men, walking three and having one error made behind him.

THOMAS HUGHES II, New York—Hughes, a right-hander, pitched 9 and 1–3 innings of hitless ball against Cleveland (George Kahler pitching), at New York on August 30, 1910, and was beaten in the eleventh, 5 to 0. In the innings in which Hughes pitched hitless ball only one man reached first—Terry Turner, in the seventh, on a wild throw by Jimmy Austin.

WALTER PERRY JOHNSON, Washington—Johnson, a right-hander, won over Boston (Harry Harper pitching), 1 to 0, at Boston on July 1, 1920, fanning 10 men, passing nobody and having one error made behind him. That was a boot by Stanley Harris on Harry Hooper in the seventh. Mike Menoskey later forced the Boston captain. Johnson whiffed two pinch hitters—Karr and Eibel—in the ninth. The only hard Washington fielding chance was a fly catch by Rice on Foster in the fifth.

ADRIAN C. JOSS, Cleveland (twice) — October 2, 1908, at Cleveland, Joss, a right-hander, won over Chicago, Ed Walsh pitching, 1 to 0, not one of the White Sox reaching first. This game alluded to previously and score printed. Joss's second appearance in the Pitcher's Hall of Fame came on April 20, 1910, in Chicago, when he won over the White Sox, Guy Harris White pitching, 1 to 0, fanning two men, passing two and having one error made behind him. Fred Parent was the Chicago player who benefited by the Cleveland mistake—a fumble by Third Baseman Bill Bradley—and at first that was called a hit for Parent.

ERNEST KOOB, St. Louis — Koob a left-hander, won over Chicago (Eddie Cicotte pitching), 1 to 0, at St. Louis on May 5, 1917, fanning two men, passing five and having two errors made behind him. This no-hit game was a tainted affair, a hit given to Weaver in the first inning being changed to an error for Austin after the official scorer (a noble critic) had arrived at the ball yard. The official scorer wasn't there when the play was made. All the other scribes, home and visiting, gave the ball hit by Weaver as a hit.

HUBERT B. LEONARD, Boston (twice) — August 30, 1916, at Boston, Leonard, a left-hander, won over St. Louis, Carl Weilman pitching, 4 to 0, fanning three men, passing two and getting errorless support. Leonard, the previous day, had lasted less than an inning against the Browns. Like Joss, Leonard pitched his second no-hit game away from home, subduing Detroit, George Dauss and George Cunningham pitching, 5 to 0, at Detroit, on June 3, 1918. Leonard then fanned four men and walked one, a pass to Bob Veach preventing him from hurling a perfect game, as he received perfect support.

GEORGE MOGRIDGE, New York — Mogridge a left-hander, won over Boston (Hub Leonard pitching), 2 to 1, at Boston on April 24, 1917, striking out three men, passing three and having three errors made behind him. Walsh's sacrifice fly in the seventh scored Boston's only run, Barry crossing the plate after having walked and gone to third on a couple of errors.

EARL L. MOORE, Cleveland — Moore, a right-hander, pitched nine hitless innings against Chicago at Cleveland on May 9, 1901, and was beaten in the tenth, 4 to 2, the White Sox then making two singles. Chicago's earlier runs came from errors and passes.

GEORGE J. MULLIN, Detroit — Mullin, a right-hander, won over St. Louis (Adams, Earl Hamilton and Roy Mitchell pitching), 7 to 0, at Detroit on July 4, 1912, (afternoon game), fanning five men, passing five and having one error made behind him—a fumble by George Moriarty, third baseman, now an American League umpire. Mullin pitched this no-hit game on his birthday. Jack Warhop acted in the same manner when he was in the Wisconsin–Illinois League. The next time the Tigers and the Browns met, Hamilton hurled a no-hit game against the Jungleites.

ROBERT B. RHOADES, Cleveland—Rhoades, a right-hander, won over Boston, 2 to 1 at Cleveland on September 18, 1908, fanning two men then, walking two, hitting one and having two errors made behind him.

JAMES SCOTT, Chicago—Scott, a right-hander, pitched nine innings of hitless and runless ball against Washington at Washington on May 14, 1914, and lost out in the tenth, 1 to 0, to Yancey Ayers. Chic Gandil opened the tenth by singling and Howard Shanks doubled him home instantly. Scott fanned two men and passed two, and three errors were made behind him.

ERNEST SHORE, Boston—Base Ruth had a run-in with Umpire Brick Owen in the first inning at Washington on June 23, 1917, after Ray Morgan had been awarded a pass, made a pass at him and was put out of the game. Manager Jack Barry put Ernest Shore, a right-hander, in to finish the game and he finished it so capably that no one reached first. Morgan, who was on when Shore went in, attempted to steal second and was killed off. Shore struck out two men. American League officials declared that Shore deserved a place along with Ward, Young, Joss and Richmond, but he never has received it. Ayers pitched against Shore. The score was 4 to 0.

FRANK ELMER SMITH, Chicago (twice)—Smith, a right-hander, and an exponent of the spit ball, won over Detroit, at Detroit, on September 6, 1905, 15 to 0, then fanning eight men, walking three and getting perfect support. His second no-hit game was reeled off in Chicago on September 20, 1908,

against Philadelphia, the score of this game being 1 to 0. Smith then fanned two men, walked one and one error was made behind him.

JESSE NILES TANNEHILL, Boston—Tannehill, a left-hander, won over Chicago, 6 to 0, at Chicago on August 17, 1904, then fanning four men, walking one and hitting one. He received perfect support.

EDWARD ARMSTRONG WALSH, Chicago—Walsh, a right-hander, won over Boston (Ray Collins pitching) 5 to 0, at Chicago, on August 27, 1911, then fanning eight men and passing one—Clyde Engle. He received perfect support. Walsh drew $60 a month when he first started to play professional ball, with the Wilkes-Barre club of the Pennsylvania State League in 1902, that club being managed by Ernest C. Landgraf, president and owner of the Syracuse Internationals now. Williamsport offered to buy Walsh for $500. Landgraf spurned the offer, then rain set in, there was a strike of the coal miners and the Pennsylvania State League blew up. Another famous pitcher who started in that league was George Leroy Wiltse, now managing Buffalo.

JOSEPH WOOD, Boston—Wood, a right-hander, won over St. Louis (Joe Lake pitching), 5 to 0, at Boston on July 29, 1911, then fanning 12 men, walking two (Lake and Hogan), hitting one (Hogan) and getting errorless support.

DENTON J. YOUNG, Boston (twice)—Young, a right-hander, retired Philadelphia without a man reaching first base at Boston on May 5, 1904, this game being alluded to previously and score printed. Like Joss and Leonard, Cy hurled his second no-hit game away from home, winning over the Yankees, 8 to 0, at New York on June 30, 1908. All that prevented Young from duplicating his perfect game against the Athletics then was a pass issued to Harry Niles, the first New York batter, the count being two and three before the deciding ball was pitched. Niles was immediately potted stealing by Lou Criger and thereafter no Yankee reached first. In this game Gavvy Cravath and Heinie Wagner, left fielding and shortstopping respectively for Boston, fielded wonderfully. Young fanned two men, walked one and got air-tight support.

Federal League's Hitless Games—5

THE HEROES

FRANK L. ALLEN, Pittsburgh—Allen, a left-hander, won over St. Louis (Robert Groom pitching), 2 to 0, at St. Louis on April 24, 1915, then fanning two men and passing four. He received perfect support.

ARTHUR DAVID DAVENPORT, St. Louis—Davenport, a right-hander, won over Chicago (Addison Brennan pitching), 3 to 0, at St. Louis on September 7, 1915, then fanning three men, passing two and having two errors made behind him.

CLAUDE RAY HENDRIX, Chicago—Hendrix, a right-hander, won over Pittsburgh (Bunny Hearne and Elmer Knetzer pitching), 10 to 0, at Pittsburgh on May 15, 1915, then fanning three men

and passing three. He received perfect support.

EDWARD FRANCIS LAFITTE, Brooklyn—Lafitte, a right-hander, won over Kansas City (Nick Cullop and Stone pitching), 6 to 0, at Brooklyn on September 19, 1914, then fanning one man, passing seven and having two errors made behind him. The Cowboys' runs were due to Lafitte's wildness.

MILES MAIN, Kansas City—Main, a right-hander, won over Buffalo (Russell Ford, inventor of the emery ball, pitching), 5 to 0, at Buffalo on August 16, 1915, then fanning seven men, passing one and having two errors made behind him. Another tainted no-hit game. A hit originally given to Walter Blair was transformed into an error for John Rawlings after the official scorer had talked to Umpires Bill Brennan and Tom Corcoran and to Kansas City players.

National League's Hitless Games—46

THE HEROES

LAWRENCE J. CORCORAN, Chicago (three times)—Larry Corcoran, right-hander, pitched his first no-hit game at Chicago against Boston on August 19, 1880, winning 6 to 0. Corcoran's second no-hit effort was revealed on the last day of the season of 1882 (September 20th), at Chicago, when he won over Worcester (Frank Mountain pitching), 5 to 0. Corcoran then fanned three men, passed one and four errors were made behind him. Corcoran's third and last no-hit game was against Providence on June 27, 1884, at Chicago, Charles Sweeney pitching against him and being beaten 6 to 0. In this game Corcoran fanned six men, passed one and six errors were made behind him.

JAMES F. GALVIN, Buffalo (twice)— James F. Galvin, right-hander, called the Little Steam Engine, when he was young, and Pudgy Jim, when he grew old, pitched his first no-hit game at Worcester, against Worcester, on August 20, 1880, winning then over Fred Corey, 1 to 0, in a game in which the Bisons made six errors and in which two of the losers fanned. Galvin's second and last no-hit game, uncovered August 4, 1884, also was revealed away from home, for he pitched it at Detroit against Detroit and Buffalo won on the lopsided basis of 18 to 0. Galvin fanned seven men that day, walked no one and two errors were made behind him.

CHRISTOPHER MATHEWSON, New York (twice)—Mathewson, a right-hander, pitched his first no-hit game at St. Louis on July 15, 1901, against St. Louis and won over Wee Willie Sudhoff, 5 to 0, fanning four men, passing four and having one error—a muffed fly ball by Centre Fielder George Van Haltren— made behind him. Mathewson's second no-hit game also was pitched away from home, being uncovered in Chicago on June 13, 1905, against Chicago. Then Big Six won over Mordecai Brown, 1 to 0, in a game in which the Three Fingered Marvel allowed only one hit up to the ninth. Mathewson struck out two men, passed none and two errors were made behind him.

LEON K. AMES, New York—Ames, a right-hander, on April 15, 1909, at New York, held Brooklyn hitless for nine innings, the Superbas winning in the thirteenth, 3 to 0. Irwin Wilhelm, now manager of the Philadelphia Nationals, pitched against Ames in this contest, which was the first of the season for both clubs.

GEORGE WASHINGTON BRADLEY, St. Louis—Bradley, a right-hander, pitched the first no-hit game in the National League over Hartford at St. Louis on July 15, 1876, this game having been commented on and the score of it being printed elsewhere.

THEODORE BREITENSTEIN, Cincinnati—Breitenstein, a left-hander, retired Pittsburgh (Charles Hastings pitching), without hit or run at Cincinnati on April 22, 1898, Hughes of Baltimore being a no-hit hero the same day. Breitenstein won his game, 11 to 0, fanning two men, passing one and having one error made behind him. Bugs Holiday, in left field, made three sensational catches that took hits away from the Pirates.

JOHN G. CLARKSON, Chicago—Clarkson, a right-hander, retired Providence without a run or it at Providence on July 27, 1885, the score of this game being 4 to 0. In it Clarkson fanned four men and five errors were made behind him.

HUGH DAILY, Cleveland—Daily, a right-hander (a one-armed right-hander, at that), retired Philadelphia without a hit or run at Philadelphia on September 13, 1883, then winning over John Coleman, 1 to 0. Daily fanned two men, passed three and two errors were made behind him. An account of this game says that the ground at Recreation Park was in a "wretchedly soggy condition and this soon made the ball so mushy it was impossible to hit it effectively."

GEORGE A. DAVIS, Boston—Davis, a right-hander, who had failed in the American League with New York, retired Philadelphia without a hit or run at Boston on September 9, 1914. Tincup Rixey and Oeschger pitching against him. Davis fanned four men, passed five and two errors were made behind him, both by Third Baseman J. Carlisle Smith. The score was 7 to 0.

FRANK L. DONAHUE, Philadelphia— Donahue, a right-hander, retired Boston without a hit or run at Philadelphia on July 8, 1898, and won over Vic Willis, 5 to 0, passing two men, striking out one and having two errors made behind him. Donahue was a very good hot weather performer. The day he pitched his no-hit game it was terribly hot.

MALCOLM WAYNE EASON, Brooklyn—Eason, a right-hander, retired St. Louis without a hit or run at St. Louis on July 20, 1906. The score of this game was 2 to 0 and in it the Superbas made one error, Eason fanning five men and passing three.

HORACE OWEN ELLER, Cincinnati— Eller, a right-hander and an American League discard, retired St. Louis without a hit or run at Cincinnati on May 11, 1919, winning over Frank Spruell (Jake) May, 6 to 0. Eller got perfect support, fanned eight men and passed three. Two of the three Cardinals walked were caught stealing by Catcher Rariden, and the reason the other wasn't nailed was that one of the thefts launched had two runners in it.

CHARLES FERGUSON, Philadelphia— Ferguson, a right-hander, retired Providence without a hit or run at Philadelphia on August 29, 1885, then winning over Dupee Shaw, 1 to 0. Ferguson fanned eight men, walked two and six errors were made behind him. Ferguson was a wonderful infielder as well as a great pitcher. He died of typhoid at Philadelphia in 1888 after having demonstrated great ability as a second baseman the previous season.

CHARLES C. FRASER, Philadelphia— Fraser, a right-hander, retired Chicago without a hit or run at Chicago on September 18, 1903, the Phillies then winning, 10 to 0. Four errors were made behind Fraser, he passed five men and fanned four.

FRANK L. (NOODLES) HAHN, Cincinnati—Hahn, a left-hander, retired Philadelphia (then the hardest hitting team in the country), without a hit or run at Cincinnati on July 12, 1900, winning over William Bernhard, 4 to 0. He fanned eight men, Ed Delahanty, and Elmer Flick each whiffing twice, and walked three, one of these on a casualty pass. One error was made behind him. The next day the Phillies, in Pittsburgh, made 24 hits, recovering their batting eyes extremely quickly.

WILLIAM V. HAWKE, Baltimore— Hawke, a right-hander, retired Washington without a hit or run at Washington on August 16, 1893, then winning over George Stephens, 5 to 0, in a game in which he got perfect support, fanned six men and walked two. This game started the fans of the country, being the first no-hit game under the new pitching rules. Hawke was a St. Louis discard. He died a couple of years later of tuberculosis.

JAY (OR JAMES) HUGHES, Baltimore— Hughes, a right-hander, retired Boston without a hit or run at Baltimore on April 22, 1898, Theodore Breitenstein of Cincinnati being a no-hit hero the same day. This was the second National League game Hughes. In his first, against Washington, on April 18th, he had blanked the Senators, 9 to 0, and dispersed them with two singles. In his no-hit game against Boston, Hughes, opposed by Ted Lewis, fanned three men, walked three and three errors were made behind him. Hughes was a discovery of Hugh Jennings's, the present Giant having seen him in action on the Coast in the fall of 1897.

THOMAS J. HUGHES II, Boston— Hughes, a right-hander, and an American League discard, retired Pittsburgh (Erwin Kantlehner and Robert Harmon pitching), without a hit or run at Boston on June 16, 1916, then winning 2 to 0. He had the Pirates hitting in the air most of the time, the Braves having only three assists. Hughes closed the game by fanning Hans Wagner for the second time.

CHARLES L. (BUMPUS) JONES, Cincinnati—Jones, who belonged to the Atlanta club, retired Pittsburgh without a hit at Cincinnati on October 16, 1892, the Pirates being beaten 7 to 1. Jones fanned one man, hit one and walked three. This was the only good game Jones ever pitched for the Reds. He was one of their greatest flivvers.

JAMES SANFORD LAVENDER, Chicago—Lavender, a right-hander, retired New York without a hit or run at New York on August 31, 1915, winning over Rube Schauer, 2 to 0, in a game in which he fanned eight men and walked one. One error was made behind him. Lavender was a Giant Nemesis for a long time. He stopped Rube Marquard after that left-hander had won 19 in a row in 1912.

THOMAS JOSEPH LOVETT, Brooklyn— Lovett, a right-hander, retired New York without a hit or run at Brooklyn on June 22, 1891, and won, 4 to 0, in a game in which he fanned four men and passed three. His support was perfect.

JOHN C. LUSH, Philadelphia—Lush, a left-hander, retired Brooklyn without a hit or run at Brooklyn on May 1, 1906, then fanning 11 men and passing three. One error was made behind him.

NICHOLAS MADDOX, Pittsburgh— Maddox, a right-hander, retired Brooklyn without a hit at Pittsburgh on September 20, 1907, the Superbas scoring once in this game and being beaten 2 to 1. Maddox fanned five men, hit one, walked three and two errors were made behind him. Maddox had only been in the National League briefly when he entered the ranks of the no-hit heroes.

RICHARD W. MARQUARD, New York—Marquard, a left-hander, retired Brooklyn without a hit or run at New York on April 15, 1915, in his first game of the year, then winning over Nap Rucker, 2 to 0. Marquard fanned two men and walked two. One error was made behind him. That same season New York intended to send Marquard to the International League, Brooklyn stepping in and claiming his on waivers.

HARRY M. MCINTIRE, Brooklyn—McIntire, a right-hander, pitched 10 innings of hitless ball against Pittsburgh at Brooklyn on August 1, 1906, and lost in the thirteenth, 1 to 0, the game's run resulting from Ganley's single, Wagner's double and Nealon's single.

FRANK XAVIER PFEFFER, Boston—Pfeffer, a right-hander and a brother of Edward J. Pfeffer, now of the St. Louis Cardinals, retired Cincinnati without a hit or run at Boston on May 8, 1907, and won over the Reds, 6 to 0. He fanned three men, walked one, hit one and one error was made behind him.

CHARLES LOUIS PHILLIPPE, Louisville—Phillippe, a right-hander, retired New York without a hit or run at Louisville on May 25, 1899, and won over Ed Doheny, 7 to 0, fanning one man, walking two and one error being made behind him.

CHARLES RADBOURNE, Providence—Radbourne, a right-hander, retired Cleveland (Hugh Daily pitching) without a hit or run at Cleveland on July 25, 1883, winning 8 to 0. One error was made behind the Iron Man and he fanned six men, walking nobody.

J. LEE RICHMOND, Worcester—Richmond, a left-hander, pitched the first perfect game in the National League against Cleveland on June 12, 1880, and the game is commented on elsewhere and the score is also printed elsewhere.

GEORGE NAPOLEON RUCKER, Brook-

lyn—Rucker, a left-hander, retired Boston without a hit or run at Brooklyn on September 5, 1908, winning over Pat Flaherty, now a Cleveland scout, 6 to 0. Rucker fanned 14 men in this game, three errors were made behind him and he passed nobody. He was responsible for the retirement of 17 of his adversaries.

AMOS W. RUSIE, New York—Rusie, a right-hander, retired Brooklyn without a hit or run at New York on July 31, 1891, and won his game, 6 to 0, fanning four men, passing eight, hitting one and having one error made behind him. Rusie now works for the Giants at the Polo Grounds. He was one of the world's speediest pitchers.

A. B. SANDERS, Louisville—Sanders, a right-hander, wasn't a no-hit hero, according to the official scorer of the game between Louisville and Baltimore, played at Louisville on August 22, 1892, and won by the Colonels, 6 to 2. The O. S. said that Voiceless Tim O'Rourke's grounder to Bassett, which the last named fumbled, was a hit, the other scorers said it was an error. Sanders passed three men and four errors were made behind him. He is said to hold the world's record for pitching the smallest number of balls in a nine inning game. Nobody knows just what this record is.

JOHN E. STIVETTS, Boston—Stivetts, a right-hander, retired Brooklyn without a hit or run at Brooklyn on August 6, 1892, the score of this game being 11 to 0. Stivetts then fanned six men, passed five and three errors were made behind him.

CHARLES MUNROE TESREAU, New

York—Tesreau, a right-hander, now baseball coach at Dortmouth, received credit for a no-hit game over Philadelphia at Philadelphia on September 6, 1912, when the Quakers were beaten 3 to 0. This no-hit game is slightly tainted, as in the middle of the game one of the Phillies apparently made an infield single. It was so recorded, anyhow, and when no hits developed later the New York war correspondents, Sid Mercer and Walter Trumbull among them, induced the Philadelphia official scorer, Stoney McLinn, to change the hit to an error—at least that is the tale. Tesreau struck out two men, walked two and two errors were made behind him.

WALTER THORNTON, Chicago— Thornton retired Brooklyn without a hit or run at Chicago on August 21, 1898, winning over Bill Kennedy, 2 to 0. He received perfect support, fanned three men and walked the same number. Chicago only had five assists in this game.

FRED TONEY, Cincinnati—Toney, a right-hander, retired Chicago without a hit or run in a ten-inning game at Chicago on May 2, 1917, this game being commented on previously and the score being printed elsewhere.

JAMES L. VAUGHN, Chicago—Vaughn, a left-hander, pitched nine innings of hitless and runless ball against Cincinnati at Chicago on May 2, 1917, this game being commented on previously and the score being printed elsewhere.

JOHN MONTGOMERY WARD, Providence—Ward, a right-hander, pitched a perfect game against Buffalo at Providence on June 17, 1880, this game being

commented on previously and the score being printed elsewhere.

ROBERT K. WICKER, Chicago— Wicker, a right-hander, pitched nine hitless and runless innings at New York against the Giants on June 11, 1904, and won over them in 12 innings, 1 to 0. Sam Mertes saved the McGrawites from hitless defeat by singling in the tenth. In the game Wicker struck out ten men and passed one. His pitching rival was Joe McGinnity, who then stubbed his toe after having won 14 games in a row. Two errors were made behind Wicker in this classic.

VICTOR G. WILLIS, Boston—Willis, a right-hander, retired Washington without a hit at Boston on August 7, 1899, but the Senators then scored a run, being beaten, 7 to 1. William Henry Dinneen, American League umpire now, pitched for them. Three errors were made behind Willis in this game, he fanned five men, passed four and hit one.

GEORGE LEROY WILTSE, New York— Wiltse, a left-hander, now manager of the Buffalo Internationals, retired Philadelphia without hit or run for ten innings at New York on the morning of July 4, 1908, and then won over George Washington McQuillan, 1 to 0. Wiltse would have gotten into the small class of perfect pitchers if he had not hit George McQuillan, 27th man at bat, in the arm with a pitched ball in the ninth after he had two strikes on him.

DENTON J. YOUNG, Cleveland— Young, a right-hander, retired Cincinnati without a hit or run at Cleveland on September 18, 1897, and then won over Billy Rhines, the Carl Mays of that time, 6 to 0. Three errors were made behind Young in this game, he fanned three men and he passed one. The only thing that looked like a hit was a grounder of Holliday's to Rhody Wallace. Wallace made a fine stop of this and then threw wild. It was charged as an error.

No-Hitless Game in Players' League

NO HERO

CHARLES KING, Chicago—King, a right-hander, is given credit for pitching a no-hit game against Brooklyn at Chicago on June 21, 1890, but this game found King pitching only eight innings and so should not be classed as a no-hit affair. The reason King did not go the full nine innings was that Brooklyn, the team that batted last, scored a run in the eighth and so it was not necessary to play the ninth, as Chicago had not scored. Seven errors were made behind King, he fanned two and he walked three.

Union's Hitless Games—3

THE HEROES

RICHARD L. BURNS, Cincinnati— Burns retired Kansas City without a hit at Kansas City on August 26, 1884, winning over Black 3 to 1. Five errors were made behind him.

EDWARD L. CUSHMAN, Milwaukee— Cushman, a left-hander, retired Washington without a hit or run at Milwau-

kee on September 28, 1884, winning over Abner Powell, 5 to 0. Cushman fanned 12 men and walked one.

CHARLES GAGUS, Washington— Gagus retired Wilmington without a hit at Washington on August 21, 1884, winning over McElroy, 12 to 1. Gagus fanned 13 men, walked three and one error was made behind him.

Boston Scene of Long Games

Boston is the favorite major league city for extended games, the longest in the American and in the National having been played there. These were, respectively, 24 and 26 innings; the game in the American was decided, that in the National wasn't.

Brooklyn clashed with Boston in the 26 inning game, played at Braves' Field on May 1, 1920, hostilities ceasing with each team possessed of a run. Joe Oeschger and Leon Cadore worked all through for the contestants, the Bostonian pitching runless ball for 21 innings and the Brooklynite for 20.

In the 24 inning game of September 1, 1906, played at the old Huntington Avenue grounds between the Athletics and the Red Sox, and won by the first named, 4 to 1, two pitchers also did all the work, John Wesley Coombs, who had entered the American League only a couple of months previously, operating for the winners and Joe Harris for the losers. Harris never pitched a good game after this, Coombs pitched a flock of them.

Harris cracked under the strain in the 24th after having denied the Mackmen a run since the third. One out then, Topsy Hartsel singled and stole second as Bris Lord Whiffed. Schreck singled Hartsel in and Socks Seybold and Danny Murphy followed with triples, good for two more runs.

For the next two days all Coombs could handle in the way of food was beef tea. The scores of these two classics:

National's Longest Game

Played at Boston—May 1, 1920

Brooklyn	AB	R	BH	PO	A	E
Olson, 2b	10	0	1	6	9	1
Neis, rf	10	0	1	9	0	0
Johnston, 3b	10	0	2	3	1	0
Wheat, lf	9	0	2	3	0	0
Myers, cf	2	0	`	1	0	0
Hood, cf	6	0	1	8	1	0
Konetchy, 1b	9	0	1	30	1	0
Ward, ss	10	0	0	5	3	1
Krueger, c	2	1	0	4	3	0
Elliott, c	7	0	0	7	3	0
Cadore, p	10	0	0	1	13	0
Totals	85	1	9	78	34	2

Boston	AB	R	BH	PO	A	E
Powell, cf	7	0	1	8	0	0
Pick, 2b	11	0	0	5	10	2
Mann, lf	10	0	2	6	0	0
Cruise, rf	9	1	1	4	0	0
Holke, 1b	10	0	2	43	1	0
Boeckel, 3b	11	0	3	1	7	0
Maranville, ss	10	0	3	1	9	0
O'Neil, c	2	0	0	4	3	0
*Christenbury	1	0	1	0	0	0
Gowdy, c	6	0	1	6	1	0
Oeschger, p	8	0	1	0	11	0
Totals	85	1	15	78	42	2

* Singled for O'Neil in 9th inning.

Brooklyn
000 010 000 000 000 000 000 000 00—1
  Boston
000 001 000 000 000 000 000 000 00—1

Two base hits—Maranville, Oeschger. Three base hit—Cruise. Stolen bases—Myers, Hood. Sacrifices—Hood, Oeschger, Powell, O'Neil, Holke, Cruise. Double plays—Olson and Konetchy; Oeschger, Gowdy, Holke and Gowdy. Bases on balls—Off Cadore 5, off Oeschger 4. Struck out—By Cadore 6, by Oeschger 5. Wild pitch—Oeschger. Umpires—McCormick and Hart. Time—3.50.

American's Longest Game

Played at Boston—September 1, 1906

Philadelphia	AB	R	BH	PO	A	E
Hartsel, lf	10	1	2	2	1	0
Lord, cf	9	0	1	6	0	0
Davis, 1b	4	0	0	12	1	0
Schreck, 1b	6	1	2	16	0	0
Seybold, rf	10	1	1	4	0	0
Murphy, 2b	9	0	2	3	7	1
Cross, ss	9	0	1	9	3	1
Knight, 3b	7	0	5	1	4	0
Powers, c	9	0	1	18	8	0
Coombs, p	9	1	1	1	9	0
Totals	82	4	16	72	33	2

Boston	AB	R	BH	PO	A	E
Heydon, rf	9	0	2	7	0	0
Parent, ss	10	1	4	6	9	0
Stahl, cf	7	0	2	5	0	0
Ferris, 2b	9	0	1	5	8	0
Hoey, lf	10	0	2	4	0	0
Grimshaw, 1b	8	0	2	25	2	0
Morgan, 3b	6	0	0	2	3	0
Carrigan, c	5	0	1	6	3	1
*Freeman	1	0	0	0	0	0
Criger, c	4	0	0	11	1	0
Harris, p	8	0	1	1	7	0
Totals	77	1	15	72	33	1

* Grounded out for Carrigan in 15th.

Philadelphia
001 000 000 000 000 000 000 003—4
Boston
000 001 000 000 000 000 000 000—1

Two base hits—Ferris, Parent. Three base hits—Knight 2. Parent, Schreck, Seybold, Murphy. Sacrifices—Lord, Knight, Ferris, Morgan. Stolen bases—Coombs 2, Cross, Lord, Stahl, Hartsel, Knight. Bases on balls—Off Coombs 6, off Harris 2. Struck out—By Coombs 18, by Harris 14. Hit by pitcher—Murphy, Stahl. Double plays—Ferris, Parent and Grimshaw; Cross Murphy and Davis. Umpire—Tim Hurst. Time—4.47. Attendance—18,084.

Another Long One for Jack

Another long game in which Coombs was involved was that at Chicago on August 4, 1910, Ed Walsh pitching against him and neither the Athletics or the White Sox being able to get a run in 16 innings. Coombs allowed three hits to Walsh's 6 and fanned 18 men to the present umpire's 10.

It was in 1910 that Coombs, graduate of Colby College, hung up the American League record for shutout games, pitching 13 of these. Six years later Grover Cleveland Alexander established the National League record for contests of this character, beating Coomb's record by three. Alexander, at the time, was with the Phillies.

Longest Runless Game— 18 Innings

The longest major league game without runs was two sessions longer than the battle between Walsh and Coombs in 1910 and was played in Detroit on July 16th of the previous year between

Detroit and Washington. Oren Edgar Summers pitched the whole game for the Tigers. William Denton Gray, left-hander, and Robert Groom, right-hander, divided the box work for the Senators. Washington made seven hits, Detroit six.

Gray, called Dolly Gray, owns the most peculiar one-hit game on record, pitched for Washington against Chicago, at Chicago, on August 28, 1909. This game the southpaw lost, 6 to 4, because in the second he gave eight bases on balls, seven of these in succession, after Patrick Henry Dougherty bounced a single over Bob Unglaub's head for the White Socks' lone swat. Chicago then made all six of its runs.

Longest 1 to 0 Games— Also 18 Innings

The longest 1 to 0 games in the major leagues also have lasted 18 innings. Providence won a contest of this type from Detroit at Providence on August 17, 1882, John Montgomery Ward pitching against George Weidman. Charles Radbourne, playing right field for the Clam Diggers, decided the contest with a home run. He was the first batter in the eighteenth. Ward allowed nine hits and fanned four men, Weidman yielded seven blows and fanned half a dozen of his opponents.

The Providence and Detroit of the American League just now, are, respectively, Washington and Chicago. On May 15, 1918, these two teams duplicated the National League contest of 36 years earlier, Walter Johnson winning over Claude Williams, left-hander. Ainsmith and Johnson singled in the eighteenth and Williams, with Shotten batting, then made a wild pitch letting Sir Walter's catcher score.

Johnson Began in 1907

Walter Perry Johnson, one of the pitching immortals, began his American League career on August 2, 1907, when he pitched eight innings against Detroit at Washington, the score of the game in which he made his debut being 2 to 1 when left it, to be replaced by Tom Hughes I. The Tigers had the two, the Senators the one. The final score was 3 to 2, with Detroit on the long end. Johnson allowed six hits, fanned three men and walked one. He reached the American League 17 days in advance of Jesse Clyde Milan, his present manager.

Johnson owns a flock of American League records. He pitched 56 consecutive runless innings from April 10 to May 15, 1913, St. Louis stopping his issuance of ciphers.

The Browns also stopped Johnson when he went after his seventeenth straight victory in 1912. Starting on July 3rd, the Idaho phenom won 16 games in a row, his last victory being over Detroit on August 23rd, by a score of 8 to 1. On August 26th, in the seventh inning of a game with St. Louis, Johnson took Hughes' place on the rubber with the score tied and with two men on the bases. Both scored and St. Louis won the game. President Johnson of the American League ruled Johnson lost this game, everybody else said he didn't.

The decision of B. B. Johnson's didn't matter for the next time out for the Washington star. August 28th, St. Louis, with Jack Powell pitching, won from him, 3 to 2. Johnson, in this defeat, fanned 12 men and allowed four hits. He was wild, however, and was poorly supported.

Joseph Wood, with Cleveland now and with Boston then, also won 16 games in succession in 1912. His string of successes began July 8th and continued until September 15th, the Browns being the last team he defeated and 2 to 1 being the score of that game.

Wood was stopped by the Tigers at Detroit on September 20th. Tex Covington and Joe Lake winning against him, 6 to 4, in a game in which Smoky Joe allowed seven hits and passed five men—Boston got only four blows—one off Covington, left-hander, and three off Lake, right-hander.

Marquard Credited with 19 Straight

Richard W. Marquard, left-handed pitcher of the giants, the year the Washington and Detroit right-handers were capturing 16 contests in succession, was credited with winning 19 games in a row, but in five of these, other boxmen were associated with him and his record does not compare with an earlier one of Tim Keefe's.

Marquard's string began April 11th and continued until July 3rd. On July 8th, he pitched against James Sanford Lavender of the Cubs in Chicago and that exponent of the spit-ball beat him,

7 to 2, Marquard being relieved at the end of the sixth, when the score was 6 to 2 in the Cubs' favor. Marquard, in this game yielded eight hits and passed seven men.

Tim Keefe Did Win 19 Straight

A National League pitcher who did win 19 straight games was Timothy Keefe, right-hander of the Giants, in 1888—June 23rd to August 10th, inclusive. On August 14th he went against the team that Hoodoed Marquard, and Gus Krock, a right-hander, beat him, 4 to 2, the Ansonites making five hits off Sir Timothy. Krock was a wonderful minor league pitcher, but he did little in the majors.

Other Streaks

Here are some of the other famous winning streaks of major league boxmen:

CHARLES RADBOURNE, Providence Nationals, 1884—Won 18 straight, August 7th to September 6th, inclusive, Buffalo, with Jim Galvin pitching, stopping him on September 9th, 2 to 0.

MICHAEL WELCH, New York Nationals, 1885—Won 17 straight, July 18th to September 4th, inclusive, Philadelphia, with Charley Ferguson pitching, stopping him on September 5th, 3 to 1.

JOHN P. LUBY, Chicago Nationals, 1890—Won 17 straight, August 6th to October 3rd, inclusive. Not stopped,

but beaten in his first game of the succeeding year by Pittsburgh.

JAMES MCCORMICK, Chicago Nationals, 1886—Won 16 straight, May 5th to July 1st, inclusive, New York, with Mickey Welch pitching, stopping him on July 3rd, 7 to 3.

In the American Association, in 1888, two young pitchers—Mickey Hughes of Brooklyn and Leon Viau of Cincinnati—each went along unbeaten from the start of the season until June 1st and then the pair hooked up in Brooklyn, Hughes winning 3 to 1. In his next game Hughes was defeated.

Giants' 26 Straight the Best

New York's Giants, finishing fourth in 1916, established the major league record for consecutive victories, that being 26. The McGrawites began this string of successes on September 7th and after winning the first game of a double header on September 30th from the Braves, lost the second, 8 to 3. George Albert Tyler, left-hander, pitched for Boston in this game; Harry Franklin Sallee, another southpaw, hurled for New York until batted out of the box in the seventh, J. Carlisle Smith and Sherwood Magee then making home runs.

The Giants' record of 26 straight shoved into the discard the exploit of the Providence team of 1884 in capturing 20 in a row, Buffalo, with Jim Galvin on the rubber, stopping the Grays on September 9th, 2 to 0.

The White Sox, in 1916, created American League history by winning 19 in a row, their triumphant career beginning on August 2nd and continuing until August 24th. On August 23rd, Chicago won over Washington, 4 to 1. It rained on August 24th and on August 25th the Sox dropped both ends of a double header to Washington. The score of the game in which Fielder Allison Jones' Hitless Wonders were stopped was 5 to 4, Washington going into the ninth two runs behind. They got these two and one more off Ed Walsh, who had relieved Frank Paderewski Smith in the seventh. Another member of the Smith family—Charles—was the winning pitcher in this controversy. He took the place of Tom Hughes I in the third inning, when the score was 3 to 0 against Washington.

Record Absolutely Unlike New York's

The Louisville American Association team of 1889 made a record absolutely unlike the New York National League team's record of 1916, when it pieced together 26 victories in succession. The Colonels of 27 years before dropped 26 in a row, their career of crime ending on June 23rd, when Tom Ramsey, left-hander, won over the St. Louis Browns, for whom Elton Chamberlain and Nat Hudson did the pitching, by a score of 7 to 3.

One of the World's Worst Ball Clubs

One of the world's worst clubs was the Pittsburgh National League team of 1890. It succeeded in dropping 23 contests in a row, including three in one day to Brooklyn on September 1st. On September 2nd the Pirates were beaten again by Brooklyn, 5 to 4, but two days later, with Varney Anderson pitching against Ed Beatin, they won over Cleveland 6 to 2, their win startling the country. The Pirates of 1890 hold the National League record for consecutive wallopings.

The American League record for successive reverses—20—in jointly owned by the Red Sox of 1906 and the Athletics of 1916. Jesse Tannehill, left-hander, stopped Boston's run of misfortune by winning over Chicago; Leslie Joseph Bush, right-hander, ended Philadelphia's most unsuccessful streak by winning over Detroit.

Keeler Hit Safely in 44 Straight Games

Histories of streaks would not be complete without some mention of the work of William H. Keeler of the Baltimore Nationals, who, in 1897, made one or more hits in 44 consecutive games. The pitcher who stopped him was Frank B. Killen, a left-hander, of Pittsburgh, and the date he did so was June 19th, Baltimore then being beaten by a score of 7 to 1.

Tyrus Raymond Cobb, in 1911, came within four games of Keeler's 1897 mark, Ed Walsh being his Killen and the date he was stopped being July 3rd.

Tyrus's First Game

In his little book, *The Baseball Bat Bag*, Al Munro Elias gives Billy Keeler's record for consecutive hitting and also gives a lot of information about Tyrus Raymond Cobb, about the only thing he doesn't give being certain information as to the Peach's first game in professional ball. That was played on April 26, 1904, at Augusta, Ga., for the Augusta club of the South Atlantic League against Columbia. In it, batting against Engel, whom Ty thinks was from the Coast, Cobb made a double and home run. He played one more game with the Georgians and then their manager inserted an ad in the *Sporting Life* that he desired a hard hitting outfielder. Said manager had ridden Ty so hard he vowed he never would return to Augusta until said manager had deserted that city and he kept his word, for when the Peach returned to Augusta, Con Struthers had vanished.

Cobb went to Anniston and a scribe there, thinking that an Atlanta paper would be interested in the wonderful work of Anniston's new player, wired 300 words about him. The hard hearted sporting editor of the Atlanta paper turned the telegram back on its sender and he had to pay the tolls.

This is the score of the Peach's first game in professional ball:

Cobb's First Game

South Atlantic League

Played at Augusta, Ga.—
April 26, 1904

Augusta	AB	R	BH	PO	A	E
Spratt, 3b	4	2	0	3	4	0
Butler, rf	5	1	1	0	0	1
McMillin, lf	4	1	0	1	0	0
Truby, 2b	4	0	1	1	1	0
Bussey, 1b	4	0	1	8	1	0
Edmunds, c	4	0	0	11	1	0
COBB, cf	4	2	2	0	0	0
Thornton, ss	3	1	0	2	1	2
Durham, p	4	0	2	1	2	0
Totals	36	7	7	27	10	3

Columbia	AB	R	BH	PO	A	E
Reardon, ss	5	1	1	1	3	1
Kuhn, 2b	5	0	0	1	3	1
Miller, 3b	4	0	1	2	3	0
Jacobs, 1b	1	1	0	13	0	0
Gunter, rf	4	2	1	0	0	0
Stewart, cf	4	1	0	2	0	0
Wilson, lf	5	1	1	3	0	0
Shea, c	4	1	2	5	2	0
Engel, p	5	1	2	0	3	0
Totals	37	8	8	27	14	2

Augusta	100	000	051—7
Columbia	103	000	013—8

Two base hits—COBB, Shea. Three base hit—Gunter. Home runs—COBB, Engel. Bases on balls—Off Durham 5, off Engel 2. Struck out—By Durham 8, by Engel 4. Passed ball—Edmonds. Stolen bases—Augusta 6. Umpire—Mace. Time 2.05.

Only Two Hundred Saw Ruth Break In

When George Herman Ruth, possible Home run King of All Time played his first championship game, said game was attended by only 200 fans. That game was played in Baltimore on April 22, 1914, between the Baltimore and Buffalo International League clubs, the reason the attendance wasn't larger being that the Ints at that time had Federal League competition.

Ruth, in his first championship game, pitched Baltimore to a 6 to 0 victory over Buffalo, giving four hits, fanning four men, walking the same number, hitting one man and making one wild pitch.

The first pitcher Ruth batted against in a championship game (he previously, on the spring trip, had batted against major league pitchers) was George Mc-Connell, right-hander, once of the New York Americans and Chicago Federals and Nationals. The Babe got two singles off Tall George, but neither counted in Baltimore's scoring. Also, just to show he was a pitcher, Ruth struck out once. The other time up he grounded to short.

Posterity may want the box score of Babe Ruth's first championship game. Here it is:

Ruth's First Championship Game

International League

Played at Baltimore, April 22, 1914

Baltimore	AB	R	BH	PO	A	E
Daniels, rf	4	1	2	3	0	0
Parent, 3b	3	0	0	1	0	0
Ball, 2b	2	2	0	1	3	0
Cree, cf	4	1	1	2	0	0
Twonbly, lf	4	1	1	1	0	0
Derrick, ss	4	1	3	1	6	0
Gleichman, 1b	4	0	0	14	1	0
Egan, c	4	0	1	4	0	0
RUTH, p	4	0	2	0	3	0
Totals	33	6	10	27	13	0

Buffalo	AB	R	BH	PO	A	E
Vaughn, 3b	5	0	2	1	4	1
McCarthy, 2b	4	0	0	0	1	0
Murray, rf	3	0	0	0	0	0
Houser, 1b	4	0	1	10	0	0
Jackson, lf	2	0	0	1	1	0
Roach, ss	4	0	1	2	4	0
Paddock, cf	4	0	1	2	0	0
Kritchell, c	4	0	1	6	2	0
McConnell, p	2	0	0	2	3	1
*Stephens	1	0	0	0	0	0
Totals	33	0	6	24	15	2

* Batted for McConnell in 9th.

Baltimore	303	000	00x—6
Buffalo	000	000	000—0

Two base hits—Daniels, Egan, Kritchell, Roach, Derrick 2. Stolen bases—Daniels, Ball, Houser. Bases on balls—Off RUTH 4, off McConnell 3. Struck out—By RUTH 4, by McConnell 6. Hit by pitched ball—Jackson. Wild pitches—RUTH 1, McConnell 1. Passed ball—Kritchell. Umpires—Nallin and Carpenter. Time—1.54.

Neal Ball Played Second

Baltimore's second baseman, the day Ruth pitched his first International League game, was Neal Ball, the first major leaguer to make an unassisted triple play. Neal did this when he was a member of the Cleveland Indians, at Cleveland, on July 19, 1909, against the Boston Red Sox, for whom he played later. Ambrose McConnell, a diminutive second baseman, who began his American League career with Boston and finished it with Chicago, hit into this triple massacre.

Paul M. Hines, Providence outfielder, is frequently given credit for having made a triple play all by his lonesome on May 8, 1878, but the late William M. Rankin, who investigated this performance, listed it among the phantom performances—and that is probably where it belongs.

William A. Wambsganss, second baseman of the Indians, also made an unassisted triple play 11 years after Neal Ball did, getting his on October 10, 1920, in a world's championship game with Brooklyn.

Quite a few minor leaguers have made unassisted triple plays, but one that the *Spalding Record Book* does not mention was that made by shortstop Walter Keating of the Buffalo Internationals against Akron in 1920. Keating, now with Syracuse, is not peeved over the matter of his omission from the Minor League Hall of Fame. "Guess I'll have to make another one," was his comment when he looked over the Little Red Book and found his name wasn't there.

Mr. Fan Not Interested

Mr. Fan does not seem to be much interested in the defensive end of the game, except so far as that end is supplied by the pitchers. The fielding records have not been as carefully combed as the batting statistics and there aren't many persons who can say with authority that So and So is a fielding top liner.

Possibly Miller Huggins, manager of the New York Americans now, set an American Association record when he was playing second for St. Paul against Louisville on September 17, 1902; pos-

sibly he didn't. Anyway, that day Huggins, who played in the old Inter-State League under the alias of Proctor, had 19 chances (11 putouts and 8 assists) at second and all the Associated Press carried on the matter was these words:

"Huggins's work was almost phenomenal."

Branch Rickey, manager of the St. Louis Nationals, was a catcher in the Dakota State League of 1902 and caught a little for the team Huggins now manages. One game in which Rickey's work was not phenomenal was that of June 28, 1907, against Washington. Then the Senators stole 13 bases on him. Rickey probably played in the Dakota State League under an alias, for that league was full of college players, among them the great Princeton pitcher, Arthur R. T. Hildebrand.

The historians seem to be fairly certain that the greatest number of errors made by a major league club in one game was 27, the Phillies having this number charged against them when they were beaten by Providence on August 21, 1883, by a score of 28 to 0—a record major league shutout score, by the way. The only Quakers who didn't err were Blondy Purcell, left fielder, and Sid Farrar, first baseman, Farrar being the father of Geraldine, the Cantatrice. The score of this game is contained in Balldom.

There, too, can be found a list of the lop sided shutouts of the majors. The most lop sided in the American League saw Detroit winning over Cleveland, 21 to 0, on September 15, 1901.

Two 24 to 0 Games

Two 24 to 0 games have been played in the major leagues, both in the National. The first was reeled off on May 27, 1885, with New York winning and Buffalo losing, Welch and Galvin being the pitchers. The second took place on June 28, 1887, Philadelphia being the conqueror and Indianapolis the conquered. Ferguson pitched for the Phillies, Morrison and Sowders being the Hoosier hurlers. This Morrison may have been the same Morrison who emitted seven wild pitches in a game against Columbus when he was working for Syracuse of the American Association on July 23, 1890, or it may have been another Morrison. There were two Morrisons and it is hard to identify them.

Easier Now

It is easier now to trace the movements of the players of Organized Ball, with the guides giving the first names of the players and the scribes extracting the middle names from them. Nobody knows what Speaker's middle name is, for he hasn't any, wishing the E on himself because when young he thought that every regular fellow should have a middle initial.

As for Speaker, he arrived in the American League on September 12, 1907 and that day helped Congalton patrol right field for the Boston Red Sox, who then were beaten by the Athletics, 7 to 1. Speaker batted twice against James Dygert, a spit ball pitcher and got no hits. He had no chances in the field, either.

Tyrus Raymond Cobb played his first game in the American League on August 30, 1905, against New York, Jack Chesbro pitching, and doubled the first time he batted.

Here are the first games of some other star players and managers of the present; their first major league games:

STEPHEN FRANCIS O'NEILL, Cleveland, catcher—September 18, 1911, against Boston, for Cleveland, when he caught George Kahler in a game that Cleveland won, 4 to 1. No hits for Steve, but he stole a base on Alva (Rip) Williams.

LEE ALEXANDER FOHL, Brown's manager—August 29, 1902, against Chicago for Pittsburgh, when he caught Cushman in a game that Pittsburgh lost, 9 to 3. No hits for Lee, he had an error and the Cubs stole six bases on him.

GEORGE GIBSON, Pirate's manager—July 2, 1905, against Cincinnati for Pittsburgh, when he caught Deacon Phillippe in a game that Pittsburgh lost, 4 to 1. No hits for Gibby, he had an error and the Reds stole three bases on him.

JOHN McINNIS, Cleveland, first baseman—April 12, 1909 (day Shibe Park was opened), against Boston for Philadelphia, when he played short in a game that the Athletics won, 8 to 1. One hit for Stuffy off Frank Arellanes and he had one error in six chances.

EVERETT SCOTT, Yankee shortstop—April 14, 1914, against Washington for Boston, when he played short in a game that Boston lost, 3 to 0. One hit for Scotty off Walter Johnson and four chances accepted. Scott had played 832 consecutive games when this season of 1922 started.

WAITE CHARLES HOYT, Yankee pitcher—July 24, 1918, against St. Louis for New York, when he pitched the ninth inning in a game that the Giants lost, 10 to 2. Three men faced the 1921 world's series hero—Betzel fanned on three pitched balls, Gonzales fanned on four pitched balls, Packard popped to Fletcher. This was the only pitching Hoyt did for the New York Nationals in championship games.

GEORGE HAROLD SISLER, Browns' first baseman—July 3, 1915 (had been in game as pinch-hitter previously), against Cleveland for St. Louis, when he pitched and won his game 3 to 1. Sisler went hitless in this game against Walker and Coumbe. He gave the Indians seven hits, fanned nine of them and walked the same number.

ARTHUR NEHF, Giant pitcher—August 13, 1915, against Philadelphia for Boston, when he pitched two hitless innings after the Phillies had knocked Rudolph out. Philadelphia won, 5 to 3. Nehf's record was all ciphers.

GEORGE HERMAN RUTH, Yankee home run king—July 11, 1914, against Cleveland for Boston, when he pitched seven innings and was taken out so that Duffy Lewis could pinch hit for him. Red Sox won this game, 4 to 3, Ruth getting credit for victory. He went hitless in two attempts against Southpaw William Mitchell, fanned one man and issued no passes.

CLARK CALVIN GRIFFITH, president Washington club—April 11, 1891, against Cincinnati for St. Louis Browns, win-

ning 13 to 5. Gave the Reds seven hits, fanned two and passed six. Failed to make a hit off either William McGill or Matthew Kilroy.

MILLER J. HUGGINS, Yankee manager—April 15, 1904, against Chicago for Cincinnati, playing second base. Singled against Frank Corridon, drew two passes, stole a base on John Kling and cared for six out of seven chances.

WILBERT ROBINSON, Superba manager—April 19, 1886, against Metropolitans for Athletics, catching Kennedy in game that Philadelphia American Association team lost 4 to 1. Scored his team's only run, made one of its three hits and stole its only base. Fielding record: Six putouts, one assist and two errors.

FRED MITCHELL, Braves' manager—April 27, 1901, against Baltimore for Boston Red Sox, in game that Orioles won, 12 to 6. Mitchell was a pitcher then and relieved Cy Young I, who was being bombarded by the Birds. He failed to stop them and made one hit off Harry Howell.

HUGH AMBROSE JENNINGS, Giants' coach—June 1, 1891, against Washington for Louisville (American Association), in game that Senators won 14 to 5. No hits for Jennings, who fanned once and sacrificed three times. Record at short: Six putouts, two assists.

EDWARD J. ROUSH, Reds' outfielder—August 20, 1913, against Boston for Chicago White Sox. Caught two fly balls, but made no hits in three trips to plate against Fred Anderson and Charles Hall.

JOHN MCGRAW, Giants' manager—

August 26, 1891, against Columbus for Baltimore (American Association), covering second in game that Orioles won, 6 to 5. The Little Napoleon, then 18 years old, made one hit off Phil Knell, scored a run, sacrificed and had two putouts, three assists and one error.

CONNIE MACK, Athletics' manager—September 16, 1886, against New York for Washington, catching Shadow Gilmore in eight innings 1 to 1 tie game. Made one of five hits of his club's off Tim Keefe, started the only double play made in the game and had nine putouts and two assists.

Al Munro Elias probably can tell the exact date when each of the famous major leaguers played their first games in fast company and another gentleman who can do the same thing is Bradshaw H. Swales of Washington, who has a very complete roster of all the major and minor league clubs from 1883 on.

PART V

World's Series' Facts and Figures from 1884 to 1921, Inclusive

Between National and American Leagues	18
Between National League and American Association	7
Total Series	25

Won by American League clubs	11
Won by National League clubs	11
Won by American Association club	1
Series undecided	2
Total Series	25

World's Series Facts

National League cities competing for world's championship	9
American League cities competing for world's championship	6
American Association cities competing for world's championship	4
Total	19

Club winning most series— Boston American League	5
Club losing most series—Chicago and New York National League	4
Manager winning most series— Connie Mack	3
Manager losing most series— John McGraw	4

First recognized World's Series	1884
First World's Series between National and American Leagues	1903
First World's Series under National Commission control	1905

For Glory—and for Lucre

Series for the championship of the baseball world date back to 1884, according to most of the authorities. Two years previously, however, Chicago, winner of the National League championship, and Cincinnati, finishing first in the American Associations pennant pursuit, met in the fall in a couple of combats and those two games may have constituted the first World's Series. The National League didn't recognize the Association then and the Association had no use for the National and the games probably only had the sanction of the club presidents and no world's title was involved. A person still in the land of the living who saw these games and who covered them is Ren Mulford, for years one of the best baseball writers of Cincinnati and now associated with the Thompson-Koch Co. advertising agency of that city. The Reds won one of these games, the White sox the other. A job for some baseball archaeologist is to procure these scores from the files of some Cincinnati paper, for both games were played in the Queen City.

From 1884 to 1890, inclusive, the National League and American Association flag winners met annually to determine which club had the right to the title of world's champions. Twice the issue was not settled, the series of 1885 between the Chicago National and the St. Louis Association teams ending in a tie and a scrap and the series of 1890, with Brooklyn representing the senior league and Louisville the junior organization, winding up with each team possessed of three victories and with the public not a bit interested who won or lost. So the parties responsible for the series called said series off and announced it would be resumed in the spring of 1891. It never was, for then the organizations were at war.

Early Series Pretentious

Some of the early series for the championship of the universe was pretentious—one of them, that of 1887, decidedly so. Then the Detroit Wolverines, managed by William Henry Watkins and captained by Ned Hanlon, played 15 games with the St. Louis Browns, whose manager and captain was Charles A. Comiskey. Fans of cities other than St. Louis and Detroit were able to see the two champion combinations in action, for contests were played in Pittsburgh, Brooklyn, New York, Philadelphia, Boston, Baltimore, Washington and Chicago.

The National Leaguers won this series, 10 games to five, and it is the longest on record. The shortest was the set between the Providence Nationals and the Metropolitans of New York and of the American Association in 1884. That set consisted of three games, with the Grays winning all three.

Some tabloid information regarding the seven series between the National League and the American Association for the world's honors:

1884—Providence captured the World's Championship for the National League by defeating the Metropolitans of the American Association in three straight games, the scores being 6 to 0, 3 to 1 and 12 to 2. Charles Radbourne officiated in all three contests for the winners. Said contests all were played at the Polo Grounds and little interest was manifested in the series, which was informal, the attendance averaging 2000 daily. The clubs seemed in no hurry to start the games, the dates on which they were played being October 23rd, 24th and 25th.

1885—There was no World's Champion, the series of seven games between the Chicago National League and St. Louis American Association teams resulting in three victories for each, with one contest a draw. The St. Louis' victories were by scores of 7 to 4, 3 to 2, and 13 to 4 and Chicago's 5 to 4 and 9 to 2 (twice). Besides playing in St. Louis

and Chicago, the teams visited Pittsburgh and Cincinnati for games, both
cities then being on the American Association circuit. The first of the games
was played on October 14th and the last
on October 24th.

1886—Charley Comiskey's St. Louis
Browns, of the American Association,
won from Anson's Chicago National
Leaguers in a six game series, taking four
contests by scores of 12 to 0, 8 to 5, 10
to 3, and 4 to 3.

Chicago's victories, both pitched by
John Clarkson, were by scores of 6 to 0
and 11 to 4. The first three contests were
played in Chicago and the last three in
St. Louis, the series starting on October
18th and ending on October 23rd. The
Windy City team won two out of the
three games played on its home lot, but
lost all three run off at Sportsman's Park
in St. Louis, a passed ball by Mike Kelly
losing Chicago a chance to tie the series
in the final game, which went ten innings and in which the slabmen were
Caruthers and Clarkson.

1887—Detroit wrested from St. Louis
the World's Championship by winning
10 out of 15 games in the most ambitious series that ever was arranged between two pennant winning teams. The
series began on October 10th and lasted
until October 26th, and games were
played in St. Louis, Detroit, Pittsburgh,
Brooklyn, New York, Philadelphia (one
on the League grounds and one on the
Association green), Boston, Baltimore,
Washington and Chicago. The St. Louis'
victories were all twirled by "Parisian
Bob" Caruthers and were by scores of 6
to 1, 5 to 2, 16 to 4, 5 to 1 and 9 to 2.

Detroit won in this fashion: 5 to 3, 2 to
1, (13 innings), 8 to 0, 9 to 0, 3 to 1, 9
to 2, 4 to 2, 13 to 3, 6 to 3 and 4 to 3.
Two things that tended to give the
Michiganders the series in such a deci-
sive manner were the pitching of
Charles (Lady) Baldwin, a left hander,
who trimmed the Browns in six out of
seven games, and the throwing of
Charley Bennett. The Detroit backstop
flagged nearly all the Comiskeyites who
attempted to steal and made them hug
their bases closely. The 15 games were
attended by 51,455 spectators, Brooklyn
furnishing the largest turnout, 6,796.
Conditions have changed since then.

1888—The New York National
League Club fought for the honors of
the universe for the first time and won
six out of 10 games from Comiskey's St.
Louis aggregation, which had again
finished first in the American Association race. The series started on October
16th and was completed on October
27th, four games being played in New
York and St. Louis and one each in
Brooklyn and in Philadelphia. The Giants won five out of the first six games
and made little effort to subdue the
Browns in the contests that were fought
in the Mound City. New York's triumphs were by scores of 2 to 1, 4 to 2,
6 to 3, 6 to 4 (10 innings), 12 to 5 and
11 to 3, while St. Louis won by scores of
3 to 0, 7 to 5, 14 to 11 and 18 to 7. Buck
Ewing took Charley Bennett's place as
a backstop able to stop the Browns on
the bases and Tim Keefe was even more
effective than Baldwin had been the previous year, beating the Missourains all
four times he faced them. The one

shutout of the series was twirled by Elton Chamberlain, who won over Mickey Welch, 3 to 0.

1889—The Giants and Brooklyns were winners in their respective organizations and met in a series of nine games, which were played between October 18th and 29th, New York winning six and losing three. The games were confined to the Metropolitan district, five being played in New York and four in Brooklyn. Brooklyn won three of the first four games and then New York took the next five. Brooklyn's triumphs were by scores of 12 to 10, 8 to 7 and 10 to 7, while the New York successes were on the basis of 6 to 2, 11 to 3, 2 to 1 (11 innings), 11 to 7, 16 to 7 and 3 to 2. Hank O'Day, National League umpire now, was the most effective of the New York pitchers, winning both his games and figuring in the one excess round affair of the set.

1890—Really the best club in America during the year of the Brotherhood's existence was the Boston Players' League team. Being outside the pale of the National Agreement, it could not compete for the World's Championship, for which honor the Brooklyns of the National League and the Louisvilles of the American Association contended. There was no result to the seven-game series, which was played between October 17th and 28th, one of the contests being a 7 to 7 draw. Four contests were played in the Falls City and three in Brooklyn and there was no mad rush on the part of the populace to be present, the country having had more exhibitions of the national pastime than it could possibly digest.

Brooklyn won by scores of 9 to 0, 5 to 3, and 7 to 2; Louisville by scores of 5 to 4, 9 to 8 and 6 to 2. Red Ehret twirled in all three of the Kentuckians' wins.

War On—No Series

The National League and American Association were at war in 1891 and there was no series, and when the two organizations consolidated that fall naturally the games for the championship of the world automatically went into the discard, for the champion team of the world would be the team that finished first in the pennant race of the National League and American Association of Professional Baseball Clubs, as the new organization termed itself.

In the first year (1892) of the consolidated organization it had a split season, with Boston winning in the first half and Cleveland in the second and with Boston on top for the year. Boston was averse to playing off for the supremacy, but the League solons insisted that they do so. The first game between the clans of Selee and Tebeau was an 11-inning runless draw and then the Seleeities showed their class by winning five contests in a row, the scores of these being 4 to 3, 3 to 2, 4 to 0, 12 to 7, and 8 to 3.

The National League's one year trial of the split season was enough for it and in 1893 there was a return to the old system of a campaign that went right through till fall.

In 1894 W. C. Temple, a wealthy Pittsburgh sportsman and one time president of the organization of which Barney Dreyfuss is now the head, donated to the National League a silver trophy called the Temple Cup, which was to be annually battled for by the teams finishing first and second.

There were four series for the Temple Cup and after the fourth the National League returned the trophy to its donor. There was a lot of interest in the first two series, very little in the last two, the public tiring of these games after some of the contestants agreed to split their shares no matter how the contests resulted. Baltimore was in four of the series, Cleveland in two, New York in one and Boston in one. Only once did a pennant winning team win a Temple Cup series, the Orioles turning the trick on their third attempt.

A short history of the series for the Temple Cup, these series not being for the championship of the world, which previously had been settled by the National League pennant pursuit.

Temple Cup Series

1894—New York defeated the pennant winning Baltimores in four straight games, three played in Baltimore, one in New York. The series started October 4th and ended October 8th. The scores were 4 to 1 (twice), 9 to 6 and 16 to 3. Amos Rusie and Jouett Meekin did all the pitching for the Giants, each man winning two games. Baltimore was able to score only twice on the Hoosier Thunderbolt, regarded as one of the speediest pitchers ever in baseball.

1895—The Orioles again missed the trophy, this time bowing to Pat Tebeau's Cleveland Spiders, who took four out of the five games, four being played in Cleveland and one in Baltimore. The contests were played between October 2nd and 8th and Cleveland won by scores of 5 to 4, 7 to 2, 7 to 1 and 5 to 2. Cy Young won three games for the Ohioans, George (Nig) Cuppy one. Charles Esper, a left hander, won the only game for the champion Birds, turning in a 5 to 0 effort.

1896—Baltimore took revenge on the Clevelands, this time capturing four in a row from Tebeau's men between October 2nd and 8th. Scores of the games: 7 to 1, 7 to 2, 6 to 2 and 5 to 0. The first three contests were played in Baltimore, the last combat was staged in Cleveland. Baltimore's pitching was divided by Bill Hoffer and Joe Corbett, while the Cleveland hurling was looked after by George Cuppy (two games), and Cy Young and Rhody Wallace (each one game).

1897—Hanlon's Hustlers won the trophy for the second successive time in what was destined to be the last Temple Cup series, the defeated team being Boston. The Orioles lost the first contest, which was played in Baltimore on October 4th, by a score of 13 to 12, and then won the next four games, played in Boston on October 5, 6, 9 and 11, by scores of 13 to 11, 8 to 3, 12 to 11 and 9 to 3. Jerry Nops, Joe Corbett and Bill Hoffer did the pitching for the Marylanders, Charley Nichols, Charley Hickman and Fred Klobedanz for the Massachusetts combination.

How They Handled It

This clipping, headed Grasping Spirit in Boston, shows how the comfort of the scribes was not looked after by the Boston management 25 years ago:

The management in Boston is being severely criticized for the lack of courtesy and the grasping proclivities displayed at the Temple Cup game yesterday. The fact that every crank in the country was anxious to keep in touch with the game through the corps of newspaper correspondents sent to Boston was entirely disregarded. Instead of furnishing extra facilities to accommodate this rather important service even the ordinary and entirely inadequate equipment was rendered impossible. The wires and instruments lead to the front row of the grandstand, where a miserable unscreened press stand offers opportunities to practice lively dodging of foul tips and wild pitches. This space was sold yesterday, and correspondents, who also paid the price of admission, by the way, were driven to the slanting roof of the stand, accompanied by the telegraph operators, where they perched among the rafters and trusted a kindly Providence to keep the wires clear. As the wires were carried into the regions somewhere under the horde of spectators beneath and the switches and other paraphernalia of telegraphy were entirely out of reach in case of accident, the state of mind in which correspondents were kept was unenviable. Perhaps Mr. Selee doesn't care whether the public outside of Boston gets news of the Temple Cup battles; but then the Temple Cup is a sort of national affair and baseball rooters are somewhat interested in it.

No Kicks Thereafter

That was the last chance war correspondents had to kick at the treatment accorded them when they were sent to cover near World's Series or World's Series. In the fall of 1900 the pennant winning Brooklyns and the second place Pittsburghs played a three game series for a cup offered by a Smoky City newspaper, but the scribes did not turn out in droves for this set of combats and neither did the populace.

The National League and American League were bitter enemies in 1901 and 1902 and the question as to which of the pennant winners was the best remained undecided these two seasons.

In 1903 Boston, representing the American League, and Pittsburgh, representing the National, met to determine the championship of the world, the series under the jurisdiction of the two clubs interested more than the two leagues interested. Eight contests were played—five in the Hub, three in Stogieville—between October 1st and 12th. The Red Sox, managed by Jimmy Collins, generally conceded to be the best third baseman of all time and now a resident of Buffalo and president of an amateur league there, took the Pirates into camp, five games to three. The Pennsylvanians won three of the first four engagements, but the Plymouth Rocks recovered their nerve and took the last four, shutting out Barney's

Buccaneers in the final frolic, when Big Bill Dinneen (William Henry Dinneen, American League umpire now) opposed Charles Louis Phillippe on the rubber.

In this series Deacon Phillippe was the mainstay of the National Leaguers, being on the rubber in all three of their victories and conquering Cy Young once, Tom Hughes 1, once, and Bill Dinneen once. Dinneen won three games for the Red Sox and Young two, the present American League umpire scoring a pair of shutouts. The scores of the Pittsburgh victories were 7 to 3, 4 to 2 and 7 to 4, while Boston won by margins of 3 to 0, 11 to 2, 6 to 3, 7 to 3 and 3 to 0. Pittsburgh, in a final effort to save the day, pitted Phillippe against Dinneen in what turned out to be the final game of the series. Dinneen outpitched Phillippe, confining the Pirates to four safeties and winding up the game by fanning Hans Wagner, another player who deserves a place on the greatest team of all time.

The scores of the games between Boston and Pittsburgh can be found in the Reach Guide of 1904 and the scores of all other games for the world's championship since can be found in the handbooks of the National Commission as well as in the publication Francis C. Richter has edited for so many years. The Spalding Guide also has been publishing the World's Series scores for years and so has the Record Book, but the Reach Guide is the only one that has contained all of them.

There was no World's Series in 1904, when the Giants and Red Sox won the pennant of their respective leagues,

owner John T. Brush of the New York National League club insisting that such a series should be under National Commission rules and drawing up a set of rules later. These rules still obtain. Naturally there have been changes in them, but the main scheme of the World's Series today remains John T. Brush's.

Interest Becomes General

Once the World's Series came under the jurisdiction of the National Commission, interest in the games became general and these games became fashionable, attracting people who only previously knew of the pastime by reading of it. In some ways the series has become a little too fashionable, for the fan who goes regularly to championship games has quite a time obtaining tickets to the classical contests.

These figures give a pretty good illustration of what interest has been taken in the 18 sets of games for the world's title between the American and National League pennant winners:

Total attendance—2,702,375.
Total receipts—$5,667,200.50

Winning a World's Series gives a league and a club considerable prestige, and to hear certain rabid bugs talk losing a series means that the losing club and league belongs in Class AA.

That the difference between the two major leagues is slight and always has been slight, the figures for the 18 World's Series between the American and National Leagues prove. Here they are:

	Amer. Leag.	Nat Leag.	Amer.'s Favor	Nat.'s Favor
Series won	11	7	4	
Games won	57	50	7	
Percentage series won	611	389	222	
Percentage games won	533	467	066	
Times at bat	3558	3506	52	
Runs	355	346	9	
Base hits	819	809	10	
Percentage	230	.231		.001
Two base hits	46	45	1	
Three base hits	46	45	1	
Home runs	22	13	9	
Sacrifice hits	109	128		19
Stolen bases	76	125		49
Putouts	2916	2917		1
Assists	1456	1470		14
Errors	170	171	1	
Percentage	963	.962	.001	

Tables Tell the Tale

The preceding table shows how little difference there has been between the American and National League clubs that have competed for the chief honors of the baseball world and tables to come later ought to show to the busy reader the world's champion clubs and the near world's champion clubs, in what fashion they won and in what fashion they lost the world's title or the chance to obtain it, the clubs that couldn't win and couldn't lose the blue ribbon or the chance to obtain it—in fact, they ought to show pretty nearly everything. Here they are, minus comment:

The Twenty-Three World's Champion Clubs

Year	Club	Won	Lost	Pc.	Manager
1914	Boston Nationals	4	0	1000	George Stallings
1884	Providence Nationals	3	0	1000	Frank Bancroft
1907	Chicago Nationals	4	*0	1000	Frank Chance
1905	New York Nationals	4	1	.800	John McGraw
1908	Chicago Nationals	4	1	.800	Frank Chance
1910	Philadelphia Americans	4	1	.800	Connie Mack
1913	Philadelphia Americans	4	1	.800	Connie Mack
1915	Boston Americans	4	1	.800	Bill Carrigan
1916	Boston Americans	4	1	.800	Bill Carrigan
1920	Cleveland Americans	5	2	.714	Tris Speaker
1887	Detroit Nationals	10	5	.667	W. H. Watkins
1889	New York Nationals	6	3	.667	James Mutrie
1886	St. Louis Association	4	2	.667	Charles Comiskey
1906	Chicago Americans	4	2	.667	Fielder Jones
1911	Philadelphia Americans	4	2	.667	Connie Mack
1917	Chicago Americans	4	2	.667	Clarence Rowland
1918	Boston Americans	4	3	.667	Edward Barrow
1903	Boston Americans	5	3	.625	James Collins
1919	Cincinnati Nationals	5	3	.625	Patrick Moran

Year	Club	Won	Lost	Pc.	Manager
1921	New York Nationals	5	3	.625	John McGraw
1888	New York Nationals	6	4	.600	James Mutrie
1909	Pittsburgh Nationals	4	3	.571	Fred Clarke
1912	Boston Americans	4	*3	.571	Jake Stahl

* One tie game in each of these series.

The Twenty-Three Near World's Champions

Year	Club	Won	Lost	Pc.	Manager
1909	Detroit Americans	3	4	.429	Hugh Jennings
1912	New York Nationals	*3	4	.429	John McGraw
1888	St. Louis Association	4	6	.400	Charles Comiskey
1903	Pittsburgh Nationals	3	5	.375	Fred Clarke
1919	Chicago Americans	3	5	.375	William Gleason
1921	New York Americans	3	5	.375	Miller Huggins
1887	St. Louis Association	5	10	.333	Charles Comiskey
1889	Brooklyn Association	3	6	.333	William McGunnigle
1886	Chicago Nationals	2	4	.333	Adrian C. Anson
1906	Chicago Nationals	2	4	.333	Frank Chance
1911	New York Nationals	2	4	.333	John McGraw
1917	New York Nationals	2	4	.333	John McGraw
1918	Chicago Nationals	2	4	.333	Fred Mitchell
1920	Brooklyn Nationals	2	5	.286	Wilbert Robinson
1905	Philadelphia Americans	1	4	.200	Connie Mack
1908	Detroit Americans	1	4	.200	Hugh Jennings
1910	Chicago Nationals	1	4	.200	Frank Chance
1913	New York Nationals	1	4	.200	John McGraw
1915	Philadelphia Nationals	1	4	.200	Patrick Moran
1916	Brooklyn Nationals	1	4	.200	Wilbert Robinson
1907	Detroit Americans	*0	4	.000	Hugh Jennings
1884	New York Association(a)	0	3	.000	James Mutrie
1914	Philadelphia Americans	0	4	.000	Connie Mack

* One tie game in each of these series.
(a) Team was called the Metropolitans.

Couldn't Win—Couldn't Lost
World's Series Without Winner and Without Loser

Year	Club	Won	Lost	Pc.	Manager
1885	Chicago Nationals	*3	3	.500	Adrian C. Anson
1885	St. Louis Association	3	*3	.500	Charles Comiskey
1890	Brooklyn Nationals	*3	3	.500	William McGunnigle
1890	Louisville Association	3	*3	.500	John C. Chapman

* One tie game in each of these series.

Cities That Have Had World's Champion Teams

City	National League	American League	American Asso.	Total
Boston	1	5	0	6
New York	4	0	0	4
Chicago	2	2	0	4
Philadelphia	0	3	0	3
Cincinnati	1	0	0	1
Cleveland	0	1	0	1
Detroit	1	0	0	1
Pittsburgh	1	0	0	1
Providence	1	0	0	1
St. Louis	0	0	1	1
Totals	11	11	1	23

Cities Competing for World's Championship 1884 to 1921 Inclusive

City	National League	American League	American Asso.	Total
Chicago	7	3	0	10
New York	8	1	1	10
Boston	1	5	0	6
Philadelphia	1	5	0	6
Brooklyn	3	0	1	4
Detroit	1	3	0	4
St. Louis	0	0	4	4
Pittsburgh	2	0	0	2
Cincinnati	1	0	0	1
Cleveland	0	1	0	1
Louisville	0	0	1	1
Providence	1	0	0	1
Totals	25	18	7	50

Record of Games Won and Lost by Each Club in World's Series 1884 to 1921, Inclusive

Clubs	Won	Lost	Pc.
Boston Nationals	4	0	1000
Providence Nationals	3	0	1000
Cleveland Americans	5	2	.714
Boston Americans	21	10	.677
Detroit Nationals	10	5	.667
Cincinnati Nationals	5	3	.625
Chicago Americans	11	9	.550

Clubs	Won	Lost	Pc.
Philadelphia Americans	13	12	.520
New York Nationals	29	27	.518
Louisville Association	3	3	.500
Chicago Nationals	18	20	.474
Pittsburgh Nationals	7	8	.467
St. Louis Association	16	21	.432
New York Americans	3	5	.375
Brooklyn Association	3	6	.333
Brooklyn Nationals	6	12	.333
Detroit Americans	4	12	.250
Philadelphia Nationals	1	4	.200
New York Association (a)	0	3	.000
Totals	162	162	.500
American League	57	50	.533
National League	83	79	.512
American Association	22	33	.400
Totals	162	162	.500

(a) Team was called the Metropolitans

Manager's Record in World's Series
1884 to 1921, Inclusive

Managers	Series Won	Series Lost	Series Tied	Games Won	Games Lost	Games Tied
Bill Carrigan	2	0	0	8	2	0
George Stallings	1	0	0	4	0	0
Frank Bancroft	1	0	0	3	0	0
Tris Speaker	1	0	0	5	2	0
William H. Watkins	1	0	0	10	5	0
Edward Barrow	1	0	0	4	2	0
Fielder Jones	1	0	0	4	2	0
Clarence Rowland	1	0	0	4	2	0
James Collins	1	0	0	5	3	0
Jake Stahl	1	0	0	4	3	1
James Mutrie	2	1	0	12	10	0
Connie Mack	3	2	0	13	12	0
Frank Chance	2	2	0	11	9	1
Fred Clarke	1	1	0	7	8	0
Patrick Moran	1	1	0	6	7	0
John McGraw	2	4	0	17	20	1
Charles Comiskey	1	2	1	16	21	1
John Chapman	0	0	1	3	3	1
William Gleason	0	1	0	3	5	0
Miller Huggins	0	1	0	3	5	0
Adrian C. Anson	0	1	1	5	7	1
William McGunnigle	0	1	1	6	9	1
Fred Mitchell	0	1	0	2	4	0

Managers	Series Won	Series Lost	Tied	Games Won	Games Lost	Tied
Wilbert Robinson	0	2	0	3	9	0
Hugh Jennings	0	3	0	4	12	1
Totals	23	23	4	162	162	8

Where the Rosters Are

Readers desiring the rosters of the pennant winning clubs and those who participated in the various World's Series can find them in another section of this book, they not being given here in order to avoid duplication and in order to save space.

As for everything that happened in the various sets of games for the blue ribbon of baseball, few feats are overlooked in the World's Series' record performances contained in the Spalding Official Base Ball Record.

Pitching Performances

The World's Series still is shy a no-hit game, Edward Marvin Reulbach of the Cubs having the best pitched game to his credit with a one-swat combat against the White Sox on October 10, 1906. Reulbach won this game 7 to 1, John Augustin (Jiggs) Donohue preventing him from getting into the Hall of Fame by singling. In this contest, which was played at South Side Park, Reulbach, a collegian, who pitched under the name of Lawson before getting into the National League, franked six men and fanned three.

Anything said about sensational performances in the World's Series from now on relates only to series between the American and National Leagues.

These have been the authors of two-hit games:

Held Opponents to Two Hits

October 11, 1906—Edward Armstrong Walsh, White Sox, against Cubs. Won his game, 3 to 0.

October 12, 1906—Mordecai Peter Centennial Brown, Cubs, against White Sox. Won his game, 1 to 0.

October 11, 1913—Edward S. Plank, Athletics, against Giants. Won his game, 3 to 1.

October 10, 1914—William Lawrence James, Braves, against Athletics. Won his game, 1 to 0.

October 6, 1921—Waite Charles Hoyt, Yankees, against Giants. Won his game, 3 to 0.

Notable Three-Hit Game

John Wesley Coombs of the Athletics, who coached Williams this spring (1922), turned in the best three-hit game in a series for the championship of the universe at New York on October 17, 1911, when he won over Christy Mathewson in 11 innings, 3 to 2. The Giants' safeties were made by Charles Herzog, Chief Meyers and Matty, Herzog's being a double and coming in the eleventh spasm. The other safeties came in the third inning.

Jack Was Never Beaten

John Wesley never lost a World's Series game, though one contest in which he took part went against his team. He won five classical combats—four for the Athletics and one for the Superbas. This is his record and it is a record that probably will endure:

Coombs's String of Five

October 18, 1910—Defeated Cubs, Mordecai Brown pitching, 9 to 3, allowing seven hits, striking out five men and passing nine. Men at bat, 31.

October 20, 1910—Defeated Cubs, Ed Reulbach pitching, 12 to 5, allowing six hits, striking out eight men and passing four. Men at bat, 31.

October 23, 1910—Defeated Cubs, Mordecai Brown pitching, 7 to 2, allowing nine hits, striking out seven men and passing one. Men at bat, 34.

October 17, 1911—Defeated Giants, Christy Mathewson pitching, 3 to 2 in 11 innings, allowing three hits, striking out seven men and passing four. Men at bat, 31.

October 10, 1916—Defeated Red Sox, Carl Mays pitching, 4 to 3, allowing seven hits and three runs in six and one third innings, striking out one man and passing one. Men at bat, 23.

The contest in which Coombs participated that was not a victory for his team was that of October 25, 1911. Jack then strained himself and had to retire in the tenth with the score tied. Plank, finishing the game, lost it, 4 to 3. In this game, 32 men faced Coombs in nine innings, his opponents scored three runs and made eight hits, he fanned nine men and he walked two.

This is Coomb's complete World's Series record—and it is *some* record:

Games pitched—6.
Games won—5.
Games lost—NONE.
Innings pitched—53 and 1–3.
Opponents' times at bat—182.
Opponents' runs—18.
Opponents' base hits—40.
Opponents' batting average—220.
Strikeouts—37.
Bases on balls—21.

Ironmonger One of Four

Coombs, who won for himself the title of Iron man by his work in the longest American League game on record, is one of four men who has won three games in one World's Series without meeting with a reverse. Before he had tamed the Cubs thrice in 1910, Christy Mathewson had won three games for the Giants from the Athletics in 1905 and Charles (Babe) Adams had done the same thing for the Pirates against the Tigers in 1909. Stanley Coveleskie of Cleveland, in 1920, won three games from Brooklyn.

Mathewson would get the place of honor among the three victory in one World's Series men for the reason that in all three of his triumphs he kept the Mackmen away from the plate. These are the records of the four heroes:

Won Three Games in One Series Without Losing Any

Year	Pitcher	Innings	AB	R	BH	Pc.	SO	BB	HB
1905	Mathewson	27	92	0	14	.152	18	1	1
1909	Adams	27	98	5	18	.184	11	6	1
1910	Coombs	27	96	10	22	.229	20	14	0
1920	Coveleskie	27	94	2	15	.160	8	2	0

Waite Charles Hoyt of the Yankees, winning two out of three in the series of 1921 from the Giants, pitched wonderfully, too, as these figures attest:

Innings—27.
At bat—106.
Runs—2.
Base hits—18.
Percentage—170.
Strikeouts—18.
Bases on balls—11.
Hit batsmen—0.

But all through the World's Series you will find wonderful pitching. Records only are considered here.

For a series the greatest number of runless innings pitched is 27, with Mathewson doing this for the Giants against the Athletics in 1905. Big Six's next appearance in a classical combat was on October 14, 1911, against the team he had "Chicagoed," thrice in 1905 and he pitched one more runless inning before being scored on through the medium of Baker's single, Murphy's sacrifice, Meyers's passed ball and Davis's safety, making 28 tallyless rounds.

Ruth Raises Runless Innings to 29

Along came Ruth, whose nickname,

front name and middle name are pretty well known by this time, later to raise the number of runless innings reeled off in series for the title to 29. This is how George Herman accomplished the trick:

1916, for Red Sox, 13 runless innings—October 9th, won over Brooklyn, 2 to 1 in 14 innings, Superbas getting their tally in first chapter.

1918, for Red Sox, 16 runless—September 5th, won over Chicago, 1 to 0; September 9th, won over Chicago, 3 to 2, Cubs getting their tallies in eighth period.

Walsh Fanned a Dozen

Edward Armstrong Walsh holds the strikeout record for a world's series' game, having placed it at 12 on October 11, 1906, when with the assistance of a triple by George Rohe with the bases packed, he was winning over Jack Pfiester of the Cubs, 3 to 0. The men the Big Reel fanned were Frank Schulte, three times; Jimmy Sheckard, Joe Tinker and John Evers, twice and Arthur Hofman, Jack Pfiester and Klink, once.

Horace Owen Eller, once the property of the team Walsh won so many games for, fanned half a dozen of the White Sox in order for Cincinnati in the second and third innings on

October 6, 1919, these men being Chic Gandil, Swede Risberg, Ray Schalk, Claude Williams, Harry Liebold and Eddie Collins. The next two batters sent easy grounders to the Red pitcher and he fanned the next, so he retired nine men in order—possibly a record, certainly nearly one.

Devore the Strike-Out Goat

Joshua Devore, midget outfielder of the Giants, at present is the strike-out goat of the world's series, for he was whiffed five straight times in the second and third games of the 1911 set, played on October 16th and 17th Ed Plank, left-hander of the Athletics, fanned him four times on the first mentioned date, and on the second mentioned date Jack Coombs, right-hander, fanned him the first time he batted, or rather tried to bat.

Few Batting Feats

As the pitcher generally has been the big factor in world's series naturally there has been a scarcity of batting feats. No player ever has been able to group more than four safeties in one combat, and just ten players have been able to acquire this number. The Thumping Ten are:

THOMAS W. LEACH, Pirates—Two singles and two triples off Young, Red Sox, on October 1, 1903.

CLARENCE H. BEAUMONT, Pirates—Four singles off Dinneen, Red Sox, on October 8, 1903.

FRANK ISBELL, White Sox—Four doubles off Reulbach, Pfiester and Overall, Cubs, on October 13, 1906.

EDGAR HAHN, White Sox—Four singles off Brown and Overall, Cubs, on October 14, 1906.

TYRUS RAYMOND COBB, Tigers—Three singles and one double off Pfiester and Reulbach, Cubs, on October 12, 1908.

LAWRENCE J. DOYLE, Giants—Two singles and two doubles off Coombs and Plank, Athletics, on October 25, 1911.

DANIEL F. MURPHY, Athletics—Three singles and one double off Ames, Wiltse and Marquard, Giants, on October 26, 1911.

FRANK F. FRISCH, Giants—Four singles off Mays, Yankees, on October 5, 1921.

GEORGE J. BURNS, Giants—Two singles, one double and one triple off Shawkey, Collins, Quinn and Rogers, Yankees, on October 7, 1921.

FRANK SNYDER, Giants—Four singles off Shawkey, Collins, Quinn and Rogers, Yankees, on October 7, 1921.

Harry Gowdy of the Braves climbed Joe Bush of the Athletics for two singles and a home run on October 12, 1914, and Walter Ruether of the Reds got a brace of triples off Eddie Cicotte and Grover Lowdermilk of the White Sox on October 1, 1919.

George Rohe, in the White Sox line-up because of an injury to George Davis, was the first world's series' player to clean the bases of their three tenants with a long hit, tripling on October 11, 1906, against Jack Pfiester, Cub southpaw.

Clean Up Boy No. 2 was Elmer John Smith of the Indians. He made a home run with three on against Burleigh Grimes of the Superbas on October 10, 1920.

Clean Up Boy No. 3 was Ross Young (or Youngs) of the Giants. He tripled with a full house in evidence in the seventh inning of the game with the Yankees, Warren Collins pitching, and Warren was through for the day. Earlier in the same spasm Young had doubled against Jack Quinn and the triple set him in a class by himself as being the one world's series' player to acquire two safeties in one inning—both long ones, too.

Useful Home Runs

Teams often have ridden to victory on home runs in world's series' games, two hits of this kind for one contest being the limit for one player. Patrick Henry Dougherty of the Red Sox helped himself to a brace of four baggers on October 2, 1903, at the expense of Pedagogue Samuel Leever and Fred (Bucky) Vail of the Pirates. Twelve years later Harry B. Hooper, also a Red Sox, made two belt line wallops in a game with the Phillies, Erskine Mayer and Eppa Rixey pitching. The date of this game was October 13th. Benjamin Michael Kauff of the Giants made a carbon copy of the Daugherty–Hooper exploits on October 11, 1917, Urban Charles Faber and David Charles Danforth pitching.

The real world's series' home run king, however, was not Dougherty, not

Hooper, not Kauff. It was John Franklin Baker, then of the Athletics, now of the Yankees. Baker's home runs made him and made history. There were three of them, two made in 1911, one made in 1913.

The clouts of 1911 always will be remembered. No. 1 appeared in the sixth inning of the game October 16th. Marquard was pitching for New York, each team had a run, Eddie Collins was on second and there were two out. John Franklin wafted the ball over the right field wall at Shibe Park, winning the game for the A's 3 to 1. Scribe Mathewson, the next morning, told how Marquard had pitched wrongly to the Trappe Thumper.

Scribe Marquard soon was able to inform his readers how Pitcher Mathewson pitched wrongly to the Maryland Mauler, getting occasion to do so after what happened in the ninth inning of the game of October 17th at the Polo Grounds. Big Six had this game in his possession, 1 to 0, when the ninth started, and disposed of the first batter—Eddie Collins. Baker then hit to right for the circuit, tying things up, and in the eleventh the Athletics won out.

Baker's last world's series home run was punched out in the fifth inning of the game of October 7, 1913, at the Polo Grounds, the White Elephants winning this game, 6 to 4. They had a two-run lead when the inning started, two men being out when Eddie Collins worked Marquard for transportation. The Rube pitched to Baker and J. Franklin hit the ball into the right field stands, his run eventually winning the contest.

Thirty-Five Home Runs to Date

Thirty-five home runs have been made in the world's series between the American and National Leagues, their makers and the men off whom they were made being as follows:

JAMES S. SEBRING, Pirates—Off Young, Red Sox, on October 1, 1903.

PATRICK H. DOUGHERTY (2), Red Sox—Off Leever and Vail, Pirates, on October 2, 1903.

JOSEPH B. TINKER, Cubs—Off Donovan, Tigers, on October 11, 1908, hit winning game.

FRED C. CLARKE, Pirates—Off Mullin, Tigers, on October 8, 1909.

DAVID J. JONES, Tigers—Off Adams, Pirates, on Oct. 13, 1909 hit starting game.

SAMUEL B. CRAWFORD, Tigers—Off Adams, Pirates, on October 13, 1909.

FRED C. CLARKE, Pirates—Off Summers, Tigers, on October 13, 1909, hit winning game.

DANIEL F. MURPHY, Athletics—Off McIntire, Cubs, on October 20, 1910, hit winning game.

J. FRANKLIN BAKER, Athletics—Off Marquard, Giants, on October 16, 1911, hit winning game.

J. FRANKLIN BAKER, Athletics—Off Mathewson, Giants, on October 17, 1911.

REUBEN N. OLDRING, Athletics—Off Marquard, Giants, on October 25, 1911.

LAWRENCE J. DOYLE, Giants—Off Hall, Red Sox, on October 15, 1912.

WILLIAM L. GARDNER, Red Sox—Off Tesreau, Giants, on October 15, 1912.

J. FRANKLIN BAKER, Athletics—Off Marquard, Giants, on October 7, 1913, hit winning game.

WALTER H. SCHANG, Athletics—Off Crandall, Giants, on October 9, 1913.

FRED C. MERKLE, Giants—Off Bender, Athletics, on October 10, 1913.

HARRY M. GOWDY, Braves—Off Bush, Athletics, on October 12, 1914.

HARRY B. HOOPER, (2), Red Sox—Off Mayer and Rixey, Phillies, on October 13, 1915, last hit winning game.

GEORGE E. LEWIS, Red Sox—Off Rixey, Phillies, on October 13, 1915.

FRED C. LUDERUS, Phillies—Off Foster, Red Sox, on October 13, 1915.

HARRY H. MYERS, Superbas—Off Ruth, Red Sox, on October 9, 1916.

WILLIAM L. GARDNER, Red Sox—Off Coombs, Superbas, on October 10, 1916.

WILLIAM L. GARDNER, Red Sox—Off Marquard, Superbas, on October 11, 1916, hit winning game.

OSCAR C. FELSCH, White Sox—Off Sallee, Giants, on October 6, 1917, hit winning game.

BENJAMIN M. KAUFF (2), Giants; Off Faber and Danforth, White Sox on October 11, 1917, first hit winning game.

JOSEPH JACKSON, White Sox—Off Eller, Reds, on October 9, 1919.

ELMER J. SMITH, Indians—Off Grimes, Superbas, on October 10, 1920, hit (with bases full) winning game.

JAMES C. J. BAGBY, Indians—Off Grimes, Superbas, on October 10, 1920.

GEORGE H. RUTH, Yankees—Off Douglas, Giants, on October 9, 1921.

EMIL F. MEUSEL, Giants—Off Harper, Yankees, on October 11, 1921.

FRANK J. SNYDER, Giants—Off Harper, Yankees, on October 11, 1921.

WILSON FEWSTER, Yankees—Off Barnes, Giants, on October 11, 1921.

And here is a summary of the world's series home runs:

By American Leaguers—22

Baker, Philadelphia	3
Gardner, Boston	3
Dougherty, Boston	2
Hooper, Boston	2
Bagby, Cleveland	1
Crawford, Detroit	1
Felsch, Chicago	1
Fewster, New York	1
Jackson, Chicago	1
Jones, Detroit	1
Lewis, Boston	1
Murphy, Philadelphia	1
Oldring, Philadelphia	1
Ruth, New York	1
Schang, Philadelphia	1
Smith, Cleveland	1

Off National Leaguers—22

Marquard, New York–Brooklyn	4
Adams, Pittsburgh	2
Grimes, Brooklyn	2
Rixey, Philadelphia	2
Barnes, New York	1
Coombs, Brooklyn	1
Crandall, New York	1
Douglas, New York	1
Eller, Cincinnati	1
Leever, Pittsburgh	1
Mathewson, New York	1
Mayers, Philadelphia	1
McIntire, Chicago	1
Sallee, New York	1
Tesreau, New York	1
Vail, Pittsburgh	1

By National Leaguers—13

Clarke, Pittsburgh	2
Kauff, New York	2
Doyle, New York	1
Gowdy, Boston	1
Luderus, Philadelphia	1
Merkle, New York	1
Meusel, New York	1
Myers, Brooklyn	1
Sebring, Pittsburgh	1
Snyder, New York	1
Tinker, Chicago	1

Off American Leaguers—13

Harper, New York	2
Bender, Philadelphia	1
Bush, Philadelphia	1
Danforth, Chicago	1
Donovan, Detroit	1
Faber, Chicago	1
Foster, Boston	1
Hall, Boston	1
Mullin, Detroit	1
Ruth, Boston	1
Young, Boston	1

PART VI

The Minor Leagues Operating in 1922

Salary Limit

AA	Pacific Coast League	None
AA	International League	None
AA	Pacific Coast League	None
A	Eastern League	$4,500
A	Southern Association	$4,500
A	Texas League	$4,500
A	Western League	$4,500
B	Illinois–Iowa–Indiana League	$3,200
B	Michigan–Ontario League	$3,000
B	South Atlantic Association	$3,200
B	Virginia League	$3,300
B	Western International League	$3,200
B	Central League	$2,500
C	Florida State League	$2,650
C	Piedmont League	$2,650
C	Southwestern League	$2,400
C	Western Association	$2,650
D	Blue Ridge League	$2,000
D	Kentucky–Illinois–Tennessee League	$1,800
D	Mississippi Valley League	$2,000
D	Texas–Oklahoma League	$2,000
D	Dakota League	$2,400
D	Appalachian League	$1,950
D	Nebraska State League	$1,800
D	Blue Grass League	$1,650
D	Eastern Shore League	$1,750
D	Cotton States League	$2,400
D	West Texas League	$1,800

Brave Man Not in Sight

If thousands of words are needed to tell the story of the start of the major leagues, millions are required to narrate the early days of the minor leagues, which this year (1922) numbered nearly 30 at the campaign's kick-off. No man has yet appeared on the baseball horizon brave enough to attempt a real history of the minor leagues, for that task is an impossible one. The leagues have changed their names and have changed their circuits so frequently that there probably isn't anyone in the country who knows the names of all the organizations that have functioned or all the cities that have supported (or tried to support) clubs. Extremely small would be the State that at some time or another hasn't had a State League.

The one minor league that developed into a major league was the American League. Before it became a major league it had Class A ranking and it had a circuit practically the same as the American Association of today. Its name prior to 1900 was the Western League. It operated continuously from 1894 to 1899 under this title and under the watchful eye of Byron Bancroft Johnson.

The minor league that has been longest in continuous existence is the International League, which is the old Eastern League. Its career dates back to 1884, if one wants to consider the New York State League of that year the International of today.

Probably the first minor league was the Northwestern League of 1879, which had a circuit consisting of Dubuque and Davenport, Iowa; Rockford, Illinois and Omaha, Nebraska. Dubuque won the pennant, two of the Iowans' stars being Charles Comiskey, owner of the Chicago White Sox, and Thomas J. Loftus, who was an American League manager in the early days of the Johnson organization.

The Old Roman was a pitcher then as well as a first baseman and as a pitcher he is said to have held all records for crippling opponents—not on purpose, but merely through his wildness. Ted Sullivan, who probably has formed more minor leagues than anyone else unless possibly John McCloskey, can tell what kind of a curver Commy was— and has told several times.

In 1883 there was a Northwestern League, Toledo winning its pennant, and there was an Inter-State League, located in the East, with Brooklyn as its champion club.

In 1884 there was an Eastern League which had clubs in Trenton, Wilmington, Baltimore, Reading, Harrisburg and other places; there was a North-

western League; there were a couple of leagues in Connecticut and Massachusetts; there was an Iron and Oil League and there was a New York State League.

Don't think by this you are going to get a yearly list of minor leagues, because you are not.

What the writer is trying to do is to show that years ago there were plenty of minor leagues.

Here are some items from the *New York Clipper Annual of 1885* about minor leagues which then were in their infancy.

February 11th—The Eastern League held a special meeting—Jersey City, N. J.

February 12th—The Western League organized—Indianapolis, Indiana.

March 12th and 13th—The Eastern League held its schedule meeting— Philadelphia, Pa.

March 16—The New York State League organized—Albany, N. Y., (and it wasn't very many years later that John Conway Toole, now president of the International League, was umpiring in it. Toole, like President John Heydler of the National League, is an ex-umpire.)

March 31st—The Western League held its scheduled meeting—St. Louis, Mo.

April 8th—Special meeting of the Southern League—Atlanta, Ga.

April 15th—The Southern League commenced its championship season.

April 18th—Opening championship games of the Western League.

April 30th—Opening championship games of the Eastern League.

June 14th—The Western League disbanded. (Cleveland was in it.)

June 25th—The Atlantic City (formerly Wilmington) club disbanded.

July 1st—Special meeting of the New York State League—Binghamton, N. Y.

July 24th—The Eastern League held a special meeting—Baltimore, Md.

July 28th—The Albany club disbanded.

August 4th—The Lancaster club disbanded.

August 31st—The Norfolk club disbanded.

September 4th—The Birmingham club disbanded.

September 7th—The Columbus, (Ga.) club disbanded.

September 12th—The Southern League held a special meeting—Atlanta, Ga.

September 17th—The Southern League closed its championship season.

September 18th—The Virginia club of Richmond disbanded.

November 10th—Special meeting of the Southern League—Macon, Ga.

November 18th—Special meeting of the Eastern League—Meriden, Conn.

December 2nd—Annual meeting of the Ontario League—Toronto, Ont.

December 16th—Annual meeting of the New York State League—Syracuse N. Y.

And here were some of the no-hit games of 1885:

April 25th—Conway, Lawrence vs. Waltham. (This Conway probably is the Conway who pitched for Baltimore the day Guy Hecker scored seven runs and he probably was pitching in the league in which Wilbert Robinson, Superba manager now was playing).

May 11th—Kelly, Springfield vs. Erie. (Evidently Springfield, Ohio.)

May 29th—Parsons, Birmingham vs. Augusta. (This was first hitless game in Southern League.)

June 11th—Morrison, Bridgeport vs. Waterbury. (This was an Eastern League game and Connie Mack was in the Eastern League then, with Hartford.)

June 24th—Stemmyer, Toronto vs. Clipper of Hamilton.

August 22nd—Barr, National of Washington vs. Virginia of Richmond.

August 28th—Pendergrass, Utica vs. Rochester. (This was probably first hitless game in what is now the International League.)

October 3rd—J. Smith, Newark vs. Baltimore.

Not in the Same League

Newark and Baltimore were not in the same league in 1885, Newark being in the Eastern and Baltimore in the American Association. The Orioles visited Newark to play an exhibition game and not only were shut out in hits and runs by the Jerseymen, but failed to get a man to first base. Sixteen of the Birds fanned. J. Smith was John (Phenomenal) Smith, Christy Mathewson's manager at Norfolk in 1900 and a man under whom William Edward Donovan and William Oliver Gilbert, Eastern League managers now, saw service when they first were starting out.

St. Louis Maroons Held Hitless, Too

The Orioles do not happen to be the only major league team that has failed to make a safe hit when playing a minor league team. The same experience happened to the St. Louis Maroons of the National League when they stacked up against the Leavenworth team of the Western League on April 25, 1886, William F. Hart of Cincinnati (Bond Hill Billy) doing the pitching for the Kansans. Hart had a remarkably long pitching career—over 20 years. So had Theodore Breitenstein. When the iron men of the game are considered the names of both Hart and of Breitenstein should be included.

So far as the writer knows there was no league on the Pacific Slope in 1885, but they had good teams there then— the Haverlys, the Pioneers, and the Greenhood and Morans among others—and no-hit games were being released by Incell and by George Van Haltren. Probably the first hitless contest on the Coast was flung by Charley Sweeney, a native son, himself, against the Haverlys of San Francisco on December 30, 1883. Sweeney, holder of the National League strikeout record for one game, was with Providence that year and the next.

The Minors in 1886

The *Clipper Annual*, out of print long since, throws this light on the minor leagues of 1886:

SOUTHERN LEAGUE—Held special meeting at Macon, Ga., January 7th; Macon and Charleston played 13-inning 3 to 3 tie at Charleston, S. C., June 16th; special meeting held at Macon, June 28th; Augusta disbanded July 6th; Chattanooga withdrew July 8th; Eddie Knouff, left-hander of Memphis, pitched a no-hit game against Macon and struck out 15 men at Memphis, August 5th; Wells of Atlanta pitched a no hit game against Charleston at Atlanta, August 16th; Knouff of Memphis struck out 16 of the Charlestons in eight innings, September 4th.

EASTERN LEAGUE—Held special meeting at New York, January 12th; held adjourned meeting at Bridgeport, January 29th; held schedule meeting at Bridgeport, March 23rd and 24th; Providence defeated Hartford, 4 to 3, in 14 innings, at Providence, May 1st; Long Island Club disbanded, May 24th; Providence disbanded, June 3rd; new schedule adopted at meeting at Meriden, June 5th; Hartford made 14 runs in the second inning of game with Waterbury, June 19th (Connie Mack was a Hartford catcher then); Meriden disbanded July 14th; Mickey Hughes of Waterbury pitched a hitless game against Bridgeport at Bridgeport, August 12th (Hughes was with Brooklyn in 1888 and 1889); Newark made 17 runs in the second inning of the game with Hartford at Newark, October 1st (Connie Mack had joined Washington before this catastrophe had happened to his old team).

WESTERN LEAGUE—Organized at meeting held at St. Joseph, Mo., January 18th; schedule meeting held at

Leavenworth, Kansas, March 28th; game between Leadville and St. Joseph held up for 30 minutes by snow storm at Leadville, Colorado, July 4th; annual meeting held at Leavenworth, November 7th, when Leadville was expelled and Omaha admitted.

NEW ENGLAND LEAGUE—Reorganized at special meeting held at Boston, January 20th; special meeting held at Haverhill, Mass., April 7th; Conway of Lawrence, (probably Dick, Guy Hecker's friend) fanned 21 of the Tufts' collegians, including 11 in succession, in an exhibition game, April 17th, three safe hits were all that were made in Portland–Lawrence game, Hatfield and Gorman pitching, May 6th; special meeting held at Boston, May 7th; Doyle of Marlboro pitched a hitless game against the Boston Blues, June 8th; Tuckerman of Brockton pitched a hitless game against the Boston Blues, July 16th; annual meeting held at Boston, July 3rd.

ONTARIO LEAGUE—Special meeting held at Toronto, January 29th.

CALIFORNIA LEAGUE—James I. Egan, official scorer, died at San Francisco, February 6th; Van Haltren of Oakland struck out three of the Haverlys in one inning on nine pitched balls, May 30th (this was the celebrated George).

NEW YORK STATE LEAGUE—Buffalo admitted at special meeting held at Syracuse, February 18th; Toronto and Hamilton admitted to membership at special meeting held at Rochester, March 17th and 18th and name of league changed to International League.

INTERNATIONAL LEAGUE—Green of Oswego pitched no-hit game against

Hamilton at Oswego, August 17th; Morrison of Hamilton struck out 16 of the Syracuse Stars, September 1st; Morrison of Hamilton struck out 17 of the Toronto team, October 2nd; first annual meeting held at Utica, November 17th, when Newark and Jersey City were admitted to membership.

NORTHWESTERN LEAGUE—Organized at meeting held at Eau Claire, Wis., March 6th; schedule meeting held at Minneapolis, March 23rd; thirty strikeouts recorded in nine inning game between Duluth and St. Paul at Duluth, June 18th, Mark Baldwin, later with Anson's Chicagos, fanning 18 (including 12 in succession) for Duluth and Fitzimmons fanning 12 for St. Paul; Murphy of Eau Claire pitched no-hit game against Minneapolis at Eau Claire, August 26th; only two safe hits made in the Duluth–Oshkosh game, Baldwin and Harper pitching, August 30th; Sowders of Minneapolis fanned 16 of the Oshkosh team, September 8th; Des Moines and Lacrosse admitted to membership at special meeting held at St. Paul, October 13th.

HUDSON RIVER LEAGUE—Organized at meeting held at Poughkeepsie, March 30th; special meeting held at Troy, July 20th; pennant awarded to Poughkeepsie, August 30th.

PENNSYLVANIA STATE LEAGUE—(Kid Gleason graduated from this league). Organized at meeting held at Williamsport, April 1st; Billy Crowell of Altoona (afterward with Cleveland) pitched no-hit game against Wilkesbarre, his team getting only one safety off Staltz.

The dope of 1886 throws some light

on the minor leagues of 1922, and it throws a lot of light on the work necessary to trace each minor league from its organization to the present moment.

The International, as before stated, was the New York State League at the start and it operated for years as the Eastern, with its destinies ably looked after by Patrick T. Powers.

The American Association sprang into existence with the American League expanded. Its career dates from 1902. That year it went in alone, fighting the National Association and winning its fight. One of the men who engaged in this successful war on the A. A. side was Ernest S. Barnard, business manager for years of the Cleveland American League and one of the smartest men there is in baseball. Mr. Barnard, formerly sporting editor of a Columbus paper, edited an American Association guide for the A. J. Reach Company in 1902 and that book ought to be procured by anyone who desires to write a history of Thomas J. Hickey's prosperous organization. Thomas Jefferson, before he became president of the American Association, was president of the Western League and of the Western Association.

The Pacific Coast League also was an outlaw organization once. It, the International and the American Association have class AA ranking and do not have to submit to the draft.

Some writers think that because the three Class AA leagues do not desire the draft they are keeping certain players back in their advancement. This writer personally happens to know that in the case of any International League player who desires to go to the majors, he would be allowed to go, draft or no draft. But the Baltimore players like Bentley, Boley and Jacobson, supposed to be able to deliver the goods in fast company haven't yet signified any desire to leave John Dunn.

Returning to the subject of the minor leagues of the present, the Eastern League of 1922 is practically the old Connecticut State League and the O'Neil circuit contains several cities that were in the Eastern when Connie Mack was a Hartford catcher, back in 1885 and 1886. Leslie Ballard Stearns, sporting editor of the Springfield, Mass., *Evening Union*, has the history of this league pretty well at his finger tips.

The Western League of the present has several cities that were in the first Western League.

The Three Eyed League was, back in 1890 and 1891, the Two Eyed League. John McGraw came out of this organization, so did Clark Griffith, though when the Old Fox was in it the league was called the Western Inter-State.

The Southern League, as shown, dates back to 1885. It hasn't functioned steadily and once was the Southern–Texas League.

The first Texas League known of was in 1888. Nineteen years later it sent a pretty good outfielder—one Tristram E. Speaker—of the American League and he helped make that organization more solid than it was with the public.

Babe Ruth is an International League graduate and so is Urban Shocker, though the last named won his spurs first in the old Canadian League, predecessor of the Michigan–Ontario.

Baseball's Who's Who, however, shows in what minor leagues all the stars of the present made their starts and the guide books do give certain details about the minor leagues. Spalding's National Association handbooks, published in 1902 and 1903 and edited by the late Tim Murnane, throw quite a little light on the compositions of the minor league circuits in their early days.

The Baseball Blue Book, published by Louis Heilbroner, is an invaluable handbook to have for anyone who attempts the apparently impossible task of keeping up with the Class AA, A, B, C and D leagues.

As for the best performances in each of these leagues, no one knows them.

There are only a few leagues one could write histories on without getting into some other league. The American Association is one of them. The Tri-State League wouldn't be one of them. There is no Tri-State League now, but there was one in 1888 and 1889 and it gave to the major leagues such stars as Ad Gumbert, Ed Delahanty and Cy Young. That Tri-State League was the successor to the old Ohio State League.

A later Tri-State League operated with clubs in Delaware, Pennsylvania and New Jersey—and operated as a Robin Hood organization until it confessed its sins and was admitted to membership in the National Association. About the time the Tri-Staters started to behave (1907) there was an Atlantic League, a free lance organization in existence and it developed (or started) players like Stanley Coveleskie, Jack (Dots) Miller and Dick Hoblitzell on their way to the majors.

Years before there had been Atlantic Leagues and Atlantic Associations. Jesse Burkett came out of the Atlantic Association, which had an Eastern League circuit, and in the Atlantic League in 1896 a well-known novelist—Zane Gray—was trying to make a living as an outfielder with Newark. The president of the Atlantic League later was Edward Grant Barrow, business manager of the New York American League club now.

In 1897 Barrow was manager of the Paterson club of the Atlantic League and his star player was a man named John Peter Wagner, one of the great players of all time.

John Peter, better known as Honus or Hans or as the Demon Dutchman, played his first National League game for Louisville at Louisville on July 19, 1897. He wasn't known then as the Demon Dutchman or as the Flying Dutchman—he merely was called a clumsy, bow-legged rookie from Paterson.

The Colonels, on the date mentioned, downed Washington by a score of 6 to 2, the clumsy, bow-legged rookie from Paterson being in center field. He had a single in two trips to the plate, and cared for three chances—two putouts and one assist. The Kentuckians' president at that time was Harry Clay Pulliam, later president of the National League, and their principal stockholder was Barney Dreyfuss.

Honus belongs on the All Star team of All Time, so here are some more facts about him:

It was on July 21, 1897, that he got his first long wallop—a double, made off Lester German of Washington. Rather a coincidence that Napoleon Lajoie's first long hit in the National should have been off German, too. Larry's was manufactured on August 14, 1896. M. Lajoie, New England League graduate, is another pastimer who belongs on the All Star team of All Time.

Wagner made his first triple on July 22nd in a game with Boston and then participated in his first league double play. Honus had to wait for a longer time before he broke into the ranks of the home-run brigade, joining this company at the expense of Jack Dunn of Brooklyn on August 27th. The Jack Dunn of Brooklyn of 1897 is the Jack Dunn of Baltimore of the present time.

Wagner's first game in the infield was played at second base on August 25th. Hans probably, during his National League career, toiled in all nine positions, though few persons can recall just when he wore the harness of a backstop. Nineteen hundred and two was one of the seasons in which the Demon (or Flying) Dutchman performed on the rubber, for on September 5th of that year, he pitched part of a game against Boston, striking out five men, passing two and uncoiling four wild pitches.

Back in 1897, when Wagner was winning his spurs as a National Leaguer, scribes had troubles of their own in finding out the names of batteries just as they do now. Witness this clipping from a paper of 1897:

> That was a peculiar state of affairs in the Louisville club the other day, in which the pitcher did not know the catcher's name, the catcher was ignorant of the pitcher's name and the members of the team, including the manager himself, were unacquainted with the names of either of the young men composing the club's battery for the day. Waddell only joined the team in Washington and Schreckengost joined the team only a short time before the game, having been taken on trial.

This all-around ignorance of names was shown when some spectators in the grandstand at Baltimore asked the catcher who was pitching.

"I don't know; I never saw him before," was Schreckengost's reply.

Presently Waddell came to the bench and when someone asked him who the catcher was he replied: "Couldn't tell you, first time I ever saw him."

"Who will be in the points today?" was asked of Manager Clarke before the game.

"This man will pitch," he replied, pointing to the name Weddel on the score card, "and that tall fellow over there will catch. I don't know what his name is." But Clarke called to Schreckengost and got that young man to spell his name out for the newspaper men, regardless of how long it delayed the game. When asked if "Weddel" was the correct name, Manager Clarke replied; "Don't know, you will have to ask him." This was done and it was found his name was Waddell.

George Edward, the Rube, also goes on the All Star team for All Time.

Billy Keeler, another player who belongs on the All Star team for All Time, led the National League in batting with the high average of .432 the first season. Wagner was in it and there were complaints that Billy was helped to the peak by generous scoring. Hark unto what this clipping says:

> John Heydler, who is one of the best known baseball scribes in the business, says exception should be taken to this over generous scoring and that Keeler's figures of 432 will not agree with any private accounts. Frank Houseman of St. Louis also has objections to Baltimore scoring methods. He says: "Down in Baltimore, one day, Keeler sent two flies to Lally, who muffed both of them. Then he hit to Hartman and the latter fumbled and then threw wild. Then Keeler made a good single. The next morning four hits appeared to Keeler's credit in the Baltimore papers. Talk about Cleveland stuffing Burkett's average, why, they are not in it with the oyster scribes of Baltimore."

Keeler, Speaker and Cobb would be the outfield for the All Star team of All Time and the infield would be made up of Adrian Constantine Anson, at first base; Napoleon Lajoie, at second; James J. Collins, at third, and Hans Wagner, at short.

Thus far, very easy.

Catchers harder. One would be William Buckingham Ewing. Possibly his middle name wasn't Buckingham and the Buckingham was merely Buck added to. Another would be Michael J. Kelly and the third would be John G. Kling, considered the greatest money catcher of the world.

If you want to know what a money player is, ask a man who has been in a flock of world's series. No disgrace to the title.

Pitchers for this mythical combina-tion would be Denton J. Young, Edward Armstrong Walsh, Walter Perry Johnson, Christopher Mathewson, Mordecai Peter Centennial Brown and George Edward Waddell.

For a substitute take Edward N. Williamson.

And for manager have William Carrigan, now in the banking and moving picture industry at Lewiston, Maine.

All in the land of the living except Ewing, Kelly, Waddell, Williamson and Anson.

Anson died on April 14th of this year (1922) at Chicago. Charles Comiskey said of him:

> He was the greatest batter that ever walked up to hit at a baseball thrown by a pitcher.

Every scribe certainly, as well as almost every fan, indulges in the inalienable right to draw up an all-star team. Here is the All Star Team of All Time as I should draw it up, exercising my inalienable right as a fan as well as a scribe.

1st B., Anson
2nd B., Lajoie
S. S., Wagner
3rd B., Collins
O. F., Cobb
O. F., Speaker
O. F., Keeler
C., Ewing
C., Kelly
C., Kling
P., Young
P., Walsh
P., Brown
P., Mathewson
P., Johnson

P., Waddell
Sub., Williamson
Mgr., William Carrigan

Now gentle reader, if you don't like this list, remember who ever did agree with any other fan's selection of an all-star team? But that's easily remedied. Pick out your own all-star team and then you'll be sure to be suited.

◆ PART VII ◆

Brief but Comprehensive Records of More Than 3,500 Major League Ball Players

The concluding section of this book is devoted to brief, biographical reviews of more than 3,500 Major League ball players. Mr. Lanigan endeavored to include in this list every player who has worn a big league uniform for any considerable time since the American League became a "Major." The names of these players are all arranged alphabetically. In most cases the first names or initials of players are given together with the position played and the seasons spent with various Major League clubs. In some cases, due to meager data, complete information was not obtainable. Furthermore, Mr. Lanigan fears that, in spite of the enormous labor spent in compiling this list, some players may have been omitted. The Baseball Magazine, as publishers of this book, will appreciate any information which will make future editions of this list more accurate or complete. In spite, however, of a few unavoidable defects, the publishers believe that Mr. Lanigan is entitled to the thanks of every baseball scribe and of all friends of baseball for the most ambitious effort ever attempted to reduce the player records of more than twenty years to a single brief but comprehensive list. As a time-saver for delvers in the dope, as a reference for the fans, such a list is invaluable. For this list makes it possible to locate in a moment all important data on practically every National or American League player since 1901.

ABBATICCHIO, EDWARD J.   2nd B.
  Boston, N. L., 1903–1906, inc.
  Pittsburgh, N. L., 1907–1910 inc.
  Boston, N. L., 1910

ABBOTT, FREDERICK   Catcher
  Cleveland, A. L., 1903–1904
  Philadelphia, N. L., 1905

ABBOTT, O. C.   Outfielder
  St. Louis, N. L., 1910

ABLES, HARRY   Pitcher
  St. Louis, A. L., 1905
  Cleveland, A. L., 1909
  New York, A. L., 1911

ABSTEIN, WILLIAM H.   1st B.
Pittsburgh, N. L., 1906–1909
St. Louis, A. L., 1910

ACOSTA, BALMADERO   Outfielder
Washington, A. L., 1913–1916, inc., 1918
Philadelphia, A. L., 1918

ADAMS   Pitcher
St. Louis, A. L., 1912–1913
Kansas City, F. L., 1914

ADAMS   Pitcher
St. Louis, N. L., 1902

ADAMS   Pitcher
Washington, A. L., 1905

ADAMS, CHARLES B.   Pitcher
St. Louis, N. L., 1906
Pittsburgh, N. L., 1907–1909 to 1916,
inc., 1918 to date

ADAMS, JOHN B.   Catcher
Cleveland, A. L., 1910–1912, inc.
Philadelphia, N. L., 1915–1919, inc.

ADAMS, KARL T.   Pitcher
Cincinnati, N. L., 1914
Chicago, N. L., 1915

ADAMS, WILLIAM   Pitcher
Philadelphia, A. L., 1918–1919

ADKINS, MERLE THERON   Pitcher
Boston, A. L., 1902
New York, A. L., 1903

AGLER, JOSEPH ABRAM   1st B.
Washington, A. L., 1912
Buffalo, F. L., 1914–1915
Baltimore, F. L., 1915

AGNEW, SAMUEL   Catcher
St. Louis, A. L., 1913–1915, inc.
Boston, A. L., 1916–1918, inc.
Washington, A. L., 1919

AHEARN, HUGH   Catcher
Brooklyn, N. L., 1901–1903, inc.

AINSMITH, EDWARD   Catcher
Washington, A. L., 1910–1918, inc.

Detroit, A. L., 1919–1920–1921
St. Louis, N. L., 1921

AITCHISON, RALEIGH   Pitcher
Brooklyn, N. L., 1911–1914–1915

AITON   Outfielder
St. Louis, A. L., 1912

AKERS, JERRY   Pitcher
Washington, A. L., 1912

ALBERTS, F.   Pitcher
St. Louis, N. L., 1910

ALCOCK, FORBES   Infielder
Chicago, A. L., 1914

ALDRIDGE, VICTOR   Pitcher
Chicago, N. L., 1917–1918

ALEXANDER, GROVER CLEVELAND
                            Pitcher
Philadelphia, N. L., 1911–1917, inc.
Chicago, N. L., 1918 to date

ALEXANDER, WALTER E.   Catcher
St. Louis, A. L., 1912–1913
New York, A. L., 1915–1916–1917

ALLEN, ARTEMUS WARD   Catcher
Buffalo, F. L., 1914–1915
Chicago, N. L., 1916
Cincinnati, N. L., 1918–1920, inc.

ALLEN, F. M.   Catcher
St. Louis, A. L., 1910

ALLEN, FRANK L.   Pitcher
Brooklyn, N. L., 1912–1914, inc.
Pittsburgh, F. L., 1915
Boston, N. L., 1916–1917

ALLEN, HORACE TANNER   Outfielder
Brooklyn, N. L., 1919

ALLISON, MACK   Pitcher
St. Louis, A. L., 1911–1913, inc.

ALLISON, MILO H.   Outfielder
Chicago, N. L., 1913–1914
Cleveland, A. L., 1916–1917

ALMEIDA, RAFAEL D.   Infielder
Cincinnati, N. L., 1911–1913, inc.

ALPERMAN, CHARLES A.   Infielder
Brooklyn, N. L., 1906–1909, inc.

ALTEN, ERNEST   Pitcher
Detroit, A. L., 1920

ALTENBURG, JESSE HOWARD   Outfielder
Pittsburgh, N. L., 1916–1917

ALTIZER, DAVID TILDEN   Inf.—O. F.
Washington, A. L., 1906–1908, inc.
Cleveland, A. L., 1908
Chicago, A. L., 1909
Cincinnati, N. L., 1910–1911

ALTROCK, NICHOLAS   Pitcher
Boston, A. L., 1902
Chicago, A. L., 1903–1909, inc.
Washington, A. L., 1909–1912–1913–
1915–1918–1919

AMES, LEON KESSLING   Pitcher
New York, N. L., 1903–1913, inc.
Cincinnati, N. L., 1913–1915, inc.
St. Louis, N. L., 1915–1919, inc.
Philadelphia, N. L., 1919

ANDERSON, E. J.   Outfielder
Pittsburgh, N. L., 1907

ANDERSON, GEORGE   Outfielder
Brooklyn, F. L., 1914–1915
St. Louis, N. L., 1918

ANDERSON, J. FRED   Pitcher
Boston, A. L., 1909–1913
Buffalo, F. L., 1914–1915
New York, N. L., 1916–1918, inc.

ANDERSON, JOHN J.   1st B.—O. F.
Milwaukee, A. L., 1901
St. Louis, A. L., 1902–1903
New York, A. L., 1904–1905
Washington, A. L., 1905–1906–1907
Chicago, A. L., 1908

ANDERSON, W.   Pitcher
Cincinnati, N. L., 1910

ANDERSON, WALTER   Pitcher
Philadelphia, A. L., 1917–1919

ANKER   Pitcher
Philadelphia, A. L., 1915

APPLEGATE   Pitcher
Philadelphia, A. L., 1904

APPLETON, EDWARD SAMUEL   Pitcher
Brooklyn, N. L., 1915–1916

ARAGON, ANGELE   Substitute
New York, A. L., 1914–1916–1917

ARCHER, PETER JAMES   Catcher
Pittsburgh, N. L., 1904
Detroit, A. L., 1907
Chicago, N. L., 1909–1917, inc.
Pittsburgh, N. L., 1918
Cincinnati, N. L.,1918
Brooklyn, N. L., 1918

ARELLANES, FRANK   Pitcher
Boston, A. L., 1908–1910, inc.

ARMBRUSTER   Outfielder
Boston, A. L., 1905–1907, inc.
Chicago, A. L., 1907

ARMBRUSTER   Catcher
Philadelphia, A. L., 1906

ARMSTRONG   Pitcher
Philadelphia, A. L., 1911

ARNDT, HARRY   Infielder
Detroit, A. L., 1902
Baltimore, A. L.,, 1902
St. Louis, N. L., 1904–1906–1907

ASMUSSEN, THOMAS   Catcher
Boston, N. L., 1907

ATKINS, FRANK M.   Pitcher
Philadelphia, A. L., 1909–1910

ATZ, JACOB   Infielder
Washington, A. L., 1902
Chicago, A. L., 1906–1909, inc.

AUBREY, HARRY   Infielder
Boston, N. L., 1903

AUSTIN, JAMES P.   Infielder
New York, A. L., 1909–1910
St. Louis, A. L., 1911 to date

AUTRY, W. C.   Infielder
Cincinnati, N. L., 1907
Boston, N. L., 1909
Cincinnati, N. L., 1909

AYERS, YANCEY W.   Pitcher
Washington, A. L., 1913–1919, inc.
Detroit, A. L., 1919–1920–1921

BABINGTON, C. P.   Outfielder
New York, N. L., 1915

BACKMAN, LESTER JOHN   Pitcher
St. Louis, N. L., 1909–1910

BACON, ELMER   Pitcher
Philadelphia, A. L., 1917

BADER, LOREN V.   Pitcher
New York, N. L., 1912
Boston, A. L., 1917–1918

BAGBY, JAMES CHARLES JACOB   Pitcher
Cincinnati, N. L., 1912
Cleveland, A. L., 1916 to date

BAICHLEY, GROVER   Pitcher
St. Louis, A. L., 1914

BAILEY, ABRAHAM LINCOLN   Pitcher
Chicago, N. L., 1919–1920–1921
Brooklyn, N. L., 1921

BAILEY, EUGENE   Outfielder
Philadelphia, A. L., 1917
Boston, N. L., 1919–1920
Boston, A. L., 1920

BAILEY, FRED MIDDLETON   Outfielder
Boston, N. L., 1916–1918, inc.

BAILEY, WILLIAM   Pitcher
St. Louis, A. L., 1907–1910, inc.
Detroit, A. L., 1911
Baltimore, F. L., 1914–1915
Chicago, F. L., 1915
Detroit, A. L., 1918
St. Louis, N. L., 1921

BAIRD, AL W.   Substitute
New York, N. L., 1917–1919

BAIRD, H. DOUGLAS   Infielder
Pittsburgh, N. L., 1915–1917, inc.
St. Louis, N. L., 1917–1919, inc.
Philadelphia, N. L., 1919
Brooklyn, N. L., 1919–1920
New York, N. L., 1920

BAKER   Outfielder
Boston, A. L., 1911

BAKER   Pitcher
Philadelphia, A. L., 1901
Cleveland, A. L., 1901

BAKER, DEL   Catcher
Detroit, A. L., 1914–1915–1916

BAKER, ERNEST   Pitcher
Cincinnati, N. L., 1905

BAKER, HOWARD   Infielder
Cleveland, A. L., 1912
Chicago, A. L., 1914–1915
New York, N. L., 1915

BAKER, JESSE   Pitcher
Chicago, A. L., 1911

BAKER, JOHN FRANKLIN   3rd B.
Philadelphia, A. L., 1908–1914, inc.
New York, A. L., 1916–1919, inc., 1921

BALDWIN, O. F.   Pitcher
St. Louis, N. L., 1908

BALENTI, MICHAEL R.   Infielder
Cincinnati, N. L., 1911
St. Louis, A. L., 1913

BALL, JAMES C.   Catcher
Boston, N. L., 1907–1908

BALL, NEAL   Infielder
New York, A. L., 1907–1909, inc.
Cleveland, A. L., 1909–1911, inc.
Boston, A. L., 1912–1913

BANCROFT, DAVID JAMES   S. S.
Philadelphia, N. L., 1915–1916–1917–
1818–1919–1920
New York, N. L., 1920–1921

BANES   Outfielder
Chicago, A. L., 1907

BANKSTON, W. E.   Outfielder
Philadelphia, A. L., 1915

BARBARE, WALTER   Infielder
Cleveland, A. L., 1914–1916, inc.
Boston, A. L., 1918

Pittsburgh, N. L., 1919–1920
Boston, N. L., 1921

BARBEAU, WILLIAM J.   Infielder
Cleveland, A. L., 1905–1906
Pittsburgh, N. L., 1909
St. Louis, N. L., 1909–1910

BARBER, TURNER   O. F.—1st B.
Washington, A. L., 1915–1916
Chicago, N. L., 1917 to date

BARBERICH, FRANK   Pitcher
Boston, N. L., 1907
Boston, A. L., 1910

BARCLAY, GEORGE O.   Outfielder
St. Louis, N. L., 1902–1904, inc.
Boston, N. L., 1904–1905

BARGER, EROS B.   Pitcher
New York, A. L., 1906
Brooklyn, N. L., 1910–1912, inc.
Pittsburgh, F. L., 1914–1915

BARNES, JESSE L.   Pitcher
Boston, N. L., 1915–1916–1917
New York, N. L., 1918 to date

BARNES, SAMUEL THOMAS, JR.   Infielder
Detroit, A. L., 1921

BARNES, VIRGIL JENNINGS   Pitcher
New York, N. L., 1919–1920

BARNEY, EDMUND   Outfielder
New York, A. L., 1915
Pittsburgh, N. L., 1915–1916

BARNHART, CLYDE L.   Infielder
Pittsburgh, N. L., 1920–1921

BARR, HYDER   Infielder
Philadelphia, A. L., 1908–1909

BARRETT, JAMES E.   Outfielder
Detroit, A. L., 1901–1905, inc.
Boston, A. L., 1907

BARRETT, WILLIAM   P.—Inf.
Philadelphia, A. L., 1921

BARROWS, ROLAND   Outfielder
Chicago, A. L., 1909–1912, inc.

BARRY   Pitcher
Philadelphia, A. L., 1912

BARRY, EDWARD   Pitcher
Boston, A. L., 1905–1906–1907

BARRY, JOHN C.   Substitute
Boston, L. L., 1901
Philadelphia, N. L., 1901–1904, inc.
Chicago, N. L., 1904
Cincinnati, N. L., 1905–1906
St. Louis, N. L., 1906–1908, inc.
New York, N. L., 1908

BARRY, JOHN J.   Infielder
Philadelphia, A. L., 1908–1915, inc.
Boston, A. L., 1915–1919, inc., (excepting 1918)

BARRY, THOMAS   Pitcher
Philadelphia, N. L., 1904

BARTHOLD   Pitcher
Philadelphia, A. L., 1904

BARTLEY, JOHN   Pitcher
New York, N. L., 1903
Philadelphia, A. L., 1906–1907

BARTON, HARRY   Outfielder
Philadelphia, A. L., 1905

BASCHANG   Outfielder
Brooklyn, N. L., 1918

BASHANG, AL   Outfielder
Detroit, A. L., 1912

BASKETTE, JAMES   Pitcher
Cleveland, A. L., 1911–1913, inc.

BASS   Substitute
Boston, N. L., 1918

BASSLER, JOHN   Catcher
Cleveland, A. L., 1913–1914
Detroit, A. L., 1921

BATCH, EMIL   Substitute
Brooklyn, N. L., 1904–1907, inc.

BATCH, WILLIAM   Substitute
Pittsburgh, N. L., 1916

BATES, JOHN W.   Outfielder
Boston, N. L., 1906–1909, inc.
Philadelphia, N. L., 1909–1910

Cincinnati, N. L., 1911–1914, inc.
Chicago, N. L., 1914
Baltimore, F. L., 1914

BATES, RAYMOND   Infielder
Cleveland, A. L., 1913
Philadelphia, A. L., 1917

BAUER, L. W.   Pitcher
Philadelphia, A. L., 1917

BAUMANN, CHARLES L.   Substitute
Detroit, A. L., 1911–1914, inc.
New York, A. L., 1915–1917, inc.

BAUMGARDNER, GEORGE   Pitcher
St. Louis, A. L., 1912–1916, inc.

BAUMGARTNER, H.   Pitcher
Detroit, A. L., 1920

BAUMGARTNER, STANWOOD F.   Pitcher
Philadelphia, N. L., 1914–1915–1916–1921

BAXTER, JOHN   Infielder
St. Louis, N. L., 1907

BAY, HARRY D.   Outfielder
Cincinnati, N. L., 1901–1902
Cleveland, A. L., 1902–1907, inc.

BAYLESS, H.   Outfielder
Cincinnati, N. L., 1908

BAYNE, WILLIAM LEAR   Pitcher
St. Louis, A. L., 1919–1920–1921

BEALL, JOHN W.   Outfielder
Chicago, A. L., 1913
Cincinnati, N. L., 1915–1916
St. Louis, N. L., 1918

BEAN, JOSEPH W.   S. S.
New York, N. L., 1902

BEATTY, DESMOND   Infielder
New York, N. L., 1914

BEAUMONT, CLARENCE H.   Outfielder
Pittsburgh, N. L., 1901–1906, inc.
Boston, N. L., 1907–1909, inc.
Chicago, N. L., 1910

BECK, ERVE F.   2nd B.
Cleveland, A. L., 1901

Cincinnati, N. L., 1902
Detroit, A. L., 1902

BECK, FRED F.   1st B.—O. F.
Boston, N. L., 1909–1910
Cincinnati, N. L., 1911
Chicago, F. L., 1914–1915

BECK, GEORGE E.   Pitcher
Cleveland, A. L., 1914

BECK, ZINN   Infielder
St. Louis, N. L., 1913–1916, inc.
New York, A. L., 1918

BECKENDORF, HENRY W.   Catcher
Detroit, A. L., 1909–1910
Washington, A. L., 1910

BECKER, BEALS   Outfielder
Pittsburgh, N. L., 1908
Boston, N. L., 1908–1909
New York, N. L., 1910–1912, inc.
Cincinnati, N. L., 1913
Philadelphia, N. L., 1913–1915, inc.

BECKER, CHARLES   Pitcher
Washington, A. L., 1911–1912

BECKER, MARTIN HENRY   Outfielder
New York, N. L, 1915

BECKLEY, JACOB   1st B.
Cincinnati, N. L., 1901–1902–1903
St. Louis, N. L., 1904–1905–1906–1907

BEDIENT, HUGH   Pitcher
Boston, A. L., 1912–1914, inc.
Buffalo, F. L., 1915

BEEBE, FRED L.   Pitcher
Chicago, N. L., 1906
St. Louis, N. L., 1906–1909, inc.
Cincinnati, N. L., 1910
Philadelphia, A. L., 1911
Cleveland, A. L., 1916

BEECHER, ROY   Pitcher
New York, N. L., 1907–1908

BEHAN, CHARLES P.   Pitcher
Philadelphia, N. L., 1921

BELL   Pitcher
Chicago, A. L., 1912

BELL   Outfielder
New York, A. L., 1912

BELL, GEORGE G.   Pitcher
Brooklyn, N. L., 1907–1911, inc.

BEMIS, HARRY P.   Catcher
Cleveland, A. L., 1902–1910, inc.

BENDER, CHARLES ALBERT   Pitcher
Philadelphia, A. L., 1903–1914, inc.
Baltimore, F. L., 1915
Philadelphia, N. L., 1916–1917

BENN, OMER   Pitcher
Cleveland, A. L., 1914

BENNETT, J.   2nd B.
St. Louis, N. L., 1906–1907

BENNETT, J. H.   Pitcher
St. Louis, A. L., 1918

BENTLEY, JOHN NEEDLES   Pitcher
Washington, A. L., 1913–1916, inc.

BENTON, JOHN C.   Pitcher
Cincinnati, N. L., 1910–1915, inc.
Pittsburgh, N. L., 1915
New York, N. L., 1915–1921, inc.

BENZ, JOSEPH D.   Pitcher
Chicago, A. L., 1911–1919, inc.

BERGEN, WILLIAM   Catcher
Cincinnati, N. L., 1901–1902–1903
Brooklyn, N. L., 1904–1911, inc.

BERGER, C. E.   Outfielder
Pittsburgh, N. L., 1914

BERGER, CHARLES   Pitcher
Cleveland, A. L., 1907–1910, inc.

BERGHAMMER, MARTIN   Infielder
Chicago, A. L., 1911
Cincinnati, N. L., 1913–1914
Pittsburgh, F. L., 1915

BERGMAN   Infielder
Cleveland, A. L., 1916

BERMAN, ROBERT   Catcher
Washington, A. L., 1918

BERNARD   Pitcher
St. Louis, N. L., 1909

BERNARD, CURTIS   Outfielder
New York, N. L., 1901

BERNHARDT, WALTER   Pitcher
New York, A. L., 1918

BERRY   Catcher
Chicago, A. L., 1904

BERRY, CLAUDE   Catcher
Philadelphia, A. L., 1906–1907
Pittsburgh, F. L., 1914–1915

BERRY, HOWARD   Catcher
Philadelphia, N. L., 1902

BERRY, J. HOWARD, JR.   Substitute
New York, N. L., 1921

BESCHER, ROBERT H.   Outfielder
Cincinnati, N. L., 1908–1913, inc.
New York, N. L., 1914
St. Louis, N. L., 1915–1917, inc.
Cleveland, A. L., 1918

BETCHER, F.   Infielder
St. Louis, N. L., 1910

BETTS   Pitcher
St. Louis, N. L., 1903

BETTS, H. M.   Pitcher
Cincinnati, N. L., 1913

BETTS, WALTER M.   Pitcher
Philadelphia, N. L., 1920–1921

BETZEL, ALBERT   Infielder
St. Louis, N. L., 1914–1918, inc.

BEVILLE, MONTE   Catcher
New York, A. L., 1903–1904
Detroit, A. L., 1904

BIEMILLER, HARRY LEE   Pitcher
Washington, A. L., 1920

BIGBEE, CARSON LEE   Outfielder
Pittsburgh, N. L., 1916 to date

BIGBEE, LYLE   Pitcher
Philadelphia, A. L., 1920
Pittsburgh, N. L., 1921

BILLIARD, HARRY P.   Pitcher
New York, A. L., 1908
Indianapolis, F. L., 1914

BILLINGS, JOHN AUGUSTUS   Catcher
  Cleveland, A. L., 1913–1918, inc.
  St. Louis, A. L., 1919 to date
BIRD   Pitcher
  Washington, A. L., 1921
BIRMINGHAM, JOSEPH L.   Outfielder
  Cleveland, A. L., 1906–1913, inc.
BISHOP   Pitcher
  Cleveland, A. L., 1914
BISHOP   Pitcher
  Philadelphia, A. L., 1921
BISLAND, RIVINGTON M.   Infielder
  Pittsburgh, N. L., 1912
  St. Louis, A. L., 1913
  Cleveland, A. L., 1914
BLACK   Infielder
  St. Louis, A. L., 1912
BLACK, DAVID   Pitcher
  Chicago, F. L., 1915
  Baltimore, F. L., 1915
BLACKBURN   Pitcher
  Chicago, A. L., 1921
BLACKBURNE, EARL S.   Catcher
  Pittsburgh, N. L., 1912
  Cincinnati, N. L., 1912–1913
  Boston, N. L., 1915–1916
  Chicago, N. L., 1917
BLACKBURNE, RUSSELL A.   Infielder
  Chicago, A. L., 1910–1912–1914–1915
  Cincinnati, N. L., 1918
  Boston, N. L., 1919
  Philadelphia, N. L., 1919
BLACKWELL, FREDERICK W.   Catcher
  Pittsburgh, N. L., 1917–1919, inc.
BLAIR, WALTER   Catcher
  New York, N. L., 1907–1911, inc.
  Buffalo, F. L., 1914–1915
BLAKE, J. FRED   Pitcher
  Pittsburgh, N. L., 1920
BLANDING, FRED J.   Pitcher
  Cleveland, A. L., 1910–1914, inc.

BLANK   Catcher
  St. Louis, N. L., 1909
BLANKENSHIP, CLIFF   Catcher
  Cincinnati, N. L., 1905
  Washington, A. L., 1907–1909
BLEWITT, ROBERT   Pitcher
  New York, N. L., 1902
BLISS   Pitcher
  New York, A. L., 1904
BLISS, JOHN J.   Catcher
  St. Louis, N. L., 1908–1912, inc.
BLOCK, JAMES   Catcher
  Washington, A. L., 1907
  Chicago, A. L., 1910–1912, inc.
  Chicago, F. L., 1914
BLUE, BERT   Catcher
  St. Louis, A. L., 1908
  Philadelphia, A. L., 1908
BLUE, LUZERNE ATWELL   1st B.
  Detroit, A. L., 1921
BLUEJACKET, JAMES   Pitcher
  Brooklyn, F. L., 1915
  Cincinnati, N. L., 1916
BLUHM, HARVEY   Infielder
  Boston, A. L., 1918
BOARDMAN, CHARLES LOUIS   Pitcher
  Philadelphia, A. L., 1913–1914
  St. Louis, N. L., 1915
BODIE, FRANK L.   Outfielder
  Chicago, A. L., 1911–1914, inc.
  Philadelphia, A. L., 1917
  New York, A. L., 1918–1919–1920–1921
BOECKEL, NORMAN D.   Infielder
  Pittsburgh, N. L., 1917–1919
  Boston, N. L., 1919 to date
BOEHLER, GEORGE   Pitcher
  Detroit, A. L., 1912–1916, inc.
  St. Louis, A. L., 1920–1921
BOEHLING, J. JOSEPH   Pitcher
  Washington, A. L., 1912–1916, inc.
  Cleveland, A. L., 1916–1917–1920

BOGART, JOHN   Pitcher
Detroit, A. L., 1920

BOHEN, PATRICK   Pitcher
Philadelphia, A. L., 1913
Pittsburgh, N. L., 1914

BOHNE, SAMUEL ARTHUR   Infielder
St. Louis, N. L., 1916
Cincinnati, N. L., 1921

BOLAND, BERNARD ANTHONY   Pitcher
Detroit, A. L., 1915–1920, inc.
St. Louis, A. L., 1921

BOLD   Outfielder
St. Louis, A. L., 1914

BOLDEN, WILLIAM   Pitcher
St. Louis, N. L., 1919

BONNER, FRANK J.   Infielder
Cleveland, A. L., 1902
Philadelphia, A. L., 1902
Boston, N. L., 1903

BONNIN   Outfielder
Buffalo, F. L., 1914

BONO, GUS   Pitcher
Washington, A. L., 1920

BOOE, EVERETT L.   Outfielder
Pittsburgh, N. L., 1913
Buffalo, F. L., 1914
Indianapolis, F. L., 1914

BOOLES   Pitcher
Cleveland, A. L., 1909

BOONE, JAMES ALBERT   Pitcher
Philadelphia, A. L., 1919
Detroit, A. L., 1921

BOONE, LUTHER   Infielder
New York, A. L., 1913–1916, inc.
Pittsburgh, N. L., 1918

BORTON, WILLIAM BAKER   1st B.
Chicago, A. L., 1912–1913
New York, A. L., 1913
St. Louis, F. L., 1915
St. Louis, A. L., 1916

BOUCHER   Infielder
St. Louis, F. L., 1914

BOUCHER, M.   Substitute
Baltimore, F. L., 1914
Pittsburgh, F. L., 1914

BOULTES, JOHN   P. Sub.
Boston, N. L., 1907–1909, inc.

BOWCOCK, BENJAMIN F.   Infielder
St. Louis, A. L., 1903

BOWDEN, TIM   Outfielder
St. Louis, A. L., 1914

BOWEN, EMMONS J.   Outfielder
New York, N. L., 1919

BOWERMAN, FRANK   Catcher
New York, N. L., 1901–1907, inc.
Boston, N. L., 1908–1909

BOWMAN, A. E.   Pitcher
Cleveland, A. L., 1914–1915

BOWMAN, ELMER   1st B.
Washington, A. L., 1920

BOYD, R. C.   Pitcher
St. Louis, A. L., 1910
Cincinnati, N. L., 1911

BOYLE, JOHN B.   Infielder
Philadelphia, N. L., 1912

BRACKEN   Pitcher
Cleveland, A. L., 1901

BRADLEY, HUGH   Infielder
Boston, A. L., 1910–1912, inc.
Pittsburgh, F. L., 1914
Brooklyn, F. L., 1915

BRADLEY, J.   Catcher
Cleveland, A. L., 1916

BRADLEY, WILLIAM J.   3rd B.
Cleveland, A. L., 1901–1910, inc.
Brooklyn, F. L., 1914
Kansas City, F. L., 1915

BRADSHAW   Infielder
Philadelphia, A. L., 1917

BRADY   Pitcher
Boston, A. L., 1908

BRADY, CLIFFORD W.   2nd B.
Boston, A. L., 1920

BRADY, J. W.   Pitcher
Philadelphia, N. L., 1905
Pittsburgh, N. L., 1906–1907
Boston, N. L., 1912
BRADY, NEAL J.   Pitcher
New York, A. L., 1915–1917
BRADY, W. A.   Pitcher
Boston, N. L., 1912
BRAGGINS   Pitcher
Cleveland, A. L., 1901
BRAIN, DAVID L.   Infielder
Chicago, A. L., 1901
St. Louis, N. L., 1903–1904–1905
Pittsburgh, N. L., 1905
Boston, N. L., 1906–1907
Cincinnati, N. L., 1908
New York, N. L., 1908
BRAINARD, FRED   Substitute
New York, N. L., 1914–1916, inc.
BRANDOM, CHESTER M.   Pitcher
Pittsburgh, N. L., 1908–1909
BRANSFIELD, WILLIAM E.   1st B.
Pittsburgh, N. L., 1901–1904, inc.
Philadelphia, N. L., 1905–1911, inc.
Chicago, N. L., 1911
BRASHEAR, NORMAN   Infielder
St. Louis, N. L., 1902
BRASHEAR, ROY P.   Infielder
Philadelphia, N. L., 1903
BRATCHI, FRED   Infielder
Chicago, A. L., 1921
BRAXTON, F. GARLAND   Pitcher
Boston, N. L., 1921
BRAZIL, FRANK LEO Infielder
Philadelphia, A. L., 1921
BRECKENRIDGE, JOHN   Pitcher
Philadelphia, A. L., 1904
BREITENSTEIN, THEODORE P.   Pitcher
St. Louis, N. L., 1901
BRENEGAN, SAM   Catcher
Pittsburgh, N. L., 1914

BRENNAN, ADDISON F.   Pitcher
Philadelphia, N. L., 1910–1913, inc.
Chicago, F. L., 1914–1915
Washington, A. L., 1918
Cleveland, A. L., 1918
BRENNER, BERT   Pitcher
Cleveland, A. L., 1912
BRENTON, LYNN DAVIS   Pitcher
Cleveland, A. L., 1913–1915
Cincinnati, N. L., 1920–1921
BRESNAHAN, ROGER P.
    P.—C.—3rd B.—O. F.
Baltimore, A. L., 1901–1902
New York, N. L., 1902–1908, inc.
St. Louis, N. L., 1909–1912, inc.
Chicago, N. L., 1913–1915, inc.
BRESSLER, RAYMOND BLOOM
    Pitcher—Outfielder
Philadelphia, A. L., 1914–1916, inc.
Cincinnati, N. L., 1917 to date
BRETON, JAMES   Infielder
Chicago, A. L., 1913–1915, inc.
BRICKLEY, GUY V.   Outfielder
Philadelphia, A. L., 1913
BRIDWELL, ALBERT H.   Infielder
Cincinnati, N. L., 1905
Boston, N. L., 1906–1907
New York, N. L., 1908–1911, inc.
Boston, N. L., 1911–1912
Chicago, N. L., 1913
St. Louis, F. L., 1914–1915
BRIEF, ANTHONY VINCENT   1st B.
St. Louis, A. L., 1912–1913
Chicago, A. L., 1915
Pittsburgh, N. L., 1917
BRIGGS, HERBERT   Pitcher
Chicago, N. L., 1904–1905
BRINKER, W. H.   Outfielder
Philadelphia, N. L., 1912
BRITTON, G.   Infielder
Pittsburgh, N. L., 1913
BROCK, JOHN   Catcher
St. Louis, N. L., 1907–1908

BROCKETT, LOUIS   Pitcher
New York, A. L., 1909–1911

BRODERICK, MATTHEW   Infielder
Brooklyn, N. L., 1903

BRODIE, WALTER STEPHENSON
                                  Outfielder
Baltimore, A. L., 1901
New York, N. L., 1902

BRONKIE, HERMAN   nfielder
Cleveland, A. L., 1910–1912
Chicago, N. L., 1914
St. Louis, N. L., 1918
St. Louis, A. L., 1919

BROOKMILLER   Pitcher
Detroit, A. L., 1905

BROTTEM, ANTON C.   Catcher
St. Louis, N. L., 1916–1918
Washington, A. L., 1921
Pittsburgh, N. L., 1921

BROUTHERS, ARTHUR H.   Infielder
Philadelphia, A. L., 1906

BROUTHERS, DENNIS L.   1st B.
New York, N. L., 1904

BROWER, FRANK WILLARD   1st B. — O. F.
Washington, A. L., 1920–1921

BROWN, CARROLL W.   Pitcher
Philadelphia, A. L., 1911–1914, inc.
New York, A. L., 1914–1915

BROWN, CHARLES E.   Pitcher
St. Louis, N. L., 1905–1907, inc.
Philadelphia, N. L., 1907–1909, inc.
Boston, N. L. 1909–1913, inc.

BROWN, CHARLES ROY   Pitcher
St. Louis, A. L., 1911–1912–1913
Cincinnati, N. L., 1915

BROWN, DON   Outfielder
St. Louis, N. L., 1915
Philadelphia, A. L., 1916

BROWN, DRUMMOND   Catcher
Boston, N. L., 1913
Kansas City, F. L., 1914–1915

BROWN, EDWARD W.   Outfielder
New York, N. L., 1920–1921

BROWN, ELMER   Pitcher
St. Louis, A. L., 1911–1912
Brooklyn, N. L., 1913–1914–1915

BROWN, FRED H.   Outfielder
Boston, N. L., 1901

BROWN, MORDECAI PETER CENTENNIAL
                                    Pitcher
St. Louis, N. L., 1903
Chicago, N. L., 1904–1012, inc.
Cincinnati, N. L., 1913
St. Louis, F. L., 1914
Brooklyn, F. L., 1914
Chicago, F. L., 1915
Chicago, N. L., 1916

BROWN, PAUL   Pitcher
Chicago, N. L., 1909

BROWN, SAMUEL   Catcher
Boston, N. L., 1906–1907

BROWNE, GEORGE E.   Outfielder
Philadelphia, N. L., 1901–1902
New York, N. L., 1902–1907, inc.
Boston, N. L., 1908
Chicago, N. L., 1909
Washington, A. L., 1909–1910
Chicago, A. L., 1910
Brooklyn, N. L., 1911

BROWNING, FRANK   Pitcher
Detroit, A. L., 1910

BRUGE, LOUIS   Outfielder
Philadelphia, N. L., 1921

BRUGGY, FRANK L.   Catcher
Philadelphia, N. L., 1921

BRUSH, ROBERT   Outfielder
Boston, N. L., 1907

BRUYETTE   Outfielder
Milwaukee, A. L., 1901

BUCHANAN   Pitcher
St. Louis, A. L., 1905

BUCKEYE   Pitcher
Washington, A. L., 1918

BUCKLES, JESSE   Pitcher
New York, A. L., 1916

BUELOW, CHARLES   Infielder
New York, N. L., 1901

BUELOW, FRED   Catcher
Detroit, A. L., 1901–1904, inc.
Cleveland, A. L., 1904–1906, inc.
St. Louis, A. L., 1907

BUES, ARTHUR   Infielder
Boston, N. L., 1913
Chicago, N. L., 1914

BURCH, AL W.   Outfielder
St. Louis, N. L., 1906–1907
Brooklyn, N. L., 1907–1911

BURCHELL, FRED   Pitcher
Philadelphia, N. L., 1903
Boston, A. L., 1907–1909, inc.

BURG, JOSEPH P.   Infielder
Boston, N. L., 1910

BURK, C. SANFORD   Infielder
Brooklyn, N. L., 1910–1912, inc.
St. Louis, N. L., 1912–1913

BURKE, FRANK   Outfielder
New York, N. L., 1906
Boston, N. L., 1907

BURKE, JAMES TIMOTHY   3rd B.
Milwaukee, A. L., 1901
Chicago, A. L., 1901
Pittsburgh, N. L., 1901–1902
St. Louis, N. L, 1903–1904–1905

BURKE, JOHN   Pitcher
New York, N. L., 1902

BURKE, WILLIAM   Pitcher
Boston, N. L., 1910–1911

BURKETT, JESSE C.   Outfielder
St. Louis, N. L., 1901
St. Louis, A. L., 1902–1904, inc.
Boston, A. L., 1905

BURNETT, J.   Outfielder
St. Louis, N. L., 1907

BURNS   Catcher
Philadelphia, A. L., 1906

BURNS   Infielder
Detroit, A. L., 1903–1904

BURNS, EDWARD J.   Catcher
St. Louis, N. L., 1912
Philadelphia, N. L., 1913–1918, inc.

BURNS, GEORGE HENRY   1st B.—O. F.
Detroit, A. L., 1913–1917, inc.
Philadelphia, A. L., 1918–1919
Cleveland, A. L., 1920–1921

BURNS, GEORGE JOSEPH   Outfielder
New York, N. L., 1911 to date

BURNS, J. F.   Infielder
Cincinnati, N. L., 1910

BURNS, JAMES   Pitcher
St. Louis, N. L., 1901

BURNS, WILLIAM   Pitcher
Washington, A. L., 1908–1909
Chicago, A. L., 1909–1910
Cincinnati, N. L., 1911
Philadelphia, N. L., 1911
Detroit, A. L., 1912

BURR, A. T.   Outfielder
New York, A. L., 1914

BURRUS, MAURICE LENNON   1st B.
Philadelphia, A. L., 1919–1920

BURWELL, WILLIAM E.   Pitcher
St. Louis, A. L., 1920–1921

BUSH, LESLIE JOSEPH   Pitcher
Philadelphia, A. L., 1912–1917, inc.
Boston, A. L., 1918–1921, inc.

BUSH, OWEN   S. S.
Detroit, A. L., 1908–1921, inc.
Washington, A. L., 1921

BUSHELMAN, J. F.   Pitcher
Cincinnati, N. L, 1909
Boston, A. L., 1911–1912

BUTCHER, HOWARD C.   Outfielder
Cleveland, A. L., 1911–1912

BUTLER   Outfielder
St. Louis, A. L., 1907

BUTLER, ARTHUR   Infielder
Boston, N. L., 1911

Pittsburgh, N. L., 1912–1913
St. Louis, N. L., 1914–1916, inc.

BUTLER, JOHN A.   Catcher
St. Louis, N. L., 1904
Brooklyn, N. L., 1906–1907

BYERS, WILLIAM   Catcher
St. Louis, N. L., 1904

BYRNE, ROBERT M.   Infielder
St. Louis, N. L., 1907–1909, inc.
Pittsburgh, N. L., 1909–1913, inc.
Philadelphia, N. L., 1913–1917, inc.
Chicago, A. L., 1917

BYRNES   Catcher
Philadelphia, A. L., 1906

CABRERA, A.   Infielder
St. Louis, N. L., 1913

CADORE, LEON J.   Pitcher
Brooklyn, N. L., 1915 to date

CADY, FORREST L.   Catcher
Boston, A. L., 1912–1917, inc.
Philadelphia, N. L., 1919

CAFFYN, BEN   Outfielder
Cleveland, A. L., 1906

CALDWELL, RALPH   Pitcher
Philadelphia, N. L., 1904–1905

CALDWELL, RAYMOND B.   Pitcher
New York, A. L., 1910–1918, inc.
Boston, A. L., 1919
Cleveland, A. L., 1919–1920–1921

CALHOUN, W. D.   Infielder
St. Louis, N. L., 1902
Boston, N. L., 1913

CALLAHAN   Outfielder
Cleveland, A. L., 1910–1911

CALLAHAN, JAMES J.   P.—Inf.—O. F.
Chicago, A. L., 1901–1905, inc.
Chicago, A. L., 1911–1912

CALLAHAN, LEO D.   Outfielder
Brooklyn, N. L., 1913
Philadelphia, N. L., 1919

CALLAHAN, R. J.   Pitcher
Cincinnati, N. L., 1915

CALLAHAN, WESLEY   Infielder
St. Louis, N. L., 1913

CALLOWAY, FRANK BURNETT   Infielder
Philadelphia, A. L., 1921

CALVO, JACINTO   Outfielder
Washington, A. L., 1913–1915

CAMERON   P.—O. F.
Boston, N. L., 1906

CAMNITZ, HARRY   Pitcher
Pittsburgh, N. L., 1909
St. Louis, N. L., 1911

CAMNITZ, S. HOWARD   Pitcher
Pittsburgh, N. L., 1904; 1906–1913, inc.
Philadelphia, N. L., 1913
Pittsburgh, F. L., 1914

CAMP, HOWARD L.   Outfielder
New York, A. L., 1917

CAMPBELL   Infielder
Pittsburgh, N. L., 1907

CAMPBELL, A. VINCENT   Outfielder
Chicago, N. L., 1908
Pittsburgh, N. L., 1910–1911
Boston, N. L., 1912
Indianapolis, F. L., 1914
Newark, F. L., 1915

CAMPBELL, WM. J.   Pitcher
St. Louis, N. L., 1905
Cincinnati, N. L., 1907–1909, inc.

CANNELL, WIRT V.   Outfielder
Boston, N. L., 1904–1905

CANTWELL, MICHAEL JOSEPH   Pitcher
New York, A. L., 1916
Philadelphia, N. L., 1919–1920

CANTWELL, THOMAS   Pitcher
Cincinnati, N. L., 1909–1910

CAPRON, RALPH E.   Outfielder
Pittsburgh, N. L., 1912
Philadelphia, N. L., 1913

CAREY, GEORGE   1st B.
Washington, A. L., 1902–1903

CAREY, MAX G.   Outfielder
Pittsburgh, N. L., 1910 to date

CARISCH, FRED   Catcher
Pittsburgh, N. L., 1903–1906, inc.
Cleveland, A. L., 1912–1914, inc.

CARLISLE, WALTER   Outfielder
Boston, A. L., 1908

CARLSON, HAROLD GUST   Pitcher
Pittsburgh, N. L., 1917 to date

CARLSON, LEON ALTON   Pitcher
Washington, A. L., 1920

CARLSTROM, ALBIN   Infielder
Boston, A. L., 1911

CARMICHAEL, CHESTER   Pitcher
Cincinnati, N. L., 1909

CARNEY, PATRICK J.   Outfielder
Boston, N. L., 1902–1904, inc.
Chicago, N. L., 1904

CARPENTER, PAUL   Pitcher
Pittsburgh, N. L., 1916

CARR, CHARLES C.   1st B.
Philadelphia, A. L., 1901
Detroit, A. L., 1903–1904
Cleveland, A. L., 1904–1905
Cincinnati, N. L., 1906
Indianapolis, F. L., 1914

CARRICK, WILLIAM   Pitcher
Washington, A. L., 1901–1902

CARRIGAN, WILLIAM F.   Catcher
Boston, A. L., 1906; 1908–1916, inc.

CARROLL, DORSEY LEE   Outfielder
Boston, N. L., 1919

CARROLL, RALPH   Catcher
Philadelphia, A. L., 1916

CARROLL, RICHARD   Pitcher
New York, A. L., 1909

CARRUTHERS   Infielder
Philadelphia, A. L., 1913–1914

CARSEY, WILFRED   Pitcher
Brooklyn, N. L., 1901

CARSON, A. J.   Pitcher
Chicago, N. L., 1910

CARTER, EDWARD   Pitcher
Philadelphia, A. L., 1908

CARTER, PAUL   Pitcher
Cleveland, A. L., 1914–1915
Chicago, N. L., 1916–1920, inc.

CASE, CHARLES C.   Pitcher
Cincinnati, N. L., 1901
Pittsburgh, N. L., 1904–1906, inc.

CASEY, JAMES P.   3rd B.
Detroit, A. L., 1901–1902
Chicago, N. L., 1903–1905, inc.
Brooklyn, N. L., 1906–1907

CASEY, JOSEPH FELIX   Catcher
Detroit, A. L., 1909–1911, inc.
Washington, A. L., 1918

CASHION, J. CARL   Pitcher
Washington, A. L., 1911–1912–1914

CASSIDY, HARRY   Outfielder
Pittsburgh, N. L., 1904

CASSIDY, JOSEPH   Shortstop
Washington, A. L., 1905

CASTLE, JOHN F.   Outfielder
Philadelphia, N. L., 1910

CASTLETON, ROY   Pitcher
Cincinnati, N. L., 1909–1910

CASTRO, LOUIS   Infielder
Philadelphia, A. L., 1902

CATES, ELI   Pitcher
Washington, A. L., 1908

CATHER, THEODORE   Substitute
St. Louis, N. L., 1912–1914, inc.
Boston, N. L., 1914–1915

CATON, JAMES HOWARD   Infielder
Pittsburgh, N. L., 1917–1920, inc.

CATTERSON, THOMAS   Outfielder
Brooklyn, N. L., 1908–1909

CAUSEY, CECIL ALGERNON   Pitcher
New York, N. L., 1918–1919

Boston, N. L., 1919
Philadelphia, N. L., 1920–1921
New York, N. L., 1921

CAVANAUGH, PAT   Infielder
Philadelphia, N. L., 1918

CANAVAN, HUGH   Pitcher
Boston, N. L., 1918

CAVET, TELLER   Pitcher
Detroit, A. L., 1911; 1914–1915

CERVAK   Pitcher
Cleveland, A. L., 1901

CHADBOURNE, CHESTER   Outfielder
Boston, A. L., 1906–1907
Kansas City, F. L., 1914–1915
Boston, N. L., 1918

CHALMERS   Pitcher
St. Louis, N. L., 1910

CHALMERS, GEORGE   Pitcher
Philadelphia, N. L., 1910–1916, inc.

CHANCE, FRANK LEROY   1st B.
Chicago, N. L., 1901–1912, inc.
New York, A. L., 1913–1914

CHANEY   Pitcher
Boston, A. L., 1913

CHANNELL, LESTER   Outfielder
New York, A. L., 1910–1914

CHAPLIN, BERT   Catcher
Boston, A. L., 1920–1921

CHAPMAN, HARRY E.   Catcher
Chicago, N. L., 1912
Cincinnati, N. L., 1913
St. Louis, F. L., 1914–1915
St. Louis, A. L., 1916

CHAPMAN, RAYMOND JOHNSON
                             Infielder
Cleveland, A. L., 1912–1920, inc.

CHAPPELL, L.   Outfielder
Chicago, A. L., 1913–1915, inc.
Cleveland, A. L., 1916
Boston, N. L., 1916–1917

CHAPPELLE, W. H.   Pitcher
Boston, N. L., 1908–1909
Cincinnati, N. L., 1909

CHARLES, RAYMOND   Infielder
St. Louis, N. L., 1908–1909
Cincinnati, N. L., 1910

CHASE, HAROLD HOMER   1st B.
New York, A. L., 1905–1913, inc.
Chicago, A. L., 1913–1914
Buffalo, F. L., 1914–1915
Cincinnati, N. L., 1916–1918, inc.
New York, N. L., 1919

CHECH, CHARLES W.   Pitcher
Cincinnati, N. L., 1905–1906
Cleveland, A. L., 1908
Boston, A. L., 1909

CHEEK, HARRY   Catcher
Philadelphia, N. L., 1910

CHEEVES, VIRGIL   Pitcher
Chicago, N. L., 1920–1921

CHENEY, LAWRENCE D.   Pitcher
Chicago, N. L., 1911–1915, inc.
Brooklyn, N. L., 1915–1919, inc.
Boston, N. L., 1919
Philadelphia, N. L., 1919

CHESBRO, JOHN DWIGHT   Pitcher
Pittsburgh, N. L., 1901–1902
New York, A. L., 1903–1909, inc.
Boston, A. L., 1909

CHILDS, CLARENCE L.   2nd B.
Chicago, N. L., 1901

CHILDS, P.   Infielder
St. Louis, N. L., 1901
Chicago, N. L., 1901
Philadelphia, N. L., 1902

CHOUINIARD   Outfielder
Chicago, A. L., 1910
Brooklyn, F. L., 1914

CHRISTENBURY, LLOYD REID   Substitute
Boston, N. L., 1919–1920–1921

CICOTTE, EDWARD V.   Pitcher
Detroit, A. L., 1905

Boston, A. L., 1908–1912, inc.
Chicago, A. L., 1912–1920, inc.

CLAIRE, D. M.   Infielder
Detroit, A. L., 1920

CLANCY, WILLIAM   1st B.
Pittsburgh, N. L., 1905

CLARK, FRED   Infielder
Chicago, N. L., 1902

CLARK, GEORGE   Pitcher
New York, A. L., 1913

CLARK, HARRY   Infielder
Chicago, A. L., 1903

CLARK, JAMES F.   Outfielder
St. Louis, N. L., 1911–1912

CLARK, ROBERT WILLIAM   Pitcher
Cleveland, A. L., 1920–1921

CLARK, ROY   Outfielder
New York, N. L., 1902

CLARKE   Outfielder
Detroit, A. L., 1921

CLARKE, ALAN T.   Pitcher
Cincinnati, N. L., 1921

CLARKE, FRED C.   Outfielder
Pittsburgh, N. L., 1901–1911, inc., 1913–
1915, inc.

CLARKE, JOSHUA   Outfielder
St. Louis, N. L., 1905
Cleveland, A. L., 1908–1909
Boston, N. L., 1911

CLARKE, JUSTIN J.   Catcher
Cleveland, A. L., 1905–1910, inc.
St. Louis, A. L., 1911
Philadelphia, N. L., 1919
Pittsburgh, N. L., 1920

CLARKE, SUMPTER M.   Substitute
Chicago, N. L., 1920

CLARKE, THOMAS ALOYSIUS   Catcher
Cincinnati, N. L., 1909–1917, inc.
Chicago, N. L., 1918

CLARKE, WILLIAM J.   C. —1st B.
Washington, A. L., 1901–1904, inc.
New York, N. L., 1905

CLARKSON, WALTER   Pitcher
New York, A. L., 1904–1906, inc.
Cleveland, A. L., 1907

CLAUSS   Pitcher
Detroit, A. L., 1913

CLAY   Outfielder
Philadelphia, N. L., 1902

CLEMENT, WALLACE OAKES   Outfielder
Philadelphia, N. L., 1908–1909
Brooklyn, N. L., 1909

CLEMONS, CLEM L.   Catcher
Chicago, N. L., 1916

CLEMONS, R. E.   Catcher
St. Louis, A. L., 1914

CLEMONS, VERNON J.   Catcher
St. Louis, A. L., 1916
St. Louis, A. L., 1919 to date

CLINGMAN, WILLIAM   Shortstop
Washington, A. L., 1903
Cleveland, A. L., 1903

CLYMER, OTIS EDGAR   Outfielder
Pittsburgh, N. L., 1905–1907, inc.
Washington, A. L., 1907–1909, inc.
Chicago, N. L., 1913
Boston, N. L., 1913

COAKLEY, ANDREW J.   Pitcher
Philadelphia, A. L., 1902 (under name of
McAllister), 1904–1906, inc.
Cincinnati, N. L., 1907–1908
Chicago, N. L., 1908–1909
New York, A. L., 1911

COBB, TYRUS RAYMOND   Outfielder
Detroit, A. L., 1905 to date

COCHRAN, A. J.   Pitcher
Cincinnati, N. L., 1915

COCHRANE, GEORGE   Infielder
Boston, A. L., 1918

COCREHAN, EUGENE   Pitcher
Boston, N. L., 1913–1914–1915

COFFEY, JOHN FRANCIS   Infielder
Boston, N. L., 1909

Detroit, A. L., 1918
Boston, A. L., 1918

COHEN   Catcher
Washington, A. L., 1907

COLE   Outfielder
Chicago, A. L., 1909–1910

COLE, BERT   Pitcher
Detroit, A. L., 1921

COLE, LEONARD L.   Pitcher
Chicago, N. L., 1909–1912, inc.
Pittsburgh, N. L., 1912
New York, A. L., 1914–1915

COLEMAN   Infielder
New York, A. L., 1912

COLEMAN, ROBERT   Catcher
Pittsburgh, N. L., 1913–1914
Cleveland, A. L., 1916

COLES   Outfielder
Kansas City, F. L., 1914

COLLAMORE, A. E.   Pitcher
Philadelphia, A. L., 1911
Cleveland, A. L., 1914–1915

COLLINS, EDGAR   Outfielder
Pittsburgh, N. L., 1914–1915
Boston, N. L., 1915–1917, inc.

COLLINS, EDWARD TROWBRIDGE
                             Infielder
Philadelphia, A. L., 1906–1914, inc. (in
1906
   Under name of Sullivan)
Chicago, A. L., 1915 to date

COLLINS, EDWIN   Outfielder
Philadelphia, A. L., 1921

COLLINS, HARRY WARREN   Pitcher
New York, A. L., 1920–1921

COLLINS, JAMES J.   3rd B.
Boston, A. L., 1901–1902–1903–1904–
1905–1906–1907
Philadelphia, A. L., 1907–1908

COLLINS, JOHN F.   O. F.—1st B.
Chicago, A. L., 1910–1920, inc.
Boston, A. L., 1921

COLLINS, RAY W.   Pitcher
Boston, A. L., 1909–1915, inc.

COLLINS, THARON PAT   Catcher
St. Louis, A. L., 1920–1921

COLLINS, WILLIAM S.   Outfielder
Boston, N. L., 1910–1911
Chicago, N. L., 1911
Brooklyn, N. L., 1913
Buffalo, F. L., 1914

COLLINS, WILSON   Outfielder
Boston, N. L., 1913–1914

COMPTON, J.   Pitcher
Cincinnati, N. L., 1911

COMPTON, SEBASTIAN   Outfielder
St. Louis, A. L., 1910–1912, inc.
Boston, N. L., 1915–1916
Pittsburgh, N. L., 1916
New York, N. L., 1918

COMSTOCK, RALPH   Pitcher
Detroit, A. L., 1913
Boston, A. L., 1915
Pittsburgh, N. L., 1918

CONGALTON, W.   Outfielder
Chicago, N. L., 1902
Cleveland, A. L., 1905–1906
Boston, A. L., 1907

CONKWRIGHT, ALLEN HOWARD   Pitcher
Detroit, A. L., 1920

CONLEY, JAMES P.   Pitcher
Baltimore, F. L., 1914–1915
Cincinnati, N. L., 1918

CONNALLY, GEORGE WALTER   Pitcher
Chicago, A. L., 1921

CONNAUGHTON, J.   Substitute
Boston, N. L., 1906

CONNELLY, JOSEPH   Outfielder
Washington, A. L., 1915

CONNOLLY, JOSEPH   Outfielder
Boston, N. L., 1913–1916, inc.

CONNOLLY, JOSEPH   Outfielder
New York, N. L., 1921

CONNOLLY, THOMAS MARTIN
Outfielder
New York, A. L., 1920–1921

CONNOR, JOSEPH C.—Inf.
Cleveland, A. L., 1901
Milwaukee, A. L., 1901
New York, A. L., 1905

CONROY, WILLIAM S. S.—Substitute
Milwaukee, A. L., 1901
Pittsburgh, N. L., 1902
New York, A. L., 1903–1908, inc.
Washington, A. L., 1909–1911, inc.

CONWAY, J. Pitcher
Washington, A. L., 1920

CONWAY, RICHARD Infielder
Boston, N. L., 1918

CONWELL, E. J. Infielder
St. Louis, N. L., 1911

CONZELMAN, JOSEPH H. Pitcher
Pittsburgh, N. L., 1913–1914–1915

COOK, JAMES Outfielder
Chicago, N. L., 1902

COOK, LUTHER A. Outfielder
New York, A. L., 1913–1916, inc.

COOK, R. E. Pitcher
St. Louis, A. L., 1915

COOLEY, RICHARD G. O. F.—1st B.
Boston, N. L., 1901–1904, inc.
Detroit, A. L., 1905

COOMBS Outfielder
Chicago, A. L., 1914

COOMBS, JOHN WESLEY Pitcher
Philadelphia, A. L., 1906–1914, inc.
Brooklyn, N. L., 1915–1918, inc.

COONEY Infielder
New York, A. L., 1905

COONEY, JAMES E. Infielder
Boston, A. L., 1917
New York, N. L., 1919

COONEY, JOHN W. Pitcher
Boston, N. L., 1921

COONEY, WILLIAM Outfielder
Boston, N. L., 1910

COONEY, WILLIAM Pitcher
Boston, N. L., 1909

COOPER, ARLIE WILBUR Pitcher
Pittsburgh, N. L., 1912 to date

COOPER, CLAUDE Outfielder
New York, N. L., 1913
Brooklyn, F. L., 1914–1915
Philadelphia, N. L., 1916–1917

COOPER, GUY E. Pitcher
Boston, A. L., 1914–1915

CORBETT, JOSEPH Pitcher
St. Louis, N. L., 1904

CORCORAN, MICHAEL J. Infielder
Cincinnati, N. L., 1910

CORCORAN, THOMAS W. Infielder
Cincinnati, N. L., 1901–1906, inc.
New York, N. L., 1907

COREY, EDWARD Pitcher
Chicago, A. L., 1918

CORHAN, ROY Infielder
Chicago, A. L., 1911
St. Louis, N. L., 1916

CORRIDEN, JOHN M. Infielder
St. Louis, A. L., 1910
Detroit, A. L., 1912
Chicago, N. L., 1913–1915, inc.

CORRIDON, FRANK J. Pitcher
Chicago, N. L., 1904
Philadelphia, N. L., 1904–1909, inc. (excepting 1906)
St. Louis, N. L., 1910

COSTELLO, DANIEL FRANCIS Outfielder
New York, A. L., 1913
Pittsburgh, N. L., 1914–1916, inc.

COTTER, RICHARD Catcher
Philadelphia, N. L., 1911
Chicago, N. L., 1912

COTTRELL, ENSIGN S. Pitcher
Pittsburgh, N. L., 1911

Chicago, N. L., 1912
Philadelphia, A. L., 1913
Boston, N. L., 1914
New York, A. L., 1915

COUCH, JOHN   Pitcher
Detroit, A. L., 1917

COUGHLIN, WILLIAM P.   3rd B.
Washington, A. L., 1901–1903, inc.
Detroit, A. L., 1904–1908, inc.

COULSON, ROBERT J.   Outfielder
Cincinnati, N. L., 1908
Brooklyn, N. L., 1910–1911
Pittsburgh, F. L., 1914

COUMBE, FRED NICHOLAS   Pitcher
Boston, A. L., 1914
Cleveland, A. L., 1914–1919, inc.
Cincinnati, N. L., 1920–1921

COURTNEY, ERNEST E.   Infielder
Boston, N. L., 1902
Baltimore, A. L., 1902
New York, A. L., 1903
Detroit, A. L., 1903
Philadelphia, N. L., 1905–1908, inc.

COURTNEY, HARRY S.   Pitcher
Washington, A. L., 1919–1920–1921

COVELESKIE, HARRY   Pitcher
Philadelphia, N. L., 1907–1909, inc.
Cincinnati, N. L, 1910
Detroit, A. L., 1914–1918, inc.

COVELESKIE, STANLEY   Pitcher
Philadelphia, A. L., 1912
Cleveland, A. L., 1916 to date

COVENEY   Catcher
St. Louis, N. L., 1903

COVINGTON, CLARENCE   1st B.
St. Louis, A. L., 1913
Boston, N. L., 1917–1918

COVINGTON, W. W.   Pitcher
Detroit, A. L., 1911–1912

COX, PLATEAU R.   Pitcher
Detroit, A. L., 1920

CRABB   Pitcher
Philadelphia, A. L., 1912
Chicago, A. L., 1912

CRABLE, GEORGE   Pitcher
Brooklyn, N. L., 1910

CRAFT, MAURICE M.   Pitcher
Washington, A. L., 1916–1919, inc.

CRAMER, WILLIAM   Pitcher
Cincinnati, N. L., 1912

CRANDALL, OTIS   Pitcher
New York, N. L., 1908–1913, inc.
St. Louis, N. L., 1913
New York, N. L., 1913
St. Louis, F. L., 1914–1915
St. Louis, A. L., 1916
Boston, N. L., 1918

CRANE, SAMUEL BYREN   Infielder
Philadelphia, A. L., 1914–1916, inc.
Washington, A. L., 1917
Cincinnati, N. L., 1920–1921

CRAVATH, C. C.   Outfielder
Boston, A. L., 1908
Chicago, A. L., 1909
Washington, A. L., 1909
Philadelphia, N. L., 1912–1920, inc.

CRAWFORD   Substitute
Baltimore, F. L., 1915

CRAWFORD, FORREST A.   Infielder
St. Louis, N. L., 1906–1907

CRAWFORD, SAMUEL   Outfielder
Cincinnati, A. L., 1901–1902
Detroit, A. L., 1908–1915, inc.

CREE, W. FRANK   Outfielder
New York, A. L., 1908–1915, inc.

CREGAN, PETER   Outfielder
Cincinnati, N. L., 1903

CRIGER, LOUIS   Catcher
New York, A. L., 1908–1915, inc.
St. Louis, A. L., 1909
New York, A. L., 1910
St. Louis, A. L., 1912

CRISP   Catcher
St. Louis, A. L., 1910–1911

CRISS, DODE   Pitcher
St. Louis, A. L., 1908–1911, inc.

CRIST, C.   Catcher
Philadelphia, N. L., 1906

CROCKETT   1st B.
Detroit, A. L., 1901

CROFT, H. T.   Outfielder
Chicago, N. L., 1901

CROLIUS, FRED   Outfielder
Boston, N. L., 1901
Pittsburgh, N. L., 1902

CROMPTON, EDWARD   Outfielder
St. Louis, A. L., 1909
Cincinnati, N. L., 1910

CRONIN, JOHN   Pitcher
Detroit, A. L., 1901–1902
Baltimore, A. L., 1902
New York, N. L., 1902–1903
Brooklyn, N. L., 1904

CROOKS, THOMAS   1st B.
Washington, A. L., 1910

CROSS   Substitute
Cleveland, A. L., 1901

CROSS, LAFAYETTE NAPOLEON   3rd B.
Philadelphia, A. L., 1901–1905, inc.
Washington, A. L., 1906–1907

CROSS, MONTFORD MONTGOMERY
       S. S.
Philadelphia, N. L., 1901
Philadelphia, A. L., 1902–1907, inc.

CROSSIN, FRANK P.   Catcher
St. Louis, A. L., 1912–1914

CROUCH   Pitcher
St. Louis, A. L., 1910

CROWELL, MINOT J.   Pitcher
Philadelphia, A. L., 1915–1916

CRUISE, WALTON E.   Outfielder
St. Louis, N. L., 1914; 1916–1919, inc.
Boston, N. L., 1919 to date

CRUM, CAL   Pitcher
Boston, N. L., 1917–1918

CRUMPLER, RAY MAXTON   Pitcher
Detroit, A. L., 1920

CRUTCHER, RICHARD   Pitcher
Boston, N. L., 1914–1915

CUETO, MANUEL   Outfielder
St. Louis, F. L., 1914
Cincinnati, N. L., 1917–1919, inc.

CULLOP, NORMAN A.   Pitcher
Cleveland, A. L., 1913–1914
Kansas City, F. L., 1915–1916
New York, A. L., 1916–1917
St. Louis, A. L., 1921

CULP, W. E.   Pitcher
Philadelphia, N. L., 1910

CUNNINGHAM   Pitcher
Philadelphia, A. L., 1906

CUNNINGHAM, ELLSWORTH   Pitcher
Chicago, N. L., 1901

CUNNINGHAM, GEORGE H., JR.   Pitcher
Detroit, A. L., 1916–1917–1918–1919–
1921

CUNNINGHAM, WILLIAM A.   Outfielder
Washington, A. L., 1910–1912, inc.

CUPPY, GEORGE B.   Pitcher
Boston, A. L., 1901

CURRAN, SAMUEL   Pitcher
Boston, N. L., 1902

CURRIE, CLARENCE   Pitcher
Cincinnati, N. L., 1902
St. Louis, N. L., 1902–1903
Chicago, N. L., 1903

CURRIE, MURPHY   Pitcher
St. Louis, N. L., 1916

CURRY   Substitute
Philadelphia, A. L., 1909
New York, A. L., 1911

CURRY   Pitcher
St. Louis, A. L., 1911

CURTIS, CLIFTON GARFIELD   Pitcher
Boston, N. L., 1909–1911, inc.

Chicago, N. L., 1911
Philadelphia, N. L., 1911
Brooklyn, N. L., 1912–1913

CURTIS, EUGENE   Outfielder
Pittsburgh, N. L., 1903

CURTIS, HARRY   Catcher
New York, N. L., 1907

CUSHMAN, CHARLES   Pitcher
Pittsburgh, N. L., 1902

CUTSHAW, GEORGE W.   3rd B.—2nd B.
Brooklyn, N. L., 1912–1917, inc.
Pittsburgh, N. L., 1918–1919–1920–1921

CUYLER, HAZEN S.   Outfielder
Pittsburgh, N. L., 1921

DAHLEN, WILLIAM FREDERICK   S. S.
Brooklyn, N. L., 1901–1903, inc.
New York, N. L., 1904–1907, inc.
Boston, N. L., 1908–1909
Brooklyn, N. L., 1910–1911

DALE, EUGENE   Pitcher
St. Louis, 1911–1912
Cincinnati, N. L., 1915–1916

DALEY, JUD   Outfielder
Brooklyn, N. L., 1911–1912

DALEY, THOMAS F.   Outfielder
Cincinnati, N. L., 1908
Philadelphia, A. L., 1913–1914
New York, A. L., 1914–1915

DALRYMPLE, M.   Outfielder
St. Louis, A. L., 1915

DALTON, TALBOT P.   Outfielder
Brooklyn, N. L., 1910–1914
Buffalo, F. L., 1915
Detroit, A. L., 1916

DALY   Infielder
St. Louis, A. L., 1912

DALY, GEORGE J.   Pitcher
New York, N. L., 1909

DALY, THOMAS DANIEL   Catcher
Chicago, A. L., 1913–1915, inc.

Cleveland, A. L., 1916
Chicago, N. L., 1918–1921, inc.

DALY, THOMAS P.   Infielder
Brooklyn, N. L., 1901
Chicago, A. L., 1902–1903
Cincinnati, N. L, 1903

DAMM   Substitute
Boston, N. L., 1909

DANFORTH, DAVID C.   Pitcher
Philadelphia, A. L., 1911–1912
Chicago, A. L., 1916–1919, inc.

DANIELS, BERTRAM C.   Outfielder
New York, A. L., 1910–1913, inc.
Cincinnati, N. L., 1914

DANZIG, HAROLD   Infielder
Boston, A. L., 1909

DARINGER, ROLLA H.   Infielder
St. Louis, N. L., 1914–1915

DASHNER, L. C.   Pitcher
Cleveland, A. L., 1913

DAUBERT, HARRY   Infielder
Pittsburgh, N. L., 1915

DAUBERT, JACOB ELLSWORTH   1st B.
Brooklyn, N. L., 1910–1918, inc.
Cincinnati, N. L., 1919 to date

DAUSS, GEORGE   Pitcher
Detroit, A. L., 1912 to date

DAVENPORT, ARTHUR DAVID   Pitcher
Cincinnati, N. L., 1914
St. Louis, F. L., 1914–1915
St. Louis, A. L., 1916–1919, inc.

DAVENPORT, CLAUDE   Pitcher
New York, N. L., 1920

DAVENPORT, JAUBERT LUNN   Pitcher
Chicago, A. L., 1920

DAVIDSON, CLAUDE B.   Infielder
Philadelphia, A. L., 1918

DAVIDSON, W. S.   Outfielder
Cleveland, A. L., 1908
Chicago, N. L., 1908
Brooklyn, N. L., 1910–1911

DAVIES, LLOYD GARRISON Pitcher
Philadelphia, A. L., 1914

DAVIS, ALFONZO D. Outfielder
Brooklyn, N. L., 1901
Pittsburgh, N. L., 1901–1902
New York, A. L., 1903
Cincinnati, N. L., 1907

DAVIS, FRANK TALMADGE Pitcher
Cincinnati, N. L., 1912
Chicago, A. L., 1916
Philadelphia, N. L., 1918
St. Louis, A. L., 1920–1921

DAVIS, GEORGE A., JR. Pitcher
New York, A. L., 1912
Boston, N. L., 1913–1914–1915

DAVIS, GEORGE STACEY Infielder
New York, N. L., 1901
Chicago, A. L., 1902
New York, N. L., 1903
Chicago, A. L., 1904–1909, inc.

DAVIS, HARRY H. 1st B.
Philadelphia, A. L., 1901–1911, inc.
Cleveland, A. L., 1912
Philadelphia, A. L., 1912–1917, inc.

DEAL, CHARLES A. Infielder
Detroit, A. L., 1912–1913
Boston, N. L., 1913–1914
St. Louis, F. L., 1915
St. Louis, A. L., 1916
Chicago, N. L., 1916–1921, inc.

DEAL, JOHN W. 1st B.
Cincinnati, N. L., 1906

DE ARMOND, CHARLES Infielder
Cincinnati, N. L., 1903

DE BERRY, JOHN HERMAN Catcher
Cleveland, A. L., 1916–1917

DE BERRY, JOSEPH Pitcher
St. Louis, A. L., 1920–1921

DEBUS, ADAM Infielder
Pittsburgh, N. L., 1917

DEDE, ARTHUR Catcher
Brooklyn, N. L., 1916

DEE, M. L. Infielder
St. Louis, A. L., 1915

DEEGAN, JOHN Pitcher
New York, N. L., 1901

DEERING, JOHN Pitcher
New York, A. L., 1903
Detroit, A. L., 1903

DE FATE, CLYDE Infielder
Detroit, A. L., 1917
St. Louis, N. L., 1917

DEGROFF, ARTHUR Outfielder
St. Louis, N. L., 1905–1906

DEININGER, OTTO C. P. — O. F.
Boston, A. L., 1902
Philadelphia, N. L., 1909

DEISEL, PAT Catcher
Brooklyn, N. L., 1902
Cincinnati, N. L., 1903

DELAHANTY, EDWARD J. Outfielder —
Philadelphia, N. L., 1901 1st B.
Washington, A. L., 1902–1903

DELAHANTY, FRANK Outfielder
New York, A. L., 1905–1906
Cleveland, A. L., 1907
New York, A. L., 1908
Buffalo, F. L., 1914
Pittsburgh, F. L., 1914

DELAHANTY, JAMES C. Inf. — O. F.
Chicago, N. L., 1901
New York, N. L., 1902
Boston, N. L., 1904–1905
Cincinnati, N. L., 1906
St. Louis, A. L., 1907
Washington, A. L., 1907–1908–1909
Detroit, A. L., 1909–1912, inc.
Brooklyn, F. L., 1914–1915

DEMOTT, BENJAMIN HARRISON Pitcher
Cleveland, A. L., 1910–1911

DENT, E. E. Pitcher
Brooklyn, N. L., 1909; 1911–1912

DERRICK, CLAUDE Infielder
Philadelphia, A. L., 1910–1912, inc.

New York, A. L., 1913
Cincinnati, N. L., 1914
Chicago, N. L., 1914

DERRINGER   Infielder
Kansas City, F. L., 1914

DES JARDINES, PAUL   Pitcher
Cleveland, A. L., 1916

DESSAU, FRANK R.   Pitcher
Boston, N. L., 1907
Brooklyn, N. L., 1910

DEVINE, J. T. (MICKEY)   Catcher
Philadelphia, N. L., 1918
Boston, A. L., 1920

DEVINNEY   Pitcher
Boston, A. L., 1920

DEVLIN, ARTHUR   3rd B.
New York, N. L., 1904–1911, inc.
Boston, N. L., 1912–1913

DE VOGT, REX EUGENE   Catcher
Boston, N. L., 1913

DEVORE, JOSHUA   Outfielder
New York, N. L., 1908–1913, inc.
Cincinnati, N. L., 1913
Philadelphia, N. L., 1913–1914
Boston, N. L., 1914

DE VORMER, ALBERT   Catcher
Chicago, A. L., 1918
New York, A. L., 1921

DEVOY, WALTER   Outfielder
St. Louis, A. L., 1909

DEXTER, CHARLES L.   C.—Sub.
Chicago, N. L., 1901–1903
Boston, N. L., 1902–1903

DICKERSON, CLARK   Pitcher
Cleveland, A. L., 1917

DICKSON, WALTER R.   Pitcher
New York, N. L., 1910
Boston, N. L., 1912–1913
Pittsburgh, F. L., 1914–1915

DIEHL, ERNEST   Substitute
Pittsburgh, N. L., 1903–1904
Boston, N. L., 1906–1909

DILLHOEFER, WILLIAM MARTIN   Catcher
Chicago, N. L., 1917
Philadelphia, N. L., 1918
St. Louis, N. L., 1919–1921, inc.

DILLINGER, H. H.   Pitcher
Cleveland, A. L., 1914

DILLON, FRANK   1st B.
Detroit, A. L., 1901–1902
Baltimore, A. L., 1902

DINNEEN, WILLIAM HENRY   Pitcher
Boston, N. L., 1901
Boston, A. L., 1902–1906, inc.
St. Louis, A. L., 1907–1908–1909

DISCH   Pitcher
Detroit, A. L., 1905

DISTEL, GEORGE   Infielder
St. Louis, N. L., 1918

DIVIS, M.   Outfielder
Philadelphia, A. L., 1916

DOAK, WILLIAM L.   Pitcher
Cincinnati, N. L., 1912
St. Louis, N. L., 1913 to date

DOANE, WALTER   Pitcher
Cleveland, A. L., 1909–1910

DOBBS, JOHN G.   Outfielder
Cincinnati, N. L., 1901–1902
Chicago, N. L., 1902–1903
Brooklyn, N. L., 1904–1905

DODD, ONA   Infielder
Pittsburgh, N. L., 1912

DODGE, JOHN L.   Infielder
Philadelphia, N. L., 1912–1913
Cincinnati, N. L., 1913

DODGE, SAMUEL EDWARD   Pitcher
Boston, A. L., 1921

DOESCHER, JOHN   Pitcher
Chicago, N. L., 1903
Brooklyn, N. L., 1903–1906, inc.
Cincinnati, N. L., 1908

DOHENY, EDWARD   Pitcher
New York, N. L., 1901
Pittsburgh, N. L., 1901–1902–1903

DOLAN, ALVA J.   Infielder
Cincinnati, N. L., 1909
New York, A. L., 1911–1912
Philadelphia, N. L., 1912–1913
Pittsburgh, N. L., 1913
St. Louis, N. L., 1914–1915

DOLAN, E. L.   1st B.
Indianapolis, F. L., 1914

DOLAN, HARRY   Outfielder
Chicago, N. L., 1901
Brooklyn, N. L., 1901–1902
Chicago, A. L., 1903
Cincinnati, N. L., 1903–1904–1905
Boston, N. L., 1905–1906

DOLAN, JOSEPH   Infielder
Philadelphia, N. L., 1901
Philadelphia, A. L., 1901

DONAHUE, FRANK L.   Pitcher
Philadelphia, N. L., 1901
St. Louis, A. L., 1902–1903
Cleveland, A. L., 1903–1905, inc.
Detroit, A. L., 1906

DONALDS, ED   Pitcher
Cincinnati, N. L., 1912

DONLIN, MICHAEL J.   Outfielder
Baltimore, A. L., 1901
Cincinnati, N. L., 1902–1903–1904
New York, N. L., 1904–1906, inc.; 1908–
1911
Boston, N. L., 1911
Pittsburgh, N. L., 1912

DONNELLY, EDWARD   Pitcher
Boston, N. L., 1912

DONOHUE, CHARLES   Infielder
St. Louis, N. L., 1904
Philadelphia, N. L., 1904

DONOHUE, JOHN AUGUSTIN
                           Catcher—1st B.
Pittsburgh, N. L., 1901
Milwaukee, A. L., 1901
St. Louis, A. L., 1902
Chicago, A. L., 1904–1909, inc.
Washington, A. L., 1909

DONOHUE, PATRICK   Catcher
Boston, A. L., 1908–1910, inc.
Cleveland, A. L., 1910
Philadelphia, A. L., 1910

DONOHUE, PETER   Pitcher
Cincinnati, N. L., 1921

DONOHUE, TIMOTHY   Catcher
Washington, A. L., 1902

DONOVAN
Cleveland, A. L., 1901   Infielder

DONOVAN, J. F.   Catcher
Philadelphia, N. L., 1906

DONOVAN, MICHAEL   Infielder
New York, A. L., 1908

DONOVAN, PATRICK JOSEPH   Outfielder
St. Louis, N. L., 1901–1902–1903
Washington, A. L., 1904
Brooklyn, N. L., 1906

DONOVAN, WILLIAM EDWARD   Pitcher
Brooklyn, N. L., 1901–1902
Detroit, A. L., 1903–1912, inc.
New York, A. L., 1915–1917, inc.
Detroit, A. L., 1918

DOOIN, CHARLES S.   Catcher
Philadelphia, N. L., 1902–1914, inc.
New York, N. L., 1915–1916

DOOLAN, MICHAEL J.   Infielder
Philadelphia, N. L., 1905–1913, inc.
Baltimore, F. L., 1914–1915
Chicago, F. L., 1915
Chicago, N. L., 1916
New York, N. L., 1916
Brooklyn, N. L., 1918

DORAN, THOMAS   Catcher
Boston, A. L., 1904–1905
Detroit, A. L., 1905

DORNER, GUS   Pitcher
Cleveland, A. L., 1902–1903
Cincinnati, N. L., 1906
Boston, N. L., 1906–1909, inc.

DORSEY, JERRY   Outfielder
Pittsburgh, N. L., 1911

DOUGHERTY   Pitcher
Chicago, A. L., 1904

DOUGHERTY, PATRICK HENRY
    Outfielder
Boston, A. L., 1902–1904, inc.
New York, A. L., 1904–1906, inc.
Chicago, A. L., 1906–1911, inc.

DOUGLAS, ASTYANAX S.   Catcher
Cincinnati, N. L., 1921

DOUGLAS, PHILIP BROOKS   Pitcher
Chicago, A. L., 1912
Cincinnati, N. L., 1914–1915
Brooklyn, N. L., 1915
Chicago, N. L., 1915; 1917–1919, inc.
New York, N. L., 1919–1921, inc.

DOUGLAS, WILLIAM B.   C.—1st B.
Philadelphia, N. L., 1901–1904, inc.

DOWD, JAMES   Pitcher
Pittsburgh, N. L., 1910

DOWD, RAYMOND LEO
Detroit, A. L., 1919
Philadelphia, A. L., 1919

DOWD, THOMAS J.   Outfielder
Boston, A. L., 1901

DOWLING, H. PETER   Pitcher
Milwaukee, A. L., 1901
Cleveland, A. L., 1901

DOWNEY, A. C.   Outfielder
Brooklyn, N. L., 1909

DOWNEY, THOMAS   Infielder
Cincinnati, N. L., 1909–1911, inc.
Philadelphia, N. L., 1912
Chicago, N. L., 1912
Buffalo, F. L., 1914–1915

DOWNS, JEROME   Substitute
Detroit, A. L., 1907–1908
Brooklyn, N. L., 1912
Chicago, N. L., 1912

DOYLE, JAMES FRANCIS   3rd B.
Cincinnati, N. L., 1910
Chicago, N. L., 1911

DOYLE, JOHN JOSEPH   1st B.
Chicago, N. L., 1901
Washington, A. L., 1902
New York, N. L., 1902
Brooklyn, N. L., 1903–1904
Philadelphia, N. L., 1904
New York, A. L., 1905

DOYLE, JOSEPH   Pitcher
New York, A. L., 1906–1910, inc.
Cincinnati, N. L., 1910

DOYLE, LAWRENCE JOSEPH   2nd B.
New York, N. L., 1907–1916, inc.
Chicago, N. L., 1917
New York, N. L., 1918–1920, inc.

DRAKE, DELOS   Outfielder
Detroit, A. L., 1911
St. Louis, F. L., 1914–1915

DRESSEN, LEE A.   Infielder
St. Louis, N. L., 1914
Detroit, A. L., 1918

DRESSER, CHARLES A.   Pitcher
Boston, N. L., 1902

DRILL, LEWIS J.   Catcher
Washington, A. L., 1902
Baltimore, A. L., 1902
Washington, A. L., 1903–1904
Detroit, A. L., 1904–1905

DRISCOLL, J.   Pitcher
Philadelphia, A. L., 1916

DRISCOLL, JOHN L.   Substitute
Chicago, N. L., 1917

DROHAN, THOMAS   Pitcher
Washington, A. L., 1913

DRUCKE, LOUIS   Pitcher
New York, N. L., 1909–1912, inc.

DRUHOT, CARL   Pitcher
Cincinnati, N. L., 1906
St. Louis, N. L., 1906–1907

DUBUC, JEAN A.   Pitcher
Cincinnati, N. L., 1908–1909
Detroit, A. L., 1912–1913–1914–1915–1916

Boston, A. L., 1918
New York, N. L., 1919

DUFF, PATRICK J.   Outfielder
Washington, A. L., 1906

DUFFY, BARNEY A.   Pitcher
Pittsburgh, N. L., 1913

DUFFY, HUGH   Outfielder
Milwaukee, A. L., 1901
Philadelphia, N. L., 1904–1905–1906

DUGAN, JOSEPH A.   Infielder
Philadelphia, A. L., 1917 to date

DUGEY, OSCAR J.   Substitute
Boston, N. L., 1913–1914
Philadelphia, N. L., 1915–1917, inc.
Boston, N. L., 1920

DUGGAN   Infielder
St. Louis, A. L., 1911

DUGGLEBY, WILLIAM J.   Pitcher
Philadelphia, N. L., 1901
Philadelphia, A. L., 1902
Philadelphia, N. L., 1902–1907, inc.
Pittsburgh, N. L., 1907

DUMONT, GEORGE HENRY   Pitcher
Washington, A. L., 1915–1918, inc.
Boston, A. L., 1919

DUNCAN, LOUIS BAIRD   Outfielder
Pittsburgh, N. L. 1915
Cincinnati, N. L. 1919 to date

DUNCAN, VAN DUKE   Inf.—O. F.
Philadelphia, N. L., 1913
Baltimore, F. L., 1914–1915

DUNDON, AUGUST   Infielder
Chicago, A. L., 1904–1906, inc.

DUNGAN, SAMUEL M.   Outfielder
Washington, A. L., 1901

DUNHAM, H. H.   Pitcher
St. Louis, N. L., 1902

DUNKLE, EDWARD   Pitcher
Chicago, A. L., 1903
Washington, A. L., 1903–1904

DUNLAP, GEORGE H.   Infielder
Cleveland, A. L., 1913–1914

DUNLEAVY, JOHN F.   Pitcher—O. F.
St. Louis, N. L., 1903–1905, inc.

DUNN, JOHN   Pitcher—Sub.
Philadelphia, N. L., 1901
Baltimore, A. L., 1901
New York, N. L., 1902–1904, inc.

DUNN, JOSEPH   Catcher
Brooklyn, N. L., 1908–1909

DUPEE, FRANK O.   Pitcher
Chicago, A. L., 1901

DURBIN, BLAINE   Pitcher
Chicago, N. L., 1907–1908
Pittsburgh, N. L., 1909
Cincinnati, N. L., 1909

DURHAM, JAMES   Pitcher
Chicago, A. L., 1902

DURHAM, LOUIS   Pitcher
Brooklyn, N. L., 1904
Washington, A. L., 1907
New York, N. L., 1908–1909

DURNING, RICHARD K.   Pitcher
Brooklyn, N. L., 1917–1918

DYER, BENJAMIN F.   Infielder
New York, N. L., 1914–1915
Detroit, A. L., 1916–1919

DYGERT, JAMES H.   Pitcher
Philadelphia, A. L., 1905–1910, inc.

DYKES, JAMES   Infielder
Philadelphia, A. L., 1918–1921, inc.

EASON, MALCOLM WAYNE   Pitcher
Chicago, N. L., 1901–1902
Boston, N. L., 1902
Detroit, A. L., 1903
Brooklyn, N. L., 1905–1906

EAST, C.   Pitcher
St. Louis, A. L., 1915

EASTERLY, THEODORE HARRISON
Catcher—Outfielder
Cleveland, A. L., 1909–1911, inc.

Chicago, A. L., 1912–1913
Kansas City, F. L., 1914–1915

EAYRS, EDWIN   Pitcher—O. F.
Pittsburgh, N. L., 1913
Boston, N. L., 1920–1921
Brooklyn, N. L., 1921

ECCLES, H.   Pitcher
Philadelphia, A. L., 1915

ECKERT, CHARLES WILLIAM   Pitcher
Philadelphia, A. L., 1919–1920

EDINGTON, FRANK   Outfielder
Pittsburgh, N. L., 1912

EDMUNDSON   Pitcher
Washington, A. L., 1906–1907–1908

EELLS, HARRY   Pitcher
Cleveland, A. L., 1906

EGAN, ALOYSIUS J.   Pitcher
Detroit, A. L., 1902
St. Louis, N. L., 1905–1906

EGAN, ARTHUR A.   Catcher
Philadelphia, A. L., 1908–1912
Cleveland, A. L., 1914–1915

EGAN, CHAS. E.   Infielder
Pittsburgh, N. L., 1901

EGAN, RICHARD JOSEPH   Infielder
Cincinnati, N. L., 1908–1913, inc.
Brooklyn, N. L., 1914–1915
Boston, N. L., 1915–1916

EHMKE, HOWARD J.   Pitcher
Buffalo, F. L., 1915
Detroit, A. L., 1916 to date

EIBEL, HENRY H.   Substitute
Boston, A. L., 1920

ELBERFELD, NORMAN   S. S.
Detroit, A. L., 1901–1902–1903
New York, A. L., 1903–1909, inc.
Washington, A. L., 1910–1911
Brooklyn, N. L., 1914

ELLAM, ROY B.   Substitute
Cincinnati, N. L., 1909
Pittsburgh, N. L., 1918

ELLER, HORACE OWEN   Pitcher
Cincinnati, N. L., 1917–1918–1919–
1920–1921

ELLERBEE, FRANK ROGERS   Infielder
Washington, A. L., 1919–1920–1921
St. Louis, A. L., 1921

ELLIOTT, CATER WARD   Substitute
Chicago, N. L., 1921

ELLIOTT, CLAUDE   Pitcher
Cincinnati, N. L., 1904
New York, N. L., 1904–1905

ELLIOTT, EUGENE B.   3rd B.
New York, A. L., 1911

ELLIOTT, HAROLD H.   Catcher
Boston, N. L., 1910
Chicago, N. L., 1916–1918, inc.
Brooklyn, N. L., 1920

ELLIS, GEORGE W.   Outfielder
St. Louis, N. L., 1909–1912, inc.

ELLISON, GEORGE R.   Pitcher
Cleveland, A. L., 1920

ELLISON, HERBERT S.   Infielder
Detroit, A. L., 1916–1920, inc.

ELY, W. FRED   Shortstop
Pittsburgh, N. L., 1901
Philadelphia, A. L., 1901
Washington, A. L., 1902

EMERSON   Pitcher
Philadelphia, A. L., 1911–1912

EMMER, FRANK   Infielder
Cincinnati, N. L., 1916

ENGEL, JOSEPH W.   Pitcher
Washington, A. L., 1912–1915, inc.
Cincinnati, N. L., 1917
Cleveland, A. L., 1919
Washington, A. L., 1920

ENGEL, ARTHUR CLYDE   Inf.—O. F.
New York, A. L., 1909–1910
Boston, A. L., 1910–1914, inc.
Buffalo, F. L., 1914–1915
Cleveland, A. L., 1916

ENRIGHT, C. M.   Infielder
St. Louis, N. L., 1909

ENRIGHT, JOHN P.   Pitcher
New York, A. L., 1917

ENS, MUTZ   Infielder
Chicago, A. L., 1912

ENZENROTH, C. H.   Catcher
St. Louis, A. L., 1914
Kansas City, F. L., 1914

ENZMANN, JOHN   Pitcher
Brooklyn, N. L., 1914
Cleveland, A. L., 1918–1919
Philadelphia, N. L., 1920

ERICKSON, ERIC GEORGE   Pitcher
New York, N. L., 1914
Detroit, A. L., 1916; 1918–1919
Washington, A. L., 1919–1921, inc.

ERWIN, ROSS E.   Catcher
Detroit, A. L., 1907
Brooklyn, N. L., 1910–1914, inc.
Cincinnati, N. L., 1914

ESCHEN, JAMES G.   Infielder
Cleveland, A. L., 1915

ESMOND, JAMES   Infielder
Cincinnati, N. L., 1911–1912
Indianapolis, F. L., 1914
Newark, F. L., 1915

ESSICK, WILLIAM   Pitcher
Cincinnati, N. L., 1906–1907

EUBANKS, JOHN   Pitcher
Detroit, A. L., 1905–1906–1907

EUNICK, FERNANDEZ   Infielder
Cleveland, A. L., 1917

EVANS, CHARLES F.   Pitcher
Boston, A. L., 1915 to date

EVANS, LOIS R.   Substitute
New York, N. L., 1908
St. Louis, N. L., 1909–1913, inc.
Brooklyn, F. L., 1914–1915
Baltimore, F. L., 1915

EVANS, ROBERT ROY   Pitcher
New York, N. L., 1902
Brooklyn, N. L., 1902–1903
St. Louis, A. L., 1903

EVANS, WILLIAM JAMES   Pitcher
Pittsburgh, N. L., 1916–1917; 1919

EVERETT, WILLIAM   1st B.
Washington, A. L., 1901

EVERS, JOHN J.   2nd. B.
Chicago, N. L., 1902–1913, inc.
Boston, N. L., 1914–1917, inc.
Philadelphia, N. L., 1917

EVERS, JOSEPH F.   Substitute
New York, N. L., 1913

EWING, REUBEN   Outfielder
St. Louis, N. L., 1921

EWING, ROBERT   Pitcher
Cincinnati, N. L., 1902–1909, inc.
Philadelphia, N. L., 1910–1911

FABER, URBAN CHARLES   Pitcher
Chicago, A. L., 1914 to date

FABRIQUE, LAVERN   Infielder
Brooklyn, N. L., 1916–1917

FAETH, TONY JOSEPH   Pitcher
Cleveland, A. L., 1919–1920

FAHEY, FRANK   Pitcher
Philadelphia, A. L., 1918

FAHRER, PETER   Pitcher
Cincinnati, N. L., 1914

FAIRBANKS   Pitcher
Philadelphia, A. L., 1904

FAIRCLOTH, JAMES L.   Pitcher
Philadelphia, N. L. 1919

FALK, BIB AUGUST Outfielder
Chicago, A. L., 1920–1921

FALKENBERG, FRED P.   Pitcher
Pittsburgh, N. L., 1903
Washington, A. L., 1905–1908, inc.
Cleveland, A. L., 1908–1913, inc., (ex-
cept 1911)
Indianapolis, F. L., 1914

Newark, F. L., 1915
Brooklyn, F. L., 1915
Philadelphia, A. L., 1916

FALSEY, P. J.   Outfielder
Pittsburgh, N. L., 1914

FANWELL, HARRY   Pitcher
Cleveland, A. L., 1910

FARMER, A. J.   Catcher
Brooklyn, N. L., 1908

FARMER, FLOYD   Substitute
Pittsburgh, N. L., 1916
Cleveland, A. L., 1918

FARRELL, CHARLES A.   Catcher
Brooklyn, N. L., 1901–1902
Boston, A. L., 1903–1905, inc.

FARRELL, JOHN S.   2nd B.
Washington, A. L., 1901
St. Louis, N. L., 1902–1905, inc.

FARRELL, JOHN S.   2nd B.
Chicago, F. L., 1914–1915

FAUSCH   Infielder
Chicago, A. L., 1916

FAUST, CHARLES V.   Pitcher
New York, N. L., 1911

FELIX, HARRY   Pitcher
New York, N. L., 1901
Philadelphia, N. L., 1902

FELSCH, OSCAR C.   Outfielder
Chicago, A. L., 1915–1920, inc.

FENNER, HORACE A.   Pitcher
Chicago, A. L., 1921

FERGUSON, ALEXANDER   Pitcher
New York, A. L., 1918–1921

FERGUSON, CHARLES   Pitcher
Chicago, N. L., 1901

FERGUSON, GEORGE CECIL   Pitcher
New York, N. L., 1906–1907
Boston, N. L., 1908–1911, inc.

FERRIS, HOBART   2nd B.—3rd B.

Boston, A. L., 1901–1907, inc.
St. Louis, A. L., 1908–1909

FERRY, JOHN F.   Pitcher
Detroit, A. L., 1904
Cleveland, A. L., 1905
Pittsburgh, N. L., 1910–1913, inc.

FEWSTER, WILSON   Substitute
New York, A. L., 1917 to date

FIENE, LOUIS   Pitcher
Chicago, A. L., 1906–1907; 1909

FILES   Pitcher
Philadelphia, A. L., 1908

FILLINGIM, DANA   Pitcher
Philadelphia, A. L., 1915
Boston, N. L., 1918 to date

FINCHER, WILLIAM ALLEN   Pitcher
St. Louis, A. L., 1916

FINLAYSON, PEMBROKE   Pitcher
Brooklyn, N. L., 1908–1909

FINNERAN, JOSEPH IGNATIUS   Pitcher
Philadelphia, N. L., 1912–1913
Brooklyn, F. L., 1914–1915
New York, A. L., 1918
Detroit, A. L., 1918

FISCHER, WILLIAM CHARLES   Catcher
Brooklyn, N. L., 1913–1914
Chicago, F. L., 1915
Chicago, N. L., 1916
Pittsburgh, N. L., 1916–1917

FISHBURNE, SAMUEL   Infielder
St. Louis, N. L., 1919

FISHER   Outfielder
St. Louis, A. L., 1910

FISHER   Pitcher
Detroit, A. L., 1902

FISHER, CHAUNCEY   Pitcher
New York, N. L., 1901
St. Louis, N. L., 1901

FISHER, CLARENCE HENRY   Pitcher
Washington, A. L., 1919–1920

FISHER, GUS   Catcher
Cleveland, A. L., 1911

FISHER, RAYMOND L.   Pitcher
New York, A. L., 1910–1917, inc.
Cincinnati, N. L., 1919–1920

FISHER, ROBERT T.   Infielder
Brooklyn, N. L., 1912–1913
Chicago, N. L., 1914–1915
Cincinnati, N. L., 1916
St. Louis, N. L., 1918–1919

FISHER, THOMAS   Pitcher
Boston, N. L., 1904

FISHER, WILBUR M.   Substitute
Pittsburgh, N. L., 1916

FISK, M. P.   Pitcher
Chicago, F. L., 1914

FITTERY, PAUL C.   Pitcher
Cincinnati, N. L., 1914
Philadelphia, N. L., 1917

FITZGERALD, JUSTIN J.   Outfielder
New York, A. L., 1911
Philadelphia, N. L., 1918

FITZGERALD, MATTHEW   Catcher
New York, N. L., 1906–1907

FITZPATRICK, EDWARD HENRY
     Infielder
Boston, N. L., 1915–1917, inc.

FITZSIMMONS, THOMAS W.   Infielder
Brooklyn, N. L., 1919

FLACK, MAX O.   Outfielder
Chicago, F. L., 1914–1915
Chicago, N. L., 1916 to date

FLAGSTEAD, IRA   Catch—Inf.—O. F.
Detroit, A. L., 1917; 1919–1921, inc.

FLAHERTY, PATRICK JOSEPH   Pitcher
Chicago, A. L., 1903–1904
Pittsburgh, N. L., 1904–1905
Boston, N. L., 1907–1908
Philadelphia, N. L., 1910
Boston, N. L., 1911

FLANAGAN, JAMES P.   Outfielder
Pittsburgh, N. L., 1905

FLATER, JOHN   Pitcher
Philadelphia, A. L., 1908

FLEMING, THOMAS   Outfielder
Philadelphia, N. L., 1902–1904

FLETCHER, ARTHUR   Infielder
New York, N. L., 1909–1920, inc.
Philadelphia, N. L., 1920

FLETCHER, FRANK   Outfielder
Philadelphia, N. L., 1914

FLETCHER, SAM S.   Pitcher
Brooklyn, N. L., 1909
Cincinnati, N. L., 1912

FLICK, ELMER HARRISON   Outfielder
Philadelphia, N. L., 1901
Philadelphia, A. L., 1902
Cleveland, A. L., 1902–1910, inc.

FLOOD, TIM   2nd B.
Brooklyn, N. L., 1902–1903

FLUHRER, JOHN L.   Outfielder
Chicago, N. L., 1915

FLYNN, DON   Outfielder
Pittsburgh, N. L., 1917

FLYNN, JOHN ANTHONY   1st B.
Pittsburgh, N. L., 1910–1911
Washington, A. L., 1912

FOHL, LEE ALEXANDER   Catcher
Pittsburgh, N. L., 1902
Cincinnati, N. L., 1903

FONSECA, LEWIS A.   Infielder
Cincinnati, N. L., 1921

FORD, EUGENE   Pitcher
Detroit, A. L., 1905

FORD, HORACE HILLS   2nd B.—S. S.
Boston, N. L., 1919–1920–1921

FORD, RUSSELL   Pitcher
New York, A. L., 1909–1913, inc.
Buffalo, F. L., 1914–1915

FOREMAN, FRANCIS I.   Pitcher
Boston, A. L., 1901
Baltimore, A. L., 1901–1902

FORTUNE, GARY REESE   Pitcher
Philadelphia, N. L., 1916–1918
Boston, A. L., 1920

FOSS, GEORGE DUEWARD　　　　Infielder
Washington, A. L., 1921

FOSTER　　　　　　　　　　Pitcher
Cleveland, A. L., 1908

FOSTER, CLARENCE　　　　Outfielder
Washington, A. L., 1901
Chicago, A. L., 1901

FOSTER, EDWARD CUNNINGHAM
　　　　　　　　　　　　Infielder
New York, A. L., 1910
Washington, A. L., 1912–1919, inc.
Boston, A. L., 1920–1921

FOSTER, GEORGE　　　　　Pitcher
Boston, A. L., 1913–1917, inc.

FOURNIER, JACQUES FRANK　　1st B.
Chicago, A. L., 1912–1917, inc.
New York, A. L., 1918
St. Louis, N. L., 1920–1921

FOUTZ　　　　　　　　　　1st B.
Baltimore, A. L., 1901

FOX, HENRY　　　　　　　Pitcher
Philadelphia, N. L., 1902

FOX, WILLIAM H.　　　　　Infielder
Cincinnati, N. L., 1901

FOXEN, WILLIAM A.　　　　Pitcher
Philadelphia, N. L., 1908–1910, inc.
Chicago, N. L., 1910–1911

FRASER, CHARLES C.　　　　Pitcher
Philadelphia, A. L., 1901
Philadelphia, N. L., 1902–1903–1904
Boston, N. L., 1905
Cincinnati, N. L., 1906
Chicago, N. L., 1907–1908–1909

FREEMAN, ALEXANDER V.　　Pitcher
Chicago, N. L., 1921

FREEMAN, H. B.　　　　　Pitcher
Philadelphia, A. L., 1921

FREEMAN, JEREMIAH　　　　1st B.
Washington, A. L., 1908

FREEMAN, JOHN B.　　　O. F.—1st B.
Boston, A. L., 1901–1906, inc.

FRENCH　　　　　　　　　Infielder
Philadelphia, A. L., 1917

FRENCH, CHARLES　　　　Infielder
Boston, A. L., 1909–1910
Chicago, A. L., 1910

FRENCH, RAYMOND　　　　Infielder
New York, A. L., 1920

FRIBERG, BERNARD ALBERT　Outfielder
Chicago, N. L., 1919–1920

FRIED　　　　　　　　　Pitcher
Detroit, A. L., 1920

FRIEL, WILLIAM E.　　　Inf.—O. F.
Milwaukee, A. L., 1901
St. Louis, A. L., 1902–1903

FRILL, JOHN E.　　　　　Pitcher
New York, A. L., 1910
St. Louis, A. L., 1912
Cincinnati, N. L., 1912

FRISCH, FRANK FRANCIS　2nd B.—3rd B.
New York, N. L., 1919–1920–1921

FRISK, EMIL　　　　　Pitcher—O. F.
Detroit, A. L., 1901
St. Louis, A. L., 1905–1907

FRITZ　　　　　　　　　Pitcher
Philadelphia, A. L., 1907

FRITZ, HARRY K.　　　　Infielder
Philadelphia, A. L., 1913
Chicago, F. L., 1914–1915

FROCK, SAMUEL W.　　　　Pitcher
Boston, N. L., 1907
Pittsburgh, N. L., 1909–1910
Boston, N. L., 1910–1911

FROELICH　　　　　　　Catcher
Philadelphia, N. L., 1909

FROMME, ARTHUR　　　　Pitcher
St. Louis, N. L., 1906–1908, inc.
Cincinnati, N. L., 1909–1913, inc.
New York, N. L., 1913–1915, inc.

FUHR, OSCAR　　　　　Pitcher
Chicago, N. L., 1921

FULLER, CHARLES　　　　Catcher
Brooklyn, N. L., 1902

FULLER, FRANK   Infielder
Detroit, A. L., 1915–1916

FULLERTON, CURTIS H.   Pitcher
Boston, A. L., 1921

FULTZ, DAVID L.   Outfielder
Philadelphia, A. L., 1901–1902
New York, A. L., 1903–1904–1905

GAGNIER, EDWARD   Infielder
Brooklyn, F. L., 1914–1915

GAINES, W. R.   Pitcher
Washington, A. L., 1921

GAINOR, DEL C.   1st B.—O. F.
Detroit, A. L., 1909; 1911–1914, inc.
Boston, A. L., 1914–1919, inc. (excepting
1918)

GAISER, F. J.   Pitcher
St. Louis, N. L., 1908

GALLAGHER   Infielder
Baltimore, F. L., 1915

GALLAGHER   Outfielder
Cleveland, A. L., 1901

GALLIA, MELVIN ALBERT   Pitcher
Washington, A. L., 1912–1917, inc.
St. Louis, A. L., 1918
Washington, A. L., 1919
St. Louis, A. L., 1920
Philadelphia, N. L., 1920

GALLOWAY, CLARENCE EDWARD
                                 Infielder
Philadelphia, A. L., 1919 to date

GALLOWAY, J. C.   Infielder
St. Louis, N. L., 1912

GAMMONS, JOHN H.   Outfielder
Boston, N. L., 1901

GANDIL, CHARLES ARNOLD   1st B.
Chicago, A. L., 1910
Washington, A. L., 1912–1915, inc.
Cleveland, A. L., 1916
Chicago, A. L., 1917–1919, inc.

GANDY, R. B.   Outfielder
Philadelphia, N. L., 1916

GANLEY, ROBERT S.   Outfielder
Pittsburgh, N. L., 1905–1906
Washington, A. L., 1907–1909, inc.
Philadelphia, A. L., 1909

GANNON, WILLIAM   Outfielder
Chicago, N. L., 1901

GANZEL, JOHN   1st B.
New York, N. L., 1901
New York, A. L., 1903–1904
Cincinnati, N. L., 1907–1908

GARDNER, EARL   2nd B.
New York, A. L., 1908–1912, inc.

GARDNER, HARRY   Pitcher
Pittsburgh, N. L., 1911–1912

GARDNER, JAMES A.   Pitcher
Chicago, N. L., 1902

GARDNER, WILLIAM LAWRENCE
                          2nd B.—3rd B.
Boston, A. L., 1909–1917, inc.
Philadelphia, A. L., 1918
Cleveland, A. L., 1919 to date

GARRETT, C. L.   Pitcher
Cleveland, A. L., 1915

GARVIN, VIRGIL   Pitcher
Milwaukee, A. L., 1901
Chicago, A. L., 1902
Brooklyn, N. L., 1902–1904, inc.
New York, A. L., 1904

GASPAR, HARRY L.   Pitcher
Cincinnati, N. L., 1909–1912, inc.

GASTON, ALEXANDER N.   Catcher
New York, N. L., 1920–1921

GATINS, FRANK   Infielder
Brooklyn, N. L., 1901

GAW, GEORGE J.   Pitcher
Chicago, N. L., 1920

GEAR, DALE D.   Pitcher
Washington, A. L., 1901

GEARY, ROBERT   Pitcher
Philadelphia, A. L., 1918–1919
Cincinnati, N. L., 1921

GEDEON, JOSEPH   2nd B.
Washington, A. L., 1913–1914
New York, A. L., 1916–1917
St. Louis, A. L., 1918–1920, inc.

GEHRING, HENRY   Pitcher
Washington, A. L., 1907

GEIER, PHIL   Outfielder
Philadelphia, A. L., 1901
Milwaukee, A. L., 1901
Boston, N. L., 1904

GENINS, FRANK   Outfielder
Cleveland, A. L., 1901

GEORGE, THOMAS E.   Pitcher
St. Louis, A. L., 1911
Cleveland, A. L., 1912
Cincinnati, N. L., 1915
Boston, N. L., 1918

GERBER, WALTER   Infielder
Pittsburgh, N. L., 1914–1915
St. Louis, A. L., 1917–1921, inc.

GERNER, EDWARD F.   Pitcher
Cincinnati, N. L., 1919

GERTENRICH, CHARLES   Outfielder
Pittsburgh, N. L., 1903

GERVAIS, L. E.   Pitcher
Boston, N. L., 1913

GESSLER, HARRY H.   Outfielder
Detroit, A. L., 1903
Brooklyn, N. L., 1903–1906, inc.
Chicago, N. L., 1906
Boston, A. L., 1908–1909
Washington, A. L., 1909–1911, inc.

GETZ, GUSTAVE   Infielder
Boston, N. L., 1909–1910
Brooklyn, N. L., 1914–1916, inc.
Cincinnati, N. L., 1917
Cleveland, A. L., 1918
Pittsburgh, N. L., 1918

GEYER, JACOB B.   Pitcher
St. Louis, N. L., 1910–1913, inc.

GHARITY, EDWARD P.   Catcher—1st B.
Washington, A. L., 1916 to date

GIBSON, FRANK GILBERT   Catcher
Detroit, A. L., 1913
Boston, N. L., 1921

GIBSON, GEORGE   Catcher
Pittsburgh, N. L., 1905–1916, inc.
New York, N. L., 1917–1918

GIBSON, NORWOOD   Pitcher
Boston, A. L., 1903–1906, inc.

GILBERT, J. R.   Outfielder
Pittsburgh, N. L., 1904

GILBERT, LAWRENCE W.   Outfielder
Boston, N. L., 1914–1915

GILBERT, WILLIAM OLIVER
                             2nd B.—S. S.
Milwaukee, A. L., 1901
Baltimore, A. L., 1902
New York, N. L., 1903–1906, inc.
St. Louis, N. L., 1908–1909

GILHAM, GEORGE   Catcher
St. Louis, N. L., 1920–1921

GILHOOLEY, FRANK   Outfielder
St. Louis, N. L., 1911–1912
New York, A. L., 1913–1918, inc.
Boston, A. L., 1919

GILL, EDWARD J.   Pitcher
Washington, A. L., 1919

GILL, WARREN D.   1st B.
Pittsburgh, N. L., 1908

GILLIGAN, JOHN P.   Pitcher
St. Louis, A. L., 1909–1910

GILMORE   Outfielder
Kansas City, F. L., 1914–1915

GIRARD, CHARLES   Pitcher
Philadelphia, N. L., 1910

GLADE, FRED   Pitcher
Chicago, N. L., 1902
St. Louis, A. L., 1904–1907, inc.
New York, A. L., 1908

GLAISER, JOHN BURKE   Pitcher
Detroit, A. L., 1920

GLAVENICH, L. F.   Pitcher
Cleveland, N. L., 1913

GLAZE, RALPH   Pitcher
Boston, A. L., 1906–1908, inc.

GLAZNER, CHARLES F.   Pitcher
Pittsburgh, N. L., 1920–1921

GLEASON, HARRY G.   Substitute
Boston, A. L., 1901–1902
St. Louis, A. L., 1904–1905

GLEASON, JOSEPH   Pitcher
Washington, A. L., 1920

GLEASON, WILLIAM   2nd B.
Detroit, A. L., 1901–1902
Philadelphia, N. L., 1903–1908, inc.

GLEASON, WILLIAM   Infielder
Pittsburgh, N. L., 1916–1917
St. Louis, A. L., 1921

GLEICH, FRANK ELMER   Outfielder
New York, A. L., 1920

GLENDON, MARTIN   Pitcher
Cincinnati, N. L., 1902

GLENN, EDWARD   Infielder
Chicago, N. L., 1902

GLENN, HARRY M.   Catcher
St. Louis, N. L., 1915

GLENN, ROBERT   Pitcher
St. Louis, N. L., 1920

GLOCKSON, NORMAN S.   Catcher
Cincinnati, N. L., 1914

GOCHNAUER, JOHN P.   Infielder
Brooklyn, N. L., 1901
Cleveland, A. L., 1902–1903

GODWIN, JOHN   Infielder
Boston, A. L., 1905–1906

GOLDEN, ROY   Pitcher
St. Louis, N. L., 1910–1911

GONZALES, EUSIBIO   Infielder
Boston, A. L., 1918

GONZALES, MIGUEL A.   Catcher
Boston, N. L., 1912
Cincinnati, N. L., 1914
St. Louis, N. L., 1915–1918, inc.
New York, N. L., 1919–1921, inc.

GOOCH, JOHN B.   Catcher
Pittsburgh, N. L., 1921

GOOCH, L. G.   Outfielder
Cleveland, A. L., 1915
Philadelphia, A. L., 1917

GOOD, EUGENE J.   Outfielder
Boston, N. L., 1906

GOOD, R. N.   Pitcher
Boston, N. L., 1910

GOODE, WILBUR   Pitcher—O. F.
New York, A. L., 1905
Cleveland, A. L., 1908–1909
Boston, N. L., 1910–1911
Chicago, N. L., 1911–1915, inc.
Philadelphia, N. L., 1916
Chicago, A. L., 1918

GOODWIN   Infielder
Kansas City, F. L., 1914–1915

GOODWIN, CLYDE   Pitcher
Washington, A. L., 1906

GOODWIN, MARVIN MARDO   Pitcher
Washington, A. L., 1916
St. Louis, N. L., 1919–1920–1921

GORDONIER, RAYMOND CHARLES
     Pitcher
Brooklyn, N. L., 1921

GOSLIN, LEON   Outfielder
Washington, A. L., 1921

GOSSETT, JOHN   Catcher
New York, A. L., 1913–1914

GOULAIT, THEODORE   Pitcher
New York, N. L., 1912

GOULD, ABNER FRANK   Pitcher
Cleveland, A. L., 1916–1917

GOWDY, HENRY M.   1st B.—Catcher
New York, N. L., 1910–1911
Boston, N. L., to date (excepting 1918
when he was in the service).

GRADY, MICHAEL W.   Catcher—1st B.
Washington, A. L., 1901
St. Louis, N. L., 1904–1905; 1906

GRAFF, FRED   Infielder
St. Louis, A. L., 1913

GRAHAM   Catcher
Boston, A. L., 1906

GRAHAM, A.   Substitute
New York, N. L., 1905

GRAHAM, DAWSON   1st B.
Cincinnati, N. L., 1914

GRAHAM, GEORGE F.   Catcher
Cleveland, A. L., 1902
Boston, N. L., 1908–1911, inc.
Chicago, N. L., 1911
Philadelphia, N. L., 1912

GRAHAM, OSCAR   Pitcher
Washington, A. L., 1907
St. Louis, A. L., 1908–1910, inc.

GRAMINO   Outfielder
Boston, A. L., 1911

GRANEY, JOHN GLADSTONE
                          Pitcher—O. F.
Cleveland, A. L., 1908; 1910 to date

GRANT, EDWARD LESLIE   Infielder
Cleveland, A. L., 1905
Philadelphia, N. L., 1907–1910, inc.
Cincinnati, N. L., 1911–1913, inc.
New York, N. L., 1913–1915, inc.

GRAY, STANLEY   Infielder
Pittsburgh, N. L., 1912

GRAY, WILLIAM   Outfielder
Pittsburgh, N. L., 1903

GRAY, WILLIAM DENTON   Pitcher
Washington, A. L., 1909–1911, inc.

GREEN, DANIEL   Outfielder
Chicago, N. L., 1901
Chicago, A. L., 1902–1905, inc.

GREGG, DAVID   Pitcher
Cleveland, A. L., 1913

GREGG, SYLVEANUS A.   Pitcher
Cleveland, A. L., 1911–1914, inc.
Boston, A. L., 1914–1915–1916
Philadelphia, A. L., 1918

GREGORY, FRANK E.   Pitcher
Cincinnati, N. L., 1912

GREISENBECK, CARLOS T.   Catcher
St. Louis, N. L., 1920

GREMINGER, EDWARD   3rd B.
Boston, N. L., 1902–1903
Detroit, A. L., 1904

GREVELL, WILLIAM   Pitcher
Philadelphia, A. L., 1919

GRIFFIN, FRANCIS A.   1st B.
Philadelphia, A. L., 1917

GRIFFIN, FRANK   Outfielder
New York, N. L., 1920

GRIFFIN, IVY MOORE   1st B.
Philadelphia, A. L., 1919–1920–1921

GRIFFIN, J. L.   Pitcher
Chicago, N. L., 1911
Boston, N. L., 1911–1912

GRIFFIN, PATRICK   Pitcher
Cincinnati, N. L., 1914

GRIFFITH, CLARK CALVIN   Pitcher
Chicago, A. L.,1901–1902
New York, A. L., 1903–1906, inc.
Cincinnati, N. L., 1909–1910
Washington, A. L., 1912

GRIFFITH, THOMAS HERMAN   Outfielder
Boston, N. L., 1913–1914
Cincinnati, N. L., 1915–1918, inc.
Brooklyn, N. L., 1919 to date

GRIGGS, ARTHUR   1st B.—O. F.
St. Louis, A. L., 1909–1910
Cleveland, A. L., 1911–1912
Brooklyn, F. L., 1914–1915
Detroit, A. L., 1918

GRIMES, BURLEIGH A.   Pitcher
Pittsburgh, N. L., 1916–1917
Brooklyn, N. L., 1918 to date

GRIMES, OSCAR RAY   1st B.
Boston, A. L., 1920
Chicago, N. L., 1921

GRIMES, ROY   Infielder
New York, N. L., 1920

GRIMM, CHARLES JOHN   1st B.
Philadelphia, A. L., 1916
St. Louis, N. L., 1918
Pittsburgh, N. L., 1919 to date

GRIMSHAW, MYRON   1st B.
Boston, A. L., 1905–1907, inc.

GRINER, DANIEL D.   Pitcher
St. Louis, N. L., 1912–1916, inc.
Brooklyn, N. L., 1918

GROH, HENRY KNIGHT   Infielder
New York, N. L., 1912–1913
Cincinnati, N. L., 1913–1921, inc.

GROOM, ROBERT B.   Pitcher
Washington, A. L., 1909–1913, inc.
St. Louis, F. L., 1914–1915
St. Louis, A. L., 1916–1917
Cleveland, A. L., 1918

GROSART, GEORGE   Infielder
Boston, N. L., 1901

GROTHE, EDWARD J.   Pitcher
Chicago, N. L., 1904

GROVER   Pitcher
Detroit, A. L., 1913

GROVER, ROY ARTHUR   Infielder
Philadelphia, A. L., 1916–1917–1919
Washington, A. L., 1919

GRUBBS, THOMAS   Pitcher
New York, N. L., 1920

GUESE, THEODORE   Pitcher
Cincinnati, N. L., 1901

GUISTO, LOUIS J.   1st B.
Cleveland, A. L., 1916–1921

GUNKEL, WILLIAM W.   Pitcher
Cleveland, A. L., 1916

GUNNING   Outfielder
Boston, A. L., 1911

HAAS, BRUNO PHILIP   Pitcher
Philadelphia, A. L., 1915

HABERER, EMIL   Catcher
Cincinnati, N. L., 1903; 1909

HACKETT, JAMES   Pitcher
St. Louis, N. L., 1902–1903

HAEFFNER, WILLIAM B.   Catcher
Pittsburgh, N. L., 1920

HAFFORD, L.   Pitcher
Cincinnati, N. L., 1906

HAGEMAN, K. R. M.   Pitcher
Boston, A. L., 1911–1912
Chicago, N. L.,1914
St. Louis, N. L., 1914

HAGERMAN, ZERAH ZEQUIEL   Pitcher
Chicago, N. L., 1909
Cleveland, A. L., 1914–1916, inc.

HAHN, EDGAR   Outfielder
New York, A. L., 1905–1906
Chicago, A. L., 1906–1910, inc.

HAHN, FRANK   Pitcher
Cincinnati, N. L., 1901–1905, inc.
New York, A. L., 1906

HAID, HAROLD   Pitcher
St. Louis, A. L., 1919

HAINES, JESSE J.   Pitcher
Cincinnati, N. L., 1918
St. Louis, N. L., 1920–1921

HAISLIP, J. C.   Pitcher
Philadelphia, N. L., 1913

HALE, GEORGE   Catcher
St. Louis, A. L., 1914; 1916–1918, inc.

HALE, ROY   Pitcher
Baltimore, A. L., 1902
Boston, N. L., 1902

HALE, SAMUEL DOUGHLAS   Infielder
Detroit, A. L., 1920–1921

HALEY, PATRICK RAYMOND   Catcher
Boston, A. L., 1915–1916
Philadelphia, A. L., 1916–1917

HALL   Pitcher
St. Louis, A. L., 1910

HALL, CHARLES   Pitcher
Cincinnati, N. L., 1906–1907
Boston, A. L., 1909–1913, inc.
St. Louis, N. L., 1916
Detroit, A. L., 1918

HALL, HERBERT — Pitcher
Philadelphia, N. L., 1911
Detroit, A. L., 1918

HALL, MARK — Pitcher
Detroit, A. L., 1913–1914

HALL, ROBERT — Substitute
Philadelphia, N. L., 1904
New York, N. L., 1905
Brooklyn, N. L., 1905

HALL, RUSSELL P. — S. S.
Cleveland, A. L., 1901

HALL, W. B. — Pitcher
Brooklyn, N. L., 1913

HALLA, JOHN — Pitcher
Cleveland, A. L., 1905

HALLIDAY, NEWTON — Infielder
Pittsburgh, N. L., 1916

HALLINAN — Substitute
St. Louis, A. L., 1911–1912

HALLMAN, WILLIAM JR. — Outfielder
Milwaukee, A. L., 1901
Chicago, A. L., 1903
Pittsburgh, N. L., 1906–1907

HALLMAN, WILLIAM W. — Infielder
Cleveland, A. L., 1901
Philadelphia, N. L., 1901–1903, inc.

HALT, ALVA WILLIAM — Substitute
Brooklyn, F. L., 1914–1915
Cleveland, A. L., 1918

HAMILTON, EARL — Pitcher
St. Louis, A. L., 1911–1916, inc.
Detroit, A. L., 1916
St. Louis, A. L., 1916–1917
Pittsburgh, N. L., 1918 to date

HAMILTON, WM. R. — Outfielder
Boston, N. L., 1901

HAMMOND, WALTER CHARLES — 2nd B.
Cleveland, A. L., 1915

HANDIBOE — Outfielder
New York, A. L., 1911

HANFORD, CHARLES — Outfielder
Buffalo, F. L., 1914
Chicago, F. L., 1915

HANLEY, J. P. — Pitcher
New York, A. L., 1913

HANLON, WILLIAM — 1st B.
Chicago, N. L., 1903

HANNAH, JOHN HARRY — Catcher
New York, A. L., 1918–1919–1920

HANNIFAN, JOHN — Substitute
Philadelphia, A. L., 1906
New York, N. L., 1906–1908, inc.
Boston, N. L., 1908

HANSON, EARL S. — Pitcher
Chicago, N. L., 1921

HANSON, ROY — Pitcher
Washington, A. L., 1918

HARDY — Catcher
Washington, A. L., 1908–1909

HARDY, HARRY — Pitcher
Washington, A. L., 1905–1906

HARDY, THOMAS — Pitcher
Chicago, N. L., 1902

HARGRAVE, EUGENE FRANKLIN — Catcher
Chicago, N. L., 1913–1914–1915
Cincinnati, N. L., 1921

HARGROVE, W. — Infielder
Chicago, A. L., 1918

HARKNESS — Pitcher
Cleveland, N. L., 1910–1911

HARLEY, RICHARD — Outfielder
Cincinnati, N. L., 1901
Detroit, A. L., 1902
Chicago, N. L., 1903

HARLEY, RICHARD — Pitcher
Boston, N. L., 1905

HARMON, ROBERT GREEN — Pitcher
St. Louis, N. L., 1909–1913, inc.
Pittsburgh, N. L., 1914–1915; 1918

HARPER — Pitcher
St. Louis, A. L., 1911

HARPER, CHARLES W.   Pitcher
St. Louis, N. L., 1901
St. Louis, A. L., 1902
Cincinnati, N. L., 1903–1906, inc.
Chicago, N. L., 1906

HARPER, HARRY C.   Pitcher
Washington, A. L., 1913–1919, inc.
Boston, A. L., 1920
New York, A. L., 1921

HARPER, JOHN W.   Pitcher
Philadelphia, A. L., 1915

HARRELL   Pitcher
Philadelphia, A. L., 1912

HARRINGTON, FRANCIS   Pitcher
Cincinnati, N. L., 1913

HARRIS   Pitcher
Kansas City, F. L., 1914

HARRIS, JOSEPH   Pitcher
Boston, A. L., 1905–1907, inc.

HARRIS, JOSEPH   1st B.—O. F.
New York, A. L., 1914
Cleveland, A. L., 1917–1919

HARRIS, STANLEY RAYMOND   2nd B.
Washington, A. L., 1919–1920–1921

HARRIS, WILLIAM BRYAN   Pitcher
Philadelphia, A. L., 1920–1921

HARSTAD, OSCAR THEANDER   Pitcher
Cleveland, A. L., 1915

HART, JAMES H.   Catcher
Chicago, A. L., 1905–1907, inc.

HART, WARREN F.   1st B.
Baltimore, A. L., 1901

HART, WILLIAM F.   Pitcher
Cleveland, A. L., 1901

HARTER, F.   Pitcher
Cincinnati, N. L., 1912–1913

HARTFORD, BRUCE   Infielder
Cleveland, A. L., 1914

HARTLEY, GROVER CLEVELAND   Catcher
New York, N. L., 1911–1913, inc.

St. Louis, F. L., 1914–1915
St. Louis, A. L., 1916–1917

HARTMAN, FRED   Infielder
Chicago, A. L., 1901
St. Louis, N. L., 1902–1903

HARTRANFT, R. J.   Pitcher
Philadelphia, N. L., 1913

HARTSEL, T. F.   Outfielder
Chicago, N. L., 1901
Philadelphia, A. L., 1902–1911, inc.

HARTY   Catcher
Chicago, N. L., 1907

HARTZELL, ROY A.   Inf.—O. F.
St. Louis, A. L., 1906–1910, inc.
New York, A. L., 1911–1916, inc.

HARVEY, ERWIN K.   P.—O. F.
Chicago, A. L., 1901
Cleveland, A. L., 1901–1902

HASBROUCK, R. L.   Infielder
Chicago, A. L., 1916–1917

HASSELBACHER   Pitcher
Philadelphia, A. L., 1916

HASTY, ROBERT KELLER   Pitcher
Philadelphia, A. L., 1919–1920–1921

HAUSER, ARNOLD J.   S. S.
St. Louis, N. L., 1910–1913, inc.
Chicago, F. L., 1915

HAWK   Pitcher
St. Louis, A. L., 1911

HAWKS, NELSON LOUIS   Outfielder
New York, A. L., 1921

HAWLEY, EMERSON P.   Pitcher
Milwaukee, A. L., 1901

HAWORTH, HOMER   Catcher
Cleveland, A. L., 1915

HAYDEN, JOHN F.   Outfielder
Philadelphia, A. L., 1901
Boston, A. L., 1906
Chicago, N. L., 1908

HAZLETON, WILLARD C.   1st B.
St. Louis, N. L., 1902

HEALEY, T. F.   Infielder
Philadelphia, A. L., 1915–1916

HEARN   Infielder
Boston, A. L., 1910

HEARN, BUNN   Pitcher
St. Louis, N. L., 1910–1911
New York, N. L., 1913
Pittsburgh, F. L., 1915
Boston, N. L., 1918–1920

HEATH, SPENCER PAUL, JR.   Pitcher
Chicago, A. L., 1920

HEATHCOTE, CLIFTON EARL   Outfielder
St. Louis, N. L., 1918 to date

HECKINGER, MICHAEL VINCENT
                                 Catcher
Chicago, N. L., 1912–1913
Brooklyn, N. L., 1913

HEHL, HERRMAN   Pitcher
Brooklyn, N. L., 1918

HEIDRICK, J. EMMETT   Outfielder
St. Louis, N. L., 1901
St. Louis, A. L., 1902–1903–1904

HEILMAN, HARRY A.   Pitcher
Brooklyn, N. L., 1918

HEILMANN, HAROLD E.   1st B.—O. F.
Detroit, A. L., 1914; 1916 to date

HEIMACH, FRED   Pitcher
Philadelphia, A. L., 1920–1921

HEINE, WILLIAM H.   Substitute
New York, N. L., 1921

HEISMAN, CHRISTOPHER   Pitcher
Cincinnati, N. L., 1901–1902
Baltimore, A. L., 1902

HEITLING   Infielder
Detroit, A. L., 1906

HEITMULLER, H.   Outfielder
Philadelphia, A. L., 1909–1910

HELFRICH   Infielder
Brooklyn, F. L., 1915

HEMINGWAY, EDSON M.   Substitute
St. Louis, A. L., 1914

New York, N. L., 1917
Philadelphia, N. L., 1918

HEMPHILL, CHARLES J.   Outfielder
Boston, A. L., 1901
Cleveland, A. L., 1902
St. Louis, A. L., 1903–1904–1906–1907
New York, A. L., 1908–1911, inc.

HEMPHILL, FRANK   Outfielder
Chicago, A. L., 1906

HENDERSON, C. D.   Pitcher
Cleveland, A. L., 1921

HENDRICKS, ED.   Pitcher
New York, N. L., 1910

HENDRICKS, JOHN C.   Outfielder
New York, N. L., 1902
Chicago, N. L., 1902
Washington, A. L., 1903

HENDRIX, CLAUDE RAY   Pitcher
Pittsburgh, N. L., 1911–1913, inc.
Chicago, F. L., 1914–1915
Chicago, N. L., 1916–1920, inc.

HENDRYX, TIMOTHY G.   Outfielder
Cleveland, A. L., 1911–1912
New York, A. L., 1915–1917, inc.
St. Louis, A. L., 1918
Boston, A. L., 1920–1921

HENION, LAYAYETTE   Pitcher
Brooklyn, N. L., 1919

HENLEY, WELDON   Pitcher
Philadelphia, A. L., 1903–1905, inc.
Brooklyn, N. L., 1907

HENLINE, WALTER J.   Catcher
New York–Philadelphia, N. L., 1921

HENNESSY, L. B.   Infielder
Detroit, A. L., 1913

HENNING   Pitcher
Kansas City, F. L., 1914–1915

HENRICKSEN, OLAF   Outfielder
Boston, A. L., 1911–1917, inc.

HENRY, FRANK JOHN   Pitcher
St. Louis, A. L., 1921

HENRY, JOHN P.   Catcher
Washington, A. L., 1910–1917, inc.
Boston, N. L., 1918

HERBERT, E.   Pitcher
Cincinnati, N. L., 1913

HERBERT, FRED   Pitcher
New York, N. L., 1915

HERMANN   Pitcher
Brooklyn, N. L., 1918

HERRELL   Pitcher
Washington, A. L., 1911

HERRING   Infielder
Washington, A. L., 1912

HERZOG, CHARLES LINCOLN   Infielder
New York, N. L., 1908–1909
Boston, N. L., 1910–1911
New York, N. L., 1911–1913, inc.
Cincinnati, N. L., 1914–1915–1916
New York, N. L., 1916–1917
Boston, N. L., 1918–1919
Chicago, N. L., 1919–1920

HESS, OTTO   Pitcher
Cleveland, A. L., 1902; 1904–1907, inc.
Boston, N. L., 1912–1915, inc.

HESTERFER, LAWRENCE   Pitcher
New York, N. L., 1901

HEVIN, JOHN A.   Catcher
St. Louis, A. L., 1920

HEYDON, MICHAEL   Catcher
Chicago, A. L., 1904
Washington, A. L., 1905–1907

HICKEY   Pitcher
Cleveland, A. L., 1904

HICKEY, ED   Infielder
Chicago, N. L., 1901

HICKMAN, CHARLES   Inf.–O. F.
New York, N. L., 1901
Boston, A. L., 1902
Cleveland, A. L., 1902–1903
Detroit, A. L., 1904–1905
Washington, Λ. L., 1905–1907, inc.

Chicago, A. L., 1907
Cleveland, A. L., 1908

HICKMAN, DAVID JAMES   Outfielder
Baltimore, F. L., 1915
Brooklyn, N. L., 1916–1919, inc.

HIGGINBOTHAM, J. C.   Pitcher
St. Louis, N. L., 1906;1908–1909
Chicago, N. L., 1909

HIGGINS, FESTUS E.   Pitcher
St. Louis, N. L., 1909–1910

HIGGINS, ROBERT S.   Catcher
Cleveland, A. L., 1909
Brooklyn, N. L., 1911–1912

HIGH   Pitcher
Detroit, A. L., 1901

HIGH, CHARLES EDWIN   Outfielder
Philadelphia, A. L., 1919–1920

HIGH, HUGH   Outfielder
Detroit, A. L., 1913–1914
New York, A. L., 1915–1918, inc.

HILDEBRAND   Outfielder
Chicago, N. L., 1902

HILDEBRAND, GEORGE   Outfielder
Brooklyn, N. L., 1902

HILDEBRAND, HOMER   Pitcher
Pittsburgh, N. L., 1905–1906–1907

HILDEBRAND, P. M.   Catcher
St. Louis, N. L., 1913

HILL, C. T.   Pitcher
Philadelphia, A. L., 1917

HILL, CARMEN PROCTOR   Pitcher
Pittsburgh, N. L., 1915–1916; 1918–1919

HILL, H. J.   Outfielder
Cleveland, A. L., 1915

HILL, HUGH   Outfielder
Cleveland, A. L., 1903
St. Louis, N. L., 1904

HILL, HUNTER B.   Infielder
St. Louis, A. L., 1903–1904
Washington, A. L., 1904–1905

HILLER, HARVEY H.   Infielder
Boston, Λ. L., 1920–1921

HILLY, W. E.   Outfielder
Philadelphia, N. L., 1914

HIMES   Pitcher
St. Louis, N. L., 1903

HIMES, JOHN   Outfielder
St. Louis, N. L., 1905–1906

HINCHAM, WM. WHITE   Inf.—O. F.
Cincinnati, N. L., 1905–1906
Cleveland, A. L., 1907–1909, inc.
Pittsburgh, N. L., 1915–1918, inc.; 1920

HINCHMAN, HARRY   Infielder
Cleveland, A. L., 1907

HINRICHS   Pitcher
Washington, A. L., 1910

HINTON, JAMES   Infielder
Boston, N. L., 1901

HITT, BRUCE   Pitcher
St. Louis, N. L., 1917

HITT, ROY   Pitcher
Cincinnati, N. L., 1907

HOBBS, LEE   Substitute
Cincinnati, N. L., 1913; 1916

HOBLITZEL, RICHARD CARLETON   1st B.
Cincinnati, N. L., 1908–1914, inc.
Boston, A. L., 1914–1918, inc.

HOCH, HARRY K.   Pitcher
Philadelphia, N. L., 1908
St. Louis, A. L., 1914–1915

HOCK, EDWARD   Substitute
St. Louis, N. L., 1920

HODGE, CLARENCE C.   Pitcher
Chicago, A. L., 1920–1921

HOELSKOETTER, ARTHUR
                    Pitcher—Catcher—Sub.
St. Louis, N. L., 1905–1908, inc.
(Played under name of Hostetter in
1907–1908).

HOEY, JOHN   Outfielder
Boston, A. L., 1906–1908, inc.

HOFF, CHESTER   Pitcher
New York, A. L., 1911–1913, inc.
St. Louis, A. L., 1915

HOFFER, WILLIAM L.   Pitcher
Cleveland, A. L., 1901

HOFFMAN, DANIEL   Outfielder
Philadelphia, A. L., 1903–1906, inc.
New York, A. L., 1906–1907
St. Louis, A. L., 1908–1911, inc.

HOFFMAN, E.   Outfielder
Cleveland, A. L., 1915

HOFFMAN, ISAAC   Outfielder
Washington, A. L., 1904
Boston, N. L., 1907

HOFFMANN, FRED C.   Catcher
New York, A. L., 1920–1921

HOFMAN, ARTHUR F.   Inf.—O. F.
Pittsburgh, N. L., 1903
Chicago, N. L., 1904–1912, inc.
Pittsburgh, N. L., 1912–1913
Brooklyn, F. L., 1914
Buffalo, F. L., 1915
New York, A. L., 1916
Chicago, N. L., 1916

HOGAN   Outfielder
Cleveland, A. L., 1901

HOGAN   Outfielder
Philadelphia, A. L., 1911
St. Louis, A. L., 1911–1912

HOGAN, KENNETH T.   Substitute
Cincinnati, N. L., 1921

HOGG, C. BRADLEY   Pitcher
Boston, N. L., 1911–1912
Chicago, N. L., 1915
Philadelphia, N. L., 1918–1919

HOGG, WILLIAM   Pitcher
New York, A. L., 1905–1908, inc.

HOGRIEVER, GEORGE   Outfielder
Milwaukee, A. L., 1901

HOHNHURST, ED H.   1st B.
Cleveland, A. L., 1910; 1912

HOLDEN, WILLIAM P.   Outfielder
New York, A. L., 1913–1914
Cincinnati, N. L., 1914

HOLKE, WALTER L.   1st B.
New York, N. L., 1914; 1916–1917–1918
Boston, N. L., 1919 to date

HOLLAHAN, WILLIAM CHARLES   Infielder
Washington, A. L., 1920

HOLLING, CARL   Pitcher
Detroit, A. L., 1921

HOLLOCHER, CHARLES   S. S.
Chicago, N. L., 1918 to date

HOLLY, EDWARD   Infielder
St. Louis, N. L., 1906–1907
Pittsburgh, F. L., 1914–1915

HOLMES   Pitcher
Philadelphia, A. L., 1906

HOLMES, E. M.   Pitcher
Philadelphia, A. L., 1918

HOLMES, H.   Catcher
St. Louis, N. L., 1906

HOLMES, J. S.   Pitcher
Brooklyn, N. L., 1908

HOLMES, ROBERT   Catcher
Chicago, N. L., 1904

HOLMES, WILLIAM J.   Outfielder
Detroit, A. L., 1901–1902
Washington, A. L., 1903
Chicago, A. L., 1903–1905, inc.

HOOD, WALLACE   Outfielder
Brooklyn, N. L., 1920
Pittsburgh, N. L., 1920
Brooklyn, N. L., 1921

HOOKER, WM. H.   Pitcher
Cincinnati, N. L., 1902–1903

HOOPER, HARRY B.   Outfielder
Boston, A. L., 1909–1920, inc.
Chicago, A. L., 1921

HOPKINS   Catcher
Pittsburgh, N. L., 1902

HOPKINS, J. W.   Outfielder
St. Louis, N. L., 1907

HOPPER, W. BOOTH   Pitcher
St. Louis, N. L., 1913–1914
Washington, A. L., 1915

HORNSBY, ROGERS   Infielder
St. Louis, N. L. 1915 to date

HORSEY, H.   Pitcher
Cincinnati, N. L., 1912

HORSTMAN, OSCAR   Pitcher
St. Louis, N. L., 1917–1919, inc.

HOUCK, BYRON W.   Pitcher
Philadelphia, A. L., 1912–1913–1914
St. Louis, A. L., 1918

HOUSE   Pitcher
Detroit, A. L., 1913

HOUSEHOLDER   Outfielder
Brooklyn, N. L., 1903

HOUSER, BEN F.   1st B.
Philadelphia, A. L., 1910
Boston, N. L., 1911–1912

HOVLIK, EDWARD   Pitcher
Washington, A. L., 1918–1919

HOVLIK, JOSEPH   Pitcher
Washington, A. L., 1910
Chicago, A. L., 1911

HOWARD   Outfielder
Boston, A. L., 1909

HOWARD   Substitute
Brooklyn, F. L., 1915

HOWARD, EARL   Pitcher
St. Louis, N. L., 1918

HOWARD, GEORGE E.   Substitute
Pittsburgh, N. L., 1905
Boston, N. L., 1906–1907
Chicago, N. L., 1907–1909, inc.

HOWARD, IVAN CHESTER   Substitute
St. Louis, A. L., 1914–1915
Cleveland, A. L., 1916–1917

HOWELL, HARRY   Pitcher—Inf.
Baltimore, A. L., 1901–1902

New York, A. L., 1903
St. Louis, A. L., 1904–1910, inc.

HOWELL, ROLAND B.   Pitcher
St. Louis, N. L., 1912

HOWLEY, DANIEL PHILIP   Catcher
Philadelphia, N. L., 1913

HOY, WILLIAM E.   Outfielder
Chicago, A. L., 1901
Cincinnati, N. L., 1902

HOYT, WAITE CHARLES   Pitcher
New York, N. L., 1918
Boston, A. L., 1919–1920
New York, A. L., 1921

HUBBELL, WILBUR WILLIAM   Pitcher
New York, N. L., 1919–1920
Philadelphia, N. L., 1920–1921

HUBER, C. B.   Infielder
Detroit, A. L., 1920–1921

HUELSMAN, FRANK   Outfielder
Washington, A. L., 1904
Chicago, A. L., 1904
St. Louis, A. L., 1904
Detroit, A. L., 1904

HUENKE, A., JR.   Pitcher
New York, N. L., 1914

HUGG, JOE   Catcher
Brooklyn, N. L., 1903

HUGGINS, MILLER JAMES   2nd B.
Cincinnati, N. L., 1904–1909, inc.
St. Louis, N. L., 1910–1916, inc.

HUGHES   Pitcher
Boston, A. L., 1905–1906

HUGHES, E.   Outfielder
Chicago, N. L., 1902

HUGHES, EDWARD   Catcher
Chicago, A. L., 1902

HUGHES, JAMES   Pitcher
Brooklyn, N. L., 1901–1902

HUGHES, THOMAS   Pitcher
New York, A. L., 1904; 1907; 1909–1910
Boston, N. L., 1914–1918, inc.

HUGHES, THOMAS J.   Pitcher
Chicago, N. L., 1901
Baltimore, A. L., 1902
Boston, A. L., 1902–1903
New York, A. L., 1904
Washington, A. L., 1904–1913, inc., (excepting 1910).

HUGHES, WILLIAM N.   Pitcher
Pittsburgh, N. L., 1921

HUHN, EMIL   Catcher—1st B.
Newark, F. L., 1915
Cincinnati, N. L., 1916–1917

HULSWITT, RUDOLPH E.   Shortstop
Philadelphia, N. L., 1902–1904, inc.
Cincinnati, N. L., 1916–1917
St. Louis, N. L., 1909–1910

HUMMEL, JOHN EDWIN   Inf.—O. F.
Brooklyn, N. L., 1905–1915, inc.
New York, A. L., 1918

HUMPHREY, A.   Outfielder
Brooklyn, N. L., 1911

HUMPHRIES, ALBERT   Pitcher
Philadelphia, N. L., 1910–1911
Cincinnati, N. L., 1911–1912
Chicago, N. L., 1913–1914–1915

HUNT, BENJAMIN F.   Pitcher
Boston, A. L., 1910
St. Louis, N. L., 1913

HUNTER   Outfielder
Cleveland, A. L., 1912

HUNTER   Substitute
Boston, A. L., 1920

HUNTER, FRED C.   1st B.
Pittsburgh, N. L., 1911

HUNTER, GEORGE H.   Pitcher—O. F.
Brooklyn, N. L., 1909–1910

HUNTER, HERBERT H.   Inf.—O. F.
New York, N. L., 1916
Chicago, N. L., 1916–1917
St. Louis, N. L., 1921

HURLEY, JERRY   Catcher
Cincinnati, N. L., 1901
Brooklyn, N. L., 1907

HUSTING, BERTHOLD J.   Pitcher
Milwaukee, A. L., 1901
Boston, A. L., 1902
Philadelphia, A. L., 1902

HUSTON, H.   Catcher
Philadelphia, N. L., 1906

HYATT, HAMILTON   Substitute
Pittsburgh, N. L., 1909–1910; 1912–1914, inc.
St. Louis, N. L., 1915
New York, A. L., 1918

HYNES   Pitcher
St. Louis, A. L., 1904

IBERG, HAMMOND E.   Pitcher
Philadelphia, N. L., 1902

IMLAY, HARRY M.   Pitcher
Philadelphia, N. L., 1913

INGERSOLL, R. R.   Pitcher
Cincinnati, N. L., 1914

INGERTON, WILLIAM JOHN   3rd B.
Boston, N. L, 1911

IRELAN, HAROLD   Infielder
Philadelphia, N. L., 1914

IRWIN   Infielder
Detroit, A. L., 1912

IRWIN, CHARLES   3rd B.
Cincinnati, N. L., 1901
Brooklyn, N. L., 1901–1902

IRWIN, WALTER K.   Substitute
St. Louis, N. L., 1921

ISBELL, FRANK   1st B.—2nd B.
Chicago, A. L., 1901–1909, inc.

JACKLITSCH, FRED   Catcher
Philadelphia, N. L., 1901–1902
Brooklyn, N. L., 1903–1904
New York, A. L., 1905
Philadelphia, N. L., 1907–1910, inc.
Baltimore, F. L., 1914–1915
Boston, N. L., 1917

JACKSON   Pitcher
Detroit, A. L., 1905

JACKSON, C.   Outfielder
Chicago, A. L., 1915

JACKSON, CHARLES HERBERT   Outfielder
Pittsburgh, N. L., 1917

JACKSON, GEORGE C.   Outfielder
Boston, N. L., 1911–1913, inc.

JACKSON, JAMES   Outfielder
Baltimore, A. L., 1901
New York, N. L., 1902
Cleveland, A. L., 1905–1906

JACKSON, JOSEPH JEFFERSON   Outfielder
Philadelphia, A. L., 1908–1909
Cleveland, A. L., 1910–1915, inc.
Chicago, A. L., 1915–1920, inc.

JACKSON, R.   1st B.
Chicago, F. L., 1914–1915

JACOBS   Catcher
Chicago, A. L., 1918

JACOBS, MICHAEL   Infielder
Chicago, N. L., 1902

JACOBS, WILLIAM ELMER   Pitcher
Philadelphia, N. L., 1914
Pittsburgh, N. L., 1916–1918, inc.
Philadelphia, N. L., 1918–1919
St. Louis, N. L., 1919–1920

JACOBSON, A.   Pitcher
Washington, A. L., 1904–1905
St. Louis, A. L., 1906–1907

JACOBSON, MERWIN   Outfielder
New York, N. L., 1915
Chicago, N. L., 1916

JACOBSON, WILLIAM C.   Outfielder
Detroit, A. L., 1915
St. Louis, A. L., 1915–1921, inc., (excepting 1916 and 1918).

JACOBUS, STUART   Pitcher
Cincinnati, N. L., 1918

JAEGER   Pitcher
Detroit, A. L., 1904

JAEGER, JOSEPH   Pitcher
  Chicago, N. L., 1920

JAMES   Outfielder
  St. Louis, N. L., 1909

JAMES, WILLIAM HENRY   Pitcher
  Cleveland, A. L., 1911–1912
  St. Louis, A. L., 1914–1915
  Detroit, A. L., 1915–1919, inc.
  Boston, A. L., 1919
  Chicago, A. L., 1919

JAMES, WILLIAM LAWRENCE   Pitcher
  Boston, N. L., 1913–1914–1915; 1919

JAMES, WILLIAM (LEFTY)   Pitcher
  Cleveland, A. L., 1912–1914, inc.

JAMIESON, CHARLES D.   Pitcher—O. F.
  Washington, A. L., 1915–1917, inc.
  Philadelphia, A. L., 1918–1919
  Cleveland, A. L., 1919–1921, inc.

JANTZEN   Infielder
  St. Louis, A. L., 1910–1912

JANVRIN, HAROLD C.   Infielder
  Boston, A. L., 1911; 1913–1917, inc.
  Washington, A. L., 1919
  St. Louis, N. L., 1919–1920–1921
  Brooklyn, N. L., 1921

JASPER, H. W.   Pitcher
  Chicago, A. L., 1914–1915
  St. Louis, N. L., 1916
  Cleveland, N. L., 1919

JEANES, ERNEST   Outfielder
  Cleveland, A. L., 1921

JENKINS, JOSEPH   Catcher
  Chicago, A. L., 1917

JENNINGS, HUGH AMBROSE   1st B.
  Philadelphia, N. L., 1901–1902
  Detroit, A. L., 1907; 1909; 1912

JENSEN   Pitcher
  Detroit, A. L., 1912
  Philadelphia, A. L., 1914

JOHNS, OLIVER   Pitcher
  Cincinnati, N. L., 1905

JOHNS, WILLIAM PETER   Infielder
  Chicago, A. L., 1915
  St. Louis, A. L., 1918

JOHNSON   Substitute
  Boston, N. L., 1918

JOHNSON, ADAM RANKIN   Pitcher
  Boston, A. L., 1914
  Chicago, F. L., 1914
  Baltimore, F. L., 1915
  St. Louis, N. L., 1918

JOHNSON, CHARLES   Outfielder
  Philadelphia, N. L., 1908

JOHNSON, E. R.   Pitcher
  Chicago, A. L., 1915

JOHNSON, EDWIN   Outfielder
  Washington, A. L., 1920

JOHNSON, ELLIS W.   Pitcher
  Chicago, A. L., 1915
  Philadelphia, A. L., 1917

JOHNSON, ELMER   Catcher
  New York, N. L., 1914

JOHNSON, ERNEST R.   Infielder
  Chicago, A. L., 1912
  St. Louis, F. L., 1915
  St. Louis, A. L., 1916–1918, inc.
  Chicago, A. L. 1921

JOHNSON, GEORGE H.   Pitcher
  Cincinnati, N. L., 1913–1914
  Kansas City, F. L., 1914–1915
  Chicago, A. L., 1915

JOHNSON, OTIS   Infielder
  New York, A. L., 1911

JOHNSON, PAUL OSCAR   Outfielder
  Philadelphia, A. L., 1920–1921

JOHNSON, RUSSELL CONWELL   Pitcher
  Philadelphia, A. L., 1916–1917

JOHNSON, W.   Outfielder
  Philadelphia, A. L., 1916–1917

JOHNSON, WALTER PERRY   Pitcher
  Washington, A. L., 1907 to date

JOHNSTON, J. T.   Outfielder
  St. Louis, A. L., 1913

JOHNSTON, JAMES HARL   Inf.—O. F.
Chicago, A. L., 1911
Chicago, N. L., 1914
Brooklyn, N. L., 1916 to date

JOHNSTON, WHEELER ROGERS   1st B.
Cincinnati, N. L., 1909
Cleveland, A. L., 1912–1913–1914
Pittsburgh, N. L., 1915–1916
Cleveland, A. L., 1918–1919–1920–1921

JONES   Pitcher
Detroit, A. L., 1903

JONES, BERT   Pitcher
St. Louis, N. L., 1901

JONES, CARROLL   Pitcher
Detroit, A. L, 1916–1918, inc.

JONES, CHARLES C.   Outfielder
Boston, A. L., 1901
Washington, A. L., 1905–1906–1907
St. Louis, A. L., 1908

JONES, DAVID JEFFERSON   Outfielder
St. Louis, A. L., 1902
Chicago, N. L., 1902–1904, inc.
Detroit, A. L., 1906–1912, inc.
Chicago, A. L., 1913
Pittsburgh, F. L., 1914
Detroit, A. L., 1918

JONES, ELIJAH   Pitcher
Detroit, A. L., 1901–1908, inc.

JONES, FIELDER ALLISON   Outfielder
Chicago, A. L., 1901–1908, inc.

JONES, HOWARD   Outfielder
St. Louis, N. L., 1921

JONES, JAMES   Outfielder
New York, N. L., 1901–1902

JONES, JOHN PAUL   Pitcher
New York, N. L., 1919
Boston, N. L., 1920

JONES, OSCAR   Pitcher
Brooklyn, N. L., 1903–1904–1905

JONES, PERCY L.   Pitcher
Chicago, N. L., 1920–1921

JONES, ROBERT W.   Infielder
Detroit, A. L., 1917 to date

JONES, SAMUEL POND   Pitcher
Cleveland, A. L., 1914–1915
Boston, A. L., 1916–1921, inc.

JONES, TEX   1st B.
Chicago, A. L., 1911

JONES, THOMAS   1st B.
Baltimore, A. L., 1902
St. Louis, A. L., 1904–1909, inc.
Detroit, A. L., 1909–1910

JONES, WILLIAM D.   Outfielder
Boston, N. L., 1911–1912

JONNARD, CLARENCE JAMES   Catcher
Chicago, A. L., 1920

JONNARD, CLAUDE   Pitcher
New York, N. L., 1921

JORDAN   Pitcher
Chicago, A. L., 1912

JORDAN, OTTO   Infielder
Brooklyn, N. L., 1903–1904

JORDAN, RAY   Pitcher
Washington, A. L., 1919

JORDAN, TIMOTHY JOSEPH
Outfielder—1st B.
Baltimore, A. L., 1901–1902
Brooklyn, N. L., 1906–1910, inc.

JOSS, ADRIAN C.   Pitcher
Cleveland, A. L., 1902–1910, inc.

JOURDAN, T. C.   Infielder
Chicago, A. L., 1916–1918, inc.; 1920

JOYCE   Infielder
Detroit, A. L., 1913

JUDE, FRANK   Outfielder
Cincinnati, N. L., 1906

JUDGE, JOSEPH IGNATIUS   1st B.
Washington, A. L., 1915 to date

JUSTIS   Pitcher
Detroit, A. L., 1905

JUUL, HERBERT V.   Pitcher
Cincinnati, N. L., 1911

KADING, J.   Infielder
Pittsburgh, N. L., 1910

KAFORA, FRANK   Catcher
Pittsburgh, N. L., 1913–1914

KAHL, GEORGE R.   1st B.
Cleveland, A. L., 1905

KAHLER, GEORGE R.   Pitcher
Cleveland, A. L., 1910–1914, inc.

KAHOE, MICHAEL   Catcher
Cincinnati, N. L., 1901
Chicago, N. L., 1901–1902
St. Louis, A. L., 1903–1904
Philadelphia, N. L., 1905
Chicago, N. L., 1907
Washington, A. L., 1907–1908

KAISER, AL   Outfielder
Chicago, N. L., 1911
Boston, N. L., 1911–1912
Indianapolis, F. L., 1914

KAISERLING, GEORGE   Pitcher
Indianapolis, F. L., 1914
Newark, F. L., 1915

KALLIO, RUPERT   Pitcher
Detroit, A. L., 1918–1919

KANE, HARRY   Pitcher
St. Louis, A. L., 1902
Detroit, A. L., 1903
Philadelphia, N. L., 1905–1906

KANE, J. J.   1st B.
Pittsburgh, N. L., 1908

KANE, JOHN F.   Substitute
Cincinnati, N. L., 1907–1908
Chicago, N. L., 1909–1910

KANTLEHNER, E. L.   Pitcher
Pittsburgh, N. L., 1914–1915–1916
Philadelphia, N. L., 1916

KARGER, EDWARD   Pitcher
Pittsburgh, N. L., 1906
St. Louis, N. L., 1906–1908, inc.
Cincinnati, N. L., 1909
Boston, A. L., 1909–1911, inc.

KARR, BENJ. J.   Pitcher
Boston, A. L., 1920–1921

KARST, JOHN   Infielder
Brooklyn, N. L., 1915

KATOLL, JOHN   Pitcher
Chicago, A. L., 1901–1902
Baltimore, A. L., 1902

KAUFF, BENJAMIN MICHAEL   O. F.
New York, A. L., 1912
Indianapolis, F. L., 1914
Brooklyn, F. L., 1915
New York, N. L., 1916–1920, inc.

KAUFFMAN, HOWARD RICHARD   1st B.
St. Louis, A. L., 1914–1915

KAUFMAN, TONY C.   Pitcher
Chicago, N. L., 1921

KAVANAUGH, MARTIN J.   Substitute
Detroit, A. L., 1914–1916, inc.
Cleveland, A. L., 1916–1918, inc.
Detroit, A. L., 1918
St. Louis, N. L., 1918

KAY, WILLIAM   Outfielder
Washington, A. L., 1907

KEARNS   Pitcher
Baltimore, A. L., 1901

KEATING, RAYMOND HERBERT   Pitcher
New York, A. L., 1912–1918, inc., (excepting 1917)
Boston, N. L., 1919

KEATING, WALTER   Infielder
Chicago, N. L., 1913–1914–1915

KEEFE, DAVID E.   Pitcher
Philadelphia, A. L., 1917 to date

KEEFE, ROBERT   Pitcher
New York, A. L., 1907
Cincinnati, N. L., 1911–1912

KEELER, WILLIAM H.   Outfielder
Brooklyn, N. L., 1901–1902
New York, A. L., 1903–1909, inc.
New York, N. L., 1910

KEELEY, BERT   Pitcher
Washington, A. L., 1908

KEEN, W. B.   Infielder
Pittsburgh, N. L., 1911

KEENAN, JAMES WILLIAM   Pitcher
Philadelphia, N. L., 1920–1921

KEENE, HOWARD VICTOR   Pitcher
Chicago, N. L., 1921

KEISTER, WILLIAM   Inf.—O. F.
Baltimore, A. L., 1901
Washington, A. L., 1902
Philadelphia, N. L., 1903

KELIHER, MAURICE M.   1st B.
Pittsburgh, N. L., 1911–1912

KELLEHER, J. P.   Infielder
St. Louis, N. L., 1912

KELLEHER, JOHN P.   Infielder
Brooklyn, N. L., 1916
Chicago, N. L., 1921

KELLEY, JOSEPH JAMES
             Outfielder—1st B.
Brooklyn, N. L., 1901
Baltimore, A. L., 1902
Cincinnati, N. L., 1902–1906, inc.
Boston, N. L., 1908

KELLIHER, A. A.   Catcher
New York, N. L., 1916

KELLOGG   Pitcher
Philadelphia, A. L., 1908

KELLOGG, W. D.   Infielder
Cincinnati, N. L., 1914

KELLUM, WINFORD   Pitcher
Boston, A. L., 1901
Cincinnati, N. L., 1904
St. Louis, N. L., 1905

KELLY   Outfielder
Chicago, A. L., 1910

KELLY, ED L.   Pitcher
Boston, A. L., 1914

KELLY, GEORGE LANGE   1st B.
New York, N. L., 1915–1916–1917
Pittsburgh, N. L., 1917
New York, N. L., 1919 to date

KELLY, HERBERT B.   Pitcher
Pittsburgh, N. L., 1914–1915

KELLY, JOHN B.   Outfielder
St. Louis, N. L., 1907

KELLY, JOSEPH HERBERT   Outfielder
Pittsburgh, N. L., 1914
Chicago, N. L., 1916
Boston, N. L., 1917–1919, inc.

KELLY, WILLIAM   Catcher
St. Louis, N. L., 1910
Pittsburgh, N. L., 1911–1913, inc.

KELLY, WILLIAM   1st B.
Philadelphia, A. L., 1920

KELSEY   Catcher
Pittsburgh, N. L., 1907

KENNA, EDWARD B.   Pitcher
Philadelphia, A. L., 1902

KENNEDY, RAY   Catcher
St. Louis, A. L., 1916

KENNEDY, SHERMAN   Outfielder
Brooklyn, N. L., 1901
New York, N. L., 1902
Pittsburgh, N. L., 1903

KENT, M. A.   Pitcher
Brooklyn, N. L., 1912–1913

KENWORTHY, WILLIAM B.   Infielder
Washington, A. L., 1912
Kansas City, F. L., 1914–1915
St. Louis, A. L., 1917

KERNS   Pitcher
Philadelphia, A. L., 1920

KERR   Catcher
Pittsburgh, F. L., 1914
Baltimore, F. L., 1914

KERR, RICHARD   Pitcher
Chicago, A. L., 1919 to date

KERWIN, DAN   Outfielder
Cincinnati, N. L., 1903

KETCHAM, FRED B.   Outfielder
Philadelphia, A. L., 1901

KIEFER, JOSEPH   Pitcher
Chicago, A. L., 1920

KILDUFF, PETER J.   Infielder
New York, N. L., 1917
Chicago, N. L., 1917–1918–1919
Brooklyn, N. L., 1919–1920–1921

KILHULLEN, J. T.   Catcher
Pittsburgh, N. L., 1914

KILLEFER, WADE HAMPTON
                          Infielder—O. F.
Detroit, A. L., 1907–1909, inc.
Washington, A. L., 1909–1910
Cincinnati, N. L., 1914–1916, inc.
New York, N. L., 1916

KILLEFER, WILLIAM, JR.   Catcher
St. Louis, A. L., 1909–1910
Philadelphia, N. L., 1911–1917, inc.
Chicago, N. L., 1918 to date

KILLIAN, EDWARD H.   Pitcher
Cleveland, A. L., 1903
Detroit, A. L., 1904–1910, inc.

KILLILAY   Pitcher
Boston, A. L., 1911

KIME, HAROLD LEE   Pitcher
St. Louis, N. L., 1919
Cincinnati, N. L., 1921

KIMMICK, WALTER LEE   Infielder
St. Louis, N. L., 1919
Cincinnati, N. L., 1921

KING   Outfielder
Milwaukee, A. L., 1901

KING, EDWARD L.   Outfielder
Philadelphia, A. L., 1916
Boston, N. L., 1919

KING, LEE   Outfielder
Pittsburgh, N. L., 1916–1917–1918
New York, N. L., 1919–1920–1921
Philadelphia, N. L., 1921

KINNEY, WALTER WILLIAM   Pitcher
Boston, A. L., 1918
Philadelphia, A. L., 1919–1920

KINSELLA, EDWARD   Pitcher

Pittsburgh, N. L., 1905
St. Louis, A. L., 1910

KINSELLA, ROBERT FRANCIS   Outfielder
New York, N. L., 1919–1920

KIPPERT, E.   Outfielder
Cincinnati, N. L., 1914

KIRBY, LARUE V.   Pitcher—O. F.
New York, N. L., 1912
St. Louis, F. L., 1914–1915

KIRCHER, MICHAEL ANDREW   Pitcher
Philadelphia, A. L., 1919
St. Louis, N. L., 1920–1921

KIRKE, JAYSON   Infielder—O. F.
Detroit, A. L., 1910
Boston, N. L., 1911–1913, inc.
Cleveland, A. L., 1914–1915
New York, N. L., 1918

KIRKPATRICK, ENOS   Infielder
Brooklyn, N. L., 1912–1913
Baltimore, F. L., 1914–1915

KIRSCH, HARRY   Pitcher
Cleveland, A. L., 1910

KISSINGER, CHAS. S.   Pitcher
Detroit, A. L., 1902–1903

KITSON, FRANK   Pitcher
Brooklyn, N. L., 1901–1902
Detroit, A. L., 1903–1904–1905
Washington, A. L., 1906–1907
New York, A. L., 1907

KITTREDGE, MALACHI JEDEDIAH
                               Catcher
Boston, N. L., 1901–1902–1903
Washington, A. L., 1903–1906, inc.

KLAWITTER, ALBERT   Pitcher
New York, N. L., 1909–1910
Detroit, A. L., 1913

KLEINOW, JOHN P.   Catcher
New York, A. L., 1904–1910, inc.
Boston, A. L., 1910–1911
Philadelphia, N. L., 1911

KLEPFER, EDWARD LLOYD   Pitcher
New York, A. L., 1911; 1913

Chicago, A. L., 1915
Cleveland, A. L., 1915–1916–1917; 1919

KLING, JOHN G.   Catcher
Chicago, N. L., 1901–1911, inc.; (excepting 1909)
Boston, N. L., 1911–1912
Cincinnati, N. L., 1913

KLING, ROBERT A.   Infielder
St. Louis, N. L., 1902

KLOBEDANZ, FRED   Pitcher
Boston, N. L., 1902

KLUGMAN, JOSEPH   2nd B.
Chicago, N. L., 1921

KNABE, FRANZ OTTO   Infielder
Pittsburgh, N. L., 1905
Philadelphia, N. L., 1907–1913, inc.
Baltimore, F. L., 1914–1915
Pittsburgh, N. L., 1916
Chicago, N. L., 1916

KNAUPP   Infielder
Cleveland, A. L., 1910–1911

KNETZER, ELMER E.   Pitcher
Brooklyn, N. L., 1909–1912, inc.
Pittsburgh, F. L., 1914–1915
Boston, N. L., 1916
Cincinnati, N. L., 1917

KNIGHT, JOHN W.   Infielder
Philadelphia, A. L., 1905–1907, inc.
Boston, A. L., 1907
New York, A. L., 1909–1911, inc.
Washington, A. L., 1912
New York, A. L., 1913

KNISELY, PETER C.   Outfielder
Cincinnati, N. L., 1912
Chicago, N. L., 1913–1915, inc.

KNODE, KENNETH T.   Substitute
St. Louis, N. L., 1920

KNOLL, "PUNCH"   Outfielder
Washington, A. L., 1905

KNOLLS, OSCAR   Pitcher
Brooklyn, N. L., 1906

KNOTTS, JOSEPH   Catcher
Boston, N. L., 1907

KNOWLSON, T.   Pitcher
Philadelphia, A. L., 1915

KNOWLTON   Pitcher
Philadelphia, A. L., 1920

KOCHER, BRADLEY W.   Catcher
Detroit, A. L., 1912
New York, N. L., 1915–1916

KOEHLER   Substitute
St. Louis, A. L., 1905–1906

KOENIGSMARK, WILLIS T.   Pitcher
St. Louis, N. L., 1919

KOESTNER, ELMER   Pitcher
Cleveland, A. L., 1910
Chicago, N. L., 1914
Cincinnati, N. L., 1914–1916

KOLP, RAY   Pitcher
St. Louis, A. L., 1921

KOMMERS, R.   Outfielder
Pittsburgh, N. L., 1913
Baltimore, F. L., 1914
St. Louis, F. L., 1914

KONETCHY, EDWARD J.   1st B.
St. Louis, N. L., 1907–1913, inc.
Pittsburgh, N. L., 1914
Pittsburgh, F. L., 1915
Boston, N. L., 1916–1918, inc.
Brooklyn, N. L., 1919–1920–1921
Philadelphia, N. L., 1921

KONNICK, MICHAEL A.   Catcher
Cincinnati, N. L., 1909–1910

KOOB, ERNEST   Pitcher
St. Louis, A. L., 1915–1919, inc. (excepting 1918)

KOPF, WALTER H.   Substitute
New York, N. L., 1921

KOPF, WILLIAM LORENZ   Infielder
Cleveland, A. L., 1913
Philadelphia, A. L., 1914–1915
Cincinnati, N. L., 1916–1917; 1919 to date

KOPP, MERLIN   Outfielder
  Washington, A. L., 1915
  Philadelphia, A. L., 1918–1919
KORES   Infielder
  St. Louis, F. L., 1915
KOUKALIK, JOHN   Pitcher
  Brooklyn, N. L., 1904
KRAFT, C. O.   Substitute
  Boston, N. L., 1914
KRAPP, EUGENE   Pitcher
  Cleveland, N. L., 1911–1912
  Buffalo, F. L., 1914–1915
KRAUSE, HARRY W.   Pitcher
  Philadelphia, A. L., 1908–1911, inc.
  Cleveland, A. L., 1912
KREITZ   Catcher
  Chicago, A. L., 1911
KRITCHELL, PAUL   Catcher
  St. Louis, A. L., 1911–1912
KROH, FLOYD M.   Pitcher
  Boston, A. L., 1907
  Chicago, N. L., 1908–1910, inc.
  Boston, N. L., 1912
KRUEGER   Substitute
  Boston, N. L., 1910
KRUEGER, A.   Outfielder
  Cincinnati, N. L., 1907
  Cleveland, A. L., 1915
  Kansas City, F. L., 1914–1915
KRUEGER, ERNEST GEORGE   Catcher
  Cleveland, A. L., 1913
  New York, A. L., 1915
  New York, N. L., 1917
  Brooklyn, N. L., 1917, to date
KRUEGER, OTTO A.   Infielder
  St. Louis, N. L., 1901–1902
  Pittsburgh, N. L., 1903–1904
  Philadelphia, N. L., 1905
KRUG, HENRY   Infielder
  Philadelphia, N. L., 1902

KRUGER, ABE   Pitcher
  Brooklyn, N. L., 1908
KRUGG   Infielder
  Boston, A. L., 1912
KUEPPER   Pitcher
  St. Louis, F. L., 1914
KUHN, WALTER   Catcher
  Chicago, A. L., 1912–1914, inc.
KULL, JOHN   Pitcher
  Philadelphia, A. L., 1909
KUSEL   Pitcher
  St. Louis, A. L., 1909
KUSTUS, JULIUS   Outfielder
  Brooklyn, N. L., 1909
KUTINA   1st B.
  St. Louis, A. L., 1911–1912
KYLE, ANDREW E.   Outfielder
  Cincinnati, N. L., 1912
LACHANCE, GEORGE   1st B.
  Cleveland, A. L., 1901
  Boston, A. L., 1902–1905, inc.
LAFITTE, EDWARD FRANCIS   Pitcher
  Detroit, A. L., 1909; 1911–1912
  Brooklyn, F. L., 1914
  Buffalo, F. L., 1915
LAJOIE, NAPOLEON
  Philadelphia, A. L., 1901–1902
  Cleveland, A. L., 1902–1914, inc.
  Philadelphia, A. L., 1915–1916
LAKE, FRED   Substitute
  Boston, N. L., 1910
LAKE, JOSEPH   Pitcher
  New York, A. L., 1907–1909, inc.
  St. Louis, A. L., 1910–1912, inc.
  Detroit, A. L., 1912–1913
LAMAR, PETER   Catcher
  Cincinnati, N. L., 1907
LAMAR, R.   Catcher
  Chicago, N. L., 1902
LAMAR, WILLIAM H.   Outfielder
  New York, A. L., 1917–1918

Boston, A. L., 1919
Brooklyn, N. L., 1920–1921

LAMB, LYMAN RAYMOND Substitute
St. Louis, A. L., 1920–1921

LAMBETH, SAMUEL OTIS Pitcher
Cleveland, A. L., 1916–1917–1918

LAMLINE, FRED Pitcher
Chicago, A. L., 1912
St. Louis, N. L., 1915

LA MOTTE, R. E. Infielder
Washington, A. L., 1920–1921

LAND, GROVER CLEVELAND Catcher
Cleveland, A. L., 1908–1911, inc; 1913
Brooklyn, F. L., 1914–1915

LANGE Pitcher
Chicago, F. L., 1914

LANGE, FRANK Pitcher
Chicago, A. L., 1910–1912, inc.

LANNING, LESTER A. Pitcher
Philadelphia, A. L., 1916

LAPORTE, FRANK Infielder
New York, A. L., 1905–1908, inc.
Boston, A. L., 1908
New York, A. L., 1909–1910
St. Louis, A. L., 1911
Washington, A. L., 1912–1913
Indianapolis, F. L., 1914
Newark, F. L., 1915

LAPP, JOHN W. Catcher
Philadelphia, A. L., 1909–1915, inc.
Chicago, A. L., 1916

LARKIN Catcher
Philadelphia, A. L., 1909

LARMORE, ROBERT Infielder
St. Louis, N. L., 1918

LAROSS, HARRY Outfielder
Cincinnati, N. L., 1914

LATHAM, WALTER ARLINGTON
Substitute
New York, N. L., 1909

LATHERS, C. T. Infielder
Detroit, A. L., 1910–1911

LATHROP, WILLIAM G. Pitcher
Chicago, A. L., 1914

LATIMER, CLIFFORD W. Catcher
Baltimore, A. L., 1901
Brooklyn, N. L., 1902

LATTIMORE, WILLIAM Pitcher
Cleveland, A. L., 1908

LAUDER, WILLIAM 3rd B.
Philadelphia, A. L., 1901
New York, N. L., 1902–1903

LAUTERBORN, WILLIAM Infielder
Boston, N. L., 1904–1905

LAVAN, JOHN LEONARD Shortstop
St. Louis, A. L., 1913
Philadelphia, A. L., 1913
St. Louis, A. L., 1913–1917, inc.
Washington, A. L., 1918
St. Louis, N. L., 1919 to date

LAVENDER, JAMES SANFORD Pitcher
Chicago, N. L., 1912–1916, inc.
Philadelphia, N. L., 1917

LAVIGNE Catcher
Buffalo, F. L., 1914

LAWRY, OTIS C. Infielder—O. F.
Philadelphia, A. L., 1916–1917

LAYDEN, EUGENE Outfielder
New York, A. L., 1915

LEACH, THOMAS W. Infielder—O. F.
Pittsburgh, N. L., 1901–1912, inc.
Chicago, N. L., 1912–1914, inc.
Cincinnati, N. L., 1915
Pittsburgh, N. L., 1918

LEAHY, THOMAS J. Catcher
Philadelphia, A. L., 1901
Milwaukee, A. L., 1901
St. Louis, N. L., 1905

LEAR, CHARLES B. Pitcher
Cincinnati, N. L., 1914–1915

LEAR, FRED F. Infielder
Philadelphia, A. L., 1915

Chicago, N. L., 1918–1919
New York, N. L., 1920

LEARD, WILLIAM W.   Infielder
Brooklyn, N. L., 1917

LEARY, F. P.   Pitcher
Cincinnati, N. L., 1907

LEARY, JOHN L.   1st B.
St. Louis, A. L., 1914–1915

LEATHERS, HAROLD   Infielder
Chicago, N. L., 1920

LE BOURVEAU, DE WITT WILEY
                                 Outfielder
Philadelphia, N. L., 1919–1920–1921

LECLAIRE, GEORGE   Pitcher
Pittsburgh, F. L., 1914
Baltimore, F. L., 1915

LEDBETTER, R. O.   Pitcher
Detroit, A. L., 1915

LEE, CLIFFORD   Catcher—O. F.
Pittsburgh, N. L., 1919–1920
Philadelphia, N. L., 1921

LEE, ERNEST D.   Infielder
St. Louis, A. L., 1920–1921
(Played in 1920 under name of Dudley)

LEE, W. J.   Outfielder
St. Louis, A. L., 1915–1916

LEE, WYATT ARNOLD   Pitcher
Washington, A. L., 1901–1903, inc.
Pittsburgh, N. L., 1904

LEES, GEORGE E.   Catcher
Chicago, A. L., 1921

LEEVER, SAMUEL A.   Pitcher
Pittsburgh, N. L., 1901–1910, inc.

LEFEVRE, ALFRED   Infielder
New York, N. L., 1920

LEHR   Infielder
Cleveland, A. L., 1905

LEHR, C. E.   Infielder
Philadelphia, N. L., 1911

LEIBOLD, HARRY LORAN   Outfielder

Cleveland, A. L., 1913–1914–1915
Chicago, A. L., 1916–1920, inc.
Boston, A. L., 1921

LEIFER, ELMER EDWIN   Outfielder
Chicago, A. L., 1921

LEIFIELD, ALBERT PETER   Pitcher
Pittsburgh, N. L., 1905–1912, inc.
Chicago, N. L., 1912–1913
St. Louis, A. L., 1918–1920, inc.

LEITNER, GEORGE   Pitcher
Philadelphia, A. L., 1901
New York, N. L., 1901
Cleveland, A. L., 1902
Chicago, A. L., 1902

LEJEUNE, SHELDON A.   Outfielder
Brooklyn, N. L., 1911
Pittsburgh, N. L., 1915

LELIVELT, JOHN F.   Outfielder
Washington, A. L., 1909–1911, inc.
New York, A. L., 1912
Cleveland, A. L., 1913–1914

LELIVELT, WILLIAM J.   Pitcher
Detroit, A. L., 1909–1910

LENCHEN   Infielder
Boston, A. L., 1910

LENNOX, EDGAR   Infielder
Philadelphia, A. L., 1906
Brooklyn, N. L., 1909–1910
Chicago, N. L., 1912
Pittsburgh, F. L., 1914–1915

LEONARD, HUBERT B.   Pitcher
Philadelphia, A. L., 1911
Boston, A. L., 1913–1918, inc.
Detroit, A. L., 1919 to date

LEONARD, JOSEPH H.   Infielder
Pittsburgh, N. L., 1914
Cleveland, A. L., 1916
Washington, A. L., 1916–1917; 1919

LEPINE, LOUIS   Outfielder
Detroit, A. L., 1902

LEROY, LOUIS   Pitcher

New York, A. L., 1905–1906
Boston, A. L., 1910

LESLIE, ROY   1st B.
Chicago, N. L., 1917
St. Louis, N. L., 1919

LEVERENZ, WALTER F.   Pitcher
St. Louis, A. L., 1913–1914–1915

LEVERETTE, HORACE W.   Pitcher
St. Louis, A. L., 1920

LEWIS, EDWARD M.   Pitcher
Boston, A. L., 1901

LEWIS, GEORGE EDWARD   Outfielder
Boston, A. L., 1910–1917, inc.
New York, A. L., 1919–1920
Washington, A. L., 1921

LEWIS, J.   Infielder
Boston, A. L., 1911
Pittsburgh, F. L., 1914–1915

LEWIS, PHIL   Shortstop
Brooklyn, N. L., 1905–1908, inc.

LIEBHARDT, GLEN   Pitcher
Cleveland, A. L., 1906–1908, inc.

LIESE, FRED R.   Pitcher
Boston, N. L., 1910

LINDAMAN, VIVIAN ALSACE   Pitcher
Boston, N. L., 1906–1909, inc.

LINDERMAN, ERNEST   Pitcher
Boston, N. L., 1907

LINDERMANN   Pitcher
Philadelphia, A. L., 1901

LINDSAY   Infielder
Detroit, A. L., 1905–1906

LINDSAY   Infielder
Cleveland, A. L., 1911

LINDSTROM, A. O.   Pitcher
Philadelphia, A. L., 1916

LINKE, FREDERICK T.   Pitcher
Cleveland, A. L., 1910
St. Louis, A. L., 1910

LINNHAUSER   Outfielder
Detroit, A. L., 1912

LISTER, PETER   1st B.
Cleveland, A. L., 1907

LIVELY   Pitcher
Detroit, A. L., 1911

LIVINGSTON, PATRICK JOSEPH Catcher
Cleveland, A. L., 1901
Cincinnati, N. L., 1906
Philadelphia, A. L., 1909–1911, inc.
Cleveland, A. L., 1912
St. Louis, N. L., 1917

LIVINGSTONE, A.   Pitcher
New York, N. L., 1901

LOAN, H.   Catcher
Philadelphia, N. L., 1912

LOBERT, JOHN   Infielder
Pittsburgh, N. L., 1903
Chicago, N. L., 1905
Cincinnati, N. L., 1906–1910, inc.
Philadelphia, N. L., 1911–1914, inc.
New York, N. L., 1915–1917, inc.

LOCKHEAD, HARRY P.   Shortstop
Philadelphia, A. L., 1901
Detroit, A. L., 1901

LOHR, HOWARD S.   Substitute
Cincinnati, N. L., 1914
Cleveland, A. L., 1916

LONERGAN   Infielder
Boston, A. L., 1911

LONG   Pitcher
Philadelphia, A. L., 1911

LONG, HERMAN   Shortstop
Boston, N. L., 1901–1902
New York, A. L., 1903
Detroit, A. L., 1903
Philadelphia, N. L., 1904

LONG, NELSON   Pitcher
Boston, N. L., 1902

LONG, THOMAS AUGUSTUS   Outfielder
Washington, A. L., 1911
St. Louis, N. L., 1915–1917, inc.

LOOS, PETER   Pitcher
Philadelphia, A. L., 1901

LORD, BRISTOL   Outfielder
Philadelphia, A. L., 1905–1907, inc.
Cleveland, A. L., 1910
Philadelphia, A. L., 1910–1912, inc.
Boston, N. L., 1913

LORD, HARRY   3rd B.
Boston, A. L., 1907–1910, inc.
Chicago, A. L., 1910–1914, inc.
Buffalo, F. L., 1915

LORENZ   Pitcher
Detroit, A. L., 1913

LOTZ, JOSEPH   Pitcher
St. Louis, N. L., 1916

LOUDELL, ARTHUR   Pitcher
Detroit, A. L., 1910

LOUDEN, WILLIAM   Infielder
New York, A. L., 1907
Detroit, A. L., 1912–1913
Buffalo, F. L., 1914–1915
Cincinnati, N. L., 1916

LOUDENSLAGER, CHARLES   Infielder
Brooklyn, N. L., 1904

LOUDERMILK, LOUIS   Pitcher
St. Louis, N. L., 1911–1912
Chicago, N. L., 1912

LOVE, EDWARD C.   Pitcher
Washington, A. L., 1913
New York, A. L., 1916–1917–1918
Detroit, A. L., 1919–1920

LOVETT   Pitcher
St. Louis, N. L., 1903

LOW, FLETCHER   Infielder
Boston, N. L., 1915

LOWDERMILK, GROVER CLEVELAND
                                 Pitcher
St. Louis, N. L., 1909–1911
Chicago, N. L., 1912
St. Louis, A. L., 1915
Detroit, A. L., 1915–1916
Cleveland, A. L., 1916
St. Louis, A. L., 1917–1918
Chicago, A. L., 1919–1920

LOWE, GEORGE W.   Pitcher
Cincinnati, N. L., 1920

LOWE, ROBERT LINCOLN   2nd B.—O. F.
Boston, N. L., 1901
Chicago, N. L., 1902–1903
Pittsburgh, N. L., 1904
Detroit, A. L., 1904–1907, inc.

LUCEY, JOSEPH   Infielder
New York, A. L., 1920

LUDERUS, FRED W.   1st B.
Chicago, N. L., 1909–1910
Philadelphia, N. L., 1910–1920, inc.

LUDWIG, W.   Catcher
St. Louis, N. L., 1908

LUHRSEN, WILLIAM F.   Pitcher
Pittsburgh, N. L., 1913

LUMLEY, HARRY G.   Outfielder
Brooklyn, N. L., 1905; 1910

LUNDBOOM, JOHN   Pitcher
Cleveland, A. L., 1902

LUNDGREN, CARL L.   Pitcher
Chicago, N. L., 1902–1909, inc.

LUNTE, HARRY   Substitute
Cleveland, A. L., 1919–1920

LUQUE, ADOLFO   Pitcher
Boston, N. L., 1914
Cincinnati, N. L., 1918 to date

LUSH, ERNEST   Outfielder
St. Louis, N. L., 1910

LUSH, JOHN C.   Pitcher
Philadelphia, N. L., 1904–1907, inc.
St. Louis, N. L., 1907–1910, inc.

LUSH, WILLIAM L.   Outfielder
Boston, N. L., 1902
Detroit, A. L., 1903
Cleveland, A. L., 1904

LYNCH, ADRIAN RYAN   Pitcher
St. Louis, A. L., 1920

LYNCH, M. J.   Outfielder
Chicago, N. L., 1902

LYNCH, MICHAEL   Pitcher
Pittsburgh, N. L., 1904–1907, inc.
New York, N. L., 1907

LYNN, BYRD   Catcher
Chicago, A. L., 1916–1920, inc.

LYONS, GEORGE   Pitcher
St. Louis, N. L., 1920

MACK, EARL   Catcher
Philadelphia, A. L., 1910–1911–1914

MACK, W. F.   Pitcher
Chicago, N. L., 1908

MADDEN, EUGENE   Outfielder
Pittsburgh, N. L., 1916

MADDEN, LEONARD J.   Pitcher
Chicago, N. L., 1912

MADDEN, THOMAS   Outfielder
New York, A. L., 1910

MADDEN, THOMAS FRANCIS   Catcher
Boston, A. L., 1909–1911, inc.
Philadelphia, N. L., 1911

MADDOX, NICHOLAS   Pitcher
Pittsburgh, N. L., 1907–1910, inc.

MAGART   Outfielder
St. Louis, A. L., 1905

MAGEE,   LEO   CHRISTOPHER
Infielder—Outfielder
St. Louis, N. L., 1911–1914, inc.
Brooklyn, F. L., 1915
New York, A. L., 1916–1917
St. Louis, A. L., 1917
Cincinnati, N. L., 1918
Brooklyn, N. L., 1919
Chicago, N. L., 1919

MAGEE, SHERWOOD ROBERT   Outfielder
Philadelphia, N. L., 1904–1914, inc.
Boston, N. L., 1915–1917, inc.
Cincinnati, N. L., 1917–1919, inc.

MAGEE, WILLIAM   Pitcher
New York, N. L., 1902
Philadelphia, N. L., 1902

MAGGERT, HARL V.   Outfielder

Pittsburgh, N. L., 1907
Philadelphia, A. L., 1912

MAGNER, S. S.   Shortstop
New York, A. L., 1911

MAGOON, GEORGE MENRY
2nd B.—S. S.
Cincinnati, N. L., 1901–1903, inc.
Chicago, A. L., 1903

MAHADY, JAMES B.   Substitute
New York, N. L., 1921

MAHARG, WILLIAM   Inf.—O. F.
Detroit, A. L., 1912
Philadelphia, N. L., 1916

MAHER, THOMAS   Infielder
Philadelphia, N. L., 1902

MAHONEY   Pitcher
Boston, N. L., 1908
Boston, A. L., 1910

MAHONEY, D. J.   Infielder
Cincinnati, N. L., 1911

MAILS, JOHN WALTER   Pitcher
Brooklyn, N. L., 1915–1916
Cleveland, A. L., 1920–1921

MAIN, MILES   Pitcher
Detroit, A. L., 1914
Kansas City. F. L., 1915
Philadelphia, N. L., 1918

MAISEL, FREDERICK C.   Infielder
New York, A. L., 1913–1917, inc.
St. Louis, A. L., 1918

MAISEL, GEORGE JOHN   Inf.—O. F.
St. Louis, A. L., 1913
Detroit, A. L., 1916
Chicago, N. L., 1921

MALARKEY, JOHN   Pitcher
Boston, N. L., 1902–1903

MALARKEY, WILLIAM J.   Pitcher
New York, N. L., 1908

MALAY, CHARLES   Outfielder
Brooklyn, N. L., 1905

MALLONEE, H. V.   Outfielder
Philadelphia, A. L., 1921

MALLOY, HERMAN Pitcher
Detroit, A. L., 1907
St. Louis, A. L., 1910
Boston, A. L., 1913

MALONE, LEWIS A. Infielder
Philadelphia, A. L., 1915–1916
Brooklyn, N. L., 1917–1919

MALONEY Outfielder
New York, A. L., 1912

MALONEY, WILLIAM A. C.—O. F.
Milwaukee, A. L., 1901
St. Louis, A. L., 1902
Cincinnati, N. L., 1902
Chicago, N. L., 1905
Brooklyn, N. L., 1906–1907–1908

MAMAUX, ALBERT LEON Pitcher
Pittsburgh, N. L., 1913–1917, inc.
Brooklyn, N. L., 1918 to date

MANGUS, GEORGE Outfielder
Philadelphia, N. L., 1912

MANION, CLYDE JENNINGS Catcher
Detroit, A. L., 1920–1921

MANN, LESLIE Outfielder
Boston, N. L., 1913–1914
Chicago, F. L., 1915
Chicago, N. L., 1916–1917–1918–1919
Boston, N. L., 1919–1920
St. Louis, N. L., 1921

MANNING, ERNEST Pitcher
St. Louis, A. L., 1914

MANNING, WALTER S. Pitcher
New York, A. L., 1907–1910, inc.

MANSKE, LOUIS Pitcher
Pittsburgh, N. L., 1906

MANUEL Pitcher
Washington, A. L., 1905
Chicago, A. L., 1908

MANUSH, FRANK Infielder
Philadelphia, A. L., 1908

MAPLE, ROLLA Pitcher
St. Louis, A. L., 1919

MARANVILLE, WALTER JAMES VINCENT
S. S.
Boston, N. L., 1912–1920, inc.
Pittsburgh, N. L., 1921

MARBET, W. Pitcher
St. Louis, N. L., 1913

MARION, DON Pitcher
Brooklyn, F. L., 1915

MARIOTT, WILLIAM EARL Infielder
Chicago, N. L., 1917–1920–1921

MARKLE, CLIFFORD M. Pitcher
New York, A. L., 1915–1916
Cincinnati, N. L., 1921

MARONEY, J. F. Pitcher
Boston, N. L., 1906
Philadelphia, N. L., 1910
Chicago, N. L. 1912

MARQUARD, RICHARD W. Pitcher
New York, N. L., 1908–1915, inc.
Brooklyn, N. L., 1915–1920
Cincinnati, N. L., 1921

MARSANS, ARMANDO Outfielder
Cincinnati, N. L., 1911–1914, inc.
St. Louis, F. L., 1915
St. Louis, A. L., 1916–1917
New York, A. L., 1917–1918

MARSHALL, J. H. Outfielder
Pittsburgh, N. L., 1902
St. Louis, N. L., 1906

MARCHALL, ROY Pitcher
Philadelphia, N. L., 1912–1913–1914

MARSHALL, WILLIAM R. Catcher
Boston, N. L., 1904
Philadelphia, N. L., 1904
New York, N. L., 1904–1906
St. Louis, N. L., 1906–1908, inc.
Chicago, N. L., 1908
Brooklyn, N. L., 1909

MARTEL, LEON A. Catcher
Philadelphia, N. L., 1909
Boston, N. L., 1910

MARTIN Infielder

Washington, A. L., 1903
St. Louis, A. L., 1903

MARTIN, DAVID   Pitcher
Philadelphia, A. L., 1908–1911–1912

MARTIN, ELWOOD G.   Pitcher
St. Louis, A. L., 1917
Chicago, N. L., 1918 to date

MARTIN, JOHN C.   Infielder
New York, A. L., 1912
Boston, N. L., 1914
Philadelphia, N. L., 1914

MARTIN, PATRICK F.   Pitcher
Philadelphia, A. L., 1919–1920

MARTIN, W. G.   Infielder
Boston, N. L., 1914

MASON, DEL   Pitcher
Washington, A. L., 1904
Cincinnati, N. L., 1906–1907

MASSEY, ROY O.   Outfielder
Boston, N. L., 1918

MASSEY, W. H.   Infielder
Boston, N. L., 1917

MATHES, J. J.   Infielder
Philadelphia, A. L., 1912
St. Louis, F. L., 1914
Boston, N. L., 1916

MATHEWS, WILLIAM   Pitcher
Boston, A. L., 1909

MATHEWSON, CHRISTOPHER   Pitcher
New York, N. L., 1901–1916, inc.
Cincinnati, N. L., 1916

MATHEWSON, HENRY   Pitcher
New York, N. L., 1907–1908

MATHISON   Infielder
Baltimore, A. L., 1902

MATTERN, ALONZO A.   Pitcher
Boston, N. L., 1908–1912, inc.

MATTESON, H. E.   Pitcher
Philadelphia, N. L., 1914
Washington, A. L., 1918

MATTICKS, W. J.   Outfielder

Chicago, A. L., 1912
St. Louis, N. L., 1918

MATTIS   Outfielder
Pittsburgh, F. L., 1914

MAUL, ALBERT   Pitcher
New York, N. L., 1901

MAXWELL, J. A.   Pitcher
Pittsburgh, N. L., 1906
Philadelphia, A. L., 1908
New York, N. L., 1911

MAY, FRANK SPRUELL   Pitcher
St. Louis, N. L., 1917–1918–1919–1920–
  1921

MAYER, J. ERSKINE   Pitcher
Philadelphia, N. L., 1912–1918, inc.
Pittsburgh, N. L., 1918–1919
Chicago, A. L., 1919

MAYER, SAMUEL   Outfielder
Washington, A. L., 1915

MAYER, WALTER   Catcher
Chicago, A. L., 1914–1915
Boston, A. L., 1917–1918
St. Louis, A. L., 1919

MAYNARD, RICHARD   Outfielder
St. Louis, N. L., 1918

MAYS, CARL WILLIAM   Pitcher
Boston, A. L., 1915–1919, inc.
New York, A. L., 1919 to date

McADAMS, J.   Pitcher
St. Louis, N. L., 1911

McALEER, JAMES ROBERT   Substitute
Cleveland, A. L., 1901
St. Louis, A. L., 1902

McALEESE, JOHN   P.—O. F.
Chicago, A. L., 1901
St. Louis, A. L., 1909

McALLISTER, LEWIS J.   C.—Sub.
Detroit, A. L., 1901–1902–1903

McALLISTER, W. L.   Catcher
St. Louis, A. L., 1913

McARTHUR, OLIVER A.   Pitcher
Pittsburgh, N. L., 1914

McAULEY, JAMES   Infielder
Pittsburgh, N. L., 1914–1916, inc.
St. Louis, N. L., 1917

McAULIFFE, JAMES   Catcher
Boston, N. L., 1904

McAVOY, G. R.   Outfielder
Philadelphia, N. L., 1914

McAVOY, JAMES   Catcher
Philadelphia, A. L., 1913–1919, inc. (excepting 1916)

McBRIDE, ALGERNON   Outfielder
New York, N. L., 1901

McBRIDE, GEORGE FLORIAN   S. S.
Milwaukee, A. L., 1901
Pittsburgh, N. L., 1905
St. Louis, N. L., 1905–1906
Washington, A. L., 1908–1920, inc.

McCABE, ARTHUR   Outfielder
Cincinnati, N. L., 1909–1910

McCABE, RICHARD JAMES   Pitcher
Boston, A. L., 1918

McCABE, TIM   Pitcher
St. Louis, A. L., 1915–1918, inc.

McCABE, WILLIAM FRANCIS   Sub.
Chicago, N. L., 1918–1920, inc.
Brooklyn, N. L., 1920

McCANDLESS   Outfielder
Baltimore, F. L., 1915

McCANN, H. EUGENE   Pitcher
Brooklyn, N. L., 1901–1902

McCANN, ROBERT EMMETT   Infielder
Philadelphia, A. L., 1920–1921

McCARTHY   Catcher
Cincinnati, N. L., 1907

McCARTHY   Catcher
New York, A. L., 1905

McCARTHY, A.   Pitcher
Detroit, A. L., 1902

McCARTHY, ALEXANDER C.   Infielder
Pittsburgh, N. L., 1910–1915, inc.
Chicago, N. L., 1915–1916
Pittsburgh, N. L., 1916–1917

McCARTHY, J. N.   Catcher
St. Louis, N. L., 1906

McCARTHY, JOHN   Outfielder
Cleveland, A. L., 1901–1902–1903
Chicago, N. L., 1903–1904–1905
Brooklyn, N. L., 1906–1907

McCARTHY, W. T.   Pitcher
Boston, N. L., 1906–1908
Pittsburgh, N. L., 1908
Cincinnati, N. L., 1908
Boston, N. L., 1909

McCARTY, G. LEWIS   Catcher
Brooklyn, N. L., 1913–1916, inc.
New York, N. L., 1916–1919, inc.
St. Louis, N. L., 1919–1920–1921

McCHESNEY, HENRY   Outfielder
Chicago, N. L., 1904

McCLELLAN, HARRY McDOWELL
                            Infielder
Chicago, A. L., 1919 to date

McCLOSKEY, J. J.   Pitcher
Philadelphia, N. L., 1906–1907

McCLURE, LAWRENCE   Pitcher
New York, A. L., 1910

McCLUSKEY, HARRY   Pitcher
Cincinnati, N. L., 1915

McCLUSKEY, J.   Infielder
Boston, N. L., 1913

McCONNELL, AMBROSE FRANCIS
                             2nd B.
Boston, A. L., 1908–1910, inc.
Chicago, A. L., 1910–1911

McCONNELL, GEORGE N.   Pitcher
New York, A. L., 1909–1912–1913
Chicago, N. L., 1914
Chicago, F. L., 1915
Chicago, A. L., 1916

McCONNELL, SAMUEL F.　　Infielder
Philadelphia, A. L., 1915

McCORMICK, HARRY E.　　Outfielder
Pittsburgh, N. L., 1904
New York, N. L., 1904
Philadelphia, N. L., 1908
New York, N. L., 1908–1909–1912–1913

McCORMICK, W.　　Infielder
Brooklyn, N. L., 1904

McCORMICK, WM. J.　　Infielder
Chicago, N. L., 1901
St. Louis, A. L., 1902–1903
Washington, A. L., 1903–1904

McCORRY, WILLIAM　　Pitcher
St. Louis, A. L., 1909

McCREEDIE, WALTER　　Outfielder
Brooklyn, N. L., 1903

McCREERY, E. B.　　Pitcher
Detroit, A. L., 1914

McCREERY, THOS. LEAVENWORTH
　　1st B.—O. F.
Brooklyn, N. L., 1901–1902–1903
Boston, N. L., 1903

McDERMOTT　　Outfielder
Detroit, A. L., 1912

McDONALD　　Infielder
St. Louis, A. L., 1910

McDONALD　　Infielder
Pittsburgh, F. L., 1914
Buffalo, F. L., 1915

McDONALD, CHARLES　　Infielder
Cincinnati, N. L., 1912–1913
Boston, N. L., 1913

McDONALD, EDWARD　　Infielder
Boston, N. L., 1911–1912
Chicago, N. L., 1913

McDONOUGH, E.　　Catcher
Philadelphia, N. L., 1909–1910

McDOUGHALL, J. A.　　Pitcher
St. Louis, N. L., 1905

McELVEEN, PRYOR M.　　3rd B.
Brooklyn, N. L., 1909–1911, inc.

McELWEE, L. S.　　Infielder
Philadelphia, A. L., 1916

McFADDEN, J. BERNARD　　Pitcher
Cincinnati, N. L., 1901
Philadelphia, N. L., 1902

McFARLAND, CHARLES E.　　Pitcher
St. Louis, N. L., 1902–1906, inc.
Pittsburgh, N. L., 1906
Brooklyn, N. L., 1906

McFARLAND, EDWARD W.　　Catcher
Philadelphia, N. L., 1901
Chicago, A. L., 1902–1907, inc.
Boston, A. L., 1908

McFARLAND, HERMAN　　Outfielder
Chicago, A. L., 1901–1902
Baltimore, A. L., 1902
New York, A. L., 1903

McFETRIDGE, JOHN　　Pitcher
Philadelphia, N. L., 1903

McGAFFIGAN, MARTIN A.　　Infielder
Philadelphia, N. L., 1917–1918

McGAMWELL, E. M.　　Infielder
Brooklyn, N. L., 1905

McGANN, DANIEL L.　　1st B.
St. Louis, N. L., 1901
Baltimore, A. L., 1902
New York, N. L., 1902–1907, inc.
Boston, N. L., 1908

McGARR　　Infielder
Detroit, A. L., 1912

McGARVEY　　Outfielder
Detroit, A. L., 1912

McGEEHAN, D. D.　　Infielder
St. Louis, N. L., 1911

McGILL, WILLIAM　　Pitcher
St. Louis, A. L., 1907

McGILVRAY, W. A.　　Outfielder
Cincinnati, N. L., 1908

McGINLEY, JAMES　　Pitcher
St. Louis, N. L., 1904–1905

McGINNITY, JOSEPH JEROME　　Pitcher

Baltimore, A. L., 1901–1902
New York, N. L., 1902–1908, inc.

McGLYNN, GRANT   Pitcher
St. Louis, N. L., 1906–1908, inc.

McGOVERN   Catcher
Boston, A. L., 1905

McGRANER, HOWARD   Pitcher
Cincinnati, N. L., 1912

McGRAW, JOHN J.   3rd B.
Baltimore, A. L., 1901–1902
New York, N. L., 1902–1903–1904–
1905–1906

McGRAW, ROBERT E.   Pitcher
New York, A. L., 1917–1918–1919
Boston, A. L., 1919
New York, A. L., 1920

McGUIRE, THOMAS   Infielder
Cleveland, A. L., 1901

McGUIRE   Pitcher
Chicago, F. L., 1914
Chicago, A. L., 1919

McGUIRE, JAMES THOMAS   Catcher
Brooklyn, N. L., 1901
Detroit, A. L., 1902–1903
New York, A. L., 1904–1906, inc.
Boston, A. L., 1907
Detroit, A. L., 1912

McHALE   Outfielder
Boston, A. L., 1908

McHALE, MARTIN J.   Pitcher
Boston, A. L., 1910–1911
New York, A. L., 1913–1915, inc.
Boston, A. L., 1916
Cleveland, A. L., 1916

McHENRY, AUSTIN BUSH   Outfielder
St. Louis, N. L., 1918 to date

McILVEEN, W.   Pitcher—Outfielder
Pittsburgh, N. L., 1906
New York, A. L., 1908

McINNIS, JOHN   Infielder
Philadelphia, A. L., 1909–1917, inc.
Boston, A. L., 1918–1921, inc.

McINTIRE, HARRY M.   Pitcher
Brooklyn, N. L., 1905–1909, inc.
Chicago, N. L., 1910–1912, inc.
Cincinnati, N. L., 1913

McINTYRE, MATTHEW   Outfielder
Philadelphia, A. L., 1901
Detroit, A. L., 1904–1910, inc.
Chicago, A. L., 1911–1912, inc.

McIVOR, E.   Outfielder
St. Louis, N. L., 1911

McJAMES, JAMES   Pitcher
Brooklyn, N. L., 1901

McKECHNIE, WILLIAM B.   Infielder
Pittsburgh, N. L., 1907; 1910–1911–1912
Boston, N. L., 1913
New York, A. L., 1913
Indianapolis, F. L., 1914
Newark, F. L., 1915
New York, N. L., 1916
Cincinnati, N. L., 1916–1917
Pittsburgh, N. L., 1918–1920

McKEE, RAYMOND   Catcher
Detroit, A. L., 1913–1916, inc.

McKENRY, F. G.   Pitcher
Cincinnati, N. L., 1915–1916

McKINNEY   Infielder
Philadelphia, A. L., 1901

McLANE, E.   Outfielder
Brooklyn, N. L., 1907

McLARRY, POLLY HOWARD   Infielder
Chicago, A. L., 1912
Chicago, N. L., 1915

McLAUGHLIN, J. A.   Outfielder
Cincinnati, N. L., 1914

McLAUGHLIN, WARREN A.   Pitcher
Pittsburgh, N. L., 1902
Philadelphia, N. L., 1903

McLAURIN, R. E.   Outfielder
St. Louis, N. L., 1908

McLEAN, JOHN B.   Catcher
Boston, A. L., 1901
Chicago, N. L., 1903

St. Louis, N. L., 1904
Cincinnati, N. L., 1906–1912, inc.
St. Louis, N. L., 1913
New York, N. L., 1913–1915, inc.

McMACKIN, SAMUEL   Pitcher
Chicago, A. L., 1902
Detroit, A. L., 1902

McMAKIN, JOHN W.   Pitcher
Brooklyn, N. L., 1902

McMANUS, A.   Pitcher
Cincinnati, N. L., 1913

McMANUS, FRANK   Catcher
Brooklyn, N. L., 1903
Detroit, A. L., 1904
New York, A. L., 1904

McMANUS, M. J.   Infielder
St. Louis, A. L., 1920–1921

McMILLAN, THOMAS LAW   S. S.
Brooklyn, N. L., 1908–1910, inc.
Cincinnati, N. L., 1910
New York, A. L., 1912

McMULLIN, FRED   Infielder
Detroit, A. L., 1914
Chicago, A. L., 1916–1920, inc.

McNALLY, MICHAEL J.   Infielder
Boston, A. L., 1915–1920, inc. (excepting 1918)
New York, A. L., 1921

McNEAL   Pitcher
Cleveland, A. L.,1901

McNICHOL, EDWARD   Pitcher
Boston, N. L., 1904–1905

McPHERSON   Pitcher
Philadelphia, A. L., 1901

McPERSON, JOHN   Pitcher
Philadelphia, N. L., 1904

McQUILLAN, GEORGE WASHINGTON
     Pitcher
Philadelphia, N. L., 1907–1910, inc.
Cincinnati, N. L., 1911
Pittsburgh, N. L., 1913–1915, inc.

Philadelphia, N. L., 1915–1916
Cleveland, N. L., 1918

McQUILLAN, HUGH A.   Pitcher
Boston, N. L., 1918–1919–1920–1921

McTIGUE, W. P.   Pitcher
Boston, N. L., 1911–1912–1913
Detroit, A. L., 1916

McWEENEY DOUGLAS   Pitcher
Chicago, A. L., 1921

MEADOWS, HENRY LEE   Pitcher
St. Louis, N. L., 1915–1916–1917–1918–1919
Philadelphia, N. L., 1919 to date

MEANEY   Infielder
Detroit, A. L., 1912

MEARA, CHARLES   Outfielder
New York, A. L., 1914

MEE   Infielder
St. Louis, A. L., 1910

MEIER, ARTHUR E.   Substitute
Pittsburgh, N. L., 1906

MEINKE, R. B.   Infielder
Cincinnati, N. L., 1910

MEISTER, KARL   Outfielder
Cleveland, A. L., 1912

MEIXEL   Outfielder
Cleveland, A. L., 1912

MELLOR, WILLIAM   Infielder
Baltimore, A. L., 1902

MELOAN, PAUL   Outfielder
Chicago, A. L., 1910–1911
St. Louis, A. L., 1911

MELTER, STEPHEN   Pitcher
St. Louis, N. L., 1909

MENAFEE, JOHN   Pitcher
Chicago, N. L., 1901–1903, inc.

MENOSKEY, J. C.   Outfielder
Pittsburgh, F. L., 1914
Washington, A. L., 1916–1917–1919
Boston, A. L., 1920–1921

MENSOR, EDWARD   Outfielder
Pittsburgh, N. L., 1912–1914, inc.

MENZE, TED   Outfielder
St. Louis, N. L., 1918

MERCER, J.   Pitcher
Pittsburgh, N. L., 1910

MERCER, J. G.   Infielder
St. Louis, N. L., 1912

MERCER, WINNIFRED B.   P.—Inf.
Washington, A. L., 1901
Detroit, A. L., 1902

MERKLE, FRED C.   1st B.
New York, N. L., 1907–1916, inc.
Brooklyn, N. L., 1916–1917
Chicago, N. L., 1917–1920, inc.

MERRITT, GEORGE   P.—O. F.
Pittsburgh, N. L., 1902–1903

MERRITT, H.   Infielder
Detroit, A. L., 1921

MERRITT, HERMAN   Infielder
New York, N. L., 1913

MERTES, SAMUEL   2nd B.—O. F.
Chicago, A. L., 1901–1902
New York, N. L., 1903–1906, inc.
St. Louis, N. L., 1906

MESSENGER, C. W.   Outfielder
Chicago, A. L., 1909–1910–1911
St. Louis, A. L., 1914

METCALF, R. F.   Infielder
Cincinnati, N. L., 1909

MEUSEL, EMIL F.   Outfielder
Washington, A. L., 1914
Philadelphia, N. L., 1918–1919–1920–
1921
New York, N. L., 1921

MEUSEL, ROBERT WILLIAM   Outfielder
New York, A. L., 1920–1921

MEYER, BENNY   Outfielder
Brooklyn, N. L., 1913
Baltimore, F. L., 1914
Buffalo, F. L., 1915

MEYER, LEE   Infielder
Brooklyn, N. L., 1909

MEYER, WILLIAM A.   Catcher
Chicago, A. L., 1913
Philadelphia, A. L., 1905

MEYERS   Pitcher
Philadelphia, A. L., 1905

MEYERS, JOHN T.   Catcher
New York, N. L., 1909–1915, inc.
Brooklyn, N. L., 1916–1917
Boston, N. L., 1917

MEYERS, RALPH   1st B.
Boston, A. L., 1910–1911
St. Louis, A. L., 1911
Boston, N. L., 1913
Brooklyn, N. L., 1914–1915

MICHAELSON, AUGUST   Pitcher
Chicago, A. L., 1921

MIDDLETON, JOHN B.   Pitcher
New York, N. L., 1917
Detroit, A. L., 1921

MIDKIFF, EZRA B.   Infielder
New York, A. L., 1912–1913

MILAN, HORACE   Oufielder
Washington, A. L., 1915–1917

MILAN, JESSE CLYDE   Outfielder
Washington, A. L., 1907 to date

MILJUS, JOHN KENNETH   Pitcher
Brooklyn, N. L., 1917; 1920–1921

MILLER   Outfielder
Washington, A. L., 1909; 1911

MILLER, C. ROSCOE   Pitcher
Detroit, A. L., 1901–1902
New York, N. L., 1902–1903
Pittsburgh, N. L., 1904

MILLER, CHARLES   Outfielder
St. Louis, N. L., 1913–1914

MILLER, DAKIN E.   Outfielder
Chicago, N. L., 1902

MILLER, EDMUND JOHN   Outfielder
Washington, A. L., 1921

MILLER, EDWARD J.   1st B.
St. Louis, A. L., 1914
Cleveland, A. L., 1918

MILLER, ELMER   Outfielder
St. Louis, N. L., 1912
New York, A. L., 1915–1918, inc.; 1921

MILLER, FRANK LEE   Pitcher
Chicago, A. L., 1913
Pittsburgh, N. L., 1916–1919, inc.

MILLER, HUGH S.   1st B.
Philadelphia, N. L., 1911
St. Louis, F. L., 1914

MILLER, JAMES   Infielder
New York, N. L., 1901

MILLER, JOHN BARNEY   2nd B.–1st B.
Pittsburgh, N. L., 1909–1913, inc.
St. Louis, N. L., 1914–1919, inc.
Philadelphia, N. L., 1920–1921

MILLER, LAWRENCE   Pitcher
St. Louis, N. L., 1903

MILLER, LAWRENCE   Outfielder
Brooklyn, N. L., 1916
Boston, A. L., 1918

MILLER, OTTO LOWELL   Catcher
Brooklyn, N. L., 1910 to date

MILLER, R.   Pitcher
Brooklyn, N. L., 1910

MILLER, RALPH HENRY   Pitcher
Washington, A. L., 1921

MILLER, RALPH J.   Infielder
Philadelphia, N. L., 1920–1921

MILLER, RAYMOND   1st B.
Pittsburgh, N. L.,1917
Cleveland, A. L., 1917

MILLER, ROY O.   Outfielder
Chicago, N. L., 1910
Boston, N. L., 1910–1912, inc.
Philadelphia, N. L., 1912–1913
Cincinnati, N. L., 1914

MILLER, THOMAS ROYALL   Outfielder
Boston, N. L., 1918–1919

MILLER, W. W.   Pitcher
Brooklyn, N. L., 1911

MILLER, WARD TAYLOR   Outfielder
Pittsburgh, N. L., 1909
Cincinnati, N. L., 1909–1910
Chicago, N. L., 1912–1913
St. Louis, F. L., 1914–1915
St. Louis, A. L., 1916–1917

MILLER, WILLIAM   Outfielder
Pittsburgh, N. L., 1902

MILLIGAN, WILLIAM J.   Pitcher
Philadelphia, A. L., 1901
New York, N. L., 1904

MILLS   Infielder
Cleveland, A. L., 1910; 1914

MILLS, RUPERT   Infielder
Newark, F. L., 1915

MINAHAN, E. J.   Pitcher
Cincinnati, N. L., 1907

MINOR   Pitcher
Philadelphia, A. L., 1921

MISSE   Infielder
St. Louis, F. L., 1914

MITCHELL, A. ROY   Pitcher
St. Louis, A. L., 1911–1912–1913–1914
Chicago, A. L., 1918
Cincinnati, N. L., 1918–1919

MITCHELL, CLARENCE E.   Pitcher
Detroit, A. L., 1911
Cincinnati, N. L., 1916–1917
Brooklyn, N. L., 1918 to date

MITCHELL, FRED L.   P.—Sub.
Boston, A. L., 1901–1902
Philadelphia, A. L., 1902
Philadelphia, N. L., 1903–1904
Brooklyn, N. L., 1904–1905
New York, A. L., 1910
Boston, N. L., 1913

MITCHELL, JOHN   Infielder
New York, A. L., 1921

MITCHELL, MICHAEL F.   Outfielder
Cincinnati, N. L., 1907–1912, inc.

Chicago, N. L., 1913
Pittsburgh, N. L., 1913–1914
Washington, A. L., 1914

MITCHELL, WILLIAM   Pitcher
Cleveland, A. L., 1909–1916, inc.
Detroit, A. L., 1916–1919, inc.

MITTERLING   Outfielder
Philadelphia, A. L., 1916

MOELLER, DANIEL E.   Outfielder
Pittsburgh, N. L., 1907–1908
Washington, A. L., 1914–1916, inc.
Cleveland, A. L., 1916

MOGRIDGE, GEORGE   Pitcher
Chicago, A. L., 1911–1912
New York, A. L., 1915–1920, inc.
Washington, A. L., 1921

MOHART, GEORGE B.   Pitcher
Brooklyn, N. L., 1920–1921

MOKAN, JOHN L.   Outfielder
Pittsburgh, N. L., 1921

MOLLENKAMP   Infielder
Philadelphia, N. L., 1914

MOLLWITZ, FRED   1st B.
Chicago, N. L., 1913–1914
Cincinnati, N. L., 1914–1916, inc.
Chicago, N. L., 1916
Pittsburgh, N. L., 1917–1919, inc.
St. Louis, N. L., 1919

MOLYNEAUX, VINCENT   Pitcher
St. Louis, A. L., 1917
Boston, A. L., 1918

MONROE, ED   Pitcher
New York, A. L., 1917–1918

MONROE, JOHN A.   Infielder
New York, N. L., 1921
Philadelphia, N. L., 1921

MOORE   Infielder
St. Louis, A. L., 1917

MOORE, EARL L.   Pitcher
Cleveland, A. L., 1901–1907, inc.
New York, A. L., 1907
Philadelphia, N. L., 1908–1913, inc.

Chicago, N. L., 1913
Buffalo, F. L., 1914

MOORE, EUGENE   Pitcher
Pittsburgh, N. L., 1909–1910
Cincinnati, N. L., 1912

MOORE, G. W.   Infielder
Chicago, N. L., 1912

MOORE, GEORGE   Pitcher
Pittsburgh, N. L., 1905

MOORE, ROY DANIEL   Pitcher
Philadelphia, A. L., 1920–1921

MORAN, CHARLES   Infielder
Washington, A. L., 1903–1904
St. Louis, A. L., 1904–1905

MORAN, CHARLES B.   P.—C.
St. Louis, N. L., 1903; 1908

MORAN, HARRY   Pitcher
Detroit, A. L., 1912
Buffalo, F. L., 1914
Newark, F. L., 1915

MORAN, J. HERBERT   Outfielder
Philadelphia, A. L., 1908
Boston, N. L., 1908–1910, inc.
Brooklyn, N. L., 1912–1913
Cincinnati, N. L., 1914
Boston, N. L., 1914–1915

MORAN, PATRICK JOSEPH   C.—Inf.
Boston, N. L., 1901–1905, inc.
Chicago, N. L., 1906–1909, inc.
Philadelphia, N. L., 1910–1914, inc.

MORE, FOREST   Pitcher
Boston, N. L., 1909
St. Louis, N. L., 1909

MOREN, LEWIS H.   Pitcher
Pittsburgh, N. L., 1903–1904
Philadelphia, N. L., 1907–1910, inc.

MOREY, DAVID B.   Pitcher
Philadelphia, A. L., 1913

MORGAN, CYRIL ARLON   Pitcher
Boston, N. L., 1921

MORGAN, HARRY R.   Pitcher
St. Louis, A. L., 1903–1905, inc.; 1907

Boston, A. L., 1907–1909, inc.
Philadelphia, A. L., 1909–1912, inc.
Cincinnati, N. L., 1913

MORGAN, RAYMOND CARYLL   Infielder
Washington, A. L., 1911–1918, inc.

MORIARTY, GEORGE JOSEPH   Infielder
Chicago, N. L., 1903–1904
New York, A. L., 1906–1908, inc.
Detroit, A. L., 1909–1915, inc.
Chicago, A. L., 1916

MORIARTY, W. J.   Infielder
Cincinnati, N. L., 1909

MORRIS, J. WALTER   Infielder
St. Louis, N. L., 1908

MORRISETTE, WILLIAM   Pitcher
Philadelphia, A. L., 1915–1916
Detroit, A. L., 1920

MORRISON, JOHN D.   Pitcher
Pittsburgh, N. L., 1920–1921

MORRISON, PHILIP   Pitcher
Pittsburgh, N. L., 1921

MORRISSEY, FRANK   Pitcher
Boston, A. L., 1901
Chicago, N. L., 1902

MORRISSEY, JOHN   Infielder
Cincinnati, N. L., 1902–1903

MORSE, P. R.   Outfielder
St. Louis, N. L., 1911

MORTON, GUY   Pitcher
Cleveland, A. L., 1914 to date

MOSELY, EARL VICTOR   Pitcher
Boston, A. L., 1913
Indianapolis, F. L., 1914
Newark, F. L., 1915
Cincinnati, N. L., 1916

MOSER, W. F.   Pitcher
Philadelphia, N. L., 1906
Boston, A. L., 1911
St. Louis, A. L., 1911

MOSKIMAN, W. B.   Pitcher
Boston, A. L., 1910

MOSTIL, JOHN ANTHONY   Outfielder
Chicago, A. L., 1918–1921

MOTT   Outfielder
Cleveland, A. L., 1903

MOULTON   Infielder
St. Louis, A. L., 1911

MOWE, RAY B.   Infielder
Brooklyn, N. L., 1913

MOWREY, H. H.   Infielder
Cincinnati, N. L., 1905–1909, inc.
St. Louis, N. L., 1909–1913, inc.
Pittsburgh, N. L., 1914
Pittsburgh, F. L., 1915
Brooklyn, N. L., 1916–1917

MOYER, CHARLES EDWARD   Pitcher
Washington, A. L., 1910

MUELLER, CLARENCE FRANKLIN
    Outfielder
St. Louis, N. L., 1920–1921

MUENCH, JACOB   1st B.
Philadelphia, A. L., 1918

MULLEN   Infielder
St. Louis, A. L., 1920

MULLEN, CHARLES   Infielder
Chicago, A. L., 1910–1911
New York, A. L., 1914–1916, inc.

MULLIGAN, EDWARD J.   Infielder
Chicago, N. L., 1915–1916
Chicago, A. L., 1921

MULLIN, GEORGE   Pitcher
Detroit, A. L., 1902–1913, inc.
Washington, A. L., 1913
Indiannapolis, F. L., 1914

MULLIN, JAMES   Infielder
Philadelphia, A. L., 1904
Washington, A. L., 1904–1905

MULRENNAN, DOMINICK JOSEPH
    Pitcher
Chicago, A. L., 1921

MUNDY, WILLIAM E.   Infielder
Boston, A. L., 1913

MUNSON, CLARENCE   Catcher
Philadelphia, N. L., 1905

MURCH, SIMEON   Infielder
St. Louis, N. L., 1904–1905
Brooklyn, N. L., 1908

MURCHISON, TIM   Pitcher
St. Louis, N. L., 1917
Cleveland, A. L., 1920

MURDOCK, W. E.   Outfielder
St. Louis, N. L., 1908

MURPHY, DANIEL L.   Inf.—O. F.
New York, N. L., 1901
Philadelphia, A. L., 1902–1913, inc.
Brooklyn, F. L., 1914–1915

MURPHY, EDWARD J.   Pitcher
St. Louis, N. L., 1901–1902–1903

MURPHY, FRED   Inf.—O. F.
Boston, N. L., 1901
New York, N. L., 1901
Boston, N. L., 1902

MURPHY, H.   Outfielder
St. Louis, N. L., 1909

MURPHY, H. C.   Infielder
Philadelphia, N. L., 1914

MURPHY, J. EDWARD   Outfielder
Philadelphia, A. L., 1912–1915, inc.
Chicago, A. L., 1915–1921, inc.

MURPHY, JOHN P.   Infielder
St. Louis, N. L., 1902

MURPHY, LEO J.   Catcher
Pittsburgh, N. L., 1915

MURPHY, J. J.   Catcher
St. Louis, N. L., 1912

MURPHY, MICHAEL J.   Catcher
Philadelphia, A. L., 1916

MURPHY, PATRICK J.   Pitcher
Philadelphia, N. L., 1919

MURPHY, ROBERT R.   Outfielder
Boston, N. L., 1918
Washington, A. L., 1919

MURRAY, EDWARD   Infielder
St. Louis, A. L., 1917

MURRAY, J.   Outfielder
Chicago, N. L., 1902

MURRAY, JAMES   Outfielder
St. Louis, A. L., 1911
Boston, N. L., 1914

MURRAY, JOHN J.   Outfielder
St. Louis, N. L., 1906–1908, inc.
New York, N. L., 1909–1914, inc.
Chicago, N. L., 1915
New York, N. L., 1915–1917

MUSSER, PAUL   Pitcher
Washington, A. L., 1912
Boston, A. L., 1919

MYATT, GLEN C.   Catcher
Philadelphia, A. L., 1920–1921

MYERS, ELMER GLEN   Pitcher
Philadelphia, A. L., 1915–1918, inc.
Cleveland, A. L., 1919–1920
Boston, A. L., 1920–1921

MYERS, HENRY HARRISON   Outfielder
Brooklyn, N. L., 1909; 1911–1914 to date

NABORS, JOHN   Pitcher
Philadelphia, A. L., 1915–1916–1917

NAGELSON   Catcher
Cleveland, A. L., 1912

NAGLE, WALTER DANIEL   Pitcher
Boston, A. L., 1911
Pittsburgh, N. L., 1911

NANCE, WILLIAM G.   Outfielder
Detroit, A. L., 1901

NAPIER, SAMUEL L.   Pitcher
St. Louis, A. L., 1912
Chicago, N. L., 1918
Cincinnati, N. L., 1920–1921

NASH, KENNETH M.   Infielder
Cleveland, A. L., 1912
St. Louis, N. L., 1914

NAYLOR, ROLEINE C.   Pitcher
Philadelphia, A. L., 1917; 1919–1920–
1921

NEAL, OFFA   Infielder
New York, N. L., 1905

NEALE, ALFRED EARLE   Outfielder
Cincinnati, N. L., 1916–1917–1918–1919–
1920
Philadelphia, N. L., 1921
Cincinnati, N. L., 1921

NEALON, JAMES   1st B.
Pittsburgh, N. L., 1906–1907

NEEDHAM, THOMAS J.   Catcher
Boston, N. L., 1904–1907, inc.
New York, N. L., 1908
Chicago, N. L., 1909–1914, inc.

NEFF, DOUGLAS WILLIAM   Infielder
Washington, A. L., 1914–1915

NEHER   Pitcher
Cleveland, A. L., 1912

NEHF, ARTHUR N.   Pitcher
Boston, N. L., 1915–1916–1917–1918–
1919
New York, N. L., 1919–1920–1921

NEIGHBORS, CECIL   Outfielder
Pittsburgh, N. L., 1908

NEIS, BERNIS EDMUND   Outfielder
Brooklyn, N. Y., 1920–1921

NELSON   Infielder
New York, N. L., 1901

NELSON   Pitcher
Chicago, A. L., 1908

NELSON, ALBERT   Pitcher
St. Louis, A. L., 1910–1912, inc.
Philadelphia, N. L., 1912–1913
Cincinnati, N. L., 1913

NELSON, LUTHER   Pitcher
New York, A. L., 1919

NESS, JOHN CHARLES   1st B.
Detroit, A. L., 1911
Chicago, A. L., 1916

NETZEL   Infielder
Cleveland, A. L., 1909

NEUER, J. S.   Pitcher
New York, A. L., 1907

NEWELL   Pitcher
St. Louis, A. L., 1907

NEWKIRK, JOE IVAN   Pitcher
Chicago, N. L., 1919–1920

NEWMAN, PAT   1st B.
St. Louis, A. L., 1910–1911

NEWTON, EUSTACE JAMES   Pitcher
Cincinnati, N. L., 1901
Brooklyn, N. L., 1901–1902
New York, A. L., 1905–1909, inc.

NICHOLS, SIMON   Infielder
Detroit, A. L., 1903
Philadelphia, A. L., 1907–1908–1909

NICHOLS   Infielder
Cleveland, A. L., 1910

NICHOLS, ARTHUR   Catcher—1st B.
St. Louis, N. L., 1901–1902–1903

NICHOLS, CHARLES A.   Pitcher
Boston, N. L., 1901
St. Louis, N. L., 1904–1905
Philadelphia, N. L., 1905–1906

NICHOLSON, F.   Pitcher
Philadelphia, N. L., 1912

NICHOLSON, FRED   Outfielder
Detroit, A. L., 1917
Pittsburgh, N. L., 1919–1920
Boston, N. L., 1921

NICHOLSON, OVID   Outfielder
Pittsburgh, N. L., 1912

NICKLAN   Outfielder
Cleveland, A. L., 1908

NIEBERGALL, CHARLES ARTHUR   Catcher
St. Louis, N. L., 1921

NIEHAUS, RICHARD J.   Pitcher
St. Louis, N. L., 1913–1914
Cleveland, A. L., 1920

NIEHOFF, JOHN ALBERT   Infielder
Cincinnati, N. L., 1913–1914
Philadelphia, N. L., 1915–1917, inc.
New York, N. L., 1918
St. Louis, N. L., 1918

NIETZKE, ERNEST   Pitcher
Boston, A. L., 1921

NILES, HARRY   Inf.—O. F.
St. Louis, A. L., 1906–1907
New York, A. L., 1908
Boston, A. L., 1908–1910, inc.
Cleveland, A. L., 1910

NILL, GEORGE C.   Infielder
Washington, A. L., 1904–1907, inc.
Cleveland, A. L., 1907

NIXON, ALBERT R.   Outfielder
Brooklyn, N. L., 1916; 1918
Boston, N. L., 1921

NOONAN, PETER   Catcher
Philadelphia, A. L., 1904
Chicago, N. L., 1906
St. Louis, N. L., 1906–1907

NOPS, JEREMIAH   Pitcher
Baltimore, A. L., 1901

NORDYKE, LOUIS   Infielder
St. Louis, A. L., 1906

NORTH, LOUIS ALEXANDER   Pitcher
Detroit, A. L., 1913
St. Louis, N. L., 1920–1921

NORTHERN, HUBBARD E.   Outfielder
St. Louis, A. L., 1910
Cincinnati, N. L., 1911
Brooklyn, N. L., 1911–1912

NORTHROP, GEORGE H.   Pitcher
Boston, N. L., 1918–1919

NOURSE, CHESTER L.   Pitcher
Boston, A. L., 1909

NOYES, WINFIELD C.   Pitcher
Boston, N. L., 1913
Philadelphia, A. L., 1917; 1919
Chicago, A. L., 1919

NUNAMAKER, LESLIE G.   Catcher
Boston, A. L., 1911–1914, inc.
New York, A. L., 1914–1917, inc.
St. Louis, A. L., 1918
Cleveland, A. L., 1919 to date

NUTTER, EVERETT   Outfielder
Boston, N. L., 1919

NYE   Infielder
St. Louis, N. L., 1917

OAKES, ENNIS T.   Outfielder
Cincinnati, N. L., 1909
St. Louis, N. L., 1910–1913, inc.
Pittsburgh, F. L., 1914–1915

OBERLIN, FRANK   Pitcher
Boston, A. L., 1906
Washington, A. L., 1907–1909–1910

O'BRIEN, JOHN   Infielder
St. Louis, A. L., 1906
Washington, A. L., 1907
Cleveland, A. L., 1907

O'BRIEN, JOHN J.   Outfielder
Washington, A. L., 1901
Cleveland, A. L., 1901
Boston, A. L., 1903

O'BRIEN, PETER J.   Infielder
Cincinnati, N. L., 1901

O'BRIEN, RAY   Outfielder
Pittsburgh, N. L., 1916

O'BRIEN, THOMAS J.   Pitcher
Boston, A. L., 1911–1912–1913
Chicago, A. L., 1913

O'CONNELL, JOHN   Infielder
Detroit, A. L., 1902

O'CONNOR, J.   Catcher
Chicago, N. L., 1916

O'CONNOR, JOHN   Catcher
Pittsburgh, N. L., 1901–1902
New York, A. L., 1903
St. Louis, A. L., 1904; 1906–1907; 1909–
1910

O'CONNOR, PATRICK FRANCIS Catcher
Pittsburgh, N. L., 1908–1910, inc.
St. Louis, N. L., 1914
Pittsburgh, F. L., 1915
New York, A. L., 1918

ODENWALD, THEODORE JOSEPH   Pitcher
Cleveland, A. L., 1921

O'DOUL, FRANK J.   Pitcher
New York, A. L., 1919–1920

ODWELL, FRED   Outfielder
Cincinnati, N. L., 1904–1907, inc.

OESCHGER, JOSEPH   Pitcher
Philadelphia, N. L., 1914–1919, inc.
New York, N. L, 1919
Boston, N. L., 1919 to date

O'FARRELL, ROBERT A.   Catcher
Chicago, N. L., 1915–1921, inc.

OGDEN, JOHN MAHLON   Pitcher
New York, N. L., 1918

O'HAGAN, HAROLD P.   1st B.
Chicago, N. L., 1902
New York, N. L., 1902
Cleveland, A. L., 1902

O'HARA, THOMAS   Outfielder
Boston, N. L., 1904
St. Louis, N. L., 1906–1907

O'HARA, WILLIAM   Outfielder
New York, N. L., 1909
St. Louis, N. L., 1910

OKRIE, FRANK MALCOLM   Pitcher
Detroit, A. L., 1920

OLDHAM, JOHN C.   Pitcher
Detroit, A. L., 1914–1915; 1920–1921

OLDRING, REUBEN NOSHIER   Outfielder
New York, A. L., 1905
Philadelphia, A. L., 1906–1916, inc.
New York, A. L., 1916
Philadelphia, A. L., 1918

O'LEARY, CHARLES T.   Infielder
Detroit, A. L., 1904–1911, inc.
St. Louis, N. L., 1913

OLMSTEAD, FRED   Pitcher
Boston, A. L., 1905
Chicago, A. L., 1909–1911, inc.

OLSON, IVAN M.   Infielder
Cleveland, A. L., 1911–1914, inc.
Cincinnati, N. L., 1915
Brooklyn, N. L., 1914–1916, inc.

O'MARA, OLIVER EDWARD   Infielder
Detroit, A. L., 1912
Brooklyn, N. L., 1914–1916, inc.; 1918–1919

O'NEIL, GEORGE M.   Catcher
New York, N. L., 1902

O'NEILL, JACK   Catcher
New York, N. L., 1902

O'NEILL, JAMES LEO   Infielder
Washington, A. L., 1920

O'NEILL, JOHN J.   Catcher
St. Louis, N. L., 1902–1903
Chicago, N. L., 1904–1905
Boston, N. L., 1906

O'NEILL, MICHAEL JOYCE   P.—O. F.
St. Louis, N. L., 1901–1904, inc.
Cincinnati, N. L., 1907

O'NEILL, PHILIP   Catcher
Cincinnati, N. L., 1904

O'NEILL, STEPHEN FRANCIS   Catcher
Cleveland, A. L., 1911 to date

O'NEILL, WILLIAM JOHN   Substitute
Boston, A. L., 1904
Washington, A. L., 1904
Chicago, A. L., 1906

ONSLOW, EDWARD HENRY   1st B.
Detroit, A. L., 1912–1913
Cleveland, A. L., 1918

ONSLOW, JOHN   Catcher
Detroit, A. L., 1912
New York, N. L., 1917

ORME, GEORGE   Outfielder
Boston, A. L., 1920

ORNDORF, JESSE   Catcher
Boston, N. L., 1907

PERRIN, JOHN S.   Outfielder
Boston, A. L., 1921

PERRING, GEORGE   Infielder
Cleveland, A. L., 1908–1910, inc.
Kansas City, F. L., 1914–1915

PERRITT, WILLIAM DAYTON   Pitcher

St. Louis, N. L., 1912–1914, inc.
New York, N. L., 1915–1921, inc.
Detroit, A. L., 1921

PERRY   Outfielder
Detroit, A. L., 1912

PERRY, SCOTT   Pitcher
St. Louis, A. L., 1915
Chicago, N. L., 1916
Cincinnati, N. L., 1917
Philadelphia, A. L., 1918–1921, inc.

PERRYMAN, EMMETT KEY   Pitcher
St. Louis, A. L., 1915

PERTICA, WILLIAM   Pitcher
Boston, A. L., 1918
St. Louis, N. L., 1921

PETERS, JOHN   Catcher
Detroit, A. L., 1915

PETERS, JOHN   Catcher
Cleveland, A. L., 1918
Philadelphia, N. L., 1921

PETERS, O. C.   Pitcher
Chicago, A. L., 1912

PETERSON   Catcher
Boston, A. L., 1906–1907

PETTY, JESSE LEE   Pitcher
Cleveland, A. L., 1921

PEZOLD, LORENZ   Infield
Cleveland, A. L., 1914

PFEFER, EDWARD JOSEPH   Pitcher
St. Louis, A. L., 1911
Brooklyn, N. L., 1913–1921, inc.
St. Louis, N. L., 1921

PFEFFER, FRANK XAVIER   Pitcher
Chicago, N. L., 1905
Boston, N. L., 1906–1908, inc.
Chicago, N. L., 1910
Boston, N. L., 1911

PFIESTER, JOHN A.   Pitcher
Pittsburgh, N. L., 1903–1904
Chicago, N. L., 1906–1911, inc.

PFYLE, MONTE   Substitute
New York, N. L., 1907

PHELAN, ARTHUR   Infielder
Cincinnati, N. L., 1910; 1912
Chicago, N. L., 1913–1915, inc.

PHELPS, EDWARD J.   Catcher
Pittsburgh, N. L., 1902–1903–1904
Cincinnati, N. L., 1905–1906
Pittsburgh, N. L., 1906–1908, inc.
St. Louis, N. L., 1909–1910
Brooklyn, N. L., 1912–1913

PHILLIPPE, CHARLES LOUIS   Pitcher
Pittsburgh, N. L., 1901–1911, inc.

PHILLIPS, THOMAS   Pitcher
St. Louis, A. L., 1915
Cleveland, A. L., 1919
Washington, A. L., 1921

PHILLIPS, WILLIAM C.   Pitcher
Cincinnati, N. L., 1901–1902–1903

PHYLE, WILLIAM   Pitcher—Inf.
New York, N. L., 1901
St. Louis, N. L., 1906

PIATT, WILEY   Pitcher
Philadelphia, A. L., 1901
Chicago, A. L., 1901–1902
Boston, N. L., 1903

PICINICH, VALENTINE J.   Catcher
Philadelphia, A. L., 1916–1917
Washington, A. L., 1918–1921, inc.

PICK, CHARLES   Infielder—O. F.
Washington, A. L., 1914–1915
Philadelphia, A. L., 1916
Chicago, N. L., 1918–1919
Boston, N. L., 1919–1920

PICKERING, OLIVER D.   Outfielder
Cleveland, A. L., 1901–1902
Philadelphia, A. L., 1903–1904
St. Louis, A. L., 1907
Washington, A. L., 1908

PICKETT, C. A.   Pitcher
St. Louis, N. L., 1910

PICKUP, CLARENCE   Outfielder
Philadelphia, N. L., 1918

PIEH, JOHN   Pitcher
New York, A. L., 1913–1915, inc.

PIERCE, GEORGE T.   Pitcher
Chicago, N. L., 1912–1916, inc.
St. Louis, N. L., 1917

PIERCY, WILLIAM   Pitcher
New York, A. L., 1917; 1921

PIEROTTI, ALBERT F.   Pitcher
Boston, N. L., 1920–1921

PIERSON, WILLIAM   Pitcher
Philadelphia, A. L., 1918–1919

PIEZ, CHARLES W.   Substitute
New York, N. L., 1914

PILLETT, HERMAN   Pitcher
Cincinnati, N. L., 1917

PINELLI, RALPH ARTHUR   Infielder
Chicago, A. L., 1918
Detroit, A. L., 1920

PIPP, WALTER CHARLES   1st B.
Detroit, A. L., 1913
New York, A. L., 1915–1921, inc.

PITLER, JACOB   Infielder
Pittsburgh, N. L., 1917–1918

PITTENGER, CLARK   Infielder
Boston, A. L., 1921

PITTENGER, CHARLES   Pitcher
Boston, N. L., 1901–1904, inc.
Philadelphia, N. L., 1905–1907, inc.

PLANK, EDWARD S.   Pitcher
Philadelphia, A. L., 1901–1914, inc.
St. Louis, F. L., 1915
St. Louis, A. L., 1916–1917

PLATTE, ALFRED   Outfielder
Detroit, A. L., 1913

PLITT, NORMAN   Pitcher
Brooklyn, N. L., 1918

POLCHOW, LOUIS   Pitcher
Cleveland, A. L., 1902

POND   Infielder
Boston, A. L., 1910

PONDER, CHAS. ELMER   Pitcher
Pittsburgh, N. L., 1917; 1919–1920–1921
Chicago, N. L., 1921

POOLE, EDWARD   Pitcher
Pittsburgh, N. L., 1901–1902
Cincinnati, N. L., 1902–1903
Brooklyn, N. L., 1904

POPP, WILLIAM   Pitcher
St. Louis, N. L., 1902

PORTER   Pitcher
Philadelphia, A. L., 1902

POTTS   Outfielder
Kansas City, F. L., 1914

POUNDS, CHARLES   Pitcher
Brooklyn, N. L., 1903
Cleveland, A. L., 1903

POWELL, JOHN   Pitcher
St. Louis, N. L., 1901
St. Louis, A. L., 1902–1903
New York, A. L., 1904–1905
St. Louis, A. L., 1905–1913, inc.

POWELL, RAYMOND R.   Outfielder
Detroit, A. L., 1913
Boston, N. L., 1917 to date

POWELL, W.   Pitcher
Chicago, N. L., 1912

POWELL, WILLIAM B.   Pitcher
Pittsburgh, N. L., 1909–1910
Cincinnati, N. L., 1913

POWERS, MAURICE R.   Catcher
Philadelphia, A. L., 1901–1909, inc.;
loaned to New York briefly in 1905

PRATT, DERRILL B.   2nd B.
St. Louis, A. L., 1912–1917, inc.
New York, N. L., 1918–1920, inc.
Boston, A. L., 1921

PRATT, L. J.   Catcher
Brooklyn, F. L., 1915
Newark, F. L., 1915

PRATT, W.   Substitute
Chicago, A. L., 1921

PRENDERGAST, MICHAEL   Pitcher
Chicago, F. L., 1914–1915
Chicago, N. L., 1916–1917
Philadelphia, N. L., 1918–1919

PRENTISS, GEORGE   Pitcher
  Boston, A. L., 1902
  Baltimore, A. L, 1902

PRIEST, JOHN C.   Infielder
  New York, A. L., 1911–1912

PROTHRO, JAMES THOMPSON   Infielder
  Washington, A. L., 1902

PROUGH, C.   Pitcher
  Cincinnati, N. L., 1912

PRUESS, EARL HENRY   Outfielder
  St. Louis, A. L., 1921

PRUITT, CHARLES   Pitcher
  Boston, A. L., 1907–1908
  Cleveland, A. L., 1908

PUCKETT, T.   Pitcher
  Philadelphia, N. L., 1911

PURTELL, WILLIAM P.   Infielder
  Chicago, A. L., 1908–1910, inc.
  Boston, A. L., 1910–1911
  Detroit, A. L., 1914

PUTTMAN, AMBROSE   Pitcher
  New York, A. L., 1903–1905, inc.
  St. Louis, N. L., 1906

QUILLEN, LEE   Infielder
  Chicago, A. L., 1906–1907

QUINLAN, THOMAS F.   Outfielder
  St. Louis, N. L., 1913
  Chicago, A. L., 1915

QUINN, CLARENCE   Pitcher
  Philadelphia, A. L., 1902–1903

QUINN, J. E.   Catcher
  Philadelphia, N. L., 1911

QUINN, JOHN   Pitcher
  New York, A. L., 1909–1912, inc.
  Boston, N. L., 1913
  Baltimore, F. L., 1914–1915
  Chicago, A. L., 19
  New York, A. L., 1919–1921

QUINN, JOSEPH   Infielder
  Washington, A. L., 1901

RADABAUGH, R.   Pitcher
  St. Louis, N. L., 1911

RADER, DON R.   S. S.
  Philadelphia, N. L., 1921

RADER, DREW L.   Pitcher
  Pittsburgh, N. L., 1921

RAFTER, JOHN J.   Catcher
  Pittsburgh, N. L., 1904

RAFTERY, THOMAS   Outfielder
  Cleveland, A. L., 1909

RAGAN, DON CARLOS PATRICK   Pitcher
  Cincinnati, N. L., 1909
  Chicago, N. L., 1909
  Brooklyn, N. L., 1911–1915, inc.
  Boston, N. L., 1915–1919, inc.
  New York, N. L., 1919
  Chicago, A. L., 1919

RALEIGH, J. A.   Pitcher
  St. Louis, N. L., 1909–1910

RALSTON   Outfielder
  Washington, A. L., 1910

RANDALL, NEWTON   Outfielder
  Chicago, N. L., 1907
  Boston, N. L., 1907

RAPP, JOSEPH ALOYSIUS   Infielder
  New York–Philadelphia, N. L., 1921

RARIDEN, WILLIAM AMUEL   Catcher
  Boston, N. L., 1909–1913, inc.
  Indianapolis, F. L., 1914
  Newark, F. L., 1915
  New York, N. L., 1916–1918, inc.
  Cincinnati, N. L., 1919–1920

RASMUSSEN, HENRY   Pitcher
  Chicago, F. L., 1915

RATH, MAURICE C.   Infielder
  Philadelphia, A. L., 1909–1910
  Cleveland, A. L., 1910
  Chicago, A. L., 1912–1913
  Cincinnati, N. L., 1919–1920

RAUB, THOMAS J.   Catcher
  Chicago, N. L., 1903
  St. Louis, N. L., 1906

RAWLINGS, JOHN WILLIAM   Infielder
  Cincinnati, N. L., 1914

Kansas City, F. L., 1914–1915
Boston, N. L., 1917–1920, inc.
Philadelphia, N. L., 1920–1921
New York, N. L., 1921

RAY   Pitcher
St. Louis, A. L., 1910

RAY, C. G.   Pitcher
Philadelphia, A. L., 1915–1916

RAYMER, FRED C.   Infielder
Chicago, N. L., 1901
Boston, N. L., 1904–1905

RAYMOND, ARTHUR L.   Pitcher
Detroit, A. L., 1904
St. Louis, N. L., 1907–1908
New York, N. L., 1909–1911, inc.

RAYMOND, LOUIS A.   Infielder
Philadelphia, N. L., 1919

REAGAN, ARTHUR   Pitcher
Cincinnati, N. L., 1903

REARDON, P.   Outfielder
Brooklyn, N. L., 1906

REDDING, PHIL   Pitcher
St. Louis, N. L., 1912–1913

REDMOND, H. J.   Infielder
Brooklyn, N. L., 1909

REED, MILTON, JR.   Infielder
St. Louis, N. L., 1911
Philadelphia, N. L., 1913–1914
Newark, F. L., 1915

REESE, STANLEY   Pitcher
Washington, A. L., 1918

REGAN, MICHAEL JOHN   Pitcher
Cincinnati, N. L., 1917–1919, inc.

REHG, WALTER P.   Outfielder
Pittsburgh, N. L., 1912
Boston, A. L., 1913–1914
Boston, N. L., 1917–1918
Cincinnati, N. L., 1919

REIDY, WILLIAM   Pitcher
Milwaukee, A. L., 1901
St. Louis, A. L., 1902–1903
Brooklyn, N. L., 1903–1904

REILLEY   Outfielder
Cleveland, A. L., 1909

REILLY, A. E.   Infielder
Pittsburgh, N. L., 1917

REILLY, BARNEY   Infielder
Chicago, A. L., 1909

REILLY, HAROLD J.   Outfielder
Chicago, N. L., 1919

REILLY, THOMAS H.   Infielder
St. Louis, N. L., 1908–1909
Cleveland, A. L., 1914

REINHART, ARTHUR C.   Pitcher
St. Louis, N. L., 1908–1909

REIS, H. C.   Pitcher
St. Louis, N. L., 1911

REISIGL   Pitcher
Cleveland, A. L., 1911

REISLING, F. C.   Pitcher
Brooklyn, N. L., 1904–1905
Washington, A. L., 1909–1910

REMENTER   Catcher
Philadelphia, N. L., 1905

REMNEAS, A.   Pitcher
Detroit, A. L., 1912
St. Louis, A. L., 1915

RENFER   Pitcher
Detroit, A. L., 1913

REULBACH, EDWARD MARVIN   Pitcher
Chicago, N. L., 1905–1913, inc.
Brooklyn, N. L., 1913–1914
Newark, F. L., 1915
Boston, N. L., 1916–1917

REYNOLDS, E. R.   Pitcher
Detroit, A. L., 1914–1915

RHEAM   Infielder—O. F.
Pittsburgh, F. L., 1914–1915

RHOADES, ROBERT S.   Pitcher
Chicago, N. L., 1902
St. Louis, N. L., 1903
Cleveland, A. L., 1903–1909, inc.

RHODES, C. A.   Pitcher

Cincinnati, N. L., 1908
St. Louis, N. L., 1903

RHODES, CHARLES   Pitcher
St. Louis, N. L., 1906

RICE, EDGAR SAMUEL   Pitcher—O. F.
Washington, A. L., 1915 to date

RICHARDSON, J. W.   Pitcher
Philadelphia, A. L., 1915–1916

RICHARDSON, W. H.   Infielder
St. Louis, N. L., 1901

RICHBOURG, LANCE   Infielder
Philadelphia, N. L., 1921

RICHIE, LEWIS A.   Pitcher
Philadelphia, N. L., 1906–1909, inc.
Boston, N. L., 1909–1910
Chicago, N. L., 1910–1913, inc.

RICHMOND, RAYMOND   Pitcher
St. Louis, A. L., 1920–1921

RICHTER, EMIL HENRY   Pitcher
Chicago, N. L., 1911

RICKEY, C. BRANCH   Catcher
St. Louis, A. L., 1905–1906
New York, A. L., 1907
St. Louis, A. L., 1914

RICO, ARTHUR F.   Catcher
Boston, N. L., 1916–1917

RIEGER, E.   Pitcher
St. Louis, N. L., 1910

RIGGERT, JOSEPH   Outfielder
Boston, A. L., 1911
St. Louis, N. L., 1914
Boston, N. L., 1919

RILEY, JAMES   Outfielder
Boston, N. L., 1910

RILEY, JAMES   Infielder
St. Louis, A. L., 1921

RING, JAMES J.   Pitcher
Cincinnati, N. L., 1917–1920, inc.
Philadelphia, N. L., 1921

RISHBERG, CHARLES AUGUST   Infielder
Chicago, A. L., 1917–1920, inc.

RISING   Outfielder
Boston, A. L., 1905

RITCHEY, CLAUDE C.   2nd B.
Pittsburgh, N. L., 1901–1906, inc.
Boston, N. L., 1907–1909, inc.

RITTER, LOUIS   Catcher
Brooklyn, N. L., 1902–1908, inc.

RITTER, W. H.   Pitcher
Philadelphia, N. L., 1912
New York, N. L., 1914–1916, inc.

RIVIERE, ARTHUR B.   Pitcher
St. Louis, N. L., 1921

RIXEY, EPPA J.   Pitcher
Philadelphia, N. L., 1912–1920, inc.
Cincinnati, N. L., 1921

ROACH, WILBUR   Infielder
New York, A. L., 1910–1911
Washington, A. L., 1912
Buffalo, F. L., 1915

ROBERTAILLE, ANTHONY   Pitcher
Pittsburgh, N. L., 1904–1905

ROBERTS, C. A.   Catcher
St. Louis, N. L., 1913
Pittsburgh, F. L., 1914

ROBERTS, RAY   Pitcher
Philadelphia, A. L., 1919

ROBERTSON, CHARLES   Pitcher
Chicago, A. L., 1919

ROBERTSON, DAVIS A.   Outfielder
New York, N. L., 1912; 1914–1917, inc.;
1919
Chicago, N. L., 1919–1921, inc.
Pittsburgh, N. L., 1921

ROBERTSON, RICHARD J.   Pitcher
Cincinnati, N. L., 1913
Brooklyn, N. L., 1918
Washington, A. L., 1919

ROBINSON, CLYDE   Infielder
Washington, A. L., 1903
Detroit, A. L., 1904
Cincinnati, N. L., 1910

ROBINSON, JACK　　　　Catcher
New York, N. L., 1902

ROBINSON, JOHN HENRY　　Pitcher
Pittsburgh, N. L., 1911–1913, inc.
St. Louis, N. L., 1914–1915
New York, A. L., 1918

ROBINSON, WILBERT　　　Catcher
Baltimore, A. L., 1901–1902

ROCHE, JACK　　　　　Catcher
St. Louis, N. L., 1914–1915; 1917

ROCKENFELD, ISAAC　　　Infielder
St. Louis, A. L., 1905–1906

RODGERS, WILLIAM K.　　Infielder
Cleveland, A. L., 1915
Boston, A. L., 1915
Cincinnati, N. L., 1915–1916, inc.

RODRIGUEZ, JOSE　　　Infielder
New York, N. L., 1916–1918, inc.

ROGERS, THOMAS　　　Pitcher
St. Louis, A. L., 1917–1919, inc.
Philadelphia, A. L., 1919
New York, A. L., 1921

ROGGE, CLINTON　　　Pitcher
Pittsburgh, F. L., 1915
Cincinnati, N. L., 1921

ROHE, GEORGE　　　　3rd B.
Baltimore, A. L., 1901
Chicago, A. L., 1905–1907, inc.

ROHWER, RAY　　　　Substitute
Pittsburgh, N. L., 1921

ROLLING, R. C.　　　　Infielder
St. Louis, N. L., 1912

ROMMEL, EDWIN AMERICUS　Pitcher
Philadelphia, A. L., 1920–1921

RONDEAU, HENRI　Catcher—O. F.
Detroit, A. L., 1913
Washington, A. L., 1915–1916

ROSE　　　　　　　Pitcher
St. Louis, A. L., 1909

ROSS, SIDNEY　　　　Pitcher
New York, N. L., 1918

ROSSMAN, CLAUDE　　　1st B
Cleveland, A. L., 1906
Detroit, A. L., 1907–1909, inc.
St. Louis, A. L., 1909

ROTH, FRANK　　　　Catcher
Philadelphia, N. L., 1903–1904
St. Louis, N. L., 1905
Cincinnati, N. L., 1909–1910

ROTH, ROBERT FRANK　　Outfielder
Chicago, A. L., 1914–1915
Cleveland, A. L., 1915–1918, inc.
Philadelphia, A. L., 1919
Boston, A. L., 1919
Washington, A. L., 1920
New York, A. L., 1921

ROUSH, EDD J.　　　　Outfielder
Chicago, A. L., 1913
Indianapolis, F. L., 1914
Newark, F. L., 1915
New York, N. L., 1916
Cincinnati, N. L., 1916 to date

ROWAN, DAVID　　　　1st B.
St. Louis, A. L., 1911
Boston, A. L., 1911

ROWAN, JOHN A.　　　Pitcher
Detroit, A. L., 1906
Cincinnati, N. L., 1908–1910, inc.
Philadelphia, N. L., 1911
Chicago, N. L., 1911
Cincinnati, N. L., 1913–1914

ROWE, HARLAN S.　　　Infielder
Philadelphia, A. L., 1916

ROY, CHARLES　　　　Pitcher
Philadelphia, N. L., 1906

RUCKER, GEORGE NAPOLEON　Pitcher
Brooklyn, N. L., 1907–1916, inc.

RUDLEY　　　　　　Infielder
Cleveland, A. L., 1905

RUDOLPH, JOHN　　　Outfielder
Philadelphia, N. L., 1903
Chicago, N. L., 1904

RUDOLPH, RICHARD　　　Pitcher
New York, N. L., 1910–1911

Boston, N. L., 1913 to date (did not pitch in 1921)

RUEL, HAROLD   Catcher
St. Louis, A. L., 1915
New York, A. L., 1917–1920, inc.
Boston, A. L., 1921

RUETHER, WALTER HENRY   Pitcher
Chicago, N. L., 1917
Cincinnati, N. L., 1917–1918–1919–1920
Brooklyn, N. L., 1921

RUMLER, WILLIAM G.   Catcher—O. F.
St. Louis, A. L., 1914; 1916–1917

RUSIE, AMOS W.   Pitcher
Cincinnati, N. L., 1901

RUSSELL, ALLAN   Pitcher
New York, A. L., 1915–1919, inc.
Boston, A. L., 1919 to date

RUSSELL, CLARENCE DICKSON   Pitcher
Philadelphia, A. L., 1910–1911–1912

RUSSELL, EWELL A.   Pitcher
Chicago, A. L., 1912–1919, inc.

RUSSELL, HARVEY HOLMES   Catcher
Baltimore, F. L., 1914–1915

RUSSELL, JOHN   Pitcher
Chicago, A. L., 1921

RUSSELL, JOHN A.   Pitcher
Brooklyn, N. L., 1917–1918

RUTH, GEORGE HERMAN
            Pitcher—Outfielder—1st B.
Boston, A. L., 1914–1919, inc.
New York, A. L., 1920–1921

RYAN, J. BUD   Outfielder
Cleveland, A. L., 1912–1913

RYAN, JOHN   Pitcher
Cleveland, A. L., 1908
Boston, A. L., 1909
Brooklyn, N. L., 1911

RYAN, JOHN BENNETT   Catcher
St. Louis, N. L., 1901–1902–1903
Washington, A. L., 1912

RYAN, WILFRED D.   Pitcher
New York, N. L., 1919–1920–1921

SAIER, VICTOR SYLVESTER   1st B.
Chicago, N. L., 1911–1917, inc.
Pittsburgh, N. L., 1919

SALISBURY, WILLIAM A.   Pitcher
Philadelphia, N. L., 1902

SALLEE, HARRY F.   Pitcher
St. Louis, N. L., 1908–1916, inc.
New York, N. L., 1916–1917–1918
Cincinnati, N. L., 1919–1920
New York, N. L., 1920–1921

SALMON, ROGER   Pitcher
Philadelphia, A. L., 1912

SALVE   Pitcher
Philadelphia, A. L., 1908

SANDERS, ROY   Pitcher
New York, A. L., 1918
St. Louis, A. L., 1929

SANDERS, ROY GARVIN   Pitcher
Cincinnati, N. L., 1917
Pittsburgh, N. L., 1918

SANDERS, WAR   Pitcher
St. Louis, N. L., 1903–1904

SARGENT, JOSEPH A., JR.   Infielder
Detroit, A. L., 1921

SAVAGE, H. J.   Infielder
Philadelphia, N. L., 1912
Pittsburgh, F. L., 1914

SAVIDGE, R. A.   Pitcher
Cincinnati, N. L., 1908–1909

SAWYER, CARL   Infielder
Washington, A. L., 1915–1916

SCANLAN, WILLIAM DENNIS   Pitcher
Pittsburgh, N. L., 1903–1904
Brooklyn, N. L., 1904–1911, inc.; (except 1908)

SCANLAN, FRANK   Pitcher
Philadelphia, N. L., 1909

SCHACHT, ALBERT   Pitcher
Washington, A. L., 1919 to date

SCHAEFER, HERMAN Infielder
Chicago, N. L., 1902
Detroit, A. L., 1905–1909, inc.
Washington, A. L., 1909–1914, inc.
Newark, F. L., 1915
New York, A. L., 1916
Cleveland, A. L., 1918

SCHALK, RAYMOND W. Catcher
Chicago, A. L., 1912 to date

SCHALLER, WALTER Outfielder
Detroit, A. L., 1911
Chicago, A. L., 1913

SCHANG, ROBERT M. Catcher
Pittsburgh, N. L., 1914–1915
New York, N. L., 1915

SCHANG, WALTER H. C.—Inf.—O. F.
Philadelphia, A. L., 1913–1917, inc.
Boston, A. L., 1918–1919–1920
New York, A. L., 1921

SCHARDT, WILBUR Pitcher
Brooklyn, N. L., 1911–1912

SCHAUER, ALEXANDER J. Pitcher
New York, A. L., 1913–1916, inc.
Philadelphia, A. L., 1917

SCHEER, AL Outfielder
Brooklyn, N. L., 1913
Indianapolis, F. L., 1914
Newark, F. L., 1915

SCHEEREN, FRITZ Outfielder
Pittsburgh, N. L., 1914–1915

SCHEGG Pitcher
Washington, A. L., 1912

SCHENEBERG Pitcher
St. Louis, A. L., 1920

SCHENEBERG, J. B. Pitcher
Pittsburgh, N. L., 1913

SCHETTLER, L. Pitcher
Philadelphia, N. L., 1910

SCHICK, MAURICE Outfielder
Chicago, N. L., 1917

SCHINDLER, WM. G. Catcher
St. Louis, N. L., 1920

SCHLAFLY, H. LAWRENCE Infielder
Chicago, N. L., 1902
Washington, A. L., 1906–1907
Buffalo, F. L., 1914

SCHLEI, GEORGE H. Catcher
Cincinnati, N. L., 1904–1908, inc.
New York, N. L., 1909–1911, inc.

SCHLITZER, VICTOR Pitcher
Philadelphia, A. L., 1908–1909
Boston, A. L., 1909

SCHMANDT, RAYMOND, H. Infielder
St. Louis, A. L., 1915
Brooklyn, N. L., 1918–1921, inc.

SCHMIDT Pitcher
St. Louis, A. L., 1913

SCHMIDT, CHARLES Catcher
Detroit, A. L., 1906–1911, inc.

SCHMIDT, CHARLES JOHN
Pitcher—1st B.
New York, A. L., 1909
Boston, N. L., 1913–1915, inc.

SCHMIDT, FRED Pitcher
Baltimore, A. L., 1901

SCHMIDT, HARRY M. Pitcher
Brooklyn, N. L., 1903

SCHMIDT, WALTER JOSEPH Catcher
Pittsburgh, N. L., 1916 to date

SCHMUTZ, CHARLES O. Pitcher
Brooklyn, N. L., 1914–1915

SCHNEIBERG, F. Pitcher
Brooklyn, N. L., 1910

SCHNEIDER, PETER JOSEPH Pitcher
Cincinnati, N. L., 1915–1918, inc.
New York, A. L., 1919

SCHORR, E. W. Pitcher
Chicago, N. L., 1915

SCHRECKENGOST, OSSEE 1st B.—C.
Boston, A. L., 1901
Cleveland, A. L., 1902
Philadelphia, A. L., 1902–1908, inc.
Chicago, A. L., 1908

SCHREIBER, B.   Pitcher
Cincinnati, N. L., 1911

SCHREIBER, HENRY W.   Substitute
Chicago, A. L., 1914
Boston, N. L., 1917
Cincinnati, N. L., 1919
New York, N. L., 1921

SCHRIVER, WILLIAM   Catcher
St. Louis, N. L., 1901

SCHULTE, DAVID   Substitute
Boston, N. L., 1906

SCHULTE, FRANK   Outfielder
Chicago, N. L., 1904–1916, inc.
Pittsburgh, N. L., 1916–1917
Philadelphia, N. L., 1917
Washington, A. L., 1918

SCHULTZ, JOSEPH CHARLES
     Infielder—Outfielder
Boston, N. L., 1912–1913
Brooklyn, N. L., 1915
Chicago, N. L., 1915
Pittsburgh, N. L., 1916
St. Louis, N. L., 1919–1921, inc.

SCHULZ, ALBERT   Pitcher
New York, A. L., 1912–1914, inc.
Buffalo, F. L., 1914–1915
Cincinnati, N. L., 1916

SCHULZ, WALTER FREDERICK   Pitcher
St. Louis, N. L., 1920

SCHUMANN   Pitcher
Philadelphia, A. L., 1906

SCHUPP, FERDINAND M.   Pitcher
New York, N. L., 1913–1919, inc.
St. Louis, N. L., 1919–1920–1921
Brooklyn, N. L., 1921

SCHWARTZ, WILLIAM   Infielder
Cleveland, A. L., 1904

SCHWEITZER, ALBERT   Outfielder
St. Louis, A. L., 1908–1911, inc.

SCHWENCK, R. C.   Pitcher
Chicago, N. L., 1909
St. Louis, A. L., 1913

SCHWERT, PIUS X.   Catcher
New York, A. L., 1914–1915

SCHWIND, A. E.   Infielder
Boston, N. L., 1912

SCOTT, AMOS   Pitcher
Cincinnati, N. L., 1901

SCOTT, EDWARD   Pitcher
Cleveland, A. L., 1901

SCOTT, GEO. W.   Pitcher
St. Louis, N. L., 1920

SCOTT, JAMES   Pitcher
Chicago, A. L., 1909–1917, inc.

SCOTT, JOHN WILLIAM   Pitcher
Pittsburgh, N. L., 1916
Boston, N. L., 1917; 1919–1920–1921

SCOTT, L. EVERETT   S. S.
Boston, A. L., 1914 to date

SCROGGINS, JAMES L.   Pitcher
Chicago, A. L., 1913

SEATON, THOMAS   Pitcher
Philadelphia, N. L., 1912–1913
Brooklyn, F. L., 1914
Newark, F. L., 1915
Chicago, N. L., 1916–1917

SEBRING, JAMES D.   Outfielder
Pittsburgh, N. L., 1902–1904, inc.
Cincinnati, N. L., 1904–1905
Brooklyn, N. L., 1909

SEDGWICK, H. KENNETH   Pitcher
Philadelphia, N. L., 1921

SEE, CHARLES H.   Outfielder
Cincinnati, N. L., 1919–1920–1921

SIEBOLD, HARRY S.   Pitcher
Philadelphia, A. L., 1915–1916–1917; 1919

SELBACH, ALBERT C.   Outfielder
New York, N. L., 1901
Baltimore, A. L., 1902
Washington, A. L., 1903
Boston, A. L., 1904–1905–1906

SELLERS, OLIVER   Outfielder
Boston, N. L., 1910

SENTELLE, PAUL　　　　　Infielder
Philadelphia, N. L., 1906–1907

SEVEREID, HENRY　　　　Catcher
Cincinnati, N. L., 1911–1912
St. Louis, A. L., 1914 to date

SEWELL, JOSEPH WHEELER　　S. S.
Cleveland, A. L., 1920–1921

SEWELL, LUKE　　　　　　Catcher
Cleveland, A. L., 1921

SEYBOLD, RALPH O.　　　Outfielder
Philadelphia, A. L., 1901–1908, inc.

SEYMOUR, J. BENTLEY　　Outfielder
Baltimore, A. L., 1901–1902
Cincinnati, N. L., 1902–1906, inc.
New York, N. L., 1906–1910, inc.
Boston, N. L., 1913

SHAFER, ARTHUR J.　　　Substitute
New York, N. L., 1909–1010; 1912–1913

SHAFER, RALPH　　　　　Outfielder
Pittsburgh, N. L., 1914

SHANKS, HOWARD S.　Infielder—O. F.
Washington, A. L., 1912 to date

SHANLEY　　　　　　　Infielder
St. Louis, A. L., 1912

SHANNER　　　　　　　Pitcher
Philadelphia, A. L., 1920

SHANNON　　　　　　　Catcher
Washington, A. L., 1907

SHANNON, JOSEPH　　　Outfielder
Boston, N. L., 1914
Philadelphia, A. L., 1917

SHANNON, MAURICE J　　Infielder
Boston, N. L., 1914
Philadelphia, A. L., 1917–1918–1919
Boston, A. L., 1919
Washington, A. L., 1920
Philadelphia, A. L., 1920–1921

SHANNON, PORTER B.　　Outfielder
St. Louis, N. L., 1904–1906, inc.
New York, N. L., 1906–1908, inc.
Pittsburgh, N. L., 1908

SHARMAN, RALPH　　　Outfielder
Philadelphia, A. L., 1917

SHARPE, BAYARD H.　　　　1st B.
Boston, N. L., 1905–1910
Pittsburgh, N. L., 1910

SHAUGHNESSY, FRANK JOSEPH
　　　　　　　　　　Outfielder
Washington, A. L., 1905
Philadelphia, A. L., 1908

SHAW, AL　　　　　　Outfielder
St. Louis, N. L., 1907–1909, inc.
Brooklyn, F. L., 1914
Kansas City, F. L., 1915

SHAW, ALFRED　　　　　Catcher
Detroit, A. L., 1901
Boston, A. L., 1907
Chicago, A. L., 1908
Boston, N. L., 1909

SHAW, BEN W　　　　　Catcher
Pittsburgh, N. L., 1917–1918

SHAW, JAMES ALOYSIUS　　Pitcher
Washington, A. L., 1913–1921, inc.

SHAW, ROYAL　　　　　Outfielder
Pittsburgh, N. L., 1908

SHAWKEY, J. ROBERT　　　Pitcher
Philadelphia, A. L., 1913–1915, inc.
New York, A. L., 1915 to date

SHAY, ARTHUR J.　　　　Infielder
Chicago, N. L., 1916

SHIELDS, CHARLES　　　　Pitcher
St. Louis, A. L., 1902
Baltimore, A. L., 1902

SHIELDS, FRANCIS LEROY　　1st B
Cleveland, A. L., 1915

SHINAULT, ENOCH ERSKINE　Catcher
Cleveland, A. L., 1921

SHIPKE, TONY　　　　　Infielder
Cleveland, A. L., 1906
Washington, A. L., 1907–1908

SHIREY, C. L.　　　　　Pitcher
Washington, A. L., 1920

SHOCKER, URBAN J.   Pitcher
New York, A. L., 1916–1917
St. Louis, A. L., 1918 to date

SHOOK   Pitcher
Chicago, A. L., 1916

SHORE, ERNEST G.   Pitcher
New York, N. L., 1912
Boston, A. L., 1914–1917, inc.
New York, A. L., 1919–1920

SHORTEN, CHARLES H.   Outfielder
Boston, A. L., 1915–1917, inc.
Detroit, A. L., 1919 to date

SHOTTEN, BURTON EDWIN   Outfielder
St. Louis, A. L., 1909; 1911–1917, inc.
Washington, A. L., 1918
St. Louis, N. L., 1919–1921, inc.

SHOVELIN, J.   Infielder
Pittsburgh, N. L., 1911
St. Louis, A. L., 1920

SHUGART, FRANK   S. S.
Chicago, A. L., 1901

SHULTZ, WALLACE L.   Pitcher
Philadelphia, N. L., 1911–1912

SICKING, EDWARD J.   Substitute
Chicago, N. L., 1916
New York, N. L., 1918–1919
Cincinnati, N. L., 1919
New York, N. L., 1920
Cincinnati, N. L., 1920

SIEGLE, J. H.   Outfielder
Cincinnati, N. L., 1905–1906

SIEVER, EDWARD
Detroit, A. L., 1901–1902
St. Louis, A. L., 1903–1904
Detroit, A. L., 1906–1907–1908

SIGLIN, WESLEY PETER   Infielder
Pittsburgh, N. L., 1914–1916, inc.

SIMMONS, GEORGE WASHINGTON
                                   Substitute
Detroit, A. L., 1910
New York, A. L., 1912
Baltimore, F. L., 1914–1915

SIMON, MICHAEL E.   Catcher
Pittsburgh, N. L., 1909–1913, inc.
St. Louis, F. L., 1914
Brooklyn, F. L., 1915

SIMS, C.   Pitcher
St. Louis, A. L., 1915

SINCOCK, HERBERT S.   Pitcher
Cincinnati, N. L., 1908

SINER, HOSEA   Infielder
Boston, N. L., 1909

SISLER, GEORGE HAROLD
                              Pitcher—1st B.
St. Louis, A. L., 1915 to date

SITTON C. VEDDER   Pitcher
Cleveland, A. L., 1909

SKEELS, DAVID   Pitcher
Detroit, A. L., 1910

SKIFF, WM. F.   Catcher
Pittsburgh, N. L., 1912

SLAGLE, JAMES F.   Outfielder
Philadelphia, N. L., 1901
Boston, N. L., 1901
Chicago, A. L., 1902–1908, inc.

SLAGLE, W. J.   Pitcher
Cincinnati, N. L., 1910

SLAPNICKA, CYRIL CHARLES   Pitcher
Chicago, N. L., 1911
Pittsburgh, N. L., 1918

SLAPPEY, J. H.   Pitcher
Philadelphia, A. L., 1920

SLATTERY   Outfielder
Chicago, A. L., 1903

SLATTERY, JOHN F.   Catcher
Chicago, A. L., 1903
St. Louis, N. L., 1906
Washington, A. L., 1909

SLATTERY, JOSEPH   Catcher
Boston, A. L., 1901

SLATTERY, PHILIP   Pitcher
Pittsburgh, N. L., 1915

SLAUGHTER, B. A.   Pitcher
Philadelphia, N. L., 1910

SLOAN, YALE Y.   Outfielder
St. Louis, A. L., 1913; 1917–1919

SMALLWOOD, WALTER   Pitcher
New York, A. L., 1917–1919

SMITH   Infielder
Detroit, A. L., 1912

SMITH   Substitute
Boston, A. L., 1920

SMITH, ALEXANDER   Catcher
Baltimore, A. L., 1902
Boston, A. L., 1903
Chicago, N. L., 1904
New York, N. L., 1906

SMITH, CHARLES E.   Pitcher
Cleveland, A. L., 1902
Washington, A. L., 1906–1909, inc.
Boston, A. L., 1909–1911, inc.
Chicago, N. L., 1911–1914, inc.

SMITH, CLARENCE   Pitcher
Chicago, A. L., 1913
Cleveland, A. L., 1916–1917

SMITH, EARL   Catcher
New York, N. L., 1919–1920–1921

SMITH, EARL O.   Substitute
Chicago, N. L., 1916
St. Louis, A. L., 1917–1921, inc.
Washington, A. L., 1921

SMITH, EDWARD   Pitcher
St. Louis, A. L., 1906

SMITH, ELMER E.   Outfielder
Pittsburgh, N. L., 1901
Boston, N. L., 1901

SMITH, ELMER JOHN   Outfielder
Cleveland, A. L., 1915–1916
Washington, A. L., 1916–1917
Cleveland, A. L., 1917; 1919–1921, inc.

SMITH, FRANK ELMER   Pitcher
Chicago, A. L., 1904–1910, inc.
Boston, A. L., 1910–1911

Cincinnati, N. L., 1911–1912
Baltimore, F. L., 1914
Brooklyn, F. L., 1915

SMITH, FRED   Pitcher
Cincinnati, N. L., 1907

SMITH, FRED V.   Infielder
Boston, N. L., 1913
Buffalo, F. L., 1914
Brooklyn, F. L., 1915
St. Louis, N. L., 1917

SMITH, GEORGE ALLEN   Pitcher
New York, N. L., 1916–1917–1918
Cincinnati, N. L., 1918
Brooklyn, N. L., 1918
New York, N. L., 1919
Philadelphia, N. L., 1919 to date

SMITH, GEORGE HENRY   2nd B.
New York, N. L., 1901–1902
Detroit, A. L., 1903

SMITH, H. J.   Outfielder
Brooklyn, N. L., 1910

SMITH, HARRY   Catcher
Philadelphia, A. L., 1901
Pittsburgh, N. L., 1902–1907, inc.
Boston, N. L., 1908–1910, inc.

SMITH, J.   Catcher
New York, A. L., 1913

SMITH, J. CARLISLE   3rd B.
Brooklyn, N. L., 1911–1914, inc.
Boston, N. L., 1914–1919, inc.

SMITH, J. HARRY   Catcher
New York, N. L., 1914–1915
Brooklyn, F. L., 1915
Cincinnati, N. L., 1916–1918

SMITH, JACOB   Pitcher
Philadelphia, N. L., 1911

SMITH, JAMES LAWRENCE   Infielder
Chicago, F. L., 1915
Baltimore, F. L., 1915
Pittsburgh, N. L., 1916
New York, N. L., 1917
Cincinnati, N. L., 1919
Philadelphia, N. L., 1921

SMITH, JOHN   Outfielder
St. Louis, N. L., 1916 to date

SMITH, JOHN W.   Pitcher
Cincinnati, N. L., 1913

SMITH, JUDSON   Infielder
Pittsburgh, N. L., 1901

SMITH, L. O.   Substitute
Pittsburgh, N. L., 1904
Chicago, N. L., 1906

SMITH, PAUL STONER   Outfielder
Cincinnati, N. L., 1916

SMITH, R.   Pitcher
Chicago, A. L, 1913

SMITH, S. S.   Pitcher
Pittsburgh, N. L., 1912

SMITH, SHERROD M.   Pitcher
Pittsburgh, N. L., 1911
Brooklyn, N. L., 1915–1916–1917; 1919 to
date

SMITH, SID   Catcher
Philadelphia, A. L., 1908
St. Louis, A. L., 1908–1909
Cleveland, A. L., 1910–1911
Pittsburgh, N. L., 1914–1915

SMITH, TONY   Infielder
Brooklyn, N. L., 1910–1911

SMITH, WALLACE   Infielder
St. Louis, N. L., 1911–1912

SMITH, WILLARD J.   Catcher
Pittsburgh, N. L., 1917–1918

SMOOT, HOMER   Outfielder
St. Louis, N. L., 1902–1906, inc.
Cincinnati, N. L., 1907

SMYKAL, FRANK J.   Infielder
Pittsburgh, N. L., 1916

SMYTH, JAMES DANIEL   Outfielder
Brooklyn, N. L., 1915–1917, inc.
St. Louis, N. L., 1917–1918

SNELL, WALTER H.   Catcher
St. Louis, A. L., 1912
Boston, A. L., 1913

SNODGRASS   Outfielder
Baltimore, A. L., 1901

SNODGRASS, FREDERICK C.
                    Catcher—Outfielder
New York, N. L., 1908–1915, inc.
Boston, N. L., 1915–1916

SNOVER, COLONEL LESTER   Pitcher
New York, N. L., 1919

SNYDER, FRANK   Catcher
St. Louis, N. L., 1912–1919, inc.
New York, N. L., 1919 to date

SNYDER, J. W.   Catcher
Brooklyn, N. L., 1917

SNYDER, WILLIAM NICHOLS   Pitcher
Washington, A. L., 1919–1920

SOMERLOTT, J. W.   1st B.
Washington, A. L., 1910–1911

SOTHORON, ALLEN   Pitcher
St. Louis, A. L., 1915; 1917–1921, inc.
Boston, A. L., 1921
Cleveland, A. L., 1921

SOUTHWICK   Catcher
St. Louis, A. L., 1911

SOUTHWORTH, WM. H.   Outfielder
Cleveland, A. L., 1915
Pittsburgh, A. L., 1918–1919–1921
Boston, A. L., 1921

SPADE, ROBERT   Pitcher
Cincinnati, N. L., 1907–1910, inc.
St. Louis, A. L., 1910

SPARKS, FRANK   Pitcher
Milwaukee, A. L., 1901
New York, N. L., 1902
Boston, A. L., 1902
Philadelphia, N. L., 1903–1910, inc.

SPEAKER, TRIS E.   Outfielder
Boston, A. L., 1907–1915, inc.
Cleveland, A. L., 1916 to date

SPEER, GEORGE H.   Pitcher
Detroit, A. L., 1909

SPENCER, CHARLES   Substitute
Boston, N. L., 1906

SPENCER, EDWARD R.   Catcher
St. Louis, A. L., 1905–1908, inc.
Boston, A. L., 1909
Philadelphia, N. L., 1911
Detroit, A. L., 1916–1918, inc.

SPENCER, L. B.   Infielder
Washington, A. L., 1913

SPENCER, ROY HAMPTON   Catcher
Detroit, A. L., 1921

SPENCER, VERNON MURRAY   Outfielder
New York, N. L., 1920

SPERAUW, PAUL B.   Infielder
St. Louis, A. L., 1920

SPONSBERG   Pitcher
Chicago, N. L., 1908

SPRATT, H. L.   Infielder
Boston, N. L., 1911–1912

ST. VRAIN, JAMES L.   Pitcher
Chicago, N. L., 1902

STACK, WILLIAM EDWARD   Pitcher
Philadelphia, N. L., 1910–1911
Brooklyn, N. L., 1912–1913
Chicago, N. L., 1913–1914

STAFFORD, HENRY A.   Infielder
New York, N. L., 1916

STAHL, CHARLES SYLVESTER   Outfielder
Boston, A. L., 1901–1902–1903–1904–
1905–1906

STAHL, GARLAND JACOB
                    Catcher—1st B.—O. F.
Boston, A. L., 1903
Washington, A. L., 1904–1906, inc.
New York, A. L., 1908
Boston, A. L., 1908–1913, inc.; (except
1911)

STANAGE, OSCAR HARLAN   Catcher
Cincinnati, N. L., 1906
Detroit, A. L., 1909–1920, inc.

STANDRIDGE, ALFRED PETER   Pitcher
St. Louis, N. L., 1911
Chicago, N. L., 1915

STANKARD, THOMAS   Infielder
Pittsburgh, N. L., 1904

STANLEY   Infielder
Chicago, F. L., 1914

STANLEY, J. L.   Pitcher
Philadelphia, N. L., 1911

STANLEY, JOSEPH B.   Outfielder
Washington, A. L., 1902
Boston, N. L., 1903–1904
Washington, A. L., 1905–1906
Chicago, A. L., 1909

STANSBURY, JOHN   Infielder
Boston, A. L., 1918

STANTON, ANDREW   Catcher
Chicago, N. L., 1904

STARK, M. R.   Infielder
Brooklyn, N. L., 1910–1912, inc.

STARKE   Infielder
Cleveland, A. L., 1909

STARKELL   Pitcher
Washington, A. L., 1906

STARNAGLE, GEORGE   Catcher
Cleveland, A. L., 1902

STARR, CHARLES W.   Infielder
St. Louis, A. L., 1905
Pittsburgh, N. L., 1908
Boston, N. L., 1909
Philadelphia, N. L., 1909

STATZ, ARNOLD JOHN   Outfielder
New York, N. L., 1919–1920
Boston, A. L., 1921

STEELE, ELMER E.   Pitcher
Boston, A. L., 1907–1909, inc.
Pittsburgh, N. L., 1910–1911
Brooklyn, N. L., 1911

STEELE, ROBERT W.   Pitcher
St. Louis, N. L., 1916–1917
Pittsburgh, N. L., 1917–1918
New York, N. L., 1918–1919

STEELE, WM. M.   Pitcher
St. Louis, N. L., 1910–1914, inc.
Brooklyn, N. L., 1914

STEELMAN, MORRIS J.   Catcher
Philadelphia, A. L., 1901–1902

STEEN, WILLIAM J.   Pitcher
Cleveland, A. L., 1912–1915, inc.
Detroit, A. L., 1915

STEINBRENNER, EUGENE   Infielder
Philadelphia, N. L., 1912

STEINFELDT, HARRY   3rd B.
Cincinnati, N. L., 1901–1905, inc.
Chicago, N. L., 1906–1910, inc.
Boston, N. L., 1911

STELLBAUER, W. J.   Substitute
Philadelphia, A. L., 1916

STEM, FRED B.   1st B.
Boston, N. L., 1908–1909

STENGEL, CHARLES D.   Outfielder
Brooklyn, N. L., 1912–1917, inc.
Pittsburgh, N. L., 1918–1919
Philadelphia, N. L., 1920–1921
New York, N. L., 1921

STEPHENS, JAMES   Catcher
St. Louis, A. L., 1907–1912, inc.

STEPHENSON, JACKSON RIGGS   2nd B.
Cleveland, A. L., 1921

STERRETT, C. H.   Catcher
New York, A. L., 1912–1913

STEVENS   Pitcher
Washington, A. L., 1914

STEWART   Infielder
St. Louis, A. L., 1921

STEWART, ASA   Pitcher
Boston, N. L., 1904

STEWART, C. P.   Outfielder
Chicago, N. L., 1913–1914

STEWART, JOHN F.   Infielder
St. Louis, N. L., 1916–1917

STEWART, MACK   Catcher
Cincinnati, N. L., 1913

STEWART, WALTER CLEVELAND   Pitcher
Detroit, A. L., 1921

STIMMELL, ARCHIBALD   Pitcher
Cincinnati, N. L., 1901–1902

STOCK, MILTON JOSEPH   Infielder
New York, N. L., 1913–1914
Philadelphia, N. L., 1915–1918
St. Louis, N. L., 1919–1921, inc.

STONE   Pitcher
St. Louis, A. L., 1913
Kansas City, F. L., 1914

STONE, GEORGE ROBERT   Outfielder
Boston, A. L., 1903
St. Louis, A. L., 1905–1910, inc.

STORKE, ALAN D.   Substitute
Pittsburgh, N. L., 1906–1909
St. Louis, N. L., 1909

STOVALL, GEORGE THOMAS   1st B.
Cleveland, A. L., 1904–1911, inc.
St. Louis, A. L., 1912–1913
Kansas City, F. L., 1914–1915

STOVALL, JESSE   Pitcher
Cleveland, A. L., 1903
Detroit, A. L., 1904

STRAND, PAUL   Pitcher
Boston, N. L., 1913–1914–1915

STRANDS, L.   Substitute
Newark, F. L., 1915

STRANG, SAMUEL NICKLIN   Infielder
New York, N. L., 1901
Chicago, N. L., 1902
Chicago, A. L., 1902
Brooklyn, N. L., 1903–1904
New York, N. L., 1905–1908, inc.

STREET, CHARLES E.   Catcher
Cincinnati, N. L., 1904–1905
Boston, N. L., 1905
Washington, A. L., 1908–1911, inc.
New York, A. L., 1912

STREIT, OSCAR   Pitcher
Cleveland, A. L., 1902

STREMMELL   Pitcher
St. Louis, A. L., 1909–1910

STRICKLETT, ELMER   Pitcher
Chicago, A. L., 1904
Brooklyn, N. L., 1905–1907, inc.

STROBEL, ALBERT   Infielder
Boston, N. L., 1905–1906

STROUD, RALPH   Pitcher
Detroit, A. L., 1910
New York, N. L., 1915–1916

STRUNK, AMOS   Outfielder
Philadelphia, A. L., 1908–1917, inc.
Boston, A. L., 1918–1919
Philadelphia, A. L., 1919–1920
Chicago, A. L., 1920–1921

STUELAND, GEORGE ANTON   Pitcher
Chicago, N. L., 1921

STUMP, WILLIAM   Substitute
New York, A. L., 1912–1913

STURGIS, DEAN D.   Catcher
Philadelphia, A. L., 1914

STYLES, WILLIAM GRAVES   Catcher
Philadelphia, A. L., 1920–1921

STUDHOFF, WILLIAM   Pitcher
St. Louis, N. L., 1901
St. Louis, A. L., 1902–1905, inc.
Washington, A. L., 1906

SUGDEN, JOSEPH   Catcher
Chicago, A. L., 1901
St. Louis, A. L., 1902–1905, inc.
Detroit, A. L., 1912

SUGGS, GEORGE FRANKLIN   Pitcher
Detroit, A. L., 1909
Cincinnati, N. L., 1910–1913, inc.
Baltimore, F. L., 1914–1915

SULLIVAN, DENNIS   Outfielder
Washington, A. L., 1905
Boston, A. L., 1907–1908
Cleveland, A. L., 1908–1909

SULLIVAN, H. A.   Pitcher
St. Louis, N. L., 1909

SULLIVAN, J.   Catcher
Detroit, A. L., 1905

SULLIVAN, J.   Catcher
Pittsburgh, N. L., 1908

SULLIVAN, JOHN JEREMIAH   Pitcher
Chicago, A. L., 1919

SULLIVAN, JOHN LAWRENCE   Outfielder
Boston, N. L., 1920–1921
Chicago, N. L., 1921

SULLIVAN, WILLIAM D.   Catcher
Chicago, A. L., 1901–1914, inc.
Detroit, A. L., 1916

SUMMA, HOMER WAYNE   Outfielder
Pittsburgh, N. L., 1920

SUMMERS, OREN EDGAR   Pitcher
Detroit, A. L., 1908–1912, inc.

SUMMERS, RUDOLPH   Pitcher
Chicago, N. L., 1912

SUTHERLAND, HARVEY S.   Pitcher
Detroit, A. L., 1921

SUTOR, HARRY G.   Pitcher
Chicago, A. L., 1909

SUTTHOFF, JOHN G.   Pitcher
Cincinnati, N. L., 1901–1903–1904
Philadelphia, N. L., 1904–1905

SWACINA, HARRY   1st B.
Pittsburgh, N. L., 1907–1908
Baltimore, F. L., 1914–1915

SWANDER, EDWARD   Outfielder
St. Louis, A. L., 1903

SWARTZ, MONROE   Pitcher
Cincinnati, N. L., 1920

SWEENEY, EDWARD   Catcher
New York, A. L., 1908–1915, inc.
Pittsburgh, N. L., 1919

SWEENEY, WILLIAM J.   2nd B.
Chicago, N. L., 1907
Boston, N. L., 1907–1913, inc.
Chicago, N. L., 1914

SWIGLER, ADAM   Pitcher
New York, N. L., 1917

SWINDELL, CHARLES   Catcher
St. Louis, N. L., 1904

SWINDELL, J. E.   Pitcher
Cleveland, A. L., 1911

SWORMSTEDT, LEONARD JORDAN
                                   Pitcher
Cincinnati, N. L., 1901–1902
Boston, A. L., 1906

TAFF, J. G.   Pitcher
Philadelphia, A. L., 1913

TAGGART, ROBERT JOHN   Outfielder
Pittsburgh, N. L., 1914
Pittsburgh, F. L., 1915
Boston, N. L., 1918

TANNEHILL, JESSE NILES   Pitcher
Pittsburgh, N. L., 1901–1902
New York, A. L., 1903
Boston, A. L., 1904–1908, inc.
Washington, A. L., 1908
Cincinnati, N. L., 1911

TANNEHILL, LEEFORD   Infielder
Chicago, A. L., 1903–1912, inc.

TATE   Outfielder
Washington, A. L., 1905

TAVENER, JACK   Infielder
Detroit, A. L., 1921

TAYLOR, BEN   Pitcher
Cincinnati, N. L., 1912

TAYLOR, JAMES WREN   Catcher
Brooklyn, N. L., 1920–1921

TAYLOR, JOHN W.   Pitcher
Chicago, N. L., 1901–1903, inc.
St. Louis, N. L., 1903–1905, inc.
Chicago, N. L., 1906–1907, inc.

TAYLOR, LUTHER H.   Pitcher
New York, N. L., 1901
Cleveland, A. L., 1902
New York, N. L., 1902–1908, inc.

TAYLOR, WILEY   Pitcher
St. Louis, A. L., 1913–1914

TEDROW   Pitcher
Cleveland, A. L., 1914

TENNANT, THOMAS   Infielder
St. Louis, A. L., 1912

TENNEY, FRED C.   1st B.
Boston, N. L., 1901–1907, inc.
New York, N. L., 1908–1909
Boston, N. L., 1911

TERRY, JOHN   Pitcher
Detroit, A. L., 1902
St. Louis, A. L., 1903

TERRY, ZEBULON A.   Infielder
Chicago, A. L., 1902
Boston, N. L., 1918
Pittsburgh, N. L., 1919
Chicago, N. L., 1920–1921

TESREAU, CHARLES MONROE   Pitcher
New York, N. L., 1912–1918, inc.

TEXTER, GEORGE   Catcher
Indianapolis, F. L., 1914
Newark, F. L., 1915

THATCHER, GRANT   Pitcher
Brooklyn, N. L., 1903–1904

THEIS, JOHN L.   Pitcher
Cincinnati, N. L., 1920

THIELMAN, HENRY   Pitcher
New York, N. L., 1902

THIELMAN, JOHN P.   Pitcher
St. Louis, N. L., 1905–1906
Cleveland, A. L., 1907–1908
Boston, A. L., 1908

THOMAS   Outfielder
Cleveland, A. L., 1908

THOMAS   Pitcher
Washington, A. L., 1916

THOMAS   Pitcher
Detroit, A. L., 1905

THOMAS, CHESTER D.   Catcher
Boston, A. L., 1911–1917, inc.
Cleveland, A. L., 1905

THOMAS, FRED   Infielder
Boston, A. L., 1918
Philadelphia, A. L., 1919
Washington, A. L., 1920

THOMAS, J. IRA   Catcher
New York, A. L., 1906–1907

Detroit, A. L., 1908
Philadelphia, A. L., 1909–1915, inc.

THOMAS, ROBERT W.   Infielder
Chicago, N. L., 1921

THOMAS, ROY   Outfielder
Philadelphia, N. L., 1901–1908, inc.
Pittsburgh, N. L., 1908
Boston, N. L., 1909
Philadelphia, N. L., 1910–1911

THOMAS, W. W.   Infielder
Boston, N. L., 1908

THOMAS, WILLIAM   Outfielder
Philadelphia, N. L., 1902

THOMASEN   Outfielder
Cleveland, A. L., 1910

THOMPSON, C.   Outfielder
Philadelphia, A. L., 1914–1916, inc.

THOMPSON, F. W.   Pitcher
Boston, N. L., 1911

THOMPSON, FRANK   Infielder
St. Louis, A. L., 1920

THOMPSON, HARRY   Pitcher—O. F.
Washington, A. L., 1919
Philadelphia, A. L., 1919

THOMPSON, J. D.   Pitcher
Chicago, A. L., 1921

THOMPSON, J. D.   Pitcher
Pittsburgh, N. L., 1903
St. Louis, N. L., 1906

THONEY, JOHN   Infielder—O. F.
Cleveland, A. L., 1902
Baltimore, A. L., 1902
Cleveland, A. L., 1903
Washington, A. L., 1904
New York, A. L., 1904
Boston, A. L., 1908–1909; 1911

THORMAHLEN, HERBERT E.   Pitcher
New York, A. L., 1917–1920, inc.
Boston, A. L., 1921

THORPE, JAMES   Substitute
New York, N. L., 1913–1914–1915

Cincinnati, N. L., 1917
New York, N. L., 1917–1918–1919
Boston, N. L., 1919

THRASHER, FRANK   Outfielder
Philadelphia, A. L., 1916–1917

TIEMEYER, EDWARD   Substitute
Cincinnati, N. L., 1906–1907
New York, A. L., 1909

TIERNEY, JAMES A.   Infielder
Pittsburgh, N. L., 1920–1921

TILLMAN, JOHN   Pitcher
St. Louis, A. L., 1915

TINGUP, BEN   Pitcher
Philadelphia, N. L., 1914–1915–1916; 1918

TINKER, JOSEPH B.   Shortstop
Chicago, N. L., 1902–1912, inc.
Cincinnati, N. L., 1913
Chicago, F. L., 1914–1915
Chicago, N. L., 1916

TIPPLE, DANIEL   Pitcher
New York, A. L., 1915

TITUS, JOHN   Outfielder
Philadelphia, N. L., 1903–1912, inc.
Boston, N. L., 1912–1913
St. Louis, N. L., 1918–1921

TOBIN, JOHN   Outfielder
St. Louis, F. L., 1914–1915
St. Louis, A. L., 1916; 1918 to date

THOMPKINS, C. H.   Pitcher
Cincinnati, N. L., 1912

TONEY, FRED   Pitcher
Chicago, N. L., 1911–1913, inc.
Cincinnati, N. L., 1915–1918, inc.
New York, N. L., 1918–1921, inc.

TONNEMAN, CHARLES R.   Catcher
Boston, A. L., 1911

TOOLEY, BERT   Shortstop
Brooklyn, N. L., 1911–1912

TOPORCER, GEORGE   2nd B.
St. Louis, N. L., 1921

TORKELSON, CHESTER   Pitcher
Cleveland, A. L., 1917

TORMER, GEORGE   1st B.
St. Louis, A. L., 1913

TORRES, RICARDO   Catcher
Washington, A. L., 1920

TOWNE, JAY KING   Catcher
Chicago, A. L., 1906

TOWNSEND, IRA DANCE   Pitcher
Boston, N. L., 1920–1921

TOWNSEND, JOHN   Pitcher
Philadelphia, N. L., 1901
Washington, A. L., 1902–1905, inc.
Cleveland, A. L., 1906

TOWNSEND, LEO   Pitcher
Boston, N. L., 1920–1921

TOZER, W. L.   Pitcher
Cincinnati, N. L., 1908

TRAGESSER, J. WALTER   Catcher
Boston, N. L., 1912; 1915–1919, inc.
Philadelphia, N. L., 1919–1920

TRAVERS   Pitcher
Detroit, A. L., 1912

TRAYNOR, HAROLD J.   Infielder
Pittsburgh, N. L., 1920–1921

TREKELL, H.   Pitcher
St. Louis, N. L., 1913

TROY   Pitcher
Detroit, A. L., 1912

TRUESDALE, FRANK H.   Infielder
St. Louis, A. L., 1910–1911
New York, A. L., 1914
Boston, A. L., 1918

TUCKEY, THOMAS   Pitcher
Boston, N. L., 1908–1909

TUERO, OSCAR   Pitcher
St. Louis, N. L., 1918–1920, inc.

TURNER, TERRENCE LAMONT   Infielder
Pittsburgh, N. L., 1901
Cleveland, A. L., 1904–1919, inc.
Philadelphia, A. L., 1919

TURNER, THEODORE   Pitcher
Chicago, N. L., 1920

TUTWILER, GUY ISBELL   Outfielder
Detroit, A. L., 1911; 1913

TWINING, H. E.   Pitcher
Cincinnati, N. L., 1916

TWOMBLY, CLARENCE E.   Outfielder
Chicago, N. L., 1920–1921

TWOMBLY, E. P.   Pitcher
Chicago, A. L., 1921

TWOMBLY, GEORGE F.   Outfielder
Cincinnati, N. L., 1914–1916, inc.
Boston, N. L., 1917

TYLER, FRED   Catcher
Boston, N. L., 1914

TYLER, GEORGE ALBERT   Pitcher
Boston, N. L., 1910–1917, inc.
Chicago, N. L., 1918–1919–1920–1921

TYREE, EARL   Catcher
Chicago, N. L., 1914

UHLE, GEORGE ERNEST   Pitcher
Cleveland, A. L., 1919 to date

UHLER, M. W.   Outfielder
Cincinnati, N. L., 1914

UNGLAUB, ROBERT A.   Infielder—O. F.
New York, A. L., 1904
Boston, A. L., 1904–1905; 1907–1908
Washington, A. L., 1908–1910, inc.

UPHAM, WILLIAM   Pitcher
Brooklyn, F. L., 1915
Boston, N. L., 1918

UPP, JERRY   Pitcher
Cleveland, A. L., 1909

URY, BERT   Infielder
St. Louis, N. L., 1903

VAIL, ROBERT S.   Pitcher
Pittsburgh, N. L., 1908

VAN BUREN, E. E.   Outfielder
Philadelphia, N. L., 1904
Brooklyn, N. L., 1904

VANCE, ARTHUR C.   Pitcher
New York, A. L., 1915

Pittsburgh, N. L., 1915
New York, A. L., 1918

VANDAGRIFT, CARL   Infielder
Indianapolis, F. L., 1914

VAN DYKE, B. H.   Pitcher
Philadelphia, N. L., 1909
Boston, A. L., 1912

VAN GILDER, ELAM   Pitcher
St. Louis, A. L., 1919–1920–1921

VAN HALTREN, GEORGE S.   Outfielder
New York, N. L., 1901–1902–1903

VANN   Substitute
St. Louis, N. L., 1913

VAN ZANDT   Pitcher
New York, N. L., 1901

VAN ZANT, ALEX   Outfielder
Chicago, N. L., 1904
St. Louis, A. L., 1905

VARNEY, LAWRENCE D.   Pitcher
Cleveland, A. L., 1902

VASBINDER   Pitcher
Cleveland, A. L., 1902

VAUGHN, JAMES L.   Pitcher
New York, A. L., 1908; 1910–1912, inc.
Washington, A. L., 1912
Chicago, N. L., 1913 to date

VAUGHN, ROBERT   Infielder
New York, A. L., 1909
St. Louis, F. L., 1915

VEACH, ROBERT H.   Outfielder
Detroit, A. L., 1912 to date

VEDDER   Pitcher
Detroit, A. L., 1920

VEIL, FRED W.   Pitcher
Pittsburgh, N. L., 1903–1904

VERNON, J. H.   Pitcher
Chicago, N. L., 1912

VICK, SAMUEL B.   Outfielder
New York, A. L., 1917–1920, inc.
Boston, A. L., 1921

VICKERS, HARRY P.   Pitcher
Cincinnati, N. L., 1902

VINSON, ERNEST   Outfielder
Cleveland, A. L., 1904–1905
Chicago, A. L., 1906

VIOX, JAMES HARRY   2nd B.
Pittsburgh, N. L., 1912–1916, inc.

VITT, OSCAR J.   Infielder
Detroit, A. L., 1912–1918, inc.
Boston, A. L., 1919 to date

VOLZ, JACOB P.   Pitcher
Boston, A. L., 1901
Boston, N. L., 1905
Cincinnati, N. L., 1908

VON KOLNITZ, ALFRED HOLMES
Catcher—Infielder
Cincinnati, N. L., 1914–1915
Chicago, A. L., 1916

VOORHEES, HENRY BURKE   Pitcher
Washington, A. L., 1902
Philadelphia, N. L., 1902

VOWINKEL, JOHN H.   Pitcher
Cincinnati, N. L., 1905

WACHTEL, PAUL   Pitcher
Brooklyn, N. L., 1917

WACKER, C.   Pitcher
Pittsburgh, N. L., 1909

WADDELL, GEORGE EDWARD   Pitcher
Chicago, N. L., 1901
Philadelphia, A. L., 1902–1907, inc.
St. Louis, A. L., 1908–1909–1910

WADE, S.   Outfielder
New York, N. L., 1907

WAGNER, CHARLES   Infielder
New York, N. L., 1902
Boston, A. L., 1906–1918, inc.; (except 1917)

WAGNER, JOHN PETER   Shortstop
Pittsburgh, N. L., 1901–1917, inc.

WAGNER, JOSEPH   Infielder
Cincinnati, N. L., 1915

WAGNER, WILLIAM   Pitcher
Brooklyn, N. L., 1913–1914

WAGNER, WILLIAM J.   Catcher
Pittsburgh, N. L., 1914–1917, inc.
Boston, N. L., 1918

WAKEFIELD, HOWARD J.   Catcher
Cleveland, A. L., 1905
Washington, A. L., 1906
Cleveland, A. L., 1907

WALDBAUER, A. C.   Pitcher
Washington, A. L., 1917

WALDRON, ERVE   Outfielder
Milwaukee, A. L., 1901
Washington, A. L., 1901

WALKER, C. FRANK   Outfielder
Detroit, A. L., 1917–1918
Philadelphia, A. L., 1921

WALKER, CLARENCE T.   Outfielder
Washington, A. L., 1911–1912
St. Louis, A. L., 1913–1915, inc.
Boston, A. L., 1916–1917
Philadelphia, A. L., 1918 to date

WALKER, CURTIS   Outfielder
New York, N. L., 1920–1921
Philadelphia, N. L., 1921

WALKER, EDWARD   Pitcher
Cleveland, A. L., 1902–1903

WALKER, ERNEST   Outfielder
St. Louis, A. L., 1914–1915

WALKER, EWART   Pitcher
Washington, A. L., 1909–1912, inc.

WALKER, FRED   Pitcher
Cincinnati, N. L., 1910
Brooklyn, N. L., 1913
Pittsburgh, F. L., 1914

WALKER, JAMES ROY   Pitcher
Cleveland, A. L., 1912–1915
Chicago, N. L., 1917–1918
St. Louis, N. L., 1921

WALKER, JOHN MILES   Catcher—1st B.
Philadelphia, A. L., 1919 to date

WALKER, THOMAS W.   Pitcher
Philadelphia, A. L., 1902
Cincinnati, N. L., 1904–1905

WALL, JOSEPH   Catcher
New York, N. L., 1901
Brooklyn, N. L., 1902

WALLACE, C. E.   Catcher
Chicago, N. L., 1915

WALLACE, F. R.   Infielder
Philadelphia, F. L., 1919

WALLACE, H. C.   Pitcher
Philadelphia, N. L., 1912

WALLACE, JAMES   Outfielder
Pittsburgh, N. L., 1905

WALLACE, RHODERICK J.
                        Shortstop—3rd B.
St. Louis, N. L., 1901
St. Louis, A. L., 1902–1916, inc.
St. Louis, N. L., 1917–1918

WALSH, A.   Outfielder
Chicago, F. L., 1914–1915

WALSH, DEE   Infielder
St. Louis, A. L., 1913–1915, inc.

WALSH, EDWARD ARMSTRONG   Pitcher
Chicago, A. L., 1904–1916, inc.
Boston, N. L., 1917

WALSH, JAMES   Pitcher
Detroit, A. L., 1921

WALSH, JAMES   Outfielder
Philadelphia, A. L., 1912–1913
New York, A. L., 1914
Philadelphia, A. L., 1914–1916, inc.
Boston, A. L., 1916–1917

WALSH, JAMES J.   Catcher
New York, A. L., 1910–1911

WALSH, JOHN   Pitcher
Pittsburgh, N. L., 1907

WALSH, THOMAS J.   Catcher
Chicago, N. L., 1906

WALSH, WALTER W.   Substitute
Philadelphia, N. L., 1920

WALSH, WILLIAM R.   Substitute
Philadelphia, N. L., 1910–1913, inc.
Baltimore, F. L., 1914–1915
St. Louis, F. L., 1915

WALTERS, ALFRED J.   Catcher
New York, A. L., 1915–1918, inc.
Boston, A. L., 1919 to date

WALTON   Pitcher
Philadelphia, A. L., 1918

WAMBSGANSS, WILLIAM A.   Infielder
Cleveland, A. L., 1914 to date

WANNER, C. C.   Infielder
New York, A. L., 1909

WARD   Outfielder
Detroit, A. L., 1912

WARD, AARON LEE   Infielder
New York, A. L., 1917–1921, inc.

WARD, CHARLES W.   Infielder
Pittsburgh, N. L., 1917
Brooklyn, N. L., 1918–1921, inc.

WARD, JOHN A.   Outfielder
Brooklyn, N. L., 1902

WARD, JOSEPH A.   Infielder
Philadelphia, N. L., 1906
New York, A. L., 1909
Philadelphia, N. L., 1909–1910

WARES, CLYDE   Infielder
St. Louis, A. L., 1913–1914

WARHOP, JOHN M.   Pitcher
New York, A. L., 1908–1915, inc.

WARMOTH, W. W.   Pitcher
St. Louis, N. L., 1916

WARNER, E. E.   Pitcher
Pittsburgh, N. L., 1912

WARNER, HOKE   Infielder
Pittsburgh, N. L., 1916, 1917; 1919
Chicago, N. L., 1921

WARNER, JOHN J.   Catcher
New York, N. L., 1901
Boston, A. L., 1902
New York, N. L., 1903–1904

St. Louis, N. L., 1905
Detroit, A. L., 1905–1906
Washington, A. L., 1906–1907–1908

WARREN, W. H.   Catcher
Indianapolis, F. L., 1914
Newark, F. L., 1915

WARWICK, FIRMIN N.   Catcher
Pittsburgh, N. L., 1921

WASHBURN, LIBE   Pitcher—O. F.
New York, N. L., 1902
Philadelphia, N. L., 1903

WASHER, WILL   Pitcher
Philadelphia, N. L., 1905

WATSON   Catcher
Brooklyn, F. L., 1914–1915
Buffalo, F. L., 1915

WATSON, C. Z.   Pitcher
Chicago, N. L., 1913

WATSON, CHARLES   Pitcher
Chicago, F. L., 1914
St. Louis, F. L., 1914

WATSON, JOHN R.   Pitcher
Philadelphia, A. L., 1918–1919
Boston, N. L., 1920
Pittsburgh, N. L., 1920
Boston, N. L., 1920–1921

WATSON, MILTON   Pitcher
St. Louis, N. L., 1916–1917
Philadelphia, N. L., 1918–1919

WATT   Infielder
Washington, A. L., 1920

WEAVER, A. C.   Catcher
St. Louis, N. L., 1902–1903
Pittsburgh, N. L., 1903
St. Louis, A. L., 1905
Chicago, A. L., 1908

WEAVER, GEORGE DAVIS   3rd B.—S. S.
Chicago, A. L., 1912–1920, inc.

WEAVER, HARRY A.   Pitcher
Philadelphia, A. L., 1915–1916
Chicago, N. L., 1917–1919, inc.

WEAVER, ORLIE F.   Pitcher
Chicago, N. L., 1910–1911
Boston, N. L., 1911

WEBB, CLEON E.   Pitcher
Pittsburgh, N. L., 1910

WEBB, WILLIAM JOSEPH   Infielder
Pittsburgh, N. L., 1917

WEEDEN, ALBERT   Substitute
Boston, N. L., 1911

WEEKS, ED   Pitcher
Boston, N. L., 1904

WEILMAN, CARL   Pitcher
St. Louis, A. L., 1921–1920, inc.; except
1919

WEIMER, JACOB   Pitcher
Chicago, A. L., 1903–1905, inc.
Cincinnati, N. L., 1906–1908, inc.
New York, N. L., 1909

WEINERT, PHILIP   Pitcher
Philadelphia, N. L., 1919–1920–1921

WEISER, HARRY   Outfielder
Philadelphia, N. L., 1915–1916

WEISS   Infielder
Chicago, F. L., 1915

WELDAY, MICHAEL   Outfielder
Chicago, A. L., 1909

WELF, O.   Outfielder
Cleveland, A. L., 1916

WELSH, FRANCIS TIGUER   Outfielder
Philadelphia, A. L., 1919 to date

WENDELL, LOUIS C.   Catcher
New York, N. L., 1915–1916

WEST, JAMES   Pitcher
Cleveland, A. L., 1905–1911

WESTERBERG, O.   Substitute
Boston, N. L., 1907

WESTERZIL, GEORGE J.   Infielder
Brooklyn, F. L., 1914–1915
St. Louis, F. L., 1915
Chicago, F. L., 1915

WETZEL, FRANKLIN BURTON   Outfielder
St. Louis, A. L., 1920–1921

WEYHING, AUGUST P.   Pitcher
Cleveland, A. L., 1901
Cincinnati, N. L., 1901

WHALEN, THOMAS   Infielder
Boston, N. L., 1920

WHALING, ALBERT   Catcher
Boston, N. L., 1920

WHEAT, MCKINLEY D.   Catcher
Brooklyn, N. L., 1915–1919, inc.
Philadelphia, N. L., 1920–1921

WHEAT, ZACHARY D.   Outfielder
Brooklyn, N. L., 1909 to date

WHEATLEY   Pitcher
Detroit, A. L., 1912

WHEELER, EDWARD   Infielder
Brooklyn, N. L., 1902

WHEELER, FLOYD   Pitcher
Pittsburgh, N. L., 1921

WHEELER, GEORGE   Outfielder
Cincinnati, N. L., 1910

WHELAN, J. F.   Outfielder
St. Louis, N. L., 1913

WHITAKER, W.   Pitcher
Philadelphia, N. L., 1901–1902

WHITE   Pitcher
Washington, A. L., 1912

WHITE, GUY HARRIS   Pitcher
Philadelphia, N. L., 1901–1902
Chicago, A. L., 1903–1913, inc.

WHITE, KIRB   Pitcher
Boston, N. L., 1909–1910
Pittsburgh, N. L., 1910–1911

WHITE, STEPHEN   Pitcher
Boston, N. L., 1912

WHITEHOUSE, CHARLES E.   Pitcher
Indianapolis, F. L., 1914
Newark, F. L., 1915

WHITEHOUSE, GEORGE   Catcher—O. F.

Boston, N. L., 1912
Newark, F. L., 1915

WHITEHOUSE, GEORGE   Pitcher
Washington, A. L., 1919

WHITEMAN, GEORGE   Outfielder
Boston, A. L., 1907
New York, A. L., 1913
Boston, A. L., 1918

WHITING, JESSE W.   Pitcher
Philadelphia, N. L., 1902
Brooklyn, N. L., 1906–1907

WHITTED, GEORGE B.   Infielder — O. F.
St. Louis, N. L., 1912–1914, inc.
Boston, N. L., 1914
Philadelphia, N. L., 1915–1919, inc.
Pittsburgh, N. L., 1919–1921, inc.

WICKER, ROBERT K.   Pitcher
St. Louis, N. L., 1901–1902–1903
Chicago, N. L., 1903–1906, inc.
Cincinnati, N. L., 1906

WICKLAND, ALBERT   Outfielder
Cincinnati, N. L., 1913
Chicago, F. L., 1914–1915
Pittsburgh, F. L., 1915
Boston, N. L., 1918
New York, A. L., 1919

WIENECKE, J.   Pitcher
Chicago, A. L., 1921

WIGGS, JAMES A.   Pitcher
Cincinnati, N. L., 1903
Detroit, A. L., 1905–1906

WILHELM, IRVIN K.   Pitcher
Pittsburgh, N. L., 1903
Boston, N. L., 1904–1905
Brooklyn, N. L., 1908–1910, inc.
Baltimore, F. L., 1914
Philadelphia, N. L., 1921

WILHOIT, JOSEPH WILLIAM   O. F.
Boston, N. L., 1916–1917
Pittsburgh, N. L., 1917
New York, N. L., 1917–1918

WILIE, DENNIS E.   Outfielder

St. Louis, N. L., 1911–1912
Cleveland, A. L., 1915

WILKINSON   Outfielder
New York, A. L., 1911

WILKINSON, ROY HAMILTON   Pitcher
Cleveland, A. L., 1918
Chicago, A. L., 1919 to date

WILLETT, ROBERT EDGAR   Pitcher
Detroit, A. L., 1907–1913, inc.
St. Louis, F. L., 1914

WILLIAMS, ALVA G.   Catcher
Boston, A. L., 1911
Washington, A. L., 1912–1916, inc.
Cleveland, A. L., 1918

WILLIAMS, ARTHUR F.   Infielder
Chicago, N. L., 1902

WILLIAMS, CLAUDE PRESTON   Pitcher
Detroit, A. L., 1913–1914
Chicago, A. L., 1916–1920, inc.

WILLIAMS, DAVID L.   Pitcher
Boston, A. L., 1902

WILLIAMS, DENNIS   Outfielder
Cincinnati, N. L., 1921

WILLIAMS, FRED C.   Outfielder
Chicago, N. L., 1912–1917, inc.
Philadelphia, N. L., 1918 to date

WILLIAMS, GUS   Outfielder
St. Louis, A. L., 1911–1915, inc.

WILLIAMS, H. P.   1st B.
New York, A. L., 1913

WILLIAMS, JAMES THOMAS WILLIAMS
          2nd B. — 3rd B.
Baltimore, A. L., 1901–1902
New York, A. L., 1903–1907, inc.
St. Louis, A. L., 1908–1909

WILLIAMS, JOHN BRODIE   Pitcher
Detroit, A. L., 1914

WILLIAMS, KENNETH ROY   Outfielder
Cincinnati, N. L., 1915–1916
St. Louis, A. L., 1918–1921, inc.

WILLIAMS, MALCOLM, JR.   Pitcher
Philadelphia, A. L., 1916

WILLIAMS, R.   Pitcher
Washington, A. L., 1914

WILLIAMS, R. E.   Catcher
New York, A. L., 1911–1914, inc.

WILLIAMS, REES G.   Pitcher
St. Louis, N. L., 1914–1916

WILLIAMS, WALTER M.   Pitcher
Chicago, N. L., 1902–1903
Boston, N. L., 1903
Philadelphia, N. L., 1903

WILLIS   Pitcher
St. Louis, A. L., 1911

WILLIS, JOSEPH   Pitcher
St. Louis, N. L., 1911–1912–1913

WILLIS, VICTOR G.   Pitcher
Boston, N. L., 1901–1905, inc.
Pittsburgh, N. L., 1906–1909, inc.
St. Louis, N. L., 1910

WILSON   Pitcher
Boston, A. L., 1901

WILSON   Substitute
Boston, A. L., 1902

WILSON   Pitcher
Detroit, A. L., 1911

WILSON   Pitcher
Brooklyn, F. L., 1915

WILSON   Outfielder
Chicago, A. L., 1918

WILSON, A. PETER   Pitcher
New York, A. L., 1908–1909
Boston, A. L., 1911

WILSON, ARTHUR EARL   Catcher
New York, N. L., 1908–1913, inc.
Chicago, F. L., 1914–1915
Pittsburgh, N. L., 1916
Chicago, N. L., 1916–1917
Boston, N. L., 1918–1920
Cleveland, A. L., 1921

WILSON, HOWARD P.   Pitcher
Philadelphia, A. L., 1902
Washington, A. L., 1903–1904

WILSON, J. OWEN   Outfielder
Pittsburgh, N. L., 1918–1913, inc.
St. Louis, N. L., 1914–1916, inc.

WILSON, SAMUEL M.   Catcher
Pittsburgh, N. L., 1921

WILSON, WILLIAM CLARENCE   Pitcher
Detroit, A. L., 1920

WILTSE, GEORGE LEROY   Pitcher
New York, N. L., 1904–1914, inc.

WILTSE, LEWIS D.   Pitcher
Pittsburgh, N. L., 1901
Philadelphia, A. L., 1901–1902
Baltimore, A. L., 1902
New York, A. L., 1903

WINCHELL, F. R.   Pitcher
Cleveland, A. L., 1909

WINGO, EDMUND (LARIVIERE)   Catcher
Philadelphia, A. L., 1909

WINGO, IVY BROWN   Catcher
St. Louis, N. L., 1911–1914, inc.
Cincinnati, N. L., 1915 to date

WINHAM, LAFAYETTE S.   Pitcher
Brooklyn, N. L., 1902
Pittsburgh, N. L., 1903

WINN, GEORGE B.   Pitcher
Boston, A. L., 1919

WINTER, GEORGE L.   Pitcher
Boston, A. L., 1901–1908, inc.
Detroit, A. L., 1908

WINTERS, JESSE F.   Pitcher
New York, N. L., 1919–1920
Philadelphia, N. L., 1921

WIRTS, ELWOOD VERNON   Catcher
Chicago, N. L., 1921

WISNER, JOHN HENRY   Pitcher
Pittsburgh, N. L., 1919–1920

WITHERUP, LEROY   Pitcher
Boston, A. L., 1906
Washington, A. L., 1908–1909

WITHROW, FRANK B.   Catcher
Philadelphia, N. L., 1920

WITT, LAWRON WALTER   Inf.—O. F.
Philadelphia, A. L., 1916 to date; (except
1918, when he was in the service)

WOOD, JOSEPH   Pitcher—O. F.
Boston, A. L., 1908–1915, inc.
Cleveland, A. L., 1917 to date

WOOD, ROBERT   Catcher
Cleveland, A. L., 1901–1902

WOODALL, LAWRENCE   Catcher
Detroit, A. L., 1920–1921

WOLF, WALTER F.   Pitcher
Philadelphia, A. L., 1921

WOLFE   Pitcher
Cleveland, A. L., 1912

WOLFE, HARRY   Infielder
Chicago, N. L., 1917
Pittsburgh, N. L., 1917

WOLFE, ROY   Infielder
Chicago, A. L., 1914

WOLFE, WILLIAM   Pitcher
Philadelphia, N. L., 1902

WOLFE, WILLIAM   Pitcher
New York, A. L., 1903–1904
Washington, A. L., 1904–1905

WOLFGANG, MELDON G.   Pitcher
Chicago, A. L., 1914–1918, inc.

WOLTER, HARRY M.   Pitcher—O. F.
Cincinnati, N. L., 1907
Pittsburgh, N. L., 1907
St. Louis, N. L., 1907
Boston, A. L., 1909
New York, A. L., 1910–1913, inc.

WOLVERTON, HARRY S.   3rd B.
Philadelphia, N. L., 1901
Washington, A. L., 1902
Philadelphia, N. L., 1902–1904, inc.
Boston, A. L., 1905
New York, N. L., 1912

WOOD, HARRY   Outfielder
Cincinnati, N. L., 1903

WOOD, JOSEPH   Pitcher—O. F.
Boston, A. L., 1908–1915, inc.
Cleveland, A. L., 1917 to date

WOOD, ROBERT   Catcher
Cleveland, A. L., 1901–1902

WOOD, ROY   Infielder
Pittsburgh, N. L., 1913
Cleveland, A. L., 1914–1915

WOODALL, LAWRENCE   Catcher
Detroit, A. L., 1920–1921

WOODBURN, EUGENE S.   Pitcher
St. Louis, N. L., 1911–1912

WOODRUFF, ORVILLE   Infielder
Cincinnati, N. L., 1904–1910

WOODWARD, FRANK RUSSELL   Pitcher
Philadelphia, N. L., 1918–1919
St. Louis, N. L., 1919
Washington, A. L., 1921

WORKS, RALPH TECUMSEH   Pitcher
Detroit, A. L., 1909–1912, inc.
Cincinnati, N. L., 1912–1913

WORTMAN, WILLIAM L.   Infielder
Chicago, N. L., 1916–1918, inc.

WRIGHT, CLARENCE EUGENE   Pitcher
Brooklyn, N. L., 1901
Cleveland, A. L., 1902–1903
St. Louis, A. L., 1993–1904

WRIGHT, EDWARD   Infielder
Chicago, A. L., 1916

WRIGHT, ROBERT C.   Pitcher
Chicago, N. L., 1915

WRIGHT, W. S.   Pitcher
Cleveland, A. L., 1909

WRIGHT, WAYNE B.   Pitcher
St. Louis, A. L., 1917–1919, inc.

WRIGHTSTONE, RUSSELL G.   Infielder
Philadelphia, N. L., 1920–1921

WYCKOFF, J. WELDON   Pitcher
Philadelphia, A. L., 1913–1916, inc.
Boston, A. L., 1916–1918, inc.

YALE, AD   Infielder
Brooklyn, N. L., 1905

YANTZ, GEORGE   Catcher
Chicago, N. L., 1912

YARYAN, EVERETT   Catcher
Chicago, A. L., 1921

YEABSLEY, BERT N.   Catcher
Philadelphia, N. L., 1919

YEAGER, GEORGE   Catcher
Cleveland, A. L., 1901
Pittsburgh, N. L., 1901
New York, N. L., 1902
Baltimore, A. L., 1902

YEAGER, JOSEPH   Pitcher—Inf.
Detroit, A. L., 1901–1902–1903
New York, A. L., 1905–1906
St. Louis, A. L., 1907–1908

YELLE, ARCHIE   Catcher
Detroit, A. L., 1917–1918

YELLOWHORSE, MOSES   Pitcher
Pittsburgh, N. L., 1921

YERKES, STANLEY   Pitcher
Baltimore, A. L., 1901
St. Louis, N. L., 1901–1903, inc.

YERKES, STEPHEN   Infielder
Boston, A. L., 1909–1914, inc.; except
1910
Pittsburgh, F. L., 1914–1915
Chicago, N. L., 1916

YINGLING, EARL H.   Pitcher
Cleveland, A. L., 1911
Brooklyn, N. L., 1912–1913
Cincinnati, N. L., 1914
Washington, A. L., 1918

YOHE   Infielder
Washington, A. L., 1909

YORK, JAMES E.   Pitcher
Philadelphia, A. L., 1919
Chicago, N. L., 1921

YOTER, E. E.   Shortstop
Philadelphia, A. L., 1921

YOUNG, D. D.   Outfielder
Cincinnati, N. L., 1909

YOUNG, DENTON J.   Pitcher
Boston, A. L., 1901–1908, inc.
Cleveland, A. L., 1909–1911, inc.
Boston, N. L., 1911

YOUNG, G. J.   Outfielder
Cleveland, A. L., 1913
Buffalo, F. L., 1914

YOUNG, H. E.   Pitcher
Pittsburgh, N. L., 1908
Boston, N. L., 1908

YOUNG, H. J.   Infielder
Boston, N. L., 1911

YOUNG, IRVING MELROSE   Pitcher
Boston, N. L., 1905–1908, inc.
Pittsburgh, N. L., 1908
Chicago, A. L., 1910–1911

YOUNG, RALPH STUART   Infielder
New York, A. L., 1913
Detroit, A. L., 1915 to date

YOUNGS, ROSS   Outfielder
New York, N. L., 1917–1918–1919–1920–
1921

ZABEL, GEORGE WASHINGTON   Pitcher
Chicago, N. L., 1913–1914–1915

ZACHARY, JAMES THOMPSON   Pitcher
Washington, A. L., 1919 to date

ZACHER, E. H.   Outfielder
New York, N. L., 1910
St. Louis, N. L., 1910

ZACKERT, G.   Pitcher
St. Louis, N. L., 1911–1912

ZAMLOCH, CARL   Pitcher
Detroit, A. L., 1913

ZEARFOSS, DAVE W.   Catcher
St. Louis, N. L., 1904–1905

ZEIDER, ROLLA H.   Infielder
Chicago, A. L., 1910–1913, inc.
New York, A. L., 1913
Chicago, F. L., 1914–1915
Chicago, N. L., 1916–1918, inc.

ZEISER, MATTHEW J.   Pitcher
Boston, A. L., 1914

ZIMMER, CHARLES L.   Catcher
Pittsburgh, N. L., 1901–1902
ZIMMERMAN, EDWARD DESMOND
                           Infielder
St. Louis, N. L., 1906
ZIMMERMAN, HENRY   Infielder
Chicago, N. L., 1907–1916, inc.
New York, N. L., 1916–1919, inc.

ZIMMERMAN, WILLIAM   Outfielder
Brooklyn, N. L., 1915

ZINK, WALTER   Pitcher
New York, N. L., 1921

ZINN, GUY   Outfielder
New York, A. L., 1911–1912

ZINN, JAMES EDWARD   Pitcher
Philadelphia, A. L., 1919
Pittsburgh, N. L., 1920–1921

ZITZMANN, WILLIAM A.   Outfielder
Pittsburgh, N. L., 1919
Cincinnati, N. L., 1919

ZMICH, ED A.   Pitcher
St. Louis, N. L., 1910–1911

ZWILLING, EDWARD H.   Outfielder
Chicago, A. L., 1910
Chicago, F. L., 1914–1915
Chicago, N. L., 1916

Baseball Cyclopedia

For Season of 1922—47th Year for National League and 22nd for American

The Pennant Races

National League

Club	Won	Lost	Pc.	Manager
New York	93	61	.604	J. J. McGraw
Cincinnati	86	68	.558	P. J. Moran
Pittsburgh	85	69	.552	G. Gibson, W. B. McKechnie
St. Louis	85	69	.552	B. Rickey
Chicago	80	74	.519	W. Killefer
Brooklyn	76	78	.494	W. Robinson
Philadelphia	57	96	.373	L. Wilhelm
Boston	53	100	.346	F. L. Mitchell
Totals	615	615	.500	

American League

Club	Won	Lost	Pc.	Manager
New York	94	60	.610	M. Huggins
St. Louis	93	61	.604	L. Fohl
Detroit	79	75	.513	T. R. Cobb
Cleveland	78	76	.507	T. E. Speaker
Chicago	77	77	.500	W. Gleason
Washington	69	85	.448	J. C. Milan
Philadelphia	65	89	.422	C. Mack
Boston	61	93	.396	H. Duffy
Totals	616	616	.500	

It was the tenth pennant for the New York National League club, the second for the New York American League club. These teams—Giants and Yankees—met for the second year in succession in the World's Series, the Giants winning again, this time gaining four victories and not losing a game, though they were tied once. This was the 24th World's Series, and the result of the set made these changes in the World's Series dope (See page 100.)

Series Won—American League   11
   National League   8
   (American–National series only.)
Cities having World's Champion Teams
   New York   5
Cities competing for World's Series
   Championship—New York   12

Record of games won and lost by World's Series clubs: New York Nationals, Won 33; lost 27; percentage .650; New York Americans, won 3; lost 9; percentage .250.

Managers' records in World's Series—John J. McGraw, series won, 3; series lost, 4; games won, 21; games lost, 20; games tied, 2. Miller J. Huggins, series lost, 2; games won, 3; games lost, 9; games tied, 1.

The players on the pennant winning clubs during the year were as follows:

NEW YORK NATIONALS—John J. McGraw, manager; Jesse L. Barnes, Virgil Jennings Barnes, Clinton Blume, Cecil Algernon Causey, Michael Cvengros, Philip Brooks Douglas, Carmen Proctor Hill, Fred Johnson, Claude Jonnard, Hugh A. McQuillan, Arthur N. Nehf, Wilfred D. Ryan, John William Scott, Patrick J. Shea, Fred A. Toney, pitch-

ers; Alexander N. Gaston, Earl Smith, Frank J. Snyder, catchers; David James Bancroft, Frank Francis Frisch, Henry Knight Groh, Travis Jackson, George Lange Kelly, Fred Maguire, Walter Scott MacPhee; John William Rawlings, infielders; William A. Cunningham, Mahlon Higbee, Lee King, Emil Frederick Meusel, Ralph Shinners, Charles D. Stengel, Ross Young, outfielders; J. Howard Berry, Isaac M. Boone, Alvin J. Dolan, Davis O. Robertson, substitutes.

NEW YORK AMERICANS—Miller James Huggins, manager; Leslie Joseph Bush, Waite Charles Hoyt, Samuel Pond Jones, C. Manley Llewellyn, Carl William Mays, George King Murray, Francis Joseph O'Doul, James Robert Shawkey, pitchers; Albert DeVormer, Fred C. Hoffmann, Walter H. Schang, catchers; John Franklin Baker, Joseph A. Dugan, Norman Alexis McMillan, John Franklin Mitchell, Walter Charles Pipp, Lewis Everett Scott, Aaron Lee Ward, infielders; Robert William Meusel, Elmer Miller, George Herman Ruth, E. Camp Skinner, Elmer John Smith, Lawton Walter Witt, outfielders; Wilson Fewster, Michael Joseph McNally, substitutes.

Just one of the 16 Major League clubs set a new record for itself during 1922. That was St. Louis of the American League. A Brown team, managed by James R. McAleer, ran second in 1902 with a percentage of .574. The Browns of 1922, managed by Lee Alexander Fohl, also finished second, but with an average of 30 points better than the McAleer directed team of twenty years previously.

The pennant won by New York in the National League was its tenth, by New York in the American League its second.

As for cellar championships, it was the sixth for the Boston Nationals and the second for the Boston Americans.

Leaders of 1922

BATTERS*—Page 46

Player	Club	League	
George H. Sisler	St. Louis	American	420
Rogers Hornsby	St. Louis	National	401

BASE STEALERS—Page 48

George H. Sisler	St. Louis	American	51
Max G. Carey	Pittsburgh	National	51

SACRIFICE HITTERS—Page 49

William A. Wambsganss	Cleveland	American	42
Zebulon A. Terry	Chicago	National	39

SCORERS—Page 50

Rogers Hornsby	St. Louis	National	141
George H. Sisler	St. Louis	American	134

MANUFACTURERS OF BASE HITS—Page 51

Rogers Hornsby	St. Louis	National	250
George H. Sisler	St. Louis	American	246

DEMON DOUBLERS—Page 53

Tris E. Speaker	Cleveland	American	48
Rogers Hornsby	St. Louis	National	46

DEMON TRIPLERS—Page 54

Jacob E. Daubert	Cincinnati	National	22
George H. Sisler	St. Louis	American	18

DEMON HOME RUNNISTS—Page 55

Rogers Hornsby	St. Louis	National	42
Kenneth R. Williams	St. Louis	American	39

BATTING IN RUNS—Page 56

| Kenneth R. Williams | St. Louis | American | 155 |
| Rogers Hornsby | St. Louis | National | 152 |

DEMON WHIFFERS—Page 56

| James Dykes | Philadelphia | American | 98 |
| Frank J. Parkinson | Philadelphia | National | 93 |

DEMON WALKERS—Page 56

| Lawton W. Witt | New York | American | 89 |
| Max G. Carey | Pittsburgh | National | 80 |

THROWN OUT OFTENEST—Page 56

C. J. Hollocher	Chicago	National	29
George H. Sisler	St. Louis	American	19
Kenneth R. Williams	St. Louis	American	19

STRIKE OUT KINGS—Page 57

| Urban J. Shocker | St. Louis | American | 149 |
| Arthur C. Vance | Brooklyn | National | 134 |

There were no Major League records created in 1922, but there were American and National League records created or equaled, these being as follows:

AMERICAN LEAGUE

Sisler's batting mark of 420 equaled Cobb's 1911 performance—bettered it a bit, fractions considered.

NATIONAL LEAGUE

Hornsby set new records in hits, with 250 in home runs with 42 and in runs batted in with 152.

FAMOUS GAMES, FAMOUS PLAYERS, FAMOUS FEATS THREE HOME RUNS IN GAME—PAGE 61

KENNETH R. WILLIAMS, St. Louis Americans, did this on April 22, 1922, at St. Louis, in game with Chicago (off Acosta in first and sixth innings, off Davenport in seventh.) Walter J. Henline, Philadelphia Nationals, did this on September 15, 1922, at Philadelphia, in game with St. Louis (off Sell in fourth inning, off Doak in seventh inning and off Sherdel in ninth inning.)

TWO HOME RUNS IN INNING—
PAGE 63

KENNETH R. WILLIAMS, St. Louis Americans, did this on August 7, 1922, at St. Louis, in game with Washington in sixth inning (first off Mogridge, second off Erickson.) A winter-time discovery was that Jacob Stenzel, Pittsburgh center fielder, made two home runs in the third inning of the game in Boston on June 6, 1894, off a pitcher named Lampe, who now is a policeman in Boston.

THREE HOME RUNS IN ONE INNING—PAGE 65

This no longer is a record for the Major Leagues, for a winter-time discovery was that on June 6, 1894, the Pittsburgh Pirates had assembled four four-baggers in the third inning on Lampe of Boston. Stenzel then made two, Elmer Smith one and Louis Bierbauer one.

GAME CONTAINING MOST RUNS—PAGE 68

The Brooklyn–Buffalo Players' League game of July 12, 1890, won by Brooklyn, 28 to 16, goes into the discard by reason of the game played in Chicago by the Cubs and Phillies on August 25, 1922. This the Cubs won, 26 to 23.

THE SIX HIT MANUFACTURERS— PAGE 71

GUY HECKER does not belong in this list, for he batted seven times. Max G. Carey of Pittsburgh made six hits (one a double) in six times at bat in an 18-inning game against New York, July 7, 1922.

NO HIT HEROES—PAGE 82

CHARLES ROBERTSON of Chicago Americans pitched an absolutely perfect no-hit game against Detroit on April 30, 1922, no one reaching first. He won this game, 2 to 0. A week later, on May 7th, Jesse Barnes of the New York Nationals pitched a no-hit game against Philadelphia, winning 6 to 0.

ONE OF WORLD'S WORST BALL CLUBS—PAGE 96

The Louisville American Association club of 1889, by losing 26 straight, still remains the team dropping the most combats in a row, but a winter-time discovery shows Cleveland, in 1899, to have lost 25 games in sequence, Cleveland being in the National League then and dopesters losing track of this stunt. The Pittsburgh Pirates of 1890 lost 23 one after the other.

KEELER HIT SAFELY IN 44 STRAIGHT GAMES—PAGE 96

George Sisler of the St. Louis Americans hit safely in 41 straight games in 1922, beating Tyrus Cobb's record of 1911 by one game and coming within three games of Keeler's record. Sisler was stopped by Bush of New York, on September 18th.

Addenda to Part VII

Major Leagues of 1922
Players Starting Major League Careers in 1922

ADAMS, EARL — Infielder Chicago Nationals	CALLAGHAN, MARTIN — Outfielder Chicago Nationals
BARFOOT, CLYDE RAYMOND — Pitcher St. Louis Nationals	CAVENEY, JAMES CHRISTOPHER — Infielder Cincinnati
BEDGOOD, PHILIP — Pitcher Cleveland	CLANTON, EUCAL — 1st B. Cleveland
BENTON, SIDNEY WRIGHT — Pitcher St. Louis Nationals	CLARK, DANIEL CURRAN — Utility Detroit
BENTON, STANLEY — Infielder Philadelphia Nationals	COTTER, HARVEY — Utility Chicago Nationals
BERGER, JOHN Philadelphia Nationals	COX, E. T. — Pitcher Chicago Americans
BLADES, RAYMOND — Inf.—O. F. St. Louis Nationals	CVENGROS, MICHAEL — Pitcher New York Nationals
BLANKENSHIP, HOMER — Pitcher Chicago Americans	DECATUR, ARTHUR — Pitcher Brooklyn
BLANKENSHIP, TED — Pitcher Chicago Americans	DORAN, WILLIAM J. Cleveland
BLUEGE, OSWALD L. — Infielder Washington	DRAKE, LOGAN Cleveland
BLUME, CLINTON — Pitcher New York Nationals	DUFF, CECIL ELBA — Pitcher Chicago Americans
BOONE, ISAAC M. — Outfielder New York Nationals	DURST, CEDRIC MONTGOMERY — O. F. St. Louis Americans
BOTTOMLEY, JAMES LEROY — 1st B. St. Louis Nationals	DYER, EDWIN HAWLEY — Pitcher St. Louis Nationals
BOWLES, E. J. Chicago Americans	EDMONDSON, GEORGE H. — Pitcher Cleveland
BRILLHEART, J. B. — Pitcher Washington	EDWARDS, JAMES C. — Pitcher Cleveland
BROWN, MYRL — Pitcher Pittsburgh	ENS, JEWEL — Infielder Pittsburgh
BUBSER, HAROLD Chicago Americans	EUBANKS, UEL — Pitcher Chicago Nationals

FITZGERALD, HOWARD C. Chicago Nationals	Outfielder
FOTHERGILL, ROBERT Detroit	Outfielder
FRANCIS, RAY Washington	Pitcher
FREIGAU, HOWARD EARL St. Louis Nationals	Infielder
FUHRMAN, OLLIE Philadelphia Americans	Catcher
FUSSELL, FRED Chicago Nationals	Pitcher
GAGNON, HAROLD DENNIS Detroit	Infielder
GALLAGHER, LAWRENCE K. Boston Nationals	Infielder
GENEWICH, JOSEPH E. Boston Nationals	Pitcher
GILLESPIE, JOHN Cincinnati	Pitcher
GOEBEL, EDWIN Washington	Outfielder
GOLVIN, WALTER G. Chicago Nationals	1st B.
GRAHAM, R. V. Chicago Americans	
GRANTHAM, GEORGE Chicago Nationals	Infielder
GRIFFITH, BERT J. Brooklyn	Outfielder
HAMON Cleveland	Pitcher
HANEY, FRED JOHN Detroit	Infielder
HARPER, GEORGE WASHINGTON Cincinnati	Outfielder
HARTNETT, CHARLES L. Chicago Nationals	Catcher
HAUSER, JOSEPH Philadelphia Americans	1st B.

HENRY, FRED M. Boston Nationals	1st B.
HIGBEE, MAHLON New York Nationals	Outfielder
HIGH, ANDREW AIRD Brooklyn	Infielder
HOLLINGSWORTH, JOHN Pittsburgh	Pitcher
HOLLOWAY, KENNETH E. Detroit	Pitcher
HULIHAN, HARRY J. Detroit	Pitcher
HUNGLING, BERNARD Brooklyn	Catcher
JACKSON, TRAVIS New York Nationals	S. S.
JEANES, ERNEST Cleveland	Outfielder
JENKINS, J. R. Chicago Americans	
JOHNSON, FRED New York Nationals	Pitcher
JOHNSON, SYLVESTER W. Detroit	Pitcher
KAHDOT, I. Cleveland	Pitcher
KECK, FRANK Cincinnati	Pitcher
KETCHUM, GUSS FRANKLIN Philadelphia Americans	Pitcher
KNIGHT, JACK St. Louis Nationals	Pitcher
KRUG, MARTIN Chicago Nationals	Infielder
LANSING, EUGENE HEWETT Boston Nationals	Pitcher
LAPAN, PETER NELSON Washington	Catcher
LEVERETTE, GORMAN V. Chicago Americans	Pitcher

LINDSEY, JAMES K. Cleveland	Pitcher	MAYNARD, L. E. Boston Americans	Infielder
LLEWELLYN, MANLEY C. New York Americans	Pitcher	MEINE, HENRY St. Louis Americans	Pitcher
LONG, JAMES Chicago Americans	Pitcher	MEREWEATHER, ARTHUR Pittsburgh	
LOVELACE, GROVER T. Pittsburgh		METIVIER, GEORGE DEWEY Cleveland	Pitcher
LUTZ, LOUIS Cincinnati	Catcher	MIDDLETON, WAYNE Cleveland	Pitcher
LYNCH, W. E. Boston Americans	Catcher	MILLER, JACOB G. Pittsburgh	Outfielder
MACPHEE, WALTER S. New York Nationals	Infielder	MOHARDT, JOHN HENRY Detroit	Outfielder
MCCURDY, HARRY H. St. Louis Nationals	Catcher—1st B.	MORRIS, WALTER E. Chicago Americans	Pitcher
MCCURE, FRANK Philadelphia Americans		MUELLER, WALTER Pittsburgh	Outfielder
MCGOWAN, FRANK BERNARD Philadelphia Americans	O. F.	MURRAY, GEORGE KING New York Americans	Pitcher
MCGREW, WALTER H. Washington	Pitcher	MURRAY, JAMES Brooklyn	Pitcher
MCMILLAN, NORMAN ALEXIS New York Americans	Inf.	OGDEN, WARREN HARVEY Philadelphia Americans	Pitcher
MCNAMARA, G. F. Washington	Outfielder	OLSEN, ARTHUR Detroit	Pitcher
MCNAMARA, THOMAS H. Pittsburgh		O'NEILL, J. H. Philadelphia Americans	Pitcher
MCNAMARA, TIMOTHY A. Boston Nationals	Pitcher	OSBORNE, ERNEST P. Chicago Nationals	Pitcher
MCNULTY, PATRICK Cleveland	Outfielder	PINTO, LERTON Philadelphia Nationals	Pitcher
MACK, FRANK GEORGE Chicago Americans	Pitcher	POST, SAMUEL G. Brooklyn	Infielder
MAGUIRE, FRED New York Nationals	Infielder	POTT, NELSON A. Cleveland	Pitcher
MATTHEWS, JAMES Boston Nationals	Pitcher	PRUETT, HERBERT St. Louis Americans	Pitcher
MATTOX, JAMES P. Pittsburgh	Catcher	RABBITT, JOSEPH Cleveland	Outfielder

REICHLE, RICHARD Boston Americans	Outfielder	SINGLETON, JOHN EDWARD Philadelphia Nationals	Pitcher
RETTIG, ADOLPH Philadelphia Americans	Pitcher	SKINNER, E. CAMP New York Americans	Outfielder
RIGNEY, ELMER ELMO Detroit	Infielder	SORRELLS, R. E. Cleveland	
ROBERTSON, EUGENE E. St. Louis Americans	Infielder	STONER, L. E. Detroit	Pitcher
ROSER, JOHN JOSEPH Boston Nationals	Outfielder	STUART, JOHN DAVIS St. Louis Nationals	Pitcher
SCHAUTE, JOSEPH BEN Cleveland	Pitcher	SULLIVAN, THOMAS A. Philadelphia Nationals	Pitcher
SCHEER, HENRY W. Philadelphia Americans	Infielder	SWENTOR, A. W. Chicago Americans	
SCHILLING, ELY Philadelphia Americans	Pitcher	TURK, I. N. Washington	Pitcher
SCHNELL, KARL Cincinnati	Pitcher	VICK, HENRY ARTHUR St. Louis Nationals	Catcher
SCHREIBER, PAUL F. St. Louis Nationals	Pitcher	WEIS, ARTHUR J. Chicago Nationals	
SHINNERS, RALPH New York Nationals	Outfielder	YARRISON, BYRON W. Philadelphia Americans	Pitcher
SHRIVER, HARRY G. Brooklyn	Pitcher	YEARGIN, JAMES A. Boston Nationals	Pitcher

Baseball Cyclopedia

For Season of 1923—48th Year for National League and 23rd for American

The Pennant Races

American League

Club	Won	Lost	Pc.	Manager
New York	98	54	.645	M. J. Huggins
Detroit	83	71	.539	T. R. Cobb
Cleveland	82	71	.536	T. E. Speaker
Washington	75	78	.490	O. Bush
St. Louis	74	78	.487	L. A. Fohl
				J. P. Austin
Philadelphia	69	83	.454	C. Mack
Chicago	69	84	.448	W. Gleason
Boston	61	91	.401	F. L. Chance
Totals	611	611	.500	

National League

Club	Won	Lost	Pc.	Manager
New York	95	58	.621	J. J. McGraw
Cincinnati	91	63	.591	P. J. Moran
Pittsburgh	87	67	.565	W. B. McKechnie
Chicago	83	71	.539	W. Killefer
St. Louis	79	74	.516	B. Rickey
Brooklyn	76	78	.494	W. Robinson
Boston	54	100	.351	F. L. Mitchell
Philadelphia	50	104	.325	A. Fletcher
Totals	615	615	.500	

It was the third pennant for the New York American League club, the eleventh for the New York National League club. These teams—Yankees and Giants—met for the third year in succession in the World's Series, and for the first time the American Leaguers won, the Huggins combination winning four games and encountering two defeats. This was the 25th World's Series, and the result of the set made these changes in the World's Series dope (See page 100.):

Series Won—American League	12
National League	8
(American–National series only)	
Cities having World's Champion Teams	
New York	6
Cities competing for World's Series	
Championship—New York	14

Record of games won and lost by World's Series clubs: New York Nationals, Won 35; lost 31; percentage .530; New York Americans, won 7; lost 11; percentage .389.

Managers' records in World's Series—John J. McGraw, series won, 3; series lost, 5; games won, 23; games lost, 24; games tied, 2. Miller J. Huggins, series won, 1; series lost, 2; games won, 7; games lost, 11; games tied, 1.

The players on the pennant winning clubs during the year were as follows:

NEW YORK AMERICANS—Miller James Huggins, manager; Leslie Joseph Bush, Waite Charles Hoyt, Samuel Pond Jones, Carl William Mays, Herbert J. Pennock, George William Pipgras, Oscar F. L. Roettger, James Robert Shawkey, pitchers; Bernard Oliver Bengough,

Fred C. Hofmann, Walter H. Schang, catchers; Walter Charles Pipp, Joseph A. Dugan, Lewis Everett Scott, Aaron Lee Ward, infielders; Robert William Meusel, George Herman Ruth, Lawton Walter Witt, Elmer John Smith, outfielders; Michael Gazella, Henry Louis Gehrig, Henry Luther Haines, Harvey Hendrick, Michael Joseph McNally, Ernest R. Johnson, substitutes.

NEW YORK NATIONALS—John Joseph McGraw, manager; Jesse L. Barnes, Virgil Jennings Barnes, John Needles Bentley, Clinton W. Blume, Dennis John Gearin, Walter Huntzinger, Fred E. Johnson, Claude Jonnard, Fred Lucas, Hugh A. McQuillan, Arthur N. Nehf, Wilfred D. Ryan, John William Scott, George Walberg, John R. Watson, pitcher; Alexander N. Gaston, Harry M. Gowdy, Earl Smith, Frank Snyder, catchers; David James Bancroft, Frank Francis Frisch, Henry Knight Groh, George Lange Kelly, Travis C. Jackson, infielders; William A. Cunningham, Emil Frederick Meusel, Charles D. Stengel, Ross Young, outfielders; Fred Maguire, William Harold Terry, James Joseph O'Connell, Ralph Shinners, Mose Solomon, Lewis Robert Wilson, substitutes.

Just one of the 16 Major League clubs set a new record for itself during 1923, the New York Americans, managed by Miller James Huggins, turning in a percentage of .645 in winning their third pennant. This percentage was .004 in excess of the best previous percentage for a Yankee team, made in 1921.

As before related, the pennant won by New York in the American League

was its third, by New York in the National League its eleventh.
As for cellar championships, it was the sixth for the Philadelphia Nationals and the third for the Boston Americans.

Leaders of 1923

BATTERS—Page 46

Player	Club	League	
Harold E. Heilmann	Detroit	American	403
Rogers Hornsby	St. Louis	National	384

BASE STEALERS—Page 48

Max G. Carey	Pittsburgh	National	51
Edward T. Collins	Chicago	American	49

SACRIFICE HITTERS—Page 49

Edward T. Collins	Chicago	American	39
John P. McInnis	Boston	National	37

SCORERS—Page 50

George H. Ruth	New York	American	151
Max G. Carey	Pittsburgh	National	120

MANUFACTURERS OF BASE HITS—Page 51

Frank J. Frisch	New York	National	223
Charles D. Jamieson	Cleveland	American	222

DEMON DOUBLERS—Page 53

Tris E. Speaker	Cleveland	American	59
Edd J. Roush	Cincinnati	National	41

DEMON TRIPLERS—Page 54

Max G. Carey	Pittsburgh	National	19
Harold J. Traynor	Pittsburgh	National	19
Leon A. Goslin	Washington	American	18
Edgar Samuel Rice	Washington	American	18

DEMON HOME RUNNISTS—Page 55

George H. Ruth	New York	American	41
Fred C. Williams	Philadelphia	National	41

BATTING IN RUNS—Page 56

George H. Ruth	New York	American	130
Tris E. Speaker	Cleveland	American	130
Emil F. Meusel	New York	National	125

DEMON WHIFFERS—Page 56

George H. Ruth	New York	American	93
George F. Grantham	Chicago	National	92

DEMON WALKERS—Page 56

George H. Ruth	New York	American	170
George H. Burns	Cincinnati	National	101

THROWN OUT OFTENEST—Page 56

Edward T. Collins	Chicago	American	29
George F. Grantham	Chicago	National	28

STRIKE OUT KINGS—Page 57

Arthur C. Vance	Brooklyn	National	197
Walter P. Johnson	Washington	American	126

FAMOUS GAMES, FAMOUS PLAYERS, FAMOUS FEATS THREE HOME RUNS IN GAME—PAGE 61

FRED C. WILLIAMS, Philadelphia Nationals, did this on May 11, 1923, at Philadelphia in game with St. Louis (off Sherdel in third inning, and off North in seventh and eighth innings.) George Lange Kelly, New York Nationals, did this on September 17, 1923, at Chicago, in game with Chicago (off Aldridge in third, fourth and fifth innings). Kelly's home runs, kindly note, were made in successive innings.

THE SIX HIT MANUFACTURERS— PAGE 71

JACQUES FRANK FOURNIER, Brooklyn Nationals, made six hits in six times at bat in game at Philadelphia on June 29, 1923, against the pitching of Glazner and Head, three singles, two doubles and one home run being in collection of clouts. Frank Willard Brower, Cleveland

Americans, batting six times at Washington on August 7, 1923, made five singles and one double off Mitchell, Friday and Potter.

UNASSISTED TRIPLE PLAYS—
PAGE 97

GEORGE HENRY BURNS, first baseman of Boston Americans, made an unassisted triple play at Boston in the second inning of the game with Cleveland on September 14, 1923. He caught Brower's liner, tagged Lutzke off first and then ran to second and reached that bag before Stephenson could get back from third. On October 6, 1923, in the same city and in the fourth inning of the game with Philadelphia, Ernest Kitchen Padgett, shortstop of Boston Nationals, retired three men without assistance in this fashion: He caught Holke's liner, ran to second to retire Tierney and then tagged Lee before he could get back to first.

NO HIT HEROES—PAGE 82

SAMUEL POND JONES, New York Americans, retired Philadelphia without hit or run at Philadelphia on September 4, 1923. Three days later, in the same city, Howard J. Ehmke, Boston Americans, got credit for duplicating Jones' feat, being assisted in his hitless-runless game by Pitcher Bryan Harris of the Athletics, who hit the wall with a safe hit in the sixth inning, but was declared out for not touching first base. Jones won his game, 2 to 0; Ehmke, 4 to 0.

There were two major league records created in 1923, as follows:

FOR PASSES

George H. Ruth, New York Americans, received 170 bases on balls. Highest previous number in one season for major league player—148, received by Ruth in 1920.

FOR TWO BASE HITS

Tris E. Speaker, Cleveland Americans, made 59. Highest previous number in one season for major league player—56, made by Edward J. Delehanty, Philadelphia Nationals, in 1899. Unofficial records show Delehanty to have hit 57 doubles that year.

Addenda to Part VII
Major Leagues of 1922
Players Starting Major League Careers in 1922

ADAMS, GEORGE   Pitcher
Cincinnati N. L.

ADAMS, SPENCER   Infielder
Pittsburgh N. L.

ARCHDEACON, MAURICE JOHN
     Outfielder
Chicago A. L.

BAGWELL, WILLIAM M.   Outfielder
Boston N. L.

BARNES, EVERETT DUANE Pittsburgh N. L.	Infielder	CONROY, WILLIAM F. Washington A. L.	Infielder
BARRETT, ROBERT S. Chicago N. L.	Substitute	CORTAZZO, JOHN Chicago A. L.	Infielder
BATCHELDER, JOSEPH EDMUND Boston N. L.	Pitcher	COUSINEAU, EDWARD T. Boston N. L.	Catcher
BELL, LESTER ROWLAND St. Louis N. L.	Infielder	CROUSE, CLYDE E. Chicago A. L.	Catcher
BENGOUGH, BERNARD OLIVER New York A. L.	Catcher	DICKERMAN, LEO L. Brooklyn N. L.	Pitcher
BENNETT, HERSCHEL E. St. Louis A. L.		DONAHUE, JOHN FRANCES Boston A. L.	Infielder
BENNETT, J. Philadelphia N. L.	Infielder	DONNEHY, THOMAS Philadelphia N. L.	Outfielder
BENTON, LAWRENCE J. Boston N. L.	Pitcher	DORMAN, C. Chicago A. L.	Catcher
BERG, MORRIS Brooklyn N. L.	Infielder	DOUTHIT, TAYLOR LEE St. Louis N. L.	Outfielder
BISHOP, JAMES Philadelphia N. L.	Pitcher	DUMOVICH, NICK Chicago N. L.	Pitcher
BLACK, DAVE Boston A. L.		ELLIOTT, JAMES THOMAS St. Louis A. L.	Pitcher
BLETHEN, CLARENCE W. Boston A. L.	Pitcher	ELSH, EUGENE ROY Chicago A. L.	Outfielder
BLETHEN, CLARENCE W. Boston A. L.	Pitcher	EMBREY, CHARLES Chicago A. L.	Pitcher
BURKE, LESLIE K. Detroit A. L.	Infielder	EMMERICH, ROBERT G. Boston N. L.	Outfielder
BURNS, JR., DENNIS Philadelphia A. L.	Pitcher	EZZELL, HOMER ESTELLE St. Louis A. L.	Infielder
BUSH, GUY F. Chicago N. L.	Pitcher	FELIX, AUGUST G. Boston N. L.	Outfielder
CASTNER, PAUL Chicago A. L.	Pitcher	FISHER, GEORGE A. Washington A. L.	Outfielder
CLARKE, RUFUS RIVERS Detroit A. L.	Pitcher	FLOWERS, D'ARCY RAYMOND St. Louis N. L.	Infielder
COLLINS, PHILIP E. Chicago N. L.	Pitcher	FOWLER, JOSEPH CHESTER Cincinnati N. L.	Infielder
CONLON, ARTHUR J. Boston N. L.	Infielder	FRENCH, W. E. Philadelphia A. L.	Outfielder

FRIDAY, GRIER Washington A. L.	Pitcher	HERRMANN, ALBERT Boston N. L.	Infielder
FRY, Cleveland A. L.	Pitcher	HOWE, LESTER C. Boston A. L.	Pitcher
GARDINIER, ARTHUR C. Philadelphia N. L.	Pitcher	HUDGENS, JAMES St. Louis N. L.	Infielder
GALLAGHER, Cleveland A. L.		HULVEY, HENSEL Philadelphia A. L.	Pitcher
GAZELLA, MICHAEL New York A. L.	Infielder	HUNTZINGER, WALTER New York N. L.	Pitcher
GEARIN, DENNIS JOHN New York N. L.	Pitcher	JONES, JESSE F. Philadelphia N. L.	Pitcher
GEHRIG, HENRY LOUIS New York A. L.	Infielder	JONES, JESSE F. Philadelphia N. L.	Pitcher
GILL, HAROLD EDMUND Cincinnati N. L.	Pitcher	JONES, J. W. Philadelphia A. L.	Outfielder
GILLENWATER, Chicago A. L.	Pitcher	KALLETT, Philadelphia A. L.	Pitcher
GRANT, GEORGE A. St. Louis A. L.	Pitcher	KAMM, WILLIAM EDWARD Chicago A. L.	Infielder
GRANT, JAMES Philadelphia N. L.	Pitcher	KERR, JOHN FRANCIS Detroit A. L.	Infielder
GRIGSBY, DENVER CLARENCE Chicago N. L.	Outfielder	KELLY, REYNOLDS CLARENCE Philadelphia A. L.	Pitcher
GULLEY, THOMAS JEFFERSON Cleveland A. L.	Outfielder	KNODE, ROBERT TROXELL Cleveland A. L.	Infielder
HAINES, HENRY LUTHER New York A. L.	Outfielder	KOPSHAW, GEORGE St. Louis N. L.	Catcher
HAPPENNY, JOHN CLIFFORD Chicago A. L.	Infielder	KUNZ, EARL DEWEY Pittsburgh N. L.	Pitcher
HARGRAVE, WILLIAM MCKINLEY Washington A. L.	Utility	LEACH, FRED M. Philadelphia N. L.	Outfielder
HARGREAVES, CHARLES RUSSELL Brooklyn N. L.	Catcher	LEVSEN, EMIL HENRY Cleveland A. L.	Pitcher
HARRIS, WILLIAM M. Cincinnati N. L.	Pitcher	LORD, CARLTON Philadelphia N. L.	Infielder
HEAD, RALPH Philadelphia N. L.	Pitcher	LUCAS, FRED New York N. L.	Pitcher
HENDRICK, HARVEY New York A. L.	Outfielder	LUCE, FRANK EDWARD Pittsburgh N. L.	Outfielder

LUTZKE, WALTER JOHN Cleveland A. L.	Infielder	PICK, EDGAR EVERETT Cincinnati N. L.	Infielder
LYONS, THEODORE A. Chicago A. L	Pitcher	PIPGRAS, GEORGE WILLIAM New York A. L.	Pitcher
MANUSH, HENRY EMMETT Detroit A. L.	Outfielder	POTTER, R. H. Washington A. L.	
MARBERY, FRED Washington A. L.	Pitcher	PROBST, JAKE Washington A. L.	Infielder
MATTHEWS, WID CURRY Philadelphia A. L.	Outfielder	PROCTOR, RICHARD Chicago A. L.	Pitcher
MCCARREN, WILLIAM JOSEPH Brooklyn N. L.	Infielder	RICE, HARRY FRANCIS St. Louis A. L.	
MEEKER, ROY Philadelphia A. L.	Pitcher	RICONDA, HARRY PAUL Philadelphia A. L.	Infielder
METZ, LEONARD RAY Philadelphia N. L.	Infielder	ROE, J. C. Washington A. L.	Pitcher
MILLER, LEO Philadelphia N. L.	Pitcher	ROETTGER, OSCAR F. L. New York A. L.	Pitcher
MITCHELL, MONROE BARR Washington A. L.	Pitcher	ROOT, CHARLES H. St. Louis A. L.	Pitcher
MIZEUR, WILLIAM St. Louis A. L.	Outfielder	ROSENBERG, LOUIS Chicago A. L.	Infielder
MOORE, EDWARD Pittsburgh N. L.	Infielder	ROWLAND, CHARLES L. Philadelphia A. L.	Catcher
MCQUAID, HERBERT Cincinnati N. L.	Pitcher	SANBERG, GUSTAVE E. Cincinnati N. L.	Catcher
MURRAY, ANTHONY J. Chicago N. L.	Outfielder	SAND, JOHN HENRY Philadelphia N. L.	Infielder
MURRAY, ROBERT Washington A. L.	Infielder	SCHEMANSKE, FREDERICK GEORGE Detroit A. L.	Pitcher
O'BRIEN, FRANK A. Philadelphia N. L.	Catcher	SCHLIEBNER, FRED PAUL Brooklyn N. L. and St. Louis A. L.	Infielder
O'CONNELL, JAMES JOSEPH New York N. L.	Outfielder	SCHULTE, JOHN St. Louis A. L.	Infielder
OZMER, HORACE Philadelphia A. L.	Pitcher	SHANER, D. W. Cleveland A. L.	Infielder
PADGETT, ERNEST KITCHEN Boston N. L.	Infielder	SIMON, SYLVESTER St. Louis A. L.	Infielder
PARKER, DIXIE Philadelphia N. L.	Catcher		

SMITH, CARR Washington A. L.	Outfielder	WADE, RICHARD F. Washington A. L.	Outfielder
SMITH, ROBERT E. Boston N. L.	Infielder	WALBERG, GEORGE New York N. L. and Philadelphia A. L.	Pitcher
SNIPES, ROXY Chicago A. L.	Outfielder	WALKER, JOHN St. Louis N. L.	Infielder
SOLOMON, MOSE New York N. L.	Outfielder	WELLS, EDWIN L. Detroit A. L.	Pitcher
STAUFFER, CHARLES E. Chicago N. L.	Pitcher	WHALEY, W. C. St. Louis A. L.	
STEINEDER, RAYMOND Pittsburgh N. L.	Pitcher	WHITEHILL, EARL Detroit A. L.	Pitcher
STIMSON, CARL Boston A. L.	Pitcher	WIGINTON, FRED THOMAS St. Louis N. L.	Pitcher
STONE, ARNOLD Pittsburgh N. L.	Pitcher	WILSON, JAMES Philadelphia N. L.	Catcher
STONE, WILLIAM A. St. Louis N. L.	Outfielder	WILSON, LEWIS ROBERT New York N. L.	Outfielder
TAYLOR, LEO Chicago A. L.		WINGFIELD, FRED Washington A. L.	Pitcher
TERRY, WILLIAM HAROLD New York N. L.	Infielder	WOEHRS, ANDREW Philadelphia N. L.	Infielder
THURSTON, HOLLIS JOHN St. Louis and Chicago A. L.	Pitcher	WOLFE Philadelphia A. L.	
TURGEON, E. J. Chicago N. L.	Infielder	WOODS, C. S. Philadelphia A. L.	Infielder
VOGEL, OTTO H. Chicago, N. L.	Outfielder	ZAHNISER, PAUL Washington A. L.	Pitcher

◆ THIRD SUPPLEMENT TO ◆

Baseball Cyclopedia

For Season of 1924—49th Year for National League and 24th for American

The Pennant Races

American League

Club	Won	Lost	Pc.	Manager
Washington	92	62	.597	Stanley Raymond Harris
New York	89	63	.586	Miller James Huggins
Detroit	86	68	.558	Tyrus Raymond Cobb
St. Louis	74	78	.487	George Harold Sisler
Philadelphia	71	81	.467	Connie Mack
Cleveland	67	86	.438	Tris Speaker (A)
Boston	67	87	.435	Lee Alexander Fohl
Chicago	66	87	.431	John Joseph Evers (B)
Totals	612	612	.500	

National League

Club	Won	Lost	Pc.	Manager
New York	93	60	.608	John Joseph McGraw (C)
Brooklyn	92	62	.597	Wilbert Robinson
Pittsburgh	90	63	.588	William Boyd McKechnie
Cincinnati	83	70	.542	John Charles Hendricks
Chicago	81	72	.530	William Killefer
St. Louis	65	89	.422	Branch Wesley Rickey (D)
Philadelphia	55	96	.364	Arthur Fletcher
Boston	53	100	.346	David James Bancroft
Totals	612	612	.500	

A—Jack McCallister, scout, managed Cleveland club while Speaker was ill with tonsillitis.

◆ **307** ◆

B—Evers was appointed manager, April 19, succeeding Frank Chance, who was ill. During Evers' absence from White Sox because of attack of appendicitis, Eddie Collins handled team.
C—Hugh Jennings directed play of Giants while McGraw was absent from team on account of an injury.
D—Bert Shotton managed Cardinals on Sunday and during Rickey's absence on extended scouting trip through California, Texas and other States.

It was the first pennant for the Washington American League club, the twelfth (and the fourth in succession) for the New York National League club, which therefore set up a new record for the parent organization. The other four-time winner in the Majors was St. Louis of the American Association, 1885 to 1888, inclusive, managed by Charles A. Comiskey. In the 28th World's Series, the 21st between the American and National Leagues, Washington won four games to New York's three, the result of the set making these changes in the dope of the classics (See page 100.):

Series Won—American League   13
      National League   8
      (American–National series only)
Cities having World's Champion Teams
      Washington   1
Cities competing for World's Series
      Championship—New York   15
      Washington   1

Record of games won and lost by World's Series clubs: New York Nationals, Won 38; lost 35; percentage .521; Washington Americans, won 4; lost 3; percentage .571.
Managers' records in World's Series—John J. McGraw, series won, 3; series lost, 6; games won, 26; games lost, 28; games tied, 2. Stanley R. Harris, series won, 1; games lost, 4; games lost, 3.
The players on the pennant winning

clubs during the year were as follows:
WASHINGTON—Stanley Raymond Harris, manager; Nicholas Altrock, Walter Perry Johnson, Joseph J. Martina, George Mogridge, Fred Marberry, Walter H. McGrew, Warren Harvey Ogden, Allan Russell, Byron Speece, Fred Davis Wingfield, James Thompson Zachary, Paul Vernon Zahniser, pitchers; William McKinley Hargrave, Harold Ruel, B. Tatek, catchers; Oswald L. Bluege, Harold Dennis Gagnon, Stanley Raymond Harris, Joseph Ignatius Judge, Wade Hampton Lefler, Ralph Joseph Miller, James Thompson Prothro, Roger Peckinpaugh, E. R. Shirley, T. C. Taylor, infielders; Carl East, George A. Fisher, Leon Allen Goslin, Bert J. Griffith, Harry Loran Leibold, Wid Curry Matthews, George Earl McNeely, Edgar Samuel Rice, Lance Richbourg, Carr Smith, outfielders.
NEW YORK NATIONALS—John Joseph McGraw, manager; Virgil Jennings Barnes, John Needles Bentley, Howard E. Baldwin, Leon J. Cadore, Wayland Ogden Dean, Dennis John Gearin, Kent Greenfield, Walter Huntzinger, Claude Jonnard, Ernest G. Maun, Hugh A. McQuillan, Arthur N. Nehf, Joseph Oeschger, Wilfred D. Ryan, John R. Watson, pitchers; Edward Wilbur Ainsmith, Harry M. Gowdy, Grover

Cleveland Hartley, Frank Snyder, catchers; Frank Francis Frisch, Henry Knight Groh, Travis C. Jackson, George Lange Kelly, Fred Lindstrom, William Harold Terry, infielders; Arthur E. Crump, Emil Frederick Meusel, James Joseph O'Connell, William H. Southworth, Lewis Robert Wilson, Ross Young, outfielders.

New York, as before related, set a new mark for the National League by win-ning its fourth flag in succession, all four having been acquired under the direction of John McGraw. Washington, winning its first Major League pennant, prevented the New York Yankees from doing the Comiskey–Browns and McGraw–Giants act.

As for cellar championships, it was the seventh for the Boston Nationals and the first for the Chicago Americans.

Leaders of 1924

BATTERS—Page 46

Player	Club	League	Pct. Or No.
George Herman Ruth	New York	American	.378
Rogers Hornsby	St. Louis	National	.4235

BASE STEALERS—Page 48

| Edward Trowbridge Collins | Chicago | American | 42 |
| Max G. Carey | Pittsburgh | National | 49 |

SACRIFICE HITTERS—Page 49

| Stanley Raymond Harris | Washington | American | 46 |
| Ralph Pinelli | Cincinnati | National | 33 |

SCORERS—Page 50

George Herman Ruth	New York	American	143
Frank Francis Frisch	New York	National	121
Rogers Hornsby	St. Louis	National	121

MANUFACTURERS OF BASE HITS—Page 51

| Edgar Samuel Rice | Washington | American | 216 |
| Rogers Hornsby | St. Louis | National | 227 |

DEMON DOUBLERS—Page 53

Harold E. Heilmann	Detroit	American	45
Joseph Wheeler Sewell	Cleveland	American	45
Rogers Hornsby	St. Louis	National	43

DEMON TRIPLERS—Page 54

Leon Allen Goslin	Washington	American	17
Edd Roush	Cincinnati	National	21

DEMON HOME RUNNISTS—Page 55

George Herman Ruth	New York	American	46
Jacques F. Fournier	Brooklyn	National	27

BATTING IN RUNS—Page 56

Leon Allen Goslin	Washington	American	129
George L. Kelly	New York	National	136

DEMON WHIFFERS—Page 56

George Herman Ruth	New York	American	81
George Grantham	Chicago	National	63

DEMON WALKERS—Page 56

George Herman Ruth	New York	American	142
Rogers Hornsby	St. Louis	National	89

THROWN OUT OFTENEST—Page 56

Edward Trowbridge Collins	Chicago	American	17
George Harold Sisler	St. Louis	American	17
Bernard Friberg	Chicago	National	27

STRIKE OUT KINGS—Page 57

Walter Perry Johnson	Washington	American	158
Arthur C. Vance	Brooklyn	National	262

FAMOUS GAMES, FAMOUS PLAYERS, FAMOUS FEATS THREE HOME RUNS IN GAME—PAGE 61

GEORGE LANGE KELLY, New York Nationals, did this on June 14, 1924, at New York in game with Cincinnati (off Sheehan in second and third innings, off Donohue in ninth). This was the second feat of this kind for Kelly. Joseph Hauser, Philadelphia Americans, did this on August 2, 1924, at Cleveland in game with Cleveland (off Shaute in second and third innings, off Roy in eighth).

THE SIX HIT MANUFACTURERS—
PAGE 71

GEORGE HENRY BURNS, Cleveland, made six hits in six times at bat in game at Detroit (first game of double header) on June 19, 1924, against the pitching of Whitehill and Holloway, his hits being as follows and in this order: Double in second inning, double in fourth, single and triple in fifth, double in seventh, single in ninth. Hazen S. Cuyler, Pittsburgh, made six hits in six times at bat in game at Philadelphia (first game of double header) on August 9, 1924, against the pitching of Oeschger, Couch and Carlson, his hits being as follows and in this order: Double in first inning, double in third, single in fourth, single in sixth, double in seventh, triple in ninth. Frank Francis Frisch, New York Nationals, made six hits in six times at bat in game at New York (first game of double header) on September 10, 1924, against the pitching of Cooney, McNamara and Muich of Boston, his hits being as follows and in this order: Sin-

gle in first inning, single in second, single in third, home run in fourth, single in sixth, single in seventh. On Frisch's seventh time at bat, in eighth inning, he bunted and was thrown out, Muich to McInnis. James Leroy Bottomley, St. Louis Nationals, made six hits in six times at bat in game at Brooklyn on September 16, 1924, against the pitching of Ehrhardt, Hollingsworth, Decatur, Wilson and Roberts, his hits being as follows and in this order: Single in first inning, double in second, home run in fourth, home run in sixth, single in seventh, single in ninth.

NEW RUNS BATTED IN RECORD—
PAGE 67

JAMES LEROY BOTTOMLEY, St. Louis Nationals, when he made six hits against Brooklyn on September 16, 1924, established a new Major League record for batting in runs in one game, knocking in 12 and thus eclipsing by one the 1892 accomplishment of Wilbert Robinson; Bottomley singled in two runs in the first inning against Ehrhardt; doubled in one in the second against Hollingsworth; hit for the circuit with the bases filled in the fourth against Decatur (Hornsby previously had been purposely passed); hit for the circuit in the sixth with one on against Decatur; singled in two runs in the seventh against Wilson and singled in one in the ninth against Roberts.

NO HIT HEROES—PAGE 82

JESSE JOSEPH HAINES, St. Louis Nationals, retired Boston without hit or run at St. Louis on July 17, 1924, receiving perfect support. Haines fanned five men and walked three, the pass getters being McNamara, in the third inning, and McNamara and Cunningham, in the sixth.

Addenda to Part VII
Players Starting Their Major League Careers During the Season of 1924

AUTREY, MARTIN New York A. L.	Catcher	CHURRY, JOHN Chicago N. L.	Catcher
BALDWIN, HOWARD E. New York N. L.	Pitcher	CLANCY, JOHN W. Chicago A. L.	Infielder
BARNES, R. A. Chicago A. L.	Pitcher	CLARK, WATSON Cleveland A. L.	Pitcher
BARNHART, EDGAR VERNON St. Louis A. L.	Pitcher	CLOUGH, EDGAR GEORGE St. Louis N. L.	Pitcher
BEALL, WALTER E. New York A. L.	Pitcher	COMBS, EARL BRYAN New York A. L.	Outfielder
BECK, WALTER St. Louis A. L.	Pitcher	CRITZ, HUGH MELVILLE Cincinnati N. L.	Infielder
BEGLEY, JAMES LAWRENCE Cincinnati N. L.	Infielder	CRUMP, ARTHUR E. New York N. L.	Outfielder
BELL, HERMAN S. St. Louis N. L.	Pitcher	DASHIELL, J. W. Chicago A. L.	Infielder
BISHOP, MAX Philadelphia A. L.	Infielder	DAVIS, I. M. Chicago A. L.	Infielder
BLOTT, JACK L. Cincinnati N. L.	Catcher	DAY, CLYDE St. Louis N. L.	Pitcher
BRETT, H. J. Chicago N. L.	Pitcher	DAWSON, JOSEPH Cleveland A. L.	Pitcher
BURKE, PATRICK E. St. Louis A. L.	Infielder	DEAN, WAYLAND OGDEN New York N. L.	Pitcher
BURNS, J. F. Chicago A. L.	Catcher	DELANEY, ARTHUR St. Louis N. L.	Pitcher
CHAPMAN, JOHN J. Philadelphia A. L.	Infielder	DEVIVEROS, B. Chicago A. L.	Infielder

DIBUT, PEDRO Cincinnati N. L.	Pitcher	HENRICH, FRANK W. Philadelphia A. L.	Outfielder
DOBBS, JOHN Chicago A. L.	Pitcher	HILLIS, MACK D. New York A. L.	Infielder
EAST, CARL Washington A. L.	Outfielder	HOLM, ROSCOE ALBERT St. Louis N. L.	Outfielder
EHRHARDT, W. C. Brooklyn, N. L.	Pitcher	HORAN, JOSEPH New York A. L.	Outfielder
ELMORE, VERDO St. Louis A. L.	Outfielder	JAMERSON, CHARLES Boston A. L.	Pitcher
EMERY, H. Philadelphia N. L.	Outfielder	JOHNSON, WILFRED IVY Brooklyn N. L.	Infielder
FITZKE, PAUL F. Cleveland A. L.	Pitcher	JONES, JOHN Brooklyn N. L.	Infielder
FORMAN, GUS Chicago A. L.	Pitcher	JONES Detroit A. L.	Pitcher
FOWLER, JESS St. Louis N. L.	Pitcher	KAMP, ALPHONSE F. Boston N. L.	Pitcher
GASTON, MILTON New York A. L.	Pitcher	KEARNS, EDWARD JOSEPH Chicago N. L.	Infielder
GEHRINGER, CHARLES Detroit A. L.	Infielder	KNOX, CLIFFORD H. Pittsburgh N. L.	Catcher
GEYGAN, JAMES E. Boston A. L.	Infielder	KREMER, RAY Pittsburgh, N. L.	Pitcher
GIBSON, CHARLES G. Philadelphia A. L.	Catcher	KUHN, BERNARD D. Cleveland A. L.	Pitcher
GRABOWSKI, JOHN Chicago A. L.	Catcher	LANE, JAMES HUNTER Boston N. L.	Infielder
GRAHAM, KYLE Boston N. L.	Pitcher	LARENCE, R. A. Chicago A. L.	Pitcher
GRAY, SAMUEL Philadelphia A. L.	Pitcher	LASLEY, WILLARD St. Louis A. L.	Pitcher
GREEN Philadelphia A. L.	Infielder	LEFLER, WADE HAMPTON Boston N. L.—Washington A. L.	Inf.—Of.
GREENE, NELSON GEORGE Brooklyn, N. L.	Pitcher	LEWIS, BURT Philadelphia N. L.	Pitcher
GREENFIELD, KENT New York N. L.	Pitcher	LINDSTROM, FRED New York N. L.	Infielder
HAFEY, CHARLES JAMES St. Louis N. L.	Outfielder	LOFTUS, RICHARD JOSEPH Brooklyn N. L.	Outfielder

LONG, THOMAS F. Brooklyn N. L.	Pitcher	ROBERTS, J. W., JR. Brooklyn N. L.	Pitcher
LUCAS, CHARLES FRED Boston N. L.	Pitcher	ROSS, CHESTER Boston A. L.	Pitcher
LUDOLPH, WILLIAM Detroit A. L.	Pitcher	ROY, LUTHER Cleveland A. L.	Pitcher
LUNDGREN, DELMAR Pittsburgh N. L.	Pitcher	RUFFING, CHARLES HERBERT Boston A. L.	Pitcher
MANGUM, LEON ALLEN Chicago A. L.	Pitcher	SALE, FRED L. Pittsburgh, N. L.	Pitcher
MARTINA, JOSEPH J. Washington A. L.	Pitcher	SCHULTZ Chicago A. L.	Pitcher
MAUN, ERNEST New York N. L.	Pitcher	SHAY, ARTHUR J. Boston N. L.	Infielder
MAY, HERBERT Pittsburgh N. L.	Pitcher	SHEPARDSON St. Louis N. L.	Catcher
M'NEELY, GEORGE EARL Washington A. L.	Outfielder	SHERLING, ED. C. Philadelphia A. L.	Outfielder
MESSENGER, ANDREW Cleveland A. L.	Pitcher	SHIELDS, BEN C. New York A. L.	Pitcher
MICHAELS, RALPH J. Chicago N. L.	Infielder	SHIELDS, VINCENT A. St. Louis N. L.	Pitcher
MILLER, J. WALTER Cleveland A. L.	Pitcher	SHIRLEY, E. R. Washington A. L.	Infielder
MILSTEAD, G. E. Chicago N. L.	Pitcher	SIMMONS, AL H. Philadelphia A. L.	Outfielder
MOREHART, RAY Chicago A. L.	Infielder	SONGER, DON C. Pittsburgh N. L.	Pitcher
MUICH, JOSEPH (FRED) Boston N. L.	Pitcher	SPEECE, BYRON Washington A. L.	Pitcher
NALEWAY, FRANK Chicago A. L.	Infielder	SPERBER, EDWIN Boston N. L.	Outfielder
PHILLIPS, EDWARD D. Boston N. L.	Catcher	SPURGEON, FRED Cleveland A. L.	Infielder
PIERCE, RAYMOND LESTER Chicago N. L.	Pitcher	STEENGRAFE, MILTON H. Chicago A. L.	Pitcher
REGO, ANTHONY St. Louis A. L.	Catcher	STRYKER, STERLING AL Boston N. L.	Pitcher
RHEM, CHARLES FLINT St. Louis N. L.	Pitcher	TATE, B. Washington A. L.	Catcher

TAYLOR, T. C. Washington A. L.	Infielder	WINGARD, ERNEST St. Louis A. L.	Pitcher
THEVENOW, THOMAS St. Louis N. L.	Infielder	WINTERS, C. J. Boston A. L.	Pitcher
THOMAS, HERBERT M. Boston N. L.	Outfielder	WOODS, J. F. Boston A. L.	Pitcher
TODT, PHIL J. Boston A. L.	Inf.—Of.	WORKMAN, H. H. Boston A. L.	Pitcher
VINES, ROBERT EARL St. Louis N. L.	Pitcher	WRIGHT, FOREST GLEN Pittsburgh N. L.	Infielder
VOIGT, OLIN St. Louis A. L.	Pitcher	WYATT, L. J. Cleveland N. L.	Outfielder
WAYNEBURG, FRANK Cleveland A. L.	Pitcher	YDE, EMIL OGDEN Pittsburg N. L.	Pitcher
WILSON, FRANCIS E. Boston N. L.	Outfielder	YOTER, ELMER Cleveland A. L.	Infielder
WILSON, GORMER Brooklyn N. L.	Pitcher	YOWELL, CARL C. Cleveland A. L.	Pitcher

Baseball Cyclopedia

For Season of 1925—50th Year for National League and 25th for the American

The Pennant Races

American League

Club	Won	Lost	Pc.	Manager
Washington	96	55	.636	Stanley Raymond Harris
Philadelphia	88	64	.579	Connie Mack
St. Louis	82	71	.537	George Harold Sisler
Detroit	81	73	.527	Tyrus Raymond Cobb
Chicago	79	75	.513	Edward Trowbridge Collins
Cleveland	70	84	.455	Tris Speaker
New York	69	85	.444	Miller James Huggins
Boston	47	105	.309	Lee Alexander Fohl
Totals	612	612	.500	

National League

Club	Won	Lost	Pc.	Manager
Pittsburgh	95	58	.621	William Boyd McKechnie
New York	86	66	.566	John Joseph McGraw (A)
Cincinnati	80	73	.523	John Charles Hendricks
St. Louis	77	76	.503	Branch Wesley Rickey and Rogers Hornsby (B)
Boston	70	83	.458	David James Bancroft
Brooklyn	68	85	.444	Wilbert Robinson (C)
Philadelphia	68	85	.444	Arthur Fletcher
Chicago	68	86	.442	William Killefer, Walter James Vincent Maranville and George Gibson (D)
Totals	612	612	.500	

A—Hugh Jennings managed New York club while McGraw as ill.
B—Hornsby became manager of St. Louis club May 31.
C—Zach Wheat appointed acting manager of Brooklyn club June 13.
D—Maranville became manager of Chicago club July 7 and was succeeded by George Gibson September 3.

It was the second pennant for the Washington American League club, the fifth for the Pittsburgh National League club. Washington's pennant was its second in succession and Pittsburg's its first since 1909. By finishing first the Pirates prevented New York from setting up a new record of five successive flags for the parent organization. In the 29th World's Series, the 22nd between the American and National Leagues, Pittsburg won four games to Washington's three, the result of the set making these changes in the dope of the classics. (See page 100.):

Series Won—American League	13
National League	9
Cities having World's Champion Teams	
Pittsburg	2
Cities competing for World's Series	
Championship—Pittsburg	3
Washington	2

Record of games won and lost by World's Series clubs: Pittsburg Nationals, won 11; lost 11; percentage 500; Washington Americans, won 7; lost 7; percentage 500.

Managers' records in World's Series—William Boyd McKechnie, series won, 1; games won, 4; games lost, 3; Stanley R. Harris, series won, 1; series lost, 1; games won 7, games lost, 7.

The players on the pennant winning clubs during the year were as follows:

PITTSBURG—William Boyd McKech-nie, manager; Charles Benjamin Adams, Victor Aldrich, Bernard A. Culloton, Louis Koupal, Ray Kremer, Henry Lee Meadows, John Dewey Morrison, John Cyrus Oldham, Thomas Clancy Shee-han, Don Songer, Emil Ogden Yde, pitchers; John Beverly Gooch, Earl Smith, Roy Hampton Spencer, catchers; Jewel Ens, George Farley Grantham, John Phelan McInnis, Edward Moore, Albert Bernard Niehaus, John William Rawlings, Lafayette Fresco Thompson, Jr., Harold J. Traynor, Forest Glenn Wright, infielders; Clyde L. Barnhart, Carson Lee Bigbee, Max G. Carey, Hazen S. Cuyler, George W. Haas, outfielders.

WASHINGTON—Stanley Raymond Harris, manager; Noble Winfred Bal-lou, Stanley Coveleskie, Alexander Fer-guson, Sylvaneus Gregg, Walter Perry Johnson, Harry Kelly, James C. Lyle, Fred Marberry, George Mogridge, War-ren Harvey Ogden, _____ Pumpelly, Walter Henry Reuther, Allan Russell, Clarence F. Thomas, pitchers; William McKinley Hargrave, Harold Ruel, Henry Severeid, Bennett Tate, catchers; Spencer Dewey Adams, Oswald L. Bluege, Stanley Raymond Harris, Jo-seph Ignatius Judge, Frank McGhee, Michael J. McNally, Charles S. Myers, Roger Peckinpaugh, Ernest R. Shirley, L. Everett Scott, John F. Stewart, infiel-ders; Roy Edward Carlyle, Leon Allen Goslin, Joseph Harris, Ernest Jeanes,

Harry Loran Leibold, George Earl Mc-
Neely, Edgar Samuel Rice, Robert
Henry Veach, outfielders.

For the Boston American it was their
fourth cellar championship and for the
Chicago Nationals their first.

Leaders of 1925

BATTERS — Page 46

Player	Club	League	Pct. Or No.
Rogers Hornsby	St. Louis	National	403
Harry Edwin Heilmann	Detroit	American	393

BASE STEALERS — Page 48

Max G. Carey	Pittsburgh	National	46
John Anthony Mostil	Chicago	American	43

SACRIFICE HITTERS — Page 49

Stanley Raymond Harris	Washington	American	41
Ralph Arthur Pinelli	Cincinnati	National	34

SCORERS — Page 50

Hazen S. Cuyler	Pittsburg	National	144
John Anthony Mostil	Chicago	American	135

MANUFACTURERS OF BASE HITS — Page 51

Al Harry Simmons	Philadelphia	American	253
James Leroy Bottomley	St. Louis	National	227

DEMON DOUBLERS — Page 53

Martin Joseph McManus	St. Louis	American	44
James Leroy Bottomley	St. Louis	National	44

DEMON TRIPLERS — Page 54

Hazen S. Cuyler	Pittsburg	National	26
Leon Allen Goslin	Washington	American	19

DEMON HOME RUNNISTS—Page 55

Rogers Hornsby	St. Louis	National	39
Robert William Meusel	New York	American	33

BATTING IN RUNS—Page 56

Rogers Hornsby	St. Louis	National	143
Robert William Meusel	New York	American	138

DEMON WHIFFERS—Page 56

Charles Leo Hartnett	Chicago	National	77
Martin Joseph McManus	St. Louis	American	69

DEMON WALKERS—Page 56

William Edward Kamm	Chicago	American	90
John Anthony Mostil	Chicago	American	90
Jacques Frank Fournier	Brooklyn	National	86

THROWN OUT OFTENEST—Page 56

John Anthony Mostil	Chicago	American	21
Edd J. Roush	Cincinnati	National	20

STRIKE OUT KINGS—Page 57

Arthur C. Vance	Brooklyn	National	221
Robert Moses Groves	Philadelphia	American	116

FAMOUS GAMES, FAMOUS PLAYERS, FAMOUS FEATS
THREE HOME RUNS IN GAME—PAGE 61

TYRUS RAYMOND COBB, of Detroit, Gordon Cochrane of Philadelphia and Leon Allen Goslin of Washington, American Leaguers all of them accomplished this feat once in 1925. Cobb made his home runs at St. Louis on May 5 off Bush in the first inning, Van Gilder in the second and Gaston in the eighth; Cochrane in the same city on May 21 off Gaston in the third and fourth innings and Blaeholder in the seventh, and Goslin at Cleveland on June 19 off Karr in the second inning and Shaute in the eighth and twelfth.

TWO HOME RUNS IN ONE INNING—PAGE 63

LEWIS ROBERT WILSON of the New York Nationals made two home runs in the third inning of the second game at

Philadelphia on July 1 against the pitching of Mitchell and Knight.

THE SIX HIT MANUFACTURERS—
PAGE 71

TYRUS RAYMOND COBB of Detroit made two singles, one double and three home runs in the game at St. Louis on May 5 against the pitching of Bush, Van Gilder, Giard, Stauffer, Gaston and Springer, Stauffer being the only Brown hurler he did not bat against.

NO HIT HEROES—PAGE 82

ARTHUR C. VANCE, of Brooklyn pitched a not hit game at Brooklyn on September 13 in the first part of a dou-

ble header against Philadelphia, winning this event 10 to 1. Three errors were made behind him and these prevented his having a shutout. Vance fanned 9 men and walked one.

UNASSISTED TRIPLE PLAYS—
PAGE 97

FOREST GLENN WRIGHT made an unassisted triple play in the ninth inning of the game of May 7 against St. Louis. The Pirate shortstop absorbed a liner from Bottomley's bat and touched second, retiring Cooney who was on his way to third. Then he ran down Hornsby, who was en route to second

FINIS

Addenda to Part VII

Players Starting Major League Careers During the Season of 1925

(With Birth Dates and Birth Places of Some)

ADAMS, DALE   Pitcher
Boston A. L.
Born Bedford, Ind., June 21, 1899

ANDERSON, WILLIAM E.   Pitcher
Boston N. L.

ANDREWS JR., ELBERT D.   Pitcher
Philadelphia A. L.
Born Greenwood, S. C., Dec. 11, 1903

ASH, KENNETH LOWTHER   Pitcher
Chicago A. L.
Born Clarksburg, W. Va., Sept. 16, 1901

BALLOU, NOBLE WINFRED   Pitcher
Washington A. L.
Born Williamsburg, Ky., Nov. 30, 1899

BEDFORD   Infielder
Cleveland A. L.

BENGE, RAY   Pitcher
Cleveland A. L.

BERRY, CHARLES   Catcher
Philadelphia A. L.

BISCHOFF, JOHN GEORGE   Catcher
Chicago–Boston A. L.
Born Edwardsville, Ill., Oct. 28, 1897

BLAEHOLDER, GEORGE   Pitcher
St. Louis A. L.

BROOKS, JOHN   Outfielder
Chicago N. L.
Born Milwaukee, Wis., Aug. 18, 1898

BROWN, LLOYD ANDREW   Pitcher
Brooklyn N. L.
Born Beeville, Texas, Dec. 25, 1904

BROWN, WALTER   Pitcher
Chicago N. L.

CALDWELL, CHARLES   Pitcher
Brooklyn N. L.
Born Clarita, Okla., April 9, 1904

CARLYLE, ROY EDWARD   Outfielder
Washington–Boston A. L.
Born Buford, Ga., Dec. 10, 1900.

CARROLL, OWEN   Pitcher
Detroit A. L.

CARTER, OTIS L.   Outfielder
New York N. L.

COCHRANE, GORDON   Catcher
Philadelphia A. L.
Born Bridgewater, Mass., April 6, 1903

CONNALLY, MERVIN T.   Infielder
Boston A. L.
Born San Francisco, Cal., April 25, 1901

CORGAN, CHARLES H.   Infielder
Brooklyn N. L.
Born Wagoner, Okla., Dec. 3, 1903

COX, ELMER JOSEPH   Outfielder
Brooklyn N. L.
Born Pasadena, Cal., Sept. 30, 1897

CULLOTON, BERNARD A.   Pitcher
Pittsburg N. L.

DIXON, LEO M.   Catcher
St. Louis A. L.
Born Chicago, Ill., Sept. 6, 1899

DOYLE, JESSE HERBERT   Pitcher
Detroit A. L.
Born Knoxville, Tenn., April 14, 1898

DRESSEN, CHARLES WALTER   Infielder
Cincinnati, N. L.
Born Decatur, Ill., Sept. 20, 1898

DURNING, GEORGE WARREN   Outfielder
Philadelphia N. L.
Born Philadelphia, Pa., May 9, 1902

DUROCHER, LEO ERNEST   Infielder
New York A. L.
Born W. Springfield, Mass., July 27, 1905

EDWARDS, FOSTER H.   Pitcher
Boston N. L.

EICHRODT, FRED   Outfielder
Cleveland A. L.

ENGLE, CHARLES   Infielder
Philadelphia A. L.

FALK, CHESTER   Pitcher
St. Louis A. L.

FARRELL, EDWARD   Infielder
New York N. L.

FITZSIMMONS, FRED L.   Pitcher
New York N. L.
Born Mislawaka, Ind., July 28, 1901

FREEZE, CARL A.   Pitcher
Chicago A. L.

FOX, JAMES EMERY   Catcher
Philadelphia A. L.
Born Sudlersville, Md., Oct. 22, 1907

GAUTREAU, WALTER   Infielder
Philadelphia A. L.—Boston N. L.

GIARD, JOSEPH   Pitcher
St. Louis A. L.

GLASS, THOMAS   Pitcher
Philadelphia A. L.
Born Greensboro, N. C., April 29, 1902

GROSS, EWELL   Infielder
Boston A. L.
Born Mesquite, Tex., Feb. 23, 1896

GROVES, ROBERT MOSES   Pitcher
Philadelphia A. L.
Born Lonaconing, Md., March 6, 1900

HAAS, GEORGE W.   Outfielder
Pittsburg N. L.

HALLAHAN, WM. ANTHONY   Pitcher
St. Louis N. L.
Born Binghamton, N. Y., Aug. 4, 1904

HARRINGTON, ANDREW M.   Infielder

Detroit A. L.
Born Mt. View, Cal., Feb. 12, 1904

HARRIS, DANIEL S.   Outfielder
Boston N. L.
Born Greensboro, N. C., July 27, 1902

HARRIS, SPENCER A.   Outfielder
Chicago A. L.

HERRERA, RAMON   Infielder
Boston A. L.

HODAPP, URBAN JOHN   Infielder
Cleveland A. L.
Born Cincinnati, Ohio, Sept. 26, 1905

HOGAN, J. FRANCIS   Outfielder
Boston N. L.

HOLT, JAMES E. M.   Infielder
Philadelphia A. L.

HOOD, AUBREY L.   Infielder
Boston N. L.

HUSTA, CARL   Infielder
Philadelphia A. L.

HUTSON, ROY L.   Outfielder
Brooklyn N. L.

JAHN, ARTHUR C.   Outfielder
Chicago N. L.

JENKINS, THOMAS G.   Outfielder
Boston A. L.

JOHNSON, HENRY   Pitcher
New York A. L.

KANE, JOHN FRANCIS   Infielder
Chicago A. L.
Born Chicago, Ill., Feb. 19, 1900

KEESEY, JAMES WARD   Infielder
Philadelphia A. L.
Born Perryville, Md., Oct. 27, 1903

KELLY, HARRY   Pitcher
Washington A. L.
Born Parkin, Ark., Feb. 13, 1906

KERR, J. MELVIN   Substitute
Chicago N. L.

KIBBIE, HORACE K.   Infielder
Boston N. L.

KLEE, OLIVER   Outfielder
Cincinnati N. L.

KOEHLER, HENRY C.   Outfielder
New York N. L.

KOENIG, MARK A.   Infielder
New York A. L.

KOUPAL, LOUIS   Pitcher
Pittsburg N. L.

LUEBBE, ROY   Catcher
New York A. L.

LYLE, JAMES C.   Pitcher
Washington A. L.

MCCREA, FRANK   Catcher
Cleveland A. L.

MCGEE, FRANK   Infielder
Washington A. L.

MCMULLEN, HUGH   Catcher
New York N. L.

MALLONEE, JULES W.   Outfielder
Chicago A. L.

MARQUIS, JAMES MILBURN   Pitcher
New York A. L.

METZLAR, ALEXANDER   Outfielder
Chicago N. L.

MOORE, ALBERT T.   Outfielder
New York N. L.

MOORE, WILLIAM C.   Pitcher
Detroit A. L.
Born Corning, N. Y., Sept. 3, 1902

MUNSON, JOSEPH   Outfielder
Chicago N. L.

MYER, CHARLES S.   Infielder
Washington A. L.

NEUBAUER, HAROLD C.   Pitcher
Boston A. L.

NEUN, JOHN H.   Infielder
Detroit, A. L.
Born Baltimore, Md., Oct. 28, 1901

NIEHAUS, ALBERT B.   Infielder
Pittsburg—Cincinnati
Born Cincinnati, Ohio, June 1, 1901

O'NEAL, ORAN H.   Pitcher
Philadelphia N. L.

ODOM, HERMAN   Infielder
New York A. L.

OGRODOWSKI, JOSEPH   Pitcher
Boston N. L.

OSBORN, FRANK ROBERT   Pitcher
Chicago N. L.
Born Weatherby, Mo., Nov. 30,1898

PAULSON, GUILFORD   Pitcher
St. Louis N. L.
Born Graettinger, Iowa, Jan. 15, 1904

POOLE, JAMES RALPH   Infielder
Philadelphia A. L.

PUMPELLY, _____   Pitcher
Washington A. L.

ROGELL, WM. GEORGE   Infielder
Boston A. L.
Born Springfield, Ill., Nov. 24, 1904

ROSENTHAL, SIMON   Outfielder
Boston A. L.

ROTHROCK, JOHN H.   Infielder
Boston A. L.

RUSH, JESSE HOWARD   Pitcher
Brooklyn N. L.
Born New Haven, W. Va., Dec. 26, 1896

SIEMER, OSCAR   Catcher
Boston N. L.
Born St. Louis, Mo., Aug. 14, 1902

SMITH, MARVIN H.   Infielder
Philadelphia A. L.
Born Ashley, Ill., July 17, 1900

SPRINGER, BRADFORD L.   Pitcher
St. Louis A. L.
Born Detroit, Mich., May 9, 1904

STALEY, GALE   Infielder
Chicago N. L.

STANDAERT, JERRY JOHN   Infielder
Brooklyn N. L.
Born Chicago, Ill., Nov. 2, 1902

STOKES, ALBERT C.   Catcher
Boston A. L.

STOKES, ARTHUR   Pitcher
Philadelphia A. L.
Born Emmittsburg, Md., Sept. 13, 1897

SULLIVAN, HAROLD A   Catcher
Cincinnati N. L.

TANKERSLEY, LAWRENCE   Catcher
Chicago A. L.
Born Terrell, Texas, June 8, 1901

THOMAS, CLARENCE F.   Pitcher
Washington A. L.

THOMPSON, JR., LAF. F.   Infielder
Pittsburg N. L.
Born Centerville, Ala., June 6, 1903

TOLSON, CHARLES S.   Infielder
Cleveland A. L.

ULRICH, FRANK   Pitcher
Philadelphia N. L.
Born Baltimore, Md., Nov. 18, 1899

USSAT, WILLIAM   Infielder
Cleveland A. L.

VACHE, ERNEST   Outfielder
Boston A. L.
Born Santa Monica, Cal., Nov. 17, 1895

VARGUS, WILLIAM FAY   Pitcher
Boston N. L.
Born N. Scituate, Mass., Nov. 11, 1900

WANNINGER, PAUL LOUIS   Infielder
New York A. L.
Born Birmingham, Ala., Dec. 12, 1904

WARNER, JACK RALPH   Infielder
Detroit A. L.
Born Evansville, Ind., Aug. 28, 1903

WEBB, EARL   Outfielder
New York N. L.

WELCH, H. M.   Infielder
Boston A. L.

WELSH, JAMES D.   Outfielder
Boston N. L.

WILLIS, CHARLES WM.   Pitcher
Philadelphia A. L.
Born Leetown, W. Va., Nov. 4, 1905

WILLOUGHBY, CLAUDE   Pitcher
Philadelphia N. L.

◆ FIFTH SUPPLEMENT TO ◆

Baseball Cyclopedia
For Season of 1926—51st Year for National League and 26th for the American

The Pennant Races
American League

Club	Won	Lost	Pc.	Manager
New York	91	63	.591	Miller James Huggins
Cleveland	88	66	.571	Tris Speaker
Philadelphia	83	67	.553	Connie Mack
Washington	81	69	.540	Stanley Raymond Harris
Chicago	81	72	.529	Edward Trowbridge Collins
Detroit	79	75	.513	Tyrus Raymond Cobb
St. Louis	62	92	.403	George Harold Sisler
Boston	46	107	.301	Lee Alexander Fohl
Totals	611	611	.500	

National League

Club	Won	Lost	Pc.	Manager
St. Louis	89	65	.578	Rogers Hornsby
Cincinnati	87	67	.565	John Charles Hendricks
Pittsburgh	84	69	.549	William Boyd McKechnie
Chicago	82	72	.532	Joseph V. McCarthy
New York	74	77	.490	John Joseph McGraw
Brooklyn	71	82	.464	Wilbert Robinson
Boston	66	86	.434	David James Bancroft
Philadelphia	58	93	.384	Arthur Fletcher
Totals	611	611	.500	

It was the first pennant for the St. Louis National League club, the fourth for the New York American League club. The Mound City's last previous flag winner was in 1888, that team being in the American Association and being managed by Charles A. Comiskey. In the 23rd World's Series between the American and National Leagues, St. Louis won four games to New York's three, the result of the set making these changes in the dope of the classics. (See page 100.):

Series Won—American League   13
            National League   10
Cities having World's Champion Teams
St. Louis   2
Cities competing for World's Series
Championship—St. Louis   5
            New York   16

Record of games won and lost by World's Series clubs: St. Louis Nationals, won 4; lost 3; percentage .571; New York Americans, won 10; lost 15; percentage .400.

Managers' records in World's Series: Rogers Hornsby, series won, 1; games won, 4; games lost, 3; Miller J. Huggins, series won, 1; series lost, 3; games won 10, games lost, 15, games tied, 1.

The players on the pennant winning clubs during the year were as follows:

ST. LOUIS NATIONALS—Rogers Hornsby, manager; Grover Cleveland Alexander (obtained from Cubs), Herman Bell, Edgar George Clough, Edwin Hawley Dyer, (optioned to Syracuse), William Anthony Hallahan, Jesse Joseph Haines, Walter Henry Huntzinger (released to Cubs), Sylvester Johnson, Howard Victor Keen, John

Walter Mails (optioned to Syracuse), Arthur Conrad Reinhart, Charles Flint Rhem, William Henry Sherdel, Allen Sutton Sothoren, pitchers; Robert Arthur O'Farrell, Henry Arthur Vick, Firmin N. Warwick, catchers; James Leroy Bottomley, Lester Rowland Bell, Rogers Hornsby, Thomas Joseph Thevenow, infielders; Francis Raymond Blades, Taylor Lee Douthit, Roscoe Albert Holm, Charles James Hafey, Clarence Franklin Mueller (traded to Giants), William H. Southworth (obtained from Giants), outfielders; D'Arcy Raymond Flowers, George Toporcer, John Smith (released to Braves), substitutes.

NEW YORK AMERICANS—Miller James Huggins, manager; Walter Beale, Edgar Garland Braxton, Waite Charles Hoyt, Samuel Pond Jones, Henry Johnson (sent to St. Paul), Herbert McQuaid, Herbert J. Pennock, Walter Henry Ruether (obtained from Nationals), James Robert Shawkey, Urban J. Shocker, Myles Lewis Thomas, pitchers; Bernard Oliver Bengough, John F. Barnes (sent to Buffalo), Tharon Pat Collins, William E. Skiff, Henry Severeid (obtained from Washington), catchers; Joseph A. Dugan, Henry Louis Gehrig, Mark Antony Koenig, Anthony Michael Lazzeri, infielders; Earl Bryan Combs, Robert William Meusel, Benjamin E. Paschal, George Herman Ruth, outfielders; Spencer Dewey Adams, Michael Gazella, Aaron Lee Ward, Roy Edward Carlyle (obtained from Boston), Henry Cullop (sent to Newark), Fred Merkle, substitutes.

Leaders of 1926

BATTERS—Page 46

Player	Club	League	Pct. Or No.
Henry Emmett Manush	Detroit	American	.377
Eugene F. Hargrave	Cincinnati	National	.353

BASE STEALERS—Page 48

John Anthony Mostil	Chicago	American	35
Hazen S. Cuyler	Pittsburgh	National	35

SACRIFICE HITTERS—Page 49

Fred Spurgeon	Cleveland	American	35
Taylor L. Douthit	St. Louis	National	37

SCORERS—Page 50

George Herman Ruth	New York	American	139
Hazen S. Cuyler	Pittsburg	National	113

MANUFACTURERS OF BASE HITS—Page 51

George H. Burns	Cleveland	American	216
Edgar Samuel Rice	Washington	American	216
Edward W. Brown	Boston	National	201

DEMON DOUBLERS—Page 53

George H. Burns	Cleveland	American	64
James L. Bottomley	St. Louis	National	40

DEMON TRIPLERS—Page 54

Henry Louis Gehrig	New York	American	20
Paul G. Waner	Pittsburgh	National	22

DEMON HOME RUNNISTS—Page 55

George Herman Ruth	New York	American	47
Lewis R. Wilson	Chicago	National	21

BATTING IN RUNS—Page 56

George Herman Ruth	New York	American	155
James L. Bottomley	St. Louis	National	120

DEMON WHIFFERS—Page 56

Anthony Michael Lazzeri	New York	American	96
Bernard A. Friberg	Philadelphia	National	77

DEMON WALKERS—Page 56

George Herman Ruth	New York	American	144
Lewis R. Wilson	Chicago	National	69

THROWN OUT OFTENEST—Page 56

Edgar Samuel Rice	Washington	American	23

STRIKE OUT KINGS—Page 57

Robert Moses Groves	Philadelphia	American	194
Arthur C. Vance	Brooklyn	National	140

*New American and Major League Record.

FAMOUS GAMES, FAMOUS PLAYERS, FAMOUS FEATS
THREE HOME RUNS IN GAME— PAGE 61

JACQUES FRANK FOURNIER, of Brooklyn and George Herman Ruth of New York (American League) each accomplished this feat once, St. Louis being the scene of each stunt. Ruth's performance came in a World's Series game. Fournier made his three home runs on July 13 off Sherdel, in the fourth, sixth and ninth innings. One man was on in the fourth, none was on in the sixth and one was on in the ninth. Ruth made his three home runs on October 6, the first and second off Rhem in the first and third innings, with no one on, and the third off Bell in the sixth, with one on.

THE SIX HIT MANUFACTURERS— PAGE 71

PAUL CLEE WANER of Pittsburg made three singles, two doubles and one triple in six times at bat in the game on August 26 at Pittsburg against New York, the hits being in this sequence: Single in first inning off Fitzsimmons; double in second off Ring; single in third off Ring, scoring Gooch; single in fifth off Ring; triple in sixth off Scott, scoring Gooch; double in eighth off Porter.

No Hit Heroes—Page 82

Theodore Amar Lyons of Chicago (American League) pitched a no hit game at Boston on August 21, winning 6 to 0. Two of the Red Sox reached first—Tobin on a pass in the first inning and Jacobson on a fumble by Third

Baseman Hunnefield in the eighth. In 1925 Lyons pitched hitless ball for right and two thirds innings in a game against Washington, Robert Veach then keeping him out of the Pitchers' Hall of Fame by singling.

Addenda to Part VII
Players Starting Their Major League Careers During the Season of 1926
(With Birth Dates and Birth Places of Some)

ALLEN, Ethan Nathan   Outfielder
Cincinnati N. L.
Born Cincinnati, O., Jan. 1, 1904

ATTREAU, Richard   Infielder
Philadelphia N. L.

BAECHT, Edward J.   Pitcher
Philadelphia N. L.

BARBEE, David Monroe   Outfielder
Philadelphia A. L.
Born Greensboro, N. C., May 7, 1905

BARNES, John F.   Catcher
New York A. L.

BECK, Clyde Eugene   Infielder
Chicago N. L.
Born El Monte, Cal., Jan. 6, 1902

BOLEN, Stewart O'Neal   Pitcher
St. Louis A. L.
Born Jackson, Ala., Oct. 12, 1903

BOYLE, James   Catcher
New York N. L.

BRICKNELL, Fred   Outfielder
Pittsburg N. L.

BUSKEY, Joseph Henry   Infielder

Philadelphia N. L.
Born Cumberland, Md., Dec. 18, 1902

BUTLER, John Stephen   Infielder
Brooklyn N. L.
Born Eureka, Kan., March 20, 1896

CARTER, Howard   Infielder
Cincinnati N. L.

CHRISTENSEN, Walter Niels   Outfielder
Cincinnati N. L.
Born San Francisco, Cal., Oct. 24, 1899

CLABAUGH, John W.   Outfielder
Brooklyn N. L.

CLOWERS, W. P.   Pitcher
Boston A. L.

COHEN, Andrew Howard   Infielder
New York N. L.
Born Baltimore, Md., Oct. 25, 1904

COMOROSKY, Adam   Outfielder
Pittsburg, N. L.
Born Swoyersville, Pa., Dec. 9, 1904

CONNELL, Joseph   Infielder
New York N. L.

COTE, WARREN P.
New York N. L.

COTTER, EDWARD C.   Infielder
Philadelphia N. L.

COX, LESLIE   Pitcher
Chicago A. L.

CRONIN, JOSEPH   Infielder
Pittsburg N. L.

CROWDER, ALVIN FLOYD   Pitcher
Washington A. L.
Born Winston-Salem, N. C., Jan. 11, 1900

CULLOP, HENRY   Outfielder
New York A. L.
Born St. Louis, Mo., Oct. 16, 1900

CUMMINGS, JOHN WILLIAM   Catcher
New York N. L.
Born Pittsburg, Pa., April 1, 1904

DAVIS, GEORGE W.   Outfielder
New York A. L.

DUNHAM, LELAND H.   Infielder
Philadelphia N. L.
Born Atlanta, Ill., June 9, 1902

ENGLE, CHARLES   Infielder
Philadelphia A. L.
Born Brooklyn, N. Y., August 27, 1905

ENNIS, RUSSELL   Catcher
Washington A. L.

FLORENCE, PAUL ROBERT   Catcher
New York N. L.
Born Chicago, Ill., April 23, 1901

GIBSON, SAMUEL BRAXTON   Pitcher
Detroit A. L.
Born High Point, N. C., August 5, 1900

GOLDSMITH, HAROLD EUGENE   Pitcher
Boston N. L.
Born Peconic, N. Y., Aug. 18, 1898

GRAVES, _____   Infielder
Chicago N. L.

HADLEY, IRVING DARIUS   Pitcher
Washington A. L.
Born Lynn, Mass., July 5, 1904

HAMBY, SANFORD   Catcher
New York N. L.

HAYWORTH, RAYMOND PAUL   Catcher
Detroit A. L.
Born High Point, N. C., Jan. 29, 1905

HEARN, ELMER LAFAYETTE   Pitcher
Boston N. L.
Born Brooklyn, N. Y., Jan. 13, 1904

HERMAN, FLOYD CAVES   Infielder
Brooklyn N. L.
Born Buffalo, N. Y., June 26, 1903

HOLLAND, HOWARD ARTHUR   Pitcher
Cincinnati N. L.
Born Franklin, Va., Jan. 6, 1903

HUDLIN, GEORGE WILLIS   Pitcher
Cleveland A. L.
Born Wagener, Okla., May 23, 1906

HUNNEFIELD, WILLIAM   Infielder
Chicago A. L.
Born Dedham, Mass., Jan. 4, 1901

JOHNS, AUGUSTUS FRANCIS   Pitcher
Detroit A. L.
Born St. Louis, Mo., Sept. 10, 1899

JONES, DECATUR   Pitcher
Washington A. L.
Born Meadville, Miss., May 22, 1904

KELLY, JOSEPH JAMES   Outfielder
Chicago N. L.
Born New York City, April 23, 1901

KELLY, MIKE   Pitcher
Philadelphia N. L.

KNEISCH, RUDOLPH FRANK   Pitcher
Detroit A. L.
Born Baltimore, Md., April 10, 1900

LACY, OSCEOLA GUY   Infielder
Cleveland A. L.
Cleveland, Tenn., June 12, 1898

LANGFORD, ELTON   Outfielder
Boston A. L.
Born Briggs, Tex., May 21, 1901

LAZZERI, ANTHONY MICHAEL   Infielder

New York A. L.
Born San Francisco, Cal., Dec. 6, 1904

LEHR, NORMAN KING   Pitcher
Cleveland A. L.
Born Rochester, N. Y., May 28, 1902

LOFTUS, FRANK P.   Pitcher
Washington A. L.
Born Scranton, Pa., March 10, 1900

MACFAYDEN, DANIEL   Pitcher
Boston A. L.
Born Provincetown, Mass., June 10, 1906

MAHAFFEY, LEROY   Pitcher
Pittsburg N. L.

MCBEE, PRYOR EDWARD   Pitcher
Chicago A. L.
Born McAlester, Okla., June 20, 1902

MEADOWS, RUFUS RIVERS   Pitcher
Cincinnati N. L.

MELILLO, OSCAR DONALD   Infielder
St. Louis A. L.
Born Chicago, Ill., Aug. 4, 1902

MOORE, WILLIAM H.   Catcher
Boston A. L.
Born Kansas City, Mo., Dec. 12, 1903

MORRELL, WILLARD   Pitcher
Washington A. L.
Born Wayland, Mass., April 9, 1901

MOSS, RAYMOND EARL   Pitcher
Brooklyn N. L.
Born Chattanooga, Tenn., Dec. 5, 1902

NEVERS, ERNEST   Pitcher
St. Louis A. L.
Born Willow Grove, Minn., June 11, 1903

NICHOLS, CHESTER R.   Pitcher
Pittsburg N. L.

OTT, MELVIN THOMAS   Catcher
New York N. L.

PATE, JOSEPH   Pitcher
Philadelphia A. L.
Born Corpus Christi, Tex., June 6, 1893

POETZ, _____   Pitcher
New York N. L.

PORTER, NED S.   Pitcher
New York N. L.

PURDY, EVERETT   Outfielder
Chicago A. L.

RAMBO, WARREN   Pitcher
Philadelphia N. L.

REGAN, WILLIAM   Infielder
Boston A. L.

REEVES, ROBERT E.   Infielder
Washington A. L.

RICE, ROBERT   Infielder
Philadelphia N. L.

RHYNE, HAROLD   Infielder
Pittsburg N. L.

RUSSELL, JACK   Pitcher
Boston A. L.
Born Paris, Tex., Oct. 24, 1905

SCOTT, FLOYD   Outfielder
Chicago N. L.

SIGAFOOS, FRANCIS LEONARD   Infielder
Philadelphia A. L.
Born Easton, Pa., March 21, 1904

SLAYBACK, ELBERT   Infielder
New York N. L.

SMITH, ALFRED K.   Pitcher
New York N. L.

SMITH, ELWOOD H.   Outfielder
New York N. L.

SMITH, GEORGE SELBY   Pitcher
Detroit A. L.
Born Louisville, Ky., Oct. 27, 1901

SOMMERS, RUDY   Pitcher
Boston A. L.

SOTHERN, DENNIS   Outfielder
Philadelphia N. L.

STUTZ, _____   Infielder
Philadelphia N. L.

SUKEFORTH, CLYDE LEROY   Catcher
Cincinnati N. L.
Born Washington, Me., Nov. 30, 1902

TABER, EDWARD — Pitcher
Philadelphia N. L.

TAYLOR, DAN — Outfielder
Washington A. L.
Born Lash, Pa., Dec. 23, 1902

TAYLOR, EDWARD JAMES — Infielder
Boston N. L.
Born Chicago, Ill., Nov. 17, 1902

THOMAS ALPHONSE — Pitcher
Chicago A. L.
Born Baltimore, Md., Dec. 23, 1899

THOMAS, MYLES LEWIS — Pitcher
New York A. L.
Born State College, Pa., Oct. 22, 1899

TYSON, ALBERT THOMAS — Outfielder
New York N. L.
Born Wilkesbarre, Pa., June 1, 1896

UCHRINSKO, JOSEPH — Pitcher
Washington A. L.

VELTMAN, ARTHUR (PAT) — Outfielder
Chicago A. L.
Born Mobile, Ala., March 24, 1906

WANER, PAUL CLEE — Outfielder
Pittsburg N. L.
Born Harrah, Okla., April 16, 1903

WELCH, JOHN VERNON — Pitcher
Chicago N. L.
Born Washington, D. C., Dec. 2, 1906

WELZER, TONY — Pitcher
Boston A. L.

WERTZ, HENRY LEVI — Pitcher
Boston N. L.

WILLIAMS, LEON T. — Pitcher
Brooklyn N. L.

WILTSE, HAROLD JAMES — Pitcher
Boston A. L.
Born Clay City, Ill., Aug. 6, 1903

WOMACK, SIDNEY KIRK — Catcher
Boston N. L.
Born Greensburg, La., Oct. 2, 1897

YARNELL, _____ — Pitcher
Philadelphia N. L.

Baseball Cyclopedia

For Season of 1927—52nd Year for
National League and 27th for the American

The Pennant Races

National League

Club	Won	Lost	Pc.	Manager
Pittsburgh	94	60	.610	Owen J. Bush
St. Louis	92	61	.601	Robert Arthur O'Farrell
New York	92	62	.597	John Joseph McGraw (A)
Chicago	85	68	.556	Joseph V. McCarthy
Cincinnati	75	78	.490	John Charles Hendricks
Brooklyn	65	88	.425	Wilbert Robinson
Boston	60	94	.390	David James Bancroft
Philadelphia	51	103	.331	John Phelan McInnis
Totals	614	614	.500	

American League

Club	Won	Lost	Pc.	Manager
New York	*110	44	*.714	Miller James Huggins
Philadelphia	91	63	.591	Connie Mack
Washington	85	69	.552	Stanley Raymond Harris
Detroit	82	71	.536	George Joseph Moriarty (B)
Chicago	70	83	.458	Raymond W. Schalk
Cleveland	66	87	.431	Jack McCallister
St. Louis	59	94	.385	Daniel Philip Howley
Boston	51	103	.322	William F. Carrigan
Totals	614	614	.500	

A—Rogers Hornsby managed Giants during McGraw's absence.
B—Albert Leifield, Coach, and Frank Shaughnessy, scout managed Tigers during Moriarty's absence.
*—New American League records.

It was the sixth pennant for the Pittsburg National League club, the fifth for the New York American League club. In the 24th World's Series between the National and American Leagues, New York made a clean sweep of the four games played, the result of the set making these changes in the dope of the classics. (See page 100.):

Series Won—American League	14
National League	10
Cities having World's Champion Teams	
New York	7
Cities competing for World's Series	
Championship—Pittsburg	4
New York	17

Record of games won and lost by World's Series clubs: Pittsburg Nationals, won 11; lost 15; percentage .423; New York Americans, won 14; lost 15; percentage .483.

Managers' records in World's Series: Owen J. Bush, series lost 1; games lost, 4; Miller J. Huggins, Series won, 2; Series lost, 3; games won 14, games lost, 15, games tied, 1.

The players on the pennant winning teams during the year were as follows:

NEW YORK AMERICANS—Miller James Huggins, manager; Walter E. Beale (optioned to St. Paul), Joseph Giard, Waite Charles Hoyt, William Wilcy Moore, Herbert Jefferis Pennock, George William Pipgras, Walter H. Ruether, Robert J. Shawkey, Myles Lewis Thomas, pitchers; Bernard Oliver Bengough, Tharon Pat Collins, John P. Grabowski, catchers; Joseph A. Dugan, Henry Louis Gehrig, Michael Gazella, Mark A. Koenig, Anthony Frank Lazzeri, Ray Morehart, Julian Walentine Wera, infielders; Earl Bryan Combs, Cedric Montgomery Durst, Robert William Meusel, Benjamin E. Paschal, George Herman Ruth, outfielders.

PITTSBURG NATIONALS—Owen J. Bush, manager; Victor S. Aldridge, Leslie Joseph Bush (released), Louis Michael Cvengros, Ralph Dawson, Carmen Proctor Hill, Ray Kremer, Henry Lee Meadows, Leroy Mehaffey (optioned to New Haven), John Kenneth Miljus, John Dewey Morrison (left club), Chester R. Nichols (optioned to New Haven), George A. Peery, Don C. Songer (released to Giants), Emil Ogden Yde, pitchers; John Beverly Gooch, Earl S. Smith, Roy Hampton Spencer, catchers; Richard Bartell, Joseph Cronin, Henry Knight Groh, George Farley Grantham, Joseph Harris, Harold Rhyne, Edward J. Sicking (returned to Indianapolis), Harold Joseph Traynor, Forest Glenn Wright, infielders; Clyde Barnhart, Fred Brickell, Adam Comoroskey, Hazen S. Cuyler, Herman Layne (optioned to Indianapolis), Paul Clee Waner, Lloyd James Waner, outfielders.

Leaders of 1927

BATTERS—Page 46

Player	Club	League	Pct. Or No.
Paul Clee Waner	Pittsburg	National	.380
Harry Edwin Heilmann	Detroit	American	.398

BASE STEALERS—Page 48

Frank Francis Frisch	St. Louis	National	48
George Harold Sisler	St. Louis	American	27

SACRIFICE HITTERS—Page 49

Harold J. Traynor	Pittsburg	National	35
Stanley Raymond Harris	Washington	American	30

SCORERS—Page 50

Rogers Hornsby	New York	National	133
Lloyd James Waner	Pittsburg	National	133
George Herman Ruth	New York	American	158

MANUFACTURERS OF BASE HITS—Page 51

Paul Clee Waner	Pittsburg	National	237
Earl Bryan Combs	New York	American	231

DEMON DOUBLERS—Page 53

Jackson Riggs Stephenson	Chicago	National	46
Henry Louis Gehrig	New York	American	52

DEMON TRIPLERS—Page 54

Paul Clee Waner	Pittsburg	National	17
Earl Bryan Combs	New York	American	23

DEMON HOME RUNNISTS—Page 55

Lewis Robert Wilson	Chicago	National	30
Fred C. Williams	Philadelphia	National	30
George Herman Ruth	New York	American	*60

BATTING IN RUNS—Page 56

Paul Clee Waner	Pittsburg	National	131
Henry Louis Gehrig	New York	American	*175

DEMON WHIFFERS—Page 56

Lewis Robert Wilson	Chicago	National	50
George Herman Ruth	New York	American	89

DEMON WALKERS—Page 56

Rogers Hornsby	New York	National	86
George Herman Ruth	New York	American	138

STRIKE OUT KINGS—Page 57

Arthur C. Vance	Brooklyn	National	184
Robert Moses Grove	Philadelphia	American	174

*New American and Major League Records.

FAMOUS GAMES, FAMOUS PLAYERS, FAMOUS FEATS
THREE HOME RUNS IN GAME—
PAGE 61

ANTHONY FRANK LAZERRI and Henry Louis Gehrig of New York (American League) each hit three home runs in games—Lazerri in New York on June 8 in game with Chicago (second inning off Faber, eighth off Faber and ninth off Connally) and Gehrig in Boston on June 23 (second inning off Lundgren, sixth off McFayden and eighth off McFayden).

UNASSISTED TRIPLE PLAYS—
PAGE 97

JAMES EDWARD COONEY, shortstop of Chicago (National League), made an unassisted triple play in the fourth inning of the morning game at Pittsburg on May 30 and in Detroit the next day John H. Neun, Tiger first baseman, retired three men on one play in the ninth inning of the game with Cleveland.

Addenda to Part VII
Players Starting Major League Careers During the Season of 1927
(With Birth Data on Some of Them)

ATKINSON, HUBERT
Washington

BAKER, NEAL V.   Pitcher
Philadelphia A. L.

BALDWIN, HOWARD C.   Infielder
Philadelphia N. L.

BARNABE, CHARLES EDWARD   Pitcher
Chicago A. L.
Born Russell Gulch, Col., June 12, 1900

BARNES, EMILE   Outfielder
Washington

BARTELL, RICHARD   Infielder
Pittsburgh
Born Chicago, Ill., Nov. 22, 1908

BATES, CHARLES WILLIAM   Outfielder
Philadelphia A. L.
Born Philadelphia, Pa., Sept. 17, 1905

BATTLE, JAMES   Infielder
Chicago A. L.
Born Celeste, Tex., March 26, 1904

BECKMAN, JAMES   Pitcher
Cincinnati

Bennett, Francis A.   Pitcher
Boston, A. L.

BILLINGS, HASKELL   Pitcher
Detroit

BOLEY, JOHN P.   Infielder
Philadelphia A. L.
Born Mahanoy City, Pa., July 27, 1898

BONEY, HENRY T.   Pitcher
New York N. L.

BRADLEY, HERBERT T.   Pitcher
Boston A. L.
Born Agenda, Kan., Jan. 3,1904

BRANOM, DUDLEY   Infielder
Philadelphia A. L.

BROWN, JOSEPH   Pitcher
Chicago A. L.

BURKE, R. J.   Pitcher
Washington

BURNETT, JOHN   Infielder
Cleveland

BUSHEY, FRANK   Pitcher
Boston A. L.

CANTWELL, BEN CALDWELL   Pitcher
New York N. L.
Born Milan, Tenn., April 13, 1902

CARLYLE, HIRAM CLEO   Outfielder
Boston A. L.
Born Fairburn, Ga., Sept. 7, 1903

CLARK, JR., BAILEY EARL   Outfielder
Boston N. L.
Born Washington, D. C., Nov. 6, 1907

CLARKSON, WILLIAM H.   Pitcher
New York N. L.

COFFMAN, SAMUEL RICHARD   Pitcher
Washington
Born Veto, Ala., Dec. 18, 1906

COLLARD, EARL CLINTON   Pitcher
Cleveland
Born Williams, Ariz., August 29, 1900

CREMINS, ROBERT   Pitcher
Boston A. L.

DEAR, PAUL S.   Infielder
Washington

DEITRICK, WILLIAM ALEXANDER
                             Infielder

Philadelphia N. L.
Born Hanover Co., Va., April 30, 1902

EGGERT, ELMER   Infielder
Boston A. L.

ENGLISH, ELWOOD   Infielder
Chicago N. L.
Born Fredonia, Ohio, March 2, 1907

FAULKNER, JAMES LEROY   Pitcher
New York N. L.
Born Beatrice, Neb., July 27, 1900

FERRELL, WESLEY C.   Pitcher
Cleveland

FLASKAMPER, RAYMOND HAROLD
                                 Infielder
Chicago A. L.
Born St. Louis, Mo., October 31, 1901

FRANKHOUSE, FRED MELOY   Pitcher
St. Louis N. L.
Born Port Royal, Pa., April 9, 1904

FREEMAN, JOHN   Outfielder
Boston A. L.

GANZEL, FOSTER PERE   Outfielder
Washington
Born Malden, Mass., May 22, 1902

GERKEN, GEORGE HERBERT   Outfielder
Cleveland
Born Chicago, Ill., July 28, 1903

GILL, JOHN WESLEY   Outfielder
Cleveland
Born Nashville, Tenn., March 27, 1906

GILLIS, GRANT   Infielder
Washington
Born Grove Hill, Ala., January 24, 1902

GRAMPP, HENRY   Pitcher
Chicago N. L.

GRAVES, SIDNEY   Infielder
Boston N. L.

HANKINS, DONALD WAYNE   Pitcher
Detroit
Born Pendleton, Ind., Feb. 9, 1903

HAYES, MINTER CARNEY   Infielder

Washington
Born Clanton, Ala., July 19, 1906

HOHMAN, WILLIAM   Outfielder
Philadelphia N. L.

HOPKINS, PAUL HENRY   Pitcher
Washington
Born Chester, Conn., Sept. 25, 1904

JABLONOWSKI, PETER WILLIAM   Pitcher
Cincinnati
Born Terryville, Conn., May 20, 1904

JOHNSON, ARTHUR GILBERT   Pitcher
New York N. L.

JORDAN, BAXTER BARELY   Infielder
New York N. L.
Born Cooleemee, N. C., Jan. 16, 1907

JUDD, RALPH   Pitcher
Washington

KAROW, MARTIN G.   Infielder
Boston A. L.

KLINGER, JOSEPH   Outfielder
New York N. L.

KRESS, RALPH   Infielder
St. Louis A. L.
Born Columbia, Cal., Jan. 2, 1907

LAYNE, HERMAN   Outfielder
Pittsburg
Born New Haven, W. Va., Feb. 13, 1902

LIND, H. CARL   Infielder
Cleveland
Born New Orleans, La., Sept. 19, 1904

LISENBEE, HORACE MILTON   Pitcher
Washington
Born Clarksville, Tenn., Sept. 23, 1901

LITTLEJOHN, CARLISLE   Pitcher
St. Louis N. L.
Born Irene, Tex., October 6, 1901

M'KAIN, HAROLD LEROY   Pitcher
Cleveland
Born Logan, Iowa, July 10, 1908

M'NAMARA, JOHN   Outfielder
Boston N. L.

MELLANO, JOSEPH   Infielder
Philadelphia A. L.

MILLER, OTIS LOUIS   Infielder
St. Louis A. L.
Born on a farm in Illinois, Feb. 2, 1901

MILLER, RUSSELL LEWIS   Pitcher
Philadelphia N. L.
Born Etna, Ohio, March 25, 1901

MILLS, ARTHUR   Pitcher
Boston N. L.
Born Utica, N. Y., March 2, 1904

MOORE, RANDOLPH   Outfielder
Chicago A. L.
Born Naples, Texas, June 21, 1906

MOORE, WILLIAM WILCEY   Pitcher
New York A. L.
Born Bonetta, Texas, May 20, 1897

MORRISON, W. GUY   Pitcher
Boston N. L.
Born Hinton W. Va., August 29, 1898

O'DONNELL, HARRY H.   Catcher
Philadelphia N. L.

ORSATTI, ERNEST R.   Outfielder
St. Louis N. L.
Born Los Angeles, Cal., Sept. 8, 1904

PARTRIDGE, JAMES   Infielder
Brooklyn
Born Mountville, Ga., Nov. 15, 1902

PEEL, HOMER HEFNER   Outfielder
St. Louis N. L.
Born Port Sullivan, Texas, Oct. 10, 1902

PEERY, GEORGE A.   Pitcher
Pittsburg

POWERS, LLOYD   Pitcher
Philadelphia A. L.

REESE, ANDREW JACKSON   Of-Inf
New York N. L.
Born Tupelo, Miss., Feb. 7, 1904

REYNOLDS, CARL   Outfielder
Chicago A. L.

ROETTGER, WALTER HENRY   Outfielder

St. Louis N. L.
Born St. Louis, Mo., August 28, 1902

ROLLINGS, WILLIAM RUSSELL   Infielder
Boston A. L.
Born Mobile, Ala., March 31, 1906

RUBLE, WILLIAM ARTHUR   Outfielder
Detroit
Born Knoxville, Tenn., March 11, 1903

SAUNDERS, RUSSELL   Outfielder
Philadelphia A. L.

SCHUBEL, HENRY G.   Infielder
St. Louis N. L.

SCHULTE, FRED WILLIAM   Outfielder
St. Louis A. L.
Born Belvidere, Ill., January 13, 1903

SEWELL, THOMAS WESLEY   Infielder
Chicago N. L.
Born Titus, Ala., April 16, 1906

SHEA, MERVYN J.   Catcher
Detroit

SMITH, RUFUS FRAZIER   Pitcher
Detroit
Born Guilford College, N. C., Jan. 24, 1906

SMITH, RICHARD P.   Catcher
New York N. L.

SPALDING, C. H.   Outfielder
Philadelphia N. L.

STEWART, FRANK   Pitcher
Chicago A. L.

STURDY, GUY   Infielder
St. Louis A. L.

SWEETLAND, LESTER L.   Pitcher
Philadelphia N. L.

TARBERT, W. A.   Outfielder
Boston A. L.

THOMAS, FAY WESLEY   Pitcher
New York N. L.
Born Wichita, Kan., October 10, 1904

TREMPER, OVERTON   Outfielder
Brooklyn

TUCKER, OLIVER D.   Outfielder
Washington

UNDERHILL, VERNE   Pitcher
Cleveland

URBAN, LUKE J.   Catcher
Boston N. L.

VANALSTYNE, CLAYTON   Pitcher
Washington

WALKER, WILLIAM   Pitcher
New York N. L.

WALKUP, JAMES HUEY   Pitcher
Detroit
Born Havana, Ark., Nov. 3, 1897

WALSH, AUGUST   Pitcher
Philadelphia N. L.
Born Wilmington, Del., August 9, 1904

WANER, LLOYD JAMES   Outfielder
Pittsburg
Born Harrah, Okla., March 16, 1906

WAY, ROBERT CLINTON   Infielder
Chicago A. L.
Born Emlenton, Penna., April 2, 1906

WERA, JULIAN WALENTINE   Infielder

New York N. L.
Born Winona, Minn., Feb. 9, 1905

WEST, SAMUEL   Outfielder
Washington

WETZEL, CHARLES   Pitcher
Philadelphia A. L.

WHITE, JOHN F.   Infielder
Cincinnati

WILKE, HARRY JOSEPH   Infielder
Chicago N. L.
Born Cincinnati, Ohio, Dec. 14, 1901

WILSON, FRANK   Outfielder
Chicago A. L.

WILSON, JOHN S.   Pitcher
Boston A. L.
Born Coal City, Ala., April 25, 1905

WOLF, RAYMOND   Infielder
Cincinnati

WRIGHT, JAMES   Pitcher
St. Louis A. L.

YERKES, C. CARROLL   Pitcher
Philadelphia A. L.

Baseball Cyclopedia

For Season of 1928—53rd Year for National League and 28th for the American

The Pennant Races

American League

Club	Won	Lost	Pc.	Manager
New York	101	53	.656	Miller James Huggins
Philadelphia	98	55	.641	Connie Mack
St. Louis	82	72	.532	Daniel Philip Howley
Washington	75	79	.487	Stanley Raymond Harris
Chicago	72	82	.468	Raymond W. Schalk
				Russell A. Blackburne
Detroit	68	86	.442	George Joseph Moriarty
Cleveland	62	92	.403	Roger Peckinpaugh
Boston	57	96	.373	William F. Carrigan
Totals	615	615	.500	

National League

Club	Won	Lost	Pc.	Manager
St. Louis	95	59	.617	William Boyd McKechnie
New York	93	61	.604	John Joseph McGraw
Chicago	91	63	.591	Joseph V. McCarthy
Pittsburgh	85	67	.559	Owen J. Bush
Cincinnati	78	74	.513	John Charles Hendricks
Brooklyn	77	76	.503	Wilbert Robinson
Boston	50	103	.327	John Slattery, Rogers Hornsby
Philadelphia	43	109	.283	Burton Edwin Shotton
Totals	612	612	.500	

Russell A. Blackburne became manager of Chicago Americans on July 4th.
Rogers Hornsby became manager of Boston Nationals on May 25th.

It was the second pennant for the St. Louis National League club, the sixth for the New York American League club. In the 25th World's Series between the National and

American Leagues, New York made a clean sweep of the four games played, the Yankees treating the Cardinals just as they had the Pirates in 1927. The result of this set made the following changes in the dope of the classics. (See page 100.):

Series Won—American League	15
National League	10
Cities having World's Champion Teams	
New York	8
Cities competing for World's Series	
Championship—St. Louis	2
New York	18

Record of games won and lost by World's Series clubs: St. Louis Nationals, won 4; lost 7; percentage .364; New York Americans, won 18; lost 15; percentage .545.

Managers' records in World's Series: Miller J. Huggins, Series won 3, Series lost 3; games won 18, games lost, 15, games tied, 1. William Boyd McKechnie, Series won, 1; lost, 1; games won 4, games lost, 7.

The players on the pennant winning teams during the year were as follows:

NEW YORK AMERICANS—Miller James Huggins, manager; Archie Stewart Campbell, Stanley Coveleskie, Fred A. Heimach, Waite Charles Hoyt, Henry Ward Johnson, William Wilcy Moore, Herbert Jefferis Pennock, George William Pipgras, Wilfred D. Ryan, Albert

B. Shealey, Urban J. Shocker, Myles Lewis Thomas and Jonathan Thompson Walton Zachary, pitchers; Bernard Oliver Bengough, Tharon Pat Collins, William Dickey and John P. Grabowski, catchers; George Henry Burns, Joseph Anthony Dugan, Leo Ernest Durocher, Michael Gazella, Henry Louis Gehrig, Mark Anthony Koenig, Anthony Michael Lazzeri and Eugene Robertson, infielders; Earl Bryan Combs, Cedric Montgomery Durst, Robert William Meusel, Benjamin Paschal and George Herman Ruth, outfielders.

ST. LOUIS NATIONALS—William Boyd McKechnie, manager; Grover Cleveland Alexander, Fred Meloy Frankhouse, Harold Augustin Haid, Jesse Joseph Haines, Sylvester W. Johnson, Tony Charles Kaufman, Charles Carlisle Littlejohn, Clarence E. Mitchell, Arthur Conrad Reinhart, Charles Flint Rhem and William Henry Sherdel, pitchers; Virgil Lawrence Davis, Gus Rodney Mancuso, Robert Arthur O'-Farrell, Earl S. Smith and James Wilson, catchers; James Leroy Bottomley, Frank Francis Frisch, Andrew Aird High, Roscoe Albert Holm, Walter James Vincent Maranville, Thomas Joseph Thevenow and George Toporcer, infielders; Francis Raymond Blades, Taylor Lee Douthit, Charles James Hafey, George Washington Harper, John Leonard Martin, Ernest R. Orsatti, Walter Henry Roettger and Nathaniel Howard Williamson, Jr., outfielders.

Leaders of 1928

BATTERS—Page 46

Player	Club	League	Pct. Or No.
Rogers Hornsby	Boston	National	.387
Leon Allen Goslin	Washington	American	.379

BASE STEALERS—Page 48

Hazen S. Cuyler	Chicago	National	37
Charles Solomon Myer	Boston	American	30

SACRIFICE HITTERS—Page 49

Harold J. Traynor	Pittsburg	National	42
John William Clancy	Chicago	American	29

SCORERS—Page 50

George Herman Ruth	New York	American	163
Paul Clee Waner	Pittsburg	National	142

MANUFACTURERS OF BASE HITS—Page 51

Henry Emmett Manush	St. Louis	American	241
Fred Charles Lindstrom	New York	National	231

DEMON DOUBLERS—Page 53

Paul Clee Waner	Pittsburg	National	50
Henry Louis Gehrig	New York	American	47
Henry Emmett Manush	St. Louis	American	47

DEMON TRIPLERS—Page 54

Earl Bryan Combs	New York	American	21
James Leroy Bottomley	St. Louis	National	20

DEMON HOME RUNNISTS—Page 55

George Herman Ruth	New York	American	54
James Leroy Bottomley	St. Louis	National	31
Lewis Robert Wilson	Chicago	National	31

Batting in Runs—Page 56

Henry Louis Gehrig	New York	American	142
George Herman Ruth	New York	American	142
James Leroy Bottomley	St. Louis	National	136

Demon Whiffers—Page 56

Lewis Robert Wilson	Chicago	National	*94
George Herman Ruth	New York	American	87

Demon Walkers—Page 56

George Herman Ruth	New York	American	135
Rogers Hornsby	Boston	National	107

Strike Out Kings—Page 57

Arthur C. Vance	Brooklyn	National	200
Robert Moses Grove	Philadelphia	American	183

*New National League Record.

Famous Games, Famous Players, Famous Feats
Three Home Runs in Game—Page 61

Lester Rowland Bell, of Boston Nationals, George Washington Harper of St. Louis Nationals and George Herman Ruth of New York Americans each hit three home runs in games—Bell in Boston against Cincinnati on June 2; Harper in New York on September 20, and Ruth in St. Louis on October 9 (world series game).

Two Home Runs in One Inning—Page 63

William W. Regan of Boston American League Club, in Chicago on June 16 in the fourth inning—the first off Ted Blankenship, the second off George Walter Connally.

Addenda to Part VII

Players Starting Major League Careers During the Season of 1928

(With Birth Data on Some of Them)

ASBJORNSON, ROBERT   Catcher
Boston A. L.
Born Concord, Mass., June 19, 1909

BALLINGER, PELHAM A.   Infielder
Washington A. L.

BARNHART, LESLIE   Pitcher
Cleveland A. L.

BARTHOLOMEW, LESTER JUSTIN   Pitcher
Pittsburgh N. L.
Born Madison, Wis., April 4, 1905

BETTENCOURT, LARRY   Infielder
St. Louis A. L.

BISSONETTE, DELPHIA LOUIS   Infielder
Brooklyn N. L.
Born Winthrop, Maine, Sept. 6, 1899

BLACKERBY, GEORGE FRANCIS   Outfielder
Chicago A. L.
Born Wichita Falls, Texas, Nov. 10, 1906

BOGGS, RAY J.   Pitcher
Boston N. L.

BOLTON, CECIL GLENN   Infielder
Cleveland A. L.
Born Booneville, Miss., Feb. 13, 1904

BOOL, ALBERT   Catcher
Washington A. L.
Born Lincoln, Neb., Aug. 24, 1897

BOSS, ELMER HARLEY   Infielder
Washington A. L.

BRAME, ERWIN BECKHAM   Pitcher
Pittsburg N. L.
Born Weaver's Store, Tenn., Oct. 12, 1901

BRANNON, OTIS   Infielder
St. Louis A. L.

BRANDT, EDWARD ARTHUR   Pitcher
Boston N. L.
Born Spokane, Wash., Feb. 17, 1905

BROWN, CLINT   Pitcher
Cleveland A. L.
Born Grays Mills, Penna., July 8, 1905

CALDWELL, BRUCE   Utility
Cleveland A. L.

CALDWELL, EARL W.   Pitcher
Philadelphia N. L.

CAMPBELL, ARCHIE STEWART   Pitcher
New York A. L.
Born Maplewood, N. J., Oct. 30, 1903

CHAPLIN, JAMES BAILEY   Pitcher
New York N. L.
Born Los Angeles, Cal., July 13, 1905

CISSELL, CHALMER WILLIAM   Infielder
Chicago A. L.
Born Perryville, Mo., Jan. 3, 1904

COX, GEORGE MARVIN   Pitcher
Chicago A. L.
Born Sherman, Texas, Nov. 15, 1904

CRONIN, WILLIAM P.   Catcher
Boston N. L.
Born Newton, Mass., Dec. 26, 1903

CROWLEY, EDGAR J.   Infielder
Washington A. L.

DANEY, LEE   Pitcher
Philadelphia A. L.

DANNING, IKE   Catcher
St. Louis A. L.

DAVIS, VIRGIL LAWRENCE   Catcher
St. Louis–Philadelphia N. L.
Born Birmingham, Ala., Dec. 20, 1904

DICKEY, WILLIAM   Catcher
New York A. L.

DORMAN, CHARLES   Outfielder
Cleveland A. L.

DUGAN, DAN   Pitcher
Chicago A. L.

EARNSHAW, GEORGE LIVINGSTON
     Pitcher
Philadelphia A. L
Born New York City, Feb. 15, 1900

EASTERLING, PAUL   Outfielder
Detroit A. L.
Born Reidsville, Ga., Sept. 28, 1905

FITZBERGER, CHARLES CASPAR   Infielder
Boston N. L.

FOLEY, RAYMOND W.   Utility
New York N. L.

FULLIS, CHARLES PHILIP   Infielder
New York N. L.
Born Girardville, Penna., Feb. 27, 1904

GARRISON, CLIFFORD   Pitcher
Boston A. L.

GILBERT, WALTER   Infielder
Brooklyn N. L.

GOLDMAN, JONAH   Infielder
Cleveland A. L.

GOODELL, J. WILLIAM   Pitcher
Chicago A. L.

GREENE, JUNE F.   Pitcher
Philadelphia N. L.
Born Greensboro, N. C., June 25, 1902

GRIFFIN, MARTIN JOHN   Pitcher
Boston A. L.
Born San Francisco, Cal., Sept. 2, 1905

HARDER, MELVIN LAROY   Pitcher
Cleveland A. L.
Born Beemer, Neb., Oct. 15, 1909

HARVEL, LUTHER   Outfielder
Cleveland A. L.

HASSLER, JOSEPH FREDRICK   Infielder

Philadelphia A. L
Born Ft. Smith, Ark., April 7, 1906

HEMSLEY, RALSTON   Catcher
Pittsburg N. L.

HINSON, JAMES PAUL   Infielder
Boston A. L.
Born Van Leer, Tenn., May 9, 1907

HOLLEY, EDWARD   Pitcher
Chicago N. L.

HUBBELL, CARL OWEN   Pitcher
New York N. L.
Born Kansas City, Mo., June 22, 1903

HURST, FRANK O'DONNELL   Infielder
Philadelphia N. L.
Born Maysville, Ky., Aug. 12, 1905

JACOBS, RAY   Infielder
Chicago N. L.

JOHNSON, SILAS KENNETH   Pitcher
Cincinnati N. L.
Born Marseilles, Ill., Oct. 5, 1908

JONES, COBURN   Infielder
Pittsburg N. L.
Born Denver, Colo., Aug. 21, 1907

KENNA, EDWARD B.   Catcher
Washington A. L.

KLEIN, CHARLES HERBERT   Outfielder
Philadelphia N. L
Born Indianapolis, Ind., Oct. 7, 1905

LENNON, EDWARD   Pitcher
Philadelphia N. L

LEOPOLD, RUDOLPH M.   Pitcher
Chicago A. L.

LERIAN, WALTER   Catcher
Philadelphia N. L

LOEPP, GEORGE HERBERT   Outfielder
Boston A. L.
Born Detroit, Mich., Sept. 11, 1903

LOPEZ, ALFONZO RAMON   Catcher
Brooklyn N. L.
Born Tampa, Fla., Aug. 20, 1908

M'DONALD, HARVEY   Outfielder
Philadelphia N. L

MALONE, PERSE PAT   Pitcher
Chicago N. L.
Born Altoona, Penna., Sept. 23, 1902

MANCUSO, GUS RODNEY   Catcher
St. Louis N. L.
Born Galveston, Texas, Dec. 5, 1905

MARTIN, JOHN LEONARD   Outfielder
St. Louis N. L.
Born Temple, Okla., Feb. 29, 1904

MILLIGAN, JOHN   Pitcher
Philadelphia N. L

MONCEWICZ, FRED A.   Infielder
Boston A. L.

MONTAGUE, EDWARD FRANCIS   Infielder
Cleveland A. L.
Born San Francisco, Cal., July 24, 1906

MOORE, JAMES STANFORD   Pitcher
Cleveland A. L.
Born Prescott, Ark., Dec. 14, 1906

MOORE, JOHN F.   Outfielder
Chicago N. L.
Born Waterville, Conn., March 23, 1903

MORGAN, EDDIE CARRE   Outfielder
Cleveland A. L.
Born Cairo, Ill., May 22, 1905

O'CONNELL, JOHN CHARLES   Catcher
Pittsburg N. L.
Born Pittsburg, Penna., June 13, 1905

ORWOLL, OSWALD CHRISTIAN   Pitcher
Philadelphia A. L
Born Portland, Oregon, Nov. 17, 1902

PAGE, PHILIP RAUSAC, JR.   Pitcher
Detroit A. L.
Born Springfield, Mass., Aug. 23, 1905

PRICE, JOSEPH   Outfielder
New York N. L.

PYLE, HARLIN   Pitcher
Cincinnati N. L.

REDFERN, GEORGE HOWARD   Infielder
Chicago A. L.
Born Ashville, N. C., April 7, 1903

REINHOLZ, A. R.   Infielder
Cleveland A. L.

SAX, ERICK OLIVER   Infielder
St. Louis A. L.
Born Branford, Conn., Nov. 5, 1906

SETTLEMIRE, MERLE   Pitcher
Boston A. L.
Born Santa Fe, Ohio, Jan. 19, 1903

SHEA, JOHN J.   Pitcher
Boston A. L.

SHEALY, ALBERT B.   Pitcher
New York A. L.

SHIRES, CHARLES ARTHUR   Infielder
Chicago A. L.
Born Milford, Mass., August 13, 1907

SHORES, WILLIAM   Pitcher
Philadelphia A. L
Born Abilene, Texas, May 26, 1905

SIMMONS, PATRICK C.   Pitcher
Boston A. L.

SLAYTON, FOSTER H.   Pitcher
Boston A. L.

SORRELL, VICTOR GARLAND   Pitcher
Detroit A. L.
Born Morrisville, N. C., April 9, 1902

SPENCER, GLENN EDWARD   Pitcher
Pittsburg N. L.
Born Corning, N. Y., Sept. 11, 1905

SPOHRER, ALFRED   Catcher
New York N. L. Boston N. L.
Born Philadelphia, Pa., Dec. 3, 1902

STONE, J. T.   Outfielder
Detroit A. L.
Born Mulberry, Tenn., Oct. 10, 1906

STRELECKI, EDWARD HENRY   Pitcher
St. Louis A. L.
Born Newark, N. J., April 10, 1903

STRIPP, JOSEPH   Infielder
Cincinnati N. L.

SULLIVAN, CHARLES EDWARD   Pitcher
Detroit A. L.
Born Yadkin Valley, N. C., 1905

SUMNER, CARL   Outfielder
Boston A. L.

SWANSON, KARL E.   Infielder
Chicago A. L.

SWEENEY, WILLIAM JOSEPH   Infielder
Detroit A. L.
Born Cleveland, Ohio, Dec. 29, 1905

TAITT, DOUGLAS JOHN   Outfielder
Boston A. L.
Born Bay City, Mich., Aug. 3, 1903

TAUSCHER, WALTER EDWARD   Pitcher
Pittsburg N. L.
Born LaSalle, Ill., Nov. 22, 1904

TOUCHSTONE, CLAYLAND MAFFITT
          Pitcher
Boston N. L.
Born Moore, Penna., Jan. 24, 1905

TUTWILER, E. S.   Pitcher
Pittsburg N. L.

VAN CAMP, AL   Pitcher
Cleveland A. L.
Born Moline, Ill., Sept. 7, 1904

WALSH, EDWARD A., JR.   Pitcher
Chicago A. L.

WALKER, MARTIN V.   Pitcher
Philadelphia N. L

WEAVER, JOHN D.   Pitcher
Washington A. L.

WEILAND, ROBERT   Pitcher
Chicago A. L.

WEST, WALTER MAXWELL   Outfielder
Brooklyn N. L.
Born Sunset, Texas, July 14, 1904

WILLIAMS, EARL BAXTER   Catcher
Boston N. L.
Born Cumberland Gap, Tenn., Jan. 27,
1903

WILLIAMSON, NATHANIEL HOWARD
          Outfielder
St. Louis N. L.
Born Little Rock, Ark., Dec. 23, 1904

WILLIAMSON, ALBERT   Pitcher
Chicago A. L.

WILSON, ROY E.   Pitcher
Chicago A. L.

WINDLE, WILLIS BREWER   Infielder
Pittsburg N. L.
Born Galena, Kansas, Dec. 13, 1905

Baseball Cyclopedia

For Season of 1929—54th Year for
National League and 29th for the American

The Pennant Races

American League

Club	Won	Lost	Pc.	Manager
Philadelphia	104	46	.693	Connie Mack
New York	88	66	.571	Miller J. Huggins
Cleveland	81	71	.533	Roger Peckinpaugh
St. Louis	79	73	.520	Daniel Philip Howley
Washington	71	81	.467	Walter Perry Johnson
Detroit	70	84	.455	Stanley Raymond Harris
Chicago	59	93	.388	Russell A. Blackburne
Boston	58	96	.377	William F. Carrigan
Totals	610	610	.500	

National League

Club	Won	Lost	Pc.	Manager
Chicago	98	54	.645	Joseph Vincent McCarthy
Pittsburgh	88	65	.575	Owen J. Bush, Jewel Ens
New York	84	67	.556	John Joseph McGraw
St. Louis	78	74	.513	William H. Southworth
Philadelphia	71	82	.464	Burton Edwin Shotton
Brooklyn	70	83	.458	Wilbert Robinson
Cincinnati	66	88	.429	John Charles Hendricks
Boston	56	98	.364	Emil Fuchs
Totals	611	611	.500	

MILLER J. HUGGINS died September 25.
JEWEL ENS became temporary manager of Pittsburg on August 28.
WILLIAM BOYD MCKECHNIE became manager of St. Louis Nationals on July 24. On July 23 the Cardinals played under the direction of CHARLES EVERARD STREET, who will be their leader in 1930.

It was the seventh pennant for the Philadelphia American League club, the eleventh for the Chicago National League club. In the 26th World's Series between the National and American Leagues, Philadelphia won four games to Chicago's one. The result of this set made the following changes in the dope of the classics. (See page 100.):

Series Won—American League   16
      National League   10
Cities having World's Champion Teams
      Philadelphia   4
Cities competing for World's Series
      Championship—Philadelphia   7
      Chicago   11

Record of games won and lost by World's Series clubs: Philadelphia Americans, won 17; lost 13; percentage .567; Chicago Nationals, won 19, lost 24, percentage .442.

Managers' records in World's Series: Connie Mack, Series won 4, Series lost 2; games won 17, games lost, 13. Joseph Vincent McCarthy, Series lost, 1; games won 1, games lost, 4.

The players on the pennant winning teams during the year were as follows:

PHILADELPHIA AMERICANS—William Breckenridge, George Livingston Earnshaw, Howard J. Ehmke, Robert Moses Grove, Oswold Christian Orwoll, John P. Quinn, Edwin Americus Rommel, William Shores, George E. Walberg and C. Carroll Yerkes, pitchers; Gordon Stanley Cochrane, Clay Mitchell Mattox and Ralph Perkins, catchers; Max Frederick Bishop, John P. Boley, George Henry Burns, Edward Trowbridge Collins, James Cronin, James J. Dykes, James Emory Foxx, Samuel Douglas Hale, Joseph Fredrick Hassler, Donald Eric McNair, R. Miller and Newell Obadiah Morse, infielders; Roger Cramer, Walter E. French, George William Haas, DeWitt Wiley LeBourveau, Edmund John Miller, Al Harry Simmons and Homer Wayne Summa, outfielders.

CHICAGO NATIONALS—John Fred Blake, Guy T. Bush, Harold Gust Carlson, Louis Michael Cvengros, Henry Grampp, Berlyn Dale Horne, Claude Alford Jonnard, Perce Lay Malone, Arthur Neukom Nehr, John Robert Osborn, Kenneth William Penner, and Charles Henry Root, pitchers; Thomas Samuel Angley, Miguel Angel Gonzales, Robert Earl Grace, Charles Leo Hartnett, John C. Schulte and James Wren Taylor, catchers; Clyde Eugene Beck, Clarence Vick Blair, Elwood English, Charles John Grimm, Rogers Hornsby, Norman Alexis McMillan and Charles Julius Tolson, infielders; Hazen S. Cuyler, Clifton Earl Heathcote, John Francis Moore, Jackson Riggs Stephenson, Dan Taylor and Lewis Robert Wilson, outfielders.

Leaders of 1929

BATTERS—Page 46

Player	Club	League	Pct. Or No.
Frank J. O'Doul	Philadelphia	National	.398
Lewis A. Fonseca	Cleveland	American	.369

BASE STEALERS—Page 48

Hazen S. Cuyler	Chicago	National	43
Charles Gehringer	Detroit	American	27

SACRIFICE HITTERS—Page 49

Frederick Edward Maguire	Boston	National	26
Joe Sewell	Cleveland	American	41

SCORERS—Page 50

Rogers Hornsby	Chicago	National	156
Charles Gehringer	Detroit	American	131

MANUFACTURERS OF BASE HITS—Page 51

Frank J. O'Doul	Philadelphia	National	254
Dale Alexander	Detroit	American	215
Charles Gehringer	Detroit	American	215

DEMON DOUBLERS—Page 53

John Henry Frederick	Brooklyn	National	52
Charles Gehringer	Detroit	American	45
Dale Alexander	Detroit	American	45
Henry Manush	St. Louis	American	45

DEMON TRIPLERS—Page 54

Lloyd James Waner	Pittsburgh	National	20
Charles Gehringer	Detroit	American	19

DEMON HOME RUNNISTS—Page 55

Charles Herbert Klein	Philadelphia	National	*43
George H. Ruth	New York	American	46

BATTING IN RUNS—Page 56

Lewis Robert Wilson	Chicago	National	*159
Al Simmons	Philadelphia	American	157

DEMON WHIFFERS—Page 56

Lewis Robert Wilson	Chicago	National	83
James Foxx	Philadelphia	American	70

DEMON WALKERS—Page 56

Melvin Thomas Ott	New York	National	113
Max Bishop	Philadelphia	American	128

STRIKE OUT KINGS—Page 57

Perce Lay Malone	Chicago	National	166
Robert Grove	Philadelphia	American	170

*New National League Record.

FAMOUS GAMES, FAMOUS PLAYERS, FAMOUS FEATS
THREE HOME RUNS IN GAME— PAGE 61

HENRY LOUIS GEHRIG, New York Americans, hit three home runs in game at Chicago on May 4—in the second inning off Urban Faber, in the seventh off Harold McKain and in the ninth off Dan Dugan.

NO HIT HEROES—PAGE 82

CARL OWEN HUBBELL, New York Nationals, retired Pittsburg without hit or run in game at New York on May 8, the score being 11 to 0. Hubbell walked one man (Adams, in the third inning) and fanned four. Three errors were made behind him, as follows: Wild throw by Jackson in first inning on Adams, muffed fly by Fullis in ninth on Riconda, and wild throw by Jackson in ninth on Adams.

Addenda to Part VII

Players Starting Major League Careers During the Season of 1929

(With Birth Data on Some of Them)

AKERS, BILL   Infielder
Detroit A. L.
Born Chattanooga, Tenn., Dec. 25, 1905

ALEXANDER, DAVID DALE   Catcher
Detroit A. L.
Born Greeneville, Tenn., April 26, 1903

ANGLEY, THOMAS SAMUEL   Catcher
Chicago N. L.
Born Baltimore, Md., Oct. 2, 1904

AVERILL, HOWARD EARL   Outfielder
Cleveland A. L.
Born Snohomish, Wash., May 21, 1903

BADGRO, MORRIS   Infielder
St. Louis A. L.
Born Orilla, Wash., Dec. 1, 1904

BARNES, FRANK SAMUEL   Pitcher
Detroit A. L.
Born Dallas, Tex., Jan. 9, 1901

BARRON, DAVID IRENUS   Outfielder
Boston N. L.
Born Clarksville, Ga., June 21, 1900

BIGELOW, ELLIOTT   Outfielder
Boston A. L.
Born Tarpon Springs, Fla., Oct. 13, 1898

BLAIR, CLARENCE VICK   Infielder
Chicago, N. L.
Born Texarkana, Tex., July 13, 1903

BOYLE, RALPH   Outfielder
Boston N. L.
Born Cincinnati, Ohio, Feb. 9, 1910

BRADSHAW, JAMES   Pitcher
Brooklyn, N. L.

BRECKENRIDGE, WILLIAM   Pitcher

PHILADELPHIA A. L.
Born Tulsa, Okla., Oct. 27, 1906

BYRD, SAMUEL DEWEY   Outfielder
New York A. L.
Born Carrilton, Ga., Oct. 15, 1908

BYRNE, GERALD W.   Pitcher
Chicago A. L.

CARROLL, EDGAR F.   Pitcher
Boston A. L.
Born Baltimore, Md., July 27, 1908

CHAGNON, LEON WILBUR   Pitcher
Pittsburg N. L.
Born Pittsfield, N. H., Sept. 28, 1905

CICERO, JOSEPH DOUGHTY   Outfielder
Boston A. L.

CLARKE, W. STUART   Infielder
Pittsburg N. L.

COBB, HERBERT EDWARD   Pitcher
St. Louis A. L.
Born Pinetops, N. C., Aug. 6, 1904

CONNOLLY, EDWARD   Catcher
Boston A. L.
Born Brooklyn, N. Y., July 17, 1908

CRABTREE, ESTEL CRAYTON   Outfield
Cincinnati N. L.
Born Lucasville, Ohio, Aug., 19, 1905

CRAMER, ROGER   Outfielder
Philadelphia A. L.
Born Beach Haven, N. J., July 22, 1907

CRAWFORD, CLIFFORD   Infielder
New York N. L.
Born Society Hill, S. C., Jan. 28, 1902

CRONIN, JAMES   Infielder

Philadelphia A. L.
Born Oakland, Cal., Aug. 7, 1906

CUNNINGHAM, BRUCE LEE   Pitcher
Boston N L.
Born San Francisco, Cal., Sept. 29, 1906

DAILEY, SAMUEL   Pitcher
Philadelphia N. L.

DELKER, EDDIE ALBERTS   Infielder
St. Louis N. L.

DOBENS, RAYMOND J.   Pitcher
Boston A. L.

DONDERO, LEONARD P.   Infielder
St. Louis A. L.
Born Newark, Cal., Sept. 12, 1905

DUNLAP, WILLIAM J.   Outfielder
Boston N. L.
Born Three Rivers, Mass., May 1, 1909

DURHAM, EDWARD F.   Pitcher
Boston A. L.
Born Chester, S. C., Aug. 17, 1908

ELLIOTT, HOWARD WILLIAM   Pitcher
Philadelphia N. L.
Born Mt. Clemens, Mich., May 29, 1903

ERICKSON, RALPH   Pitcher
Pittsburg N. L.

ESTRADA, OSCAR   Pitcher
St. Louis A. L.
Born Havana, Cuba, Feb. 15, 1904

FERRELL, RICHARD BENJAMIN   Catcher
St. Louis A. L.
Born Dunham County, N. C., Oct. 12,
1905

FREDERICK, JOHN HENRY   Outfielder
Brooklyn N. L.
Born Denver, Col., Jan. 26, 1901

FRENCH, LAWRENCE   Pitcher
Pittsburg N. L.
Born Visalia, Cal., Nov. 1, 1908

FREY, BENJAMIN   Pitcher
Cincinnati N. L.
Born Dexter, Mich., April 6, 1905

FUNK, ELIAS CALVIN   Outfielder
New York A. L.
Born Lacene, Kan., Oct. 28, 1904

GARDNER, RAY VINCENT   Infielder
Cleveland A. L.
Born Fredrick, Md., Oct. 25, 1901

GELBERT, CHARLES MAGNUS   Infielder
St. Louis N. L.
Born Scranton, Penna., Jan. 26, 1906

GOOCH, CHARLES FURMAN   Infielder
Washington A. L.
Born Smyrna, Tenn., June 5, 1904

GRABOWSKI, ALBERT   Pitcher
St. Louis N. L.
Born Syracuse, N. Y., Sept. 4, 1901

GRACE, ROBERT EARL   Catcher
Chicago N. L.

GUDAT, MARVIN JOHN   Pitcher
Cincinnati N. L.
Born Wester, Tex., Aug. 27, 1904

HERRING, ARTHUR L.   Pitcher
Detroit A. L.

HOFFMAN, CLARENCE   Outfielder
Chicago A. L.
Born Belleville, Ill., Jan. 28, 1904

HOGSETT, ELON CHESTER   Pitcher
Detroit A. L.
Born Brownell, Kan., Nov. 2, 1903

HOLLOWAY, JAMES   Pitcher
Philadelphia N. L.

HORNE, BERLYN DALE   Pitcher
Chicago N. L.
Born Bachman, Ohio, April 12, 1900

INGRAM, MELVIN D.   Outfielder
Pittsburg N. L.
Born Asheville, N. C., July 4, 1905

JAMES, ROBERT BYRNE   Infielder
Boston N. L.
Born Angleton, Tex., Sept. 2, 1905

JESSEE, DANIEL EDWARD   Infielder
Cleveland A. L.
Born Louisville, Ky., Feb. 22, 1904

JOHNSON, ROY CLEVELAND   Outfielder
Detroit A. L.
Born Venita, Okla., Feb. 23, 1904

JORGENS, ARNDT   Catcher
New York A. L.
Born Norway, May 18, 1905

KEMNER, HERMAN JOHN   Pitcher
Cincinnati N. L.
Born Quincy, Ill., March 4, 1899

KIMSEY, CLYDE K.   Pitcher
St. Louis A. L.
Born Copper Hill, Tenn., Aug. 6, 1906

LAND, W. L.   Outfielder
Washington A. L.

LARY, LYNFORD HOBART   Infielder
New York A. L.
Born Armona, Cal., Jan. 28, 1906

LEGETT, LOUIS ALFRED   Catcher
Boston N. L.
Born New Orleans, La., June 1, 1902

LESLIE, SAMUEL ANDREW   Infielder
New York N. L.
Born Moss Point, Miss., July 26, 1906

LISKA, ADOLPH JAMES   Pitcher
Washington A. L.
Born Dwight, Neb., July 10, 1906

LUCAS, RAY   Pitcher
New York N. L.
Born Springfield, Ohio, Oct. 2, 1908

LYONS, TERRY   Infielder
Philadelphia N. L.

M'CULLOUGH, PAUL   Pitcher
Washington A. L.
Born Newcastle, Penna., July 28, 1903

M'NAIR, DONALD ERIC   Infielder
Philadelphia A. L.
Born Meridian, Miss., April 12, 1909

MARSHALL, EDWARD H.   Infielder
New York N. L.

MATTOX, CLAY MITCHELL   Catcher
Philadelphia A. L.
Born Leesville, Va., Nov. 24, 1905

MILLER, ELMER   Pitcher
Philadelphia N. L.

MILLER, R.   Infielder
Philadelphia A. L.

MOORE, WILLIAM AUSTIN   Pitcher
Brooklyn N. L.
Born Elberton, Ga., Feb. 7, 1906

MORSE, NEWELL OBADIAH   Infielder
Philadelphia A. L.
Born Berkeley, Cal., Sept. 4, 1905

MOSOLF, JAMES F.   Outfielder
Pittsburg N. L.

NARLESKY, WILLIAM EDWARD   Infielder
Boston A. L.
Born Perth Amboy, N. J., June 9, 1901

NEKOLA, FRANCIS J.   Pitcher
New York A. L.

NEWSOME, LOUIS N.   Pitcher
Brooklyn N. L.

O'ROURKE, JOSEPH   Infielder
Philadelphia N. L.

PARMELEE, LEROY EARL   Pitcher
New York N. L.
Born Lambertville, Mich., April 25, 1907

PATTISON, JAMES   Pitcher
Brooklyn N. L.

PEPLOSKI, HENRY STEPHEN   Infielder
Boston N. L.
Born Wilmington, Del., Sept. 15, 1907

PORTER, RICHARD TWILLEY   Outfielder
Cleveland N. L.
Born Princess Anne, Md., Dec. 30, 1901

PRUDHOMME, JOHN OLGUS   Pitcher
Detroit A. L.
Born Shreveport, La., Nov. 20, 1902

RHIEL, WILLIAM JOSEPH   Infielder
Brooklyn N. L.
Born Youngstown, Ohio, Sept. 30, 1904

RHODES, JOHN GORDON   Pitcher
New York A. L.
Born Salt Lake City, Utah, Aug. 11, 1907

RICHARDSON, CLIFFORD NOLEN
Infielder
Detroit A. L.
Born Chattanooga, Tenn., Jan. 18, 1904

ROETZ, EDWARD   Infielder
St. Louis A. L.
Born Philadelphia, Pa., Sept. 6, 1905

RYAN, JOHN FRANCIS   Outfielder
Boston A. L.

SANKEY, BENJAMIN TURNER   Infielder
Pittsburg N. L.
Born Nauvoo, Ala., Sept 2, 1907

SAVIDGE, DON   Pitcher
Washington A. L.
Born Berwick, Penna., Aug. 28, 1908

SCARRITT, RUSSELL MALLORY   Outfielder
Boston A. L.
Born Pensacola, Fla., Jan. 17, 1904

SELPH, CAREY   Infielder
St. Louis N. L.
Born Donaldson, Ark., Dec. 5, 1902

SHERID, ROYDAN R.   Pitcher
New York A. L.
Born Norristown, Penna., Jan. 25, 1908

SHOFFNER, MILBURN   Pitcher
Cleveland A. L.

SIGMAN, TRIP   Outfielder
Philadelphia N. L.
Born Mooresville, N. C., Jan. 17, 1905

SMYTHE, WILLIAM HARRY   Pitcher
Philadelphia N. L.
Born Augusta, Ga., Oct. 24, 1904

STIELY, FRED   Pitcher
St. Louis A. L.
Born Pillow, Penna., June 1, 1901

STRONER, JAMES M.   Infielder
Pittsburg N. L.
Born Chicago, Ill., May 29, 1904

SUSCE, GEORGE   Catcher
Philadelphia N. L.

SWANSON, ERNEST EVAR   Outfielder
Cincinnati N. L.
Born DeKalb, Ill., Oct. 15, 1902

SWETONIC, STEPHEN A.   Pitcher
Pittsburg N. L.

TENNANT, JAMES MCDONNELL   Pitcher
New York N. L.
Born Shepherdstown, W. Va., Mar. 3, 1907

VOYLES, PHILIP   Outfielder
Boston N. L.

WATWOOD, JOHN C.   Outfielder
Chicago A. L.
Born Alexander City, Ala., Aug. 17, 1906

WESTON, ALFRED   Outfielder
Boston N. L.

WINEAPPLE, EDWARD   Pitcher
Washington A. L.
Born Salem, Mass., Aug. 10, 1907

WUESTLING, GEORGE   Infielder
Detroit A. L.

WYATT, WHITLOW, JOHN   Pitcher
Detroit A. L.
Born Kensington, Ga., Sept. 27, 1907

Baseball Cyclopedia

For Season of 1930—55th Year for National League and 30th for the American

The Pennant Races

American League

Club	Won	Lost	Pc.	Manager
Philadelphia	102	52	.662	Connie Mack
Washington	94	60	.610	Walter Perry Johnson
New York	86	68	.558	Robert J. Shawkey
Cleveland	81	73	.527	Roger Peckinpaugh
Detroit	75	79	.487	Stanley Raymond Harris
St. Louis	64	90	.417	William Killefer Jr.
Chicago	62	92	.403	Owen J. Bush
Boston	52	102	.338	Charles Wagner
Totals	616	616	.500	

National League

Club	Won	Lost	Pc.	Manager
St. Louis	92	62	.597	Charles E. Street
Chicago	90	64	.584	Joseph Vincent McCarthy
				Rogers Hornsby
New York	87	67	.565	John Joseph McGraw
Brooklyn	86	68	.558	Wilbert Robinson
Pittsburgh	80	74	.519	Jewel Ens
Boston	70	84	.455	William Boyd McKechnie
Cincinnati	59	95	.383	Daniel Philip Howley
Philadelphia	52	102	.338	Burton Edwin Shotton
Totals	616	616	.500	

DAVID BANCROFT managed New York Nationals when John McGraw was forced to absent himself from them because of illness.

It was the eighth pennant for the Philadelphia American League club, the third for the St. Louis National League club. In the 27th World's Series between the National and American Leagues, Philadelphia won four games to St. Louis's two. The result of this set made the following changes in the dope of the classics. (See page 100.):

Series Won—American League	17
National League	10
Cities having World's Champion Teams	
Philadelphia	5
Cities competing for World's Series	
Championship—Philadelphia	8
St. Louis	3

Record of games won and lost by World's Series clubs: Philadelphia Americans, won 21; lost 15; percentage .583; St. Louis Nationals, won 6, lost 11, percentage .353.

Managers' records in World's Series: Connie Mack, Series won 5, Series lost 2; games won 21, games lost, 15. Charles E. Street, Series lost, 1; games won 2, games lost, 4.

The players on the pennant winning teams during the year were as follows:

PHILADELPHIA AMERICANS—George Livingston Earnshaw, Howard J. Ehmke, Robert Moses Grove, Glenn Liebhardt Jr., Leroy Mahaffey, Alfred Mahon, Charles Perkins, John P. Quinn, Edwin Americus Rommel, William Shores and George E. Walberg, pitchers; Gordon Stanley Cochrane, Ralph Perkins and Walter H. Schang, catchers; Max Frederick Bishop, John P. Boley, Edward Trowbridge Collins, James J. Dykes, James Emory Foxx, Michael Francis Higgins, James Ward Keesey, Donald Eric McNair and Edwin Dibrell Williams, infielders; Roger Cramer, George William Haas, Spencer Anthony Harris, Edmund John Miller, James William Moore, Al Harry Simmons and Homer Wayne Summa, outfielders.

ST. LOUIS NATIONALS—Herman S. Bell, Jerome Dean, Fred Meloy Frankhouse, Albert Grabowski, Burleigh A. Grimes, Harold Augustin Haid, Jesse Joseph Haines, William Anthony Hallahan, Carmen Proctor Hill, Sylvester W. Johnson, Tony Charles Kaufmann, James Kendrick Lindsey, Clarence E. Mitchell, Charles Flint Rhem and William Sherdell, pitchers; Gus Rodney Mancuso, Earl Smith and James Wilson, catchers; Earl John Adams, James Leroy Bottomley, Edward Stephen Farrell, Frank Francis Frisch, Charles Magnus Gelbert, Andrew Aird High and Ernest R. Orsatti, infielders; Francis Raymond Blades, Taylor Lee Douthit, George A. Fisher, Charles James Hafey, John Leonard Martin, Creonti Puccinelli, Homer Hefner Peel and George Archibald Watkins, outfielders.

Leaders of 1930

BATTERS—Page 46

Player	Club	League	Pct. Or No.
William H. Terry	New York	National	.401
Al Harry Simmons	Philadelphia	American	.381

BASE STEALERS—Page 48

Hazen S. Cuyler	Chicago	National	37
Martin J. McManus	Detroit	American	23

SACRIFICE HITTERS—Page 49

Adam Comorosky	Pittsburgh	National	33
George William Haas	Philadelphia	American	33

SCORERS—Page 50

Charles Herbert Klein	Philadelphia	National	158
Al Harry Simmons	Philadelphia	American	152

MANUFACTURERS OF BASE HITS—Page 51

William H. Terry	New York	National	254
Urban John Hodapp	Cleveland	American	225

DEMON DOUBLERS—Page 53

Charles Herbert Klein	Philadelphia	National	59*
Urban John Hodapp	Cleveland	American	51

DEMON TRIPLERS—Page 54

Adam Comorosky	Pittsburgh	National	23
Earl Bryan Combs	New York	American	22

DEMON HOME RUNNISTS—Page 55

Lewis Robert Wilson	Chicago	National	56*
George Herman Ruth	New York	American	49

BATTING IN RUNS—Page 56

Lewis Robert Wilson	Chicago	National	190†
Henry Louis Gehrig	New York	American	174

DEMON WHIFFERS—Page 56

Lewis Robert Wilson	Chicago	National	84
James Emory Foxx	Philadelphia	American	66
Edward Morgan	Cleveland	American	66

DEMON WALKERS—Page 56

George Herman Ruth	New York	American	136
Lewis Robert Wilson	Chicago	National	105

STRIKE OUT KINGS—Page 57

Robert Moses Grove	Philadelphia	American	214
William Anthony Hallahan	St. Louis	National	177

*New National League Record.
†New major league record.

FAMOUS GAMES, FAMOUS PLAYERS, FAMOUS FEATS
THREE HOME RUNS IN GAME—
PAGE 61

Feat of hitting three home runs in one game was accomplished seven times in 1930, as follows:

American League—May 21, George Herman Ruth, New York, at Philadelphia; May 22, Henry Louis Gehrig, New York, at Philadelphia; July 3, Carl Nettles Reynolds, Chicago, at New York; August 19, Leon Allen Goslin, St. Louis, at Philadelphia; September 17, Howard Earl Averill, Cleveland, at Cleveland against Washington. Reynolds' home runs came in successive innings—the first, second and third.

National League—July 26, Lewis Robert Wilson, Chicago, at Philadelphia; August 31, Melvin T. Ott, New York, at New York against Boston.

Addenda to Part VII

Players Starting Their Major League Careers During the Season of 1930

(With birth dates of some of them)

APPLING, LUKE B.   Shortstop
Chicago A. L.

BEAN, BELVE BENTON   Pitcher
Cleveland A. L.
Born Alvarado, Tex., April 22, 1906

BEDNAR, ANDREW F.   Pitcher
Pittsburgh N. L.
Born Streator, Ill., August 16, 1909

BERGER, WALTER ANTONE   Outfielder
Boston N. L.
Born Chicago, Ill., October 10, 1905

BRIDGES, THOMAS   Pitcher
Detroit A. L.
Born Gordonsville, Tenn., Dec. 28, 1906

BROWN, ROBERT M.   Pitcher
Boston N. L.
Born Dorchester, Mass., April 1, 1911

BURNS, IRVING JOHN   Infielder
St. Louis A. L.
Born Cambridge, Mass., August 31, 1907

CAMPBELL, BRUCE   Outfielder
Chicago A. L.
Born Chicago, Ill., Oct. 20, 1909

CARAWAY, CECIL PAT   Pitcher
Chicago A. L.
Born Gordon, Texas, Sept. 26, 1908

CHAPMAN, WILLIAM BEN   Infielder
New York A. L.
Born Nashville, Tenn., Dec. 25, 1908

CHATHAM, CHARLES   Infielder
Boston N. L.
Born West Texas, Dec. 25, 1904

CHILD, HARRY   Pitcher
Washington A. L.

COOKE, ALLEN LINDSEY   Outfielder
New York A. L.
Born Swepsonville, N. C., June 23, 1907

CROUCH, JACK ALBERT   Catcher
St. Louis A. L.
Born Salisbury, N. C., October 12, 1905

CUCCINELLO, ANTHONY FRANK
                                 Infielder
Cincinnati N. L.
Born Astoria, N. Y., Nov. 8, 1907

DEAN, JEROME   Pitcher
St. Louis N. L.

DESAUTELS, EUGENE A.   Catcher
Detroit A. L.
Born Worcester, Mass., June 13, 1908

DETORE, GEORGE FRANCIS   Infielder
Cleveland A. L.
Born Utica, N. Y., November 11, 1908

DOLJACK, JOHN FRANK   Outfielder
Detroit A. L.

DUGAS, AUGUSTIN LEO   Outfielder
Pittsburgh N. L.
Born St. Jean de Mathe, Joliette, Quebec, March 24, 1909

ECKERT, ALBERT G.   Pitcher
Cincinnati N. L.
Born Milwaukee, Wis., May 17, 1909

FINN, NEAL   Infielder
Brooklyn N. L.

FISCHER, CHARLES WILLIAM   Pitcher
Washington A. L.
Born Medina, N. Y., Nov. 5, 1905

GALVIN, JAMES J.   Substitute
Boston A. L.

GLIATTO, SALVADOR MICHAEL   Pitcher
Cleveland A. L.
Born Chicago, Ill., May 7, 1905

GOMEZ, VERNON   Pitcher
New York A. L.
Born Rodeo, Cal., November 26, 1909

GREENBERT, HENRY   Infielder
Detroit, A. L.
Born New York City, January 1, 1911

GROSKLOSS, HOWARD H.   Substitute
Pittsburgh N. L.

GULLIC, TED   Outfielder
St. Louis A. L.
Born Oklahoma, January 2, 1907

HANSEN, ROY EMIL   Pitcher
Philadelphia N. L.
Born Chicago, Ill., February 21, 1907

HEALEY, FRANCIS   Catcher
New York N. L.

HENDERSON, WILLIAM   Pitcher
New York A. L.

HEVING, JOSEPH WILLIAM   Pitcher
New York N. L.
Born Covington, Ky., September 2, 1901

HIGGINS, MICHAEL FRANCIS   Infielder
Philadelphia A. L.
Born Red Oak, Texas, May 27, 1909

HOLSHOUSER, HERMAN ALEXANDER
                          Pitcher
St. Louis A. L.
Born Rockwell, N. C., Jan. 20, 1907

HUGHES, III, THOMAS FRANKLIN
                      Outfielder
Detroit A. L.
Born Emmett, Ark., August 6, 1907

JEFFRIES, IRVING FRANKLIN   Infielder
Chicago A. L.
Born Louisville, Ky., September 10, 1909

JOLLEY, SMEAD POWELL   Outfielder
Chicago A. L.
Born Wesson, Ark., January 14, 1904

KAHN, OWEN EARLE   Infielder
Boston N. L.
Born Richmond, Va., June 11, 1905

KARLON, WILLIAM JOHN   Catcher
New York A. L.
Born April 8, 1909

KLINE, ROBERT   Pitcher
Boston A. L.
Born Enterprise Ohio, December 1, 1910

KUHEL, JOSEPH   Infielder
Washington A. L.
Born Cleveland, Ohio, June 25, 1906

LANG, MARTIN J.   Pitcher
Pittsburgh N. L.
Born Hooper, Neb., September 27, 1907

LAWSON, ROXIE   Pitcher
Cleveland A. L.
Born Stockport, Iowa, April 13, 1909

LEE, HAL BURNHAM   Outfielder
Brooklyn N. L.
Born Ludlow, Miss., February 15, 1906

LEVEY, JAMES JULIUS   Infielder
St. Louis A. L.
Born Pittsburgh, Pa., September 13, 1907

LIEBHARDT JR., GLENN   Pitcher
Philadelphia A. L.
Born Cleveland, O., July 31, 1910

M'AFEE JR., WILLIAM FORT   Pitcher
Boston N. L.
Born September 7, 1907

M'EVOY, LOUIS ANTHONY   Pitcher
New York A. L.
Born Williamsburg, Kan., May 30, 1903

M'LEOD, SOULE JAMES   Infielder
Washington A. L.
Born Wilmot, Ark., September 12, 1910

MAHON, ALFRED GEORGE   Pitcher
Philadelphia A. L.
Born St. Edward, Neb., Sept. 23, 1910

MOORE, CARLOS WITMAN   Pitcher
Washington A. L.
Born Clinton, Tenn., August 13, 1907

MOORE, JAMES WILLIAM   Outfielder
Chicago A. L., Philadelphia A. L.
Born Paris, Tenn., April 24, 1903

MOORE, JOE GREGG   Outfielder
New York N. L.
Born Gause, Texas, December 25, 1908

MOSS, CHARLES MALCOLM   Pitcher
Chicago A. L.
Born April 18, 1905

MULLEAVY, GREGORY THOMAS   Infielder
Chicago A. L.
Born Detroit, Mich., September 25, 1907

MULRONEY, FRANK J.   Pitcher
Boston A. L.
Born Mallard, Iowa, April 8, 1906

NELSON, LYNN BIRCHARD   Pitcher
Chicago N. L.
Born February 24, 1907

OLIVER, THOMAS N.   Outfielder
Boston A. L.
Born Montgomery, Ala., January 15, 1904

PERKINS, CHARLES S.   Pitcher
Philadelphia A. L.
Born Birmingham, Ala., September 9, 1905

PHELPS, RAYMOND C.   Pitcher
Brooklyn N. L.
Born Dunlap, Tenn., December 11, 1903

PHILLIPS, ALBERT ABERNETHY   Pitcher
Philadelphia N. L.
Born Newton, N. C., May 25, 1904

POWELL, ALVIN J.   Outfielder
Washington A. L.
Born Silver Springs, Md., July 15, 1908

PUCCINELLI, CREONTI   Outfielder
St. Louis N. L.
Born San Francisco, Cal., June 22, 1907

REESE, JIMMIE   Infielder
New York A. L.
Born Los Angeles, Cal., October 1, 1905

RENSA, GEORGE   Catcher
Detroit A. L., Philadelphia N. L.
Born Parsons, Pa., September 29, 1901

RIDDLE, JOHN L.   Catcher
Chicago A. L.
Born Clinton, S. C., October 3, 1905

ROSENBERG, HARRY   Outfielder
New York N. L.

RYAN, JOHN C.   Infielder
Chicago A. L.

SAMUELS, JOSEPH JONAH   Pitcher
Detroit A. L.
Born Scranton, Pa., March 21, 1908

SEEDS, ROBERT I.   Outfielder
Cleveland A. L.
Born Ringgold, Texas, February 24, 1908

SHERLOCK, JOHN C.   Infielder
Philadelphia N. L.
Born Buffalo, N. Y., October 26, 1904

SHEVLIN, JAMES C.   Infielder
Detroit A. L.

SLADE, GORDON   Infielder
Brooklyn N. L.

SMALL, CHARLES A.   Outfielder
Boston A. L.

SMITH, ERNEST H.   Infielder
Chicago A. L.
Born Paterson, N. J., October 11, 1901

SPOTTS, JAMES   Catcher
Philadelphia N. L.

SPRINZ, JOSEPH   Catcher
Cleveland A. L.
Born St. Louis, Mo., August 3, 1902

STILES, ROLLAND   Pitcher
St. Louis A. L.
Born Ratcliff, Ark., November 17, 1907

STORTI, LIN   Infielder
St. Louis A. L.
Born Santa Monica, Cal., Dec. 24, 1906

SUHR, AUGUST   Infielder
Pittsburgh N. L.
Born San Francisco, Cal., January 3, 1906

TEACHOUT, ARTHUR JOHN   Pitcher
Chicago N. L.
Born Los Angeles, Cal., February 27,
1904

TREADAWAY, RAY   Outfielder
Washington A. L.

VOSMIK, JOSEPH FRANKLIN   Outfielder
Cleveland A. L.
Born Cleveland, O., April 4, 1910

WALTER, JAMES BERNARD   Pitcher
Pittsburgh N. L.
Born August 15, 1908

WARNEKE, LONIE   Pitcher
Chicago N. L.
Born Mt. Ida, Ark., March 17, 1909

WARSTLER, HAROLD B.   Infielder
Boston A. L.

WATKINS, GEORGE ARCHIBALD
Outfielder
St. Louis N. L.
Born Palestine, Tex., June 4, 1902

WATSON, JOHN   Infielder
Detroit A. L.
Born Tazewell, Va., January 16, 1909

WEHDE, WILBUR   Pitcher
Chicago A. L.

WERBER, WILLIAM   Infielder
New York A. L.
Born Berwyn, Maryland, June 20, 1908

WILLINGHAM, HUGH   Infielder
Chicago A. L.

WILLIAMS, EDWIN DIBRELL   Infielder
Philadelphia A. L.
Born Greenbrier, Ark., January 19, 1911

WINEGARNER, RALPH LEE   Infielder
Cleveland A. L.
Born Benton, Kan., October 29, 1909

WINSETT, JOHN THOMAS   Outfielder
Boston A. L.
Born McKenzie, Tenn., Nov. 24, 1909

WISE, HUGH EDWARD   Catcher
Detroit A. L.
Born Campbellsville, Ky., March 9, 1907

WOOD JR., CHARLES ASHER   Pitcher
Pittsburgh N. L.
Born Spartanburg, S. C., January 13, 1910

WYSONG, HARLAN   Pitcher
Cincinnati N. L.

Baseball Cyclopedia

For Season of 1931—56th Year for
National League and 31st for the American

The Pennant Races

American League

Club	Won	Lost	Pc.	Manager
Philadelphia	107	45	.704	Connie Mack
New York	94	59	.614	Joseph Vincent McCarthy
Washington	92	62	.597	Walter Perry Johnson
Cleveland	78	76	.506	Roger Peckinpaugh
St. Louis	63	91	.409	William Killefer Jr.
Boston	62	90	.408	John Francis Collins
Detroit	61	93	.396	Stanley Raymond Harris
Chicago	56	97	.366	Owen J. Bush
Totals	613	613	.500	

National League

Club	Won	Lost	Pc.	Manager
St. Louis	101	53	.656	Charles E. Street
New York	87	65	.572	John Joseph McGraw
Chicago	84	70	.545	Rogers Hornsby
Brooklyn	79	73	.520	Wilbert Robinson
Pittsburgh	75	79	.487	Jewel Ens
Philadelphia	66	88	.429	Burton Edwin Shotton
Boston	64	90	.416	William Boyd McKechnie
Cincinnati	58	96	.377	Daniel Philip Howley
Totals	614	614	.500	

It was the ninth pennant for the Philadelphia American League club, the fourth for the St. Louis National League club. In the 28th World's Series between the National and American Leagues, St. Louis won four games to Philadelphia's three. The result of this set made the following changes in the dope of the classics. (See page 100.):

Series Won—American League	17
National League	11
Cities having World's Champion Teams	
St. Louis	2
Cities competing for World's Series	
Championship—Philadelphia	9
St. Louis	4

Record of games won and lost by World's Series clubs: Philadelphia Americans, won 24; lost 19; percentage .558; St. Louis Nationals, won 10, lost 14, percentage .417.

Managers' records in World's Series: Connie Mack, Series won 5, Series lost 3; games won 24, games lost, 19. Charles E. Street, Series won 1, series lost, 1; games won 6, games lost, 7.

The players on the pennant winning teams during the year were as follows: PHILADELPHIA AMERICANS—Sollie M. Carter, George Livingston Earnshaw, Robert Moses Grove, Waite Charles Hoyt, Lewis B. Krausse, Henry McDonald, Leroy Mahaffey, James N. Peterson, Edwin Americus Rommel, William Shores and George E. Walberg, pitchers; Gordon Stanley Cochrane, John A. Heving and Joseph Palmisano, catchers; Max Frederick Bishop, John Peter Boley, James Joseph Dykes, James Emory Foxx, Donald Eric McNair, Philip Julius Todt and Edwin Dibrell Williams, infielders; Roger Cramer, Louis Klopsche Finney, George William Haas, Edmund John Miller, James William Moore, Al Harry Simmons, outfielders.

ST. LOUIS NATIONALS—Paul Derringer, Burleigh A. Grimes, Jesse Joseph Haines, William Anthony Hallahan, Tony Charles Kaufmann, Sylvester W. Johnson, James Kendrick Lindsey, Charles Flint Rhem and Allyn McClelland Stout, pitchers; Miguel Angel Gonzales, Gus Rodney Mancuso, Charles E. Street and James Wilson, catchers; Earl John Adams, Joseph Anthony Benes, James Leroy Bottomley, James Anthony Collins, Lee Cunningham, Edward Alberts Delker, D'Arcy Raymond Flowers, Frank Francis Frisch, Charles Magnus Gelbert, Andrew Aird High, infielders; Francis Raymond Blades, Taylor Lee Douthit, Charles James Hafey, Oliver Joel Hunt, John Leonard Martin, Ernest R. Orsatti, Walter Henry Roettger and George Archibald Watkins, outfielders.

Leaders of 1931

BATTERS—Page 46

Player	Club	League	Pct. Or No.
Al Harry Simmons	Philadelphia	American	.390
Charles James Hafey	St. Louis	National	.349

BASE STEALERS—Page 48

William Ben Chapman	New York	American	61
Frank Francis Frisch	St. Louis	National	28

SACRIFICE HITTERS—Page 49

Frederick E. Maguire	Boston	National	31
George William Haas	Philadelphia	American	19

SCORERS—Page 50

Henry Louis Gehrig	New York	American	163
Charles Herbert Klein	Philadelphia	National	121
William H. Terry	New York	National	121

MANUFACTURERS OF BASE HITS—Page 51

Lloyd James Waner	Pittsburgh	National	214
Henry Louis Gehrig	New York	American	211

DEMON DOUBLERS—Page 53

Earl Webb	Boston	American	67*
Earl J. Adams	St. Louis	National	46

DEMON TRIPLERS—Page 54

William H. Terry	New York	National	20
Roy Johnson	Detroit	American	19

DEMON HOME RUNNISTS—Page 55

Henry Louis Gehrig	New York	American	46
George Herman Ruth	New York	American	46
Charles Herbert Klein	Philadelphia	National	31

BATTING IN RUNS—Page 56

Henry Louis Gehrig	New York	American	184**
Charles Herbert Klein	Philadelphia	National	121

DEMON WHIFFERS—Page 56

Henry N. Cullop	Cincinnati	National	86
James Emory Foxx	Philadelphia	American	84

DEMON WALKERS—Page 56

George Herman Ruth	New York	American	128
Melvin Thomas Ott	New York	National	80

STRIKE OUT KINGS—Page 57

Robert Moses Grove	Philadelphia	American	175
William Anthony Hallahan	St. Louis	National	159

*New Major League Record.
**New American League Record.

FAMOUS GAMES, FAMOUS PLAYERS, FAMOUS FEATS

THREE HOME RUNS IN GAMES
PAGE 61

Feat of hitting three home runs in one game was accomplished twice in 1931, as follows:

National League—April 24, Rogers Hornsby, Chicago, at Pittsburgh (third, fifth and sixth innings); June 24, George Archibald Watkins, St. Louis, at Philadelphia (fourth, sixth, and ninth innings). Each player attained his trio of circuit hits in successive appearances at the plate.

NO-HIT GAMES
PAGE 82

Two no-hit, no-run games were pitched in 1931, as follows:

American League—April 29, Wesley Cheek Ferrell, Cleveland, at Cleveland, against St. Louis, score 9 to 0; August 8, Robert J. Burke, Washington, at Washington, against Boston, score 5 to 0. Three errors were made behind Ferrell, who walked 3 and fanned 8. Perfect support was accorded Burke, who walked 5 and fanned 8.

Addenda to Part VII
Players Starting Their Major League Careers During the Season of 1931
(With birth dates of most of them)

ADAIR, JAMES AUDREY   Infielder
Chicago N. L.
Born Waxahachie, Tex., January 25, 1908

ADAMS, ROBERT   Pitcher
Philadelphia N. L.
Born Birmingham, Ala., January 20, 1910

ANDREWS, IVY PAUL   Pitcher
New York A. L.
Born Dora, Ala., May 6, 1907

ANDRUS, WILLIAM MORGAN   Infielder
Washington A. L.
Born Beaumont, Tex., July 25, 1907

ARLETT, RUSSELL P.   Outfielder
Philadelphia N. L.
Born Oakland, Cal., 1899

BARTON, VINCENT   Outfielder
Chicago N. L.
Born Edmonton, Alberta, 1908

BENES, JOSEPH ANTHONY   Infielder
St. Louis N. L.
Born Long Island City, N. Y., January 8, 1901

BOLTON W. CLIFF   Catcher
Washington A. L.
Born High Point, N. C., April 10, 1907

BOWLER, GRANT TIERNEY   Pitcher
Chicago A. L.
Born Denver Col., October 24, 1909

BROWER, LOUIS   Shortstop
Detroit A. L.
Born Cleveland, Ohio, June 6, 1907

CARTER, SOLLIE M.   Pitcher
Philadelphia A. L.
Born Picayune, Miss., December 23, 1909

COHEN, ALBERT H.   Outfielder
Brooklyn N. L.
Born New York City, December 25,1910

COLLIER, ORLIN EDWARD   Pitcher
Detroit A. L.
Born East Prairie, Mo., February 17, 1908

COLLINS, JAMES ANTHONY
First Baseman
St. Louis N. L.
Born Altoona, Pa., March 30, 1905

CONNATSER, BRUCE M.   First Baseman
Cleveland A. L.
Born Sevierville, Tenn., September 19, 1905

CONNELL, EUGENE   Catcher
Philadelphia N. L.

COONEY, ROBERT DANIEL   Pitcher
St. Louis A. L.
Born Glens Falls, N. Y., July 12, 1907

CRAGHEAD, HOWARD OLIVER   Pitcher
Cleveland A. L.
Born Fresno, Cal., May 25 1908

CREEDEN, PATRICK F.   Substitute
Boston A. L.

CUNNINGHAM, LEE   Infielder
St. Louis N. L.
Born Mesquite, Tex., January 17, 1908

DERRINGER, PAUL   Pitcher
St. Louis N. L.
Born Springfield, Ky., October 17, 1906

DREESEN, WILLIAM   Infielder
Boston N. L.
Born New York City, July 26, 1904

ENGLISH, GILBERT RAYMOND   Infielder
New York N. L.
Born Trinity, N. C., July 2, 1910

FALLENSTIN, EDWARD JOSEPH   Pitcher
Philadelphia N. L.
Born Newark, N. J., December 22, 1908

FINNEY, HAROLD WILSON   Catcher
Pittsburgh N. L.
Born Lafayette, Ala., August 13, 1910

FINNEY, LOUIS KLOPSCHE   Outfielder
Philadelphia A. L.
Born Buffalo, Ala., August 13, 1910

FITZGERALD, RAYMOND FRANCIS
                        Outfielder
Cincinnati N. L.
Born Westfield, Mass., December 5, 1906

FRAZIER, VICTOR   Pitcher
Chicago N. L.
Born Houston, Tex., August 5, 1906

GALLIVAN, PHILIP J.   Pitcher
Brooklyn N. L.
Born Seattle, Wash., May 29, 1907

GARLAND, LOUIS LYMAN   Pitcher
Chicago A. L.
Born Archie, Mo., July 16, 1905

GARRITY, FRANK JOSEPH   Catcher
Chicago, A. L.
Born Boston, Mass., February 4, 1908

GRIMES, EDWARD ADELBERT   Infielder
St. Louis A. L.
Born Chicago, Ill., September 8, 1905

GRUBE, FRANK THOMAS   Catcher
Chicago A. L.
Born Easton, Pa., January 7, 1909

HALE, ARNELL ODELL   Infielder
Cleveland A. L.
Born Hosston, La., August 10, 1909

HEATH, MINOR WILSON   First Baseman
Cincinnati N. L.
Born Toledo, Ohio, October 30, 1903

HERBERT, WALLACE PREUCHER   Pitcher

St. Louis A. L.
Born Lake Charles, La., August 24, 1909

HERMAN, WILLIAM   Infielder
Chicago N. L.
Born New Albany, Ind., July 7, 1909

HILCHER, JR., WALTER FRANK   Pitcher
Cincinnati N. L.
Born Chicago, Ill., February 28, 1909

HILDEBRAND, ORAL CLYDE   Pitcher
Cleveland A. L.
Born Indianapolis, Ind., April 13, 1907

HOAG, MYRIL   Outfielder
New York A. L.
Born Davis, Cal., March 9, 1909

HUNT, OLIVER JOEL   Outfielder
St. Louis N. L.
Born Texaco, N. M., October 11, 1905

JENSEN, FORREST   Outfielder
Pittsburgh N. L.

JURGES, WILLIAM FREDERICK   Infielder
Chicago N. L.
Born New York City, May 9, 1908

KLOZA, JOHN CLARENCE   Outfielder
St. Louis A. L.
Born Milwaukee, Wis., November 2,
1904

KOSTER, FRED C.   Outfielder
Philadelphia N. L.
Born Louisville, Ky., December 21, 1906

KRAUSSE, LEWIS B.   Pitcher
Philadelphia A. L.
Born Media, Pa., June 8, 1912

KREEVICH, MIKE   Outfielder
Chicago N. L.
Born Mount Olive, Ill., June 10, 1910

LOMBARDI, ERNESTO JELLOPI   Catcher
Brooklyn N. L.
Born Oakland, Cal., April 6, 1908

LUCAS, JOHN CHARLES   Outfielder
Boston A. L.
Born Glen Carbon, Ill., February 10, 1908

M'CLANAHAN, PETE   Outfielder
Pittsburgh N. L.
Born Cold Springs, Tex., October 24, 1906

M'DONALD, HENRY   Pitcher
Philadelphia A. L.
Born Santa Monica, Cal., January 16, 1911

M'LAUGHLIN, JUSTIN   Pitcher
Boston A. L.

M'WILLIAMS, WILLIAM HENRY
                       Outfielder
Boston A. L.

MALLON, LESLIE CLYDE   Infielder
Philadelphia N. L.
Born Dallas, Tex., November 21, 1907

MARQUARDT, ALBERT LUDWIG   Infielder
Boston A. L.
Born Toledo, Ohio, September 22, 1905

MARSHALL, WILLIAM   Infielder
Boston A. L.

MASTERS, WALTER THOMAS   Pitcher
Washington A. L.
Born Pen Argyl, Pa., March 29, 1907

MATTINGLY, L. EARL   Pitcher
Brooklyn N. L.
Born Charles County, Md., November 4, 1904

MOONEY, JAMES IRVING   Pitcher
New York N. L.
Born Mooresburg, Tenn., September 4, 1906

MOORE, JR., EUGENE   Outfielder
Cincinnati N. L.
Born Lancaster, Tex., August 26, 1909

MUNGO, VAN L.   Pitcher
Brooklyn N. L.
Born Pageland, S. C., June 9, 1911.

MURPHY, WALTER JOSEPH   Pitcher
Boston A. L.
Born New York City, September 27, 1909

NORMAN, WILLIS PATRICK   Outfielder
Chicago A. L.
Born St. Louis, Mo., July 16, 1910

OLSON, MARVIN CLEMENT   Infielder
Boston A. L.
Born Gayville, S. D., May 28, 1907

OWEN, MARVIN JAMES   Infielder
Detroit A. L.
Born San Jose, Cal., March 22, 1908

PALMISANO, JOSEPH   Catcher
Philadelphia A. L.
Born West Point, Ga., November 19, 1904

PETERSON, JAMES N.   Pitcher
Philadelphia A. L.
Born Philadelphia, Pa., August 18, 1908

PHELPS, ERNEST GORDON   Catcher
Washington A. L.
Born Odenton, Md., April 19, 1908

PICKERING, URBANE   Infielder
Boston A. L.
Born Modesto, Cal., 1903

PIET, ANTHONY F.   Infielder
Pittsburgh N. L.
Born Chicago, Ill., December 7, 1906

PLANETA, EMIL   Pitcher
New York N. L.
Born Middletown, Conn., 1910

QUELLICH, GEORGE WILLIAM
                       Outfielder
Detroit A. L.
Born Johnsville, Cal., February 10, 1903

REIS, ROBERT JOSEPH THOMAS
                       Infielder
Brooklyn N. L.
Born New York City, January 2, 1910

ROLFE, ROBERT ABIAL   Infielder
New York A. L.
Born Penacook, N. H., October 17, 1908

ROSENFELD, MAX   Outfielder
Brooklyn N. L.
Born New York City, December 23, 1904

RYE, EUGENE   Outfielder
Boston A. L.
Born Chicago, Ill., November 15, 1908

SCALZI, JOHN   Infielder
Boston N. L.

SCHESLER, CHARLES   Pitcher
Philadelphia N. L.

SCHULMERICH, WESLEY   Outfielder
Boston N. L.

SCHUMACHER, HAROLD HENRY   Pitcher
New York N. L.
Born Hinckley, N. Y., November 23, 1910

SHIVER, IVEY MERWIN   Outfielder
Detroit A. L.
Sylvester, Ga., January 23, 1907

SIMONS, MELBURN   Outfielder
Chicago A. L.
Born Carlyle, Ill., July 1, 1902

SMITH, JOHN MARSHALL   First Baseman
Boston A. L.
Born Washington, D. C., September 27,
1906

STANTON, GEORGE W.   First Baseman
St. Louis A. L.
Born Stantonsburg, N. C., June 19, 1906

STEINECKE, WILLIAM ROBERT   Catcher
Pittsburgh N. L.
Born Cincinnati, Ohio, February 7, 1907

STEVENS, ROBERT JORDAN   Shortstop
Philadelphia N. L.
Born Chevy Chase, Md., April 17, 1910

STORIE, HOWARD EDWARD   Catcher
Boston A. L.
Born Pittsfield, Mass., May 15, 1911

STOUT, ALLYN McCLELLAND   Pitcher
St. Louis N. L.
Born Peoria, Ill., October 31, 1904

STUMPF, GEORGE FREDERICK   Outfielder
Boston A. L.
Born New Orleans, La., December 15,
1910

SULLIVAN, WILLIAM J.   Infielder
Chicago A. L.
Born Chicago, Ill., October 23, 1910

URBANSKI, WILLIAM MICHAEL
                               Infielder
Boston N. L.
Born Linoleumville, N. Y., June 15, 1904

VERGEZ, JOHNNY LOUIS   Infielder
New York N. L.
Born Oakland, Cal., July 9, 1906

WADDEY, FRANK ORUM   Outfielder
St. Louis A. L.
Born Memphis, Tenn., August 21, 1905

WALKER, FRED   Outfielder
New York A. L.
Born Villa Ricka, Ala., September 24,
1910

WALKER, GERALD H.   Outfielder
Detroit A. L.
Born Gulfport, Miss., March 19, 1909

WALKER, HARVEY W.   Outfielder
Detroit A. L.
Born Gulfport, Miss., August 17, 1907

WALTERS, WILLIAM HENRY   Infielder
Boston N. L.
Born Philadelphia, Pa., 1910

WATT, FRANK MARION   Pitcher
Philadelphia N. L.
Born Washington, D. C., December 15,
1903

WEAVER, MONTE MORTON   Pitcher
Washington A. L.
Born Holton, N. C., June 15, 1906

WILSON, CHARLES WALKER   Infielder
Boston N. L.
Born Clinton, S. C, January 5, 1906

WORTHINGTON, ROBERT   Outfielder
Boston N. L.
Born Alhambra, Cal., April 24, 1906

YOUNG, RUSSELL CHARLES   Catcher
St. Louis A. L.

Baseball Cyclopedia
For Season of 1932—57th Year for
National League and 32nd for the American

The Pennant Races
American League

Club	Won	Lost	Pc.	Manager
New York	107	47	.695	Joseph Vincent McCarthy
Philadelphia	94	60	.610	Connie Mack
Washington	93	61	.604	Walter Perry Johnson
Cleveland	87	65	.572	Roger Peckinpaugh
Detroit	76	75	.503	Stanley Raymond Harris
St. Louis	63	91	.409	William Killefer Jr.
Chicago	49	102	.325	Lewis A. Fonseca
Boston	43	111	.279	John Francis Collins and Martin J. McManus
Totals	612	612	.500	

National League

Club	Won	Lost	Pc.	Manager
Chicago	90	64	.584	Rogers Hornsby and Charles J. Grimm
Pittsburgh	86	68	.558	George Gibson
Brooklyn	81	73	.526	Max G. Carey
Philadelphia	78	76	.506	Burton Edwin Shotton
Boston	77	77	.500	William Boyd McKechnie
New York	72	82	.468	John Joseph McGraw and William Harold Terry
St. Louis	72	82	.468	Charles E. Street
Cincinnati	60	94	.390	Daniel Philip Howley
Totals	616	616	.500	

Martin J. McManus took charge of Red Sox on June 20.
Charles John Grimm took charge of Cubs on August 4.
William Harold Terry took charge of Giants on June 4.

It was the twelfth pennant for the Chicago National League club, the seventh for the New York American League club. In the 29th World's Series between the National and American League clubs, New York won all four games. The result of this set made the following changes in the dope of the classics. (See page 100.):

Series Won—American League	18
National League	11
Cities having World's Champion Teams	
New York	9
Cities competing for World's Series	
Championship—New York	19
Chicago	12

Record of games won and lost by World's Series clubs: New York Americans, won 22; lost 15; percentage .595; Chicago Nationals, won 19, lost 28, percentage .404.

Managers' records in World's Series: Joseph Vincent McCarthy, Series won 1, Series lost 1; games won 5, games lost, 4. Charles John Grimm, games lost 4, series lost 1.

The players on the pennant winning teams during the year were as follows: NEW YORK AMERICANS—John Thomas Allen, Ivy Paul Andrews, Walter George Brown, Charles Devens, Vernon Gomez, Henry Ward Johnson, Daniel Knowles MacFayden, William Wiley Moore, John J. Murphy, Herbert J. Pennock, George William Pipgras, John Gordon Rhodes, Charles Herbert Ruffing and Edwin L. Wells, pitchers; William Dickey, Joseph Charles Glenn, Arndt Jorgens and Edward David Phillips, catchers; Frank Peter Crosetti, Edward S. Farrell, Henry Louis Gehrig, Lynford Hobart Lary, Anthony Michael Lazerri, Jack Saltsgaver, Leroy Schalk and Joseph Wheeler Sewell, infielders; Samuel Dewey Byrd, William Ben Chapman, Earl Bryan Combs, Allen Lindsey Cooke, Myril Hoag and George Herman Ruth, outfielders.

CHICAGO NATIONALS—Edward J. Baecht, Guy Bush, Burley Grimes Leroy Herrmann, Perce Lay Malone, Frank Spuriell May, Louis N. Newsom, Charles Henry Root, Robert Eldredge Smith, Lyle F. Tinning, Lonie Warneke and Charles Carroll Yerkes, pitchers; Charles Leo Hartnett, Ralston B. Hemsley and James Wren Taylor, catchers; Elwood English, Charles John Grimm, Stanley Camfield Hack, William Herman, Rogers Hornsby, William Frederick Jurges, Mark Antony Koenig and Harry Warren Taylor, infielders; Vincent Barton, Hazen S. Cuyler, Joseph Franklin Demaree, Marvin John Gudat, John Francis Moore, Lancelot Clayton Richbourg, Jackson Riggs Stephenson, Dan Taylor, outfielders.

Leaders of 1932

BATTERS—Page 46

Player	Club	League	Pct. Or No.
Frank J. O'Doul	Brooklyn	National	368
David Dale Alexander	Detroit–Boston	American	367

BASE STEALERS—Page 48

William Ben Chapman	New York	American	38
Charles Herbert Klein	Philadelphia	National	20

SACRIFICE HITTERS—Page 49

Richard Bartell	Philadelphia	National	35
George William Haas	Philadelphia	American	27

SCORERS—Page 50

Charles Herbert Klein	Philadelphia	National	152
James Emory Foxx	Philadelphia	American	151

MANUFACTURERS OF BASE HITS—Page 51

Charles Herbert Klein	Philadelphia	National	226
Al Harry Simmons	Philadelphia	American	216

DEMON DOUBLERS—Page 53

Paul Clee Waner	Pittsburgh	National	62*
Donald Eric McNair	Philadelphia	American	47

DEMON TRIPLERS—Page 54

Floyd Caves Herman	Cincinnati	National	19
Joseph Cronin	Washington	American	18

DEMON HOME RUNNISTS—Page 55

James Emory Foxx	Philadelphia	American	58
Charles Herbert Klein	Philadelphia	National	38
Melvin Thomas Ott	New York	National	38

BATTING IN RUNS—Page 56

| James Emory Foxx | Philadelphia | American | 169 |
| Frank O'Donnell Hurst | Philadelphia | National | 143 |

DEMON WHIFFERS—Page 56

| Bruce Douglas Campbell | Chicago–St. Louis | American | 104 |
| Lewis Robert Wilson | Brooklyn | National | 85 |

DEMON WALKERS—Page 56

| George Herman Ruth | New York | American | 130 |
| Melvin Thomas Ott | New York | National | 100 |

STRIKE OUT KINGS—Page 57

| Jerome Herman Dean | St. Louis | National | 191 |
| Charles Herbert Ruffing | New York | American | 190 |

*New National League Record.

FAMOUS GAMES, FAMOUS PLAYERS, FAMOUS FEATS
FOUR HOME RUNS IN GAME
PAGE 59

HENRY LOUIS GEHRIG, New York Americans, hit four home runs in succession in game of June 3 at Philadelphia, obtaining these hits first four times he batted and driving in 6 runs with them. Fifth time up GEHRIG grounded out and sixth time up he flied out.

THREE HOME RUNS IN GAMES
PAGE 61

Feat of hitting three home runs in one game was accomplished five times in 1932, as follows:

AMERICAN LEAGUE—June 23, Leon Allen Goslin, St. Louis, at St. Louis against New York; July 9, William Ben Chapman, New York, at New York against Detroit; July 10, James Emory Foxx, Philadelphia, at Cleveland (18-inning game); July 15, Al Harry Simmons, Philadelphia, at Philadelphia against Detroit (11 inning game).

SIX HIT MANUFACTURERS
PAGE 71

ROGER CRAMER, Philadelphia Americans, made six singles in six times at bat at Chicago on June 20.

Addenda to Part VII

Players Starting Their Major League Careers During the Season of 1932

(With birth dates of most of them)

ALLEN, JOHN THOMAS   Pitcher
New York A. L.
Born Lenoir, N. C., September 30, 1908

ANDERSON, HAROLD   *Outfielder
Chicago A. L.
Born St. Louis, Mo., February 10, 1906

BERGER, LOUIS W.   Infielder
Cleveland A. L.
Born Baltimore, Md., May 13, 1910

BIGGS, CHARLES   Pitcher
Chicago A. L.

BLUEGE, OTTO K.   Infielder
Cincinnati N. L.

BOERNER, LAURENCE HYER   Pitcher
Boston A. L.
Born Staunton, Va., January 21, 1908

BOWMAN, JOSEPH EMIL   Pitcher
Philadelphia A. L.
Born Kansas City, Mo., June 17, 1910

BRENZEL, WILLIAM RICHARD   Catcher
Pittsburgh N. L.
Born Oakland, Cal., March 3, 1910

BRUBAKER, WILBUR LEE   Infielder
Pittsburgh N. L.
Born Cleveland, O., November 7, 1910

CAIN, MERRITT PATRICK   Pitcher
Philadelphia A. L.
Born Macon, Ga., April 5, 1908

CARLETON, JAMES OTTO   Pitcher
St. Louis N. L.
Born Comanche, Tex., August 19, 1906

CHAMBERLAIN, WILLIAM VINCENT
                                    Pitcher

Chicago A. L.
Born Stoughton, Mass., April 21, 1912

CIHOCKI, EDWARD J.   Infielder
Philadelphia A. L.
Born Wilmington, Del., May 9, 1909

COLEMAN, EDWARD PARKE   Outfielder
Philadelphia A. L.
Born Canby, Ore., December 1, 1906

CROSETTI, FRANK PETER   Infielder
New York A. L.
Born San Francisco, Cal., Oct. 4, 1910

DAGLIA, PETE GEORGE   Pitcher
Chicago A. L.
Born Napa, Cal., February 29, 1907

DAVIS, HARRY ALBERT   Infielder
Detroit A. L.
Born Shreveport, La., May 7, 1910

DELANCEY, WILLIAM P.   Catcher
St. Louis N. L.
Born Greensboro, N. C., Nov. 28, 1912

DEMAREE, JOSEPH F.   Outfielder
Chicago N. L.
Born Woodland, Cal., June 10, 1910

DESHONG, JAMES   Outfielder
Philadelphia A. L.
Born Harrisburg, Pa., Nov. 30, 1910

DEVENS, CHARLES   Pitcher
New York A. L.
Born Milton, Mass., January 1, 1910

ECKHARDT, OSCAR G.   Outfielder
Boston N. L.
Born Yorktown, Tex., Dec. 3, 1903

EDELEN, JR., EDWARD J.   Pitcher

Washington A. L.
Born Bryantown, Md., March 16, 1912

ENGLISH, CHARLES D.   Infielder
Chicago A. L.
Born Darlington, S. C., April 8, 1909

EVANS, WILLIAM ARTHUR   Pitcher
Chicago A. L.

FIEBER, CLARENCE   Pitcher
Chicago A. L.
Born San Francisco, Cal., Sept. 4, 1913

FREITAS, TONY   Pitcher
Philadelphia A. L.

FRIEDRICHS, ROBERT G.   Pitcher
Washington A. L.
Born Cincinnati, Ohio, August 30, 1910

GALLAGHER, EDWARD M.   Pitcher
Boston A. L.
Born Boston, Mass., Nov., 28, 1911

GARMS, DEBS   Infielder
St. Louis, A. L.
Born Bangs, Tex., June 26, 1908

GLENN, JOSEPH CHARLES   Catcher
New York A. L.
Born Dickson City, Pa., Nov. 9, 1909

GOLDSTEIN, ISIDORE   Pitcher
Detroit A. L.
Born New York City, June 8, 1908

GRABOWSKI, REGINALD J.   Pitcher
Philadelphia N. L.
Born Syracuse, N. Y., July 16, 1909

GREGORY, PAUL EDWIN   Pitcher
Chicago A. L.
Born Webster County, Miss., July 9, 1908

HACK, STANLEY C.   Infielder
Chicago N. L.
Born Sacramento, Cal., Dec. 6, 1909

HERRMANN, LEROY   Pitcher
Chicago N. L.
Born February 27, 1908

HOLLAND, ROBERT C.   Outfielder

Boston N. L.
Born Nashville, N. C., October 12, 1904

JONES, ARTHUR LENOX   Pitcher
Brooklyn N. L.
Bosn Kershaw, S. C., February 7, 1910

KINGDON, WESTCOTT W.   Infielder
Washington A. L.
Born Los Angeles, Cal., July 4, 1901

KNOTHE, GEORGE B.   Infielder
Philadelphia N. L.
Born Passaic, N. J., January 12, 1900

KNOTHE, WILFRED E.   Infielder
Boston N. L.
Born Passaic, N. J., May 1, 1905

KOENECKE, LEONARD G.   Outfielder
New York N. L.
Born Baraboo, Wis., January 18, 1907

KOWALIK, FABIAN L.   Pitcher
Chicago A. L.
Born Falls City, Tex., April 22, 1910

LUCAS, JOHN CHARLES   Outfielder
Boston A. L.
Born Glen Carbon, Ill., February 10, 1908

LAWRENCE, WILLIAM H.   Outfielder
Detroit A. L.
Born San Mateo, Cal., March 11, 1909

LEHENY, REGIS   Pitcher
Boston A. L.

MADJESKI, EDWARD W.   Catcher
Philadelphia A. L.
Born Far Rockaway, N. Y., July 24, 1909

MAPLE, HOWARD   Catcher
Washington A. L.
Born Adrian, Mo., July 20, 1906

MARROW, CHARLES K.   Pitcher
Detroit A. L.
Born Tarboro, N. C., August 29, 1909

M'KEITHAN, EMMET J.   Pitcher
Philadelphia A. L.
Born Bostic, N. C., November 2, 1910

M'LARNEY, ARTHUR J.   Infielder
New York N. L.
Born Fort Worden, Wash., Dec. 20, 1909

M'LAUGHLIN, JIMMY   Infielder
St. Louis A. L.
Born St. Louis, Mo., Jan. 3, 1902

M'NAUGHTON, GORDON J.   Pitcher
Boston A. L.
Born Chicago, Ill., July 31, 1910

MEDWICK, JOSEPH M.   Outfielder
St. Louis N. L.
Born Carteret, N. J., Nov. 24, 1911

MICHAELS, JOHN JOSEPH   Pitcher
Boston A. L.
Born Bridgeport, Conn., July 10, 1907

MOON, LEO   Pitcher
Cleveland A. L.

MORRISSEY, JOSEPH A.   Infielder
Cincinnati N. L.
Born Warren, R. I., January 16, 1905

MURPHY, JOHN J.   Pitcher
New York A. L.
Born New York City, July 14, 1908

MUSSER, WILLIAM D.   Infielder
Washington A. L.
Born Zion, Pa., March 5, 1910

PADDEN, THOMAS F.   Catcher
Pittsburgh N. L.
Born Manchester, N. H., Oct. 6, 1908

PATTERSON, HENRY J.   Catcher
Boston A. L.
Born San Francisco, Cal., July 17, 1908

PEARSON, MARCELLUS M.   Pitcher
Cleveland A. L.
Born Oakland, Cal., Sept. 2, 1902

PEPPER, RAYMOND W.   Outfielder
St. Louis N. L.
Born Decatur, Ala., August 5, 1906

PIPGRAS, EDWARD   Pitcher
Brooklyn N. L.
Born Slayton, Minn., June 15, 1904

POLLI, LOUIS AMERICO   Pitcher
St. Louis A. L.
Born Goddart, Vt., July 9, 1903

POSER, JOHN FALK   Pitcher
Chicago A. L.
Born Columbia, Wis., March 10, 1910

POWERS, ELLIS FOREE   Outfielder
Cleveland A. L.
Born Crestwood, Ky., March 2, 1906

PYTLAK, FRANK A.   Catcher
Cleveland A. L.
Born Buffalo, N. Y., July 30, 1908

RAGLAND, FRANK R.   Pitcher
Washington A. L.
Born Paris, Miss., May 26, 1905

REDER, JOHN   Infielder
Boston A. L.

REISS, ALBERT   Infielder
Philadelphia A. L.
Born Elizabeth, N. J., Jan. 8, 1910

RICHARDS, PAUL RAPIER   Catcher
Brooklyn N. L.
Born Waxahachie, Tex., Nov. 21, 1908

SALTSGAVER, JACK   Infielder
New York A. L.
Born Farmington, Ia., Jan. 23, 1908

SCHALK, LEROY   Infielder
New York A. L.
Born Chicago, Ill., November 9, 1908

SCHAREIN, ARTHUR O.   Infielder
St. Louis A. L.
Born Decatur, Ill., June 30, 1905

SEWELL, TRUETT BANKS   Pitcher
Detroit A. L.
Born Decatur, Ala., May 11, 1908

SIEBERT, RICHARD W.   Infielder
Brooklyn N. L.
Born Fall River, Mass., Feb. 19, 1912

SMITH, ARTHUR LAIRD   Pitcher
Chicago A. L.
Born Boston, Mass., June 21, 1906

SMITH, HAROLD L.   Pitcher
Pittsburgh N. L.
Born Creston, Iowa, June 30, 1905

SPOGNARDI, ANDREW E.   Infielder
Boston A. L.
Born East Boston, Mass., Oct. 18, 1910

STARR, RAYMOND F.   Pitcher
St. Louis N. L.
Born Nowata, Okla., April 23, 1907

STEIN, IRVING M.   Pitcher
Philadelphia A. L.

SWIFT, WILLIAM   Pitcher
Pittsburgh N. L.

TAYLOR, HARRY W.   nfielder
Chicago N. L.
Born McKeesport, Pa., Dec. 26, 1908

TERWILLIGER, RICHARD   Pitcher
St. Louis N. L.

THOMAS, LUTHER BAXTER   Pitcher
Washington A. L.
Born Faber, Va., September 9, 1910

TINNING, LYLE F.   Pitcher
Chicago N. L.
Born Pilger, Neb., March 12, 1907

TOBIN, JOHN   Infielder
New York N. L.

TODD, ALFRED CHESTER   Catcher
Philadelphia N. L.
Born Memphis, Tenn., August 21, 1905

WALKER, FRED   Outfielder
New York A. L.
Born Villa Ricka, Ala., September 24, 1910

WALKER, GERALD H.   Outfielder
Detroit A. L.
Born Gulfport, Miss., March 19, 1909

WALKER, HARVEY W.   Outfielder
Detroit A. L.
Born Gulfport, Miss., August 17, 1907

WALTERS, WILLIAM HENRY   Infielder
Boston N. L.
Born Philadelphia, Pa., 1910

WATT, FRANK MARION   Pitcher
Philadelphia N. L.
Born Troy, N. Y., January 7, 1906

VAUGHAN, FLOYD   Infielder
Pittsburgh N. L.
Born Clifty, Ark., March 9, 1912

WEBB, JAMES LEVERNE   Infielder
St. Louis N. L.
Born Meridian, Miss., Nov. 4, 1911

WHITE, JOYNER   Outfielder
Detroit A. L.
Born Red Oak, Ga., June 1, 1909

WINFORD, JAMES H.   Pitcher
St. Louis N. L.
Born Shelbyville, Tenn., Oct. 9, 1909

WISE, ARCHIE   Pitcher
Chicago A. L.

Baseball Cyclopedia

For Season of 1933—58th Year for National League and 33rd for the American

The Pennant Races

National League

Club	Won	Lost	PC	Manager
New York	91	61	.599	William Harold Terry
Pittsburgh	87	67	.565	George Gibson
Chicago	86	68	.553	Charles John Grimm
Boston	83	71	.539	William Boyd McKechnie
St. Louis	82	71	.536	Charles E. Street and
Brooklyn	65	88	.425	Frank Francis Frisch
Philadelphia	60	92	.395	Max G. Carey
Cincinnati	58	94	.382	Burton Edwin Shotton
Totals	612	612	.500	Owen J. Bush

American League

Club	Won	Lost	PC	Manager
Washington	99	53	.651	Joseph Edward Cronin
New York	91	59	.607	Joseph Vincent McCarthy
Philadelphia	79	72	.523	Connie Mack
Cleveland	75	76	.497	Roger Peckinpaugh and
Detroit	75	79	.487	Walter Perry Johnson
Chicago	67	83	.447	Stanley Raymond Harris
Boston	63	86	.423	Lewis A. Fonseca
St. Louis	55	96	.364	Martin J. McManus
Totals	604	604	.500	William Killefer Jr. and
				Rogers Hornsby

Frank Francis Frisch took charge of Cardinals on July 24.
Walter Perry Johnson took charge of Indians on June 9.
Rogers Hornsby took charge of Browns on July 26.

It was the thirteenth pennant for the New York National League club, the third for the Washington American League Club. In the 30th World's Series between the National and American League clubs, New York acquired four victories to Washington's one. The result of this set made the following changes in the dope of the classic: (See Page 100).

Series Won—American League	18
National League	12
Cities Having World's Champion Teams—New York	10
Cities Competing for World's Series Championships—New York	20
Washington	3

Record of games won and lost by World's Series clubs: New York Nationals, won 42, lost 36, percentage .538; Washington Americans, won 8, lost 11, percentage .421.

Managers' record in World's Series: William Harold Terry, series won 1, games won 4, games lost 1. Joseph Edward Cronin, series lost 1, games won 1, games lost 4.

The players on the pennant winning teams during the year were as follows:

NEW YORK NATIONALS—Herman Bell, William Watson Clark, Fred Landis Fitzsimmons, Carl Owen Hubbell, Adolfo Luque, Leroy Carl Parmelee, John Theodore Salveson, Harold Henry Schumacher, William Shores, Glenn Edward Spencer, Raymond Francis Starr and George Ernest Uhle, pitchers; Harry Danning, Gus Rodney Mancuso and Paul Rapier Richards, catchers; Hugh Melville Critz, Charles Walter Dressen, Travis Calvin Jackson, Robert Byrne James, Samuel Andrew Leslie, Joseph Malay, John Collins Ryan, William Harold Terry and Johnny Louis Vergez, infielders; George Willis Davis, Henry Leiber, Joe Gregg Moore, Francis Joseph O'Doul, Melvin Thomas Ott, Homer Hefner Peel and Philip Weintraub, outfielders.

WASHINGTON AMERICANS—Robert J. Burke, John Milard Campbell, Edwin Volney Chapman, Alvin Floyd Crowder, Edward Linke, William Fort McAffee Jr., Alex B. McColl, Raymnd Lee Prim, Jack Russel, Walter Cleveland Stewart, Alphonse Thomas, Luther Baxter Thomas, Monte Morton Weaver and Earl O. Whitehill, pitchers; Morris Berg, William Clifton Bolton and Luther Sewell, catchers; Robert Anthony Boken, Oswald Louis Bluege, Joseph Edward Cronin, John Francis Kerr, Joseph Kuhel, Charles Solomon Myer, Jr., and Cecil Travis, infielders; Leon Allen Goslin, David S. Harris, Henry Emmett Manush, Edgar Charles Rice and Fred William Schulte, outfielders.

Leaders of 1933

BATTERS—Page 46

Player	Club	League	Pct. or No.
Charles Herbert Klein	Philadelphia	National	368.
James Emory Foxx	Philadelphia	American	356.

BASE STEALERS—Page 48

William Ben Chapman	New York	American	27.
John Leonard Martin	St. Louis	National	26.

SACRIFICE HITTERS—Page 49

Richard Bartell	Philadelphia	National	37.
George William Haas	Chicago	American	30.

SCORERS—Page 50

Henry Louis Gehrig	New York	American	138.
John Leonard Martin	St. Louis	National	122.

MANUFACTURERS OF BASE HITS—Page 52

Charles Herbert Klein	Philadelphia	National	223.
Henry Emmett Manush	Washington	American	221.

DEMON DOUBLERS—Page 53

Joseph Edward Cronin	Washington	American	45.
Charles Herbert Klein	Philadelphia	National	44.

DEMON TRIPPLERS—Page 54

Floyd Vaughan	Pittsburgh	National	19.
Henry Emmett Manush	Washington	American	17.

DEMON HOME RUNNISTS—Page 55

James Emory Foxx	Philadelphia	American	48.
Charles Herbert Klein	Philadelphia	National	28.

BATTING IN RUNS—Page 56

James Emory Foxx	Philadelphia	American	163.
Charles Herbert Klein	Philadelphia	National	120.

DEMON WHIFFERS—Page 56

James Emory Foxx	Philadelphia	American	93.
Walter Antone Berger	Boston	National	77.

DEMON WALKERS—Page 56

George Herman Ruth	New York	American	114.
Melvin Thomas Ott	New York	National	75.

STRIKEOUT KINGS—Page 57

Jerome Herman Dean	St. Louis	National	191.
Vernon Gomez	New York	American	163.

FAMOUS GAMES, FAMOUS PLAYERS—FAMOUS FEATS

THREE HOME RUNS IN GAMES PAGE 61

Feat of hitting three home runs in one games was accomplished twice in 1933, as follows:

AMERICAN LEAGUE—June 8, James Emory Foxx, of Philadelphia, at Philadelphia against New York, in first three times at bat. In last time at bat, June 7, against Washington, at Philadelphia, Foxx hit home run. So on two dates he hit four home runs in succession, tying major league record.

NATIONAL LEAGUE—July 20, Floyd Caves Herman, at Chicago, against Philadelphia, player just having been restored to duty after warming bench for four days for light hitting.

RUNS BATTED IN PAGE 68

JAMES EMORY FOXX, Philadelphia Americans, created new American League record for runs batted in one game by hitting in nine at Cleveland, on August 14. Tripled two men home in first inning, hit for circuit with packed house in second, doubled man home in fourth and singled two men over in sixth. Batted against Hudlin in first two trips to plate, against Bean other times.

SIX HIT MANUFACTURERS PAGE 71

SAM WEST, St. Louis Americans, made five singles and one double in six times at bat against Chicago at St. Louis on April 13, this being his second game as a Brown.

Addenda to Part VII

Players Starting Their Major League Careers During the Season of 1933

(With birth dates of most of them)

ALMADA, MELO   Outfielder
Boston A. L.
Born Los Angeles, Cal., Feb. 7, 1915.

AUKER, ELDON LEROY   Pitcher
Detroit A. L.
Born Norcatur Kan., Sept. 21, 1910.

BARRETT, RICHARD OLIVER   Pitcher
Philadelphia A. L.
Born Montoursville, Pa., Sept. 28, 1907.

BIRKOFFER, RALPH   Pitcher
Pittsburgh N. L.
Born Cincinnati, O., Nov. 5, 1909.

BOCEK, MILTON F.   Outfielder
Chicago A. L.
Born Chicago, Ill., July 16, 1912.

BOKEN, ROBERT ANTHONY   Infielder
Washington, A. L.
Born Augusta, Me., Dec. 2, 1903.

BRENNAN, JAMES DONALD   Pitcher
New York A. L.
Born Augusta, Me., Dec. 2, 1903.

BUTLER, CHARLES T.   Pitcher
Philadelphia N.L.
Born Green Cave Springs, Fla., May 12, 1906

CAMILLI, ADOLPH   Infielder
Chicago N. L.
Born San Francisco, Cal., Apr. 23, 1907.

CAMPBELL, JOHN MILLARD   Pitcher
Washington A. L.
Born Washington, D. C., Sept. 3, 1908.

CAMPBELL, WILLIAM GILTHORPE
    Catcher
Chicago N. L.
Born Kansas City, Kan., Feb. 13, 1908.

CHAPMAN, EDWIN VOLNEY   Pitcher
Washington A. L.
Born Courtland, Miss., Nov. 28, 1906.

CLASET, GOWELL SYLVESTER   Pitcher
Philadelphia A. L.
Born Battle Creek, Mich., Nov. 26, 1908.

COOMBS, RAYMOND FRANK   Pitcher
Philadelphia A. L.
Born Goodwins Mills, Maine, Feb. 2, 1903.

DANNING, HENRY   Catcher
New York N. L.
Born Los Angeles, Cal., Sept. 6, 1911.

DELMAS, BERT C.   Infielder
Brooklyn N. L.
Born

DIETRICH, WILLIAM JOHN   Pitcher
Philadelphia A. L.
Born Philadelphia, Pa., March 29, 1910.

FOX, ERVIN   Outfielder
Detroit A. L.
Born Evansville, Ind., March 8, 1909.

FREY, LINUS REINHARD   Infielder
Brooklyn N. L.
Born St. Louis, Mo., August 23, 1912.

GALATZER, MILTON   Outfielder
Cleveland A. L.
Born Chicago, Ill., May 4, 1904.

GYSELMAN, RICHARD RENALD   Infielder
Boston N. L.
Born San Francisco, Cal., Apr. 6, 1911.

HAMLIN, LUKE B.   Pitcher
Detroit A. L.
Born Terris Center, Mich., July 3, 1906.

HASLIN, MICHAEL J.   Infielder
Philadelphia N. L.
Born Wilkesbarre, Pa., Oct. 31, 1910.

HAYES, FRANK W.   Pitcher
Philadelphia A. L.
Born Jamesburg, N. J., Oct. 13, 1915.

HENSHAW, ROY   Pitcher
Chicago N. L.
Born Chicago, Ill., June 29, 1911.

HUNTER, EDDIE   Infielder
Cincinnati N. L.
Born

HUTCHESON, JOSEPH JOHNSON
        Outfielder
Brooklyn N. L.
Born Springtown, Tex., Feb. 5, 1905.

HURCHINSON, IRA   Pitcher
Chicago A. L.
Born Chicago, Ill., August 21, 1912.

JACKSON, JOHN   Pitcher
Philadelphia N. L.
Born

JOHNSON, ROBERT LEE   Outfielder
Philadelphia A. L.
Born Sporinon, Okla., Nov. 26, 1906.

JORDAN, JAMES WILLIAM   Infielder
Brooklyn N. L.
Born Spartanburg, S. C., Jan. 13, 1908.

KNICKERBOCKER, JR., WILLIAM HART
        Infielder
Cleveland, A. L.
Born Los Angeles, Cal., Dec. 29, 1912.

KNOTT, JACK H.   Pitcher
St. Louis A. L.
Born Dallas, Tex., March 2, 1907.

LEE, THORNTON STARR   Pitcher
Cleveland A. L.
Born Sonoma, Cal., Sept. 13, 1907.

LEIBER, HENRY   Outfielder
New York N. L.
Born Phoenix, Ariz., Jan. 17, 1912.

LEONARD, EMIL   Pitcher
Brooklyn N. L.
Born Auburn, Ill., March 25, 1909.

LEWIS, WILLIAM H.   Catcher
St. Louis N. L.
Born Ripley, Tenn., Oct. 15, 1905.

LINKE, EDWARD   Pitcher
Washington A. L.
Born Chicago, Ill., Nov. 9, 1912.

LOVETT, MERRITT M.
Chicago A. L.
Born

MALAY, JOSEPH   Infielder
New York N. L.
Born Brooklyn, N. Y., Oct. 25, 1906.

MARCUM, JOHN ALFRED   Pitcher
Philadelphia A. L.
Born Eminence, Ky., Sept. 9, 1909.

M'COLL, ALEXANDER B.   Pitcher
Washington A. L.
Born Eagleville, O., March 29, 1896.

MEOLA, EMIL   Pitcher
Boston A. L.
Born New York City, Oct. 19, 1908.

MOWRY, JOSEPH A.   Outfielder
Boston N. L.
Born St. Louis, Mo., April 6, 1910.

MULLER, FRED W.   Infielder
Boston A. L.
Born Newark, Cal., Dec. 21, 1909.

NONNENKAMP, LEE WILLIAM
        Outfielder
Pittsburgh N. L.
Born St. Louis, Mo., July 7, 1911.

OULLIBER, JOHN ANDREW   Outfielder
Cleveland A. L.
Born New Orleans, La., Feb. 25, 1911

OUTEN, WILLIAM AUSTIN   Catcher
Brooklyn, N. L.
Born Mount Holly, N. C., June 17, 1905.

PASEK, JOHN PAUL   Catcher
Detroit A. L.
Born Niagara Falls, N. Y., June 26, 1906.

PEARCE, FRANKLIN THOMAS   Pitcher
Philadelphia N. L.
Born Shelby County, Ky., Aug. 31, 1905.

PICKREL, CLARENCE DOUGLAS   Pitcher
Philadelphia N. L.
Born Gretna, Va., March 28, 1911.

PRIM, RAY   Pitcher
Washington A. L.
Born Saliepa, Ala., Dec. 30, 1909.

REIBER, FRANK BERNARD   Catcher
Detroit A. L.
Born Huntington, W. Va., September
19, 1909.

RICHMOND, BERYL   Pitcher
Chicago N. L.
Born Cameron, W. Va., Aug. 24, 1907.

ROBELLO, TOM   Infielder
Cincinnati N. L.
Born Oakland, Cal., Feb. 9, 1913.

ROY, EMIL A.   Pitcher
Philadelphia A. L.
Born Brighton, Mass., 1910.

ROWE, LYNWOOD THOMAS   Pitcher
Detroit A. L.
Born Waco, Tex., Jan. 11, 1912.

SALVESON, JOHN THEODORE   Pitcher
New York N. L.
Born Fullerton, Cal., Jan. 5, 1914.

STONEHAM, JOHN A.   Outfielder
Chicago A. L.
Born Wood River, Ill., Nov. 8, 1908.

THOMPSON, RUPERT LUCKHART

Outfielder
Boston N. L.
Born Lincoln, Ill., May 19, 1910.

TIETJE, LESLIE WILLIAM   Pitcher
Chicago A. L.
Born Sumner, Pa., Sept. 11, 1911.

TRAVIS, CECIL   Infielder
Washington A. L.
Born Riverdale, Ga., Aug. 8, 1913.

TROSKY, HAROLD ARTHUR   Infielder
Cleveland A. L.
Born Norway, Ia., Nov. 11, 1912.

VANATTA, RUSELL   Pitcher
New York A. L.
Born Augusta, N. J., June 21, 1906.

WEINTRAUB, PHILIP   Outfielder
New York N. L.
Born Chicago, Ill., Oct. 12, 1907.

WHITEHEAD, BURGESS URQUHART
                              Infielder
St. Louis N. L.
Born Tarboro, N. C., June 29, 1910.

WINSTON, HENRY R.   Pitcher
Philadelphia A. L.
Born Youngsville, N. C., June 15, 1909.

WRIGHT, ALBERT   Infielder
Boston N. L.
Born San Francisco, Cal., November 11,
1912.

YOUNG, LINWELL FLOYD   Infielder
Pittsburgh N. L.
Born Jamestown, N. C., Aug. 28, 1907.

ZAPUSTAS, JOSEPH   Outfielder
Philadelphia A. L.
Born July 25, 1911.

Index

Compiled by Roger Erickson of the Bibliography
Committee of the Society for American Baseball Research.